Blue Crimes and International Criminal Law

Edited by
Regina M. Paulose
International Criminal Law Attorney

Series in Law

VERNON PRESS

www.vernonpress.com

In the Americas:
Vernon Press
1000 N West Street, Suite 1200
Wilmington, Delaware, 19801
United States

In the rest of the world:
Vernon Press
C/Sancti Espiritu 17,
Malaga, 29006
Spain

Series in Law

Library of Congress Control Number: 2025935444

ISBN: 979-8-8819-0240-7

Cover design by Vernon Press. Cover image by Sagina Vadakal.

Table of Contents

List of Abbreviations

AU	African Union
EEZ	Exclusive Economic Zone
ICC	International Criminal Court
ICCPR	International Covenant on Civil and Political Rights
ICJ	International Court of Justice
ICTY	International Criminal Tribunal for the Former Yugoslavia
ICW	International Whaling Commission
ILC	International Law Commission
ILO	International Labour Organization
ITLOS	International Tribunal on the Law of the Sea
IUU	Illegal, unreported, and unregulated (fishing)
SIDS	Small Island Developing States
UN	United Nations
UNCLOS	UN Convention on the Law of the Sea

Introduction
Through the Looking Glass

Regina M. Paulose
International Criminal Law Attorney

Blue Crimes and International Criminal Law is a companion volume to *Green Crimes and International Criminal Law*, which was published in 2021 by Vernon Press. While this volume incorporates some themes from *Green Crimes* the main purpose of this volume is to provide a link between international criminal law and water (which includes water for consumption, our oceans, and other bodies of water).

This volume explores three overarching questions. The first question explored is what constitutes blue crimes? I define blue crimes as an umbrella category of crimes which are linked in some manner to water. Within the broad category of blue crimes, there are two subcategories: ocean crimes, or crimes of the sea, and water crimes. These two subcategories are covered in this book. The contributors in this volume have been given leeway to define and interpret blue crimes as they see appropriate. The other question explored is how can the international community respond to blue crimes? The damage being inflicted on life around and within our oceans, the way water is used as a weapon against civilians, or diverted from civilians and wildlife under the guise of green energy, and the potential collapse of our marine ecosystem due to overfishing and in some cases – slaughter for sport - should encourage a prompt re-examination of the place of blue crimes within international criminal law. We already know the important role that water plays on earth. Our rivers, lakes, and oceans are catalysts for producing and providing for all life. These bodies of water, particularly our oceans, are now at the epicenter of fighting human-induced climate change. Despite the laws, regulations, and treaties that appear to regulate water and water bodies, there is little to no enforcement of these laws. Which brings us to the third question explored: how do we appropriately enforce these legal regimes to protect water and the life around it?

The following chapters discuss important issues within the arena of blue crimes, and the editor remains hopeful that entities such as the International Seabed Authority, parties to the UN Convention on the Law of the Sea, and the ICC will consider how to address blue crimes in an effective manner. Further, it is hoped that the topics covered in this book will also inspire focused discussion during the UN Ocean Decade (2021 – 2030).

In Chapter 1, Dr. Zoi Aliozi continues the conversation she started in *Green Crimes,* examining a definition of blue crimes and its intersection with the rights of nature, climate justice, and ecocide. Dr. Aliozi's chapter will orient the reader to some of the philosophical underpinnings of the issues presented throughout this book. In Chapter 2, Lu Shegay furthers the discussion on the rights of nature by examining the horrific slaughter of whales for commercial purposes and why these frameworks need to be re-evaluated to protect marine mammals.

In Chapter 3, Dr. Pierpaolo Petrelli takes the reader through the UN Convention on the Law of the Sea, highlighting the multiple shortcomings of UNCLOS in its current form, particularly given challenges such as migrant deaths and damage to environmentally sensitive areas such as the Arctic. Connected to UNCLOS reform is the discussion in Chapter 4, where co-authors Lancaster, Erinosho, Hamukuaya, and Sanni discuss fisheries crimes with a specific focus on the Caribbean and African regions. Their chapter introduces the concept of blue justice and how blue justice can be a more inclusive means of allowing communities to participate in ocean governance. Dr. Mark Chadwick also raises questions about the need for UNCLOS reform and brings us back to the original crime of the sea – piracy - where he explores why the crime of piracy is in need of a make-over in Chapter 5.

The next two chapters in the book move the conversation away from traditional concepts of blue crimes and narrow the focus on blue crimes in specific contexts. In Chapter 6, Ronald Rogo and Christine Okidi examine the situation of the El Molo people who continue to face challenges to water access as a result of hydropower projects. This chapter connects back to the discussion started in the *Green Crimes* volume regarding the growth of hydropower in Asia and its link to violations of human rights and international criminal law. In the same vein, in Chapter 7, Dr. Shabnam Moinipour presents a very grim picture of challenges involving water security and corruption in the water governance sector in the Islamic Republic of Iran. She suggests incorporating a human rights framework to water governance challenges in order to ensure water access and water security for people in Iran.

Finally, the last two chapters examine avenues for accountability for blue crimes within the international arena. In Chapter 8, Henna Shah explores corporate accountability and blue crimes by surveying the effectiveness of international corporate accountability instruments and in Chapter 9, Vy Nguyen questions what role, if any, the ICC could have in prosecuting blue crimes.

On a final and important note, I wanted to thank Dr. Narissa Ramsundar for her valuable peer review feedback to the contributors. In addition, special thanks again go to Sagina Vadakal, who created the cover art for this book and to Tim Franklin, who assisted with technical edits. In addition, I am grateful to Sherri A. White for her feedback. Last but never least, thank you to all the contributors to this volume who worked diligently to make this book a wonderful companion volume to *Green Crimes.*

Chapter 1

Exploring Ecocide as a Blue Crime Through the Lens of Climate Justice

Dr. Zoi Aliozi

Human Rights & Climate Justice Expert

Abstract: This chapter is an examination of the concept of *blue crimes* (meaning *crimes at sea* within the theory of *blue criminology)*, through the lens of *climate justice*. The examination is undertaken through an interdisciplinary exploration that blends law and philosophy while attempting to highlight the urgency of integrating climate justice into international criminal law, human rights, and global justice discourse. Focusing on ecocide as a blue crime, it examines existing legal frameworks and considers the incorporation of ecocide into international criminal law. The chapter delves into the philosophical dimensions of climate justice, highlighting its significance as a social, ethical, and legal concern in addressing crimes at sea with special legal firmness. Acknowledging the strong link between international criminal law, human rights, and climate justice is vital for ensuring global justice and in tackling climate change.

Keywords: Blue Crimes, Blue Criminology, Climate Justice, Ecocide, The Rights of Nature, International Law, Criminal Law, Philosophy, Human Rights, Interdisciplinarity, legal philosophy, environmental ethics, eco-philosophy.

Prolegomena

The first question that demands exploration is: **What is climate justice?**

An ideal definition of climate justice would be: Climate justice is the fair treatment of all people, living beings, ecosystems, and the biosphere, extending to the cosmos. It emphasizes equity, accountability, human rights, and the rights of future generations, animals, and nature.

Thus, climate justice could also be articulated as: Climate justice, in essence, is the fair treatment of all people (from an anthropocentric perspective) and/or all life and the biosphere (from an ecocentric perspective) in addressing climate change. It focuses on equity, accountability, human rights, support for vulnerable communities, the rights of future generations, animal rights, and the rights of nature.

There can be numerous and diverse definitions of climate justice, depending on the discipline through which we choose to analyze the concept. However, the common denominator across all interpretations of climate justice is its root cause, its starting point: climate change itself. In every definition, climate change is traced back to human activities. Humanity is the common thread, both the cause and the reason behind climate change, which serves as the foundation for any legal inquiry into accountability. At the same time, humans are not only responsible and accountable for climate injustices but also the subjects and beneficiaries of climate justice.

While seemingly straightforward, this question opens the door to a cascade of further inquiries, much like the mythical Hydra—each answer giving rise to multiple new questions. This is because climate justice as a concept can be translated in many different ways, depending on which discipline we view the phenomenon, concept, idea, or movement. I like to think of this flexibility and inclusivity of the definition of climate justice in terms of an initiation into Socratic questioning, where finding the true answer leads us to deeper, more complex considerations.

For example, a couple of years ago, in 2022, the United Nations finally and officially recognized the *human right to a healthy environment,*[1] a significant step in framing climate justice within the human rights discourse, but pragmatically too little too late; since it took 77 years for the UN to recognize the universal applicability of the human right to a clean environment. International law, in essence, has been weak concerning climate justice enforceability, which is the defining factor for a number of inadequacies and misconceptions surrounding our understanding of climate justice. The most striking to me, and a common misconception that I believe requires clarification, is the notion of separating climate justice from human rights. In my view, climate justice is inherently linked to human rights. In recent years, there has been a noticeable shift, with human rights increasingly being framed in the context of environmental issues.[2] In my view, the two are inseparable, interlinked, interdependent and complementary. To turn away from climate justice is, in essence, to turn away from human rights itself, and vice versa. This disconnect underscores the critical need for deeper understanding and the

[1] U.N. Human Rights Council, Res. 48/13, U.N. Doc. A/HRC/RES/48/13 (Oct. 8, 2021).
[2] John H. Knox, *Climate Change and Human Rights Law*, 50 VA. J. INT'L L. 163 (2009).

integration of climate justice across policy, law, and education—particularly during this time of climate emergency.[3]

A notable case that highlights the intersection of climate justice and human rights is *Urgenda Foundation v. The State of the Netherlands* (2015). In this case, a Dutch court ruled that the government had a legal duty to reduce greenhouse gas emissions in order to protect its citizens from the impacts of climate change. This decision marked a watershed moment, as it framed climate change as not only an environmental issue but also a human rights issue. Similarly, the *Juliana v. United States* case, although ultimately dismissed on procedural grounds, raised the critical question of whether the U.S. government had violated young people's constitutional rights by failing to take adequate action on climate change. This case, as an example, demonstrates the gradual but meaningful progress in aligning legal frameworks with the principles of climate justice and ecocentrism. By integrating the concepts of green criminology, ecocide, and the rights of nature, there is potential to move toward a legal system that more effectively addresses the interconnected crises of environmental degradation, human rights violations, and social inequality.

From the perspective of critical legal studies, this emphasis is not merely theoretical—it challenges entrenched power structures that marginalize climate issues and treat them as secondary to human rights. Similarly, it questions the devaluation of animal rights, positioning them as inferior to human rights within the unspoken legal and moral hierarchy in international law. Critical legal scholars argue that the law is often complicit in maintaining structures of oppression, and in this case, the reluctance to fully embrace climate justice reflects the legal system's failure to address the intertwined crises of environmental degradation and social injustice.[4] This chapter argues that ecocide should be recognized as an international crime to establish legal consequences for environmental destruction, particularly in oceans, which have been overlooked in climate and legal discussions despite their vital role in sustaining life. Oceans are severely impacted by pollution, overfishing, and habitat destruction, affecting marine life and vulnerable communities. By promoting ecocentric ideas, stronger protection of marine animals, and the rights of nature, this approach offers a powerful basis for reform through climate justice considerations in law and policy.

Similarly, *feminist legal scholarship* offers valuable insights into why climate justice must be central to human rights. Feminist scholars have long critiqued

---

[3] U.N. Framework Convention on Climate Change, Report of the Conference of the Parties, U.N. Doc. FCCC/CP/2015/10/Add.1 (2016).

[4] Robert M. Cover, *Violence and the Word*, 95 YALE L.J. 1601, 1606 (1986).

the law for its tendency to marginalize vulnerable communities, particularly women and indigenous populations, who are disproportionately affected by climate change.[5] Climate justice, from a feminist perspective, involves recognizing and addressing these intersecting inequalities. It demands that we prioritize the principle of vulnerability and the needs of those most impacted by climate-related harms, rather than maintaining legal frameworks that reinforce existing power dynamics.[6]

This chapter seeks to contribute to the evolving discourse on climate justice by offering a new perspective: the legal construction of *ecocide* as a form of *blue crime*. While ecocide has been traditionally understood as the widespread destruction of ecosystems, here, I aim to examine it through the lens of crimes committed against marine environments—often overlooked in mainstream legal and policy discussions. By exploring the legal and moral implications of treating ecocide as a blue crime, I hope to provide fresh insights into how climate justice can be advanced in both human rights law, environmental law,[7] and criminal law, through integration of these concepts into international criminal justice legal frameworks.

To properly address *what climate justice is,* we must first ask: *Who is asking the question?* From which perspective are we approaching this concept? And why are we seeking a definitive answer? In philosophical research circles, we know that most of the time, it is not the answer that is wrong, but the question. So, are we asking the right question? The interpretation of climate justice varies depending on the context:

> Philosophically, it can be understood as a theory of justice concerned with fairness in addressing climate change.[8]

Morally, it reflects the idea that destroying nature violates both ecological balance and human rights, positioning environmental destruction as a moral and legal wrong on par with crimes against humanity.[9]

---

[5] Susan Schneider, *Feminist Perspectives on Environmental Law*, 31 HARV. ENVTL. L. REV. 61, 77 (2007).

[6] V. G. M. R. K. Singh, *Intersectionality and Climate Justice*, 45 U. PA. J. INT'L L. 451, 465 (2023).

[7] Polly Higgins, *Eradicating Ecocide: Laws and Governance to Stop the Destruction of Our Planet*, 4 CLIMATE L. 237, 245 (2013).

[8] John Rawls, *A Theory of Justice* (Harvard University Press 1971).

[9] Richard Falk, *Human Rights and the Environment*, 10 AM. U. INT'L L. REV. 1079, 1095 (1995).

Legally, climate justice refers to the application of laws, treaties, and legal principles to address the impacts of climate change, often through frameworks like international environmental law, human rights law, and emerging criminal law focused on environmental harm.[10]

Politically and socially, it represents a movement driven by activists advocating for environmental protection and opposing the fossil fuel industry.[11]

Academically, climate justice flourishes as a human-rights-based research topic, and it can be interdisciplinary, or applied across multiple disciplines, from law and economics to environmental science and ethics, or even architecture, biology, and so on and so forth, where its meaning transforms and adjusts according to the field of study.[12]

In this scholarly work, climate justice is intertwined with these various perspectives, reflecting its flexible, evolving nature. However, at its core, climate justice is structured by a legal framework deeply rooted in philosophical principles. This chapter will examine climate justice as an issue fundamentally linked to the legal responses to anthropogenic climate change, particularly through the lens of human rights and criminal law. This intersection of legal, ethical, and environmental factors shapes the exploration of climate justice in this chapter, guided by the following definition:

> Climate justice is essentially the blueprint for a fair and sustainable future of life on this planet. Climate justice can be understood as a lens for looking at climate change as a social, ethical and legal issue, rather than solely an environmental one.[13]

The following paragraphs aim to explore the concept of blue crimes through the lens of climate justice. The primary focus is on analyzing whether ecocide, as the worst and most severe blue crime, can meaningfully contribute to international criminal justice. Ecocide represents one of the most significant legal developments of our time—an effort to establish a law designed to protect our planet. This is a critical issue, as ecocide is poised to be recognized as one of the most serious crimes of our era. Ecocide, as a blue crime, would involve severe environmental harm to oceans and marine ecosystems, prosecutable

---

10 *Report of the Conference of the Parties*, *supra* note 3.

11 Bill McKibben, *The End of Nature* (Random House 1989).

12 J. B. Ruhl, *Climate Change and the Law: A Primer for Legal Scholars*, 44 ENVTL. L. 95 (2014).

13 Zoi Aliozi, *Policy Brief: Climate Justice and Human Rights in a World in Climate Emergency*, GLOBAL CAMPUS OF HUMAN RIGHTS (2021).

under international law. Examples include large-scale oil spills or illegal dumping, which threaten marine life and human communities.[14]

To fully appreciate the brilliance of this legal construction, it's essential to recognize that when ecocide becomes legally applicable universally, any form of human-driven mass harm to nature will become illegal and prosecutable under international criminal law.[15] This shift represents a powerful extension of legal protection, where environmental destruction—whether through deforestation, ocean pollution, or industrial practices—would no longer go unpunished.[16]

Ecocide in the oceans, driven by human activities such as pollution, overfishing, and habitat destruction, poses a severe threat to marine ecosystems and biodiversity. Recognizing ecocide as an international crime could pave the way for holding individuals and corporations accountable, regardless of where these actions occur, effectively overcoming the challenges of extraterritoriality. By applying universal jurisdiction through international criminal law, this legal framework could ensure that the destruction of ocean ecosystems is prosecuted globally, ensuring that no nation can shield perpetrators from responsibility. This approach would strengthen global environmental justice, offering a more robust mechanism for protecting our oceans. This legal revolution not only offers hope for safeguarding the planet but also redefines our moral and ethical responsibilities toward the environment, aligning human rights with the rights of nature.[17] It signals a transformative step toward ensuring that environmental protection becomes a core tenet of international justice, prioritizing the well-being of both humanity and the natural world. What is important to highlight is that, philosophically, it invites a reconsideration of human's role within the cosmos. It calls for a departure from the outdated anthropocentrism in law and a progression toward an ecocentric perspective on what law and justice ought to be. But through an ecocentric standpoint, where humans are not at the top of the value hierarchy, but rather part of an ecosystem interdependent for our well-being, humanity is not the entitled ruler of nature. Instead, we are part of it, with our best interest lying in protecting nature, as we depend on it. This perspective rejects the unregulated exploitation of natural resources simply because we live in a free market ruled by capitalist systems.

Moving the reflecting path from philosophy to law, it is arguable that from a legal perspective, including ecocide within the mandate of the ICC would

---

[14] Higgins, 237.

[15] International Law Commission, *Draft Principles on the Protection of the Environment in Relation to Armed Conflicts*, U.N. Doc. A/74/10 (2019).

[16] Janusz Symonides, *Human Rights and the Environment: The Need for Global Governance*, 18 INT'L J. ENV'T & SUSTAINABLE DEV. 77, 85 (2019).

[17] Cormac Cullinan, *Wild Law: A Manifesto for Earth Justice* (2002).

elevate it to the level of the other gravest crimes, such as genocide, war crimes, and crimes against humanity.[18] The ICC's purpose is to prosecute the worst crimes against humanity and ensure accountability on a global scale.[19] Recognizing ecocide as a crime would address the devastating impact environmental destruction has on human rights, as ecosystems underpin human survival, health, and well-being.[20] By prosecuting ecocide, the ICC could help protect vulnerable communities from the catastrophic effects of environmental degradation, which often disproportionately affect marginalized populations, and further reinforce the principle that environmental protection is inseparable from the protection of human rights.[21]

In light of the urgent climate crisis, integrating ecocide into international criminal law could be a crucial step in securing justice for both the planet and humanity.[22]

This chapter, as explained above, employs an interdisciplinary methodology, drawing on the dual disciplines of law and philosophy as its analytical foundation. Within this framework, climate justice is approached as a multifaceted concept, whose scope and interpretation vary depending on the disciplinary lens applied. From a legal perspective, climate justice is closely tied to criminal law and human rights, emphasizing the need for accountability and protection in the face of environmental harm. Conversely, when viewed through a philosophical lens, climate justice engages with political theory and global justice frameworks, offering a basis for the emergence of transformative ideas, such as the rights of nature and the recognition of ecocide. These evolving concepts align with the pressing ethical and environmental challenges humanity faces today, underscoring the need for new paradigms in both theory and practice.

Our planet is suffering a climate emergency, a crisis officially recognized by the United Nations in 2019.[23] In this urgent global context, the necessity for

---

18 David R. Boyd, *The Rights of Nature: A Legal Revolution That Could Save the Planet* (2017).

19 International Criminal Court, Rome Statute of the International Criminal Court, art. 1, July 17, 1998, 2187 U.N.T.S. 90.

20 Dinah Shelton, *Human Rights and the Environment: The Right to a Healthy Environment,* 27 PACE ENVTL. L. REV. 161, 175 (2010).

21 Shyami P. S. Jayasuriya, *Environmental Degradation and Human Rights: A Case for Ecocide,* 9 J. INT'L Humanitarian Legal Studies 233 (2018).

22 Polly Higgins, *Eradicating Ecocide: Laws and Governance to Stop the Destruction of Our Planet,* 4 Climate L. 237 (2013).

23 U.N. Climate Action Summit, *Climate Emergency: An Urgent Call for Action* (2019), available at: https://www.un.org/en/climatechange/urgency-action.

immediate and transformative climate action has become undeniable, as evidenced by rising sea levels, extreme weather events, and the rapid loss of biodiversity.[24] These challenges have prompted a significant global shift towards sustainability and greener practices across all sectors—whether it's in education through climate curricula, in industry through the adoption of renewable energy, or in policy through frameworks like the Paris Agreement.[25]

Most importantly for our discussion, this shift is also reflected in law. Legal systems around the world are increasingly acknowledging the need to protect not only human rights but also the rights of animals, and nature. This is evident in groundbreaking developments such as New Zealand granting legal personhood to the Whanganui River[26] and Ecuador enshrining the rights of nature in its constitution.[27] These legal precedents align with growing ecocentric debates on green criminology,[28] which expand the definition of crime to include criminal harm against the environment itself, a concept often referred to as ecocide.[29]

I. Codifying Ecocide as a Blue Crime

Climate justice has emerged as a crucial force within the movement advocating for the legal codification and recognition of ecocide, emphasizing the disproportionate impact of environmental harm on vulnerable communities. It plays a pivotal role in advancing the principles of green criminology by holding corporations and states accountable for environmental damage. Moreover, it integrates the language of human and environmental rights into mainstream discourse, as seen in lawsuits like the *Urgenda* case[30] in the Netherlands, where the government was held legally responsible for failing to meet its climate commitments. These developments highlight the growing recognition that environmental protection is not only a scientific or policy issue but a legal and moral imperative.

---

[24] Intergovernmental Panel on Climate Change, *Global Warming of 1.5°C* (2018), available at: https://www.ipcc.ch/sr15/.

[25] Paris Agreement, Dec. 12, 2015, 55 U.N.T.S. 359.

[26] Te Awa Tupua (Whanganui River Claims Settlement) Act 2017, No. 7 (N.Z.).

[27] Ecuador Const. arts. 71-74 (2008).

[28] REGINA M. PAULOSE, GREEN CRIMES AND INTERNATIONAL CRIMINAL LAW 123 (Vernon Press 2021).

[29] Zoi Aliozi, *Green Criminology: A Rights-Based Approach*, in R. Paulose ed., GREEN CRIMES AND INTERNATIONAL CRIMINAL LAW 1 (Vernon Press 2021).

[30] Urgenda Foundation v. The Netherlands, [2015] HAZA C/09/00456689 (June 24, 2015); aff'd, (Oct. 9, 2018) (District Court of The Hague and The Hague Court of Appeal) (affirmed by the Supreme Court, Dec. 20, 2019).

The recognition of ecocide and blue crimes in international law has seen notable growth in recent years, signaling an increasing commitment to environmental justice. For instance, Belgium introduced ecocide as a criminal offense in its legal framework in 2024, aiming to address severe environmental harm such as large-scale oil spills and other acts of significant ecological destruction.[31] Similarly, France's Climate & Resilience Act (2021) criminalizes ecocide under national law, with penalties for those causing serious and lasting environmental damage.[32] The European Union has also made strides, with the European Council adopting a directive that criminalizes environmental offenses comparable to ecocide, setting a precedent for other member states to follow.[33] These examples reflect a broader trend toward incorporating blue crimes—such as ocean pollution, overfishing, and destruction of marine habitats—into legal frameworks, highlighting the growing importance of protecting marine ecosystems within international law.

A. Ecocide as an International Crime

If the Rome Statute, the treaty that established the ICC, were to be written today, it is highly likely that ecocide—mass environmental destruction—would have been included among the list of the gravest international crimes such as genocide, crimes against humanity, and war crimes. The momentum to classify ecocide as a crime under international law has been steadily growing, with countries such as France, Belgium, and Vanuatu advocating for its inclusion. This would empower the ICC to hold individuals, corporations, and governments accountable for severe environmental damage on a global scale.

Blue crimes, a term rooted in the emerging field of blue criminology, refer to crimes that occur at sea or have significant impacts on marine environments. These crimes can include illegal fishing, pollution, human trafficking, piracy, and, as this chapter emphasizes, ecocide. Blue criminology, as a discipline, seeks to address the unique challenges posed by crimes at sea, which often occur in areas beyond national jurisdiction and involve multiple state and non-state actors. The concept of blue crimes recognizes that the ocean is a critical

---

[31] Belgium Federal Parliament, "Act Introducing the (New) Book II of the Belgian Criminal Code," February 2024.

[32] Law No. 2021-1104 of August 22, 2021, on Combating Climate Change and Strengthening Resilience to its Effects, Journal Officiel de La République Française (Aug. 24, 2021), available at https://www.vie-publique.fr/loi/278460-loi-22-aout-2021-climat-et-resilience-convention-citoyenne-climat.

[33] European Council, "Directive on Environmental Crimes," European Union, March 2023.

global common that requires robust legal protections to safeguard its ecosystems and the human populations that depend on them.

The intersection of these concepts—climate justice, ecocide, and blue crimes—forms the foundation of this chapter's exploration of how international criminal law can and should evolve to address the pressing issue of environmental destruction at sea. By defining these terms and understanding their interconnections, we can better appreciate the importance of integrating climate justice into the legal frameworks that govern our global environment. This integration is not only a matter of legal necessity but also of moral and ethical responsibility to current and future generations.

B. From Anthropocentrism to Ecocentrism: A Shift in Legal Philosophy

In recent decades, legal and philosophical debates have increasingly shifted from an anthropocentric to an ecocentric understanding of law. Anthropocentrism, the traditional view that places human beings at the center of legal and moral consideration, has long dominated international and domestic legal systems.[34] As mentioned briefly above, this perspective often regards nature as a resource for human use, leading to its exploitation without adequate safeguards for the environment itself.[35] However, the rise of climate justice and green criminology has begun to challenge this anthropocentric focus, pushing toward an ecocentric framework where the environment, ecosystems, and non-human life forms are recognized as having intrinsic value and legal rights.[36]

An example of this shift is seen in the emergence of "Rights of Nature" legal frameworks. Ecuador became the first country to enshrine the rights of nature in its constitution in 2008, recognizing ecosystems as legal entities with rights to exist, persist, and regenerate. Similarly, in 2017, the Whanganui River in New Zealand was granted legal personhood, affording it the same rights as a human being under New Zealand law.[37] These developments represent a major move away from anthropocentrism and toward ecocentrism, where nature is not merely protected for the sake of human benefit but acknowledged as a subject of law in its own right.[38]

---

[34] Patrick Glenn, *Legal Traditions of the World* 26 (3d ed. 2010).
[35] Richard A. Posner, *The Law and Economics of Climate Change*, 5 YALE J. OF REGULATION 159 (1988).
[36] Rob White, *Green Criminology: An Introduction to the Concept*, 14 CRIMINOLOGY & CRIM. JUST. 267 (2014).
[37] Te Awa Tupua (Whanganui River Claims Settlement) Act 2017, No. 7 (N.Z.).
[38] David R. Boyd, *The Rights of Nature: A Legal Revolution That Could Save the Planet* 41 (2017).

In the context of climate justice, this shift has important implications. Climate justice advocates for addressing the unequal distribution of environmental harm, often disproportionately affecting vulnerable populations and ecosystems.[39] Through an ecocentric lens, climate justice expands beyond human-centered concerns to include the rights of non-human life and the environment itself. This approach can lead to more holistic legal frameworks that address the root causes of environmental degradation and its broader impacts.

C. The Role of Criminology in Addressing Ecocide

Criminology[40] plays a key role in this transformation, providing a critical analysis of environmental harm as a form of crime, whether or not it is recognized by existing legal systems. It expands the concept of crime to include harms against ecosystems and species, challenging traditional legal definitions that focus solely on human victims. The number one landmark case that illustrates this shift is the ongoing effort to classify "ecocide" as an international crime. Ecocide refers to mass environmental destruction that threatens to destroy ecosystems and harm human populations alike. The international push to include ecocide as a crime under the Rome Statute of the ICC is a significant step toward holding corporations and governments accountable for large-scale environmental harm.

D. The Emergence of Blue Crimes: Environmental Harm at Sea

The concept of "blue crimes" has recently gained prominence in the realm of international criminal law, reflecting an urgent need to address unlawful activities committed at sea that have far-reaching consequences for climate justice and human rights. Traditionally, the corpus of international criminal law has been primarily concerned with *hostis humani generis*[41] crimes, such as genocide, war crimes, and crimes against humanity. However, as environmental degradation intensifies and oceanic ecosystems face unprecedented threats, it has become imperative to broaden the scope of international criminal law to include offenses that directly impact marine environments and the global sea commons they constitute.

Blue crimes are understood as unlawful acts that result in significant harm to marine environments, thereby breaching international legal norms. These

---

[39] J. B. Ruhl, *Climate Change and the New Ecological Paradigm*, 46 ENVTL. L. 133 (2016).

[40] Paulose, GREEN CRIMES, *supra* note 12, at 45.

[41] *Hostis humani generis* is a Latin term that is used as a principle of international law and means "enemy of all mankind." It refers to individuals committing universally condemned crimes, like piracy or terrorism, subject to prosecution by any nation. See: *United States v. Smith*, 18 U.S. (5 Wheat.) 153, 162 (1820).

crimes encompass a spectrum of activities, including but not limited to IUU fishing, hunting of cetacean animals (dolphins and whales), marine pollution, human trafficking across international waters, piracy, and the nascent but increasingly salient concept of ecocide. The prosecution of such crimes presents unique challenges, largely due to their occurrence in areas beyond national jurisdiction—*terra nullius*—and the involvement of multiple actors whose actions have transboundary effects.[42] Given that the oceans comprise over 70% of the Earth's surface and play a vital role in regulating the global climate, sustaining biodiversity, and providing livelihoods, the degradation of these marine ecosystems through blue crimes has profound implications.[43] These implications extend beyond environmental harm to include violations of fundamental human rights, the destabilization of economic systems, and the exacerbation of global inequalities.

E. Ecocide and Blue Crimes: Legal Challenges and Opportunities

In recent scholarship, there has been a growing acknowledgment of the necessity for a more *comprehensive* and *holistic* approach to addressing blue crimes within the international legal framework. This necessitates not only the fortification of existing legal instruments but also the consideration of new legal paradigms that would encompass emerging crimes, such as ecocide—a term that denotes the extensive destruction of ecosystems, particularly marine environments. The inclusion of ecocide as a crime under international law would mark a significant development in holding individuals and entities accountable for environmental harm that threatens the ecological balance of the planet.

Integrating blue crimes into the *jus cogens* of international criminal law is essential for advancing climate justice. This integration underscores the *principle of non-discrimination*, especially in protecting vulnerable populations who bear the brunt of environmental degradation and ensuring accountability for those who perpetrate such harm. As the global community confronts escalating environmental crises, the expansion of international criminal law to address blue crimes represents a crucial step toward ensuring the long-term health of our planet and safeguarding the rights of future generations. The importance of such legal evolution has been emphasized in recent academic discourse.

---

42 David Freestone, *The Role of International Law in the Conservation of Marine Biodiversity*, 16 INT'L J. OF MARINE AND COASTAL LAW 439, 442 (2001).

43 Intergovernmental Panel on Climate Change, *Climate Change and Oceans: 2021 Report*, 2 (2021).

For legal scholars, exploring climate justice through the lens of ecocide as a blue crime is both challenging and worthwhile.

The emerging discourse on blue criminology introduced the concept of "blue crimes," focusing on crimes committed at sea and their far-reaching impacts on global ecosystems, human rights, and international justice. Among these blue crimes, ecocide, the extensive destruction of marine environments, stands out as a critical area of concern. As the world faces escalating environmental crises, the concept of ecocide has gained prominence, particularly in the context of climate justice. Ecocide, by its nature, intersects with various disciplines, including law, philosophy, environmental science, and human rights. Its classification as a blue crime within international criminal law is a recent development that underscores the urgency of addressing environmental harm on a global scale. The sea, as a vast and largely unregulated space, presents unique challenges for legal frameworks that seek to protect both human and non-human entities. Traditional international law has often fallen short in addressing the complexities of crimes that transcend national boundaries, particularly when it comes to environmental destruction at sea. This chapter aims to fill that gap.

The concept of ecocide, while gaining prominence, is not yet codified in binding international law, which complicates its application to "blue crimes" such as illegal fishing, marine pollution, and habitat destruction. Current frameworks, including the Rome Statute of the ICC and regional legal systems, provide limited avenues to address harm to marine ecosystems. However, domestic and regional cases from the United States and the EU, including decisions by the European Court of Human Rights (ECtHR), offer insights into the gaps and possibilities for recognizing ecocide.

In the U.S., cases like *United States v. Viking Resources*[44] demonstrate the enforcement of environmental laws concerning marine ecosystems. Viking Resources was penalized under the Clean Water Act for oil spills that caused significant damage to aquatic ecosystems. While effective within national jurisdictions, these statutes lack the capacity to classify such acts as international crimes akin to ecocide.

In the EU, *European Commission v. Spain*[45] exemplifies how regional law addresses marine degradation. The European Court of Justice (ECJ) found Spain in violation of EU environmental directives, specifically Directive

---

[44] *United States v. Viking Resources* 607 F. Supp. 2d 808 (E.D. Mich. 2009).

[45] *European Commission v. Spain* (Case C-223/12, 2014).

2008/56/EC on marine strategy,[46] for failing to prevent industrial pollution affecting marine waters. Similarly, under the European Convention on Human Rights (ECHR), the case of *Tătar v. Romania*[47] highlighted state responsibility for environmental harm affecting human health, which could be extended to marine harm where ecosystems directly support livelihoods.

Despite these precedents, none explicitly criminalize marine destruction as ecocide. Existing provisions under the UNCLOS address state responsibilities but lack punitive measures for individuals or entities committing severe marine ecosystem damage. To fill these gaps, the development of ecocide laws must explicitly include marine-specific provisions, drawing from such precedents to establish accountability and deterrence mechanisms under international and regional legal frameworks.

F. Advancing Climate Justice through Legal Reform

Climate justice, which seeks to address the ethical and legal dimensions of climate change, provides a crucial lens through which to examine ecocide as a blue crime. The concept of climate justice emphasizes the need to protect vulnerable populations who are disproportionately affected by environmental degradation and climate change. These populations often lack the resources and political power to seek redress for the harms they suffer, making the incorporation of climate justice into international criminal law not only necessary but urgent.

The framing of ecocide within blue criminology highlights the importance of recognizing environmental harm as a serious violation of international law. This chapter argues that the current legal frameworks must evolve to incorporate ecocide as an international crime, reflecting the interconnectedness of human rights, environmental protection, and global justice. By doing so, the international community can better address the complex and multifaceted challenges posed by environmental crimes at sea, ensuring that justice is not only served for the victims of these crimes but also for the environment itself.

Blue crimes refer to criminal offenses that specifically target marine ecosystems, such as illegal fishing, ocean pollution, and the destruction of coral reefs. Traditionally, these crimes have been framed in utilitarian terms, focusing on the economic or environmental damage to humans. However, from a Rights of

---

[46] Directive 2008/56 of the European Parliament and of the Council of 17 June 2008, establishing a framework for community action in the field of marine environmental policy, 2008 O.J. (L 164) 19 (EC).

[47] *Tătar v. Romania* (App. No. 67021/01, 2009).

Nature and climate justice perspective, blue crimes also represent a violation of the intrinsic rights of marine ecosystems themselves.

The maxim *sic utere tuo ut alienum non laedas* (use your property in such a way that it does not harm others) applies not only to interactions between humans but can also be extended to interactions with nature. Just as human actions should not harm other individuals, human use of the oceans must not infringe upon the rights of marine ecosystems. This legal reasoning offers a compelling argument for prosecuting blue crimes as violations of the personhood of marine environments. For example, recognizing the Great Barrier Reef as a legal entity would allow for legal action against industries or states that contribute to its degradation, holding them liable not only for economic damage but for violations of the reef's right to exist and thrive.

From a climate justice perspective, the rights of nature represent a profound shift in legal and moral philosophy, recognizing natural entities as subjects of law with juridical standing—locus standi—to have their interests represented and protected. This legal recognition operates within a framework of ecocentrism, where the focus is not on human benefit but on the intrinsic value of nature. This departure from traditional anthropocentric legal models parallels the emerging field of environmental constitutionalism, where nature itself is granted constitutional rights, as seen in the legal frameworks of Ecuador and Bolivia.

In the context of climate justice, this legal transformation is essential because it addresses the disproportionate impacts of environmental destruction on marginalized communities, particularly indigenous peoples and those in the Global South. The maxim *ubi jus ibi remedium* (where there is a right, there is a remedy) underscores that by recognizing nature's rights, legal systems are obligated to provide remedies when those rights are violated, thus reinforcing the pursuit of equity and sustainability in international law.

The legal maxim *salus populi suprema lex esto* (the welfare of the people shall be the supreme law) also applies here but must be reinterpreted in a climate justice context as *salus terrae suprema lex esto* (the welfare of the Earth shall be the supreme law). This maxim reflects the understanding that human welfare is intrinsically tied to the health of ecosystems, and any legal system that seeks to protect human rights must also protect the rights of the environment.

The rights of nature also have significant implications for international law, particularly in relation to *erga omnes* obligations—duties owed to the international community. Environmental protection, like the prevention of genocide or the prohibition of slavery, is increasingly recognized as an *erga omnes* obligation. The climate justice movement pushes for *jus cogens* norms (peremptory norms from which no derogation is permitted) to be extended to include the protection of ecosystems, recognizing that environmental harm, such as the destruction of rainforests or the acidification of oceans, affects all of humanity.

In this light, the recognition of the rights of nature could be viewed as a *jus cogens* norm, implying that states and non-state actors have a non-derogable duty to protect the Earth's ecosystems, even in the absence of specific treaties or national legislation. This principle could empower international bodies like the ICJ to adjudicate cases where the rights of nature are violated, potentially establishing customary international law in this domain.

Ecocide is defined as the large-scale destruction of ecosystems, resulting in significant harm to the environment and the life it supports.[48] The term *ecocide* is derived from the Greek word *oikos,* meaning *home* or *habitat,* and the Latin word *caedere,* meaning *to kill* or *to destroy.* Thus, ecocide means etymologically: *the killing of our home or destruction of our natural habitat on a large scale.* To grasp its importance, impact, and possible function in international law, it's helpful to see through linguistics how *ecocide* etymologically parallels *genocide.* The term ecocide essentially reflects the term genocide, which is a deeply *anthropocentric* crime against humanity, and propagates it from an *ecocentric* lens, giving rise to the term ecocide which aspires to be a crime against humanity and nature.[49]

Ecocide developed further as a concept in response to the climate crisis and escalating environmental degradation caused by human activities, particularly industrialization and modern warfare, during the twentieth century. It gained traction as environmentalists and climate justice scholars sought to address the devastating impacts of large-scale environmental destruction on ecosystems and biodiversity. Initially, ecocide primarily referred to the deliberate destruction of ecosystems during wartime, as seen in cases such as the use of Agent Orange in Vietnam. Over time, the concept has evolved to encompass a broader range of human-induced environmental harms occurring in peacetime. Today, ecocide encompasses not only acts of environmental destruction committed during armed conflict but also those occurring in non-conflict situations, such as industrial pollution, deforestation, and habitat destruction. Ecocide is essentially the activation of a law to protect the Earth from humans.

The recognition of ecocide as a serious environmental crime has gained momentum in recent years, driven by the urgent need to address the global climate emergency. Climate justice advocates argue that criminalizing ecocide at the international level would hold individuals and corporations accountable for

---

[48] Zoi Aliozi, *The Definition of Ecocide,* in DICTIONARY OF CLIMATE LAW/CLIMATE JUSTICE (2024), available at: https://www.direitointernacionalsemfronteiras.com.
[49] *Id.*

their role in causing harm to the environment. This includes not only direct perpetrators but also those who finance, enable, or benefit from ecocidal activities. Efforts to establish ecocide as an international crime aim to provide a legal framework for prosecuting and deterring actions that result in the destruction of ecosystems.

Ecocide, intersecting with legal doctrines like environmental law, human rights, and criminal law, represents a severe form of environmental crime. It aligns with climate justice and the rights of nature, aiming to address the disproportionate harm on marginalized communities and ecosystems' intrinsic value. Despite gaining recognition in some countries and efforts toward international acknowledgment, its legal standing remains weak. Beyond legality, ecocide reflects a philosophical concern, as human-driven destruction of nature can lead to self-harm and biodiversity loss. Discussions often touch on environmental violence and slow violence, describing gradual harm to ecosystems and communities. Prosecuting ecocide faces challenges in establishing the *mens rea*, as it often involves recklessness or negligence. Ecocide's legal and philosophical dimensions underscore the interconnectedness of human actions, environmental damage, and the consequences for individuals and the planet.

While ecocide is not yet recognized as an international crime under existing treaties or conventions, there have been significant developments at the national and international levels to address environmental destruction. Some countries have enacted domestic legislation criminalizing ecocide, imposing penalties for significant environmental harm. Additionally, efforts are underway to include ecocide within the jurisdiction of the ICC, alongside genocide, war crimes, and crimes against humanity. Proposals to amend the Rome Statute of the ICC to include ecocide as a punishable offense are being actively discussed, reflecting the growing recognition of the need to hold individuals and entities accountable for ecocidal activities.

International law is not explicitly addressing ecocide; however, it is increasingly being considered within the framework of international environmental law and criminal law.

In 2020, the Stop Ecocide Foundation formed an Independent Expert Panel for the Legal Definition of Ecocide. The proposed legal definition of ecocide states that:

> For the purpose of this Statute, 'ecocide' means unlawful or wanton acts committed with knowledge that there is a substantial likelihood of

> severe and either widespread or long-term damage to the environment being caused by those acts.[50]

The proposed legal definition of ecocide, as articulated by the Independent Expert Panel for the Legal Definition of Ecocide in late 2020, includes actions that cause "severe and either widespread or long-term damage to the environment." While this definition is broadly applicable to environmental harm, it does not explicitly address the ocean or marine ecosystems. The inclusion of "the environment" could theoretically encompass marine environments if they experience significant damage, but this remains ambiguous without explicit language in the definition referring to oceans or marine life.

This definitional gap suggests that a further debate may be necessary. While ecocide law is framed to target significant and lasting environmental harm, the current definition doesn't clarify whether marine ecosystems fall within its scope. The definition of "environment" could be interpreted as including both terrestrial and marine environments, but the lack of specificity around "blue crimes" such as marine pollution, overfishing, or coral reef destruction leaves some uncertainty.[51]

Ecocide, often regarded as a form of "green crime," presents significant challenges in legal prosecution due to its complex nature. Unlike conventional crimes, where the guilty act (*actus reus*) and guilty mind (*mens rea*) are usually more straightforward to establish, ecocide involves environmental harm that is gradual, often subtle, and difficult to trace to a single moment or individual.[52] This complexity makes it difficult to pinpoint the specific actions and intentions that result in large-scale environmental destruction.

G. Actus Reus and Mens Rea

One of the central challenges in prosecuting ecocide is determining the *actus reus*—the physical act that constitutes the crime. Environmental destruction, particularly that leading to ecocide, is frequently a slow process that occurs over years or even decades. For instance, activities like deforestation, industrial pollution, and large-scale mining may cause widespread environmental damage that unfolds over time, making it difficult to establish a direct connection

---

[50] Stop Ecocide Foundation, *Legal Definition of Ecocide*, 2021, available at: https://www.stopecocide.earth/legal-definition-of-ecocide.

[51] United Nations Environment Programme, *The Emissions Gap Report 2020* 12 (2020), available at https://www.unep.org/emissions-gap-report.

[52] WILLIAM SCHABAS, THE INTERNATIONAL CRIMINAL COURT: A COMMENTARY 320 (2010).

between specific actions and their consequences.[53] This gradual harm complicates the legal process, as there is no singular moment in which the destruction can be clearly attributed to a specific act. Take, for example, the case of large-scale deforestation, where the damage to biodiversity and carbon sequestration may not be immediately apparent but becomes catastrophic over time. Similarly, industrial pollution often does not manifest its full harm immediately, complicating efforts to hold perpetrators accountable for long-term environmental degradation. The challenge, therefore, lies in identifying and proving the direct cause of such destruction, a task that traditional legal frameworks struggle to address.[54]

Establishing a *mens rea*, or the guilty mind, is another hurdle in ecocide cases. Unlike other crimes, where the intent to cause harm is often clear, ecocide does not always involve direct malicious intent. Many of the actors involved in activities that lead to environmental destruction—such as corporations or governmental bodies—do not necessarily set out to cause harm but are driven by economic or developmental interests. In some cases, the individuals or organizations responsible may not have explicitly sought to damage the environment but rather prioritized economic gain or growth at the expense of ecological sustainability. This raises important questions about whether negligence or recklessness should be sufficient to establish criminal liability in ecocide cases. While it is difficult to prove intent in environmental cases, some have argued that individuals and corporations should be held accountable for the foreseeable consequences of their actions, even if they did not intend for the harm to occur.

The challenge lies in proving the mental state behind environmental harm, which may not always be obvious or malicious, but which still results in significant, often irreversible damage.

The intersection of *actus reus, mens rea,* and the concept of "slow violence" presents significant hurdles for legal systems attempting to address ecocide. The gradual nature of environmental destruction means that the full extent of the damage may not become apparent for years or even decades. As a result, those responsible for ecocide may avoid legal repercussions simply because the harm was not immediately recognizable. Traditional legal frameworks are often ill-equipped to address such slow-moving, yet devastating, forms of violence. Furthermore, current laws lack the foresight and flexibility needed to adequately address the complexities of modern environmental issues. While

---

53 KAI AMBOS, TREATISE ON INTERNATIONAL CRIMINAL LAW: VOLUME I – FOUNDATIONS AND GENERAL PART 175–78 (2013).

54 International Criminal Court, *Policy Paper on Case Selection and Prioritisation* 12 (2016), available at: https://www.icc-cpi.int.

international law has made some strides in holding individuals accountable for crimes such as war crimes or genocide, it remains less developed when it comes to environmental crimes. As a result, ecocide—especially in the form of large-scale, long-term environmental degradation—often goes unpunished, perpetuating environmental destruction and reinforcing patterns of injustice.[55]

In the face of these challenges, it becomes evident that traditional legal approaches are insufficient to tackle the unique nature of ecocide. There is a need for new frameworks that account for both the gradual nature of environmental harm and the complex dynamics of responsibility in cases of large-scale ecological destruction. Developing effective legal mechanisms to address ecocide, and to hold perpetrators accountable, is essential to preventing further harm to the environment.

H. Recent Legal Developments on Ecocide

In recent years, there has been a growing push for legal recognition of ecocide as a crime under both national and international law. Several countries and regions have made significant strides in incorporating ecocide into their legal frameworks, signaling a shift towards greater accountability for environmental crimes. Belgium made a notable move in February 2024 when its Federal Parliament introduced ecocide as a criminal offense as part of the reform of the Belgian criminal code. The new law, which applies to both individuals in positions of decision-making power and corporations, aims to address severe environmental degradation, including oil spills and other major incidents. Under the law, individuals could face up to 20 years in prison, while corporations could face fines of up to 1.6 million euros. France also took a significant step with its "Climate & Resilience Act," passed in 2021.[56] The Act introduced ecocide as a "délit," or offense, under national law, which could result in up to 10 years of imprisonment for actions causing serious and lasting harm to the environment. Additionally, the French government is mandated to report to parliament on its efforts to recognize ecocide as an international crime. At the European Union level, the European Council adopted a new environmental crime directive that criminalizes offenses comparable to ecocide. This marks a significant step towards legal recognition of ecocide within EU law. The directive has gained momentum following support from the European Parliament in March 2023, and member states are now required to align their national laws with this new framework within the next two years. Several countries outside of Europe have also taken action. In Ecuador, the Penal Code includes provisions for crimes against the environment, referred to as "crimes

[55] Cormac McCarthy, *Slow Violence and the Environmental Future* 134 (2021).
[56] Directive 2008/56, *supra* note 46.

against nature or Pacha Mama," reflecting the nation's deep connection to environmental protection.[57] Similarly, Vietnam has incorporated ecocide into its Penal Code, specifically under Article 278, which criminalizes the destruction of the natural environment as a crime against humanity, whether committed during peace or war. Other countries, including Uzbekistan, Russia, Kazakhstan, Kyrgyzstan, and Tajikistan, have introduced laws that punish actions capable of causing ecological catastrophes, such as mass destruction of flora or fauna and contamination of air or water resources. These nations have enacted penalties ranging from prison terms of 10 to 20 years, further signaling a growing global commitment to tackling environmental harm through criminal law. Chile recently joined the ranks with the introduction of Law 21.595 in 2023, which amended the Penal Code to include provisions against "attacks against the environment." This new law incorporates elements of the legal definition of ecocide as formulated by the Independent Expert Panel convened by the Stop Ecocide Foundation.

The growing body of legal reforms recognizing ecocide as a crime marks a significant shift in global environmental governance. However, the challenges of establishing clear definitions, pinpointing the guilty act, and proving intent in ecocide cases remain substantial. As national and international legal systems continue to evolve, it is essential that they develop the capacity to address the complexities of ecocide, including the gradual and often invisible nature of environmental harm. The recognition of ecocide as a criminal offense is an important step toward holding individuals and corporations accountable for environmental degradation, but further work is needed to ensure that the law adequately addresses the full scope of ecological destruction, including marine and oceanic environments.

II. Ecocide and the Need for Legal Innovation

Through continued legal innovation and global cooperation, ecocide can become a meaningful tool in the fight against environmental degradation, providing a deterrent to those who prioritize economic gain over the preservation of the planet's ecosystems. By providing stronger legal protections for marine environments, we can advance both environmental justice and climate

---

[57] *Delitos contra el ambiente y la naturaleza o Pacha Mama* ["Crimes against the environment and nature or Pacha Mama (Mother Earth)"], Código Orgánico Integral Penal [Organic Comprehensive Penal Code], Ministerio de Justicia, Derechos Humanos y Cultos [Ministry of Justice, Human Rights, and Worship], Serie Justicia y Derechos Humanos, Neoconstitucionalismo y Sociedad [Justice and Human Rights Series, Neoconstitutionalism and Society] (Ecuador).

justice, ensuring that the oceans—our planet's lifeblood—are safeguarded for future generations.

As the world grapples with the mounting pressures of environmental degradation, the legal recognition of "blue crimes"—criminal acts that harm oceans and marine life—has emerged as an increasingly urgent area of focus in international criminal law and global justice. The protection of oceans and marine ecosystems is no longer just an environmental issue but a matter of global security, economic stability, and human rights. With oceans covering over 70% of the Earth's surface and playing a critical role in regulating climate, the importance of safeguarding marine life and preventing environmental harm in the seas cannot be overstated. Blue crimes, including overfishing, marine pollution, habitat destruction, and illegal dumping, not only threaten biodiversity but also jeopardize the livelihoods of millions of people who depend on the oceans for food and income. As such, the legal framework for addressing these crimes must evolve to reflect their scale and significance.

Ecocide, as a crime of environmental destruction, provides an important legal tool to hold perpetrators accountable for harmful acts that lead to widespread and long-term damage. However, the current legal definition of ecocide and its application in international criminal law often overlooks the specific threats faced by marine ecosystems. While there is growing recognition of the need to address environmental harm more broadly, marine environments are not sufficiently protected under current ecocide frameworks, leaving a significant gap in legal accountability.

The inclusion of ecocide within international criminal law and climate justice should specifically incorporate the protection of oceans and marine life. The term "environment" in the definition of ecocide, though comprehensive, remains ambiguous, making it unclear whether marine ecosystems are adequately covered. For ecocide to serve its purpose in safeguarding our planet's ecological integrity, it must explicitly account for the damage caused to oceans, as well as the critical role that marine ecosystems play in climate regulation, biodiversity, and the survival of vulnerable communities. [58]

Thus, to truly protect the Earth's ecosystems and promote climate justice, it is essential to broaden the scope of ecocide to include blue crimes. This expansion would align international criminal law with the urgent need to address marine environmental destruction and foster a more just and sustainable future. The time has come for legal systems to adapt to the realities of the climate crisis and include robust protections for our oceans and marine life in

---

[58] United Nations Framework Convention on Climate Change (UNFCCC), May 9, 1992, 1771 U.N.T.S. 107, art. 3, ¶1.

the fight against environmental harm. Only through comprehensive legal frameworks can we ensure accountability and preservation for the oceans, their ecosystems, and the communities that depend on them.

The legal protection of marine life, including iconic species such as dolphins and whales, has long been a focus of environmental law. International agreements such as the International Whaling Commission and the Convention on International Trade in Endangered Species have played key roles in curbing the hunting and exploitation of these species. However, the enforcement of such protections remains difficult, with significant gaps in addressing the broader range of marine threats, including habitat destruction, pollution, and overfishing.

In the case of *Whaling in the Antarctic (Australia v. Japan: New Zealand Intervening)*, the ICJ ruled in 2014 that Japan's whaling program, conducted under the guise of scientific research, violated the International Convention for the Regulation of Whaling.[59] The Court found that Japan had failed to demonstrate that its whaling activities were for genuine scientific purposes, highlighting the importance of international law in the protection of marine species such as whales. This case underscores the role of international law in curbing practices that directly harm marine life and ecosystems, aligning with the broader goal of preventing ecocide.

Further supporting the notion of environmental protection under international law, the UNCLOS provides a robust framework for protecting marine environments. The convention mandates the protection and preservation of marine biodiversity, requiring states to take necessary measures to prevent, reduce, and control pollution in marine areas under their jurisdiction (UNCLOS Articles 192-196). The expansion of ecocide law to encompass marine ecosystems could strengthen these protections, making it a criminal offense to engage in activities that lead to large-scale harm in the oceans.

In recent years, the International Tribunal for the Law of the Sea has addressed several cases concerning marine pollution, such as in the case of The M/V "Saiga" (No. 2) Case (*Saint Vincent and the Grenadines v. Guinea*), where the tribunal ruled that Guinea violated the rights of Saint Vincent and the Grenadines by arresting the crew of a tanker. This case emphasized the legal responsibility of states to protect the marine environment, aligning with the principles that should guide the prosecution of ecocide.

As the urgency to address climate change intensifies; and given that the climate change, climate justice is relevant to is always linked to anthropogenic harms and hence to legal responsibility, while the need for legal accountability is

---

[59] *Whaling in the Antarctic* (Australia v. Japan: New Zealand Intervening), Judgment, 2014 I.C.J. 226 (Mar. 31).

in our times clear and necessary; new legal frameworks are needed to hold perpetrators accountable for environmental harm. One such framework is the codification of ecocide as a "blue crime" within the realm of climate justice. Ecocide refers to the mass destruction of ecosystems, and its recognition as a criminal act has been proposed to enforce accountability on both national and international levels. As a blue crime, ecocide would fall under the category of environmental crimes affecting oceanic and marine ecosystems, aligning with the broader goal of protecting global commons and addressing climate justice. Acknowledging ecocide as a blue crime is crucial for protecting oceanic environments, ensuring accountability, and fostering sustainable practices to maintain the health and vitality of the world's oceans. One of the key reasons for advocating the codification of ecocide as a crime is the growing recognition that environmental harm disproportionately affects vulnerable communities, particularly those in developing countries and Indigenous populations. Climate change, deforestation, ocean pollution, and resource extraction often devastate ecosystems that these communities rely on for their livelihoods, exacerbating poverty and displacing populations. In this context, the codification of ecocide could serve as a powerful tool for climate justice by holding corporations, governments, and individuals accountable for their role in environmental degradation. The Rome Statute, which established the ICC, recognizes genocide, crimes against humanity, war crimes, and aggression, but ecocide is notably absent. Advocates have called for amending the Rome Statute to include ecocide as a crime, similar to how environmental destruction was addressed in the prosecution of war crimes in *Prosecutor v. Tadić* at the ICTY.[60]

A. The Role of Ecocide in Climate Justice

The legal recognition of ecocide would also address a critical gap in the current international legal system, which largely focuses on individual human rights rather than the rights of nature or the environment. While human rights law has evolved to include protections for those affected by environmental harm, there is still no comprehensive legal framework that holds perpetrators accountable for the destruction of ecosystems themselves. Ecocide, if recognized as an international crime, could fill this gap by prioritizing the protection of ecosystems and the global commons over short-term economic interests. Given the critical role that oceans play in regulating the global climate, protecting marine ecosystems is essential for achieving climate justice. Oceans act as carbon sinks, absorbing around 25% of the CO_2 emissions produced by human

[60] *Prosecutor v. Tadić*, Case No. IT-94-1, Judgment, ¶¶ 587-93 (Int'l Crim. Trib. for the Former Yugoslavia July 15, 1999).

activities.[61] They also support marine biodiversity, which is essential for maintaining the health of ecosystems and the services they provide. However, the continued degradation of marine environments, through activities like illegal fishing, plastic pollution, and oil spills, threatens the ability of oceans to perform these vital functions.

The integration of ecocide as a blue crime would strengthen the legal framework for protecting marine ecosystems by recognizing the large-scale destruction of oceanic environments as a criminal act. This would not only deter environmental harm but also provide a legal mechanism for holding those responsible for marine destruction accountable. For instance, oil spills caused by negligent or reckless actions could be prosecuted as ecocide, ensuring that corporations are held liable for the damage they cause to marine ecosystems.[62] Furthermore, recognizing ecocide as a blue crime would elevate the importance of protecting oceans in the broader conversation about climate justice, highlighting the interconnectedness of terrestrial and marine ecosystems in mitigating climate change.

Climate justice is a framework that emphasizes the intersection of human rights, environmental protection, and social equity in addressing climate change. It seeks to address the disproportionate impacts of climate change on marginalized communities and to promote the fair distribution of the benefits and burdens associated with environmental protection. In this context, the codification of ecocide as a blue crime aligns with the principles of climate justice by holding those who cause large-scale environmental harm accountable and by prioritizing the protection of ecosystems for the benefit of all.[63]

The recognition of ecocide as a crime would provide a legal basis for prosecuting individuals and entities that contribute to environmental destruction, ensuring that the costs of environmental harm are not borne solely by vulnerable communities. By criminalizing ecocide, the law would shift the focus from compensating victims after the fact to preventing environmental harm in the first place. This preventive approach is essential for achieving climate justice, as it recognizes the intrinsic value of ecosystems and the need to protect them for future generations.

---

[61] IPCC, 2019: Summary for Policymakers, in *IPCC Special Report on the Ocean and Cryosphere in a Changing Climate* 3, 3-35 (H.-O. Pörtner et al. eds., Cambridge University Press 2019), https://doi.org/10.1017/9781009157964.001.

[62] *Prosecutor v. Blagojević*, Case No. IT-02-60, ICTY Trial Judgment, ¶ 832 (Jan. 17, 2005).

[63] Sumudu Atapattu, *Climate Justice and Human Rights: International and Domestic Perspectives* 152 (2021).

Moreover, the codification of ecocide as a blue crime could help bridge the gap between environmental law and human rights law by recognizing that the destruction of ecosystems undermines the fundamental rights to life, health, and a clean environment.[64] Many international human rights bodies, including the United Nations, have acknowledged the link between environmental degradation and human rights violations, but there is still a lack of legal accountability for those responsible for environmental harm. Ecocide could serve as a means to hold corporations, governments, and individuals accountable for actions that not only harm the environment but also violate the rights of affected communities.

While the case for codifying ecocide as a blue crime is compelling, there are several challenges that must be addressed to make this legal framework effective. One of the primary challenges is the lack of consensus among nations on the definition of ecocide and the thresholds for criminal liability. Some countries may resist the recognition of ecocide as a crime due to concerns about the impact on their economic interests, particularly in industries like oil and gas, mining, and industrial agriculture. Additionally, there may be challenges in enforcing ecocide laws, particularly in countries with weak legal systems or limited resources for environmental protection.[65]

However, the potential benefits of codifying ecocide as a blue crime far outweigh these challenges. By recognizing ecocide as a criminal act, the international community would send a strong message that environmental destruction will no longer be tolerated. This could lead to greater accountability for environmental crimes, increased investment in sustainable practices, and stronger protections for vulnerable communities and ecosystems. Furthermore, the codification of ecocide would contribute to the broader goal of achieving climate justice by addressing the root causes of environmental harm and promoting a more equitable distribution of environmental benefits and burdens.[66]

Conclusion: The Growing Importance of Blue Crimes in International Criminal Law and Climate Justice

As the world grapples with the mounting pressures of environmental degradation, the legal recognition of "blue crimes"—criminal acts that harm oceans and

---

[64] UNHRC Res. 48/13, The Human Right to a Clean, Healthy, and Sustainable Environment, U.N. Doc. A/HRC/RES/48/13 (Oct. 18, 2021).

[65] Meinhard Doelle & Sara L. Seck, *International Climate Law and Human Rights: What Are the Prospects for Effective Cooperation?*, 12(1) MCGILL INT'L J. SUST. DEV. L. & POL'Y 53 (2016).

[66] International Criminal Court, Assembly of States Parties, *Report of the Independent Expert Panel for the Legal Definition of Ecocide*, U.N. Doc. ICC-ASP/19/INF.3 (Dec. 2020).

marine life—has emerged as an increasingly urgent area of focus in international criminal law and global justice. The protection of oceans and marine ecosystems is no longer just an environmental issue but a matter of global security, economic stability, and human rights. With oceans covering over 70% of the Earth's surface and playing a critical role in regulating climate, the importance of safeguarding marine life and preventing environmental harm in the seas cannot be overstated.[67] Blue crimes, including overfishing, marine pollution, habitat destruction, and illegal dumping, not only threaten biodiversity but also jeopardize the livelihoods of millions of people who depend on the oceans for food and income. As such, the legal framework for addressing these crimes must evolve to reflect their scale and significance.

Ecocide, as a crime of environmental destruction, provides an important legal tool to hold perpetrators accountable for harmful acts that lead to widespread and long-term damage. However, the current legal definition of ecocide and its possible application in international criminal law often overlooks the specific threats faced by marine ecosystems. While there is growing recognition of the need to address environmental harm more broadly, marine environments are not sufficiently protected under current ecocide frameworks, leaving a significant gap in legal accountability.

In modern legal systems, individuals have often avoided criminal responsibility for causing significant environmental harm, like major spills or deforestation. Ecocide laws aim to prevent individuals from hiding behind corporate or governmental immunity and extraterritorial issues. This legal shift puts protecting natural ecosystems, vital for human survival and prosperity, at the forefront. Recognizing ecocide as a crime signals a deep understanding of the essential link between human well-being and ecological health, urging immediate action to safeguard nature for future generations. Embracing ecocide legislation marks a crucial step towards global environmental fairness and long-term sustainability. Addressing the economic complexities of ecocide as an international crime is.vital, especially concerning potential impacts on global employment. In our capitalist profit-driven economy, where financial gains often override environmental concerns, criminalizing ecocide faces significant challenges. Industries reliant on natural resources, like fossil fuels, agriculture, and fisheries, resist such measures, fearing operational and financial consequences. These industries actively lobby against climate justice, impeding

---

67 IPCC, 2019: Summary for Policymakers, in *IPCC Special Report on the Ocean and Cryosphere in a Changing Climate* 3, 3-35 (H.-O. Pörtner et al. eds., Cambridge University Press 2019), https://doi.org/10.1017/9781009157964.001.

progress. Balancing environmental preservation with economic interests requires dialogue and collaboration among stakeholders to find sustainable solutions.

An obstacle hindering the recognition and adoption of ecocide as a punishable offense within international legal frameworks is the prevailing anthropocentric orientation of these systems. Anthropocentrism, deeply entrenched within legal doctrines and practices, prioritizes human interests over the intrinsic value of non-human entities, including ecosystems and biodiversity. This human-centered perspective often limits the acknowledgment of environmental harms and the significance of ecocide within legal discourse. International law, historically rooted in anthropocentric principles, tends to prioritize human concerns and economic interests, thereby marginalizing environmental considerations. Legal structures shaped by anthropocentrism may struggle to fully recognize the value and rights of nature, viewing environmental protection primarily through the lens of human utility and exploitation.

In contrast to anthropocentrism, ecocentrism represents a paradigm shift towards recognizing the intrinsic value and rights of the natural world independent of human interests. Ecocentric perspectives emphasize the interconnectedness and interdependence of all life forms, advocating for the protection and preservation of ecosystems for their inherent worth. Embracing ecocentrism within legal frameworks could provide a foundation for prioritizing environmental conservation and addressing ecocide as a fundamental offense against the integrity of the Earth's ecosystems. In essence, activating ecocide as a law to protect our home planet earth will serve both anthropocentric and ecocentric perspectives.

The codification of ecocide as a blue crime represents a significant step forward in advancing climate justice and protecting the planet's ecosystems. By holding individuals and entities accountable for the large-scale destruction of marine and terrestrial environments, this legal framework would contribute to the prevention of environmental harm, the promotion of sustainability, and the protection of vulnerable communities. While challenges remain in defining and enforcing ecocide as a crime, the potential benefits of achieving climate justice make it a worthy endeavor for legal scholars, policymakers, and environmental advocates. The recognition of ecocide as a blue crime would not only strengthen environmental law but also serve as a powerful tool for protecting the global commons in the face of the climate crisis.

Ecocide, the large-scale destruction of ecosystems, represents a significant threat to global environmental health and human well-being. As climate change accelerates the degradation of natural environments, the need to address ecocide through robust legal frameworks has become increasingly apparent. Within the context of international law and blue criminology, codifying ecocide as a "blue crime"—a crime that impacts marine and aquatic ecosystems—

emerges as a crucial element in advancing climate justice. This section explores how integrating ecocide as a blue crime into international legal frameworks can enhance climate justice, drawing on existing legal instruments, case law, and the principles of blue criminology.

Ecocide refers to the extensive and systematic destruction of ecosystems, causing severe and irreversible harm. As a concept, ecocide aligns with the principles of climate justice by addressing the disproportionate impacts of environmental degradation on vulnerable communities. Climate justice aims to rectify these inequalities by integrating human rights with environmental protection and holding perpetrators accountable for the harm they inflict.[68]

Recognizing ecocide as a blue crime involves framing it as a significant threat to marine and coastal environments, which are critical to both global biodiversity and human livelihoods.

In the context of international law, climate justice seeks to balance the scales between those who suffer the most from environmental harm and those who contribute significantly to it. By incorporating ecocide into legal frameworks as a blue crime, the international community can address both the environmental and social dimensions of climate change.[69]

International criminal law has traditionally focused on crimes against humanity, war crimes, and genocide. However, incorporating ecocide as a crime under international law would address significant gaps in accountability for large-scale environmental harm. Proposals to include ecocide in the Rome Statute highlight the need to address environmental destruction with the same gravity as other international crimes.[70] Recognizing ecocide as a blue crime would specifically target crimes affecting marine environments, thereby aligning with the principles of international criminal law. The current definition of ecocide primarily focuses on land-based environmental crimes, and this is one of the main challenges when it comes to its application to oceanic and marine environments. Ecocide, as it is understood today, generally refers to large-scale environmental destruction that can cause widespread harm to ecosystems, often with a focus on terrestrial ecosystems such as forests, rivers, and lands. While the scope of ecocide, as articulated by some legal scholars and advocates, is broad enough to encompass the destruction of the

---

68 *Tadić*, Case No. IT-94-1, ¶¶ 587-93.

69 See, e.g., *Climate Justice: A Guide to the Law and Policy of Climate Change* (Peter M. Martin ed., 2020).

70 Report of the Independent Expert Panel for the Legal Definition of Ecocide, *supra* note 63.

environment, the legal frameworks currently in place have been more centered on land-based harm rather than marine ecosystems.

The current definition of ecocide struggles to include oceans for several reasons. Ecocide, as a crime, as explained above, has typically focused on land-based activities like deforestation, mining, and pollution that harm terrestrial ecosystems. Although oceanic pollution, such as oil spills and plastic waste, may be considered environmental harm, they are not always directly categorized as ecocide. The definition of ecocide is often vague when it comes to marine ecosystems, leaving uncertainty about whether damage to oceanic environments like coral reefs or whale populations fits the criteria. Additionally, while international frameworks like the UNCLOS regulate marine biodiversity and pollution, they do not specifically recognize ecocide related to oceans. Another challenge is jurisdiction, as it can be difficult to pinpoint responsibility for marine destruction, especially in international waters. Despite this, there is increasing advocacy for including marine ecosystems within the scope of ecocide, recognizing the growing threat posed by ocean pollution, overfishing, and habitat destruction. Legal scholars suggest expanding ecocide to specifically address these marine issues, given their importance to global climate systems and biodiversity.

Marine life, including endangered species like dolphins and whales, plays a vital role in maintaining the health of global ecosystems. Their protection should be central to any international legal efforts to safeguard the environment.

To make ecocide a truly global tool for environmental justice, it is necessary to expand its definition to explicitly cover marine ecosystems. Oceans play a fundamental role in regulating the Earth's climate, supporting biodiversity, and sustaining human life, yet they remain vulnerable to exploitation and degradation. Legal frameworks must evolve to hold accountable those responsible for destroying marine life and habitats, making ecocide a broader crime that includes blue crimes. Through this extension, international criminal law can more effectively protect the oceans and marine life, contributing to global climate justice and safeguarding our planet's biodiversity for future generations.

The integration of ecocide as a blue crime also intersects with human rights law. The UN Human Rights Council has recognized the right to a healthy environment as a fundamental human right, underscoring the link between environmental health and human rights.[71]

---

[71] Human Rights Council Res. 10/4, The Human Right to a Safe, Clean, Healthy, and Sustainable Environment, U.N. Doc. A/HRC/RES/10/4 (Mar. 26, 2009).

Incorporating ecocide into international law as a blue crime would enhance the protection of these rights by providing a mechanism for holding perpetrators accountable for environmental harm that impacts human health and well-being.

To advance climate justice, it is crucial to integrate ecocide as a blue crime into international legal frameworks. This would involve amending existing treaties and agreements, to explicitly address ecocide and its impacts on marine and coastal ecosystems. Strengthening these frameworks would enhance global efforts to protect the environment and ensure accountability for large-scale environmental harm. Establishing robust accountability mechanisms is essential for enforcing laws against ecocide. This includes creating international and national legal provisions for prosecuting ecocide, enhancing transparency in environmental impact assessments, and ensuring that those responsible for environmental harm are held accountable. Incorporating ecocide into the Rome Statute and developing specialized tribunals or mechanisms could further strengthen these efforts.

Legal precedents and case law play a critical role in advancing climate justice. By recognizing ecocide as a blue crime, international courts and tribunals can establish important legal standards for environmental protection and accountability. Ongoing efforts to address environmental harm through international jurisprudence will contribute to the development of a more comprehensive legal framework for climate justice. International law should support the rights of Indigenous and marginalized communities by recognizing their role in environmental stewardship and ensuring their participation in decision-making processes. This includes protecting their rights against environmental degradation and integrating their traditional knowledge into environmental governance.

Integrating ecocide as a blue crime into international law represents a significant advancement in climate justice and environmental protection. By addressing the large-scale destruction of marine and coastal ecosystems, this approach aligns with the principles of blue criminology and enhances accountability for environmental harm. Strengthening international legal frameworks, developing accountability mechanisms, and supporting vulnerable communities are essential steps in achieving a just and equitable response to the climate crisis. As the international community continues to address the challenges of climate change, recognizing ecocide as a blue crime will be a crucial element in advancing climate justice.

The recognition of ecocide as an international crime represents a profound evolution in environmental law, offering a powerful mechanism for addressing the escalating threats to planetary ecosystems. Defined as the extensive destruction of natural environments through human activities, ecocide not only devastates biodiversity but also exacerbates the global climate crisis. The term's etymology, *Home-Killing*, underscores the catastrophic impacts of such actions on humanity's shared home, drawing an ethical parallel to atrocities like genocide.

Ecocide aligns seamlessly with the principles of climate justice, which seeks to address the disproportionate burden of environmental harm on vulnerable communities and ecosystems. Climate justice goes beyond addressing the consequences of climate change; it also emphasizes holding accountable those who drive environmental degradation. Ecocide provides a crucial legal framework to combat these injustices by criminalizing severe and widespread environmental harm, particularly in contexts where vulnerable populations and ecosystems bear the brunt of exploitation and destruction. Recognizing ecocide as a crime strengthens the international community's commitment to both ecological preservation and the protection of marginalized communities disproportionately affected by environmental harm.

Moreover, the inclusion of ecocide within the framework of blue crimes addresses the unique vulnerabilities of marine and coastal ecosystems, which are critical for regulating the Earth's climate and sustaining biodiversity. Blue crimes—acts that threaten the health and sustainability of oceanic systems—represent a distinct and urgent category of international environmental harm. Oceans are integral to the global climate system, yet they face relentless threats from overfishing, pollution, seabed mining, and habitat destruction. By criminalizing ecocide as a blue crime, the international legal system acknowledges the vital importance of marine ecosystems and creates mechanisms to deter and punish large-scale environmental harms that disproportionately affect these critical areas.

The integration of ecocide into international law has been championed by organizations like the Stop Ecocide Foundation, which has proposed a robust definition: "unlawful or wanton acts committed with knowledge that there is a substantial likelihood of severe and either widespread or long-term damage to the environment." This definition not only captures the gravity of environmental destruction but also provides a clear standard for accountability. Such recognition would represent a transformative shift in international law by treating environmental degradation not merely as a policy failure but as a serious criminal act.

Nevertheless, significant challenges remain in determining the most effective legal mechanism to address ecocide and advance climate justice. While the ICC has been proposed as a forum for prosecuting ecocide, doubts persist about its capacity and willingness to prioritize environmental crimes within its mandate.

Recognizing ecocide as an international crime, particularly within the scope of blue crimes, underscores the moral, ethical, and legal imperatives of protecting the global commons. Criminalizing ecocide not only deters future harm but also affirms a broader commitment to climate justice, ensuring that environmental degradation is addressed with the urgency and seriousness it demands. By holding individuals, corporations, and states accountable for severe environmental destruction, the international community can bridge gaps in environmental governance and strengthen the resilience of ecosystems critical to planetary health.

In conclusion, the recognition of ecocide as the most severe blue crime as part of the international legal framework represents a crucial step toward achieving climate justice. These legal innovations highlight the interconnectedness of human and ecological well-being and affirm the intrinsic value of nature. By criminalizing large-scale environmental destruction, the international community can take a decisive stand against exploitation, uphold the principles of justice, and safeguard the planet for present and future generations. At the end of it all, ecocide is activating a law to save our home planet.

Bibliography

Zoi Aliozi, *Climate Justice: Climate Change and Human Rights*, in Denialism and Human Rights (N. Moerland ed., Intersentia, 2017).

Zoi Aliozi, *Climate Justice: Human Rights and Animal Rights*, The Resolution Journal (Jersey Law Commission, 2020).

Zoi Aliozi, *Climate Justice, Environmental Law and the Case of Ecocide*, The Resolution Journal (Jersey Law Commission, forthcoming 2025).

Zoi Aliozi, *Green Criminology: A Rights-Based Approach*, in Green Crimes and International Criminal Law (R. Paulose ed., Vernon Press, 2021).

Zoi Aliozi, Policy Brief: *Climate Justice and Human Rights in a World in Climate Emergency*, Global Campus of Human Rights (2021).

Zoi Aliozi, *The Legal Definition of Ecocide.* Dictionary of Climate Law/Climate Justice. (Direito Internacional Sem Fronteiras, forthcoming 2025).

Zoi Aliozi, *The Rights of Nature Through the Lens of Climate Justice*, The Resolution Journal (forthcoming 2025).

Zoi Aliozi & Kalliopi Chainoglou, *Human Rights: A Comparative Approach* (Law & Soc. Sci., Kallipos, 2024).

Kai Ambos, Treatise on International Criminal Law: Volume I – Foundations and General Part 175–78 (2013). https://doi.org/10.1093/law/9780199657926.001.0001.

Sumudu Atapattu, Climate Justice and Human Rights: International and Domestic Perspectives 152 (2021).

Belgium Federal Parliament, "Act Introducing the (New) Book II of the Belgian Criminal Code," February 2024.

David Boyd, *The Rights of Nature: A Legal Revolution That Could Save the World* (ECW Press 2017).

Climate Justice: A Guide to the Law and Policy of Climate Change (Peter M. Martin ed., 2020).

Constitution of Ecuador (2008), arts. 71-74.

Robert M. Cover, *Violence and the Word*, 95 Yale L.J. 1601, 1606 (1986). https://doi.org/10.2307/796468.

Cormac Cullinan, Wild Law: A Manifesto for Earth Justice (Chelsea Green Pub 2011).

Delitos contra el ambiente y la naturaleza o Pacha Mama ["Crimes against the environment and nature or Pacha Mama (Mother Earth)"], Código Orgánico Integral Penal [Organic Comprehensive Penal Code], Ministerio de Justicia, Derechos Humanos y Cultos [Ministry of Justice, Human Rights, and Worship], Serie Justicia y Derechos Humanos, Neoconstitucionalismo y Sociedad [Justice and Human Rights Series, Neoconstitutionalism and Society] (Ecuador).

Directive 2008/56 of the European Parliament and of the Council of 17 June 2008, establishing a framework for community action in the field of marine environmental policy, 2008 O.J. (L 164) 19 (EC).

Meinhard Doelle & Sara L. Seck, *International Climate Law and Human Rights: What Are the Prospects for Effective Cooperation?*, 12(1) McGill Int'l J. Sust. Dev. L. & Pol'y 53 (2016).

European Commission v. Spain (Case C-223/12, 2014). https://doi.org/10.1016/S0262-4079(14)61336-1

European Council, "Directive on Environmental Crimes," European Union, 2023.

Richard Falk, Human Rights Horizons: The Pursuit of Justice in a Globalizing World (Routledge, 2000).

Richard Falk, *Human Rights and the Environment*, 10 Am. U. Int'l L. Rev. 1079, 1095 (1995).

"France's Climate & Resilience Act, 2021," National Assembly, France.

David Freestone, *The Role of International Law in the Conservation of Marine Biodiversity*, 16 Int'l J. of Marine and Coastal Law 439, 442 (2001).

Patrick Glenn, Legal Traditions of the World 26 (3d ed. 2010). https://doi.org/10.1093/he/9780199580804.001.0001.

Polly Higgins, Damien Short & Nigel South, *Protecting the Planet: A Proposal for a Law of Ecocide*, 59 Crime, L. & Soc. Change 251 (2013).

Polly Higgins, *Eradicating Ecocide: Laws and Governance to Stop the Destruction of Our Planet*, 4 Climate L. 237, 245 (2013). https://doi.org/10.1007/s10611-013-9413-6.

Human Rights Council Res. 10/4, The Human Right to a Safe, Clean, Healthy, and Sustainable Environment, U.N. Doc. A/HRC/RES/10/4 (Mar. 26, 2009).

Duncan French & Lavanya Rajamani (eds.), Climate Change and Human Rights: An International and Comparative Law Perspective (Oxford Univ. Press, 2020).

Human Rights Council Res. 10/4, The Human Right to a Safe, Clean, Healthy, and Sustainable Environment, U.N. Doc. A/HRC/RES/10/4 (Mar. 26, 2009).

Intergovernmental Panel on Climate Change, *Climate Change and Oceans: 2021 Report*, 2 (2021).

Intergovernmental Panel on Climate Change, Global Warming of 1.5°C (2018), https://www.ipcc.ch/sr15/.

International Criminal Court, Assembly of States Parties, *Report of Independent Expert Panel, the Legal Definition of Ecocide*, U.N. Doc. ICC-ASP/19/INF.3 (2020).

International Criminal Court, *Policy Paper on Case Selection and Prioritisation* 12 (2016), https://www.icc-cpi.int.

International Criminal Court, Rome Statute of the International Criminal Court, art. 1, July 17, 1998, 2187 U.N.T.S. 90.

International Law Commission, *Draft Principles on the Protection of the Environment in Relation to Armed Conflicts*, U.N. Doc. A/74/10 (2019).

IPCC, 2019: Summary for Policymakers, in IPCC Special Report on the Ocean and Cryosphere in a Changing Climate 3, 3-35 (H.-O. Pörtner et al. eds., Cambridge University Press 2019), https://doi.org/10.1017/9781009157964.001.

IPCC, Climate Change 2023: Synthesis Report. Contribution of Working Groups I, II and III to the Sixth Assessment Report of the Intergovernmental Panel on Climate Change, at 35-115 (Core Writing Team, H. Lee & J. Romero eds., 2023).

Shyami P. S. Jayasuriya, *Environmental Degradation and Human Rights: A Case for Ecocide*, 9 J. Int'l Humanitarian Legal Studies 233 (2018).

John H. Knox, Climate Change and Human Rights Law, 50 Va. J. Int'l L. 163 (2009).

Law No. 2021-1104 of August 22, 2021, on Combating Climate Change and Strengthening Resilience to its Effects, Journal Officiel de La République Française (Aug. 24, 2021), https://www.vie-publique.fr/loi/278460-loi-22-aout-2021-climat-et-resilience-convention-citoyenne-climat.

Peter Martin, Climate Justice: A Guide to the Law and Policy of Climate Change (2020).

Cormac McCarthy, Slow Violence and the Environmental Future 134 (2021).

Bill McKibben, The End of Nature (Random House 1989).

Regina M. Paulose, Green Crimes and International Criminal Law (Vernon Press 2021).

Paris Agreement, Dec. 12, 2015, 55 U.N.T.S. 359.

Richard A. Posner, *The Law and Economics of Climate Change*, 5 Yale J. of Regulation 159 (1988).

Prosecutor v. Blagojević, Case No. IT-02-60, Trial Judgment, 832 (Int'l Crim. Trib. for the Former Yugoslavia Jan. 17, 2005).

Prosecutor v. Tadić, Case No. IT-94-1, Judgment, 587-93 (Int'l Crim. Trib. for the Former Yugoslavia July 15, 1999).

John Rawls, A Theory of Justice (Harvard University Press 1971). https://doi.org/10.4159/9780674042605.

J. B. Ruhl, *Climate Change and the New Ecological Paradigm*, 46 Envtl. L. 133 (2016).

J. B. Ruhl, *Climate Change and the Law: A Primer for Legal Scholars*, 44 Envtl. L. 95 (2014).

García Ruiz et al., *Eco-Crimes and Ecocide at Sea: Toward a New Blue Criminology*, 66 Int'l J. Offender Therapy & Com. Criminology 407, 407-29 (2022). https://doi.org/10.1177/0306624X20967950.

Philippe Sands, East West Street: On the Origins of Genocide and Crimes Against Humanity (Alfred A. Knopf, 2016).

William A. Schabas, An Introduction to the International Criminal Court, (6th ed., Cambridge Univ. Press, 2020). https://doi.org/10.1017/9781108616157.

William Schabas, The International Criminal Court: A Commentary, 320 (2010). https://doi.org/10.1017/9781108616157.

Susan Schneider, *Feminist Perspectives on Environmental Law*, 31 Harv. Envtl. L. Rev. 61, 77 (2007).

Karen N. Scott, International Law in the Era of Climate Change (Edward Elgar Publishing, 2018).

Dinah Shelton, *Human Rights and the Environment: The Right to a Healthy Environment*, 27 Pace Envtl. L. Rev. 161, 175 (2010).

V. G. M. R. K. Singh, *Intersectionality and Climate Justice*, 45 U. Pa. J. Int'l L. 451, 465 (2023).

Stop Ecocide Foundation, *Legal Definition of Ecocide*, 2021, https://www.stopecocide.earth/legal-definition-of-ecocide.

Janusz Symonides, *Human Rights and the Environment: The Need for Global Governance*, 18 Int'l J. Env't & Sustainable Dev. 77, 85 (2019).

Mihnea Tanasescu, The Rights of Nature and the Indigenous Struggle in Ecuador, Envtl. Values (2020).

Dan Tarlock, Environmental Law, the Economy, and Sustainable Development: The United States, the European Union, and the International Community (Cambridge Univ. Press, 2000).

Tătar v. Romania (App. No. 67021/01, 2009).

Te Awa Tupua (Whanganui River Claims Settlement) Act 2017 (N.Z.).

Antonio Augusto Cançado Trindade, International Law for Humankind: Towards a New Jus Gentium (Martinus Nijhoff, 2010). https://doi.org/10.1163/ej.9789004184282.i-728.

U.N. Climate Action Summit, *Climate Emergency: An Urgent Call for Action* (2019), available at https://www.un.org/en/climatechange/urgency-action.

U.N. Human Rights Council, Resolution 48/13, U.N. Doc. A/HRC/RES/48/13 (Oct. 8, 2021).

UNHRC Res. 48/13, The Human Right to a Clean, Healthy, and Sustainable Environment, U.N. Doc. A/HRC/RES/48/13 (Oct. 18, 2021).

United Nations Environment Programme, The Emissions Gap Report 2020 12 (2020), available at https://www.unep.org/emissions-gap-report.

United Nations Framework Convention on Climate Change (UNFCCC), May 9, 1992, 1771 U.N.T.S. 107, art. 3, 1.

United Nations Framework Convention on Climate Change, Report of the Conference of the Parties on Its Twenty-First Session, U.N. Doc. FCCC/CP/2015/10/Add.1 (2016).

United States v. Smith, 18 U.S. (5 Wheat.) 153, 162 (1820).

United States v. Viking Resources, 607 F. Supp. 2d 808 (E.D. Mich. 2009).

Urgenda Foundation v. The Netherlands, [2015] HAZA C/09/00456689 (June 24, 2015); aff'd (Oct. 9, 2018) (District Court of The Hague and The Hague Court of Appeal) (affirmed by the Supreme Court, Dec. 20, 2019).

Christina Voigt (ed.), Climate Change and Environmental Hazards Related to Shipping: An International Legal Framework (Cambridge Univ. Press, 2019).

Whaling in the Antarctic (Australia v. Japan: New Zealand Intervening), Judgment, 2014 I.C.J. 226 (Mar. 31).

Rob White, *Green Criminology: An Introduction to the Concept,* 14 Criminology & Crim. Just. 267 (2014). https://doi.org/10.4324/9780203096109.

David Zierler, The Invention of Ecocide: Agent Orange, Vietnam, and the Scientists Who Changed the Way We Think About the Environment (Univ. of Ga. Press, 2011). https://doi.org/10.1353/book11509.

Chapter 2

A Global Overview of Whaling: The Application of International Treaties and *Erga Omnes* Obligations

Lu Shegay
Kazakhstani attorney and legal researcher

Abstract: Whaling is the practice of hunting whales that is exercised by States for the purposes of subsequent use of the derivatives, such as meat and blubber, for the purposes of meat consumption, and medical purposes. Whaling has been at the center of many debates on the conservation of cetaceans (specifically their intelligence and suffering), as well as sustainability and thus raised many issues in the international community. In this chapter, I will discuss the necessity to protect cetaceans and the detrimental side of whaling and its effect on these animals. I will discuss the application of and effectiveness of the International Convention for the Regulation of Whaling (ICRW) in relation to protection of whale species. Furthermore, I will address the application of international treaties and customary law under Public International Law, *erga omnes* obligations of States in relation to whaling, international liability, and the relevant case law.

Keywords: whaling, ICRW, IWC, public international law, *erga omnes*, commercial whaling, Iceland, Japan, Norway, CMS, CITES, UNCLOS, ecocide, habitat loss.

Introduction

Whaling is the practice of capturing cetaceans for scientific and medicinal purposes, entertainment, and consumption. The practice of industrial whaling dates back to 875 AD and catching whales for their meat and blubber was instrumental in the Industrial Revolution. With time the practice of commercial whaling has become popular around the world, being profitable in terms of trade and resources. Certain coastal States obviously had more accessibility to the areas with more dense populations of whales, which led to the creation of a number of whaling ships, and the industry successfully grew further into the twentieth century.[1] As a result, a lot of whale species have faced the threat of extinction. This has become a great concern among certain States. The most common species of whales that are being hunted are some of the smaller species, such as minke whales, belugas, narwhals, and pilot whales, with a smaller number of larger species, such as gray whales, sei whales, fin whales, bowhead whales, Bryde's whales, sperm whales, and humpback whales.[2] The primary concerns were cetacean intelligence and suffering, sustainability of whales, and national sovereignty.

One of the main reasons for the debate concerning whaling is centered around the suffering of cetaceans and the unnecessary practice of whaling. The overall discussion about the sentience of animals has raised a plethora of debates for the past decades. Sentience, in the general sense, is defined as the ability to experience feelings and sensations.[3] When it comes to the contemplation of animal sentience, opinions are divided. Most scientists affirm that animals are capable of feeling pain and suffering, however, some claim that only particular species of animals are sentient, such as those of a "great importance" or those who are constantly under the spotlight. Aquatic animals do not receive as much attention as land animals. However, it is important to mention that aquatic animals, including whales, play a key role in mitigating climate change,[4] which is a major issue in the modern day. Climate change not only destroys the habitat of a number of animals but also threatens people with increased natural disasters and occurrences, such as flooding, extreme heat, food and water deficiencies, etc. The question of the sentience of animals, and the urge to protect them, has led to the development of animal rights advocacy. This, in turn, led to the inclusion and recognition of animal sentience in legal instruments in different countries. Certain jurisdictions recognize the sentience of animals legally, typically in their Constitutions.[5] Internationally,

---

[1] J.N. Tønnessen & Arne Odd Johnsen, *The History of Modern Whaling* 3-6 (Univ. of California Press 1982).

[2] INTERNATIONAL WHALING COMMISSION, https://iwc.int/management-and-conservation/whaling/total-catches (last visited September 4, 2024).

[3] *Sentience*, MERRIAM-WEBSTER DICTIONARY (11th ed. 2003); *Sentience*, CAMBRIDGE LEARNER'S DICTIONARY (4th ed. 2021).

[4] UN ENVIRONMENT PROGRAMME, https://www.unep.org/news-and-stories/story/protecting-whales-protect-planet (last visited September 10, 2024);
Natàlia Amigó, *How do whales help mitigate climate change?*, SUBMON (November 18, 2021), https://www.submon.org/en/how-do-whales-help-mitigate-climate-change/.

[5] Belgium, Italy, Germany, Luxembourg, Slovenia and Austria, Switzerland, Egypt, Brazil, and India have proclaimed in their respective Constitutions that animals are recognized as sentient beings. See Prayank Jain, *Environmental Personhood Towards a Rights Based*

animals have been recognized as sentient beings in the Treaty of Lisbon.[6] The overall discussion of the sentience of animals led to debates about the legal personhood of animals and whether animals are entitled to certain rights, such as the right to life and the right to freedom. However, these are not mutually exclusive and given the novel area of animal law, what approach is more efficient to apply is dependent on a case-by-case basis.

The question of whether cetaceans specifically are sentient cannot be credibly disputed. They have been proven by scientists to be intelligent animals possessing cognitive abilities with problem-solving skills. For instance, a 2014 study found that the long-finned pilot whale has more neocortical neurons than any other mammal, including humans, examined to date. The neocortex is involved in cerebral functions, such as cognition, sensory perception, reasoning, and is a part of the brain that is responsible for high-order thinking.[7] There was neurological evidence found in the studies conducted by the scientists that the neocortex is present in cetaceans, which means that whales are capable of sophisticated thought processes. Dolphins and chimpanzees are able to use tools, engage in group and cooperative behavior, and understand abstract concepts.[8] The question of recognizing cetaceans as sentient beings, thus protecting them legally, has come under the spotlight with numerous activities conducted in relation to these animals, including but not limited to whaling, captivity for entertainment, and scientific research.

I. Rights of Nature

Rights of Nature is the concept implying that nature in itself is entitled to protection, and that trees, mountains, rivers, and animals, as separate entities, have the inherent right to be protected. This innovative perspective challenges the traditional status of nature and other entities as mere objects under the law, instead, it seeks legal recognition of the entire ecosystem. This approach seems to offer a fresh perspective on conserving and preserving not only natural entities

---

Approach for Nature and Humanity, in GREEN CRIMES AND INTERNATIONAL CRIMINAL LAW 35 (Regina M. Paulose ed., Vernon Press 2021).

[6] Treaty of Lisbon amending the Treaty on European Union and the Treaty establishing the European Community, Dec. 13, 2007, Preamble.

[7] Simona Lodato & Paola Arlotta, *Generating Neuronal Diversity in the Mammalian Cerebral Cortex*, ANNU REV CELL DEV BIOL., 705 (Sep. 11, 2015).

[8] Christophe Boesch & Hedwige Boesch, *Tool Use and Tool Making in Wild Chimpanzees*, 54 FOLIA PRIMATOL (BASEL) 89-91 (1990).

but also animals, and approximately 39 countries have implemented the rights of nature at their domestic levels.[9]

Incorporating the protection of animals within the concept of Rights of Nature is one of the efficient approaches to protecting animals at both the domestic and international levels. Within the animal rights movement the most essential issue that the advocates are working on is to achieve the possibility for animals to have a right to be protected.

Humans share 99% of their DNA with some nonhuman animals, however, nonhuman animals are not on the list of legal persons. In the past women and black slaves were limited in their rights and even did not possess them. This was created by man, and that hierarchy regulated political and legal relationships between humans and nonhuman animals.[10] Wise distinguished the definitions of a legal person and a legal thing where the legal person has the capacity for legal rights while legal thing does not have any. Jeremy Bentham discussed two major theories in granting legal rights to nonhuman animals. The first one was based on animal autonomy which means the possessing rights of nonhuman animals as humans have and as he called it "full autonomy." The second theory was based more on protection of animals, preventing animals from suffering.[11] These two theories were in contrast with the theory offered by Favre, who proposed changing the nature of ownership regarding animals.[12] Wise and Sunstein discussed that the protection of nonhuman animals should be demonstrated through the will to consider these animals as legal persons.[13] Under the standard of absolute equality nonhuman animals should possess dignity rights fully as humans who are under Kantian autonomy[14] while nonhuman animals maintaining a realistic autonomy should have dignity rights equally proportionate to those humans who maintain realistic autonomy. Moreover, Wise asserted that those nonhuman animals possessing either a Kantian autonomy or a realistic autonomy should be entitled to have dignity rights which were granted to humans who lack any autonomy.[15] On the other hand, Sunstein argued that legal personhood of animals can be

---

[9] Alex Putzer et al., *Putting the rights of nature on the map. A quantitative analysis of rights of nature initiatives across the world,* 18 J. OF MAPS 89, 93–96 (2022).

[10] Steven Wise, *The Legal Thinghood of Nonhuman Animals,* 23 ENVTL. AFF. L. REV. 471, 471-472 (1996).

[11] Jeremy Bentham, *An Introduction to the Principles of Morals and Legislation* ch. XVII (1789).

[12] David Favre, *Equitable Self-Ownership for Animals,* 50 DUKE L. J. 473, 475 (2000).

[13] Emma Maddux, *Time to Stand: Exploring the Past, Present, and Future of Nonhuman Animal Standing,* 47 WAKE FOREST L. REV. 1243, 1256 (2012).

[14] Steven Wise, *Hardly a Revolution - The Eligibility of Nonhuman Animals for Dignity Rights in a Liberal Democracy,* 22 VT. L. REV. 793, 900 (1998).

[15] *Supra* note 13, at 1257.

undoubtedly justified by the capacity of nonhuman animals,[16] particularly by the capacity to suffer.

Under the rights of nature, animals will be able to bring their claims through their guardians. Wise proposed two options in deciding who may represent animals in the court. The first was a test, which permits "a substitute decision-maker to exercise an incompetent's power rights by objectively ascertaining the relief that will result from the proposed actions."[17] The second option was the rule of substituted judgment where the court uses the "mental mantle of the incompetent" and substitutes itself for being an individual in the decision-making process.[18]

John Austin, the first Anglophone legal theorist who presented the concepts of personhood and thinghood in his works, wrote that persons, as subjects of law, could be distributed to different classes holding rights and duties with certain capacities and incapacities.[19] In modern law, the legal person is defined as someone possessing legal rights and bearing legal obligations. Western legal systems recognize children as legal persons and call animals as legal nonpersons. Supposing that children can hold rights, not being abused is related to the theory of interests that offers legal protection of interests through exercising legal obligations. The obligation not to exercise violence towards children is in the interests of children, and this constitutes a right for children. If such a protection creates what might be called a legal right, such rights could and should be granted to animals as well because the interests of nonhuman animals can be protected in the same manner.[20]

II. Controversy Surrounding Whaling

The major concern that arose with regard to whaling came from conservationists arguing that numerous whale species were on the edge of extinction, mainly due to historic commercial whaling practices. Even though, since then, the population of whales has been restored, cetaceans still face many other threats, such as habitat loss, climate change, and direct anthropogenic activities, which are caused by whaling internationally. Not only does whaling directly affect cetaceans through capture, but it also affects other aquatic animals. Cetaceans play a significant role in the marine ecosystem; preserving whales specifically

---

[16] Cass R. Sunstein, *The Rights of Animals*, 70 U. CHI. L. REV. 387, 400-401 (2003).

[17] Joseph Mendelson, *Should Animals Have Standing? A Review of Standing Under the Animal Welfare Act*, 24 B. C. ENVLT. AFF. L. REV. 795, 879 (1997).

[18] *Id.*, at 880.

[19] John Austin, *The Province of Jurisprudence Determined* XVI (1832).

[20] Visa Kurki, *Animals, Slaves, and Corporations: Analyzing Legal Thinghood*, 18 GERMAN L. J. 1069, 1080 (2017).

as beings at the top of the food chain of the oceans and some of the species as prey, is essential because these aquatic animals affect the overall food chain and the presence of other species of aquatic animals is important for the oceans. Furthermore, another concern about whaling was raised among conservationists and animal rights advocates, who claim that the practice of whaling is inhumane and that the killing of these socially complex, intelligent, and sentient animals is ethically wrong. Scientists have proved that whales demonstrate cognitive abilities, such as problem-solving skills, communication, and self-awareness. Yet, the methods that are used in whaling oftentimes involve cruelty and severe suffering caused to whales,[21] which altogether raises many debates among animal rights advocates, conservationists, and the public. However, the main issue with whaling lies in the legal framework that has loopholes and does not protect whales in a proper and sustainable manner. At the international level, the main controversy in modern days stems from the fact that most nations—even those with a history of industrial whaling—are abstaining from the practice of commercial whaling. This leads to the controversy of why a few States in the world should be allowed to continue commercial whaling, while the majority object to the practice. In this chapter, the discussion will only be limited to the issues of whaling for the purposes of commercial whaling and whaling for the purposes of scientific research.

III. Legal Framework

A. International Convention for the Regulation of Whaling

With the emergence of the animal rights movement, the attitude towards animal protection in general and whaling in particular has changed significantly, due to the enormous work done by the increasing number of animal advocates and changing State attitudes, including growing disapproval of whaling. The main international instrument that regulates the protection of whales and the prohibition of commercial whaling is the ICRW, which is aimed at the "proper conservation of whale stocks and thus make possible the orderly development of the whaling industry."[22] The ICRW was created in response to a number of cases related to catching whales for commercial purposes; its objective is to protect all whale species from overhunting and ensure proper conservation and management of the whale population. The IWC is the specialized regional

---

[21] In many countries, whaling has always been a part of their cultural and traditional practices, and many countries practice aboriginal whaling, however, this Chapter will only discuss the consequences of commercial whaling activities and will not touch upon whaling by indigenous communities.

[22] International Convention for the Regulation of Whaling, Preamble, Dec. 3, 1946.

fishery management organization, which was established under the ICRW to implement the aims prescribed by the convention; the IWC is the main decision-making body of the convention. It is also responsible for adopting a binding "schedule" that regulates the methods of catching whales, protected areas, catch limit, and the scope of the rights to catch whale species for the purposes of scientific research. Currently, there are 88 State Parties to the ICRW, with the initial signatories being Argentina, Australia, Brazil, Canada, Chile, Denmark, France, the Netherlands, New Zealand, Norway, Peru, South Africa, the Soviet Union, the United Kingdom, and the United States. Since the ratification of the ICRW, nine States have withdrawn from the convention, including Canada, Egypt, Guatemala, Greece, Jamaica, Mauritius, the Philippines, the Seychelles, and Venezuela. The most recent State Party that withdrew from the ICRW was Japan in 2019, to resume commercial whaling.

In 1972, at the United Nations Environmental Conference, where a 10-year global moratorium on commercial whaling was proposed, six States voted "no": Japan, Iceland, the Soviet Union, South Africa, Norway, and Panama.[23] Next year, the same moratorium was proposed again and the same States, with the exception of Panama, voted "no." In 1982, the moratorium on commercial whaling was finally approved and planned to enter into force in 1986. The clause on the moratorium reads as follows:

> Notwithstanding the other provisions of paragraph 10, catch limits for the killing for commercial purposes of whales from all stocks for the 1986 coastal and the 1985/86 pelagic seasons and thereafter shall be zero. This provision will be kept under review, based upon the best scientific advice, and by 1990 at the latest the Commission will undertake a comprehensive assessment of the effects of this decision on whale stocks and consider modification of this provision and the establishment of other catch limits.[24]

The moratorium is binding to all State Parties of the IWC and currently, the ban on commercial whaling is still in force. The enacted moratorium only applies to commercial whaling, but there are two exceptions under the ICRW that allow State Parties to continue whaling. First, State Parties are allowed to issue special permits to their citizens to "kill, take, and treat whales for purposes of scientific research subject to restrictions as to number and subject to such other conditions as the Contracting Government thinks fit..."[25] This exception was

---

[23] David Day & Sierra Club, *The Whale War* 29-32 (1987).

[24] *Supra* note 22, ¶ 10(e).

[25] *Id.*, art. VIII.

used by Japan when it was bound by the ICRW and exercised whaling, and more on its activities will be discussed below. Second, it is allowed for States to object to any amendments to the convention and thus exempt themselves from being bound by these amendments.[26] While the IWC allows objections to the amendments to the ICRW, other treaties have different approaches. For instance, the UN Charter has a high bar on amendments, but requires the dissenters to accept the changes eventually, while the Rome Statute of the ICC allows opting out of amendments to certain essential clauses.[27]

As in any other treaties, the scope of ICRW provisions is only limited to its State Parties and those States which are left not bound by the moratorium anymore. Japan had multiple tries to lift the commercial whaling ban with no success until it finally decided to leave the IWC. In the modern days, the main whaling countries are Japan that withdrew from the convention, Norway, that objected to the moratorium clause; and Iceland that operates under the reservation to the convention and mainly continues hunting whales for commercial purposes—all three will be discussed below.

B. United Nations Convention on the Law of the Sea

UNCLOS contains the provisions regarding the regulation in different maritime zones and establishes general duties to "protect and preserve the marine environment in the maritime zones and high seas areas."[28] UNCLOS is binding to all States, regardless of whether they adopted the treaty or not, because it has the effect of customary law enshrined in the treaty. Moreover, UNCLOS sets out the requirement for all States to exercise a "'total allowable' catch based upon an established 'maximum sustainable yield' in achieving 'optimum utilization' of marine living resources."[29] General rules of public international law provide that the coastal State has the greater authority over the closest maritime area, this maritime zone is also called territorial waters, the breadth of which shall not exceed 12 nautical miles from the baseline.[30] Beyond the territorial waters, States have limited and balanced with other States' rights and duties over the maritime zone, such as the contiguous zone, which is up to 24 nautical miles from the

---

[26] *Id.*, art. V, ¶ 3.

[27] Ian Hurd, *Almost Saving Whales: The Ambiguity of Success at the International Whaling Commission*, ETHICS & INTERNATIONAL AFFAIRS (Aug. 28, 2012), https://papers.ssrn.com/sol3/papers.cfm?abstract_id=2488609.

[28] United Nations Convention on the Law of the Sea (UNCLOS) art. 192, Dec. 10, 1982.

[29] *Id.*, art. 119;

Erika J. Techera & Natalie Klein, *International Law of Sharks: Obstacles, Options and Opportunities* 27 (2017).

[30] *Supra* note 28, art. 3.

baseline.[31] The next area is the EEZ, which is up to 200 nautical miles from the baseline, where the coastal State has a right to manage and conserve marine living resources.[32] Finally, there are high seas, the area not belonging to any State, but where any State has freedom of navigation, freedom of overflight, freedom of fishing with due regard for the interests of other States, freedom of scientific research, etc.[33] It is also allowed for all States to exercise fishing in the high seas, although an effort has been made to amend the regulations with the purpose of protecting marine living beings under UNCLOS. The concept of maritime zones, their breadth, and regulations are important for the purpose of having a better understanding of how different States can exercise their jurisdiction over the whale species and what actions can be taken by States in relation to the conservation and management of whales. However, it becomes more challenging to manage and establish conservation of highly migratory whales, or of those swimming between the EEZs of different States, or between the high seas and the EEZs. In this regard, UNCLOS contains only broad provisions and requires States to cooperate[34] directly or through international organizations. Despite the high seas allowing all States to enjoy the freedom in those areas, States shall take necessary steps for the conservation and management of living resources while exercising any activity.[35] Therefore, if any vessel violates the conservation and management requirements on the high seas, it is considered a vessel, against which the action shall be taken, and other States cannot interfere with a foreign-flagged vessel unless such flag vessel State has given its consent.[36] The ITLOS, in its Advisory Opinion for the Sub-Regional Fisheries Commission concluded that "the flag State is under the 'due diligence obligation' to take all necessary measures to ensure compliance and to prevent unregulated and unreported fishing by fishing vessels flying its flag."[37]

UNCLOS entirely is not an animal-focused treaty, rather it is centered around the regulation of actions exercised by all States within defined maritime zones. Treaties are one of the primary sources of international law, and apart from

---

[31] *Id.*, art. 33.
[32] *Id.*, art. 57.
[33] *Id.*, art. 87.
[34] *Id.*, art. 118.
[35] *Id.*, art. 117.
[36] *Id.*, art. 110.
Natalie Klein, *The Right of Visit and the 2005 Protocol on the Suppression of Unlawful Acts against the Safety of Maritime Navigation,* 35 DENVER J. OF INTL. LAW & POLICY 287, 288 (2005).
[37] Request for an Advisory Opinion Submitted by the Sub-Regional Fisheries Commission (No. 21), Case No. 21, Order of Apr. 2, 2015, 4 ITLOS Rep. 129.

UNCLOS, States adopted a number of treaties to focus on the conservation and management of marine living beings.

While there might not be problems with States being bound by this convention because of the customary law enshrined in it, this international instrument is not animal-focused and not even whale-focused. However, it establishes the rules and regulations according to which States can exercise their jurisdiction over a particular maritime zone. These rules are directly related to whales and the activities that are usually conducted by humans. For the reasons above, UNCLOS plays an important role in the issue of conservation and management of whales. Especially with whaling being one of the widespread threats for these animals, and there are some highly migratory species of whales that swim long distances, UNCLOS is a good source to regulate the activities of States attempting to hunt whales.

C. Convention on International Trade in Endangered Species of Wild Fauna and Flora

Convention on International Trade in Endangered Species (CITES) is a multilateral treaty, which protects endangered plants and animals and is intended to regulate, control, prohibit, or limit international trade of endangered or threatened species. CITES protects approximately 5,800 species of animals and 30,000 species of plants against over-exploitation through international trade.[38] CITES lists each species under one of the three Appendices dependent on the level of being threatened by international trade, thus, those Appendices provide different levels of protection for species listed under the particular Appendix.

With that being said, Appendix I lists threatened with extinction species or species that may be affected by international trade. These species cannot be used in commercial trade but are permitted only in exceptional cases with the approved license. Any other trade of the species of Appendix I requires export and import permits. Each party of the CITES has its own appointed Management Authority, Scientific Authority, Enforcement Focal Point, and other executive bodies exercising their duties. With regard to Appendix I, the Management Authority of the exporting country monitors whether the import permit has been obtained, while the Scientific Authority of the exporting country shall ensure that such export of species will not affect the wild population.[39]

Appendix II contains the list of species that may not necessarily be threatened with extinction but may become so if the trade is not strictly regulated.

---

[38] Convention on International Trade in Endangered Species of Wild Fauna and Flora Appendices I, II, III, Mar. 3, 1973.

[39] *Id.*

International trade of species listed in Appendix II can be authorized by the export permit or re-export certificate, and the export permit is required by the exporting country. The import permit is not required, however, some parties, in accordance with their domestic legislation, may request such a permit.[40] Moreover, species of animals listed in Appendix I that are bred in captivity for commercial purposes are treated as those from Appendix II.[41]

If one Parties requests other CITES parties to assist in controlling the trade of some species, these species are included in Appendix III. These species should not be necessarily threatened with extinction globally, but trade is allowed only with an export permit and a certificate of origin from the country which listed these species.[42]

D. Convention on the Conservation of Migratory Species of Wild Animals

The Convention on the Conservation of Migratory Species of Wild Animals (CMS is an international treaty aimed at the conservation of migratory species within their migratory ranges. This treaty was signed under the auspices of the United Nations Environment Programme with the main purpose of conservation of wild animals and their habitats on a global level. One of the fundamental principles is to acknowledge the importance of migratory species and the necessity to take actions to improve the conservation status, which would be favorable for the species of wild animals and their habitat.[43] As in the CITES, CMS has Appendices with different levels of protection. Appendix I lists migratory species threatened with extinction where State Parties are bound by the duty to ensure strict protection of species.[44] State Parties shall also prevent the taking of animals belonging to such species, except for the taking for scientific purposes, for accommodating the needs of traditional subsistence users of such species, for enhancing the propagation or survival of the affected species, and extraordinary circumstances.[45]

Appendix II includes migratory species that have unfavorable conservation status and that would significantly benefit from international cooperation, and these species serve as the basis for the establishment of regional or global instruments under the treaty.[46] Therefore, State Parties shall strive to conclude

---

40 *Id.*

41 *Id.*, art. VII.

42 *Id.*

43 Convention on the Conservation of Migratory Species of Wild Animals ("CMS") art. II, Nov. 6, 1979.

44 *Id.*, art. III(1).

45 *Id.*, art. III(5).

46 *Id.*, art. IV(1).

agreements that would be beneficial and would "give priority to the species in an unfavorable conservation status."[47]

As for the protection of whales, this treaty is instrumental because it is focused on whales crossing national boundaries. Appendix I lists endangered migratory species, and State Parties shall endeavor to protect the habitat of these species, take actions to prevent any impact leading to the endangerment of species. Appendix I lists 18 species of cetaceans and includes the sei whale, blue whale, humpback whale, and North Atlantic right whale, etc.[48] This convention contains beneficial provisions related to whales, although it is based on the rights and duties of State Parties and their scope of activities towards whale species. However, because migratory species of whales are usually swimming between different maritime zones, this instrument may be challenging to establish sustainable protection, conservation, and management of whales. Another issue is that the entire convention is not limited to whale species in scope and applies to all migratory species, and with the least public concern about aquatic animals and whales the regulations are not improved and challenged by State Parties or interested parties.

CMS is another international instrument that touches upon the protection of animals, but it has a special relation to whales due to their tendency to migrate. While one of the fundamental principles of this convention is to strive to provide immediate protection to those species listed under the convention, it is crucial for States mostly operating the activity related to whales to be signatories of this agreement. Although 133 States are parties[49] to the CMS, there are still those important countries that have not signed and ratified this convention yet. For instance, while the United States supported the moratorium on commercial whaling, it is a non-party to the CMS, as well as Iceland, which is not only a non-Party to the CMS but also continues hunting for whales. The convention would have a better effect if some so-called "important" countries ratified CMS due to the provision of parties to cooperate and endeavor to manage and conserve the population of whales. So-called "important" countries are indicated as those who have the interest and a "better location" for whaling.

IV. Non-Commercial Whaling Constitutes a Customary Law Rule

Not only do international treaties and conventions impose obligations on States in the international law community, but customary law is another

---

[47] *Id.*, art. IV (3).

[48] *Id.*, Appendix I.

[49] As of March 1, 2022.

primary source of international law that can be violated as specified in Article 38 of the Statute of International Court of Justice, mainly to be able to bring the lawsuit before the ICJ. The mere essence of custom is specified as the "evidence of a general practice accepted by law."[50] To establish the customary law rule, there should be two elements present, which are State practice and *opinio juris*. As the ICJ noted in the Libya/Malta case, "the substance of customary law must be 'looked for primarily in the actual practice and *opinio juris* of states.'"[51]

Animal law is an emerging area of law that develops rapidly on some issues and slower in the others and it still lacks a number of international legally binding instruments. Specifically, while touching upon the issues of the legal protection of cetaceans, only a few international conventions can be applied, such as the ICRW[52] , which only provides that whaling is allowed for the purposes of scientific research; the UNCLOS[53] that only contains the provisions on the conservation and management of whale population and cooperative measures of States; CITES[54] that solely covers the trade regulations of certain species; and CMS,[55] the scope of which is only limited by the protection of migratory species. All these above-mentioned major conventions do not directly apply to the protection of cetaceans from commercial whaling, they only are focused on either specific species of whales or aimed at the restoration of the population of whales, but they do not differentiate commercial whaling from other activities. Thus, the application of a customary law rule in the issues of commercial whaling would be an effective means to legally protect cetaceans from overhunting since the custom has the universal application and it can also be "activated by spontaneous behavior and thus mirrors the contemporary concerns of society."[56]

Certainly, what is important to take into consideration in the arising customary law rule is particular aspects, such as the duration, consistency, repetition, and generality.[57] However, within the framework of international law it is also important to note that the emerging custom depends on circumstances and issues at stake. It is not explicitly stated that the time is the

---

[50] Statute of the International Court of Justice, art. 38, June 26, 1945.

[51] Continental Shelf (Libya v Malta), Judgment, 1985 I.C.J. Rep. 13, ¶ 13, 29 (June 3). *See also* the Advisory Opinion on the Legality of the Threat or Use of Nuclear Weapons, ICJ "International Court of Justice" Reports, 1996, 226, 253; 110 ILR, 163. MALCOM SHAW, INTERNATIONAL LAW 74 (1976).

[52] *Supra* note 22, art. 8.

[53] *Supra* note 28, art. 61, 119.

[54] *Supra* note 38, art. II.

[55] *Supra* note 43, art. II.

[56] Shaw, *supra* note 51, at 73.

[57] *Id.*, at 76.

most significant factor in the formation of the custom. As for the factors of continuity and repetition, the ICJ concluded in the Asylum case that a customary law rule must be "in accordance with a constant and uniform usage practiced by the States in question."[58] However, even repetition may not be all that necessary if the *opinio juris* is clearly established.

There is no doubt that whaling as a practice itself appeared a long time ago, and commercial whaling took place approximately 875 A.D. originally in Spain and France, which later became popular across the globe. However, since the enactment of the ICRW and the formation of the IWC, it can be argued that the practice of not hunting cetaceans by States for commercial purposes constitutes a customary law rule. The practice of non-commercial whaling contains both elements required to form a customary law rule, which is State practice and *opinio juris*. The nature of the customary law is based on the usage of such practice and close relatedness to a particular issue, which implies that a customary law can be created by a few States given their influence, involvement, and interest in the issue. For instance, in the Anglo-Norwegian Fisheries case, the United Kingdom requested the court to decide the legality of Norway in measurement of its territorial sea. The United Kingdom's argument was that customary law did not allow the length of a baseline drawn across a bay to be longer than ten miles. The Court dismissed that and provided that there was insufficient uniformity to such a custom and that the actual state practice did not imply the formation of a custom.[59]

> In these circumstances the Court deems it necessary to point out that although the ten-mile rule has been adopted by certain States both in their national law and in their treaties and conventions, and although certain arbitral decisions have applied it as between these States, other States have adopted a different limit. Consequently, the ten-mile rule has not acquired the authority of a general rule of international law.[60]

While in the international community all views are acceptable, those States that carry more interest in the issue would have the higher influence in the formation of a customary law. Most States accepted the provisions outlined in the ICRW, mainly the moratorium on commercial whaling, i.e., most States ratified the convention and are parties to the IWC that makes this moratorium legally binding on parties. Since the enactment of the moratorium on commercial

---

58 *Asylum* (Colombia v Peru), Judgment, 1950 I.C.J. Rep. 266, ¶¶276-277 (Nov. 20).

59 *Fisheries* (United Kingdom v Norway), Judgment, 1951 I.C.J. Rep. ¶116, 131, 138 (Dec. 18).

60 *Id.*

whaling, all State Parties to the IWC have abstained from hunting whales for commercial purposes, even the most "whaling nations" in the past. And the non-commercial whaling since then formed a customary norm that contains all necessary elements to consider it a custom, which are state practice of not exercising the commercial whaling and *opinio juris*, a psychological factor of accepting the provisions and complying with the obligations.

State practice in international law can be expressed in numerous ways that include but are not limited to conferences, legal instruments, official statements, decisions of courts, etc. It appears that those members of the IWC that supported the moratorium on commercial whaling activities have explicitly envisaged that in their domestic regulations and official statements. In some circumstances, in international law, the domestic laws of States can create the basis for the emergence of the customary norm. For instance, in the Scotia case, where a British ship had sunk an American vessel that did not display the correct lights on the high seas, it was decided by the United States Supreme Court that the Act of Parliament "formed the basis of the relevant international custom since other states had legislated in virtually identical terms."[61] IWC members express in their domestic legislation that the hunting of cetaceans is only allowed under exceptional circumstances, which is for the purposes of scientific research. With that said, the IWC members have consistently abstained from the practice of commercial whaling since the moratorium entered into force.

As in cases with any occurrence of the customary law rule, there are always exceptions presumed, which in international law would be the persistent objector. Within the framework of international law, the persistent objector doctrine implies that a sovereign State has to consistently and clearly object to the emerging norm of customary law once it occurs.[62] The doctrine allows a State to not be bound by particular provisions of customary norms by consistently and in a timely manner objecting to the rule. Customary international law consists of practices and rules that have evolved over time and are generally accepted as binding by the international community. Even though it is possible to avoid being bound by certain customs, the doctrine of persistent objector has particular requirements, which consist of timely and consistent objection and public and clear objection. The former requires that a State willing to object to the arising customary norm must object to the formation of the customary rule while it is still in the process of being crystallized, and it must maintain this objection consistently over time. The latter requires the objection to be sufficiently clear and expressed publicly, and that the position of the State is

61 Shaw, *supra* note 51, at 83; *Nottebohm* (Liechtenstein v Guatemala), Judgment, 1955 I.C.J. Rep. ¶4, 22 (Apr. 6).

62 James A. Green, *The Persistent Objector Rule in International Law* (2016).

recognized by other States and the international community, i.e., other States shall be aware of the objecting State. The ICJ, in its decisions, recognized the doctrine of persistent objector in the Asylum case where the ICJ opined:

> The Court cannot therefore find that the Colombian Government has proved the existence of such a custom. But even if it could be supposed that such a custom existed between certain Latin-American States only, it could not be invoked against Peru which, far from having by its attitude adhered to it, has, on the contrary, repudiated it by refraining from ratifying the Montevideo Conventions of 1933 and 1939, which were the first to include a rule concerning the qualification of the offence in matters of diplomatic asylum.[63]

Moreover, in the Fisheries case, the ICJ, to the argument on the baseline delimitation of the territorial sea, it decided:

> Although the ten-mile rule has been adopted by certain States both in their national law and in their treaties and conventions, and although certain arbitral decisions have applied it as between these States, other States have adopted a different limit. Consequently, the ten-mile rule has not acquired the authority of a general rule of international law.[64]

And concluded that in any event "the ten-mile rule would appear to be inapplicable as against Norway inasmuch as she has always opposed any attempt to apply it to the Norwegian coast."[65]

One may claim that since Japan withdrew from the IWC and the convention respectively, it is not bound by the moratorium and the provisions of the conventions, which is true within the scope of treaty obligations, however, Japan violates the norms of customary law by exercising commercial whaling and it did not object to the moratorium in a timely manner, thus, the doctrine of persistent objector would not be applicable in this case. When the moratorium on commercial whaling was first proposed to the members of the IWC, there is no doubt that Japan voted against the ban. However, it did not withdraw from the convention in a timely manner and continued to be bound by the provisions enshrined in the convention.

---

[63] *Asylum, supra* note 58, at 277–278; Establishing that neither the Bolivarian Agreement of 1911, nor the Havana Convention on asylum, nor the Montevideo Convention on Political Asylum, supported Columbia's argument).

[64] *Fisheries, supra* note 59, at 131.

[65] *Id.*

V. Whaling Countries Violate International Obligations of *Erga Omnes* Concerning Commercial Whaling Activities

The concept of *erga omnes* obligations, which means the obligations towards all, in international law is defined as the obligations by a State owed to a community States.[66] For the first time, the discussion of this concept appeared in the Barcelona Traction case by the ICJ (*Belgium v. Spain*), where the court concluded the following:

> In particular, an essential distinction should be drawn between the obligations of a state towards the international community as a whole, and those arising vis-a-vis another State in the field of diplomatic protection. By their very nature the former are the concern of all States. In view of the importance of the rights involved, all States can be held to have a legal interest in their protection; they are obligations *erga omnes*.
>
> Such obligations derive, for example, in contemporary international law, from the outlawing of acts of aggression, and of genocide, as also from the principles and rules concerning the basic rights of human person, including protection from slavery and racial discrimination.[67]

While initially, the *erga omnes* obligations were applied in cases of crimes against humanity, genocide, and the prohibition of slavery, with the emerging areas of law, such as animal law and environmental law, the application of this concept is considered acceptable and non-compliance with these obligations form the violation of law. The efficient side of the application of *erga omnes* obligations in the questions of commercial whaling, as well as in any other case, is that it has a universal effect, i.e, it does not affect the bilateral relationship between States. The violation of *erga omnes* obligations is not the violation directed towards a certain State, rather it is centered around the harm to the interests of the whole international community.[68] Given that the huge number of States abstained from exercising commercial whaling and only 3 States continuing this practice, it can be stated that the current whaling States violate the *erga omnes* obligations.

With that said, I would like to discuss the reasoning why these States can continue whaling commercially and the case study held in the ICJ.

---

[66] Ardit Memeti & Bekim Nuhija, *The Concept of Erga Omnes Obligations in International Law*, 14 New Balkan Politics 31, 33-34 (2013).

[67] *Barcelona Traction, Light and Power Company Limited* (Belgium v Spain), Judgment, 1970 I.C.J. Rep. 3, ¶¶ 33-34 (Feb. 5).

[68] Christian J. Tams, *Enforcing Obligations Erga Omnes in International Law* 17 (2005).

VI. Icelandic Whaling

Icelandic whaling activities date back to the twelfth century and continued to the nineteenth century when the modern whaling practices were introduced. Iceland is now one of three countries that continues hunting for whales, both commercially and for the purposes of scientific research, which are allowed under its domestic jurisdiction,[69] and it does catch whales for the subsequent export to Japan. Iceland paused its whaling activities during 2019 and 2021 due to the COVID-19 restrictions, but recently, the Ministry of Food, Agriculture and Fisheries of Iceland announced that it issued special permits that would allow whale hunting and is estimated at catching 209 fin whales and 217 minke whales during each year's whaling season until 2029.[70]

At the international level, since the adoption of the moratorium on commercial whaling, a number of IWC members objected to this decision, but not Iceland, instead, it left the IWC in 1992. However, in 2002, Iceland re-adhered to the ICRW with the instrument that contained the reservation to the commercial whaling moratorium. The text of the reservation reads as follows:

> Notwithstanding this, the Government of Iceland will not authori[z]e whaling for commercial purposes by Icelandic vessels before 2006 and, thereafter, will not authori[z]e such whaling while progress is being made in negotiations within the IWC on the R[evised] M[anagement] S[cheme]. This does not apply, however, in case of the so-called moratorium on whaling for commercial purposes, contained in paragraph 10(e) of the Schedule not being lifted within a reasonable time after the completion of the RMS. Under no circumstances will whaling for commercial purposes be authori[z]ed without a sound scientific basis and an effective management and enforcement scheme.[71]

VII. Japanese Whaling and the Antarctic Case

In the international community, Japan is seen as the main antagonist in questions related to whaling activities. Its whale hunting activities began roughly in the twelfth century, but on an industrial scale, the conduct took place in the 1800s. Japan was actively engaged in commercial whaling during the twentieth century until the IWC imposed a moratorium on commercial whaling in 1986, with Japan

[69] THE WHALING ACT (No. 64/1989).

[70] Amy Walker, *Iceland issues permits allowing whale hunting until 2029*, BBC (Dec. 5, 2024), https://www.bbc.com/news/articles/ced896w96w3o.

[71] *Supra* note 23, Icelandic Instruments of Adherence, International Convention for the Regulation of Whaling, Dec. 2, 1946, 161 U.N.T.S. 72, filed on Jun. 8, 2001; May 10, 2002; Oct. 10, 2002, https://iwc.int/iceland#instruments.

becoming a signatory of the ICRW and a member of the IWC in 1951.[72] Japan was under a lot of pressure in the international community for commercial whaling and for having high quotas on catching whales. This led to a number of concerns among the IWC members and advocates.

In 2010, Australia initiated the proceedings in the ICJ against Japan alleging[73] that the Japanese-launched program "JARPA II" in the Southern Ocean and inside the Australian Whale Sanctuary does not comply with the clause of scientific purposes under the ICRW and that Japan continues to breach three substantive obligations under the Schedule, which included the obligation to respect the moratorium setting zero catch limits for the killing of whales from all stocks for commercial purposes,[74] the obligation not to undertake commercial whaling of fin whales in the Southern Ocean Sanctuary,[75] and the obligation to observe the moratorium on the taking, killing or treating of whales, except minke whales, by factory ships or whale catchers attached to factory ships.[76] Furthermore, Australia alleged that Japan violated the procedural requirements for proposed scientific permits outlined in paragraph 30 of the Schedule of the ICRW. Japan contested all allegations, claiming that its programs were designed for catching and killing cetaceans for the purposes of scientific research, thus, it did not violate the provisions of the convention.[77]

The Court examined the language of the ICRW, specifically Article VIII, taking into consideration other aspects, such as the object and purpose of the convention, preamble, and other provisions. The Court noted in its analysis that the programs designed for the purposes of scientific research shall "foster scientific knowledge; they may pursue an aim other than either conservation or sustainable exploitation of whale stocks."[78] One of the distinguished actions of Japan in relation to whaling was its lethal methods. The Court ought to examine whether the "JARPA II" program involved scientific research purposes and whether the implementation of the program and lethal methods were reasonable. The Court provided that the two elements of the phrase "scientific research" and "for purposes of" in the convention are cumulative. Thus, even if the conduct of whaling involved scientific research, "the killing, taking and

---

[72] Ministry of Foreign Affairs of Japan, https://www.mofa.go.jp/policy/economy/fishery/whales/iwc/what.html#:~:text=The%20International%20Whaling%20Commission%20(IWC,joined%20the%20IWC%20in%201951 (last visited Sep. 30, 2024).

[73] *Whaling in the Antarctic* (Australia v. Japan: New Zealand Intervening), Judgment, 2014 I.C.J. 226, 42-50 (Mar. 31).

[74] *Supra* note 22, Schedule, ¶10(e).

[75] *Id.*, ¶7 (b).

[76] *Id.*, ¶10(d).

[77] *Whaling in the Antarctic, supra* note 73, ¶ 50.

[78] *Id.*, ¶¶51-60.

treating of whales pursuant to such a programme does not fall within Article VIII unless these activities are 'for purposes of' scientific research."[79] The term "scientific research" is, unfortunately, by no means defined by the ICRW, and Australia, in its allegations, relied on the opinion of the scientific expert who claimed that the conduct of scientific research has four essential characteristics, which include "defined and achievable objectives that aim to contribute to knowledge important to the conservation and management of stocks; 'appropriate methods,' including the use of lethal methods only where the objectives of the research cannot be achieved by any other means; peer review; and the avoidance of adverse effects on stock."[80] However, the Court was not persuaded by this argument and stated it was unnecessary to offer a general definition of the term of "scientific research."[81]

In the end, in 2014, the ICJ decided that the Japanese whaling program, "JARPA II" in the Southern Ocean and inside the Australian Whale Sanctuary did not comply with the provisional clause of scientific purposes under the ICRW and was not conducted for scientific purposes. The ICJ also considered the Japanese research program to be unnecessary and lacking scientific merit and provided that this program implied a thinly disguised commercial whaling operation. As a result, Japan was ordered to immediately cease its operations under this program. However, in response to such a ruling, Japan launched a new program "NEWREP-A" as a replacement for its previous program "JARPA II." Its program "NEWREP-A" led to the hunting of 333 Antarctic minke whales annually during the period of 2015-2018.[82]

In addition to losing the case in the ICJ, the Standing Committee of CITES also found Japan's activities of moving the sei whale[83] meat from the high seas into Japan violating the provisions of the convention, mainly prohibiting[84] trade of species and their body parts listed under Appendix I of CITES for commercial purposes. In 2018, Japan withdrew from the IWC, explaining that the IWC lost its original goal to sustainable whaling, implying that the idea of the ICRW was initially to conserve and manage the whale population due to the decline of these animals as opposed to the complete ban on commercial

---

[79] *Id.*, ¶¶60-70.
[80] *Id.*
[81] *Id.*
[82] ICR, *Overview of the New Scientific Whale Research Project in the Antarctic (NEWREP-A)*, https://web.archive.org/web/20240219005119/https://www.icrwhale.org/NEWREP-Agaiyou.html (last visited Oct. 1, 2024).
[83] *Supra* note 38, Appendix I.
[84] *Id.*, art. III.

whaling, and announced that it would resume commercial whaling in 2019.[85] These days, Japan exercises commercial whaling in its territorial waters and EEZ to avoid any potential violations under international law, hunting up to 25 sei whales, 187 Bryde's whales, and 142 minke whales annually, as well as 59 fin whales.[86]

The remaining whaling countries violate *erga omnes* obligations, which raises a huge and critical issue that highlights the tension between national sovereignty and global responsibility. Justifying commercial whaling through cultural and economic arguments, these nations undermine global efforts to protect endangered species and uphold international norms and the legal coherence of international conservation efforts. Apart from that, the whaling nations also fail to recognize the ethical imperative of the issue. While animal protection has not been incorporated fully on an international level, the movement is growing, bringing many more issues on the table that mainly affect not only animals themselves, but also humans and the planet in general. With the methods involved in commercial whaling, these nations violate a rapidly growing ethical consensus that animals are entitled to inherent rights, have intrinsic value, and should be protected from unnecessary suffering and harm. Furthermore, by continuing commercial whaling, these nations contradict the concept of State duties to cooperate, sustainable development, and environmental justice. By disregarding their *erga omnes* obligations, these States provide that their national interests outweigh the global commitments to preserve biodiversity, conserve species of animals, and address the shared global challenges.

VIII. Ecocide

Ecocide is one of the emerging forms of crimes that was proposed by environmentalists, animal rights activists, and advocates due to the emergence of issues that the planet and its inhabitants are facing today. Ecocide implies the extended destruction and damage to the ecosystems to the extent where supporting the life of both humans and non-humans is becoming a question and is associated with global environmental impact, such as the destruction of habitats of species of animals, deforestation, pollution, etc. In 2021, the

---

85 Michal Kolmaš, *When Shaming Fails: Japanese Withdrawal from the International Whaling Commission*, AUSTL. OUTLOOK (Nov. 18, 2020), https://www.internationalaffairs.org.au/australianoutlook/when-shaming-fails-japanese-withdrawal-from-the-international-whaling-commission/.

86 Chris Wold, *Japan Expands Its Whale Hunt to Include Fin Whales and Violates Its Duty to Cooperate* (June 26, 2024), https://www.ejiltalk.org/japan-expands-its-whale-hunt-to-include-fin-whales-and-violates-its-duty-to-cooperate/.

Independent Expert Panel for the Legal Definition of Ecocide, established by environmental advocates and legal scholars, provided a definition of ecocide, which includes the cause of a "serious and widespread harm" to the environment.[87] The term has not been formally recognized as a crime in international law yet, however, a lot of efforts have been made to implement this concept in practice.[88]

In discussing the application of the concept of an ecocide to commercial whaling, it can be easily asserted that the practice has all the elements to consider it an act of ecocide because, in the past, the practice has led to the near extinction of several whale species and with no necessary measures these days the issue might come back since a few species, such as North Atlantic right whale and fin whale while being on the edge of extinction, are still being hunted by the whaling nations, not to mention that the catching of whales greatly affect the entire marine ecosystem as it was discussed in the beginning of the chapter. Whales face all threats mostly from anthropogenic activities and the practices of hunting that also lead to many other issues arising, such as noise pollution, overfishing, habitat loss, and all these actions altogether can cause irreversible damage to the species and their place in the ecosystem. Even with an immediate action to stop commercial whaling, the population of these animals will not be restored fast, thus, the impact of commercial whaling has a long-term harm on the animals and the ecosystem. Whales have long life cycles and slow reproductive rates, as well as they are migratory animals, so their patterns span across national boundaries, and that adds up to the other element of an ecocide.

The depletion of whale populations, in particular, those species that are endangered and on the verge of extinction, disrupts marine ecosystems, contributes greatly to climate change, and causes irreversible and long-term damage to biodiversity. The continued practice of commercial whaling represents a global environmental crime and without necessary steps the situation may turn fatal.

Conclusion

Ending commercial whaling is an urgent and imperative step that needs to be undertaken by the international community. As global awareness of animal law and environmental issues increases along with the disappearance of numerous species of animals and climate change, the urge to take necessary steps comes

---

[87] Stop Ecocide International, https://stopecocide.earth/legal-definition (last visited Oct. 12, 2024).

[88] Jojo Mehta & Julia Jackson, *To stop climate disaster, make ecocide an international crime. It's the only way*, THE GUARDIAN (Feb. 24, 2021), https://www.theguardian.com/commentisfree/2021/feb/24/climate-crisis-ecocide-international-crime.

into place. Whales, as some of the largest and most intelligent creatures on Earth, play a significant role in the entire marine ecosystem and keep the oceans healthy. The continued exploitation of these animals for commercial purposes is a reminder of a world where nature is still viewed as a commodity rather than a shared heritage that needs to be protected. The economic justification for whaling has become increasingly untenable in the modern realities. While some States claim that whaling is an integral part of their cultural traditions, this argument overlooks the fact that cultures evolve and adapt over time, and with even high market demands, a lot of individuals are turning against this cruel and unethical practice.

Continued commercial whaling is also incompatible with established international treaties that are aimed at the protection of endangered species, such as CITES and CBD, which highlight the importance of conserving threatened species. Whaling nations like Japan, Norway, and Iceland, which defy the global moratorium, undermine these international instruments, taking the risk in the credibility of international law.

Bibliography

Advisory Opinion on the Legality of the Threat or Use of Nuclear Weapons, ICJ Reports, 1996, 226, 253; 110 ILR, 163.

Natàlia Amigó, *How do whales help mitigate climate change?* Submon (November 18, 2021), https://www.submon.org/en/how-do-whales-help-mitigate-climate-change/.

Asylum (*Colombia v Peru*), Judgment, 1950 I.C.J. Rep. 266, ¶ 276-277 (Nov. 20).

John Austin, The Province of Jurisprudence Determined XVI (1832).

Barcelona Traction, Light and Power Company Limited (*Belgium v Spain*), Judgment, 1970 I.C.J. Rep. 3, 33-34 (Feb. 5).

Jeremy Bentham, An Introduction to the Principles of Morals and Legislation Chapter XVII (1789). https://doi.org/10.1093/oseo/instance.00077240.

Christophe Boesch & Hedwige Boesch, *Tool Use and Tool Making in Wild Chimpanzees*, 54 Folia Primatol (Basel) 89-91 (1990). https://doi.org/10.1159/000156428.

Continental Shelf (*Libya v Malta*), Judgment, 1985 I.C.J. Rep. 13, ¶ 13, 29 (June 3).

Convention on the Conservation of Migratory Species of Wild Animals ("CMS") art. II, Nov. 6, 1979.

Convention on International Trade in Endangered Species of Wild Fauna and Flora ("CITES") Appendices I, II, III, Mar. 3, 1973.

David Day & Sierra Club, The Whale War 29-32 (1987).

David Favre, *Equitable Self-Ownership for Animals*, 50 Duke L. J. 473, 475 (2000). https://doi.org/10.2307/1373095.

Fisheries (*United Kingdom v Norway*), Judgment, 1951 I.C.J. Rep. 116, ¶ 131, 138 (Dec. 18).

James A. Green, The Persistent Objector Rule in International Law (2016). https://doi.org/10.1093/law/9780198704218.001.0001.

Ian Hurd, *Almost Saving Whales: The Ambiguity of Success at the International Whaling Commission*, Ethics & International Affairs (Aug. 28, 2012), https://papers.ssrn.com/sol3/papers.cfm?abstract_id=2488609. https://doi.org/10.2139/ssrn.2488609.

Icelandic Instruments of Adherence, International Convention for the Regulation of Whaling, Dec. 2, 1946, 161 U.N.T.S. 72, filed on Jun. 8, 2001; May 10, 2002; Oct. 10, 2002, https://iwc.int/iceland#instruments.

ICR, *Overview of the New Scientific Whale Research Project in the Antarctic (NEWREP-A)*, https://web.archive.org/web/20240219005119/. https://www.icrwhale.org/NEWREP-Agaiyou.html.

International Convention for the Regulation of Whaling, Preamble, Dec. 3, 1946.

International Whaling Commission, https://iwc.int/management-and-conservation/whaling/total-catches (last visited September 4, 2024).

Prayank Jain, *Environmental Personhood Towards a Rights Based Approach for Nature and Humanity*, in Green Crimes and International Criminal Law 35 (Regina M. Paulose ed., Vernon Press 2021).

Natalie Klein, *The Right of Visit and the 2005 Protocol on the Suppression of Unlawful Acts against the Safety of Maritime Navigation*, 35 Denver J. of Intl. Law & Policy 287, 288 (2005).

Michal Kolmaš, *When Shaming Fails: Japanese Withdrawal from the International Whaling Commission*, Australian Outlook (Nov. 18, 2020), https://www.internationalaffairs.org.au/australianoutlook/when-shaming-fails-japanese-withdrawal-from-the-international-whaling-commission/.https://doi.org/10.1080/10357718.2020.1799936

Visa Kurki, *Animals, Slaves, and Corporations: Analyzing Legal Thinghood*, 18 German L. J. 1069, 1080 (2017). https://doi.org/10.1017/S2071832200022252.

Simona Lodato & Paola Arlotta, *Generating Neuronal Diversity in the Mammalian Cerebral Cortex*, Annu Rev Cell Dev Biol., 705 (Sep. 11, 2015). https://doi.org/10.1146/annurev-cellbio-100814-125353.

Emma Maddux, *Time to Stand: Exploring the Past, Present, and Future of Nonhuman Animal Standing*, 47 Wake Forest L. Rev. 1243, 1256 (2012).

Jojo Mehta & Julia Jackson, *To stop climate disaster, make ecocide an international crime. It's the only way*, The Guardian (Feb. 24, 2021), https://www.theguardian.com/commentisfree/2021/feb/24/climate-crisis-ecocide-international-crime.

Ardit Memeti & Bekim Nuhija, *The Concept of Erga Omnes Obligations in International Law*, 14 New Balkan Politics 31, 33-34 (2013). https://doi.org/10.2139/ssrn.3502662.

Joseph Mendelson, *Should Animals Have Standing? A Review of Standing Under the Animal Welfare Act*, 24 B. C. Envlt. Aff. L. Rev. 795, 879 (1997).

Merriam-Webster Dictionary (11th ed. 2003); *Sentience*, Cambridge Learner's Dictionary (4th ed. 2021).

Ministry of Foreign Affairs of Japan, https://www.mofa.go.jp/policy/economy/fishery/whales/iwc/what.html#:~:text=The%20International%20Whaling%

20Commission%20(IWC,joined%20the%20IWC%20in%201951 (last visited Sep. 30, 2024).

Nottebohm *(Liechtenstein v Guatemala)*, Judgment, 1955 I.C.J. Rep. 4, ¶ 4, 22 (Apr. 6).

Alex Putzer et al., *Putting the rights of nature on the map. A quantitative analysis of rights of nature initiatives across the world*, 18 J. of Maps 89, 93–96 (2022). https://doi.org/10.1080/17445647.2022.2079432.

Request for an Advisory Opinion Submitted by the Sub-Regional Fisheries Commission (No. 21), Case No. 21, Order of Apr. 2, 2015, 4 ITLOS Rep. 129.

Malcolm Shaw, International Law 74 (1976). https://doi.org/10.1016/0003-2697(76)90208-6.

Statute of the International Court of Justice, art. 38, June 26, 1945.

Stop Ecocide International, https://stopecocide.earth/legal-definition (last visited Oct. 12, 2024).

Cass R. Sunstein, *The Rights of Animals*, 70 U. Chi. L. Rev. 387, 400-401 (2003). https://doi.org/10.2307/1600565.

Christian J. Tams, Enforcing Obligations Erga Omnes in International Law 17 (2005).

Erika J. Techera & Natalie Klein, International Law of Sharks: Obstacles, Options and Opportunities 27 (2017). https://doi.org/10.1163/9789004345515_003.

J.N. Tønnessen & Arne Odd Johnsen, The History of Modern Whaling 3-6 (Univ. of California Press 1982). https://doi.org/10.1525/9780520418752.

The Whaling Act (No. 64/1989) (Icld.). https://doi.org/10.1007/978-1-349-20207-2_10

Treaty of Lisbon amending the Treaty on European Union and the Treaty establishing the European Community, Dec. 13, 2007, Preamble.

United Nations Convention on the Law of the Sea ('UNCLOS') art. 192, Dec. 10, 1982.

UN Environment Programme, https://www.unep.org/news-and-stories/story/protecting-whales-protect-planet.

Amy Walker, *Iceland issues permits allowing whale hunting until 2029*, BBC (Dec. 5, 2024), https://www.bbc.com/news/articles/ced896w96w3o.

Whaling in the Antarctic *(Australia v. Japan: New Zealand Intervening)*, Judgment, 2014 I.C.J. 226 ¶ 42-50 (Mar. 31).

Steven Wise, *The Legal Thinghood of Nonhuman Animals*, 23 Envtl. Aff. L. Rev. 471, 471-472 (1996).

Steven Wise, *Hardly a Revolution - The Eligibility of Nonhuman Animals for Dignity Rights in a Liberal Democracy*, 22 Vt. L. Rev. 793, 900 (1998).

Chris Wold, *Japan Expands Its Whale Hunt to Include Fin Whales and Violates Its Duty to Cooperate* (June 26, 2024), https://www.ejiltalk.org/japan-expands-its-whale-hunt-to-include-fin-whales-and-violates-its-duty-to-cooperate.

Chapter 3

Reforming UNCLOS: Addressing Global Ocean Governance Challenges in the twenty-first Century

Dr. Pierpaolo Petrelli

Associate Professor at O.P. Jindal Global University

Abstract: UNCLOS, a cornerstone of maritime governance, has significantly shaped international ocean management through innovations like Exclusive Economic Zones and the designation of Areas Beyond National Jurisdiction (ABNJ) as the "common heritage of mankind." Despite these achievements, UNCLOS's reliance on voluntary compliance, fragmented regulations, and outdated provisions increasingly fail to address twenty-first-century challenges, such as IUU fishing, human rights abuses, and climate-induced ecological crises. These gaps jeopardize marine biodiversity, global food security, and socio-economic equity, particularly for Small Island Developing States (SIDS).

This chapter critiques UNCLOS's limitations by using regional case studies. In the Arctic, melting ice exposes governance gaps, as new shipping routes emerge. The Mediterranean region highlights the human toll of fragmented migration policies and inconsistent search and rescue (SAR) operations. The Pacific region shows SIDS vulnerabilities to weak enforcement, flag-of-convenience practices, and climate-driven shifts.

The proposed reforms include binding Article 119 bis for climate-resilient fisheries management, mandatory vessel audits overseen by Regional Fisheries Management Organizations (RFMOs), and equipping RFMOs with enforceable authority. Technological innovations such as blockchain-based seafood traceability and satellite surveillance offer transformative solutions. Reforming UNCLOS is a legal necessity and moral imperative to ensure sustainable equitable ocean governance for future generations.

Keywords: UNCLOS reform, SIDS, Regional Fisheries Management Organizations, Arctic, migrants, EEZ, Search and Rescue operations, Sustainable Development Goals.

Introduction

Oceans, covering over 70% of the Earth's surface and regulating the planet's climate, are critical for sustaining life on Earth. They support intricate ecosystems, drive global trade, and provide livelihoods to billions of people.[1] However, these vital resources face unprecedented threats, with over 35% of fish stocks being overexploited and millions being dependent on fragile marine ecosystems.[2] These escalating challenges expose critical weaknesses in global ocean governance frameworks, particularly in the UNCLOS.[3] Adopted in 1982 and enforced in 1994, UNCLOS was a groundbreaking achievement in international law, introducing principles that balanced the sovereign rights of coastal states with the collective responsibility to protect the world's oceans.[4] However, drafted during an era of Cold War geopolitics and nascent environmental awareness, its provisions now struggle to address the complexities of the rapidly evolving maritime landscape.[5]

UNCLOS's transformative framework introduced EEZs, designated Areas Beyond National Jurisdiction as the "common heritage of mankind," and

---

[1] Alok Jha, *The Ocean Is Not Just Huge but Also Hugely Important*, THE CONVERSATION (Mar. 26, 2014), https://theconversation.com/the-ocean-is-not-just-huge-but-also-hugely-important-24815; Johan Rockström, Tim Beringer, David Hole, Bronson Griscom, Michael B. Mascia, Carl Folke & Felix Creutzig, *We Need Biosphere Stewardship That Protects Carbon Sinks and Builds Resilience*, 118 PROC. NAT'L ACAD. SCI. (2021), https://doi.org/10.1073/pnas.2115218118.

[2] U.N. FOOD & AGRIC. ORG. (FAO), *The State of World Fisheries and Aquaculture 2024* (2024), https://openknowledge.fao.org/server/api/core/bitstreams/66538eba-9c85-4504-8438-c1cf0a0a3903/content/cd0683en.html.

[3] Bilawal M. Khaskheli et al., *Technology Advancement and International Law in Marine Policy, Challenges, Solutions, and Future Prospective*, 10 FRONTIERS MAR. SCI. (2023), HTTPS://DOI.ORG/10.3389/FMARS.2023.1258924.

[4] UNITED NATIONS CONVENTION ON THE LAW OF THE SEA (UNCLOS), Dec. 10, 1982, 1833 U.N.T.S. 3 (entered into force Nov. 16, 1994) https://www.un.org/depts/los/convention_agreements/texts/unclos/unclos_e.pdf; Chris Armstrong, *The United Nations Convention on the Law of the Sea, Global Justice and the Environment*, 13 GLOBAL CONSTITUTIONALISM 16, 16–20 (2023), https://doi.org/10.1017/s2045381723000151.

[5] Nilufer Oral, UNCLOS and Sea Level Rise, 149 MARINE POLICY (2023), https://doi.org/10.1016/j.marpol.2022.105454.

implemented binding dispute resolution mechanisms.[6] These innovations have laid the foundation for balancing resource exploitation, navigational rights, and environmental protection. However, decades of inaction to adapt its provisions have left UNCLOS ill-equipped to address the contemporary challenges. This chapter examines the most pressing governance challenges facing UNCLOS, focusing on the systemic gaps in enforcement, jurisdictional ambiguities, and environmental governance.[7]

One of UNCLOS's most glaring weaknesses is its reliance on flag-state jurisdiction under Article 94, which imposes detailed obligations on flag-states, but has been undermined by inadequate enforcement and flag-of-convenience practices.[8] These practices enable vessels to evade accountability by registering in states that have minimal regulatory oversight.[9] This loophole facilitates IUU fishing, resulting in global economic losses estimated between $10 billion to $23.5 billion annually, with enforcement challenges prevalent in hotspot regions such as the Indo-Pacific.[10] UNCLOS's systemic reliance on voluntary compliance underscores UNCLOS's inability to effectively enforce its principles in an interconnected maritime environment.[11]

Jurisdictional ambiguities exacerbate these problems. Articles 56 and 74 of UNCLOS, addressing EEZ rights and overlapping maritime claims, lack binding resolution mechanisms and often compel states into protracted negotiations

---

[6] The concept of CHM is particularly significant for ABNJ governance. The CHM principle aims to contribute to *"a just and equitable international economic order" that considers the interests of all nations, especially developing countries..."* see Marie Bourrel et al., *The Common Heritage of Mankind as a Means to Assess and Advance Equity in Deep Sea Mining,* 95 MARINE POL'Y 311, 311-316 (2016), https://doi.org/10.1016/j.marpol.2016.07.017.

[7] Armstrong, *supra* note 4; UNITED NATIONS GENERAL ASSEMBLY, *Transforming Our World: The 2030 Agenda for Sustainable Development,* U.N. Doc. A/RES/70/1, at 1 (Oct. 21, 2015), https://sdgs.un.org/2030agenda.

[8] "Each State shall effectively exercise its jurisdiction and control in administrative, technical, and social matters over ships flying its flag." *See* UNCLOS, *supra* note 3, Article 94; *see* also James H. Ford & Chris Wilcox, *Shedding Light on the Dark Side of Maritime Trade - A New Approach for Identifying Countries as Flags of Convenience,* 99 MARINE POL'Y 298, 298-303 (2018), https://doi.org/10.1016/j.marpol.2018.10.026.

[9] Ford & Wilcox, *supra* note 8.

[10] U.N. FOOD & AGRIC. ORG. (FAO), *The State of World Fisheries and Aquaculture 2022: Towards Blue Transformation* 57 (2022), https://www.fao.org/publications/sofia/2022 (analyzing the economic impacts of IUU fishing); INTERPOL, *Case Studies on IUU Fishing Enforcement Operations,* Rep. No. 18/SPRW, at 14–20 (2018) (documenting enforcement challenges in hotspot regions).

[11] Bourrel et al., *supra* note 6.

or reliance on alternative tribunals.[12] For instance, China's expansive nine-dash line claim in the South China Sea directly contravenes UNCLOS principles, fueling regional instability despite the 2016 arbitral ruling invalidating the claim.[13] The absence of robust enforcement mechanisms perpetuates such disputes, underscoring UNCLOS's limitations in managing geopolitical conflicts related to resource management and navigational rights.[14]

The landmark case *of Philippines v. China* (2016), adjudicated under the auspices of the Permanent Court of Arbitration, invalidated China's nine-dash-line claim in the South China Sea, reaffirming UNCLOS's principles of equitable maritime resource allocation.[15] Despite this, China's refusal to comply with the ruling demonstrates the limitations of the UNCLOS enforcement mechanisms. Similarly, in the case of *Bangladesh v. Myanmar* (2012), resolved by ITLOS, highlighted the potential of UNCLOS to peacefully settle overlapping EEZ disputes.[16] However, such success remains an exception, as many disputes, including those in the Arctic, rely on prolonged negotiations rather than binding resolutions.

Comparative international frameworks offer valuable lessons in reform. The Antarctic Treaty System demonstrates the efficacy of binding obligations with Articles 1 and 3, establishing robust frameworks for peaceful purposes and ecosystem preservation.[17] Similarly, the Paris Agreement illustrates the integration of enforceable climate commitments through mechanisms, such as Article 6, which promotes market-based approaches for emission reductions.[18]

---

[12] UNCLOS, *supra* note 3, Articles 56, 74; Alan E. Boyle, Dispute Settlement and the Law of the Sea Convention: Problems of Fragmentation and Jurisdiction, 46 INT'L & COMP. L.Q. 37, 37–54 (1997), https://doi.org/10.1017/s0020589300060103; Chie Kojima, *Integration of General Principles of International Environmental Law into the Law of the Sea: Assessment and Challenges*, 149 MARINE POL'Y (2023), https://doi.org/10.1016/j.marpol.2023.105497.

[13] PERMANENT COURT OF ARBITRATION, *South China Sea Arbitration (Philippines v. China)*, Award (July 12, 2016), paras. 75–83, https://pcacases.com/web/view/7; *see* also Douglas Guilfoyle, *The Rule of Law and Maritime Security: Understanding Lawfare in the South China Sea*, 95 INT'L AFF. 999, 999–1017 (2019), https://doi.org/10.1093/ia/iiz141.

[14] Armstrong, *supra* note 4.

[15] *South China Sea Arbitration (Philippines v. China)*, *supra* note 13.

[16] *Dispute Concerning Delimitation of the Maritime Boundary Between Bangladesh and Myanmar in the Bay of Bengal* (*Bangladesh/Myanmar*), Judgment, ITLOS REPORTS 2012.

[17] *Antarctic Treaty* arts. 1, 3, Dec. 1, 1959, 402 U.N.T.S. 71 (entered into force June 23, 1961); *see* also Joanna Yao, *An International Hierarchy of Science: Conquest, Cooperation, and the 1959 Antarctic Treaty System*, 27 EUR. J. INT'L REL. 995, 995–1019 (2021), https://doi.org/10.1177/13540661211033889.

[18] *Paris Agreement* art. 6, Dec. 12, 2015, T.I.A.S. No. 16-1104, 55 I.L.M. 743 (entered into force Nov. 4, 2016).

These models exemplify the adaptability and enforceability that UNCLOS must adopt in order to remain relevant in a rapidly changing world.[19]

Beyond governance, UNCLOS's environmental provisions, discussed further below, fail to address modern threats, such as ocean acidification, blue carbon ecosystem degradation, and climate-driven shifts in fisheries.[20] Critical habitats such as mangroves and seagrasses, which are essential for carbon sequestration and ecosystem health, face escalating threats from rising sea levels, coastal development, and unsustainable practices.[21] Despite their ecological importance, UNCLOS lacks enforceable mandates for protection, leaving states dependent on fragmented national policies that fall short of global sustainability objectives.[22]

Human rights violations in the maritime sector further underscore UNCLOS's inadequacies of UNCLOS. Industries linked to IUU fishing are often riddled with exploitative practices, including forced labor, wage theft, and human trafficking.[23] Migrant workers aboard fishing vessels endure inhumane conditions that are exacerbated by weak oversight in areas beyond national jurisdiction.[24] While UNCLOS imposes general obligations for SAR operations, these provisions are insufficient to combat labor abuse.[25] Expanding UNCLOS

---

19 Christina Voigt, *The Power of the Paris Agreement in International Climate Litigation*, 32 REV. EUR. COMP. & INT'L ENVTL. L. 237, 237–249 (2023), https://doi.org/10.1111/reel.12514.

20 UNCLOS, *supra* note 3, Part XII, Articles 192–237; *see* also Oral, *supra* note 5; Armstrong, *supra* note 4.

21 Ken W. Krauss et al., *How Mangrove Forests Adjust to Rising Sea Level*, 202 NEW PHYTOLOGIST 19, 19–34 (2013), https://doi.org/10.1111/nph.12605; Eric L. Gilman et al., *Threats to Mangroves from Climate Change and Adaptation Options: A Review*, 89 AQUATIC BOTANY 237, 237–250 (2008), https://doi.org/10.1016/j.aquabot.2007.12.009.

22 Sarah M. Watson, *Greenhouse Gas Emissions from Offshore Oil and Gas Activities—Relevance of the Paris Agreement, Law of the Sea, and Regional Seas Programmes*, 185 OCEAN & COASTAL MGMT (2019), https://doi.org/10.1016/j.ocecoaman.2019.104942.

23 Several papers highlight the connection between IUU fishing and human rights violations. For example, *see* Baris Soyer, David Miller & Georgios Leloudas, *Tackling IUU Fishing: Developing a Holistic Legal Response*, 7 TRANSNAT'L ENVTL. L. 139, 139-163 (2017), https://doi.org/10.1017/s2047102517000267; Christopher Ewell et al., *Potential Ecological and Social Benefits of a Moratorium on Transshipment on the High Seas*, 81 MARINE POL'Y 293, 293-300 (2017), https://doi.org/10.1016/j.marpol.2017.04.004; Jane Lubchenco & Peter M. Haugan, *Illegal, Unreported and Unregulated Fishing and Associated Drivers*, in 1 SPRINGER 553, 553-591 (2023), https://doi.org/10.1007/978-3-031-16277-0_15.

24 Ewell et al., *supra* note 21; *see* also Natalie A. Miller et al., *Identifying Global Patterns of Transshipment Behavior*, 5 FRONTIERS MARINE SCI. 7 (2018), https://doi.org/10.3389/fmars.2018.00240.

25 Armstrong, *supra* note 4; Watson, *supra* note 20.

to incorporate binding human rights standards would align it with contemporary ethical norms, although such reforms face resistance from states that prioritize sovereignty over accountability.[26]

UNCLOS's foundational principle of the "common heritage of mankind" offers significant potential for equitable resource management but suffers from legal ambiguities and the absence of binding obligations.[27] The lack of robust regulations for activities, such as deep-sea mining, raises concerns about environmental degradation and inequitable exploitation.[28] Recent initiatives, such as the 2023 High Seas Treaty, provide a potential roadmap for bridging these gaps but emphasize the need for harmonization with UNCLOS to ensure consistency and collective stewardship.[29]

I. UNCLOS and the Challenges of Modern Ocean Governance

UNCLOS has long served as the cornerstone of global maritime governance, establishing a framework that balances coastal state sovereignty with the

---

[26] States may be reluctant to accept binding human rights obligations within the context of maritime law, particularly given the challenges already faced in implementing existing human rights commitments. *See* Vidya V. Nadkarni & Rakesh Sinha, *Transforming Social Work Education in India: Integrating Human Rights*, 1 J. HUM. RTS. & SOC. WORK 9, 9-18 (2016), https://doi.org/10.1007/s41134-016-0002-3.

[27] UNCLOS, *supra* note 3, Article 136; *see* also Chunyan Wang, Qian Zhao & Yen-Chiang Chang, *On the Legal Status of Marine Fishery Resources: From the Perspectives of International Fishery Law*, 9 HELIYON (2023), https://doi.org/10.1016/j.heliyon.2023.e15354; Astra Zalik, *Mining the Seabed, Enclosing the Area: Ocean Grabbing, Proprietary Knowledge and the Geopolitics of the Extractive Frontier Beyond National Jurisdiction*, 68 INT'L SOC. SCI. J. 343, 343-359 (2018), https://doi.org/10.1111/issj.12159.

[28] INTERNATIONAL TRIBUNAL FOR THE LAW OF THE SEA (ITLOS), *Seabed Disputes Chamber, Advisory Opinion*, Feb. 1, 2011, ¶¶ 143–145, ITLOS Reports 2011. (highlighting regulatory challenges in seabed mining); *see* also Nélia C. Mestre et al., *Exploitation of Deep-Sea Resources: The Urgent Need to Understand the Role of High Pressure in the Toxicity of Chemical Pollutants to Deep-Sea Organisms*, 185 ENVTL. POLLUTION 369, 369-371 (2013), https://doi.org/10.1016/j.envpol.2013.10.021; Jia Wang et al., *Taking Precautionary Approaches to the Governance of Commercial Deep Seabed Mining: Law-Making of International Seabed Authority and Multi-Subject Participation*, 15 SUSTAINABILITY (2023), https://doi.org/10.3390/su15086414.

[29] UNITED NATIONS, *High Seas Treaty*, June 19, 2023, arts. 12–14, U.N. Doc. A/RES/77/249; *see* also Elisa Morgera et al., *Addressing the Ocean-Climate Nexus in the BBNJ Agreement: Strategic Environmental Assessments, Human Rights and Equity in Ocean Science*, 38 INT'L J. MARINE & COASTAL L. 447, 447-479 (2023), https://doi.org/10.1163/15718085-bja10139.

principles of shared stewardship over ABNJ.[30] However, its static provisions, designed in 1982, struggled to address the modern complexities of ocean governance.[31] IUU fishing, jurisdictional disputes, and climate-induced ecological changes are straining its framework, exposing gaps in enforcement, adaptability, and equity.[32]

One of the most pressing deficiencies lies in UNCLOS's reliance on flag state jurisdiction under Article 94, which obliges states to ensure compliance with international standards for vessels flying flags. This provision was intended to uphold state sovereignty while ensuring vessel accountability, but it has been undermined by the proliferation of flags of convenience whereby vessels register in states with minimal regulatory oversight.[33] These practices facilitate IUU fishing and labor abuse and enable evasion of oversight through mechanisms such as flag hopping.[34] Global economic losses from IUU fishing alone exceed $20 billion annually.[35]

The governance gaps identified in the Arctic, Mediterranean, and Pacific illustrate the need for systemic reforms to UNCLOS, including stricter obligations on flag states to enhance accountability.[36] For example, port state controls could require rigorous documentation checks supported by regional cooperation to mitigate loopholes in flag state jurisdiction.[37] Additionally, clarifying liability

---

30 Alexander Proelss (ed.), *United Nations Convention on the Law of the Sea: A Commentary* 12–15 (Nomos, 2017); David Anderson, *Modern Law of the Sea: Selected Essays* 89–91 (Martinus Nijhoff Publishers, 2008).

31 Elise Druel & Kristina M. Gjerde, *Sustaining Marine Life Beyond Boundaries: Options for an Implementing Agreement for Marine Biodiversity Beyond National Jurisdiction Under the United Nations Convention on the Law of the Sea*, 49 MARINE POL'Y 90, 90-97 (2013), https://doi.org/10.1016/j.marpol.2013.11.023.

32 Gohar A. Petrossian, *Preventing Illegal, Unreported and Unregulated (IUU) Fishing: A Situational Approach*, 189 BIOLOGICAL CONSERVATION 39, 39-48 (2014), https://doi.org/10.1016/j.biocon.2014.09.005.

33 UNCLOS, *supra* note 3, Article 94; *see* also Boyle, *supra* note 12; Druel & Gjerde, *supra* note 29.

34 Gohar A. Petrossian et al., *Flags for Sale: An Empirical Assessment of Flag of Convenience Desirability to Foreign Vessels*, 116 MARINE POL'Y 103937 (2020), https://doi.org/10.1016/j.marpol.2020.103937.

35 Heidi Welch et al., *Hot Spots of Unseen Fishing Vessels*, 8 SCI. ADVANCES (2022), https://doi.org/10.1126/sciadv.abq2109; Ussif Rashid Sumaila et al., *Illicit Trade in Marine Fish Catch and Its Effects on Ecosystems and People Worldwide*, 6 SCI. ADVANCES (2020), https://doi.org/10.1126/sciadv.aaz3801.

36 Druel & Gjerde. *supra* note 29.

37 Lay Fong Chuah et al., *Analyzing the Influencing Factors of Port State Control for a Cleaner Environment via Bayesian Network Model*, 14 CLEANER ENG'G & TECH. (2023), https://doi.org/10.1016/j.clet.2023.100636; Şafak Şanlıer, *Analysis of Port State Control*

frameworks for environmental damage and human rights violations would strengthen accountability for states and vessel operators in flags of convenience.[38]

The problem of jurisdictional disputes further underscores UNCLOS's limitations of UNCLOS in addressing modern ocean governance challenges.[39] Articles 56 and 74, which govern EEZs and overlapping maritime claims, rely heavily on voluntary arbitration and non-binding dispute resolution mechanisms.[40] While these provisions were intended to promote cooperation and respect state sovereignty, they have proven to be inadequate in resolving disputes in contentious regions.[41] For example, the South China Sea dispute exemplifies this inadequacy. Despite the 2016 arbitral tribunal ruling under UNCLOS invalidating China's nine-dash-line claims, China's refusal to comply highlights the treaty's lack of enforceable mechanisms.[42] This defiance undermines the rule of law, jeopardizes regional stability, and obstructs equitable resource management.[43]

Similarly, the Arctic region demonstrates how climate change and geopolitical competition exacerbate jurisdictional ambiguity.[44] As melting ice opens up previously inaccessible areas, states assert overlapping claims to maritime

---

Inspection Data: The Black Sea Region, 112 MARINE POL'Y (2019), https://doi.org/10.1016/j.marpol.2019.103757.

38 Jelena Subotic, *Expanding the Scope of Post-Conflict Justice: Individual, State and Societal Responsibility for Mass Atrocity*, 48 J. PEACE RSCH. 157, 157–169 (2011), https://doi.org/10.1177/0022343310394696.

39 Boyle, *supra* note 12.

40 *See* UNCLOS, *supra* note 3, Articles 56, 74. For example, the Convention allows for the use of joint management zones (JMZs) as an alternative to outright delimitation, particularly for shared resources like transboundary fisheries. *See* Nesli Isigi Kadagi et al., *Joint Management of Shared Resources as an Alternative Approach for Addressing Maritime Boundary Disputes: The Kenya-Somalia Maritime Boundary Dispute*, 16 J. INDIAN OCEAN REG. 348, 348–370 (2020), https://doi.org/10.1080/19480881.2020.1823169.

41 Mariachiara Melillo, *Informal Dispute Resolution in Preferential Trade Agreements*, 53 J. WORLD TRADE 95, 95–127 (2019), https://doi.org/10.54648/trad2019005.

42 *South China Sea Arbitration (Philippines v. China)*, *supra* note 13, paras. 210–212.

43 Elizabeth Mendenhall, *Making the Most of What We Already Have: Activating UNCLOS to Combat Marine Plastic Pollution*, 155 MARINE POL'Y (2023), https://doi.org/10.1016/j.marpol.2023.105786.

44 Dmitry Sharapov, *Northern Sea Route and Climate Change*, 460 E3S WEB CONF. (2023), https://doi.org/10.1051/e3sconf/202346009019; Elizabeth A. Barnes & James A. Screen, *The Impact of Arctic Warming on the Midlatitude Jet-Stream: Can It? Has It? Will It?*, 6 WIREs CLIMATE CHANGE 277, 277–286 (2015), https://doi.org/10.1002/wcc.337.

zones and resources, straining UNCLOS's governance framework.[45] Article 234, which addresses ice-covered areas, narrowly focuses on pollution control and does not adequately address broader complexities, such as environmental protection, shipping governance, or resource management.[46] Without binding dispute resolution mechanisms or enforceable legal standards, critical governance gaps persist in one of the world's most fragile ecosystems.[47]

To address these shortcomings, UNCLOS should incorporate binding arbitration mechanisms under Article 74 to resolve EEZ disputes and overlapping claims effectively.[48] Establishing a permanent maritime adjudication body within the ITLOS could provide a centralized forum for dispute resolution, offering enforceable decisions to ensure equitable outcomes.[49] Cooperative resource-sharing models, such as the Barents Sea Agreement between Norway and Russia, demonstrate the potential for joint development agreements.[50] By incentivizing such agreements and requiring their integration into UNCLOS, states can manage contested areas more effectively while fostering collaboration and stability.[51]

In addition to jurisdictional disputes, the accelerating impact of climate change highlights the limitations of UNCLOS in addressing environmental challenges.[52] Rising sea levels, ocean acidification, and shifting fish migration patterns disrupt marine ecosystems and threaten the livelihood of coastal communities.[53] Despite these profound effects, UNCLOS lacks binding

---

[45] Brendan M. Boylan, *Increased Maritime Traffic in the Arctic: Implications for Governance of Arctic Sea Routes,* 131 MARINE POL'Y (2021), https://doi.org/10.1016/j.marpol.2021.104566.

[46] UNCLOS, *supra* note 3, Article 234.

[47] Oral, *supra* note 5.

[48] UNCLOS, *supra* note 3, Article 74.

[49] Eric A. Posner & John C. Yoo, *A Theory of International Adjudication,* SSRN ELEC. J. (2004), https://doi.org/10.2139/ssrn.507003.

[50] Min Pan & Henry P. Huntington, *A Precautionary Approach to Fisheries in the Central Arctic Ocean: Policy, Science, and China,* 63 MARINE POL'Y 153, 153–157 (2015), https://doi.org/10.1016/j.marpol.2015.10.015; *see* also Arild Moe et al., *Space and Timing: Why Was the Barents Sea Delimitation Dispute Resolved in 2010?,* 34 POLAR GEOGRAPHY 145, 145–162 (2011), https://doi.org/10.1080/1088937x.2011.597887; Elena Eriksen et al., *From Single Species Surveys Towards Monitoring of the Barents Sea Ecosystem,* 166 PROG. OCEANOG. 4, 4–14 (2017), https://doi.org/10.1016/j.pocean.2017.09.007.

[51] Armstrong, *supra* note 4; Oral, *supra* note 5.

[52] Oral, *supra* note 18.

[53] "Rising atmospheric carbon dioxide (CO 2) levels, from fossil fuel combustion and deforestation, along with agriculture and land-use practices are causing wholesale increases in seawater CO 2 and inorganic carbon levels; reductions in pH; and alterations

commitment to mitigate or adapt to climate-induced changes, particularly in ABNJ.[54] This omission leaves states and regional governance frameworks ill-prepared to effectively respond to the cascading environmental and economic consequences of a warming planet.[55]

One critical area of reform is the establishment of adaptive management mechanisms.[56] Introducing a new provision, Article 119 bis, could enable UNCLOS to incorporate climate-resilient fishery management practices. This provision could include science-based quotas, predictive modelling of fish stock migration patterns, and mandatory reporting mechanisms for states. Such measures would promote the sustainable use of marine resources, particularly in regions such as the Pacific, where SIDS face disproportionate challenges from shifting fish stocks and rising ocean temperatures.[57] These reforms would also support UNCLOS's broader objective of equitable resource distribution, ensuring that vulnerable states are not left to bear the brunt of climate-induced resource scarcity.[58]

---

in acid-base chemistry of estuarine, coastal, and surface open-ocean waters. On the basis of laboratory experiments and field studies of naturally elevated CO 2 marine environments, widespread biological impacts of human-driven ocean acidification have been posited, ranging from changes in organism physiology and population dynamics to altered communities and ecosystems. Acidification, in conjunction with other climate change–related environmental stresses, particularly under future climate change and further elevated atmospheric CO2 levels, potentially puts at risk many of the valuable ecosystem services that the ocean provides to society, such as fisheries, aquaculture, and shoreline protection." *See* Scott C. Doney et al., *The Impacts of Ocean Acidification on Marine Ecosystems and Reliant Human Communities*, 45 ANN. REV. ENVIRON. & RES. 83, 83–112 (2020), https://doi.org/10.1146/annurev-environ-012320-083019; *see* also Nicolás E. Talloni-Álvarez et al., *Climate Change Impact on Canada's Pacific Marine Ecosystem: The Current State of Knowledge*, 104 MARINE POL'Y 163, 163–176 (2019), https://doi.org/10.1016/j.marpol.2019.02.035.

54 Natalie B. Gardiner, *Marine Protected Areas in the Southern Ocean: Is the Antarctic Treaty System Ready to Co-Exist with a New United Nations Instrument for Areas Beyond National Jurisdiction?*, 122 MARINE POL'Y (2020), https://doi.org/10.1016/j.marpol.2020.104212.

55 Oral, *supra* note 5.

56 This may involve developing new norms and standards for regional cooperation, as demonstrated by the Common Fisheries Resource Analysis of skipjack tuna in the South China Sea. *See* Jessica Prince et al., *Supporting Regional Co-Operation in the South China Sea with an Initial Assessment of the Data-Limited Skipjack Tuna Fishery*, 155 MARINE POL'Y (2023), https://doi.org/10.1016/j.marpol.2023.105711.

57 James M. Shultz et al., *Disaster Risk Reduction and Sustainable Development for Small Island Developing States*, 3 DISASTER HEALTH 32, 32–44 (2016), https://doi.org/10.1080/21665044.2016.1173443.

58 Druel & Gjerde. *supra* note 29; Voigt, *supra* note 17.

The protection of blue carbon ecosystems such as mangroves, seagrasses, and salt marshes represent another urgent area where UNCLOS can be strengthened.[59] These ecosystems play a dual role in mitigating climate change through carbon sequestration and preserving biodiversity.[60] However, they remain largely unprotected within the current framework.[61] Explicit provisions for their conservation would align UNCLOS with global climate agreements such as the Paris Agreement, creating synergies between marine and climate governance.[62] By safeguarding these ecosystems, UNCLOS could advance its environmental mandate while addressing the interconnected challenges of climate change and biodiversity loss.[63]

The human rights challenges within the maritime sector further illustrate the inadequacies of UNCLOS. Industries linked to IUU fishing are often marred by exploitative practices, including forced labor, wage theft, and human trafficking.[64] Migrant workers aboard fishing vessels frequently endure inhumane conditions exacerbated by the weak regulatory oversight of the ABNJ.[65] While UNCLOS

---

59 Druel & Gjerde. *supra* note 29; Charlotte Salpin et al., *Marine Scientific Research in Pacific Small Island Developing States*, 95 MARINE POL'Y 363, 363–371 (2016), https://doi.org/10.1016/j.marpol.2016.07.019.

60 For instance, in the United Arab Emirates, natural mangroves were found to hold substantial carbon in above- and belowground biomass, with total ecosystem carbon stocks ranging from 2 to 515 Mg C/ha; *see* Lisa M. Schile et al., *Limits on Carbon Sequestration in Arid Blue Carbon Ecosystems*, 27 ECOL. APPLICATIONS 859, 859–874 (2017), https://doi.org/10.1002/eap.1489. Similarly, the Gulf of Mexico's blue carbon habitats store an estimated 480.48 Tg C, with mangroves being the dominant carbon stock; *see* Anitra L. Thorhaug et al., *Gulf of Mexico Estuarine Blue Carbon Stock, Extent and Flux: Mangroves, Marshes, and Seagrasses: A North American Hotspot*, 653 SCI. TOTAL ENV'T 1253, 1253–1261 (2018), https://doi.org/10.1016/j.scitotenv.2018.10.011.

61 Druel & Gjerde. *supra* note 29; Salpin et al., *supra* note 57.

62 Voigt, *supra* note 17.

63 *Id.*

64 Multiple studies have found evidence linking IUU fishing operations to forced labor, human trafficking, and other exploitative practices. *See* Ewell et al., *supra* note 21; Mary Mackay, *The Intersection Between Illegal Fishing, Crimes at Sea, and Social Well-Being*, 7 FRONTIERS MARINE SCI. 10 (2020), https://doi.org/10.3389/fmars.2020.589000; Elizabeth R. Selig et al., *Revealing Global Risks of Labor Abuse and Illegal, Unreported, and Unregulated Fishing*, 13 NAT. COMMC'NS 1 (2022), https://doi.org/10.1038/s41467-022-28916-2.

65 INTERNATIONAL LABOUR ORGANIZATION, *Forced Labour and Human Trafficking in Fisheries*, https://www.ilo.org/topics/forced-labour-modern-slavery-and-trafficking-persons/sectors-and-topics/forced-labour-and-human-trafficking-fisheries; INTERNATIONAL TRANSPORT WORKERS' FEDERATION, *A One Way Ticket to Labour Exploitation: How Transit Visa Loopholes Are Being Used to Exploit Migrant Fishers on UK Fishing Vessels*, https://www.itfglobal.org/sites/default/files/node/resources/files/ITF_Fisheries-Briefi

imposes general obligations for safety and humane treatment, it lacks specific, enforceable provisions that address the protection of maritime workers' rights.

To address these issues, UNCLOS must explicitly integrate labor standards into its framework.[66] Amending Article 94 to require compliance with international labor conventions, such as the ILO Work in Fishing Convention (No. 188),[67] would compel flag states to enforce humane working conditions aboard their vessels.[68] Additionally, port state measures, already a proven tool in combating IUU fishing, could be expanded to include mandatory labor inspections.[69] Such measures would ensure that vessels entering ports adhere to international labor standards, fostering accountability across maritime industries.[70]

II. Real-World Impacts of UNCLOS's Limitations

As the lifeblood of global ecosystems and economies, the world's oceans demand a governance framework robust enough to address the escalating pressures of the twenty-first century.[71] For decades, the UNCLOS, often hailed

---

ng_Final.pdf; WORLD WIDE FUND FOR NATURE (WWF), *Slavery at Sea: Forced Labour, Human Rights Abuses, and the Need for the Western and Central Pacific Fisheries Commission to Establish Labour Standards for Crew*, Comm'n 18th Reg. Sess., WCPFC18-2021-OP091 (Nov. 18, 2021), https://meetings.wcpfc.int/file/10140/download.

66 Penelope J. Ridings, *Labour Standards on Fishing Vessels: A Problem in Search of a Home?*, 22 Melb. J. Int'l L. 308, 308-331 (2021), https://law.unimelb.edu.au/__data/assets/pdf_file/0017/4126004/Ridings-unpaginated.pdf.

67 INTERNATIONAL LABOUR ORGANIZATION (ILO), *C188 - Work in Fishing Convention, 2007 (No. 188)*, https://normlex.ilo.org/dyn/normlex/en/f?p=NORMLEXPUB:12100:0::NO::P12100_INSTRUMENT_ID:312333.

68 The Maritime Labour Convention (MLC) of 2006 already establishes rights and protections for seafarers, including regulations on working hours, accommodation, and repatriation; *see* Ashwin A. Hebbar & Narayan Mukesh, *COVID-19 and Seafarers' Rights to Shore Leave, Repatriation and Medical Assistance: A Pilot Study*, 71 INT'L MAR. HEALTH 217, 217-228 (2020), https://doi.org/10.5603/imh.2020.0040. However, ratification and enforcement of ILO conventions remain inconsistent across countries; *see* Joseph Ladou, *International Occupational Health*, 206 INT'L J. HYGIENE & ENVTL. HEALTH 303, 303-313 (2003), https://doi.org/10.1078/1438-4639-00226; Durmaz Peksen & Robert G. Blanton, *The Impact of ILO Conventions on Worker Rights: Are Empty Promises Worse Than No Promises?*, 12 Rev. Int'l Orgs. 75, 75-94 (2016), https://doi.org/10.1007/s11558-015-9241-9.

69 Selig et al., *supra* note 62.

70 *Id.*; *See* also Kirsten Auld et al., *The Collective Effort of the United Nations Specialised Agencies to Tackle the Global Problem of Illegal, Unreported and Unregulated (IUU) Fishing*, 243 OCEAN & COASTAL MGMT. (2023), https://doi.org/10.1016/j.ocecoaman.2023.106720.

71 Robin Warner & Rosemary Rayfuse, *Securing a Sustainable Future for the Oceans Beyond National Jurisdiction: The Legal Basis for an Integrated Cross-Sectoral Regime for*

as the cornerstone of international maritime law, has provided a foundational structure for ocean governance.[72] However, as crises such as climate change, biodiversity loss, geopolitical conflicts, and human rights abuses intensify, the treaty's reliance on voluntary commitments and weak enforcement mechanisms have come under increasing scrutiny.[73] These deficiencies jeopardize environmental health, global stability, and equitable resource management, with far-reaching consequences for both developed and developing nations.

The South China Sea clearly illustrates these limitations.[74] Marked by overlapping territorial claims and strategic significance, the region exemplifies UNCLOS's struggles to mediate disputes when powerful states refuse to comply with binding rules.[75] In the 2016 Arbitral Decision in *the Philippines v. China*, the tribunal invalidated China's expansive nine-dash line claims, reaffirming the authority of international law in maritime dispute resolution.[76] However, the absence of robust enforcement mechanisms has allowed China to disregard the ruling, perpetuate tensions, and undermine trust in UNCLOS's ability to resolve such conflicts effectively.[77] This case underscores broader tension within the treaty, balancing state sovereignty with collective responsibility. In contrast, governance frameworks such as the Antarctic Treaty demonstrate the benefits of enforceable obligations and consensus-driven approaches, which have successfully mitigated disputes and fostered cooperation in another geopolitically sensitive region.[78]

High Seas Governance for the 21st Century, 23 INT'L J. MARINE & COASTAL L. 399, 399-421 (2008), https://doi.org/10.1163/092735208x331845; Peder Hjorth & Kaveh Madani, *Adaptive Water Management: On the Need for Using the Post-WWII Science in Water Governance*, 37 WATER RES. MGMT. 2247, 2247-2270 (2023), https://doi.org/10.1007/s11269-022-03373-0; Jill Mendler De Suarez et al., *Ensuring Survival: Oceans, Climate and Security*, 90 OCEAN & COASTAL MGMT. 27, 27-37 (2013), https://doi.org/10.1016/j.ocecoaman.2013.08.007.

[72] Oral, *supra* note 5; Armstrong, *supra* note 4; Salpin et al., *supra* note 57.

[73] *Id.*

[74] Robert Beckman, *The UN Convention on the Law of the Sea and the Maritime Disputes in the South China Sea*, 107 AM. J. INT'L L. 142, 142-163 (2013), https://doi.org/10.5305/amerjintelaw.107.1.0142; Prince et al., *supra* note 54.

[75] *Id.*

[76] *South China Sea Arbitration (Philippines v. China)*, *supra* note 13.

[77] Luis A. León Arzich, *Realism and the Chinese Attitudes Toward UNCLOS: The South China Sea Arbitration as a Case Study*, No. 134 REVISTA POL. & ESTRATEGIA 21, 21-54 (2019), https://doi.org/10.26797/rpye.v0i134.786; Isaac B. Kardon, *China Can Say "No": Analyzing China's Rejection of the South China Sea Arbitration*, 13 U. PA. ASIAN L. REV. 1, 42 (2018), https://scholarship.law.upenn.edu/alr/vol13/iss2/1.

[78] Neda A. Zawahri & Sara McLaughlin Mitchell, *Fragmented Governance of International Rivers: Negotiating Bilateral versus Multilateral Treaties*, 55 INT'L STUD. Q. 835, 835-858

Beyond jurisdictional disputes, enforcement deficiencies under UNCLOS have manifested in the growing crisis of IUU fishing.[79] In West Africa, where IUU fishing is rampant, weak enforcement mechanisms have allowed the flag-of-convenience arrangements to thrive.[80] These arrangements enable shipowners to register vessels in states with minimal regulatory oversight, thereby facilitating widespread violations of international standards.[81] West Africa has become a global hotspot for IUU fishing, accounting for up to 40% of the global cases between 2010 and 2022.[82] The economic and environmental toll is devastating, with regional losses estimated between \$2.3 billion and \$9.4 billion annually.[83] These activities deplete fish stocks, undermine food security, and jeopardize the livelihoods of coastal communities.[84]

SIDS, already grappling with resource constraints, are particularly vulnerable to this exploitation.[85] Addressing these gaps requires stricter measures within

---

(2011), https://doi.org/10.1111/j.1468-2478.2011.00673.x; Karolina M. Milewicz & Duncan Snidal, *Cooperation by Treaty: The Role of Multilateral Powers*, 70 INT'L ORG. 823, 823-844 (2016), https://doi.org/10.1017/s002081831600031x.

[79] Xiujuan Chen, Qingxu Xu & Liyuan Li, *Illegal, Unreported, and Unregulated Fishing Governance in Disputed Maritime Areas: Reflections on the International Legal Obligations of States*, 8 FISHES 36 (2023), https://doi.org/10.3390/fishes8010036; Gohar A. Petrossian & Frank S. Pezzella, *IUU Fishing and Seafood Fraud: Using Crime Script Analysis to Inform Intervention*, 679 ANNALS AM. ACAD. POL. & SOC. SCI. 121, 121-139 (2018), https://doi.org/10.1177/0002716218784533.

[80] Flag-of-convenience (FOC) arrangements are a known contributor to IUU fishing globally. *See* Donald Liddick, *The Dimensions of a Transnational Crime Problem: The Case of IUU Fishing*, 17 TRENDS IN ORG. CRIME 290, 290-312 (2014), https://doi.org/10.1007/s12117-014-9228-6.

[81] Tony Alderton & Nick Winchester, *Globalisation and De-Regulation in the Maritime Industry*, 26 MARINE POL'Y 35, 35-43 (2001), https://doi.org/10.1016/s0308-597x(01)00034-3.

[82] Sam Geall et al., *Charting a Blue Future for Cooperation between West Africa and China on Sustainable Fisheries*, The Stimson Center 1, 13 (2023), https://www.stimson.org/wp-content/uploads/2023/09/IUU-Fishing-West-Africa-Report_8.30.23-1.pdf.

[83] Alassane Doumbouya et al., *Assessing the Effectiveness of Monitoring Control and Surveillance of Illegal Fishing: The Case of West Africa*, 4 FRONTIERS MARINE SCI. 50 (2017), https://doi.org/10.3389/fmars.2017.00050.

[84] "Illegal, unreported and unregulated fishing poses an enormous threat to the conservation and management of the dwindling fish stocks, causing multiple adverse consequences for fisheries, coastal and marine ecosystems and for the people who depend on these resources." *See* Alexey A. Kurekin et al., *Operational Monitoring of Illegal Fishing in Ghana through Exploitation of Satellite Earth Observation and AIS Data*, 11 REMOTE SENSING 293, 1 (2019), https://doi.org/10.3390/rs11030293.

[85] On the vulnerabilities of Small Island Developing States (SIDS). *See* Gianmoena Scandurra et al., *On the Vulnerability of Small Island Developing States: A Dynamic*

UNCLOS, such as mandatory vessel audits and enhanced integration with frameworks, such as the Port State Measures Agreement (PSMA).[86] These mechanisms could close enforcement loopholes and promote equitable resource management, ensuring that vulnerable regions are not disproportionately affected by illegal practices.[87]

The Arctic offers another stark example of UNCLOS's limitations, particularly in addressing the complex interplay between ecological and geopolitical challenges. Climate change is transforming the region, with melting sea ice opening previously inaccessible shipping routes and exposing large reserves of oil, gas, and minerals.[88] Article 234 of UNCLOS, which grants coastal states regulatory authority over ice-covered areas to address pollution concerns, falls short of managing broader dynamics, such as resource extraction, shipping disputes, and indigenous rights.[89]

The fragmented application of Article 234 by Arctic states underscores this inadequacy. While Canada emphasizes environmental protection, Russia's focus on economic development creates disparities in its regional governance approaches.[90] This divergence highlights the need for enforceable conservation

---

Analysis, 84 Ecol. Indicators 382, 382-392 (2017), https://doi.org/10.1016/j.ecolind.2017.09.016; *see* also Kristen Lowitt et al., *Environmental Change and Food Security: The Special Case of Small Island Developing States*, 15 REG'L ENVTL. CHANGE 1293, 1293-1298 (2015), https://doi.org/10.1007/s10113-015-0849-3; Jessica Mercer et al., *Ecosystem-Based Adaptation to Climate Change in Caribbean Small Island Developing States: Integrating Local and External Knowledge*, 4 SUSTAINABILITY 1908, 1908-1932 (2012), https://doi.org/10.3390/su4081908.

[86] On mandatory vessel audits: *see* Rebecca Prentiss Pskowski, *The IMO and the Implementation of Mandatory Instruments*, in LAW 2024 284, 284-303 (2024), https://doi.org/10.4337/9781802206883.00026; *see* also Deepak Raj Sharma & Sigmund Simonsen, *Ensuring the Quality of ISM Audits: The Role and Adequacy of the Legal Framework of Auditing*, 12 MAR. SAFETY & SEC. L.J. 24 (2023), https://www.marsafelawjournal.org/contributions/ensuring-the-quality-of-ism-audits-the-role-and-adequacy-of-the-legal-framework-of-auditing/. On the Port State Measures Agreement: *see* U.N. FOOD & AGRIC. ORG. (FAO), *Agreement on Port State Measures (PSMA)*, https://www.fao.org/iuu-fishing/international-framework/psma/en/; *see* also Selig et al., *supra* note 62.

[87] *Id.*

[88] Amanda H. Lynch, Charles H. Norchi & Xiangbai Li, *The Interaction of Ice and Law in Arctic Marine Accessibility*, 119 PROC. NAT'L ACAD. SCI. (2022), https://doi.org/10.1073/pnas.2202720119.

[89] *Id.*

[90] Neil Bradford & David A. Wolfe, *Governing Regional Economic Development: Innovation Challenges and Policy Learning in Canada*, 6 CAMBRIDGE J. REGIONS, ECON. & SOC'Y 331, 331-347 (2013), https://doi.org/10.1093/cjres/rst006; Vladislava Vladimirova, *Regional Environmental Governance of Protected Natural Territories in the European*

measures and the establishment of a dedicated RFMO to safeguard fragile ecosystems.[91] Such a framework could standardize policies across the Arctic, ensuring consistent management of shipping lanes and resource development, while addressing the rights and needs of indigenous populations.[92]

High seas, which extend beyond national jurisdictions, present another universal challenge. UNCLOS's provisions for conserving marine biodiversity, such as Article 119, rely heavily on voluntary cooperation and scientific evidence but lack enforceable commitments.[93] This has allowed overexploitation and ecological degradation to persist. For instance, the collapse of cod stocks in the Northwest Atlantic under the supervision of the Northwest Atlantic Fisheries Organization illustrates the devastating consequences of weak governance.[94] With approximately 30% of global fish stocks now classified as overexploited or depleted, the urgency for robust governance measures is clear.[95]

The recently adopted High Seas Treaty complements UNCLOS by mandating the creation of Marine Protected Areas (MPAs) that require Environmental Impact Assessments (EIAs).[96] These advancements provide much-needed tools for addressing biodiversity loss in ABNJ.[97] However, aligning the treaty's

---

North: Russia, Finland, and Norway, and the Case of Pasvik-Inari Trilateral Park, 176 CLIMATIC CHANGE 7 (2023), https://doi.org/10.1007/s10584-023-03559-4.

[91] Adam Soliman, *Fisheries Governance and How It Fits Within the Broader Arctic Governance*, 37 SEATTLE U. L. REV.1209, 1210 (2014), https://digitalcommons.law.seattleu.edu/sulr/vol37/iss4/5/.

[92] *Id.*

[93] UNCLOS, *supra* note 3, Article 119; *see* also Evelyn Meltzer, *Global Overview of Straddling and Highly Migratory Fish Stocks: The Nonsustainable Nature of High Seas Fisheries*, 25 OCEAN DEV. & INT'L L. 255, 255-344 (1994), https://doi.org/10.1080/00908329409546036.

[94] Carl Walters & Jean-Jacques Maguire, *Lessons for Stock Assessment from the Northern Cod Collapse*, 6 REV. FISH BIOL. & FISHERIES 125, 125-137 (1996), https://doi.org/10.1007/BF00182340; Robin M. Cook, Alex Sinclair & Guðmundur Stefánsson, *Potential Collapse of North Sea Cod Stocks*, 385 NATURE 521, 521-522 (1997), https://doi.org/10.1038/385521a0.

[95] Trevor A. Branch et al., *Contrasting Global Trends in Marine Fishery Status Obtained from Catches and from Stock Assessments*, 25 CONSERVATION BIOLOGY 777, 777-786 (2011), https://doi.org/10.1111/j.1523-1739.2011.01687.x.

[96] EUROPEAN COMMISSION, *Win for the Ocean: High Seas Treaty Signed at United Nations*, Directorate-General for Maritime Affairs and Fisheries (Sept. 20, 2023), https://oceans-and-fisheries.ec.europa.eu/news/win-ocean-high-seas-treaty-signed-united-nations-2023-09-20_en; Rui Jiang & Ping Guo, *Sustainable Management of Marine Protected Areas in the High Seas: From Regional Treaties to a Global New Agreement on Biodiversity in Areas Beyond National Jurisdiction*, 15 SUSTAINABILITY (2023), https://doi.org/10.3390/su151511575.

[97] Druel & Gjerde. *supra* note 29.

objectives with UNCLOS's principles of freedom of navigation and equitable resource use remains complex.[98] Harmonizing these frameworks requires sustained international cooperation to ensure consistency in governance and enforcement across jurisdictions.[99]

These deficiencies in UNCLOS extend beyond technical flaws, touching on the ethical and practical considerations that exacerbate global inequalities. The treaty aspires to balance state sovereignty with collective stewardship, promoting equitable access to marine resources, while protecting ocean ecosystems for future generations.[100] However, its fragmented governance framework and reliance on voluntary commitments have perpetuated inequities and ecological degradation.[101] Developing nations, often lacking the resources to enforce governance standards or exploit marine resources, bear a disproportionate burden, whereas powerful states and private actors dominate resource exploitation.[102] This disparity erodes trust in multilateral institutions and highlights the systemic need for reforms that prioritize equity, accountability, and resilience in ocean governance.[103]

Despite these challenges, the real-world impacts of UNCLOS's limitations also highlight its potential for evolution. Addressing critical gaps, such as weak enforcement mechanisms, inadequate environmental safeguards, and fragmented dispute resolution frameworks, can transform the treaty into a more effective and inclusive governance model.[104] Strengthening enforcement mechanisms, fostering inclusive governance, and ensuring adaptive management are not merely desirable but essential for revitalizing the UNCLOS.[105] Frameworks like the

---

[98] Gardiner, *supra* note 52.

[99] Gardiner, *supra* note 52; Jiang & Guo, *supra* note 94.

[100] Bourrel et al., *supra* note 6.

[101] Gardiner, *supra* note 52; Watson, *supra* note 20.

[102] Mishari Alsaleh et al., *Nature of Property Rights and Motivation for Blue Growth: An Empirical Evidence from the Fisheries Industry,* 48 NAT. RESOURCES FORUM 184, 184-210 (2023), https://doi.org/10.1111/1477-8947.12317; Andrew Merrie et al., *An Ocean of Surprises—Trends in Human Use, Unexpected Dynamics and Governance Challenges in Areas Beyond National Jurisdiction,* 27 GLOBAL ENVTL. CHANGE 19, 19-31 (2014), https://doi.org/10.1016/j.gloenvcha.2014.04.012.

[103] Ahmet Faruk Aysan et al., *Natural Resources Governance and Conflicts: Retrospective Analysis,* 85 RESOURCES POL'Y (2023), https://doi.org/10.1016/j.resourpol.2023.103942; Bruce Glavovic et al., *Living on the Margin in the Anthropocene: Engagement Arenas for Sustainability Research and Action at the Ocean–Land Interface,* 14 CURRENT OPINION ENVTL. SUSTAINABILITY 232, 232-238 (2015), https://doi.org/10.1016/j.cosust.2015.06.003; Lena Partzsch, *Alternatives to Multilateralism,* Massachusetts Institute of Technology (2020), https://doi.org/10.7551/mitpress/12610.001.0001.

[104] Mendenhall, *supra* note 41; Druel & Gjerde. *supra* note 29; Boyle, *supra* note 12.

[105] *Id.*

High Seas Treaty offer opportunities for synergy but aligning them with UNCLOS will require concerted international cooperation and a commitment to harmonizing objectives.[106]

The interconnected nature of these governance challenges - from geopolitical disputes in the South China Sea to ecological crises in the Arctic and resource exploitation in the high seas - underscores the urgency of systemic change. Drawing lessons from these examples and bridging theoretical critiques with actionable solutions can guide UNCLOS toward becoming a framework that meets the demands of a rapidly evolving world.[107] By fostering an equitable and enforceable governance model, UNCLOS can remain a cornerstone of international maritime law equipped to protect the oceans for future generations.

A. The Arctic's Struggle: Environmental Risks and Governance Failures

The Arctic epitomizes the intersection of environmental vulnerability, geopolitical competition, and inadequate governance - issues that also surface in the Mediterranean and Pacific. Once characterized by its isolation and resilience, the region now commands global attention as its rapid transformation unfolds.[108] This accelerated warming destabilizes Arctic ecosystems and reverberates globally, intensifying extreme weather events and challenging governance structures designed for a more static environment.[109]

Feedback loops, such as the loss of reflective ice surfaces, expose darker ocean waters that absorb more heat, thaw permafrost, release methane, a potent greenhouse gas, and further amplify climate change.[110] Thawing permafrost

---

[106] Kjell Grip, *International Marine Environmental Governance: A Review*, 46 AMBIO 413, 413-427 (2016), https://doi.org/10.1007/s13280-016-0847-9.
[107] Armstrong, *supra* note 4.
[108] Gregory K. Silber & Jeffrey D. Adams, *Vessel Operations in the Arctic, 2015–2017*, 6 FRONTIERS MARINE SCI. 573 (2019), https://doi.org/10.3389/fmars.2019.00573.
[109] Studies have consistently shown that Arctic temperatures are rising at a rate 3-4 times higher than the global average. *See* ARCTIC MONITORING AND ASSESSMENT PROGRAMME, *AMAP Assessment 2023: Arctic Climate Update* (2023), at 4, https://www.amap.no; *see* also Gifford H. Miller et al., *Arctic Amplification: Can the Past Constrain the Future?*, 29 QUATERNARY SCI. REV. 1779, 1779-1790 (2010), https://doi.org/10.1016/j.quascirev.2010.02.008; James A. Screen & Ian Simmonds, *Increasing Fall-Winter Energy Loss from the Arctic Ocean and Its Role in Arctic Temperature Amplification*, 37 GEOPHYS. RES. LETT. (2010), https://doi.org/10.1029/2010gl044136.
[110] The sea-ice albedo feedback (SIAF) is a key driver of Arctic amplification, where reduced sea ice decreases surface albedo, leading to greater solar absorption and further warming. This positive feedback mechanism contributes to enhanced Arctic warming under increased greenhouse gases. *See* Chad W. Thackeray & Alex Hall, *An Emergent Constraint on Future Arctic Sea-Ice Albedo Feedback*, 9 NAT. CLIMATE CHANGE 972, 972-978

alone is estimated to release up to one gigaton, or 1000 million tons of methane by 2100, further exacerbating global warming.[111] The destabilization of the polar vortex has been linked to harsher winters in Europe, intensified hurricanes in the Atlantic, and more severe monsoons in South Asia.[112] Once a stabilizing force for the Earth's climate, the Arctic amplifies global environmental risks. According to the *Arctic Report Card*, 2023 marked one of the warmest years on record, characterized by significant sea ice loss and cascading ecological impacts.[113]

The ecological consequences of these changes have been profound. Polar bears, walruses, and other species that rely on sea ice for hunting and breeding face habitat loss and declining populations.[114]

Polar bears now travel vast distances in search of food and often suffer severe health and reproductive consequences.[115] Similarly, walruses deprived of stable ice platforms are forced onto overcrowded coastlines, where human disturbances and resource competition further increase their vulnerability.[116] Marine ecosystems are equally at risk, with declining krill populations disrupting food webs and threatening fish stocks, marine mammals, and global fisheries, depending on Arctic biodiversity.[117]

(2019), https://doi.org/10.1038/s41558-019-0619-1; Matthew Jenkins & Aiguo Dai, *The Impact of Sea-Ice Loss on Arctic Climate Feedbacks and Their Role for Arctic Amplification*, 48 GEOPHYS. RES. LETT. (2021), https://doi.org/10.1029/2021gl094599.

111 ARCTIC MONITORING AND ASSESSMENT PROGRAMME, *supra* note 109; Christian Knoblauch et al., *Methane Production as Key to the Greenhouse Gas Budget of Thawing Permafrost*, 8 NAT. CLIMATE CHANGE 309, 309-312 (2018).

112 Martin Wegmann et al., *Eurasian Autumn Snow Link to Winter North Atlantic Oscillation Is Strongest for Arctic Warming Periods*, 11 EARTH SYST. DYNAM. 509, 509-524 (2020), https://doi.org/10.5194/esd-11-509-2020.

113 NATIONAL OCEANIC AND ATMOSPHERIC ADMINISTRATION (NOAA), *Arctic Report Card 2023*, https://arctic.noaa.gov/report-card/report-card-2023/.

114 U.S. FISH & WILDLIFE SERVICE, *Polar Bear Conservation Management Plan* (2020), at 22, https://www.fws.gov; Evan V. Regehr et al., *Survival and Breeding of Polar Bears in the Southern Beaufort Sea in Relation to Sea Ice*, 79 J. ANIMAL ECOLOGY 117, 117-127 (2009), https://doi.org/10.1111/j.1365-2656.2009.01603.x; Jouke Prop et al., *Climate Change and the Increasing Impact of Polar Bears on Bird Populations*, 3 FRONTIERS ECOL. & EVOLUTION 33 (2015), https://doi.org/10.3389/fevo.2015.00033.

115 *Id.*

116 Karyn D. Rode et al., *Spring Fasting Behavior in a Marine Apex Predator Provides an Index of Ecosystem Productivity*, 24 GLOBAL CHANGE BIOLOGY 410, 410-423 (2017), https://doi.org/10.1111/gcb.13933.

117 Kit M. Kovacs et al., *Impacts of Changing Sea-Ice Conditions on Arctic Marine Mammals*, 41 MARINE BIODIVERSITY 181, 181-194 (2010), https://doi.org/10.1007/s12526-010-0061-0.

Human activities exacerbate these vulnerabilities, transforming the Arctic into a contested arena for economic opportunities and geopolitical rivalry. These developments underscore the limitations of UNCLOS's provisions in addressing the complex interplay of environmental, economic, and geopolitical dynamics—a challenge mirrored in other regions, such as the Mediterranean and Pacific.

The retreat of sea ice has opened new shipping routes, such as the Northern Sea Route and the Northwest Passage, significantly reducing the transit times between Europe and Asia. For example, the Northern Sea Route can cut shipping distances by up to 40%, making it an attractive alternative to traditional routes, such as the Suez Canal.[118] However, increased maritime traffic increases environmental risks, including oil spills, ship collisions, and underwater noise pollution, all of which threaten the Arctic marine life.[119]

While the International Maritime Organization's phased ban on heavy fuel oil in Arctic waters implemented in July 2024 represents a critical step forward, exemptions granted to certain vessels until 2029 have drawn criticism for failing to address the urgency of environmental protection.[120] Enforcement challenges in the Arctic, exacerbated by its remoteness, further undermine regulatory efforts, highlighting the need for real-time monitoring technologies, such as satellite surveillance and automated reporting systems.[121]

Resource competition further complicates governance. The Arctic contains an estimated 13% of the world's undiscovered oil and 30% of its natural gas,

---

118 Harald Schøyen & Svein Bråthen, *The Northern Sea Route Versus the Suez Canal: Cases from Bulk Shipping*, 19 J. TRANSPORT GEOGRAPHY 977, 977-983 (2011), https://doi.org/10.1016/j.jtrangeo.2011.03.003.

119 Maria Nevalainen, Inka Helle & Jarno Vanhatalo, *Preparing for the Unprecedented—Towards Quantitative Oil Risk Assessment in the Arctic Marine Areas*, 114 MARINE POLLUTION BULL. 90, 90-101 (2016), https://doi.org/10.1016/j.marpolbul.2016.08.064; Travis J. Moore et al., *Exploring Ship Traffic Variability Off California*, 163 OCEAN & COASTAL MGMT. 515, 515-527 (2018), https://doi.org/10.1016/j.ocecoaman.2018.03.010.

120 IMO, *Resolution MEPC.301(72)*, *supra* note 65, at 3; Emily Blake, *As Arctic Heavy Fuel Oil Ban Comes into Force, Critics Want More*, Cabin Radio (July 1, 2024), https://cabinradio.ca/190927/news/travel/as-arctic-heavy-fuel-oil-ban-comes-into-force-critics-want-more/; Elena F. Tracy, *Despite Heavy Fuel Oil Ban, Arctic Marine Biodiversity Still Threatened*, WWF Global Arctic Programme (June 19, 2024), https://www.arcticwwf.org/newsroom/features/despite-heavy-fuel-oil-ban-arctic-marine-biodiversity-still-threatened/.

121 ARCTIC COUNCIL, *Arctic Shipping Governance Strategies: Challenges and Innovations* (2024), at 8, https://www.arcticbiodiversity.is; Kathryn Urban, *A New (Cold) Front in Polar Intelligence? Trends and Implications of Technology-Enabled Monitoring in the Arctic*, J. SCI. POL'Y & GOVERNANCE (Jan. 11, 2021), https://doi.org/10.38126/JSPG190111.

making it a hotspot for resource extraction.[122] Strategic areas such as the Lomonosov Ridge have become focal points of overlapping claims, with Russia, Canada, and Denmark asserting competing territorial rights under Article 76 of the UNCLOS.[123] Article 76, which governs the delineation of the continental shelf, provides a procedural framework for states to submit claims to the Commission on the Limits of the Continental Shelf (CLCS).[124] However, the CLCS lacks authority to resolve disputes, limiting its role in issuing non-binding recommendations.[125] This regulatory gap is evident in the ongoing Lomonosov Ridge dispute, where the lack of binding arbitration mechanisms under the UNCLOS has prolonged geopolitical tensions.

The ongoing debate over Ridge's classification as an extension of the Eurasian or North American continental shelf underscores the inadequacy of the current legal frameworks to resolve disputes.[126] Russia's militarization of the Arctic, including large-scale military exercises and infrastructure development for resource extraction, has heightened geopolitical tensions, prompting responses from NATO and the United States.[127] These developments have transformed the Arctic from a region of cooperation to one that is increasingly marked by security concerns.[128]

The involvement of non-Arctic states adds another layer of complexity to regional governance. For instance, China's Polar Silk Road initiative involves significant investments in Arctic infrastructure and research, which are framed

---

122 Mikhail Dvoynikov et al., *New Concepts of Hydrogen Production and Storage in Arctic Region,* 10 RESOURCES 3 (2021), https://doi.org/10.3390/resources10010003; Donald L. Gautier et al., *Assessment of Undiscovered Oil and Gas in the Arctic,* 324 SCIENCE 1175, 1175-1179 (2009), https://doi.org/10.1126/science.1169467.

123 Sophie Natalie Chevalier, *The Arctic: From Peace Exceptionalism to International Insecurity - Examining the Interplay Between Hydrocarbon Developments and Military Expansions.* Master's thesis, European University Institute, 2024; Robert Orttung, *Russia's Arctic Ambitions,* OXFORD RESEARCH ENCYCLOPEDIA OF POLITICS (June 18, 2024), https://oxfordre.com/politics/view/10.1093/acrefore/9780190228637.001.0001/acrefoe-9780190228637-e-2274.

124 UNCLOS, *supra* note 3, Article 76.

125 Bjarni Kunoy, *The Admissibility of a Plea to an International Adjudicative Forum to Delimit the Outer Continental Shelf Prior to the Adoption of Final Recommendations by the Commission on the Limits of the Continental Shelf,* 25(2) INT'L J. MARINE & COASTAL L. 237, 237–70 (2010), https://doi.org/10.1163/157180910x12665776638704.

126 *Id.*

127 Trends Research & Advisory, *The Arctic: A Risk of Escalating Conflicts,* TRENDS RESEARCH & ADVISORY (Dec. 6, 2024), https://trendsresearch.org/insight/the-arctic-a-risk-of-escalating-conflicts/.

128 *Id.*

as contributions to sustainable development.[129] However, these actions have raised concerns about strategic ambitions and erosion of governance structures primarily designed for Arctic states.[130] Norway's 2024 decision to block the sale of private property in the Svalbard archipelago, citing national security concerns, exemplifies its heightened sensitivity to non-Arctic actors.[131]

This shifting geopolitical landscape challenges the principle of Arctic exceptionalism–the idea that the Arctic should remain insulated from broader geopolitical tensions. Scholars have argued that Russia's invasion of Ukraine undermined this principle, demonstrating that the Arctic cannot be separated from global conflicts.[132] This shift necessitates governance frameworks capable of addressing both environmental and security challenges and ensuring that the Arctic remains a region of peace and stability.[133]

Indigenous communities in the Arctic, such as the Inuit, Saami, and Chukchi, are among those most affected by these transformations. For millennia, these communities have relied on Arctic ecosystems using traditional ecological knowledge (TEK) to sustain their livelihoods and navigate environmental changes.[134] TEK encompasses detailed observations of seasonal cycles, animal migration, and ice stability, offering critical insights that complement scientific

---

[129] Chih Yuan Woon, *Framing the "Polar Silk Road" (冰上丝绸之路): Critical Geopolitics, Chinese Scholars and the (Re)Positionings of China's Arctic Interests,* 78 POL. GEOGRAPHY (2020), https://doi.org/10.1016/j.polgeo.2019.102141.

[130] Stephanie Pezard et al., *China's Strategy and Activities in the Arctic: Implications for North American and Transatlantic Security,* RAND CORPORATION RESEARCH REPORT RRA1282-1-v2 (2022), https://www.rand.org/content/dam/rand/pubs/research_reports/RRA1200/RRA1282-1-v2/RAND_RRA1282-1-v2.pdf.

[131] NORWEGIAN GOVERNMENT, *National Security Policy on Arctic Territories: Svalbard and Beyond* (2024), https://www.regjeringen.no.

[132] Andreas Østhagen & Marco Dordoni, *Security and Defence in the Mediterranean and in the Arctic,* European University Institute, Quaderni "La Comunità Internazionale" 42, 62 (2024), https://ricerca.unistrapg.it/retrieve/ac1555c1-12f4-4b6a-ba16-7066431b34ab/SECURITY%20AND%20DEFENCE%20IN%20THE%20MEDITERRANEAN%20AND%20IN%20THE%20ARCTIC.pdf.

[133] Daniel Schneider, *Climate Change and Maritime Claims in the Arctic Region* 43 (LLM Thesis, Univ. of Iceland, 2024).

[134] James D. Ford et al., *Sea Ice, Climate Change, and Community Vulnerability in Northern Foxe Basin, Canada,* 38 CLIMATE RES. 137, 137-154 (2009), https://doi.org/10.3354/cr00777; Bindu Panikkar & Benjamin Lemmond, *Being on Land and Sea in Troubled Times: Climate Change and Food Sovereignty in Nunavut,* 9 LAND 508 (2020), https://doi.org/10.3390/land9120508.

research.[135] However, climate change and industrial activities increasingly disrupt traditional practices, threatening the ecosystems that sustain indigenous communities and their cultural identities.[136]

Hunting, fishing, and other subsistence activities are becoming less viable traditional food sources. The retreat of sea ice disrupts the migratory patterns of seals, whales, and caribou, which are vital to indigenous diets and economies.[137] Meanwhile, industrial expansion, including oil and gas exploration, mining, and shipping, encroaches on traditional territories, exacerbates ecological stress, and marginalizes indigenous populations.[138] The exclusion of indigenous voices from governance processes perpetuates historical injustices and undermines the potential for sustainable solutions informed by the TEK.[139]

Efforts to integrate indigenous perspectives into governance frameworks have been promising. The Gwich'in people's advocacy for the protection of Porcupine Caribou Herd's calving grounds in the Arctic National Wildlife Refuge (ANWR) exemplifies the power of Indigenous-led conservation initiatives.[140] These lands are essential not only for the caribou's survival, but also for Gwich'in's cultural and economic well-being. Advocacy efforts have secured significant protection, but ongoing debates over oil exploration in ANWR highlight the fragility of these gains and the need for governance frameworks that prioritize indigenous rights and environmental stewardship.[141]

---

135 James D. Ford et al., *Vulnerability to Climate Change in Igloolik, Nunavut: What We Can Learn from the Past and Present*, 42 POLAR REC. 127, 127-138 (2006), https://doi.org/10.1017/s0032247406005122.

136 *Id.*; *see* also Fikret Berkes & Derek Armitage, *Co-Management Institutions, Knowledge, and Learning: Adapting to Change in the Arctic*, 34 Études/Inuit/Studies 109, 109-131 (2011), https://doi.org/10.7202/045407ar.

137 Ningning Sun, *Land-Use Governance and Indigenous Engagement in Arctic Alaska and Norway: Successes, Current Gaps, and Paths Forward* (2024) (Environmental Studies Senior Thesis, Dartmouth College), https://digitalcommons.dartmouth.edu/environmental_studies_senior_theses/3.

138 Timo Kumpula et al., *Land Use and Land Cover Change in Arctic Russia: Ecological and Social Implications of Industrial Development*, 21 GLOBAL ENVTL. CHANGE 550, 550-562 (2011), https://doi.org/10.1016/j.gloenvcha.2010.12.010.

139 Zareen Shawoo & Thomas F. Thornton, *The UN Local Communities and Indigenous Peoples' Platform: A Traditional Ecological Knowledge-Based Evaluation*, 10 WIREs CLIMATE CHANGE (2019), https://doi.org/10.1002/wcc.575.

140 GWICH'IN STEERING COMMITTEE, *Advocating for the Porcupine Caribou Herd* (2023), at 15, https://www.gwichinsteeringcommittee.org.

141 Neil M. Dawson et al., *The Role of Indigenous Peoples and Local Communities in Effective and Equitable Conservation*, 26 ECOLOGY & SOC'Y (2021), https://doi.org/10.5751/es-12625-260319.

Ethical principles such as environmental justice and intergenerational equity are central to addressing the Arctic governance challenges. Environmental justice emphasizes the disproportionate burdens borne by Arctic Indigenous communities, which contribute minimally to global greenhouse gas emissions but face the most severe consequences of climate change and industrial exploitation.[142] Intergenerational equity underscores the moral obligation to preserve Arctic ecosystems for future generations, ensuring that governance decisions prioritize long-term sustainability over short-term economic gains.[143] Embedding these principles into Arctic governance frameworks enhances legitimacy and fosters inclusive decision making.[144]

B. The Mediterranean Migration Crisis: Human Rights Challenges at Sea

The Mediterranean migration crisis exemplifies profound tensions between Europe's political priorities, regional governance frameworks, and international human rights obligations. Each year, thousands of migrants and refugees risk their lives by crossing the sea, fleeing conflicts, persecution, and poverty. According to the International Organization for Migration, over 30,000 people have died attempting to cross the Mediterranean since 2014, making it the deadliest migration route in the world.[145] Survivors often face indefinite detention, exploitation, and deprivation of basic rights, reflecting significant failures in Europe's migration governance systems.[146]

The drivers of migration in the Mediterranean region are diverse and interconnected. Wars in Syria, Afghanistan, and Libya have displaced millions

---

[142] Sarah F. Trainor et al., *Arctic Climate Impacts: Environmental Injustice in Canada and the United States*, 12 LOCAL ENVT. 627, 627-643 (2007), https://doi.org/10.1080/13549830701657414.

[143] Tatiana S. Degai & Andrey N. Petrov, *Rethinking Arctic Sustainable Development Agenda Through Indigenizing UN Sustainable Development Goals*, 28 INT'L J. SUSTAINABLE DEV. & WORLD ECOLOGY 518, 518-523 (2021), https://doi.org/10.1080/13504509.2020.1868608; Alexander Golub, Maggie Mahoney & Jennifer Harlow, *Sustainability and Intergenerational Equity: Do Past Injustices Matter?*, 8 SUSTAINABILITY SCI. 269, 269-277 (2013), https://doi.org/10.1007/s11625-013-0201-0.

[144] Catherine Wood-Donnelly, *Evaluating Normative Capacity Through Arctic Environmental Governance*, 176 CLIMATIC CHANGE 9 (2023), https://doi.org/10.1007/s10584-023-03603-3.

[145] INT'L ORG. FOR MIGRATION (IOM), *Missing Migrants Project: Mediterranean* (2024), https://missingmigrants.iom.int/.

[146] Leoni Anna Geray, *Fortress Europe: Analysing the Human Rights Impact of EU Border Externalisation in Third Countries Since 2015* (2024) (unpublished Bachelor's thesis, Ludwig Maximilian University of Munich) (on file with author), https://epub.ub.uni-muenchen.de/121612/1/Bachelorarbeit_Geray.pdf.

of people, and entrenched socio-economic inequalities and environmental degradation exacerbate these crises.[147] Climate change intensifies these pressures, particularly in vulnerable regions such as the Sahel, where desertification and food insecurity are accelerating displacement.[148] The African Union's Great Green Wall Initiative, which aims to combat desertification, demonstrates how regional strategies can address these root causes; however, such efforts require sustained investment and international support.[149]

The principle of non-refoulement, enshrined in the 1951 Refugee Convention and reinforced by customary international law, prohibits the return of individuals to countries where they face persecution or harm. As a *jus cogens* norm (a fundamental and non-derogable principle of international law), non-refoulement binds all states regardless of treaty obligations.[150]

Non-refoulement intersects UNCLOS's provisions on SAR operations under Articles 98 and 94.[151] While these articles impose obligations on states to assist persons in distress at sea, they lack enforceable mandates to ensure compliance with human rights standards, particularly for migrants intercepted in the Mediterranean region. This principle has been undermined by EU policies, including pushback practices, externalization agreements, and mismanagement of asylum claims under the Dublin III Regulation.

---

[147] At the end of 2023, 117.3 million people worldwide were forcibly displaced as a result of persecution, conflict, violence, human rights violations and events seriously disturbing public order. *See* U.N. HIGH COMM'R FOR REFUGEES (UNHCR), *Global Trends: Forced Displacement in 2023* (June 2024), at 28, https://www.unhcr.org/. In Syria alone, about 13 million people have been displaced, including 8 million internally displaced persons. *See* Hazem G. Abdo, *Impacts of War in Syria on Vegetation Dynamics and Erosion Risks in Safita Area, Tartous, Syria*, 18 REG'L ENVTL. CHANGE 1707, 1707-1719 (2018), https://doi.org/10.1007/s10113-018-1280-3.

[148] U.N. ENV'T PROGRAMME (UNEP), *Regional Climate Change Impacts on Sub-Saharan Africa: Sahel Report* (2023), https://www.unep.org/; Riccardo Marasco et al., *Diamonds in the Rough: Dryland Microorganisms Are Ecological Engineers to Restore Degraded Land and Mitigate Desertification*, 16 Microbial Biotechnology 1603, 1603-1610 (2023), https://doi.org/10.1111/1751-7915.14216.

[149] John Cropper, *Growing a World Wonder: The Great Green Wall and the History of Environmental Decline in the Sahel, 1450–2022*, 30 ENV'T & HIST. 145 (2023), https://doi.org/10.3197/096734023X16702350656933; S. Trautman, R. Chevallier & A. Gosling, *The African Union Great Green Wall Initiative Strategy (2024-2034): A New Continental Roadmap for Restoration, Sustainable Land Management and Climate Resilient Livelihoods*, AICCRA INFO NOTE (2024), https://hdl.handle.net/10568/149059.

[150] *Convention Relating to the Status of Refugees*, July 28, 1951, 189 U.N.T.S. 137, entered into force Apr. 22, 1954.

[151] UNCLOS, *supra* note 3, Articles 96 and 98.

In *Hirsi Jamaa and Others v. Italy* (2012) and the European Court of Human Rights (ECtHR) held that Italy's maritime interceptions and forced returns to Libya violated non-refoulement.[152] Similarly, in *M.S.S. v. Belgium and Greece* (2011), the ECtHR found systemic failures in Greece's reception conditions, highlighting the incompatibility of such practices with international human rights obligations.[153] These rulings emphasize the legal framework that should guide EU migration policies, emphasizing the protection of migrants' rights.

The Global Compact for Migration (GCM) adopted in 2018 complements these principles by emphasizing humane treatment and shared responsibility for migration governance. Objective 13 of the GCM calls for the elimination of practices that violate non-refoulement and the establishment of fair asylum procedures.[154]

The structural deficiencies of the EU's migration governance systems are further exacerbated by the Dublin III Regulation, which places responsibility for asylum claims on the first EU country that a migrant enters. This policy disproportionately burdens frontline states, such as Greece, Italy, and Spain, forcing them to manage the majority of asylum applications with insufficient resources.[155] These systemic governance failures reveal the need for harmonized regional frameworks and highlight the broader inadequacies of UNCLOS in integrating human rights into maritime governance.

Overcrowded detention centers, such as the Moria camp in Greece, have come to symbolize these systemic failures, with conditions that violate international standards, including the ICCPR.[156]

---

[152] *Hirsi Jamaa and Others v. Italy*, App. No. 27765/09, Eur. Ct. H.R. (2012), at para. 81 (establishing the extraterritorial application of non-refoulement under international human rights law).

[153] *M.S.S. v. Belgium and Greece*, App. No. 30696/09, Eur. Ct. H.R. (2011), at para. 263 (addressing systemic failures in reception conditions and asylum processing).

[154] U.N. General Assembly, *Global Compact for Safe, Orderly and Regular Migration*, G.A. Res. 73/195, U.N. Doc. A/RES/73/195 (Dec. 19, 2018), https://documents.un.org/doc/undoc/gen/n18/451/99/pdf/n1845199.pdf.

[155] Camilla Cafiero, *The Dublin III Regulation: Critiques and Latest Attempts of Reform*, Univ. Juridic (2019), https://internationallawreview.ro/fisiere/pdf/01_-Law_Review_nr_1-2019_PAGINAT_BT_C_Cafiero.pdf; Dr. Francesco Maiani, *The Reform of the Dublin III Regulation*, Policy Department C – Citizens' Rights and Constitutional Affairs, European Parliament (2016), http://www.europarl.europa.eu/supporting-analyses.

[156] A cross-sectional study conducted in Moria camp found a positive association between the length of stay and the occurrence of acute mental health crises, with the odds of a crisis increasing by 1.03 for every 10% increase in days of residence. *See* Willem Van De Wiel et al., *Mental Health Consequences of Long-Term Stays in Refugee Camps: Preliminary Evidence from Moria*, 21 BMC Pub. Health (2021), https://doi.org/10.1186/s

The EU member states exhibit significant variations in their migration policies. Germany has emerged as a leader in resettlement programs, prioritizing the integration of refugees through well-funded initiatives including language training, job placement, and social services.[157] These policies contributed to Germany's reputation as a model for humane and effective migration governance. In contrast, Italy and Malta rely heavily on bilateral agreements with Libya, which have been criticized for enabling refoulement and perpetuating human rights abuses in Libyan detention centers.[158] These divergent approaches underscore the need for a harmonized EU framework that balances responsibility among member states while adhering to international legal standards.

The integration of refugees into host societies is essential for sustainable migration governance. Countries such as Sweden have demonstrated the success of comprehensive integration policies, which include education, employment, and social support systems designed to promote social cohesion and economic contributions from migrants.[159] These programs serve as models for other EU member states, highlighting the importance of long-term planning in migration management.

To address the structural deficiencies in EU migration policies, the Dublin III Regulation must be reformed to ensure a fair distribution of responsibilities among member states. Proposals for a centralized EU asylum agency could streamline the allocation process and reduce strain on frontline states, such as

---

12889-021-11301-x; *see* also Dimitra Papageorgiou & Eva Tzavala, *Migration in the Mediterranean Sea: Management Within and Beyond Borders*, in HUMAN RIGHTS ISSUES IN MIGRATION AND BORDER MANAGEMENT: CHALLENGES AND PERSPECTIVES 189 (Ivan Sammut & Ivan Mifsud eds., 2024), ISBN 978-94-6236-329-8.

157 The country adopted an 'integration' and 'welcome' politics, which, despite its imperfections, has been considered an important model for European refugee policy. *See* Nanette Funk, *A Spectre in Germany: Refugees, a "Welcome Culture" and an "Integration Politics,"* 12 J. GLOBAL ETHICS 289, 289-299 (2016), https://doi.org/10.1080/17449626.2016.1252785.

158 AMNESTY INTERNATIONAL, *The EU's Complicity in Migrant Abuse in Libya*, Amnesty International Australia (Dec. 18, 2017), https://www.amnesty.org.au/migrant-abuse-libya/; AMNESTY INTERNATIONAL, *Libya: European Governments Complicit in Horrific Abuse of Refugees and Migrants*, Amnesty International (Dec. 12, 2017), https://www.amnesty.org/en/latest/press-release/2017/12/libya-european-governments-complicit-in-horrific-abuse-of-refugees-and-migrants/.

159 For example, Sweden maintains voluntary participation in integration courses and imposes no integration requirements for long-term residence or citizenship. *See* Anja Wiesbrock, *The Integration of Immigrants in Sweden: A Model for the European Union?*, 49 INT'L MIGRATION 48, 48-66 (2011), https://doi.org/10.1111/j.1468-2435.2010.00662.x.

Greece and Italy.[160] Additionally, an EU-wide fund dedicated to migration management would provide necessary resources to improve reception conditions, expand resettlement schemes, and facilitate family reunification.[161]

Safe and legal pathways for asylum seekers, such as humanitarian corridors, are essential to reduce reliance on dangerous sea crossings and uphold international human rights obligations. Expanding resettlement quotas and creating robust family reunification frameworks will enhance the EU's compliance with the principle of non-refoulement.[162]

Climate-induced migration is one of the most pressing challenges in migration governance. Rising sea levels, desertification, and extreme weather events are driving displacement, particularly in vulnerable regions, such as the Sahel and coastal areas.[163] Regional initiatives, such as the African Union's Great Green Wall Initiative, offer promising strategies to address these root causes, but require sustained investment and international cooperation.[164]

Comparative insights from other regions underscore the need for balanced and rights-based migration governance. The United States' securitized approach at the US-Mexico border has drawn significant criticism for human rights violations, including family separations and overcrowded detention facilities.[165] Similarly, Australia's offshore detention system has been condemned

---

160 "The European Union Agency for Asylum would be responsible for the establishment and technical maintenance of the system for allocation of asylum seekers." *See* Joana Abrisketa Uriarte, *The Reform of the Dublin III Regulation: How to Build or Not to Build Further Enforcing Mechanisms*, 23 SPANISH YEAR BOOK OF INT'L LAW 263, 263-272 (2019), https://doi.org/10.17103/sybil.23.16.

161 Henrik Enderlein & Nicole Koenig, *Towards Dublin IV: Sharing Norms, Responsibility and Costs*, Policy Paper No. 169, Jacques Delors Institute (June 2016), https://institutdelors.eu/wp-content/uploads/2020/08/dubliniv-enderleinkoenig-jdib-june16-1.pdf; Nicholas R. Micinski, *Delegating Responsibility: International Cooperation on Migration in the European Union* (Univ. of Mich. Press 2022), https://dx.doi.org/10.1353/book.99519.

162 Resettlement is seen as a means of securing responsibility sharing within international refugee law, though currently less than 1% of refugees can be resettled annually due to limited places. *See* Tineke de Boer & Marjoleine Zieck, *The Legal Abyss of Discretion in the Resettlement of Refugees*, 32 INT'L J. REFUGEE L. 54, 54-85 (2020), https://doi.org/10.1093/ijrl/eeaa005.

163 Zuowei Yang et al., *Analysis of Spatiotemporal Changes and Driving Factors of Desertification in the Africa Sahel*, 213 CATENA (2022), https://doi.org/10.1016/j.catena.2022.106213.

164 Trautman, Chevallier & Gosling, *supra* note 145.

165 HUMAN RIGHTS WATCH, *US: Family Separation Harming Children, Families*, Human Rights Watch (July 11, 2019), https://www.hrw.org/news/2019/07/11/us-family-separation-harming-children-families.

for its inhumane treatment of asylum seekers, emphasizing the importance of aligning migration policies with international legal standards.[166]

To address climate-induced migration, the EU must adopt comprehensive legal frameworks that extend protection to individuals displaced by environmental change. Advocating amendments to the 1951 Refugee Convention to include climate-related displacement would establish a critical legal foundation to address this growing issue.[167]

The Mediterranean migration crisis highlights the urgent need for the EU to adopt a comprehensive and humane approach to migration governance. Reforming the Dublin III Regulation, establishing centralized mechanisms for asylum allocation, and creating an EU-wide migration management fund are critical initial steps. These reforms must be coupled with the expansion of safe pathways, such as resettlement schemes and humanitarian corridors, to uphold the EU's international legal obligations and reduce its reliance on dangerous sea crossings.[168]

By integrating climate resilience into migration policies and supporting regional adaptation strategies such as the Great Green Wall Initiative, the EU can address the root causes of displacement and set a global standard for sustainable migration governance. These efforts align with the EU's commitments under the European Green Deal [169] and the Charter of Fundamental Rights,[170] reaffirming its role as a global leader in equity, sustainability, and justice.

---

166 HUMAN RIGHTS WATCH, *Australia: Appalling Abuse, Neglect of Refugees on Nauru*, Human Rights Watch (Aug. 2, 2016), https://www.hrw.org/news/2016/08/02/australia-appalling-abuse-neglect-refugees-nauru; AMNESTY INTERNATIONAL, *Unsafe Offshore Detention Facilities Mean Asylum Seekers Must Be Processed in Australia*, Amnesty International Australia (Feb. 19, 2024), https://www.amnesty.org.au/unsafe-offshore-detention-facilities-mean-asylum-seekers-must-be-processed-in-australia/.

167 Hoang Anh Q. (Jason) Nguyen, *Are "Climate Refugees" Compatible with the 1951 Refugee Convention?*, European Parliament Research Briefing (2021), https://www.europarl.europa.eu/RegData/etudes/BRIE/2021/698753/EPRS_BRI%282021%29698753_EN.pdf.

168 Susan Fratzke et al., *Refugee Resettlement and Complementary Pathways: Opportunities for Growth*, UNHCR (Sept. 2021), https://www.unhcr.org/sites/default/files/legacy-pdf/614462c94.pdf; Chiara Ricci, *The Necessity for Alternative Legal Pathways: The Best Practice of Humanitarian Corridors Opened by Private Sponsors in Italy*, 21 GERMAN L.J. 265, 265-283 (2020), https://doi.org/10.1017/glj.2020.7.

169 EUROPEAN COMMISSION, *The European Green Deal*, European Commission (2024), https://commission.europa.eu/strategy-and-policy/priorities-2019-2024/european-green-deal_en.

170 CHARTER OF FUNDAMENTAL RIGHTS OF THE EUROPEAN UNION, European Parliament (2000), https://www.europarl.europa.eu/charter/pdf/text_en.pdf.

C. IUU Fishing and Jurisdictional Challenges in the Pacific

IUU fishing in the Pacific exposes systemic governance gaps and ethical concerns that disproportionately impact SIDS. These nations, which are heavily reliant on marine resources for food security, cultural heritage, and economic stability, face significant challenges in combating the harmful practices of distant-water fishing fleets.[171] The Pacific Ocean, a critical global resource, harbors some of the most biodiverse ecosystems and productive fisheries worldwide. For example, tuna stocks play a vital role in sustaining regional economies while meeting global food demands. However, over 192,000 tons of tuna are illegally harvested annually in the Western and Central Pacific, leading to economic losses exceeding $600 million.[172] These figures underscore the urgent need for effective governance measures to protect Pacific marine ecosystems and ensure sustainable fishery management.

The challenges faced by Pacific nations are exacerbated by jurisdictional ambiguity and enforcement limitations. Although UNCLOS grants coastal states sovereign rights to manage resources within their EEZs, enforcement remains a daunting challenge for SIDS.[173] Article 94 of UNCLOS, which tasks flag states with ensuring compliance by vessels flying their flag, is frequently undermined by the widespread use of flags of convenience.[174] These vessels exploit regulatory loopholes, undermine conservation efforts and evade accountability. In high seas, where jurisdictional oversight is minimal, these gaps are even more pronounced. Practices such as transshipment, wherein

---

[171] Hugo Lucas et al., *Critical Challenges and Capacity Building Needs for Renewable Energy Deployment in Pacific Small Island Developing States (Pacific SIDS)*, 107 RENEWABLE ENERGY 42, 42-52 (2017), https://doi.org/10.1016/j.renene.2017.01.029.

[172] Radio New Zealand, *Transhipping of Fish Costing Pacific Nations*, RNZ (Dec. 5, 2024), https://www.rnz.co.nz/international/pacific-news/528450/transhipping-of-fish-costing-pacific-nations; Pew Charitable Trusts, *Transshipment Plays a Major Role in the Global Tuna Industry*, Pew Trusts (Sept. 2024), https://www.pewtrusts.org/en/research-and-analysis/issue-briefs/2024/09/transshipment-plays-a-major-role-in-the-global-tuna-industry.

[173] UNCLOS, *supra* note 3, Article 56 (granting coastal states sovereign rights over marine resources within their EEZs).

[174] This practice often results in a lack of genuine link between vessels and their flag states, contrary to Article 91 of UNCLOS. *See* J. Henry Ford & Chris Wilcox, *Shedding Light on the Dark Side of Maritime Trade – A New Approach for Identifying Countries as Flags of Convenience*, 99 MARINE POL'Y 298, 298-303 (2018), https://doi.org/10.1016/j.marpol.2018.10.026.

catches are transferred between vessels at sea, enable illegally caught fish to infiltrate the global supply chains.[175]

Regional governance frameworks, such as the Western and Central Pacific Fisheries Commission (WCPFC)[176] and the Parties to the Nauru Agreement (PNA),[177] play critical roles in addressing these challenges. The WCPFC has implemented measures, such as vessel monitoring systems and compliance schemes, to regulate highly migratory fish stocks.[178] These initiatives have contributed to greater accountability, yet their reliance on voluntary compliance and limited jurisdiction over non-member states significantly weaken their effectiveness.[179] The PNA's Vessel Day Scheme, which allocates fishing days to prioritize sustainability and economic benefits, has substantially increased revenue for the Pacific nations.[180] However, its narrow focus on economic returns sometimes conflicts with the broader conservation goals.[181]

Localized governance approaches also play an essential role in addressing the challenges posed by IUU fishing. Community-Based Fisheries Management (CBFM) offers a promising solution by empowering local communities to

---

175 Transshipment at sea, involving the transfer of catch from fishing vessels to refrigerated cargo vessels, is a significant challenge in global fisheries management. This practice often obscures the origin of the catch, complicating sustainable fisheries management and potentially allowing illegally caught fish to enter legitimate seafood markets. *See* Ewell et al., *supra* note 21; Nathalie A. Miller et al., *supra* note 22.

176 Western & Central Pacific Fisheries Commission, *Home Page*, WCPFC (2024), https://www.wcpfc.int/home.

177 Parties to the Nauru Agreement, *Home Page*, PNA (2024), https://www.pnatuna.com.

178 In the Western and Central Pacific Ocean (WCPO), VMS data has been utilized to understand the spatial patterns of fishing activity, which is crucial for fisheries resource monitoring and spatial management. *See* Shenglong Yang et al., *The Environmental Niche of the Tuna Purse Seine Fleet in the Western and Central Pacific Ocean Based on Different Fisheries Data*, 8 FISHES 78 (2023), https://doi.org/10.3390/fishes8020078.

179 R. Watson, A. Sousa-Santos & M. Howes, *Challenges in International Fisheries Compliance: Voluntary vs. Binding Agreements*, 18 MAR. POL'Y 347, 350–52 (2021).

180 PARTIES TO THE NAURU AGREEMENT, *PNA Vessel Day Scheme*, PNA (2024), https://www.pnatuna.com/content/pna-vessel-day-scheme; *see* also Elizabeth Havice, *Rights-Based Management in the Western and Central Pacific Ocean Tuna Fishery: Economic and Environmental Change Under the Vessel Day Scheme*, 42 MARINE POL'Y 259, 259-267 (2013), https://doi.org/10.1016/j.marpol.2013.03.003.

181 Peter Arbo & Pham Thi Thu Thủy, *Use Conflicts in Marine Ecosystem-Based Management — The Case of Oil Versus Fisheries*, 122 OCEAN & COASTAL MGMT. 77, 77-86 (2016), https://doi.org/10.1016/j.ocecoaman.2016.01.008.

manage marine resources sustainably.[182] For example, in the Solomon Islands, CBFM initiatives incorporating traditional ecological knowledge have successfully reduced illegal fishing activities and enhanced fish stock recovery.[183] Ensuring that governance frameworks prioritize stakeholder participation not only improves compliance, but also aligns conservation efforts with the cultural and economic needs of affected populations.[184]

The governance gaps in the high seas further exacerbate the pressures faced by Pacific nations. The high seas, which fall outside national jurisdiction, are particularly vulnerable to exploitation owing to the limited enforcement mechanisms under UNCLOS. While Articles 116 to 119 of the Convention emphasize cooperation in conserving and managing marine resources, their reliance on voluntary compliance has allowed distant-water fleets to operate with minimal accountability.[185] Practices such as transshipment, where catches are transferred between vessels, remain a significant concern. Without robust monitoring systems and mandatory reporting requirements, transshipment facilitates the laundering of illegally caught fish into global supply chains, undermining the effectiveness of regional and national conservation efforts.[186]

MPAs offer a compelling solution to address the governance challenges posed by IUU fishing and high-sea exploitation. MPAs safeguard critical habitats, promote biodiversity, and mitigate the impacts of climate change on marine ecosystems. Expanding the network of MPAs in the Pacific, particularly in high-risk areas, will provide ecological buffer zones that contribute to the

---

[182] Marc Léopold et al., *Community-Based Management of Near-Shore Fisheries in Vanuatu: What Works?*, 42 MARINE POL'Y 167, 167-176 (2013), https://doi.org/10.1016/j.marpol.2013.02.013; Di Yang & Robert Pomeroy, *The Impact of Community-Based Fisheries Management (CBFM) on Equity and Sustainability of Small-Scale Coastal Fisheries in the Philippines*, 86 MARINE POL'Y 173, 173-181 (2017), https://doi.org/10.1016/j.marpol.2017.09.027.

[183] *Lessons Learned from Community-Based Adaptive Marine Resource Management in Solomon Islands*, Secretariat of the Pacific Regional Environment Programme (SPREP), https://www.sprep.org/att/IRC/eCOPIES/Countries/Solomon_Islands/68.pdf.

[184] The active involvement of local stakeholders in protected area management is increasingly recognized as crucial for biodiversity conservation, with formal and informal governance arrangements shaping participation. *See* M. D. López-Rodríguez et al., *Delineating Participation in Conservation Governance: Insights from the Sierra de Guadarrama National Park (Spain)*, 114 ENVTL. SCI. & POL'Y 486, 486-496 (2020), https://doi.org/10.1016/j.envsci.2020.09.019.

[185] UNCLOS, *supra note 3*, Articles 116-119 (emphasizing cooperation in conserving high seas resources but relying on voluntary compliance mechanisms, limiting enforceability).

[186] Katherine Seto et al., *Toward Transparent Governance of Transboundary Fisheries: The Case of Pacific Tuna Transshipment*, 136 MARINE POL'Y (2020), https://doi.org/10.1016/j.marpol.2020.104200.

sustainability of marine resources.[187] Integrating these MPAs into regional governance frameworks, such as the WCPFC, and aligning them with global commitments under the UNCLOS would significantly enhance their effectiveness. However, establishing and maintaining MPAs require substantial financial and technical resources.[188]

Ethical considerations must underpin any governance strategy that can address these challenges. Environmental justice highlights the inequities faced by SIDS, which bear the brunt of resource depletion and ecological degradation caused by distant-water fishing fleets.[189] While wealthier nations extract significant economic value from Pacific fisheries, they often contribute minimally to conservation or enforcement efforts. Intergenerational equity further underscores the moral obligation of future generations to preserve the ecological health of the Pacific.[190] Ensuring that governance frameworks prioritize sustainable resource management is critical for balancing the needs of current populations with those of future generations.

Equity-focused financial mechanisms are essential for bridging these gaps. Establishing an international conservation fund under the UNCLOS, supported by contributions from distant-water fishing nations, would provide critical resources for enforcement infrastructure, monitoring systems, and capacity-building initiatives.[191] Revenue-sharing agreements codified within regional frameworks such as the PNA could further ensure that Pacific nations receive a fair share of the economic benefits derived from their marine resources. By linking revenue distribution to compliance with conservation measures, these

---

[187] The expansion of MPAs, especially in high-risk areas, could create important buffer zones that help maintain spawner biomass, improve yields, and preserve genetic diversity. *See* C. G. Attwood, J. M. Harris & A. J. Williams, *International Experience of Marine Protected Areas and Their Relevance to South Africa*, 18(1) S. AFR. J. MARINE SCI. 311, 311-332 (1997), https://doi.org/10.2989/025776197784161162.

[188] Ashley McCrea-Strub et al., *Understanding the Cost of Establishing Marine Protected Areas*, 35 MARINE POL'Y 1, 1-9 (2010), https://doi.org/10.1016/j.marpol.2010.07.001.

[189] Edwin A. Hernández-Delgado, *Coastal Restoration Challenges and Strategies for Small Island Developing States in the Face of Sea Level Rise and Climate Change*, 4 COASTS 235, 235-286 (2024), https://doi.org/10.3390/coasts4020014.

[190] This concept is particularly relevant to preserving the ecological health of the Pacific, as it requires current decision-makers to act pro-socially in the best interests of future generations. *See* Stavros Syropoulos & Ezra M. Markowitz, *Perceived Responsibility Towards Future Generations and Environmental Concern: Convergent Evidence Across Multiple Outcomes in a Large, Nationally Representative Sample*, 76 J. ENVTL. PSYCHOL. (2021), https://doi.org/10.1016/j.jenvp.2021.101651.

[191] Nagisa Shiiba et al., *How Blue Financing Can Sustain Ocean Conservation and Development: A Proposed Conceptual Framework for Blue Financing Mechanism*, 139 MARINE POL'Y (2022), https://doi.org/10.1016/j.marpol.2021.104575.

agreements would incentivize sustainable fishing practices and strengthen the alignment between economic gains and ecological stewardship.[192]

III. Confronting Ocean Governance Challenges in the Arctic, Mediterranean, and Pacific

The Arctic, Mediterranean, and Pacific regions collectively illustrate the systemic and interconnected nature of the ocean governance challenges. Governance gaps across these regions jeopardize marine ecosystems, undermine economic stability, and expose human rights to violations. Issues such as IUU fishing, climate change, jurisdictional disputes, and labor exploitation highlight the urgent need for both coordinated global responses and region-specific solutions. Despite their unique circumstances, these regions have common governance failures, underscoring the pressing need for innovative strategies and multilateral cooperation to safeguard marine resources and promote sustainability. The Arctic's geopolitical rivalries, Mediterranean's human rights crises, and Pacific's IUU fishing challenges demonstrate the interconnected nature of ocean governance. Addressing these shared issues requires systemic reforms that integrate binding enforcement mechanisms, adaptive management strategies, and equitable resource-sharing models.

Climate change in the Arctic has intensified governance challenges by rapidly transforming the physical and ecological landscapes of the region. Arctic amplification, where warming occurs more than twice the global average, has resulted in accelerated sea ice melting, opening previously inaccessible areas for shipping and resource extraction. This transformation has intensified competition among Arctic states over lucrative resources, such as oil, natural gas, and minerals.[193] However, despite these stakes, the absence of a dedicated RFMO leaves vast portions of the Arctic high seas vulnerable to overfishing and IUU activities. Shifting fish stocks driven by warming waters further complicate governance as they are frequently cross-national boundaries, demanding cooperative frameworks that remain insufficient to address such transboundary issues.[194]

---

[192] Arthur D. Yeeting et al., *Implications of New Economic Policy Instruments for Tuna Management in the Western and Central Pacific*, 63 MARINE POL'Y 45, 45-52 (2015), https://doi.org/10.1016/j.marpol.2015.10.003.

[193] Warwick F. Vincent, *Arctic Climate Change: Local Impacts, Global Consequences, and Policy Implications*, in ARCTIC ECOLOGY 507, 507-526 (Springer ed., 2019), https://doi.org/10.1007/978-3-030-20557-7_31.

[194] Jose Palacios-Abrantes et al., *Timing and Magnitude of Climate-Driven Range Shifts in Transboundary Fish Stocks Challenge Their Management*, 28 GLOBAL CHANGE BIOLOGY, 2312-2326 (2022), https://doi.org/10.1111/gcb.16058; Olav Schram Stokke, *Climate Cha*

UNCLOS provides a foundational framework for regulating activities within EEZs, but it lacks the robust mechanisms required to govern high-sea fisheries or respond effectively to climate-induced ecological shifts. This regulatory void exposes critical areas to unregulated exploitation, thereby threatening efforts to balance resource use with environmental conservation. Establishing an Arctic-specific RFMO could bridge these gaps by promoting sustainable fisheries management and fostering cooperation among the Arctic states. Such a framework would also serve to mitigate geopolitical tensions surrounding resource claims. Incorporating Indigenous knowledge and traditional ecological perspectives into governance frameworks would further enhance their effectiveness. For instance, co-management agreements between indigenous communities and government agencies such as those in Alaska and Canada provide valuable lessons for integrating local ecological knowledge with scientific management.[195]

In the Mediterranean region, governance challenges are further complicated by territorial disputes, ecological pressures, and significant human rights concerns. Disagreements over maritime boundaries, particularly among Turkey, Greece, and Cyprus, impede efforts to regulate shared resources and effectively manage fisheries. While the General Fisheries Commission for the Mediterranean (GFCM) plays a central role in overseeing fisheries management, its lack of binding enforcement powers and political fragmentation among Mediterranean states undermines its ability to achieve sustainable results.[196]

The Mediterranean's human rights challenges are particularly evident in the fishing industry, where forced labor and human trafficking are rampant. Economic priorities often overshadow ethical considerations, exposing vulnerable populations to exploitation. Addressing these systemic failures requires the integration of resource management with robust human rights protection. One possible avenue is expanding the PSMA to include labor

---

nge and Institutional Resilience in Arctic Environmental Governance, 12 POL. & GOVERNANCE (2024), https://doi.org/10.17645/pag.7369.

195 These agreements aim to address natural resource conflicts and promote participatory decision-making, yet they often fall short of achieving true power-sharing and local empowerment. *See* Alfonso Peter Castro & Erik Nielsen, *Indigenous People and Co-Management: Implications for Conflict Management,* 4(4-5) ENVTL. SCI. & POL'Y 229, 229-239 (2001), https://doi.org/10.1016/s1462-9011(01)00022-3.

196 Massimiliano Cardinale et al., *Mediterranean Sea: A Failure of the European Fisheries Management System,* 4 FRONTIERS IN MARINE SCI. (2017), https://doi.org/10.3389/fmars.2017.00072; Silvia De Juan et al., *A Regional Network of Sustainable Managed Areas as the Way Forward for the Implementation of an Ecosystem-Based Fisheries Management in the Mediterranean,* 65 OCEAN & COASTAL MGMT. 51, 51-58 (2012), https://doi.org/10.1016/j.ocecoaman.2012.04.024.

protection alongside its anti-IUU fishing provisions. Strengthening the capacity of the GFCM to implement binding measures and incorporate human rights standards into its regulatory framework is an essential step toward creating a more ethical and effective governance system for the Mediterranean.[197]

In the Pacific, SIDS face unique governance challenges because of their reliance on marine resources for food security, cultural identity, and economic development. Distant-water fleets, often operating under flags of convenience, exploit legal loopholes to engage in IUU fishing, which depletes critical resources, such as tuna stocks. These activities not only threaten the sovereignty of Pacific nations, but also undermine the economic stability of their communities. Limited enforcement capacity further exacerbates these challenges, as SIDS lack the resources to effectively monitor and protect their vast EEZs. The struggle to safeguard marine resources highlights the need for greater regional cooperation and support.[198]

Regional cooperation is vital for addressing these issues. Advancements in monitoring and surveillance technologies, such as satellite tracking and real-time reporting systems, can significantly enhance the ability of Pacific nations to safeguard their EEZs. International financial support from organizations such as the Global Environment Facility (GEF) and the World Bank is crucial in building the infrastructure and capacity required for sustainable fisheries management. Investments in capacity-building programs would empower Pacific nations to manage and protect their marine resources independently, thereby reducing their reliance on external actors.[199]

---

[197] Steven W. Purcell, Alessandro Lovatelli & Kaliola Pakoa, *Constraints and Solutions for Managing Pacific Island Sea Cucumber Fisheries with an Ecosystem Approach*, 45 MARINE POL'Y 240, 240-250 (2013), https://doi.org/10.1016/j.marpol.2013.11.005; Lydia C. L. Teh et al., *The Role of Human Rights in Implementing Socially Responsible Seafood*, 14 PLOS ONE (2019), https://doi.org/10.1371/journal.pone.0210241.

[198] For example, the Benguela Current Large Marine Ecosystem (BCLME) project demonstrates the importance of regional cooperation in implementing marine conservation measures. Through a collaborative approach involving Angola, Namibia, and South Africa, the BCLME initiative refined existing Ecologically or Biologically Significant Marine Areas (EBSAs) and proposed management recommendations. *See* L. R. Harris et al., *Practical Marine Spatial Management of Ecologically or Biologically Significant Marine Areas: Emerging Lessons From Evidence-Based Planning and Implementation in a Developing-World Context*, 9 FRONTIERS IN MARINE SCI. (2022), https://doi.org/10.3389/fmars.2022.831678.

[199] Rob White, *Transnational Environmental Crime: Toward an Eco-global Criminology* 265–270 (Willan Publishing, 2011); Daniel Schneider, *Fisheries Governance and Resource Management in Pacific Islands*, 37 *J. INT'L ENVTL. L.* 134, 140–42 (2024).

Climate change further exacerbates the governance challenges faced by Pacific nations, with ocean acidification, rising sea levels, and shifting fish stocks threatening the stability of local ecosystems. Integrating climate-resilient fisheries management practices into governance frameworks is essential for enabling Pacific nations to adapt to these environmental changes. Protecting blue carbon ecosystems, such as mangroves and seagrasses, offers dual benefits: conserving biodiversity and mitigating climate change by sequestering carbon. Aligning regional fisheries governance with broader environmental strategies would bolster the resilience of Pacific nations, ensuring the sustainability of both marine ecosystems and communities that depend on them.[200]

The interconnected governance challenges in the Arctic, Mediterranean, and Pacific underscore the limitations of the existing frameworks and the urgent need for systemic reform. In the Arctic, creating a dedicated RFMO tailored to the region's ecological and geopolitical complexities could address overfishing, facilitate equitable resource sharing, and reduce tension among Arctic states.[201] Incorporating Indigenous knowledge into governance frameworks would further enhance decision-making by grounding it in both scientific data and the lived experiences of local communities.[202] This holistic approach could help to balance environmental, economic, and cultural priorities, ensuring that Arctic governance is more inclusive and adaptive to ongoing environmental changes.

In the Mediterranean, expanding the mandates of existing frameworks, such as the GFCM, to include binding enforcement mechanisms and human rights protection could foster a more holistic approach to governance. Integrating anti-IUU measures with labor protection and sustainability standards would ensure that ecological objectives are pursued alongside social and ethical considerations. Collaborative models such as the Norway-Russia Fisheries Agreement demonstrate the potential for innovative governance solutions that

---

200 Andrea Bryndum-Buchholz et al., *The Status of Climate Change Adaptation in Fisheries Management: Policy, Legislation and Implementation*, 22(6) FISH & FISHERIES 1248, 1248-1273 (2021), https://doi.org/10.1111/faf.12586; Mecki Kronen et al., *Socio-Economic Drivers and Indicators for Artisanal Coastal Fisheries in Pacific Island Countries and Territories and Their Use for Fisheries Management Strategies*, 34(6) MARINE POL'Y 1135, 1135-1143 (2010), https://doi.org/10.1016/j.marpol.2010.03.013.

201 Alex Shahbazi, *Sustaining Tomorrow's Central Arctic Ocean Today: Using Best Practices to Guide the Central Arctic Ocean Fisheries Agreement's Implementation*, WWF 10-21 (Nov. 2022), https://files.worldwildlife.org/wwfcmsprod/files/Publication/file/7zhj2wrz1i_CAOFA_Full_Report_pages_web_version.pdf.

202 Robin Bronen et al., *Usteq: Integrating Indigenous Knowledge and Social and Physical Sciences to Coproduce Knowledge and Support Community-Based Adaptation*, 43(2-3) POLAR GEOGRAPHY 188, 188-205 (2019), https://doi.org/10.1080/1088937x.2019.1679271.

balance economic development with sustainability.[203] Adapting similar frameworks in the Mediterranean could address tensions arising from resource exploitation and promote peaceful resolution to territorial disputes.

In the Pacific Ocean, empowering SIDS through targeted capacity-building initiatives, financial support, and the adoption of advanced surveillance technologies is essential to combat IUU fishing and protect marine ecosystems.[204] Aligning fisheries governance with climate-resilient strategies, including the preservation of blue carbon ecosystems, would equip Pacific nations to adapt to environmental changes while safeguarding their economic and cultural reliance on marine resources.[205] These efforts would bolster the resilience of Pacific communities and promote sustainable marine stewardship.

IV. Reforming UNCLOS: Legal Proposals for a Modern Maritime Governance Framework

UNCLOS, adopted in 1982, has established itself as the foundational framework for managing marine resources and regulating oceanic activities. However, despite its significant influence on maritime law, modern challenges such as IUU fishing, jurisdictional ambiguities, labor abuses, and climate change have significant limitations within its structure.[206] These gaps threaten global food security, marine biodiversity, and the socio-economic stability of SIDS, which depend heavily on marine resources for sustenance and economic development. With global economic losses from IUU fishing exceeding $20 billion annually and the escalating impacts of climate-driven disruptions on marine ecosystems, the comprehensive reform of UNCLOS has become an urgent necessity.[207] Aligning ocean governance with the United Nations Sustainable Development Goals (SDGs), particularly SDG 14 (Life Below

---

[203] Norway and Russia have finalized a fisheries agreement for 2025, focusing on the sustainable management of key fish stocks in the Barents Sea. The total allowable catch for Northeast Arctic cod has been set at 340,000 tonnes, marking a 25% reduction from the previous year and representing the lowest quota since 1991. *See Norway and Russia Agree on 2025 Fisheries Management Plan*, The Fishing Daily (Dec. 2024), https://thefishingdaily.com/latest-news/norway-and-russia-agree-on-2025-fisheries-management-plan.

[204] Lucas et al., *supra* note 166.

[205] For example, by implementing tailored management approaches that adapt to shifting marine resources, small island nations can improve their food self-sufficiency from the sea. *See* Lida Teneva et al., *Small Island Nations Can Achieve Food Security Benefits Through Climate-Adaptive Blue Food Governance by 2050*, 151 MARINE POL'Y (2023), https://doi.org/10.1016/j.marpol.2023.105577.

[206] Oral, *supra* note 5; Armstrong, *supra* note 4.

[207] Donald Liddick, *supra* note 78.

Water), offers a crucial opportunity to establish a more effective framework for safeguarding oceans in the 21st century.[208]

One of the most critical gaps in UNCLOS lies in its reliance on flag-state jurisdiction, as outlined in Article 94. This provision mandates that flag states ensure compliance with international maritime regulations for vessels flying their flags. However, the widespread use of "flags of convenience," where vessels register under jurisdictions with minimal enforcement standards, undermines this principle.[209] Such practices allow vessels engaged in IUU fishing or labor abuses to evade accountability, compounding regulatory failures. The persistent use of flags of convenience in the Pacific and Arctic exemplifies these governance failures, underscoring the urgency to reform Article 94 to enhance enforcement mechanisms. Comparative frameworks, such as the ILO Work in Fishing Convention (No. 188), demonstrate the potential for integrating enforceable labor standards into maritime governance.[210] The proposed Article 94 bis could mandate flag states to comply with international labor and environmental standards, with violations subject to penalties through a centralized UNCLOS enforcement body.

To close these loopholes, reforms to Article 94 mandated independent vessel audits, transparency requirements, and verification mechanisms.[211] Linking flag state compliance to economic incentives, such as preferential access to global seafood markets, could further encourage adherence to sustainable practices.[212] Legal precedents, such as *Philippines v. China* (2016), *Bangladesh v. Myanmar* (2012), demonstrated how robust legal frameworks can mediate disputes and promote equitable resource management.[213] Strengthening flag

---

208 UNITED NATIONS GENERAL ASSEMBLY, *supra* note 7.

209 Walton J. McLeod, *The Flags-of-Convenience Problem*, 16 S.C. L. REV. 409, 410–12 (1964), https://scholarcommons.sc.edu/sclr/vol16/iss3/4;_Dana D. Miller & U. Rashid Sumaila, *Flag Use Behavior and IUU Activity Within the International Fishing Fleet: Refining Definitions and Identifying Areas of Concern*, 44 MARINE POL'Y 204, 204-211 (2013), https://doi.org/10.1016/j.marpol.2013.08.027.

210 INTERNATIONAL LABOUR ORGANIZATION (ILO), *supra* note 67.

211 Md Syful Islam, *Navigating Modern Era at Sea: Legal Challenges and Opportunities of Unmanned and Autonomous Shipping*, AI & ETHICS (2024), https://doi.org/10.1007/s43681-024-00554-y.

212 Fiorenza Micheli et al., *A System-Wide Approach to Supporting Improvements in Seafood Production Practices and Outcomes*, 12 FRONTIERS IN ECOLOGY & ENV'T 297, 297-305 (2014), https://doi.org/10.1890/110257.

213 *South China Sea Arbitration (Philippines v. China)*, *supra* note 13, paras. 393–94; *Dispute Concerning Delimitation of the Maritime Boundary Between Bangladesh and Myanmar in the Bay of Bengal (Bangladesh/Myanmar)*, *supra* note 16.

State responsibilities under UNCLOS would significantly enhance transparency and accountability in global maritime governance.

Port state measures represent another critical avenue for addressing IUU fishing and labor abuse in maritime industries. The Food and Agriculture Organization PSMA has already proven effective in deterring illegal fishing by granting port states the authority to inspect vessels and deny entry to those that fail to comply with international regulations.[214] For instance, nations such as Thailand have strengthened port inspections under the PSMA framework, reducing illegal fishing activities in their waters.[215] However, the effective implementation of PSMA provisions often requires significant capacity-building, as many developing nations lack the resources to conduct inspections and enforce compliance.

Labor rights in the maritime sector, particularly within the fishing industry, demand urgent attention as part of the broader UNCLOS reforms. Migrant workers aboard fishing vessels frequently endure exploitative conditions, including forced labor, wage theft, and physical abuse.[216] Certification programs such as the Marine Stewardship Council and Fair Trade USA play a pivotal role in enabling consumers to make ethical choices and ensure fisheries comply with labor and environmental standards.[217] Introducing a new provision, Article 94 bis, into UNCLOS mandates compliance with these labor standards for all vessels under its jurisdiction. This proposed Article 94 bis would complement existing UNCLOS provisions by extending the accountability framework to include labor conditions, filling a critical gap in maritime governance.[218]

Climate change represents an overarching challenge that complicates all aspects of ocean governance. Rising sea temperatures, ocean acidification, and shifting fish stocks require adaptive governance frameworks capable of

---

[214] "The Agreement on Port State Measures (PSMA) is the first binding international agreement to specifically target illegal, unreported and unregulated (IUU) fishing. Its objective is to prevent, deter and eliminate IUU fishing by preventing vessels engaged in IUU fishing from using ports and landing their catches." See FAO, *supra* note 84.

[215] U.N. FOOD & AGRIC. ORG. (FAO), *State of World Fisheries and Aquaculture 2020*, at 32 (2020), https://www.fao.org/documents/card/en/c/cc0461en.

[216] INTERNATIONAL ORGANIZATION FOR MIGRATION (IOM), *Protection of Migrants at Sea*, 11–15 (2018), https://www.iom.int/protection-migrants-at-sea.

[217] MARINE STEWARDSHIP COUNCIL, *Sustainable Fishing*, https://www.msc.org; FAIR TRADE CERTIFIED, *Home Page*, Fair Trade USA (2024), https://www.fairtradecertified.org.

[218] Alexa Blaskowsky, *Seafarer Abandonment and the Maritime Labor Convention: An Examination of Its Effectiveness and Future Solutions*, 25 OR. REV. INT'L L. 259 (2024), https://scholarsbank.uoregon.edu/server/api/core/bitstreams/2a5a6d1b-140d-414f-b711-6dadfe3ba988/content.

addressing these dynamic and interrelated challenges.[219] Introducing a new Article 119 bis to UNCLOS could enable the integration of predictive modeling tools to forecast changes in fish populations, establish climate-resilient catch quotas, and develop conservation strategies for blue carbon ecosystems, such as mangroves and seagrasses.[220] These ecosystems play a vital role not only in supporting marine biodiversity but also in mitigating climate change through carbon sequestration.[221] Legal precedents such as the ICJ advisory opinion on climate change obligations underscore the emerging principle of ecological integrity in international law.[222] Introducing a new Article 119 bis to UNCLOS, modeled after the Paris Agreement's binding commitments under Article 6, could integrate adaptive governance mechanisms for marine biodiversity and blue carbon ecosystems.[223] This approach aligns UNCLOS with global climate governance trends, ensuring its relevance in addressing twenty-first-century environmental crises.

Integrating these protections into UNCLOS would address the cascading environmental risks seen in the Arctic and Pacific, while advancing global sustainability goals.

Aligning UNCLOS reforms with international agreements such as the Paris Agreement and the High Seas Treaty would ensure coherence in global efforts to combat climate-related threats.[224] Funding initiatives to restore blue carbon habitats and prioritize climate-adaptive fisheries management would empower nations to address the accelerating impact of climate change. These measures would also reinforce the alignment of UNCLOS with the SDGs, particularly SDG 13 (Climate Action) and SDG 14 (Life Below Water), providing a comprehensive future-proof governance framework.[225]

---

[219] Lucy Greenhill, Jasper O. Kenter & Halvor Dannevig, *Adaptation to Climate Change–Related Ocean Acidification: An Adaptive Governance Approach*, 191 OCEAN & COASTAL MGMT. (2020), https://doi.org/10.1016/j.ocecoaman.2020.105176.

[220] Ariane E. Sutton-Grier & Alexandra Moore, *Leveraging Carbon Services of Coastal Ecosystems for Habitat Protection and Restoration*, 44(3) Coastal Mgmt. 259, 259-277 (2016), https://doi.org/10.1080/08920753.2016.1160206.

[221] *Id.*

[222] *Application of the Convention on the Prevention and Punishment of the Crime of Genocide (The Gambia v. Myanmar)*, Pending Case, International Court of Justice, https://www.icj-cij.org/case/187.

[223] Article 6 of the Paris Agreement sets out how countries can pursue voluntary cooperation to reach their climate targets. It enables international cooperation to tackle climate change and unlock financial support for developing countries. See *Paris Agreement*, *supra* note 18.

[224] Morgera et al., *supra* note 27.

[225] UN, *Agenda 2030*, *supra* note 203.

RFMOs play a crucial role in governing transboundary fisheries and promoting sustainability. However, their efforts are often constrained by limited enforcement authority and fragmented cooperation among the member states.[226] Organizations such as the Western and Central Pacific Fisheries Commission [227] and the General Fisheries Commission for the Mediterranean[228] have made significant progress in managing fisheries within their regions.[229] Current initiatives, such as the High Seas Treaty negotiations and the Global Fishing Watch project, demonstrate the potential of multilateral collaboration to enhance transparency and enforce sustainable practices in areas beyond national jurisdiction.[230]

Empowering RFMOs with advanced monitoring technologies, such as satellite tracking, blockchains, and real-time data-sharing systems, would further strengthen their oversight capacity.[231]

The Arctic exemplifies the urgency of addressing governance gaps as rapid environmental changes are transforming the region. The loss of sea ice is opening new fisheries and shipping routes, increasing the risk of overfishing and resource exploitation in the absence of a robust governance framework.[232] Establishing an Arctic-specific RFMO is critical to ensuring that resource management in the region is sustainable, science-based, and cooperative.[233]

---

[226] Selina Cullis-Suzuki & Daniel Pauly, *Failing the High Seas: A Global Evaluation of Regional Fisheries Management Organizations*, 34(5) MARINE POL'Y 1036, 1036-1042 (2010), https://doi.org/10.1016/j.marpol.2010.03.002.

[227] The Western and Central Pacific Fisheries Commission (WCPFC) was established by the Convention for the Conservation and Management of Highly Migratory Fish Stocks in the Western and Central Pacific Ocean (WCPF Convention) which entered into force on 19 June 2004. *See* Western & Central Pacific Fisheries Commission, *supra* note 176.

[228] The General Fisheries Commission for the Mediterranean is a regional fisheries management organization. With 22 member countries & the EU, its main objective is to ensure the conservation and the sustainable use of living marine resources as well as the sustainable development of aquaculture in the Mediterranean and in the Black Sea. *See* U.N. FOOD & AGRIC. ORG. (FAO), *General Fisheries Commission for the Mediterranean*, FAO (2024), https://www.fao.org/gfcm/en/.

[229] Camryn Goodman et al., *Enhancing Cooperative Responses by Regional Fisheries Management Organisations to Climate-Driven Redistribution of Tropical Pacific Tuna Stocks*, 9 FRONTIERS IN MARINE SCI. (2022), https://doi.org/10.3389/fmars.2022.1046018.

[230] UNITED NATIONS, *BBNJ Agreement*, U.N., https://www.un.org/bbnjagreement/en; Global Fishing Watch, *Home Page*, https://globalfishingwatch.org.

[231] Daniel C. Dunn et al., *Empowering High Seas Governance with Satellite Vessel Tracking Data*, 19(4) FISH & FISHERIES 729, 729-739 (2018), https://doi.org/10.1111/faf.12285.

[232] Dmitry Sharapov, *supra* note 42.

[233] Alex Shahbazi, *supra* note 196.

This RFMO can be drawn from the Arctic Council's frameworks, incorporating ecosystem-based management practices to mitigate environmental risks.[234]

In the Pacific, SIDS face distinct governance challenges because of their dependence on marine resources for food security and economic stability. The pervasive threat of IUU fishing, often facilitated by distant-water fleets operating under flags of convenience, undermines these nations' sovereignty and economic resilience.[235] International funding mechanisms such as the Global Environment Facility[236] and the World Bank[237] can play a vital role in supporting SIDS' enforcement capabilities and climate-resilient fisheries management.

Adaptive measures, such as climate-resilient catch quotas, would enable SIDS to respond to the shifting marine environments caused by rising ocean temperatures and acidification. Additionally, protecting blue carbon ecosystems, such as mangroves and seagrasses, offers dual benefits: mitigating climate change through carbon sequestration and preserving biodiversity that is critical to regional economies.[238]

Reforming the UNCLOS is an ambitious yet essential endeavor that requires active participation from a diverse range of stakeholders, including governments, international organizations, civil society, indigenous communities, and the private sector. Achieving consensus among states with differing priorities demands diplomatic strategies that emphasize shared responsibilities and mutual benefits.[239] Multilateral agreements, international forums, and inclusive dialogue platforms can foster collaboration, mitigate resistance to change, and build momentum for comprehensive reform. Through sustained collaboration, adaptive innovation, and equitable reform, UNCLOS can fulfill its potential as a cornerstone of global ocean governance, securing the oceans as a vital resource for future generations.

---

[234] Tore Henriksen, *The Arctic Ocean, Environmental Stewardship, and the Law of the Sea*, 6(1) U.C. IRVINE L. REV. 61 (2016), https://escholarship.org/uc/item/725567qv.

[235] Jiwon Park et al., *Tracking Elusive and Shifting Identities of the Global Fishing Fleet*, 9(3) SCIENCE ADVANCES (2023), https://doi.org/10.1126/sciadv.abp8200; *see* also Gohar A. Petrossian, *supra* note 30.

[236] Global Environment Facility, *Home Page*, GEF (2024), https://www.thegef.org.

[237] World Bank, *Home Page*, https://www.worldbank.org/ext/en/home.

[238] Integrating blue carbon ecosystem conservation into climate change mitigation strategies and biodiversity protection plans is crucial for achieving a "triple win" for climate mitigation, adaptation, and conservation. *See* Sutton-Grier & Moore, *supra* note 214.

[239] Chris Whomersley, *How to Amend UNCLOS and Why It Has Never Been Done*, 9(1) KOREAN J. INT'L & COMP. L. 72, 72-83 (2021), https://doi.org/10.1163/22134484-12340146.

Conclusion

The ocean, which covers over two-thirds of the Earth's surface, serves as the foundation of global ecological and economic systems. It regulates the global climate, supports biodiversity, ensures food security, and sustains millions of livelihoods worldwide.[240] Despite its critical importance, accelerating threats - including illegal, unreported, and unregulated fishing, jurisdictional disputes, human rights abuses, and climate change–are testing the limits of existing governance frameworks.[241] The United Nations Convention on the Law of the Sea, which was revolutionary upon its adoption in 1982, now struggles to meet the complexities of today's interconnected maritime challenges.[242] Without timely reforms, these systemic issues have cascading consequences that endanger marine ecosystems, disrupt global food security, and compromise the economic resilience of vulnerable communities.[243]

Reforming UNCLOS is not just a legal necessity, but also a moral imperative. Addressing these limitations requires immediate attention to several critical areas, starting with flag state jurisdiction. Article 94, which tasks flag states while ensuring compliance with international regulations, is undermined by practices such as flags of convenience and flag hopping, which enable vessels to evade oversight.[244] Introducing mandatory vessel audits, transparency requirements, and stricter penalties for noncompliance would close these regulatory loopholes and restore accountability. Compliance with economic incentives, such as preferential access to global seafood markets, could further promote sustainable practices. These reforms are particularly critical for regions such as the Pacific, where Small Island Developing States face acute challenges to sovereignty and resource management due to unregulated maritime activities.

Enhancing port state measures is another cornerstone of comprehensive maritime governance reforms. Although port states play a critical role in curbing IUU fishing, their enforcement authority remains constrained under

---

[240] Roger P. Harris et al., *Marine Ecosystems and Global Change*, Oxford University Press (2010), https://doi.org/10.1093/acprof:oso/9780199558025.001.0001.

[241] Auld et al., *supra* note 68.

[242] Kojima, *supra* note 12; Oral, *supra* note 5.

[243] Joanna Mossop, *Can We Make the Oceans Greener: The Successes and Failures of UNCLOS as an Environmental Treaty*, 49 V.U.W.L. REV. 128-130 (2018), https://doi.org/10.26686/vuwlr.v49i4.5341; Emma Witbooi et al., *Organized Crime in the Fisheries Sector Threatens a Sustainable Ocean Economy*, NATURE 3 (2020), https://doi.org/10.1038/s41586-020-2913-5.

[244] UNCLOS, *supra* note 3, Article 94.

the current framework.[245] Integrating provisions from the Port State Measures Agreement into UNCLOS and broadening their scope to include labor protection would significantly strengthen port states' capabilities. Such an effort would need to balance the interests of various stakeholders, address jurisdictional concerns, and ensure compatibility with the existing UNCLOS principles and dispute settlement mechanisms.[246] Requiring vessels to maintain detailed crew documentation and verifying compliance with safe working conditions, freedom from exploitation, and access to grievance mechanisms would address labor abuses while ensuring sustainable fishing practices. These measures, particularly in high-risk regions, such as the Mediterranean, would promote transparency and accountability across the global seafood supply chain, benefiting both ecological sustainability and human rights.

Jurisdictional disputes represent a significant barrier to effective ocean governance.[247] Although UNCLOS includes mechanisms for resolving such disputes, the lack of enforceable processes and complexity of overlapping Exclusive Economic Zones often hinder cooperation. Expanding the role of the International Tribunal for the Law of the Sea to handle EEZ disputes more efficiently and introducing binding arbitration mechanisms under UNCLOS would facilitate equitable resource-sharing and conflict resolution.[248]

Ongoing negotiations for a new international legally binding instrument for biodiversity beyond national jurisdiction and the need for improved efforts to conserve and sustainably use marine resources in areas beyond national jurisdiction further highlight the importance of effective dispute resolution mechanisms.[249]

---

[245] Gohar A. Petrossian et al., *Where Do "Undocumented" Fish Land? An Empirical Assessment of Port Characteristics for IUU Fishing*, 21(3) EUR. J. CRIM. POL'Y & RES. 337, 337-351 (2014), https://doi.org/10.1007/s10610-014-9267-1.

[246] Boyle, *supra* note 12; Xiaodan Liao, *The Timor Sea Conciliation Under Article 298 and Annex V of UNCLOS: A Critique*, 18(2) CHINESE J. INT'L L. 281, 281-325 (2019), https://doi.org/10.1093/chinesejil/jmz020.

[247] The Somalia-Kenya maritime dispute illustrates how unresolved boundaries can impede resource exploitation and undermine regional stability. *See* Kadagi et al., *supra* note 38.

[248] The growing number of inter-state disputes and the need for specialized expertise in maritime law suggest that ITLOS could play a crucial role in addressing complex issues related to EEZs and resource-sharing. *See* Boyle, *supra* note 12; *see* also Edward L. Miles & William T. Burke, *Pressures on the United Nations Convention on the Law of the Sea of 1982 Arising from New Fisheries Conflicts: The Problem of Straddling Stocks*, 20(4) OCEAN DEV. & INT'L L. 343, 343-357 (1989), https://doi.org/10.1080/00908328909545900.

[249] Druel & Gjerde. *supra* note 29.

Regional agreements such as the Norway-Russia Barents Sea framework demonstrate how cooperative governance can sustainably manage shared resources while reducing geopolitical tension.[250] Applying such models to contested regions, such as the Arctic, could prevent unilateral exploitation and foster collaborative management.

The climate crisis is an overarching challenge that demands urgent reform of UNCLOS. Oceans are at the forefront of climate change, facing rising temperatures, acidification, and shifting fish stocks, all of which complicate resource management and conservation efforts.[251] Incorporating the proposed Article 119 bis into UNCLOS could address these challenges by introducing adaptive management strategies such as predictive modeling for fish stock migration, climate-resilient catch quotas, and conservation measures for blue carbon ecosystems such as mangroves and seagrasses. These ecosystems play a dual role in mitigating climate change through carbon sequestration, while supporting marine biodiversity.[252] Including specific provisions for their protection within UNCLOS would align global ocean governance with broader climate goals. Collaborative frameworks that integrate UNCLOS with agreements such as the Paris Agreement and High Seas Treaty could ensure a unified international response, mitigating the cascading effects of climate change on marine ecosystems.

Regional Fisheries Management Organizations are integral to sustainable ocean governance but often lack the authority and resources needed to address modern challenges. Expanding Article 118 of UNCLOS to grant RFMOs binding regulatory powers would significantly enhance their ability to combat IUU

---

250 The Norway-Russia agreement on marine delimitation in the Barents Sea, reached in 2010, exemplifies successful cooperative governance of shared resources. This agreement was driven primarily by Russia's broader foreign policy considerations, including efforts to reduce conflicts with neighboring states, improve its international image, and strengthen the UN Convention on the Law of the Sea as the framework for Arctic governance. *See* Moe et al., *supra* note 48.

251 Elizabeth Mendenhall et al., *Climate Change Increases the Risk of Fisheries Conflict*, 117 MARINE POL'Y (2020), https://doi.org/10.1016/j.marpol.2020.103954; Martina H. Stiasny et al., *Ocean Acidification Effects on Atlantic Cod Larval Survival and Recruitment to the Fished Population*, 11(8) PLOS ONE (2016), https://doi.org/10.1371/journal.pone.0155448; Cristina Villalobos et al., *Ocean Acidification and Ocean Warming Effects on Pacific Herring (Clupea Pallasi) Early Life Stages*, 7 FRONTIERS IN MARINE SCI. (2020), https://doi.org/10.3389/fmars.2020.597899.

252 Oscar Serrano et al., *Chapter 28 - Conservation of Blue Carbon Ecosystems for Climate Change Mitigation and Adaptation*, in COASTAL WETLANDS 965-996 (Gerardo M. E. Perillo et al. eds., Elsevier 2018), https://doi.org/10.1016/b978-0-444-63893-9.00028-9.

fishing, enforce conservation measures, and sustainably manage fisheries.[253] Establishing an Arctic-specific RFMO could address governance gaps in the region, as melting sea ice exposes new fisheries and resources to exploitation. Similarly, strengthening the capacity of RFMOs such as the Western and Central Pacific Fisheries Commission would empower Pacific nations to effectively protect their maritime territories. A centralized oversight body within UNCLOS that harmonizes RFMO activities could ensure consistency and foster global cooperation in transboundary resource management.[254]

Incorporating human rights protections into UNCLOS reforms is essential for achieving equitable ocean governance. Migrant workers in the maritime sector, particularly in the fishing industry, often endure severe exploitation, including forced labor, wage theft, and physical abuse. Introducing Article 94 bis to UNCLOS mandates adherence to international labor standards, ensuring safe and dignified working conditions for all maritime workers. Aligning UNCLOS with established human rights frameworks, such as the ILO conventions[255] and the ICCPR,[256] would provide a robust foundation for protecting workers' rights. Ensuring that fisheries are both ecologically sustainable and free from labor abuses would address the human cost of global seafood supply chains and promote justice within ocean governance.[257]

SIDS face unique challenges due to their limited resources, technological gaps, and heightened vulnerability to climate change. Reforming UNCLOS to include capacity-building programs and financial support mechanisms would empower these nations to effectively protect their resources.[258] Initiatives such

---

[253] UNCLOS, *supra* note 3, Article 118.

[254] Lorraine Elliott, *Transnational Environmental Crime in the Asia Pacific: An "Un(der)securitized" Security Problem?*, 20(4) PAC. REV. 499, 499-522 (2007), https://doi.org/10.1080/09512740701671995.

[255] INTERNATIONAL LABOUR ORGANIZATION, *ILO Conventions*, https://www.ilo.org/resource/ilo-conventions.

[256] OFFICE OF THE HIGH COMMISSIONER FOR HUMAN RIGHTS, *International Covenant on Civil and Political Rights*, https://www.ohchr.org/en/instruments-mechanisms/instruments/international-covenant-civil-and-political-rights.

[257] Gabrielle E. Lout, *Human Rights in a Sea of Market-Based Approaches: Evaluation of Market-Based Tools Integrating Social Responsibility in the Sustainable Seafood Movement*, 35 SUSTAINABLE PROD. & CONSUMP. 1, 1-12 (2023), https://doi.org/10.1016/j.spc.2022.10.020; Teh et al., *supra* note 192.

[258] The BBNJ agreement presents a critical opportunity to change the course of capacity building by strengthening the international legal framework, including funding, information-sharing, monitoring, and decision-making. *See* Harriet Harden-Davies et al., *How Can a New UN Ocean Treaty Change the Course of Capacity Building?*, 32(5) AQUATIC CONSERVATION: MARINE & FRESHWATER ECOSYSTEMS 907, 907-912 (2022), https://doi.org/10.1002/aqc.3796.

as technology transfers, satellite surveillance, and real-time monitoring systems can enhance their enforcement capabilities and safeguard marine ecosystems while strengthening resilience against climate-related impacts.[259] These reforms must prioritize the needs of SIDS, ensuring that vulnerable states are equipped to thrive despite growing environmental and economic pressures.

Reforming the UNCLOS is a comprehensive and long-term endeavor that requires collaboration among diverse stakeholders, including governments, international organizations, civil society, indigenous communities, and the private sector. Achieving consensus among states with differing priorities demands diplomatic strategies that emphasize shared responsibilities and mutual benefits. Multilateral agreements, inclusive dialogue platforms, and international forums can foster collaboration and mitigate resistance to change.[260] Framing these reforms as opportunities for sustainable development and global cooperation will further enhance their feasibility and appeal.

In conclusion, reforming UNCLOS is both a legal necessity and a moral imperative to address the multifaceted challenges threatening the world's oceans today. By integrating adaptive management strategies, robust enforcement mechanisms, climate resilience, and human rights protection, the UNCLOS can evolve into a dynamic and effective governance framework. Global cooperation is pivotal for achieving this transformation. Through inclusive reforms that prioritize equity and innovation, UNCLOS can safeguard marine biodiversity, enhance resilience to climate change, and ensure the sustainable use of marine resources by future generations. These reforms must balance ecological preservation with equitable resource distribution to ensure sustainability and justice for all nations.

Global cooperation is pivotal to the successful modernization of UNCLOS. Aligning regional innovations with broader international agreements, such as the Paris Agreement and the High Seas Treaty, can create a cohesive and unified

---

[259] Giovanni Soldi et al., *Space-Based Global Maritime Surveillance. Part I: Satellite Technologies*, 36(9) IEEE AEROSPACE & ELECTRONIC SYS. MAG. 8, 8-28 (2021), https://doi.org/10.1109/maes.2021.3070862; Robin Whytock et al., *Real-Time Alerts from AI-Enabled Camera Traps Using the Iridium Satellite Network: A Case Study in Gabon, Central Africa*, 14(3) METHODS IN ECOLOGY & EVOLUTION 867, 867-874 (2023), https://doi.org/10.1111/2041-210x.14036.

[260] For example, the use of strategies such as the Framework Convention Pathway can help states manage uncertainties and gradually deepen commitments as they learn more about the problem and potential solutions. *See* Kenneth W. Abbott & Duncan Snidal, *Pathways to International Cooperation*, in THE POLITICS OF GLOBAL REGULATION 50-84 (Cambridge Univ. Press 2004), https://doi.org/10.1017/cbo9780511494147.003.

ocean governance system. This system must prioritize the needs of vulnerable states while fostering solidarity among all nations. Ultimately, through inclusive reform efforts and a commitment to equity, UNCLOS can safeguard marine biodiversity, enhance resilience to climate change, and ensure the sustainable use of marine resources by future generations.

Bibliography

Kenneth W. Abbott & Duncan Snidal, *Pathways to International Cooperation*, in The Politics of Global Regulation 50-84 (Cambridge Univ. Press 2004), https://doi.org/10.1017/cbo9780511494147.003.

Hazem G. Abdo, *Impacts of War in Syria on Vegetation Dynamics and Erosion Risks in Safita Area, Tartous, Syria*, 18 Reg'l Envtl. Change 1707, 1707-1719 (2018), https://doi.org/10.1007/s10113-018-1280-3.

Tony Alderton & Nick Winchester, *Globalisation and De-Regulation in the Maritime Industry*, 26 Marine Pol'y 35, 35-43 (2001), https://doi.org/10.1016/s0308-597x(01)00034-3.

Mishari Alsaleh et al., *Nature of Property Rights and Motivation for Blue Growth: An Empirical Evidence from the Fisheries Industry*, 48 Nat. Resources Forum 184, 184-210 (2023), https://doi.org/10.1111/1477-8947.12317.

Amnesty International, *Libya: European Governments Complicit in Horrific Abuse of Refugees and Migrants*, Amnesty International (Dec. 12, 2017), https://www.amnesty.org/en/latest/press-release/2017/12/libya-european-governments-complicit-in-horrific-abuse-of-refugees-and-migrants/.

Amnesty International, *The EU's Complicity in Migrant Abuse in Libya*, Amnesty International Australia (Dec. 18, 2017), https://www.amnesty.org.au/migrant-abuse-libya/.

Amnesty International, *Unsafe Offshore Detention Facilities Mean Asylum Seekers Must Be Processed in Australia*, Amnesty International Australia (Feb. 19, 2024), https://www.amnesty.org.au/unsafe-offshore-detention-facilities-mean-asylum-seekers-must-be-processed-in-australia/.

David Anderson, *Modern Law of the Sea: Selected Essays* 89–91 (Martinus Nijhoff Publishers, 2008). https://doi.org/10.1163/ej.9789004158917.i-627.

Antarctic Treaty, Dec. 1, 1959, 402 U.N.T.S. 71 (entered into force June 23, 1961).

Application of the Convention on the Prevention and Punishment of the Crime of Genocide *(The Gambia v. Myanmar)*, Pending Case, International Court of Justice, https://www.icj-cij.org/case/187.

Peter Arbo & Pham Thi Thu Thủy, *Use Conflicts in Marine Ecosystem-Based Management — The Case of Oil Versus Fisheries*, 122 Ocean & Coastal Mgmt. 77, 77-86 (2016), https://doi.org/10.1016/j.ocecoaman.2016.01.008.

Arctic Council, *Arctic Shipping Governance Strategies: Challenges and Innovations* (2024), at 8, https://www.arcticbiodiversity.is.

Arctic Monitoring and Assessment Programme, *AMAP Assessment 2023: Arctic Climate Update* (2023), https://www.amap.no.

Arctic Monitoring and Assessment Programme, *AMAP Assessment 2023: Methane Emissions from Permafrost Thaw* (2023), https://www.amap.no.

Chris Armstrong, *The United Nations Convention on the Law of the Sea, Global Justice and the Environment*, 13 Global Constitutionalism 16, 16–20 (2023), https://doi.org/10.1017/s2045381723000151.

Luis A. León Arzich, *Realism and the Chinese Attitudes Toward UNCLOS: The South China Sea Arbitration as a Case Study*, No. 134 Revista Pol. & Estrategia 21, 21-54 (2019), https://doi.org/10.26797/rpye.v0i134.786.

C. G. Attwood, J. M. Harris & A. J. Williams, *International Experience of Marine Protected Areas and Their Relevance to South Africa*, 18(1) S. Afr. J. Marine Sci. 311, 311-332 (1997), https://doi.org/10.2989/025776197784161162.

Kirsten Auld et al., *The Collective Effort of the United Nations Specialised Agencies to Tackle the Global Problem of Illegal, Unreported and Unregulated (IUU) Fishing*, 243 Ocean & Coastal Mgmt. (2023), https://doi.org/10.1016/j.ocecoaman.2023.106720.

Ahmet Faruk Aysan et al., *Natural Resources Governance and Conflicts: Retrospective Analysis*, 85 Resources Pol'y (2023), https://doi.org/10.1016/j.resourpol.2023.103942.

Elizabeth A. Barnes & James A. Screen, *The Impact of Arctic Warming on the Midlatitude Jet-Stream: Can It? Has It? Will It?*, 6 WIREs Climate Change 277, 277–286 (2015), https://doi.org/10.1002/wcc.337.

Robert Beckman, *The UN Convention on the Law of the Sea and the Maritime Disputes in the South China Sea*, 107 Am. J. Int'l L. 142, 142-163 (2013), https://doi.org/10.5305/amerjintelaw.107.1.0142.

Fikret Berkes & Derek Armitage, *Co-Management Institutions, Knowledge, and Learning: Adapting to Change in the Arctic*, 34 Études/Inuit/Studies 109, 109-131 (2011), https://doi.org/10.7202/045407ar.

Emily Blake, *As Arctic Heavy Fuel Oil Ban Comes into Force, Critics Want More*, Cabin Radio (July 1, 2024), https://cabinradio.ca/190927/news/travel/as-arctic-heavy-fuel-oil-ban-comes-into-force-critics-want-more/.

Alexa Blaskowsky, *Seafarer Abandonment and the Maritime Labor Convention: An Examination of Its Effectiveness and Future Solutions*, 25 Or. Rev. Int'l L. 259 (2024), https://scholarsbank.uoregon.edu/server/api/core/bitstreams/2a5a6d1b-140d-414f-b711-6dadfe3ba988/content.

Marie Bourrel et al., *The Common Heritage of Mankind as a Means to Assess and Advance Equity in Deep Sea Mining*, 95 Marine Pol'y 311, 311-316 (2016), https://doi.org/10.1016/j.marpol.2016.07.017.

Brendan M. Boylan, *Increased Maritime Traffic in the Arctic: Implications for Governance of Arctic Sea Routes*, 131 Marine Pol'y (2021), https://doi.org/10.1016/j.marpol.2021.104566.

Alan E. Boyle, Dispute Settlement and the Law of the Sea Convention: Problems of Fragmentation and Jurisdiction, 46 Int'l & Comp. L.Q. 37, 37–54 (1997), https://doi.org/10.1017/s0020589300060103.

Neil Bradford & David A. Wolfe, *Governing Regional Economic Development: Innovation Challenges and Policy Learning in Canada*, 6 Cambridge J. Regions, Econ. & Soc'y 331, 331-347 (2013), https://doi.org/10.1093/cjres/rst006.

Trevor A. Branch et al., *Contrasting Global Trends in Marine Fishery Status Obtained from Catches and from Stock Assessments*, 25 Conservation Biology 777, 777-786 (2011), https://doi.org/10.1111/j.1523-1739.2011.01687.x.

Robin Bronen et al., *Usteq: Integrating Indigenous Knowledge and Social and Physical Sciences to Coproduce Knowledge and Support Community-Based Adaptation*, 43(2-3) Polar Geography 188, 188-205 (2019), https://doi.org/10.1080/1088937x.2019.1679271.

Andrea Bryndum-Buchholz et al., *The Status of Climate Change Adaptation in Fisheries Management: Policy, Legislation and Implementation*, 22(6) Fish & Fisheries 1248, 1248-1273 (2021), https://doi.org/10.1111/faf.12586.

Camilla Cafiero, *The Dublin III Regulation: Critiques and Latest Attempts of Reform*, Univ. Juridic (2019), https://internationallawreview.ro/fisiere/pdf/01_-Law_Review_nr_1-2019_PAGINAT_BT_C_Cafiero.pdf.

Massimiliano Cardinale et al., *Mediterranean Sea: A Failure of the European Fisheries Management System*, 4 Frontiers in Marine Sci. (2017), https://doi.org/10.3389/fmars.2017.00072.

Alfonso Peter Castro & Erik Nielsen, *Indigenous People and Co-Management: Implications for Conflict Management*, 4(4-5) Envtl. Sci. & Pol'y 229, 229-239 (2001), https://doi.org/10.1016/s1462-9011(01)00022-3.

Charter of Fundamental Rights of the European Union, European Parliament (2000), https://www.europarl.europa.eu/charter/pdf/text_en.pdf.

Xiujuan Chen, Qingxu Xu & Liyuan Li, *Illegal, Unreported, and Unregulated Fishing Governance in Disputed Maritime Areas: Reflections on the International Legal Obligations of States*, 8 Fishes 36 (2023), https://doi.org/10.3390/fishes8010036.

Sophie Natalie Chevalier, *The Arctic: From Peace Exceptionalism to International Insecurity - Examining the Interplay Between Hydrocarbon Developments and Military Expansions*. Master's thesis, European University Institute, 2024.

Lay Fong Chuah et al., *Analyzing the Influencing Factors of Port State Control for a Cleaner Environment via Bayesian Network Model*, 14 Cleaner Eng'g & Tech. (2023), https://doi.org/10.1016/j.clet.2023.100636.

Convention Relating to the Status of Refugees, July 28, 1951, 189 U.N.T.S. 137, entered into force Apr. 22, 1954.

Robin M. Cook, Alex Sinclair & Guðmundur Stefánsson, *Potential Collapse of North Sea Cod Stocks*, 385 Nature 521, 521-522 (1997), https://doi.org/10.1038/385521a0.

John Cropper, *Growing a World Wonder: The Great Green Wall and the History of Environmental Decline in the Sahel, 1450–2022*, 30 Env't & Hist. 145 (2023), https://doi.org/10.3197/096734023X16702350656933.

Selina Cullis-Suzuki & Daniel Pauly, *Failing the High Seas: A Global Evaluation of Regional Fisheries Management Organizations*, 34(5) Marine Pol'y 1036, 1036-1042 (2010), https://doi.org/10.1016/j.marpol.2010.03.002.

Neil M. Dawson et al., *The Role of Indigenous Peoples and Local Communities in Effective and Equitable Conservation*, 26 Ecology & Soc'y (2021), https://doi.org/10.5751/es-12625-260319.

Tineke de Boer & Marjoleine Zieck, *The Legal Abyss of Discretion in the Resettlement of Refugees*, 32 Int'l J. Refugee L. 54, 54-85 (2020), https://doi.org/10.1093/ijrl/eeaa005.

Silvia De Juan et al., *A Regional Network of Sustainable Managed Areas as the Way Forward for the Implementation of an Ecosystem-Based Fisheries Management in the Mediterranean*, 65 Ocean & Coastal Mgmt. 51, 51-58 (2012), https://doi.org/10.1016/j.ocecoaman.2012.04.024.

Tatiana S. Degai & Andrey N. Petrov, *Rethinking Arctic Sustainable Development Agenda Through Indigenizing UN Sustainable Development Goals*, 28 Int'l J. Sustainable Dev. & World Ecology 518, 518-523 (2021), https://doi.org/10.1080/13504509.2020.1868608.

Dispute Concerning Delimitation of the Maritime Boundary Between Bangladesh and Myanmar in the Bay of Bengal (*Bangladesh/Myanmar*), Judgment, ITLOS Reports 2012.

Scott C. Doney et al., *The Impacts of Ocean Acidification on Marine Ecosystems and Reliant Human Communities*, 45 Ann. Rev. Environ. & Res. 83, 83–112 (2020), https://doi.org/10.1146/annurev-environ-012320-083019.

Alassane Doumbouya et al., *Assessing the Effectiveness of Monitoring Control and Surveillance of Illegal Fishing: The Case of West Africa*, 4 Frontiers Marine Sci. 50 (2017), https://doi.org/10.3389/fmars.2017.00050.

Elise Druel & Kristina M. Gjerde, *Sustaining Marine Life Beyond Boundaries: Options for an Implementing Agreement for Marine Biodiversity Beyond National Jurisdiction Under the United Nations Convention on the Law of the Sea*, 49 Marine Pol'y 90, 90-97 (2013), https://doi.org/10.1016/j.marpol.2013.11.023.

Daniel C. Dunn et al., *Empowering High Seas Governance with Satellite Vessel Tracking Data*, 19(4) Fish & Fisheries 729, 729-739 (2018), https://doi.org/10.1111/faf.12285.

Mikhail Dvoynikov et al., *New Concepts of Hydrogen Production and Storage in Arctic Region*, 10 Resources 3 (2021), https://doi.org/10.3390/resources10010003.

Lorraine Elliott, *Transnational Environmental Crime in the Asia Pacific: An "Un(der)securitized" Security Problem?*, 20(4) Pac. Rev. 499, 499-522 (2007), https://doi.org/10.1080/09512740701671995.

Henrik Enderlein & Nicole Koenig, *Towards Dublin IV: Sharing Norms, Responsibility and Costs*, Policy Paper No. 169, Jacques Delors Institute (June 2016), https://institutdelors.eu/wp-content/uploads/2020/08/dubliniv-enderleinkoenig-jdib-june16-1.pdf.

Elena Eriksen et al., *From Single Species Surveys Towards Monitoring of the Barents Sea Ecosystem*, 166 Prog. Oceanog. 4, 4–14 (2017), https://doi.org/10.1016/j.pocean.2017.09.007.

European Commission, *The European Green Deal*, European Commission (2024), https://commission.europa.eu/strategy-and-policy/priorities-2019-2024/european-green-deal_en.

European Commission, *Win for the Ocean: High Seas Treaty Signed at United Nations*, Directorate-General for Maritime Affairs and Fisheries (Sept. 20, 2023), https://oceans-and-fisheries.ec.europa.eu/news/win-ocean-high-seas-treaty-signed-united-nations-2023-09-20_en.

Christopher Ewell et al., *Potential Ecological and Social Benefits of a Moratorium on Transshipment on the High Seas*, 81 Marine Pol'y 293, 293-300 (2017), https://doi.org/10.1016/j.marpol.2017.04.004.

Fair Trade Certified, *Home Page*, Fair Trade USA (2024), https://www.fairtradecertified.org.

J. Henry Ford & Chris Wilcox, *Shedding Light on the Dark Side of Maritime Trade – A New Approach for Identifying Countries as Flags of Convenience*, 99 Marine Pol'y 298, 298-303 (2018), https://doi.org/10.1016/j.marpol.2018.10.026.

James D. Ford et al., *Vulnerability to Climate Change in Igloolik, Nunavut: What We Can Learn from the Past and Present*, 42 Polar Rec. 127, 127-138 (2006), https://doi.org/10.1017/s0032247406005122.

James D. Ford et al., *Sea Ice, Climate Change, and Community Vulnerability in Northern Foxe Basin, Canada*, 38 Climate Res. 137, 137-154 (2009), https://doi.org/10.3354/cr00777.

Susan Fratzke et al., *Refugee Resettlement and Complementary Pathways: Opportunities for Growth*, UNHCR (Sept. 2021), https://www.unhcr.org/sites/default/files/legacy-pdf/614462c94.pdf.

Nanette Funk, *A Spectre in Germany: Refugees, a "Welcome Culture" and an "Integration Politics,"* 12 J. Global Ethics 289, 289-299 (2016), https://doi.org/10.1080/17449626.2016.1252785.

Natalie B. Gardiner, *Marine Protected Areas in the Southern Ocean: Is the Antarctic Treaty System Ready to Co-Exist with a New United Nations Instrument for Areas Beyond National Jurisdiction?*, 122 Marine Pol'y (2020), https://doi.org/10.1016/j.marpol.2020.104212.

Donald L. Gautier et al., *Assessment of Undiscovered Oil and Gas in the Arctic*, 324 Science 1175, 1175-1179 (2009), https://doi.org/10.1126/science.1169467.

Sam Geall et al., *Charting a Blue Future for Cooperation between West Africa and China on Sustainable Fisheries*, The Stimson Center 1, 13 (2023), https://www.stimson.org/wp-content/uploads/2023/09/IUU-Fishing-West-Africa-Report_8.30.23-1.pdf.

Leoni Anna Geray, *Fortress Europe: Analysing the Human Rights Impact of EU Border Externalisation in Third Countries Since 2015* (2024) (unpublished Bachelor's thesis, Ludwig Maximilian University of Munich) (on file with author), https://epub.ub.uni-muenchen.de/121612/1/Bachelorarbeit_Geray.pdf.

Eric L. Gilman et al., *Threats to Mangroves from Climate Change and Adaptation Options: A Review*, 89 Aquatic Botany 237, 237–250 (2008), https://doi.org/10.1016/j.aquabot.2007.12.009.

Bruce Glavovic et al., *Living on the Margin in the Anthropocene: Engagement Arenas for Sustainability Research and Action at the Ocean–Land Interface*, 14 Current Opinion Envtl. Sustainability 232, 232-238 (2015), https://doi.org/10.1016/j.cosust.2015.06.003.

Global Environment Facility, *Home Page*, GEF (2024), https://www.thegef.org.

Global Fishing Watch, *Home Page*, https://globalfishingwatch.org.

Alexander Golub, Maggie Mahoney & Jennifer Harlow, *Sustainability and Intergenerational Equity: Do Past Injustices Matter?*, 8 Sustainability Sci. 269, 269-277 (2013), https://doi.org/10.1007/s11625-013-0201-0.

Camryn Goodman et al., *Enhancing Cooperative Responses by Regional Fisheries Management Organisations to Climate-Driven Redistribution of Tropical Pacific Tuna Stocks*, 9 Frontiers in Marine Sci. (2022), https://doi.org/10.3389/fmars.2022.1046018.

Lucy Greenhill, Jasper O. Kenter, & Halvor Dannevig, *Adaptation to Climate Change–Related Ocean Acidification: An Adaptive Governance Approach*, 191 Ocean & Coastal Mgmt. (2020), https://doi.org/10.1016/j.ocecoaman.2020.105176.

Kjell Grip, *International Marine Environmental Governance: A Review*, 46 Ambio 413, 413-427 (2016), https://doi.org/10.1007/s13280-016-0847-9.

Douglas Guilfoyle, *The Rule of Law and Maritime Security: Understanding Lawfare in the South China Sea*, 95 Int'l Aff. 999, 999–1017 (2019), https://doi.org/10.1093/ia/iiz141.

Gwich'in Steering Committee, *Advocating for the Porcupine Caribou Herd* (2023), at 15, https://www.gwichinsteeringcommittee.org.

Harriet Harden-Davies et al., *How Can a New UN Ocean Treaty Change the Course of Capacity Building?*, 32(5) Aquatic Conservation: Marine & Freshwater Ecosystems 907, 907-912 (2022), https://doi.org/10.1002/aqc.3796.

L. R. Harris et al., *Practical Marine Spatial Management of Ecologically or Biologically Significant Marine Areas: Emerging Lessons From Evidence-Based Planning and Implementation in a Developing-World Context*, 9 Frontiers in Marine Sci. (2022), https://doi.org/10.3389/fmars.2022.831678.

Roger P. Harris et al., *Marine Ecosystems and Global Change*, Oxford University Press (2010), https://doi.org/10.1093/acprof:oso/9780199558025.001.0001.

Elizabeth Havice, *Rights-Based Management in the Western and Central Pacific Ocean Tuna Fishery: Economic and Environmental Change Under the Vessel Day Scheme*, 42 Marine Pol'y 259, 259-267 (2013), https://doi.org/10.1016/j.marpol.2013.03.003.

Ashwin A. Hebbar & Narayan Mukesh, *COVID-19 and Seafarers' Rights to Shore Leave, Repatriation and Medical Assistance: A Pilot Study*, 71 Int'l Mar. Health 217, 217-228 (2020), https://doi.org/10.5603/imh.2020.0040.

Edwin A. Hernández-Delgado, *Coastal Restoration Challenges and Strategies for Small Island Developing States in the Face of Sea Level Rise and Climate Change*, 4 Coasts 235, 235-286 (2024), https://doi.org/10.3390/coasts4020014.

Tore Henriksen, *The Arctic Ocean, Environmental Stewardship, and the Law of the Sea*, 6(1) U.C. Irvine L. Rev. 61 (2016), https://escholarship.org/uc/item/725567qv.

Hirsi Jamaa and Others v. Italy, App. No. 27765/09, Eur. Ct. H.R. (2012).

Peder Hjorth & Kaveh Madani, *Adaptive Water Management: On the Need for Using the Post-WWII Science in Water Governance*, 37 Water Res. Mgmt. 2247, 2247-2270 (2023), https://doi.org/10.1007/s11269-022-03373-0.

Human Rights Watch, *Australia: Appalling Abuse, Neglect of Refugees on Nauru*, Human Rights Watch (Aug. 2, 2016), https://www.hrw.org/news/2016/08/02/australia-appalling-abuse-neglect-refugees-nauru.

Human Rights Watch, *US: Family Separation Harming Children, Families*, Human Rights Watch (July 11, 2019), https://www.hrw.org/news/2019/07/11/us-family-separation-harming-children-families.

International Labour Organization (ILO), *C188 - Work in Fishing Convention, 2007 (No. 188)*, https://normlex.ilo.org/dyn/normlex/en/f?p=NORMLEXPUB:12100:0::NO::P12100_INSTRUMENT_ID:312333.

International Labour Organization (ILO), *Forced Labour and Human Trafficking in Fisheries*, https://www.ilo.org/topics/forced-labour-modern-slavery-and-trafficking-persons/sectors-and-topics/forced-labour-and-human-trafficking-fisheries.

International Labour Organization (ILO), *ILO Conventions*, available at https://www.ilo.org/resource/ilo-conventions.

International Organization for Migration (IOM), *Missing Migrants Project: Mediterranean* (2024), https://missingmigrants.iom.int/.

International Organization for Migration (IOM), *Protection of Migrants at Sea*, 11–15 (2018), https://www.iom.int/protection-migrants-at-sea.

International Transport Workers' Federation, *A One Way Ticket to Labour Exploitation: How Transit Visa Loopholes Are Being Used to Exploit Migrant Fishers on UK Fishing Vessels*, https://www.itfglobal.org/sites/default/files/node/resources/files/ITF_Fisheries-Briefing_Final.pdf.

International Tribunal For The Law Of The Sea (ITLOS), *Seabed Disputes Chamber, Advisory Opinion*, Feb. 1, 2011, ¶¶ 143–145, ITLOS Reports 2011.

INTERPOL, *Case Studies on IUU Fishing Enforcement Operations*, Rep. No. 18/SPRW, at 14–20 (2018).

Md Syful Islam, *Navigating Modern Era at Sea: Legal Challenges and Opportunities of Unmanned and Autonomous Shipping*, AI & Ethics (2024), https://doi.org/10.1007/s43681-024-00554-y.

Matthew Jenkins & Aiguo Dai, *The Impact of Sea-Ice Loss on Arctic Climate Feedbacks and Their Role for Arctic Amplification*, 48 Geophys. Res. Lett. (2021), https://doi.org/10.1029/2021gl094599.

Alok Jha, *The Ocean Is Not Just Huge but Also Hugely Important*, The Conversation (Mar. 26, 2014), https://theconversation.com/the-ocean-is-not-just-huge-but-also-hugely-important-24815.

Rui Jiang & Ping Guo, *Sustainable Management of Marine Protected Areas in the High Seas: From Regional Treaties to a Global New Agreement on Biodiversity in Areas Beyond National Jurisdiction*, 15 Sustainability (2023), https://doi.org/10.3390/su151511575.

Nesli Isigi Kadagi et al., *Joint Management of Shared Resources as an Alternative Approach for Addressing Maritime Boundary Disputes: The Kenya-Somalia Maritime Boundary Dispute*, 16 J. Indian Ocean Reg. 348, 348–370 (2020), https://doi.org/10.1080/19480881.2020.1823169.

Isaac B. Kardon, *China Can Say "No": Analyzing China's Rejection of the South China Sea Arbitration*, 13 U. Pa. Asian L. Rev. 1, 42 (2018), https://scholarship.law.upenn.edu/alr/vol13/iss2/1.

Bilawal M. Khaskheli et al., *Technology Advancement and International Law in Marine Policy, Challenges, Solutions, and Future Prospective*, 10 Frontiers Mar. Sci. (2023), https://doi.org/10.3389/fmars.2023.1258924.

Christian Knoblauch et al., *Methane Production as Key to the Greenhouse Gas Budget of Thawing Permafrost*, 8 Nat. Climate Change 309, 309-312 (2018). https://doi.org/10.1038/s41558-018-0095-z.

Chie Kojima, *Integration of General Principles of International Environmental Law into the Law of the Sea: Assessment and Challenges*, 149 Marine Pol'y (2023), https://doi.org/10.1016/j.marpol.2023.105497.

Kit M. Kovacs et al., *Impacts of Changing Sea-Ice Conditions on Arctic Marine Mammals*, 41 Marine Biodiversity 181, 181-194 (2010), https://doi.org/10.1007/s12526-010-0061-0.

Ken W. Krauss et al., *How Mangrove Forests Adjust to Rising Sea Level*, 202 New Phytologist 19, 19–34 (2013), https://doi.org/10.1111/nph.12605.

Mecki Kronen et al., *Socio-Economic Drivers and Indicators for Artisanal Coastal Fisheries in Pacific Island Countries and Territories and Their Use for Fisheries Management Strategies*, 34(6) Marine Pol'y 1135, 1135-1143 (2010), https://doi.org/10.1016/j.marpol.2010.03.013.

Bjarni Kunoy, *The Admissibility of a Plea to an International Adjudicative Forum to Delimit the Outer Continental Shelf Prior to the Adoption of Final Recommendations by the Commission on the Limits of the Continental Shelf*, 25(2) Int'l J. Marine & Coastal L. 237, 237–7 (2010), https://doi.org/10.1163/157180910x12665776638704.

Timo Kumpula et al., *Land Use and Land Cover Change in Arctic Russia: Ecological and Social Implications of Industrial Development*, 21 Global Envtl. Change 550, 550-562 (2011), https://doi.org/10.1016/j.gloenvcha.2010.12.010.

Alexey A. Kurekin et al., *Operational Monitoring of Illegal Fishing in Ghana through Exploitation of Satellite Earth Observation and AIS Data*, 11 Remote Sensing 293, 1 (2019), https://doi.org/10.3390/rs11030293.

Joseph Ladou, *International Occupational Health*, 206 Int'l J. Hygiene & Envtl. Health 303, 303-313 (2003), https://doi.org/10.1078/1438-4639-00226.

Marc Léopold et al., *Community-Based Management of Near-Shore Fisheries in Vanuatu: What Works?*, 42 Marine Pol'y 167, 167-176 (2013), https://doi.org/10.1016/j.marpol.2013.02.013.

Lessons Learned from Community-Based Adaptive Marine Resource Management in Solomon Islands, Secretariat of the Pacific Regional Environment Programme (SPREP), https://www.sprep.org/att/IRC/eCOPIES/Countries/Solomon_Islands/68.pdf.

Xiaodan Liao, *The Timor Sea Conciliation Under Article 298 and Annex V of UNCLOS: A Critique*, 18(2) Chinese J. Int'l L. 281, 281-325 (2019), https://doi.org/10.1093/chinesejil/jmz020.

Donald Liddick, *The Dimensions of a Transnational Crime Problem: The Case of IUU Fishing*, 17 Trends in Org. Crime 290, 290-312 (2014), https://doi.org/10.1007/s12117-014-9228-6.

Gabrielle E. Lout, *Human Rights in a Sea of Market-Based Approaches: Evaluation of Market-Based Tools Integrating Social Responsibility in the Sustainable Seafood Movement*, 35 Sustainable Prod. & Consump. 1, 1-12 (2023), https://doi.org/10.1016/j.spc.2022.10.020.

M. D. López-Rodríguez et al., *Delineating Participation in Conservation Governance: Insights from the Sierra de Guadarrama National Park (Spain)*, 114 Envtl. Sci. & Pol'y 486, 486-496 (2020), https://doi.org/10.1016/j.envsci.2020.09.019.

Kristen Lowitt et al., *Environmental Change and Food Security: The Special Case of Small Island Developing States*, 15 Reg'l Envtl. Change 1293, 1293-1298 (2015), https://doi.org/10.1007/s10113-015-0849-3.

Jane Lubchenco & Peter M. Haugan, *Illegal, Unreported and Unregulated Fishing and Associated Drivers*, in 1 Springer 553, 553-591 (2023), https://doi.org/10.1007/978-3-031-16277-0_15.

Hugo Lucas et al., *Critical Challenges and Capacity Building Needs for Renewable Energy Deployment in Pacific Small Island Developing States (Pacific SIDS)*, 107 Renewable Energy 42, 42-52 (2017), https://doi.org/10.1016/j.renene.2017.01.029.

Amanda H. Lynch, Charles H. Norchi & Xiangbai Li, *The Interaction of Ice and Law in Arctic Marine Accessibility*, 119 Proc. Nat'l Acad. Sci. (2022), https://doi.org/10.1073/pnas.2202720119.

Mary Mackay, *The Intersection Between Illegal Fishing, Crimes at Sea, and Social Well-Being*, 7 Frontiers Marine Sci. 10 (2020), https://doi.org/10.3389/fmars.2020.589000.

Dr. Francesco Maiani, *The Reform of the Dublin III Regulation*, Policy Department C - Citizens' Rights and Constitutional Affairs, European Parliament (2016), http://www.europarl.europa.eu/supporting-analyses.

Riccardo Marasco et al., *Diamonds in the Rough: Dryland Microorganisms Are Ecological Engineers to Restore Degraded Land and Mitigate Desertification*, 16 Microbial Biotechnology 1603, 1603-1610 (2023), https://doi.org/10.1111/1751-7915.14216.

Marine Stewardship Council, *Sustainable Fishing*, https://www.msc.org.

Ashley McCrea-Strub et al., *Understanding the Cost of Establishing Marine Protected Areas*, 35 Marine Pol'y 1, 1-9 (2010), https://doi.org/10.1016/j.marpol.2010.07.001.

Walton J. McLeod, *The Flags-of-Convenience Problem*, 16 S.C. L. Rev. 409, 410–12 (1964), https://scholarcommons.sc.edu/sclr/vol16/iss3/4.

Mariachiara Melillo, *Informal Dispute Resolution in Preferential Trade Agreements*, 53 J. World Trade 95, 95–127 (2019), https://doi.org/10.54648/trad2019005.

Evelyn Meltzer, *Global Overview of Straddling and Highly Migratory Fish Stocks: The Nonsustainable Nature of High Seas Fisheries*, 25 Ocean Dev. & Int'l L. 255, 255-344 (1994), https://doi.org/10.1080/00908329409546036.

Elizabeth Mendenhall et al., *Climate Change Increases the Risk of Fisheries Conflict*, 117 Marine Pol'y (2020), https://doi.org/10.1016/j.marpol.2020.103954.

Elizabeth Mendenhall, *Making the Most of What We Already Have: Activating UNCLOS to Combat Marine Plastic Pollution*, 155 Marine Pol'y (2023), https://doi.org/10.1016/j.marpol.2023.105786.

Jill Mendler De Suarez et al., *Ensuring Survival: Oceans, Climate and Security*, 90 Ocean & Coastal Mgmt. 27, 27-37 (2013), https://doi.org/10.1016/j.ocecoaman.2013.08.007.

Jessica Mercer et al., *Ecosystem-Based Adaptation to Climate Change in Caribbean Small Island Developing States: Integrating Local and External*

Knowledge, 4 Sustainability 1908, 1908-1932 (2012), https://doi.org/10.3390/su4081908.

Andrew Merrie et al., *An Ocean of Surprises—Trends in Human Use, Unexpected Dynamics and Governance Challenges in Areas Beyond National Jurisdiction*, 27 Global Envtl. Change 19, 19-31 (2014), https://doi.org/10.1016/j.gloenvcha.2014.04.012.

Nélia C. Mestre et al., *Exploitation of Deep-Sea Resources: The Urgent Need to Understand the Role of High Pressure in the Toxicity of Chemical Pollutants to Deep-Sea Organisms*, 185 Envtl. Pollution 369, 369-371 (2013), https://doi.org/10.1016/j.envpol.2013.10.021.

Fiorenza Micheli et al., *A System-Wide Approach to Supporting Improvements in Seafood Production Practices and Outcomes*, 12 Frontiers in Ecology & Env't 297, 297-305 (2014), https://doi.org/10.1890/110257.

Nicholas R. Micinski, *Delegating Responsibility: International Cooperation on Migration in the European Union* (Univ. of Mich. Press 2022), https://dx.doi.org/10.1353/book.99519.

Edward L. Miles & William T. Burke, *Pressures on the United Nations Convention on the Law of the Sea of 1982 Arising from New Fisheries Conflicts: The Problem of Straddling Stocks*, 20(4) Ocean Dev. & Int'l L. 343, 343-357 (1989), https://doi.org/10.1080/00908328909545900.

Karolina M. Milewicz & Duncan Snidal, *Cooperation by Treaty: The Role of Multilateral Powers*, 70 Int'l Org. 823, 823-844 (2016), https://doi.org/10.1017/s002081831600031x.

Dana D. Miller & U. Rashid Sumaila, *Flag Use Behavior and IUU Activity Within the International Fishing Fleet: Refining Definitions and Identifying Areas of Concern*, 44 Marine Pol'y 204, 204-211 (2013), https://doi.org/10.1016/j.marpol.2013.08.027.

Gifford H. Miller et al., *Arctic Amplification: Can the Past Constrain the Future?*, 29 Quaternary Sci. Rev. 1779, 1779-1790 (2010), https://doi.org/10. 1016/j.quascirev.2010.02.008.

Natalie A. Miller et al., *Identifying Global Patterns of Transshipment Behavior*, 5 Frontiers Marine Sci. 7 (2018), https://doi.org/10.3389/fmars.2018.00240.

Arild Moe et al., *Space and Timing: Why Was the Barents Sea Delimitation Dispute Resolved in 2010?*, 34 Polar Geography 145, 145–162 (2011), https://doi.org/10.1080/1088937x.2011.597887.

Travis J. Moore et al., *Exploring Ship Traffic Variability Off California*, 163 Ocean & Coastal Mgmt. 515, 515-527 (2018), https://doi.org/10.1016/j.ocecoaman.2018.03.010.

Elisa Morgera et al., *Addressing the Ocean-Climate Nexus in the BBNJ Agreement: Strategic Environmental Assessments, Human Rights and Equity in Ocean Science*, 38 Int'l J. Marine & Coastal L. 447, 447-479 (2023), https://doi.org/10.1163/15718085-bja10139.

Joanna Mossop, *Can We Make the Oceans Greener: The Successes and Failures of UNCLOS as an Environmental Treaty*, 49 V.U.W.L. Rev. 128-130 (2018), https://doi.org/10.26686/vuwlr.v49i4.5341.

M.S.S. v. Belgium and Greece, App. No. 30696/09, Eur. Ct. H.R. (2011).

Vidya V. Nadkarni & Rakesh Sinha, *Transforming Social Work Education in India: Integrating Human Rights,* 1 J. Hum. Rts. & Soc. Work 9, 9-18 (2016), https://doi.org/10.1007/s41134-016-0002-3.

National Oceanic and Atmospheric Administration (NOAA), *Arctic Report Card 2023,* https://arctic.noaa.gov/report-card/report-card-2023/ (last visited Dec. 5, 2024).

Maria Nevalainen, Inka Helle & Jarno Vanhatalo, *Preparing for the Unprecedented—Towards Quantitative Oil Risk Assessment in the Arctic Marine Areas,* 114 Marine Pollution Bull. 90, 90-101 (2016), https://doi.org/10.1016/j.marpolbul.2016.08.064.

Hoang Anh Q. (Jason) Nguyen, *Are "Climate Refugees" Compatible with the 1951 Refugee Convention?,* European Parliament Research Briefing (2021), https://www.europarl.europa.eu/RegData/etudes/BRIE/2021/698753/EPRS_BRI%282021%29698753_EN.pdf.

Norway and Russia Agree on 2025 Fisheries Management Plan, The Fishing Daily (Dec. 2024), https://thefishingdaily.com/latest-news/norway-and-russia-agree-on-2025-fisheries-management-plan.

Norwegian Government, *National Security Policy on Arctic Territories: Svalbard and Beyond* (2024), https://www.regjeringen.no.

Office of the High Commissioner for Human Rights, *International Covenant on Civil and Political Rights,* available at https://www.ohchr.org/en/instruments-mechanisms/instruments/international-covenant-civil-and-political-rights.

Nilufer Oral, UNCLOS and Sea Level Rise, 149 Marine Policy (2023), https://doi.org/10.1016/j.marpol.2022.105454.

Robert Orttung, *Russia's Arctic Ambitions,* Oxford Research Encyclopedia of Politics (June 18, 2024), https://oxfordre.com/politics/view/10.1093/acrefore/9780190228637.001.0001/acrefore-9780190228637-e-2274. https://doi.org/10.1093/acrefore/9780190228637.013.2274.

Andreas Østhagen & Marco Dordoni, *Security and Defence in the Mediterranean and in the Arctic,* European University Institute, Quaderni "La Comunità Internazionale" 42, 62 (2024), https://ricerca.unistrapg.it/retrieve/ac1555c1-12f4-4b6a-ba16-7066431b34ab/SECURITY%20AND%20DEFENCE%20IN%20THE%20MEDITERRANEAN%20AND%20IN%20THE%20ARCTIC.pdf.

Jose Palacios-Abrantes et al., *Timing and Magnitude of Climate-Driven Range Shifts in Transboundary Fish Stocks Challenge Their Management,* 28 Global Change Biology, 2312-2326 (2022), https://doi.org/10.1111/gcb.16058.

Min Pan & Henry P. Huntington, *A Precautionary Approach to Fisheries in the Central Arctic Ocean: Policy, Science, and China,* 63 Marine Pol'y 153, 153–157 (2015), https://doi.org/10.1016/j.marpol.2015.10.015.

Bindu Panikkar & Benjamin Lemmond, *Being on Land and Sea in Troubled Times: Climate Change and Food Sovereignty in Nunavut,* 9 Land 508 (2020), https://doi.org/10.3390/land9120508.

Dimitra Papageorgiou & Eva Tzavala, *Migration in the Mediterranean Sea: Management Within and Beyond Borders,* in Human Rights Issues in Migration and Border Management: Challenges and Perspectives 189 (Ivan Sammut & Ivan Mifsud eds., 2024), ISBN 978-94-6236-329-8.

Paris Agreement, Dec. 12, 2015, T.I.A.S. No. 16-1104, 55 I.L.M. 743 (entered into force Nov. 4, 2016).

Jiwon Park et al., *Tracking Elusive and Shifting Identities of the Global Fishing Fleet*, 9(3) Science Advances (2023), https://doi.org/10.1126/sciadv.abp8200.

Parties to the Nauru Agreement, *Home Page*, PNA (2024), https://www.pnatuna.com.

Parties to the Nauru Agreement, *PNA Vessel Day Scheme*, PNA (2024), https://www.pnatuna.com/content/pna-vessel-day-scheme.

Lena Partzsch, *Alternatives to Multilateralism*, Massachusetts Institute of Technology (2020), https://doi.org/10.7551/mitpress/12610.001.0001.

Durmaz Peksen & Robert G. Blanton, *The Impact of ILO Conventions on Worker Rights: Are Empty Promises Worse Than No Promises?*, 12 Rev. Int'l Orgs. 75, 75-94 (2016), https://doi.org/10.1007/s11558-015-9241-9.

Permanent Court of Arbitration, *South China Sea Arbitration (Philippines v. China)*, Award (July 12, 2016), paras. 75–83, https://pcacases.com/web/view/7.

Gohar A. Petrossian et al., *Where Do "Undocumented" Fish Land? An Empirical Assessment of Port Characteristics for IUU Fishing*, 21(3) Eur. J. Crim. Pol'y & Res. 337, 337-351 (2014), https://doi.org/10.1007/s10610-014-9267-1.

Gohar A. Petrossian & Frank S. Pezzella, *IUU Fishing and Seafood Fraud: Using Crime Script Analysis to Inform Intervention*, 679 Annals Am. Acad. Pol. & Soc. Sci. 121, 121-139 (2018), https://doi.org/10.1177/0002716218784533.

Gohar A. Petrossian et al., *Flags for Sale: An Empirical Assessment of Flag of Convenience Desirability to Foreign Vessels*, 116 Marine Pol'y 103937 (2020), https://doi.org/10.1016/j.marpol.2020.103937.

Gohar A. Petrossian, *Preventing Illegal, Unreported and Unregulated (IUU) Fishing: A Situational Approach*, 189 Biological Conservation 39, 39-48 (2014), https://doi.org/10.1016/j.biocon.2014.09.005.

Pew Charitable Trusts, *Transshipment Plays a Major Role in the Global Tuna Industry*, Pew Trusts (Sept. 2024), https://www.pewtrusts.org/en/research-and-analysis/issue-briefs/2024/09/transshipment-plays-a-major-role-in-the-global-tuna-industry.

Stephanie Pezard et al., *China's Strategy and Activities in the Arctic: Implications for North American and Transatlantic Security*, RAND Corporation Research Report RRA1282-1-v2 (2022), https://www.rand.org/content/dam/rand/pubs/research_reports/RRA1200/RRA1282-1-v2/RAND_RRA1282-1-v2.pdf.

Eric A. Posner & John C. Yoo, *A Theory of International Adjudication*, SSRN Elec. J. (2004), https://doi.org/10.2139/ssrn.507003.

Jessica Prince et al., *Supporting Regional Co-Operation in the South China Sea with an Initial Assessment of the Data-Limited Skipjack Tuna Fishery*, 155 Marine Pol'y (2023), https://doi.org/10.1016/j.marpol.2023.105711.

Alexander Proelss (ed.), *United Nations Convention on the Law of the Sea: A Commentary* 12–15 (Nomos, 2017).

Jouke Prop et al., *Climate Change and the Increasing Impact of Polar Bears on Bird Populations*, 3 Frontiers Ecol. & Evolution 33 (2015), https://doi.org/10.3389/fevo.2015.00033.

Rebecca Prentiss Pskowski, *The IMO and the Implementation of Mandatory Instruments*, in Law 2024 284, 284-303 (2024), https://doi.org/10.4337/9781802206883.00026.

Steven W. Purcell, Alessandro Lovatelli & Kaliola Pakoa, *Constraints and Solutions for Managing Pacific Island Sea Cucumber Fisheries with an Ecosystem Approach*, 45 Marine Pol'y 240, 240-250 (2013), https://doi.org/10.1016/j.marpol.2013.11.005.

Radio New Zealand, *Transhipping of Fish Costing Pacific Nations*, RNZ (Dec. 5, 2024), https://www.rnz.co.nz/international/pacific-news/528450/transhipping-of-fish-costing-pacific-nations.

Evan V. Regehr et al., *Survival and Breeding of Polar Bears in the Southern Beaufort Sea in Relation to Sea Ice*, 79 J. Animal Ecology 117, 117-127 (2009), https://doi.org/10.1111/j.1365-2656.2009.01603.x.

Chiara Ricci, *The Necessity for Alternative Legal Pathways: The Best Practice of Humanitarian Corridors Opened by Private Sponsors in Italy*, 21 German L.J. 265, 265-283 (2020), https://doi.org/10.1017/glj.2020.7.

Penelope J. Ridings, *Labour Standards on Fishing Vessels: A Problem in Search of a Home?*, 22 Melb. J. Int'l L. 308, 308-331 (2021), https://law.unimelb.edu.au/__data/assets/pdf_file/0017/4126004/Ridings-unpaginated.pdf.

Johan Rockström, Tim Beringer, David Hole, Bronson Griscom, Michael B. Mascia, Carl Folke & Felix Creutzig, *We Need Biosphere Stewardship That Protects Carbon Sinks and Builds Resilience*, 118 PROC. NAT'L ACAD. SCI. (2021), https://doi.org/10.1073/pnas.2115218118.

Karyn D. Rode et al., *Spring Fasting Behavior in a Marine Apex Predator Provides an Index of Ecosystem Productivity*, 24 Global Change Biology 410, 410-423 (2017), https://doi.org/10.1111/gcb.13933.

Charlotte Salpin et al., *Marine Scientific Research in Pacific Small Island Developing States*, 95 Marine Pol'y 363, 363–371 (2016), https://doi.org/10.1016/j.marpol.2016.07.019.

Şafak Şanlıer, *Analysis of Port State Control Inspection Data: The Black Sea Region*, 112 Marine Pol'y (2019), https://doi.org/10.1016/j.marpol.2019.103757.

Gianmoena Scandurra et al., *On the Vulnerability of Small Island Developing States: A Dynamic Analysis*, 84 Ecol. Indicators 382, 382-392 (2017), https://doi.org/10.1016/j.ecolind.2017.09.016.

Lisa M. Schile et al., *Limits on Carbon Sequestration in Arid Blue Carbon Ecosystems*, 27 Ecol. Applications 859, 859–874 (2017), https://doi.org/10.1002/eap.1489.

Daniel Schneider, *Climate Change and Maritime Claims in the Arctic Region* (LLM Thesis, Univ. of Iceland, 2024).

Daniel Schneider, *Fisheries Governance and Resource Management in Pacific Islands*, 37 *J. Int'l Envtl. L.* 134, 140–42 (2024).

Harald Schøyen & Svein Bråthen, *The Northern Sea Route Versus the Suez Canal: Cases from Bulk Shipping*, 19 J. Transport Geography 977, 977-983 (2011), https://doi.org/10.1016/j.jtrangeo.2011.03.003.

James A. Screen & Ian Simmonds, *Increasing Fall-Winter Energy Loss from the Arctic Ocean and Its Role in Arctic Temperature Amplification*, 37 Geophys. Res. Lett. (2010), https://doi.org/10.1029/2010gl044136.

Elizabeth R. Selig et al., *Revealing Global Risks of Labor Abuse and Illegal, Unreported, and Unregulated Fishing*, 13 Nat. Commc'ns 1 (2022), https://doi.org/10.1038/s41467-022-28916-2.

Oscar Serrano et al., *Chapter 28 - Conservation of Blue Carbon Ecosystems for Climate Change Mitigation and Adaptation*, in Coastal Wetlands 965-996 (Gerardo M. E. Perillo et al. eds., Elsevier 2018), https://doi.org/10.1016/b978-0-444-63893-9.00028-9.

Katherine Seto et al., *Toward Transparent Governance of Transboundary Fisheries: The Case of Pacific Tuna Transshipment*, 136 Marine Pol'y (2020), https://doi.org/10.1016/j.marpol.2020.104200.

Alex Shahbazi, *Sustaining Tomorrow's Central Arctic Ocean Today: Using Best Practices to Guide the Central Arctic Ocean Fisheries Agreement's Implementation*, WWF 10-21 (Nov. 2022), https://files.worldwildlife.org/wwfcmsprod/files/Publication/file/7zhj2wrz1i_CAOFA_Full_Report_pages_web_version.pdf.

Dmitry Sharapov, *Northern Sea Route and Climate Change*, 460 E3S Web Conf. (2023), https://doi.org/10.1051/e3sconf/202346009019.

Deepak Raj Sharma & Sigmund Simonsen, *Ensuring the Quality of ISM Audits: The Role and Adequacy of the Legal Framework of Auditing*, 12 Mar. Safety & Sec. L.J. 24 (2023), https://www.marsafelawjournal.org/contributions/ensuring-the-quality-of-ism-audits-the-role-and-adequacy-of-the-legal-framework-of-auditing/.

Zareen Shawoo & Thomas F. Thornton, *The UN Local Communities and Indigenous Peoples' Platform: A Traditional Ecological Knowledge-Based Evaluation*, 10 Wires Climate Change (2019), https://doi.org/10.1002/wcc.575.

Nagisa Shiiba et al., *How Blue Financing Can Sustain Ocean Conservation and Development: A Proposed Conceptual Framework for Blue Financing Mechanism*, 139 Marine Pol'y (2022), https://doi.org/10.1016/j.marpol.2021.104575.

James M. Shultz et al., *Disaster Risk Reduction and Sustainable Development for Small Island Developing States*, 3 Disaster Health 32, 32–44 (2016), https://doi.org/10.1080/21665044.2016.1173443.

Gregory K. Silber & Jeffrey D. Adams, *Vessel Operations in the Arctic, 2015–2017*, 6 Frontiers Marine Sci. 573 (2019), https://doi.org/10.3389/fmars.2019.00573.

Giovanni Soldi et al., *Space-Based Global Maritime Surveillance. Part I: Satellite Technologies*, 36(9) IEEE Aerospace & Electronic Sys. Mag. 8, 8-28 (2021), https://doi.org/10.1109/maes.2021.3070862.

Adam Soliman, *Fisheries Governance and How It Fits Within the Broader Arctic Governance*, 37 Seattle U. L. Rev.1209, 1210 (2014), https://digitalcommons.law.seattleu.edu/sulr/vol37/iss4/5/.

South China Sea Arbitration *(Philippines v. China)*, *supra* note 13, ¶¶. 210–212.

Baris Soyer, David Miller & Georgios Leloudas, *Tackling IUU Fishing: Developing a Holistic Legal Response*, 7 Transnat'l Envtl. L. 139, 139-163 (2017), https://doi.org/10.1017/s2047102517000267.

Martina H. Stiasny et al., *Ocean Acidification Effects on Atlantic Cod Larval Survival and Recruitment to the Fished Population*, 11(8) PLOS ONE (2016), https://doi.org/10.1371/journal.pone.0155448.

Olav Schram Stokke, *Climate Change and Institutional Resilience in Arctic Environmental Governance*, 12 Pol. & Governance (2024), https://doi.org/10.17645/pag.7369.

Jelena Subotic, *Expanding the Scope of Post-Conflict Justice: Individual, State and Societal Responsibility for Mass Atrocity*, 48 J. Peace Rsch. 157, 157–169 (2011), https://doi.org/10.1177/0022343310394696.

Ussif Rashid Sumaila et al., *Illicit Trade in Marine Fish Catch and Its Effects on Ecosystems and People Worldwide*, 6 Sci. Advances (2020), https://doi.org/10.1126/sciadv.aaz3801.

Ningning Sun, *Land-Use Governance and Indigenous Engagement in Arctic Alaska and Norway: Successes, Current Gaps, and Paths Forward* (2024) (Environmental Studies Senior Thesis, Dartmouth College), https://digitalcommons.dartmouth.edu/environmental_studies_senior_theses/3.

Ariane E. Sutton-Grier & Alexandra Moore, *Leveraging Carbon Services of Coastal Ecosystems for Habitat Protection and Restoration*, 44(3) Coastal Mgmt. 259, 259-277 (2016), https://doi.org/10.1080/08920753.2016.1160206.

Stavros Syropoulos & Ezra M. Markowitz, *Perceived Responsibility Towards Future Generations and Environmental Concern: Convergent Evidence Across Multiple Outcomes in a Large, Nationally Representative Sample*, 76 J. Envtl. Psychol. (2021), https://doi.org/10.1016/j.jenvp.2021.101651.

Nicolás E. Talloni-Álvarez et al., *Climate Change Impact on Canada's Pacific Marine Ecosystem: The Current State of Knowledge*, 104 Marine Pol'y 163, 163–176 (2019), https://doi.org/10.1016/j.marpol.2019.02.035.

Lydia C. L. Teh et al., *The Role of Human Rights in Implementing Socially Responsible Seafood*, 14 PLOS ONE (2019), https://doi.org/10.1371/journal.pone.0210241.

Lida Teneva et al., *Small Island Nations Can Achieve Food Security Benefits Through Climate-Adaptive Blue Food Governance by 2050*, 151 Marine Pol'y (2023), https://doi.org/10.1016/j.marpol.2023.105577.

Chad W. Thackeray & Alex Hall, *An Emergent Constraint on Future Arctic Sea-Ice Albedo Feedback*, 9 Nat. Climate Change 972, 972-978 (2019), https://doi.org/10.1038/s41558-019-0619-1.

Elena F. Tracy, *Despite Heavy Fuel Oil Ban, Arctic Marine Biodiversity Still Threatened*, WWF Global Arctic Programme (June 19, 2024), https://www.arcticwwf.org/newsroom/features/despite-heavy-fuel-oil-ban-arctic-marine-biodiversity-still-threatened/.

Sarah F. Trainor et al., *Arctic Climate Impacts: Environmental Injustice in Canada and the United States*, 12 Local Envt. 627, 627-643 (2007), https://doi.org/10.1080/13549830701657414.

S. Trautman, R. Chevallier & A. Gosling, *The African Union Great Green Wall Initiative Strategy (2024-2034): A New Continental Roadmap for Restoration,*

Sustainable Land Management and Climate Resilient Livelihoods, AICCRA Info Note (2024), https://hdl.handle.net/10568/149059.

Trends Research & Advisory, *The Arctic: A Risk of Escalating Conflicts*, Trends Research & Advisory (Dec. 6, 2024), https://trendsresearch.org/insight/the-arctic-a-risk-of-escalating-conflicts/.

Anitra L. Thorhaug et al., *Gulf of Mexico Estuarine Blue Carbon Stock, Extent and Flux: Mangroves, Marshes, and Seagrasses: A North American Hotspot*, 653 Sci. Total Env't 1253, 1253–1261 (2018), https://doi.org/10.1016/j.scitotenv.2018.10.011.

United Nations, *BBNJ Agreement*, U.N., https://www.un.org/bbnjagreement/en.

United Nations, *High Seas Treaty*, June 19, 2023, U.N. Doc. A/RES/77/249

United Nations Convention on the Law of the Sea (UNCLOS), Dec. 10, 1982, 1833 U.N.T.S. 3 (entered into force Nov. 16, 1994) https://www.un.org/depts/los/convention_agreements/texts/unclos/unclos_e.pdf.

U.N. Env't Programme (UNEP), *Regional Climate Change Impacts on Sub-Saharan Africa: Sahel Report* (2023), https://www.unep.org/.

U.N. Food & Agric. Org. (FAO), *Agreement on Port State Measures (PSMA)*, https://www.fao.org/iuu-fishing/international-framework/psma/en/.

U.N. Food & Agric. Org. (FAO), *General Fisheries Commission for the Mediterranean*, FAO (2024), https://www.fao.org/gfcm/en/.

U.N. Food & Agric. Org. (FAO), *State of World Fisheries and Aquaculture 2020*, at 32 (2020), https://www.fao.org/documents/card/en/c/cc0461en.

U.N. Food & Agric. Org. (FAO), *The State of World Fisheries and Aquaculture 2022: Towards Blue Transformation* 57 (2022), available at https://www.fao.org/publications/sofia/2022.

U.N. Food & Agric. Org. (FAO), *The State of World Fisheries and Aquaculture 2024* (2024), https://openknowledge.fao.org/server/api/core/bitstreams/66538eba-9c85-4504-8438-c1cf0a0a3903/content/cd0683en.html.

U.N. General Assembly, *Global Compact for Safe, Orderly and Regular Migration*, G.A. Res. 73/195, U.N. Doc. A/RES/73/195 (Dec. 19, 2018), https://documents.un.org/doc/undoc/gen/n18/451/99/pdf/n1845199.pdf.

U.N. General Assembly, *Transforming Our World: The 2030 Agenda for Sustainable Development*, U.N. Doc. A/RES/70/1, at 1 (Oct. 21, 2015), https://sdgs.un.org/2030agenda.

U.N. High Comm'r for Refugees (UNHCR), *Global Trends: Forced Displacement in 2023* (June 2024), at 28, https://www.unhcr.org/.

U.N. Security Council, Statement by the President of the Security Council, U.N. Doc. S/PRST/2023/6 (2023).

U.S. Fish & Wildlife Service, *Polar Bear Conservation Management Plan* (2020), at 22, https://www.fws.gov.

Kathryn Urban, *A New (Cold) Front in Polar Intelligence? Trends and Implications of Technology-Enabled Monitoring in the Arctic*, J. Sci. Pol'y & Governance (Jan. 11, 2021), https://doi.org/10.38126/JSPG190111.

Joana Abrisketa Uriarte, *The Reform of the Dublin III Regulation: How to Build or Not to Build Further Enforcing Mechanisms*, 23 Spanish Year Book of Int'l Law 263, 263-272 (2019), https://doi.org/10.17103/sybil.23.16.

Willem Van De Wiel et al., *Mental Health Consequences of Long-Term Stays in Refugee Camps: Preliminary Evidence from Moria*, 21 BMC Pub. Health (2021), https://doi.org/10.1186/s12889-021-11301-x.

Cristina Villalobos et al., *Ocean Acidification and Ocean Warming Effects on Pacific Herring (Clupea Pallasi) Early Life Stages*, 7 Frontiers in Marine Sci. (2020), https://doi.org/10.3389/fmars.2020.597899.

Warwick F. Vincent, *Arctic Climate Change: Local Impacts, Global Consequences, and Policy Implications*, in Arctic Ecology 507, 507-526 (Springer ed., 2019), https://doi.org/10.1007/978-3-030-20557-7_31.

Vladislava Vladimirova, *Regional Environmental Governance of Protected Natural Territories in the European North: Russia, Finland, and Norway, and the Case of Pasvik-Inari Trilateral Park*, 176 Climatic Change 7 (2023), https://doi.org/10.1007/s10584-023-03559-4.

Christina Voigt, *The Power of the Paris Agreement in International Climate Litigation*, 32 Rev. Eur. Comp. & Int'l Envtl. L. 237, 237–249 (2023), https://doi.org/10.1111/reel.12514.

Carl Walters & Jean-Jacques Maguire, *Lessons for Stock Assessment from the Northern Cod Collapse*, 6 Rev. Fish Biol. & Fisheries 125, 125-137 (1996), https://doi.org/10.1007/BF00182340.

Chunyan Wang, Qian Zhao & Yen-Chiang Chang, *On the Legal Status of Marine Fishery Resources: From the Perspectives of International Fishery Law*, 9 Heliyon (2023), https://doi.org/10.1016/j.heliyon.2023.e15354.

Jia Wang et al., *Taking Precautionary Approaches to the Governance of Commercial Deep Seabed Mining: Law-Making of International Seabed Authority and Multi-Subject Participation*, 15 Sustainability (2023), https://doi.org/10.3390/su15086414.

Robin Warner & Rosemary Rayfuse, *Securing a Sustainable Future for the Oceans Beyond National Jurisdiction: The Legal Basis for an Integrated Cross-Sectoral Regime for High Seas Governance for the 21st Century*, 23 Int'l J. Marine & Coastal L. 399, 399-421 (2008), https://doi.org/10.1163/092735208x331845.

R. Watson, A. Sousa-Santos & M. Howes, *Challenges in International Fisheries Compliance: Voluntary vs. Binding Agreements*, 18 Mar. Pol'y 347, 350–52 (2021).

Sarah M. Watson, *Greenhouse Gas Emissions from Offshore Oil and Gas Activities - Relevance of the Paris Agreement, Law of the Sea, and Regional Seas Programmes*, 185 Ocean & Coastal Mgmt (2019), https://doi.org/10.1016/j.ocecoaman.2019.104942.

Heidi Welch et al., *Hot Spots of Unseen Fishing Vessels*, 8 Sci. Advances (2022), https://doi.org/10.1126/sciadv.abq2109.

Martin Wegmann et al., *Eurasian Autumn Snow Link to Winter North Atlantic Oscillation Is Strongest for Arctic Warming Periods*, 11 Earth Syst. Dynam. 509, 509-524 (2020), https://doi.org/10.5194/esd-11-509-2020.

Western & Central Pacific Fisheries Commission, *Home Page*, WCPFC (2024), https://www.wcpfc.int/home.

Rob White, *Transnational Environmental Crime: Toward an Eco-global Criminology* 265–270 (Willan Publishing, 2011).

Chris Whomersley, *How to Amend UNCLOS and Why It Has Never Been Done*, 9(1) Korean J. Int'l & Comp. L. 72, 72-83 (2021), https://doi.org/10.1163/22134484-12340146.

Robin Whytock et al., *Real-Time Alerts from AI-Enabled Camera Traps Using the Iridium Satellite Network: A Case Study in Gabon, Central Africa*, 14(3) Methods in Ecology & Evolution 867, 867-874 (2023), https://doi.org/10.1111/2041-210x.14036.

Anja Wiesbrock, *The Integration of Immigrants in Sweden: A Model for the European Union?*, 49 Int'l Migration 48, 48-66 (2011), https://doi.org/10.1111/j.1468-2435.2010.00662.x.

Emma Witbooi et al., *Organized Crime in the Fisheries Sector Threatens a Sustainable Ocean Economy*, Nature 3 (2020), https://doi.org/10.1038/s41586-020-2913-5.

Catherine Wood-Donnelly, *Evaluating Normative Capacity Through Arctic Environmental Governance*, 176 Climatic Change 9 (2023), https://doi.org/10.1007/s10584-023-03603-3.

Chih Yuan Woon, *Framing the "Polar Silk Road" (冰上丝绸之路): Critical Geopolitics, Chinese Scholars and the (Re)Positionings of China's Arctic Interests*, 78 Pol. Geography (2020), https://doi.org/10.1016/j.polgeo.2019.102141.

World Bank, *Home Page*, https://www.worldbank.org/ext/en/home.

World Wide Fund for Nature (WWF), *Slavery at Sea: Forced Labour, Human Rights Abuses, and the Need for the Western and Central Pacific Fisheries Commission to Establish Labour Standards for Crew*, Comm'n 18th Reg. Sess., WCPFC18-2021-OP091 (Nov. 18, 2021), https://meetings.wcpfc.int/file/10140/download.

Di Yang & Robert Pomeroy, *The Impact of Community-Based Fisheries Management (CBFM) on Equity and Sustainability of Small-Scale Coastal Fisheries in the Philippines*, 86 Marine Pol'y 173, 173-181 (2017), https://doi.org/10.1016/j.marpol.2017.09.027.

Shenglong Yang et al., *The Environmental Niche of the Tuna Purse Seine Fleet in the Western and Central Pacific Ocean Based on Different Fisheries Data*, 8 Fishes 78 (2023), https://doi.org/10.3390/fishes8020078.

Zuowei Yang et al., *Analysis of Spatiotemporal Changes and Driving Factors of Desertification in the Africa Sahel*, 213 Catena (2022), https://doi.org/10.1016/j.catena.2022.106213.

Joanna Yao, *An International Hierarchy of Science: Conquest, Cooperation, and the 1959 Antarctic Treaty System*, 27 Eur. J. Int'l Rel. 995, 995–1019 (2021), https://doi.org/10.1177/13540661211033889.

Arthur D. Yeeting et al., *Implications of New Economic Policy Instruments for Tuna Management in the Western and Central Pacific*, 63 Marine Pol'y 45, 45-52 (2015), https://doi.org/10.1016/j.marpol.2015.10.003.

Astra Zalik, *Mining the Seabed, Enclosing the Area: Ocean Grabbing, Proprietary Knowledge and the Geopolitics of the Extractive Frontier Beyond National Jurisdiction*, 68 Int'l Soc. Sci. J. 343, 343-359 (2018), https://doi.org/10.1111/issj.12159.

Neda A. Zawahri & Sara McLaughlin Mitchell, *Fragmented Governance of International Rivers: Negotiating Bilateral versus Multilateral Treaties*, 55 Int'l

Stud. Q. 835, 835-858 (2011), https://doi.org/10.1111/j.1468-2478.2011.00673.x.

Chapter 4

Fisheries Crimes, Blue Justice & Small-Scale Fisheries: Experiences from Africa and the Caribbean

Alana Malinde S. N. Lancaster

The University of the West Indies (Cave Hill Campus)

Bolanle T. Erinosho

University of Derby

Hashali Hamukuaya

University of South Africa

Tajudeen Sanni

Villa College, Maldives [1]

Abstract: Blue crimes – transnational organized crime at sea – are a clear and present threat to countries dependent on the sea and its resources. Fisheries crimes, as a subset of blue crimes, pose a significant threat to maritime nations and communities reliant on ocean resources. This threat is particularly acute as the fisheries sector contributes to trade, employment, culture, and food and nutritional security. These crimes are governed by complex governance and regulatory frameworks and range from illegal, unregulated and unreported (IUU) fishing to a variety of other criminal offences such as human trafficking, drug trafficking, and money laundering. Fisheries crimes therefore impact the sustainability of the fisheries sector and are a maritime issue of growing

---

[1] All of the authors of this Chapter were members of the UKRI GCRF funded One Ocean Hub. This Chapter draws in part from research undertaken by these authors under the One Ocean Hub, which is a collaborative research program for sustainable development funded by United Kingdom Research and Innovation (UKRI) through the Global Challenges Research Fund (GCRF) (Grant Ref: NE/S008950/1).

international and regional concern, since they intersect with transnational organized crimes at sea, because of the transboundary nature of fisheries. In 2018, Global North and Global South States endorsed the Copenhagen Declaration on Transnational Organised Crime in the Global Fishing Industry, aimed at addressing criminal activities in the fisheries sector by strengthening maritime security and advancing the sustainable ocean governance agendas of Global North and Global South States. Drawing on research in the small-scale fisheries sector in Ghana, South Africa, and the CARICOM & OECS Caribbean, this chapter highlights the complexity of addressing fisheries crime in the small-scale fisheries sector. It assesses the impact of these crimes on small-scale fishing communities through a human rights and blue justice lens, and concludes with suggested approaches to combat fisheries crimes in ways that safeguard ocean sustainability and protect small-scale fisheries communities.

Keywords: Blue crimes, fisheries crimes, blue justice, human rights, small-scale fisheries, Africa, Caribbean, CARICOM, OECS, Copenhagen Declaration on Transnational Organized Crime in the Global Fishing Industry; SDG 14; SDG 16.

Introduction

Blue crimes – the collective term for transnational organized crime at sea – have become a pervasive threat for both populations and States dependent on the sea and its resources. While there is no clear consensus on the definition of blue crimes, they may be broadly categorized into three main groups.[2] The first group being crimes against mobility, which involves targeting shipping, supply chains, and maritime trade. The second category is criminal flows which involves the use of the sea as a conduit for smuggling and trafficking. The third category relates to environmental crimes which often have elements of inflicting harm on the sea and its resources, including fish stocks.[3] Blue crimes and their effect on maritime activities are gaining significance globally because of the importance of the oceans to the economies of a majority of States,[4]

---

[2] SafeSeas, P*anel - Towards a 'Blue' Criminology: How Should We Study Transnational Organised Crime at Sea?* SAFESEAS (December 2, 2021), https://www.safeseas.net/panel-towards-a-blue-criminology-how-should-we-study-transnational-organised-crime-at-sea/.

[3] Christian Bueger and Timothy Edmunds, *Blue Crime: Conceptualising Transnational Organised Crime at Sea,* MARINE POLICY 119 (2020), https://doi.org/10.1016/j.marpol.2020.104067.

[4] United Nations Office on Drugs and Crime (UNODC), *Transnational Organized Crime in the Fishing Industry* (2011), https://www.unodc.org/documents/human-trafficking/Issue_Paper_-_TOC_in_the_Fishing_Industry.pdf.

including under the blue economy development paradigm. Within this context, fisheries crime, a specific blue "environmental" crime, has increasingly risen to prominence,[5] as an umbrella term for a heterogenous group of crimes that occur across the entire fisheries sector.[6] This comes as a result of illegal, unreported, and unregulated (IUU) fishing, which accounts for annual losses of an estimated USD 23.5 billion,[7] and resultant impacts on the economies of States, food and nutrition security These crimes are governed by complex governance and regulatory frameworks and range from IUU fishing to a variety of other criminal offences such as human trafficking, drug trafficking, and money laundering. Fisheries crimes therefore impact the sustainability of the fisheries sector and are a maritime issue of growing international and regional concern, since they intersect with transnational organized crimes at sea due to the transboundary nature of fisheries. These impacts are critical, as fish, seafood, and their products form an important part of the global diet and contribute to the livelihoods and cultures of a significant percentage of coastal populations.

Overwhelmingly, as will be discussed in the Chapter, the global regulatory framework has attempted to address these issues through the criminalization of certain predatory fisheries practices, and the intersection of fisheries with a variety of other criminal offenses such as human trafficking, drug trafficking, gun trafficking and money laundering. Efforts to address the connections between blue crimes and illegal fishing have risen to prominence, notably

---

[5] Emma Witbooi et al., "Organised Crime in the Fisheries Sector Threatens a Sustainable Ocean Economy," *Nature* 588 (2020): 48–56, https://www.nature.com/articles/s41586-020-2913-5; see also André Standing, *Corruption and State-Corporate Crime in Fisheries*, U4 Issue 2015:15 (Bergen: Chr. Michelsen Institute, 2015), https://www.cmi.no/publications/5589-corruption-and-state-corporate-crime-in-fisheries.

[6] United Nations Office on Drugs and Crime (UNODC), *Transnational Organized Crime in the Fishing* Industry: *Focus on: Trafficking in Persons Smuggling of Migrants Illicit Drugs Trafficking* (2011), https://www.unodc.org/documents/human-trafficking/Issue_Paper_-_TOC_in_the_Fishing_Industry.pdf.; United Nations Office on Drugs and Crime (UNODC), *Fisheries Crime: Bringing to Light the Perfect Storm of Illegal Activities in the Fishing* Sector https://www.unodc.org/documents/about-unodc/Campaigns/Fisheries/focus_sheet_PRINT.pdf . (accessed September 29, 2024); See also . See also André Standing, *Criminality in Africa's Fishing Industry: A Threat to Human Security, ISS Africa Report,* (June 6, 2017), https://africacenter.org/publication/criminality-africa-fishing-industry-threat-human-security/.

[7] David J. Agnew et al., *Estimating the Worldwide Extent of Illegal Fishing,* PLOS ONE 4 (2) (2009): e4570, doi:10.1371/journal.pone.0004570. See also Gunnar Stølsvik, *The Development of the Fisheries Crime Concept and Processes to Address It in the International Arena,* Marine Policy 99 (2019), 243-249, doi:10.1016/j.marpol.2018.12.027.

through a 2008 Report of the Secretary-General,[8] a United Nations General Assembly Resolution which requested that States embark on measures to contribute to increasing the understanding of the close nexus between illegal fishing and transnational organized crime at sea.[9] This was reinforced by the Sustainable Development Goals (SDGs), specifically SDG 14 (life below water) and SDG 16 (peace, justice and strong institutions).[10] However, like blue crimes, fisheries crimes straddle multiple regimes, and at the international level, efforts to address it first developed through a criminal lens, largely within the context of the United Nations Convention against Transnational Organized Crime (UNTOC). This focus has obfuscated, and often adopted a criminalized approach to fisheries crimes which directly impact the sustainable management of marine living resources and can be better addressed depending on the degree of connection of crime with fisheries activity.[11] However, given the longstanding associations of marine small-scale fisheries (SSF) communities with the ocean, and the strong connection between the culture and traditional knowledge of small-scale fisherfolk communities and the ocean. A predominantly criminal law approach often leads to the marginalization of small-scale fishers, their exclusion from marine governance, and the disruption of indigenous and traditional knowledge of the ocean. Historically, the inconsistencies in many regulatory approaches and the safeguarding of the rights of coastal peoples, led to a long history of coastal peoples' fight for justice,[12] and since 2018,[13] this quest has birthed the blue justice movement, which has developed and rapidly grown alongside these efforts.[14] Within this new lens of fisheries governance, current

---

[8] United Nations General Assembly, *Oceans and the Law of the Sea*, G.A. Res. 63/111, U.N. Doc. A/RES/63/111 (Dec. 5, 2008), ¶¶ 98-105, https://sdgs.un.org/documents/ares63111-oceans-and-law-sea-19229.

[9] United Nations General Assembly, *Sustainable Fisheries, Including Through the 1995 Agreement for the Implementation of the Provisions of the United Nations Convention on the Law of the Sea of 10 December 1982 Relating to the Conservation and Management of Straddling Fish Stocks and Highly Migratory Fish Stocks, and Related Instruments*, A/RES/63/112 (Dec. 5, 2008), ¶ 59, https://sdgs.un.org/documents/ares63112-sustainable-fisheries-incl-throug-19230.

[10] United Nations, *Transforming Our World: The 2030 Agenda for Sustainable Development*, A/RES/70/1 (October 21, 2015), https://sdgs.un.org/2030agenda.

[11] Martin Isaacs, *The Role of Fisheries Crime in the Blue Economy*, MARINE POLICY 104 (2019), 123-130, doi:10.1016/j.marpol.2019.02.005.

[12] Nathan J. Bennett et al., *Environmental (in) justice in the Anthropocene ocean*, MARINE POLICY 147 (2023), 105383,

[13] Svein Jentoft et al. (eds), *Blue Justice: Small-Scale Fisheries In A Sustainable Ocean Economy*, SPRINGER NATURE (2022).

[14] Jessica L. Blythe, et al., *Blue justice: A review of emerging scholarship and resistance movements*, CAMBRIDGE PRISMS: COASTAL FUTURES 1 (2023): e15.

international, regional, and national efforts to address fisheries crimes must be examined to understand their impact on these vulnerable groups, especially since the impact of blue crimes on the fisheries sector has had far-reaching effects on the livelihoods, identity, and culture of small-scale fishers.[15] Accordingly, the conceptualization, design and enforcement of blue crimes must be fair, inclusive, equitable and recognize the culture, traditions and identities of SSF communities.[16]

In this Chapter, we utilize the approach posited by Urbina, of classifying fisheries crime into three categories: illegal fishing, illicit fisheries-related crimes, and crimes committed in the context of the fisheries sector.[17] This approach is reflected in regional and international instruments, such as the Ålesund Resolution,[18] and the Copenhagen Declaration,[19] which address the connections between fisheries crime and transnational organized crime.[20] The latter instrument to date is the only internationally endorsed instrument addressing transnational organized fisheries crime from a blue justice lens. Despite being a non-binding instrument, the Declaration has seen wide-ranging endorsement by at least sixty States across the Global North and Global South. Underpinned by a blue justice theory of practice, an approach situated

---

[15] European Institute for International Law and International Relations, *The Blue Economy and its Related Crimes* (June 8, 2023), https://www.eiir.eu/strategic-affairs/international-economy/the-blue-economy-and-its-related-crimes/. See also United Nations General Assembly, *Oceans and the Law of the Sea*, A/RES/72/72 (Dec. 5, 2017), ¶ 98, https://documents.un.org/doc/undoc/gen/n17/421/83/pdf/n1742183.pdf

[16] Holly J Niner et al., *Reflections on the Past, Present, and Potential Futures of Knowledge Hierarchies in Ocean Biodiversity Governance*, FRONTIERS IN MARINE SCIENCE 11 (2024), https://doi.org/10.3389/fmars.2024.1347494.

[17] Julio Jorge Urbina, *Towards an International Legal Definition of the Notion of Fisheries Crime*, MARINE POLICY 119 (2020): 104067, https://doi.org/10.1016/j.marpol.2022.105214.

[18] Nordic Council of Ministers, *Nordic Minister Statement on Transnational Organized Fisheries Crime*, (June 28, 2017), https://www.norden.org/en/declaration/nordic-minister-statement-transnational-organized-fisheries-crime.

[19] Blue Justice, The International Declaration on Transnational Organised Crime in the Global Fishing Industry (the Copenhagen Declaration), (October 15, 2018) https://bluejustice.org/copenhagen-declaration/; High Level Panel on a Sustainable Ocean Economy, The International Declaration on Transnational Organized Crime in the Global Fishing Industry and the Blue Justice Initiative, https://action.oceanpanel.org/initiative/norway/the-international-declaration-on-transnational-organized-crime-in-the-global-fishing-industry-and-the-blue-justice-initiative/ (accessed September 29, 2024).

[20] See Emma Witbooi et al., *Organised Crime in the Fisheries Sector*, in Jane Lubchenci and Peter M, Haugan (eds.) *The Blue Compendium, From Knowledge to Action for a Sustainable Ocean Economy*, Springer (2023, 2024), 593, https://doi.org/10.1007/978-3-031-16277-0.

in social justice for small-scale fisheries that contests the exclusion and marginalization of small-scale fishers,[21] the Declaration acknowledges that fisheries crimes have wide-ranging consequences, including impacting the sustainability of the oceans, the human rights, and the livelihoods of those dependent on the oceans. The Declaration is endorsed by Ghana, South Africa, Namibia and twelve States[22] of the CARICOM[23] and OECS[24] Caribbean (C&OC) which we discuss in this Chapter in a comparative analysis of experiences across African and Caribbean States. Against this background, the Chapter explores the manifestation of fisheries crimes across these different regions, and utilizes the fundamental tenet of blue justice as a call for collaborative research between academics, civil society, non-governmental organizations and practitioners,[25] to assess the impact of fisheries crimes on SSF communities. We conclude that approaches which originate within a human rights and blue justice framing is an approach to combatting fisheries crimes which can safeguard the sustainability of the oceans and protect small-scale fisheries communities.

---

[21] See Moenieba Isaacs, *Is The Blue Justice Concept a Human Rights Agenda?*, AFRICAN PORTAL: POLICY BRIEF, 54 (2019), 1–5; Svein Jentoft and Ratana Chuenpagdee, *Interactive Learning and Governance Transformation for Securing Blue Justice for Small-Scale Fisheries*, ADMINISTRATION & SOCIETY 54 (7) (2022), 1255-1282;. Jentoft et al., *supra* note 12.

[22] The Bahamas, Belize, Grenada, Guyana, Jamaica, Montserrat, Saint Kitts and Nevis, Saint Lucia, Saint Vincent and the Grenadines, Suriname, The Turks and Caicos Islands, and Trinidad and Tobago.

[23] The Caribbean Community (CARICOM) is a political and economic union located in the Americas, which comprises fifteen full Members and five associate Members. Full Members of CARICOM are Antigua & Barbuda, The Bahamas, Barbados, Belize, The Commonwealth of Dominica, Grenada, Guyana, Haiti, Jamaica, Montserrat, Saint Lucia, St. Christopher (St. Kitts) & Nevis, St. Vincent & the Grenadines, Suriname, and Trinidad & Tobago. The union also comprises five associate Members: Anguilla, Bermuda, The [British] Virgin Islands, Cayman Islands, and the Turks & Caicos Islands.

[24] The Organisation of Eastern Caribbean States (OECS) is an inter-governmental organization dedicated to economic harmonization and integration, protection of human and legal rights, and the encouragement of good governance between countries and territories in the Eastern Caribbean. All full Members of OECS are also full Members of CARICOM. The full Members of the OECS are Antigua & Barbuda, The Commonwealth of Dominica, Grenada, Montserrat, St. Christopher (St. Kitts) & Nevis, St. Lucia and St. Vincent & the Grenadines The union also comprises five associate Members: Anguilla, The [British] Virgin Islands, Martinique, and Guadeloupe.

[25] Isaacs, *supra* note 21.

I. Fisheries Crimes Across the Oceans

As emphasized in the introduction, the global importance of marine fisheries has led to fisheries crimes becoming the most focused upon aspect of blue crimes. In Africa and the Caribbean, fisheries constitute a historically important sector, and even with the shift to the blue economy, fisheries often remain the largest sector for small-scale operators.[26] Further, the wide-ranging impacts of fisheries crime on the environment, food, economic and social security of many States has resulted in widespread attention at the international, regional and national levels.[27] From a regional perspective, the impact of fisheries crimes is particularly severe in developing countries where fisheries play a critical role in contributing to the economy, food security, livelihood and culture.

Across Africa and the Caribbean, fisheries crimes are generally established in fisheries-specific legislation and can range from crimes related to prohibited fishing gear, licensing requirements, prohibited fishing zones including marine protected areas, exceeding catch limits, and fishing during closed seasons,[28] and moratoria. For example, in Ghana, section 52 of the Fisheries Act (Act 625) provides that a person shall not use a canoe for fishing in fishery waters unless a license has been issued for the canoe. It prescribes a fine and forfeiture upon conviction for the offense.[29] Section 84 of the Fisheries Act of Ghana further grants the Fisheries Commission the power to declare closed season, also prescribes the offense of fishing during the closed season that attracts steep fines and forfeiture of the offenders fishing vessels if convicted. Despite these measures, SSF communities in Ghana have noted that the declaration of the closed season has resulted in increased vulnerabilities, including declining incomes during the closed season, inadequacy of relief materials and

---

[26] World Bank, Oceans, Fisheries and Coastal Economies, WORLD BANK GROUP (April 3, 2024), https://www.worldbank.org/en/topic/oceans-fisheries-and-coastal-economies (accessed September 29, 2024).

[27] Eve de Coning and Emma Witbooi, *Towards a new' fisheries crime' paradigm: South Africa as an Illustrative Example*, MARINE POLICY 60 (2015), 208-215, https://doi.org/10.1016/j.marpol.2015.06.024. See also Standing, *supra* note 6; and Dana D. Miller, and U. Rashid Sumaila, *Flag Use Behavior and IUU Activity within the International Fishing Fleet: Refining Definitions and Identifying Areas of Concern*, MARINE POLICY 44 (2014), 204-211, https://doi.org/10.1016/j.marpol.2013.08.027.

[28] See Gohar A. Petrossian, *Preventing Illegal, Unreported and Unregulated (IUU) Fishing: A Situational Crime Prevention Approach*, BIOLOGICAL CONSERVATION 189 (2015), 39-48, https://doi.org/10.1016/j.biocon.2014.09.005; Standing, *supra* note 26

[29] Republic of Ghana, *Fisheries Act 2002*, https://faolex.fao.org/docs/pdf/gha34737.pdf (accessed September 29, 2024).

compensation schemes during the ban, leading to increased poverty and crime in fisheries-dependent communities.[30]

Similarly, South Africa's Marine Living Resources Act notes, among a range of offenses, that 'no person shall use, permit to be used, or attempt to use any explosive, firearm, poison, or other noxious substance for the purpose of killing, stunning, disabling, or catching fish, or in any way rendering fish to be caught more easily.' It prescribes a punishment upon conviction of a fine not exceeding two million rand or imprisonment for a period not exceeding five years.[31] The enforcement of the Marine Living Resources Act has been criticized for criminalizing many small-scale fishers and curtailing their traditional livelihoods in an increasingly militarized manner.[32]Similar provisions can be found in Namibia's Marine Resources Act of 2000, which prescribes a range of fishing offenses with fines upon conviction of up to two million Namibia dollars. Notably, this Act also includes offences such as impersonating fisheries officers or offering inducements and gifts to officers to subvert fisheries regulations, for which it prescribes fines upon conviction of up to one million Namibian dollars.[33]

Oceans apart in the Caribbean, fisheries crimes have attracted both regional enforcement and conservation measures, as well as national efforts, largely because of the region's geographical location.[34] For example, fishery reserves and closed areas are widely used for enforcement and conservation purposes. In Barbados, the Fisheries (Management) Regulations, 1998 provide that a

---

[30] See Victor Owusu et al., *Factors Influencing Compliance of Closed Fishing Season: Lessons from Small-Scale Coastal Fisheries in the Central Region of Ghana*, HUMANITIES AND SOCIAL SCIENCES COMMUNICATIONS 10 (2023), 20, https://doi.org/10.1057/s41599-023-01513-4; Samuel Nyavor et al., *Compensation Payment for Fisherfolk During Closed-Season Fishing: Lessons from Small-Scale Fisherfolk in Ghana*, COGENT SOCIAL SCIENCES, 9 (2) (2023), https://doi.org/10.1080/23311886.2023.2282502; GNA, *Closed Season: The Woes of Women and Children in Fishing Communities*, MYJOYONLINE (July 30, 2023), https://www.myjoyonline.com/closed-season-the-woes-of-women-and-children-in-fishing-communities/#google_vignette (accessed September 29, 2024).

[31] Republic of South Africa, *Marine Living Resources Act 1998*, ss. 44 (1) (a); 58(1) (b), https://www.fao.org/faolex/results/details/en/c/LEX-FAOC015984/ (accessed September 29, 2024).

[32] Marieke Norton, *The Militarisation of Marine Resource Conservation and Law Enforcement in the Western Cape, South Africa*, MARINE POLICY, 60 (2015), 338-344, https://doi.org/10.1016/j.marpol.2014.09.007.

[33] Republic of Namibia, *Marine Resources Act, 2000*, https://www.fao.org/faolex/results/details/en/c/LEX-FAOC044344/ (accessed September 29, 2024).

[34] Patrick, McConney, Hazel A. Oxenford, and Milton Haughton, Management in the Gulf and Caribbean: Mosaic or Melting Pot?, GULF AND CARIBBEAN RESEARCH, 19 (2) (2007), 103-112, https://aquila.usm.edu/cgi/viewcontent.cgi?article=1422&context=gcr.

'closed area' means 'any area declared by the Minister, by notice published in the Official Gazette, as an area within which the fishing of designated species of fish or by designated fishing methods is prohibited.'[35] Additionally, laws aimed at the conservation of marine areas, as well as species can often criminalize fisheries that have historical and cultural significance. For instance, in 2007, St. Vincent and the Grenadines, a multi-island State in the Eastern Caribbean, designated the Tobago Cays as a no-take marine reserve by law,[36] engulfing the entire fishing grounds of the islet of Mayreau.[37] In Barbados, the designation of the Folkestone Marine Reserve[38] established the island's first (and currently only legally designated) marine park, with a recreational zone, a scientific zone, two water-sports zones for tourism, and a recreational zone, but excluded traditional small-scale fishers from the reserve.[39] Likewise, the moratorium on the West Indian sea egg (*Tripneustes ventricosus*),[40] a species of

---

35 Barbados, *Fisheries (Management) Regulations 1998*, s. 2, https://www.fao.org/faolex/results/details/en/c/LEX-FAOC018057 (accessed September 29, 2024).

36 Government of St. Vincent and the Grenadines, *Fisheries Regulations 1987*, https://natlex.ilo.org/dyn/natlex2/r/natlex/fe/details?p3_isn=3608 (accessed September 29, 2024); Alba Garcia Rodriguez and Lucia M. Fanning, *Assessing Marine Protected Areas Effectiveness: A Case Study with the Tobago Cays Marine Park*, OPEN JOURNAL OF MARINE SCIENCE 7 (3) (2017), 379-408; Daniel Hoggarth, *Tobago Cays Marine Park 2007-2009 Management Plan*, ORGANISATION OF EASTERN CARIBBEAN STATES, AND ENVIRONMENT AND SUSTAINABLE DEVELOPMENT UNIT (2007).

37 See UNEP, *Factsheet: The Protocol on Specially Protected Areas and Wildlife in the Wider Caribbean (SPAW): Tobago Cays Marine Park*, UNEP/CEP/CAR SPAW RAC/CaMPAM, https://www.car-spaw-rac.org/IMG/pdf/factsheet_stvincent_grenadine_tobago_cays.pdf (accessed September 29, 2024); Bertha Simmons and Patrick McConney, *Tobago Cays Marine Park: Are The Conditions for Successful Co-Management Likely to be Met?*, CERMES Technical Report No. 6, Centre for Resources Management and Environmental Studies (CERMES) (2006), 10, https://www.cavehill.uwi.edu/cermes/docs/technical_reports/simmons_2006_tcmp_co_management_conditions_ctr_06.aspx.

38 Robin Mahon and Michael B. Mascia, The Barbados (Alias Folkestone) Marine Reserve, Barbados: A Late Bloomer?, *Gulf and Caribbean Research* 14.2 (2003): 171-180; Janice Cumberbatch, *Case Study of the Folkestone Marine Park and Reserve, Barbados*, CANARI Technical Report No. 281, Caribbean Natural Resources Institute (CANARI) (2001), https://tools.thecpag.org/sites/default/files/2021-02/Case%20Study%20of%20the%20Folkestone%20Marine%20Park%20and%20Reserve%20Barbados.pdf.

39 Jonathan Pugh, *Speaking Without Voice: Participatory Planning, Acknowledgment, and Latent Subjectivity in Barbados*, ANNALS OF THE ASSOCIATION OF AMERICAN GEOGRAPHERS, 103 (5) (2013), 1226 – 1281.

40 Barbados, *Fisheries (Sea Egg Closed Season) Notice, 2015*, https://www.barbadoslawcourts.gov.bb/assets/content/pdfs/annuals/statutoryinstrumentsannual/sIs2015/SI2015No72.pdf, (accessed November 29, 2024); Shelly-Ann Cox, Sea Egg Season Remains Closed, Barbados Fisheries Division (September 3, 2023), https://www.fisheries.gov.bb/sea-egg-season-remains-closed/

cultural and historical significance in Barbados, has had a negligible effect on conservation of the fishery and the curbing of the illegal sale of the species. Instead, the lack of consultation with fishing communities has negatively impacted fishers, and failed to prevent the crash of the fishery.[41] This is comparable on the effects of conservation and regulatory measures on small-scale fisheries (SSF), such as the use of closed fishing seasons in Ghana.[42]

One enduring feature of these laws across Africa and the Caribbean, is their origin in Westernised, colonial concepts, which often exclude the customary laws and values of the Indigenous and traditional fishers in these regions.[43] Legislative and enforcement measures often adversely impact SSF communities as stringent regulations, since while ostensibly aimed at conservation and sustainable management, often fail to consider the socio-economic realities of SSF communities. Closed seasons and licensing requirements, although necessary for resource management, can lead to significant income loss for fishers' who rely on daily catches for their livelihoods. The oversight of providing adequate compensation and relief during these periods exacerbates poverty and can drive fishers towards illegal activities out of necessity.[44] Moreover, the exclusion of customary laws and traditional practices from modern fisheries management frameworks alienates SSF communities, undermining their cultural heritage and traditional knowledge systems.[45] Consequently, these colonial, paternalistic approaches often exacerbate the conditions for fisheries crime, and, as will be discussed in the next section, underpin the need for a blue justice approach in Africa and the Caribbean.

II. Crimes Related to Illegal Fishing in the African and Caribbean Context

In addition to illegal fisheries crimes, African and Caribbean countries also experience illicit fisheries-related crimes, or as the United Nations Office on

---

[41] Patrick McConney, Robin Mahon and Christopher Parker, Barbados Case Study: The Sea Egg Fishery, CCA/CERMES/MRAG (2003), https://citeseerx.ist.psu.edu/document?repid=rep1&type=pdf&doi=de4673fa0523742322cf3ce72ca3a8ce262a9358; Robin Mahon and Christopher Parker, *Barbados Sea Eggs, Past, Present, Future*, Fisheries Management Plan, Public Information Document No. 1, Fisheries Division, Ministry of Agriculture and Rural Development, Barbados (1999), https://www.fisheries.gov.bb/content/files/2023/09/Mahon_1999_sea_eggs_past_present_future.pdf; Khemraj Parsram, *Barbados Case Study: The Sea Egg Fishery, A Summary of Lessons Learnt*, CCA/CERMES (2004), https://assets.publishing.service.gov.uk/media/57a08cbded915d3cfd00159c/R8317Barb2.pdf.

[42] Owusu, *supra* note 30.

[43] Standing, *supra* note 6.

[44] *Id.*

[45] *Id.*

Drugs and Crime (UNODC) terms it, crimes in the fisheries sector, which occur in the marine space. These are crimes, which can help facilitate the commission of illegal fishing, and can include the forgery of documents, fraud, labor exploitation, corruption, and tax evasion. Illegal fishing potentially lends itself to these crimes particularly in poorly regulated spaces, and has been increasing in both Africa and the Caribbean. For example, in Ghana, there have been multiple cases of threats, abuses, and murder of official fisheries observers, the bribery of fisheries enforcement officers, and complex schemes to evade regulations of fisheries vessels.[46] In Namibia, the Fishrot scandal involved corruption by high-ranking officials and businessmen who allegedly manipulated fishing quotas for personal gain. The scandal has had significant economic and social impacts, including job losses and reduced government revenue that should have been used for social programs.[47]

Also related to these crimes are other offences committed at sea, including transnational organized crimes linked to the fisheries sector. These are crimes, which have little or no relation with fishing activities, or are not necessarily linked to fishing, but criminal organizations make use of the transnational nature of fisheries operations as a cover for committing crimes. Examples include the smuggling of narcotics,[48] human trafficking, and terrorism,[49] and can manifest in fishing communities with few alternative livelihood options. Accordingly, low-level poaching for economic and social survival, may morph into, or co-exist alongside, organized criminal activity. In South Africa example, this is evident in the context of abalone and west coast rock lobster, where the boundaries between 'protest poaching', opportunistic poaching and the facilitation of, or involvement in, organized criminal activity, are porous, and often overlap.'[50]

---

[46] Interpol, *International Law Enforcement Cooperation in the Fisheries Sector: A Guide for Law Enforcement Practitioners*, Interpol General Secretariat (2018), https://www.interpol.int/Crimes/Environmental-crime/Fisheries-crime.

[47] See IPPR, FIAM International & ICJ, *Human Rights Violations, Transnational Corporations and a Scandal in the Fishing Industry, CIVIC264* (March 31, 2022), https://www.civic264.org.na/images/pdf/2022/3/Fishrot-humanrightsimpact_1.pdf; BBC News, *Fishrot: The Corruption Scandal Entwining Namibia and Iceland*, BBC NEWS (February 6, 2023), https://www.bbc.com/news/world-africa-64526018.

[48] UNODC, *supra* note 6

[49] Channing Mavrellis, *The Serious Impacts of Fisheries Crime*, GLOBAL FINANCIAL INTEGRITY (October 22, 2018), https://gfintegrity.org/the-serious-impacts-of-fisheries-crime/.

[50] See Hennie van As, *Poaching of Marine Living Resources: Can the Tide Be Turned?*, SOUTH AFRICAN JOURNAL OF SCIENCE, 120 (1-2) (2024), 1-5, https://doi.org/10.17159/2413-3108/2020/i69a8351; Moenieba Isaacs, *Fisheries crime, Human Rights and Small-Scale Fisheries in South Africa: A Case of Bigger Fish to Fry*, MARINE POLICY 105 (2019): 158-168,

In Nigeria, Okafor-Yarwood has demonstrated the cyclical relationship between IUU fishing, human, and national security, noting that declining livelihoods of fishing communities has led to the increase in drug trafficking, piracy, or armed robbery at sea. Proceeds obtained from fisheries-related drug and human trafficking may also be used to fund rebellion in unstable countries thus compromising national security.[51] In addition, criminal networks often use fishing vessels to smuggle drugs, weapons, and people across borders, for example, in Namibia, there have been instances where fishing vessels were used to traffic drugs, highlighting the need for a coordinated approach to combat these crimes.[52]

In the Caribbean, a strong correlation has developed between fisheries and transnational organized crime, where, for example, small fishing boats leave the Jamaican coast, carrying marijuana on a round trip to Haiti, where the marijuana is exchanged illegally for guns; the guns return to Jamaica in the fishing vessels. This is dubbed the 'drugs-for-guns' trade, and recently the bartering of marijuana for cocaine has also emerged.[53] Another example is Old Providence, a tiny island off the coast of Columbia's Caribbean Sea, where the sea is the primary source of income for the island's economy. In recent years, there has been an increase in fishers who 'disappear' or are incarcerated primarily in relation to their conversance with the surrounding waters. This familiarity, a form of traditional knowledge inherited from their privateering ancestors, which has been discovered and perverted to nefarious purposes by narco-smugglers.[54]

Although this Section has drawn on experiences from across African countries and the Caribbean, as illustrated by the action underpinning the Copenhagen

---

https://doi.org/10.1016/j.marpol.2018.12.023; Maria Hauck and Neville A. Sweijd, *A Case Study of Abalone Poaching in South Africa and its Impact on Fisheries Management,* ICES Journal Of Marine Science, 56 (6), (1999), 1024-1032.

[51] Ifesinachi Okafor-Yarwood, *The Cyclical Nature of Maritime Security Threats: Illegal, Unreported and Unregulated Fishing as a Threat to Human and National Security in the Gulf of Guinea,* African Security, 14 (2) (2021), 123-146, doi:10.1080/19392206.2021.1982241.

[52] African Defense Forum, Human Trafficking Victims Discovered on Shadowy Fishing Vessels in Namibia, ADF Magazine (October 11, 2022), https://adf-magazine.com/2022/10/human-trafficking-victims-discovered-on-shadowy-fishing-vessels-in-namibia/.

[53] Emma Witbooi, *Criminality and Resilience: An Assessment of Organized Crime in Jamaica,* Research Report, Global Initiative Against Transnational Organized Crime (February 2020), https://globalinitiative.net/wp-content/uploads/2020/02/Jamaica-report.26.02.v1.pdf.

[54] BBC News, *The Island Where Men Are Disappearing,* BBC News (October 12, 2015), https://www.bbc.com/news/magazine-34487450 .

Declaration, fisheries crimes occur across many developing and developed countries with varying levels of administrative and other forms of capacity.

III. Consequences of Fisheries Crimes on Small-Scale Fishers

As the previous section illustrates, fisheries crimes have multiple consequences for small-scale fishers. Additionally, the push by many States towards a blue economy agenda, with a focus on foreign direct investments in extractive industries (such as oil, gas, minerals, and industrial fisheries), may lead to disproportionate impacts on small-scale fishers and further fuel fisheries crimes in the small-scale sector. Therefore, without a blue justice approach in African and Caribbean fisheries therefore, the blue economy paradigm has the potential to further marginalize SSF communities.[55]

The impacts of the blue economy agenda are currently being assessed by African and Caribbean states, while the consequences of IUU fishing on small-scale fishers (SSF) are well established. SSF fishers often operate in remote and vulnerable areas, making them particularly susceptible to the impacts of IUU fishing,[56] since the depletion of fish stocks due to IUU fishing and the presence of IUU fishing vessels in their fishing grounds can lead to conflicts and competition for resources. Further, the decline in fish stocks due to IUU fishing has far-reaching consequences, including threatening the livelihoods and food security of those who rely on small-scale fisheries[57] Additionally, overfishing depletes fish populations, undermines conservation efforts, and threatens the sustainability of marine ecosystems. This decline in fish stocks has significant economic and social impacts, particularly on small-scale fishers and coastal communities. Human rights violations are also a significant concern for SSF fishers. For example, the criminalization of certain fishing practices can lead to the marginalization and criminalization of small-scale fishers who rely on these practices for their livelihoods. The criminalization of fishing practices can also result in harassment, arrests, and violence from law enforcement authorities. Furthermore, the loss of access to traditional fishing grounds and resources can

---

[55] Nathan J. Bennett et al., *Blue Growth and Blue Justice: Ten Risks and Solutions for the Ocean Economy*, MARINE POLICY, 125 (2021), 104387.

[56] Dyhia Belhabib and U. Rashid Sumaila, T*he Blue Economy–Cultural Livelihood–Ecosystem Approach: The Case of Africa*, FRONTIERS IN MARINE SCIENCE 7 (2020), 586, https://doi.org/10.3389/fmars.2020.00586.

[57] U. Rashid Sumaila et al., *Illicit Trade in Marine Resources: Impacts on Economies, Ecosystems, and Fisheries Management*, NATURE COMMUNICATIONS, 11 (1), (2020), 1-12, https://doi.org/10.1038/s41467-020-17721-2.

undermine their cultural identity, social cohesion and disrupt traditional fishing practices and undermine community structures.[58]

For example, in Ghana, IUU fishing has led to significant declines in fish stocks, threatening the livelihoods of small-scale fishers. The use of illegal fishing gear and practices has resulted in overfishing and the depletion of fish populations. This has had a devastating impact on small-scale fishers who rely on these resources for their livelihoods. In South Africa, the abalone fishery sector has been severely affected by IUU fishing, as the illegal harvesting of abalone has led to the depletion of abalone populations and has had significant economic and social impacts on small-scale fishers. The involvement of organized crime in the illegal abalone trade has further exacerbated the situation, leading to increased violence and insecurity in fishing communities.[59] In Tanzania, fisheries crimes include the use of explosives for blast fishing, which is not only illegal, but also highly destructive to marine ecosystems. This practice has led to the depletion of fish stocks and significant environmental damage. The involvement of organized crime in these activities further complicates enforcement efforts and poses a threat to maritime security.

Over in the Caribbean, IUU fishing has had a significant impact on small-scale fishers and coastal communities, and has led to actions to address it at both a regional and national level. The depletion of fish stocks due to illegal fishing practices has threatened the livelihoods of small-scale fishers and has undermined food security in the region. The presence of IUU fishing vessels in Caribbean waters has also led to conflicts and competition for resources, further exacerbating the challenges faced by small-scale fishers.[60] Another consequence of fisheries crime is the increase in 'seascape grabbing', which prejudices blue rights. Tenure, access rights, and equity issues facing small-scale fisheries are jeopardized by the blue economy development agenda. This

---

[58] *Id.*

[59] Maria Hauck and Merle Sowman, *Poaching, Security and the State in South Africa: Evolving Perspectives on Abalone Crime*, Journal Of Southern African Studies, 46 (4) (2020), 707-724. https://doi.org/10.1080/03057070.2020.1795225.

[60] See for example, Alana Malinde S. N. Lancaster Salmon et al., *De La Pesca al Cultivo del Medio Marino: El Caso Exitoso de la Gestión Comunitaria en Mayreau, Cayos de Tobago y San Vincente y Las Granadinas*, in Lina María Saavedra-Díaz y Maria Claudia Díazgranados, *Comunidades Con Voz: El Futuro De La Pesca Artesanal En LatinoamériRica Y El Caribe*, Editoral Madgalena/Conservation International Foundation/NORAD/Universidad del Magdalena (2022), 1 – 33, https://editorial.unimagdalena.edu.co/Editorial/Publicacion/4236.

is complicated by the human rights impacts at the ocean-climate nexus,[61] and exacerbated by the post-colonial preference to a top-down management strategy instead of a strong human-rights-based approach to small-scale fisheries management, as advocated by the United Nations Special Rapporteur on the Right to Food and the Voluntary Guidelines for Securing Sustainable Small-Scale Fisheries in the Context of Food Security and Poverty Eradication (SSF Guidelines).[62]

Fisheries crimes are therefore a complex and multi-faceted issue that requires a coordinated and comprehensive approach. Addressing these crimes involves not only strengthening national fisheries management and enforcement but also tackling the broader issues of transnational organized crime and ensuring that the rights of small-scale fishers and coastal communities are protected.

IV. Combatting Fisheries Crimes: From the Global to Regional Perspectives

The complexity of fisheries crimes has led to measures to combat them at international, regional, and national levels. These include binding agreements and voluntary instruments which facilitate the management of fisheries at the global and regional level. However, it is crucial to integrate the concept of blue justice into these efforts to ensure that the rights and interests of small-scale fishers and coastal communities are protected.

A. Global Perspective

Fisheries crime was not explicitly provided for at the time of the adoption of the 1982 United Nations Convention on the Law of the Sea (UNCLOS).[63] UNCLOS creates multiple obligations on State parties to conserve the living resources of the ocean, including adopting obligations to conserve fish stocks.[64] It also sets

---

[61] Environmental Justice Foundation, *A Human Rights Lens on the Impacts of Industrial Illegal Fishing and Overfishing in Ghana*, ENVIRONMENTAL JUSTICE FOUNDATION (2021), https://ejfoundation.org/resources/downloads/EJF-DIHR-socio-economic-report-2021-final.pdf.

[62] Food and Agriculture Organization of the United Nations. *Voluntary Guidelines for Securing Sustainable Small-Scale Fisheries in the Context of Food Security and Poverty Eradication*, FAO (2015), https://www.fao.org/3/a-i4356en.pdf

[63] Judith Swan, *Fisheries Crime: Bridging the Conceptual Gap and Practical Response*, MARINE POLICY, 134 (2022), 104791, https://doi.org/10.1016/j.marpol.2021.104791. See also *United Nations Convention on the Law of the Sea*, 1833 U.N.T.S. 397 (November 16, 1994), https://www.un.org/depts/los/convention_agreements/texts/unclos/unclos_e.pdf.

[64] For example, UNCLOS Article 61 requires coastal states to determine the allowable catch of living resources within their exclusive economic zones (EEZ) and to ensure that these resources are not endangered by over-exploitation. It mandates measures to maintain or restore populations of harvested species at levels that can produce the

out the enforcement powers of state parties in respect of matters including the enforcement of fisheries laws.[65] Similarly, the 1995 Straddling Fish Stocks Agreement notes the role of regional fisheries management bodies in the enforcement of fisheries management agreements.[66] Other related international laws include the Port State Management Agreement,[67] and Voluntary Guidelines for Flag State Performance.[68] The Food and Agriculture Organization (FAO) has developed guidelines and frameworks for responsible fisheries management, including the Code of Conduct for Responsible Fisheries.[69] This Code encourages sustainable practices and provides guidance on combatting IUU fishing through improved governance and enforcement mechanisms. States are to ensure compliance with national and international laws and take enforcement action against perpetrators.

---

maximum sustainable yield. Article 62 emphasizes the utilization of living resources in the EEZ, promoting the objective of optimum utilization without prejudice to Article 61. Article 63 addresses the conservation and management of shared fish stocks, including those that straddle the EEZs of two or more coastal states or occur both within the EEZ and in adjacent areas. Article 64 requires states to cooperate directly or through international organizations to conserve highly migratory species both within and beyond the EEZ Article 65 allows states to regulate the exploitation of marine mammals more strictly than provided for in the Convention. Additionally, Articles 116-120 focus on the conservation of living resources on the high seas, obligating states to adopt measures for their nationals to conserve these resources. Collectively, these provisions establish a comprehensive framework for the conservation and sustainable use of marine living resources under the LOSC.

65 See Tim Stephens and Donald R Rothwell, *The LOSC Framework for Maritime Jurisdiction and Enforcement 30 Years On*, The International Journal of Marine and Coastal Law, 27 (2012), 701 – 709, https://openresearch-repository.anu.edu.au/server/api/core/bitstreams/ba3eead3-8499-4409-b7d5-7257e5ced471/content.

66 United Nations, *Agreement for the Implementation of the Provisions of the United Nations Convention on the Law of the Sea of 10 December 1982 Relating to the Conservation and Management of Straddling Fish Stocks and Highly Migratory Fish Stocks* (Dec. 4, 1995), https://www.un.org/oceancapacity/unfsa.

67 Food and Agriculture Organization of the United Nations. *Agreement on Port State Measures to Prevent, Deter and Eliminate Illegal, Unreported and Unregulated Fishing* (November 22, 2009), https://www.fao.org/fileadmin/user_upload/legal/docs/037t-e.pdf.

68 Food and Agriculture Organization of the United Nations, *Voluntary Guidelines for Flag State Performance* (2015), https://openknowledge.fao.org/server/api/core/bitstreams/903d8997-7bc8-4c88-8d93-e6f57cf5609d/content.

69 Food and Agriculture Organization of the United Nations, *Code of Conduct for Responsible Fisheries* (1995), https://www.fao.org/3/v9878e/v9878e00.htm.

Another relevant instrument is the 2007 Work in Fishing Convention (C188).[70] The Convention was adopted by the International Labour Organization (ILO), which sets minimum standards for the treatment of workers in the fishing industry, addressing issues such as forced labor and unsafe working conditions that are often associated with fisheries crimes. These instruments forge a synergy with UNODC programs targeting fisheries-related crimes, including initiatives focused on wildlife crime, money laundering, marine pollution crime, and transnational organized crime. These programs aim to strengthen legislative frameworks and enhance law enforcement capacities globally, and if implemented in the context of a blue justice and human rights perspective, these instruments could have a transformative impact.

Although these agreements include provisions and requirements that may address illegal fisheries, with provisions and guidance relating to port State measures, flag State performance, coastal State responsibilities, market State measures, or a combination of all or some of these, it was not until the adoption of the United Nations Food and Agricultural Organization (FAO) International Plan of Action to Prevent, Deter, and Eliminate Illegal, Unreported and Unregulated Fishing (IPOA-IUU), that a comprehensive attempt was made to define the specific conduct of illegal fishing. The IPOA-IUU defines 'illegal fishing' as fishing and fishing-related activities conducted in contravention of national, regional and international laws. It further defines 'unreported fishing' as involving the non-reporting, misreporting and under-reporting of information on fishing operations and their catches. Meanwhile, 'unregulated fishing' constitutes fishing activities that are not regulated by states, fishing in areas or for fish stocks for which there are no management measures and fishing in a Regional Fisheries' Management Organization (RFMO) area by vessels of non-member states. These three make up what is now widely known as IUU fishing. Globally, illegal, unreported, and unregulated (IUU) fishing is one area of illicit activity which undermines international efforts to sustainably manage and rebuild fisheries, creating unfair market competition for fishermen who adhere to strict conservation measures.

While the FAO IPOA-IUU initially conceived addressing anti-IUU fishing as an administrative law enforcement problem through the strengthening of fisheries management and governance processes, there has been a growing emphasis on the criminalization of IUU fishing. In this respect, the connections between IUU fishing operations and transnational organized crime, which has given rise to the commission of different crimes along the fisheries value chain,

---

[70] International Labour Organization, *Work in Fishing Convention, 2007 (No. 188)*, ILO (2007), https://www.ilo.org/dyn/normlex/en/f?p=NORMLEXPUB:12100:0::NO::P12100_ILO_CODE:C188.

are now well documented. In particular, there is now a recognition that the impacts of IUU fishing are not only an economic threat to the survival of the fisheries industry, as well as a threat to maritime security, but also its scale, complexity and causal factors include weak and sometimes corrupt governance systems. This makes IUU fishing a crime that can have transnational elements.

On the other hand, fisheries crimes seen through lenses of blue justice and small-scale fisheries, raise critical questions about those international legal frameworks, including in terms of enforcement mechanisms. This conversation is particularly relevant for regions like Africa and the Caribbean, where fisheries crimes pose significant threats to marine biodiversity and the livelihoods of local communities discussed in this Chapter. There is a compelling argument for establishing to consolidate the principles in soft instruments, and the generic or inadequate provisions of different treaties, which fail to address fisheries crimes holistically, effectively and in a more contemporary context. Soft instruments, while useful for signaling some level of intent,[71] lack the enforceability required to combat IUU fishing robustly. A binding treaty would create clear legal obligations for states, enhancing cooperation and accountability in managing marine resources. While UNTOC serves as a precedent for such an approach, a similar framework focused on ocean governance from a blue justice approach – such as that proposed by the Ålesund Resolution and the Copenhagen Declaration – could significantly bolster efforts against fisheries crimes.

However, the regulation of global fisheries through binding instruments beyond the general provisions in the UNLCOS have struggled. For example, the 1995 Straddling Fish Stocks Agreement,[72] one of UNCLOS' three implementing agreements has seen a low level of uptake, especially among Global South States.[73] While UNCLOS' third implementing agreement, the recently concluded BBNJ Agreement,[74] aims to enhance conservation efforts in areas beyond national jurisdiction (ABNJ), it does not directly address enforcement

---

[71] Christine M. Chinkin, *The Challenge of Soft Law: Development and Change in International Law*, THE INTERNATIONAL AND COMPARATIVE LAW QUARTERLY, 38(4) (1989), 850–66. http://www.jstor.org/stable/759917.

[72] Straddling Stocks Agreement, *supra* note 66.

[73] Giselle Vigneron, Compliance and International Environmental Agreements: A Case Study of the 1995 United Nations Straddling Fish Stocks Agreement, GEO. INT'L ENVTL. L. REV, 10, (1997), 581.

[74] *Agreement under the United Nations Convention on the Law of the Sea on the Conservation and Sustainable Use of Marine Biological Diversity of Areas Beyond National Jurisdiction* (June 19, 2023), https://documents.un.org/doc/undoc/ltd/n23/177/28/pdf/n2317728.pdf.

mechanisms against criminal activities.[75] Further, while States have recourse to the International Tribunal for the Law of the Sea (ITLOS) over disputes concerning the interpretation and application of UNCLOS,[76] discussions regarding expanding the Tribunal's jurisdiction beyond traditional treaty interpretation are ongoing.[77] ITLOS's current jurisdictional framework allows for advisory opinions on legal questions, which could be instrumental in clarifying states' obligations concerning international agreements related to the purposes of UNCLOS,[78] including fisheries management and enforcement against IUU fishing.[79] While the Tribunal has recently signalled its desire to explore the scope of its jurisdiction in keeping with contemporary threats that were not contemplated at the time of its adoption,[80] there remains a gap in addressing criminal activities specifically. On the other hand, systems,

---

[75] International Tribunal for the Law of the Sea, *Advisory Opinion in Case No. 31, Request Submitted to the Tribunal by the Commission of Small Island States on Climate Change and International Law,* ITLOS (May 21, 2024), https://www.itlos.org/fileadmin/itlos/documents/cases/31/Advisory_Opinion/C31_Adv_Op_21.05.2024_orig.pdf.

[76] *Statute of the International Tribunal for the Law of the Sea* (December 10, 1982), Article 20, 21. See Miguel G García-Revillo, *International Tribunal for the Law of the Sea (ITLOS),* YEARBOOK OF INTERNATIONAL ENVIRONMENTAL LAW, 29 (2018), 381–383. https://doi.org/10.1093/yiel/yvz058; Tajudeen Sanni, *SDG 14: Life under water* in Ralf Michaels, Verónica Ruiz Abou-Nhim and Hans van Loon (eds), *The Private Side of Transforming Our World - UN Sustainable Development Goals 2030 and the Role of Private International Law,* https://www.intersentiaonline.com/publication/the-private-side-of-transforming-our-world-un-sustainable-development-goals-2030-and-the-role-of-p/16 (accessed November 15, 2024).

[77] See for example Julia Weston, *The International Tribunal for the Law of the Sea: Its Wide Jurisdiction and Potential to Analyse Current Law of the Sea,* CZECH YEARBOOK OF INTERNATIONAL LAW, XIII (2022), 211 – 234.

[78] *Rules of the International Tribunal for the Law of the Sea* (October 28, 1997; amended September 25, 2018), Art. 138, https://www.itlos.org/fileadmin/itlos/documents/basic_texts/Itlos_8_E_17_03_09.pdf; ITLOS, *Request for Advisory Opinion Submitted by the Sub-Regional Fisheries Commission (SRFC Advisory Opinion), Advisory Opinion* (2 April 2015), ¶¶ 54–56, https://www.itlos.org/index.php?id=252; Carlos A. Cruz Carillo, *The Advisory Jurisdiction of ITLOS: From Uncertainties to Opportunities for Ocean Governance,* in Froukje Maria Platjouw and Alla Pozdnakova (eds.), *The Environmental Rule of Law for the Oceans, Designing Legal Solutions* (Cambridge University Press: 2023).

[79] International Tribunal for the Law of the Sea, *International Agreements Conferring Jurisdiction on the Tribunal,* https://www.itlos.org/en/main/jurisdiction/international-agreements-conferring-jurisdiction-on-the-tribunal/.

[80] Alana Malinde S. N. Lancaster, *Full Seas, Floods & Fortunes? Fathoming The Impact of the ITLOS Advisory Opinion to the Future of Climate Justice for Climate Vulnerable Populations in Large Ocean States* in Ezio Costa Costa Cordella and Pilar Moraga Sariego (eds.), *State Responsibilities in the Climate Crisis: Legal Standards and Global Litigation* (Tirant Lo Blanch: 2024).

as discussed in 5.2., have developed mechanisms such as the Treaty of San José,[81] but there are a myriad of obstacles to global responses such as a global treaty or the establishment of a specialized court or tribunal dedicated to maritime crimes, which could enhance legal clarity and enforcement capabilities. We acknowledge that there are obstacles to be overcome to develop either the judicial body and implement legally binding, specialized, and globally recognized legal instruments to achieve the goal of sustainable fishery governance,[82] but this needs to be balanced with the fact that the enforcement of fisheries regulations presents significant challenges to an overwhelming majority of States. These challenges include addressing threats by third-party actors operating in international waters, and jurisdictional complexities which arise because many States may lack the capacity or political will to pursue enforcement actions against foreign vessels engaged in IUU fishing.[83]

Within this context, despite not directly addressing enforcement mechanisms against criminal activities from the global perspective, the BBNJ Agreement has the potential to influence the management of some forms of environmental criminal activity related to marine resources in the ABNJ. Most notably, the Agreement promotes cooperation among states for managing marine biodiversity beyond national jurisdiction, through a framework of clearer guidelines, which may indirectly reduce opportunities for IUU fishing.[84] However, its effectiveness will largely depend on the commitment of states to enforce these guidelines and collaborate on shared challenges. Overwhelming, therefore, the effective tackling of IUU fishing and other fisheries crimes will require cooperative frameworks which empower coastal states to take necessary

---

[81] Alana Malinde S. N. Lancaster, *A Sea of Challenges, But an Ocean of Possibilities: Examining the Nexus between Maritime Security & Safeguarding the Rights of Ocean-dependent Populations in Caribbean Small Island Developing States,* CARIBBEAN LAW REVIEW 22 (2) (2025) (forthcoming).

[82] See generally Minna Yu and Xinyu Liu, *A New Approach to Combating Illegal, Unreported, and Unregulated Fishing: Analysis of the WTO Agreement on Fisheries* Subsidies, MARINE DEVELOPMENT 2 (1), 10 (2024). https://doi.org/10.1007/s44312-024-00023-4.

[83] Shekar Bose, *Law Enforcement, Compliance, and Fisheries Sustainability* in Laith A. Jawad (ed.), *The Arabian Seas: Biodiversity, Environmental Challenges and Conservation Measures* (Springer Nature: 2021), 829-844.

[84] International cooperation is one of the fundamental principles of BBNJ. See BBNJ Agreement, *supra* note 74, Article 8.

actions against violators,[85] including enhanced surveillance technologies,[86] increased funding for enforcement agencies, and international partnerships that facilitate information sharing and joint operations.[87] While States may continue to struggle with an effective (suite of) approach(es) at the global level, they can simultaneously continue to develop and utilize regional approaches to the governance of blue crimes.

B. Regional Perspectives

Both the African and Caribbean regions have developed regional mechanisms in response to fisheries crimes and wider threats to their marine environment. For example, the African Charter on Maritime Security and Safety and Development in Africa, also known as the Lome Charter,[88] addresses a wide range of maritime issues, including fisheries crimes and small-scale fisheries. It directs state parties to prevent and combat illegal, unreported, and unregulated (IUU) fishing by establishing effective monitoring, control, and surveillance systems. The Charter also calls for cooperation to prevent and suppress piracy, armed robbery, and other illicit activities, and its recognition of the importance of small-scale fisheries to the livelihoods of coastal communities is significant. However, despite its progressive provisions, the treaty has yet to come into force due to the reluctance of most African Union (AU) states to ratify it.

Another instrument in the African region is the 2015 African Integrated Maritime Strategy (AIMS-2013), which outlines Africa's vision for a secure, safe, and prosperous maritime domain, including measures to combat IUU fishing.[89] While AIMS is a generic instrument on maritime security, there is a

---

85 Elizabeth Mendenhall, *Advancing the International Law of the Sea to Address Illegal, Unreported, and Unregulated Fishing Future Fisheries Management,* Issue Brief, Mercatus Center (October 18, 2023), https://www.mercatus.org/research/policy-briefs/advancing-international-law-sea-address-illegal-unreported-and-unregulated.

86 Sara Orofino, et.al., *Opportunities and Challenges for Improving Fisheries Management Through Greater Transparency in Vessel Tracking,* ICES JOURNAL OF MARINE SCIENCE, 80 (4) (2023), 675-689.

87 Nature Crime Alliance, *Why Multisector Collaboration is Critical in the Fight Against Illegal Fishing* (September 27, 2024), https://naturecrimealliance.org/multi-sector-action-critical-to-fight-illegal-fishing/.

88 *African Charter on Maritime Security and Safety and Development in Africa (Lomé Charter)* (October 15, 2016), https://au.int/en/treaties/african-charter-maritime-security-and-safety-and-development-africa-lome-charter.

89 African Union, *2050 Africa's Integrated Maritime Strategy (2050 AIM Strategy),* AFRICAN UNION (2012), https://www.nairobiconvention.org/clearinghouse/sites/default/files/2050%20Africa%E2%80%99s%20Integrated%20Maritime%20%28AIM%29%20Strategy.pdf.

dedicated African Union (AU) Policy Framework and Reform Strategy for Fisheries and Aquaculture in Africa that aims to ensure coherent policy development for the sustainable governance of fisheries.[90] It offers opportunities for AU member states to leverage their natural resources by implementing strategic reforms. The framework provides guidance on good governance principles and outlines strategic actions for key pillars of fisheries reform. One principle focuses on the development of small-scale fisheries to contribute to poverty alleviation, and it acknowledges the role of women in fisheries. The instrument also offers guidance on capturing the wealth of fisheries, reducing poverty, improving food and nutritional security, and ensuring equitable distribution of benefits, particularly for the poorest and most vulnerable members of society, such as women.

An important policy direction is the strengthening of South-South cooperation and developing coordinated mechanisms among Regional Economic Communities (RECs), Regional Fisheries Bodies (RFBs), and Large Marine Ecosystem (LME)-based commissions to ensure coherence in fisheries policies and aquaculture development.[91] Some initiatives addressing fisheries issues include the South-West Atlantic Commission,[92] and the Benguela Current Commission (BCC).[93] In West Africa, regional efforts to combat fisheries crimes involve collaboration among multiple countries and organizations. The Fisheries Committee for the West Central Gulf of Guinea (FCWC),[94] and the Sub-Regional Fisheries Commission (SRFC)[95] are key players in this region, working together to enhance surveillance, enforcement, and prosecution of fisheries crimes. The FCWC Regional Fisheries Monitoring Centre (RMCSC)

---

[90] African Union Commission and NEPAD Planning and Coordinating Agency, *Policy Framework and Reform Strategy for Fisheries and Aquaculture in Africa*, African Union (May 2014), https://au.int/sites/default/files/documents/30266-doc-au-ibar_-_fisheries_policy_framework_and_reform_strategy.pdf.

[91] African Union Inter-African Bureau for Animal Resources. *Policy Brief on Strategies for Institutional Coordination Between RECs and RFBs and Strengthening Their Relationships with NSAs*, AU-IBAR (2022), http://repository.au-ibar.org/bitstream/handle/123456789/1508/Policy%20Brief%20%20on%20strategies%20for%20institutional%20coordination%20%28Final%20Version%202%29141022.pdf?sequence=1.

[92] UIA, *Regional Fisheries Advisory Commission for the Southwest Atlantic*, https://uia.org/s/or/en/1100001222 (accessed September 29, 2024).

[93] Benguela Current Convention, *Overview of the Benguela Current Convention*, https://www.benguelacc.org/bcc-overview/ (accessed September 29, 2024).

[94] Fisheries Committee for the West Central Gulf of Guinea, *About Us: Fisheries Committee for the West Central Gulf of Guinea*, https://fcwc-fish.org/about-us (accessed September 29, 2024).

[95] Sub-Regional Fisheries Commission, http://spcsrp.org/en (accessed September 29, 2024).

addresses major national and regional challenges in combating IUU fishing and associated fisheries crimes.[96] The West Africa Task Force brings together six member countries – Benin, Côte d'Ivoire, Ghana, Liberia, Nigeria, and Togo – to tackle illegal fishing and fisheries crime.[97]

In the Caribbean, the Caribbean Community Common Fisheries Policy (CCCFP), a binding instrument focusing on cooperation and collaboration between Members of CARICOM, is the main regional instrument[98] to address the issue of fisheries crime. The Policy is a key tool in implementing Art. 60 of the 2001 Revised Treaty of Chaguaramas, which promotes sustainable fisheries by requiring Parties to conserve, manage, and sustainably utilize fisheries and related ecosystems.[99] The CCCFP includes improved regional fisheries monitoring, control and surveillance to reduce illegal fishing and harmonized regional and national data and information systems for better data sharing and open access to all, as well as increased regional food and nutrition security. It also aims to complement the recognition by Article 121 of the Revised Treaty, that the Caribbean Sea as a special area of sustainable development. This latter designation is buttressed by the Regional Seas Programme for the Wider Caribbean Region, the Cartagena Convention, a key instrument in promoting the blue justice approach in the Caribbean. The Regional Seas Programme is also complemented by the work of the International Commission for the Conservation of Atlantic Tunas (ICCATT), the RFMO, which includes many Caribbean Member States. Additionally, the Caribbean Large Marine Ecosystem (CLME) Project sought to improve the management of shared living marine resources in the Caribbean and North Brazil Shelf Large Marine Ecosystems, a highly productive Large Marine Ecosystems (LME)[100] through ecosystem-based management, governance and stakeholder coordination. The Project

---

[96] Fisheries Committee for the West Central Gulf of Guinea, *Regional MCS Centre – Fisheries Committee for the West Central Gulf of Guinea*, https://fcwc-fish.org/regional-mcs-centre (accessed September 29, 2024).

[97] TMT, *West Africa Task Force:TMT Targeting Illegal Fishing and Associated Crime*, https://www.tm-tracking.org/west-africa-task-force (accessed September 29, 2024).

[98] Caribbean Community, *Caribbean Community Common Fisheries Policy (CCCFP)*, https://caricom.org/documents/12304-cccf-policy.pdf (accessed September 29, 2024).

[99] *Revised Treaty of Chaguaramas Establishing the Caribbean Community including the CARICOM Single Market and Economy*, https://caricom.org/documents/4906-revised_treaty-text.pdf (accessed September 29, 2024).

[100] Kenneth Sherman, *The Large Marine Ecosystem Concept: Research and Management Strategy for Living Marine Resources*, ECOLOGICAL APPLICATIONS, 1 (4) (1991), 349-360; Lucia Fanning, Robin Mahon, and Patrick McConney, *Focusing on Living Marine Resource Governance: The Caribbean Large Marine Ecosystem and Adjacent Areas Project*, COASTAL MANAGEMENT 37 (3-4) (2009), 219-234.

emphasized regional cooperation, capacity building, and the use of both criminal and civil approaches to combat fisheries crimes.[101]

Finally, the Regional Security System (RSS) is a regional security organization in the Caribbean that addresses various security threats, including fisheries crimes. It employs a highly militarized approach, involving the use of naval and coast guard forces to enforce a wide diversity of maritime security threats, including maritime policing duties, natural and other disasters, pollution control, the protection of exclusive economic zones, as well as fisheries protection.[102] While the RSS has been tremendously important to the maintenance of maritime security in the Caribbean Region, the regional environment for security is complex and in continuous change, and the threat from maritime crime is undermining the ability of RSS and Caribbean States to achieve the Sustainable Development Goals (SDGs), especially SDGs 16 (peace, justice, and strong institutions), and SDG 14 (life below water).[103] Additionally, threats posed by maritime insecurity in the Caribbean have catalytic implications, including increasingly, climate insecurity, which are exacerbating maritime security concerns, and require contemporary and effective mechanisms to diminish the threat.[104] On such option being explored by States, is the adoption of the Agreement Concerning the Cooperation in Suppressing Illicit Maritime and Air Trafficking in Narcotic Drugs and Psychotropic Substances in the Caribbean Area (the Treaty of San José),[105] which has its origins in several U.N.–facilitated meetings in the 1990s following reports concerning the increasing level of violence and drug trafficking within the

[101] CLME+ Project, Catalysing Implementation of the Strategic Action Programme for the Sustainable Management of Shared Living Marine Resources in the Caribbean and North Brazil Shelf Large Marine Ecosystems, https://www.clmeproject.org/ (accessed September 29, 2024).

[102] Treaty Establishing the Regional Security System (RSS Agreement) (March 5, 1996), Article 4 (1), https://assets.ctfassets.net/1yxaau1iba16/6Xjf0wHdA6XB32aQiYCPci/e5bb5fae403657a184a22562d37d302f/Treaty_Establishing_the_RSS.pdf (accessed September 29, 2024).

[103] Lancaster, *supra* note 81.

[104] *Id.*

[105] *Agreement Concerning Co-Operation in Suppressing Illicit Maritime and Air Trafficking in Narcotic Drugs and Psychotropic Substances in the Caribbean Area* (Treaty of San José) (April 10, 2003), Article 25, https://zoek.officielebekendmakingen.nl/trb-2003-82.pdf (accessed November 29, 2024). See also William C. Gilmore, *Agreement Concerning Co-operation in Suppressing Illicit Maritime and Air Trafficking in Narcotic Drugs and Psychotropic Substances in the Caribbean Area, 2003*, The Stationery Office (2005), 8; Efthymios Papastavridis, *The Interception of Vessels On the High Seas*, Hart Publishing Limited (2013), 221.

Caribbean area.[106] The Agreement aims to ostensibly enhance "... cooperation to the 'fullest extent possible in combating illicit maritime (...) traffic in and over the waters of the Caribbean area (...) in conformity with the international law of the sea and applicable agreements ..."[107]

It is noteworthy that while the focus across the African and Caribbean Regions is overwhelmingly mired in a criminal approach, there is also the recognition that maritime security can lead to the oppression, marginalization and vulnerability to blue injustices for coastal communities, Indigenous and Afro-descendent peoples, and small-scale fishers intimately connected with the ocean. It is within this context that the blue justice approach, born of grassroots resistance efforts led by coastal communities, have, in many instances, successfully stopped unfair exposure to environmental harms. The blue justice approach can also preserve their livelihoods and ways of life, defend their culture and customary rights, renegotiate power distributions, and propose alternative futures[108] for the governance of marine resources. Within this context, we examine the role of the blue justice lens as an emerging approach to addressing fisheries crimes and safeguarding the human rights of small-scale fishers across the African and Caribbean Regions.

V. Small-Scale Fishers, Fisheries Crimes within the Blue Justice Lens

Blue justice has emerged as a critical framework for environmental justice in small-scale fisheries in the face of the new blue economy paradigm, and burgeoning blue growth and the uncertainties these pose for coastal futures.[109] The term blue justice was introduced into academic circles by Moenieba Isaacs[110] during the Third World Small-Scale Fisheries Congress, and has its roots in early literature focusing on securing rights for small-scale fisheries within the blue economy.[111] Within this context, blue justice is defined as 'an approach that seeks to address the injustices faced by small-scale fishers and coastal communities, and to promote their rights and interests in the context of fisheries governance and marine conservation.'[112] This framework promotes fairness, equity, and sustainability in the governance of marine resources, particularly small-scale fishers and coastal communities. Further, blue justice

---

106 United Nations General Assembly, *Cooperation between the United Nations and the Caribbean Community*, A/RES/53/17 (16 November 1998), ¶ 15.

107 Treaty of San José, *supra* note 105, Article 2.

108 Blythe et al., *supra* note 14.

109 *Id.*

110 Issacs, *supra* note 21.

111 Jentoft et al., *supra* note 13.

112 *Id.*

addresses power imbalances and inequalities in the fisheries sector, especially between small-scale fishers and industrial fishing operations, and emphasizes the need for equitable and inclusive measures that promote the sustainable use of marine resources while safeguarding the human rights of those who depend on them.[113]

Since its introduction in 2018, academic engagement with the concept has grown rapidly,[114] with connections to wider, relevant debates, such as blue injustices and grassroots resistance to these injustices.[115] Early blue justice literature has focused on securing rights for small-scale fisheries within the blue economy, while recent literature focuses on different drivers of blue injustices, including intersecting forms of oppression and marginalization, which render coastal individuals and communities vulnerable. The underlying philosophy aims to ensure a more equitable distribution of resources, benefits, and decision-making power, recognizing the rights of small-scale fishers and coastal communities.[116]

Based on conceptualizations by different scholars, blue justice is predicated on several key principles. These principles include fairness and equity in access to resources and benefits; recognition of the rights and interests of small-scale fishers and coastal communities; public participation in decision-making processes; environmental sustainability, and social justice and human well-being. In the context of these principles, blue justice aims to contribute to a more just and sustainable fisheries sector, and to support the well-being and livelihoods of small-scale fishers and coastal communities included in dealing with fisheries crimes. The principles generally align with the Food and Agriculture Organisation (FAO)'s Principles of Blue Transformation, a vision of its work on aquatic food systems, which include public participation, environmental sustainability, human rights, equity and justice.[117] In particular,

---

[113] Alicia Bugeja Said and Moenieba Isaacs. *Blue Justice: Small-Scale Fisheries in a Sustainable Ocean Economy* (Springer Nature), 2021.

[114] See for example, Issacs, *supra* note 21; Bennett et al., *supra* note 58; Svein Jentoft and Ratana Chuenpagdee, *Interactive Learning and Governance Transformation for Securing Blue Justice for Small-Scale Fisheries*, ADMINISTRATION & SOCIETY, 54(7), 1255–1282; Jentoft et al., *supra* note 12.

[115] Blythe et al., *supra* note 14.

[116] Nathan J. Bennett et al., *Towards a Blue Justice Framework: Integrating Social Equity and Environmental Sustainability in Marine Conservation*, MARINE POLICY 87 (2018), 194-204.

[117] Food and Agricultural Organisation, *Blue Transformation in Brief: Advancing Aquatic Ecosystems for Prosperity and Well-being* (2023), https://openknowledge.fao.org/server/api/core/bitstreams/ac40a573-c505-4f1d-a5a2-422e0eaf7a45/content#:~:text=Blue%20Transformation%20outlines%20a%20vision,depend%20on%20fisheries%20and%20aqu

the Blue Transformation Principles of equity and justice speak to blue justice, as it seeks to "promote justice and fair treatment of all people and communities and implement measures to accelerate the achievement of equitable outcomes, particularly for vulnerable and marginalized groups."[118] It also speaks to the blue transformation human rights principle that aims to "recognize, respect, promote and protect human rights principles of those participating in aquatic food systems, as stipulated in international human rights instruments."[119]

Before discussing the increased proliferation of human-rights-based instruments which support the blue justice approach, it must be highlighted that the blue justice framework is more than ever also relevant to the discourse on the future of sustainable aquaculture,[120] mariculture[121] and aquaponics.[122] Overwhelmingly, the majority of fish and seafood are still derived from marine capture fisheries, but with global food demand rising,[123] and for the first time in 2022, world aquaculture production surpassed capture fisheries.[124] These production systems, along with their value chains related to imports, exports

---

aculture; Food and Agricultural Organisation, *Blue Transformation: FAO's Work on Aquatic Food Systems*, https://openknowledge.fao.org/server/api/core/bitstreams/39ef1d5b-0bee-4c31-9883-1325a44c48a8/content#:~:text=Promoting%20the%20sustainable%20intensification%20and,global%20demand%20for%20aquatic%20foods.&text=Sustainable%20aquaculture%20production%20grows%20by,secure%20equitable%20livelihoods%20for%20all.&text=100%20percent%20of%20marine%20and,outcomes%20of%20aquatic%20food%20systems.&text=It%20requires%20a%20commitment%20from,food%20security%20and%20poverty%20alleviation.

118 Food and Agricultural Organisation, *Blue Transformation: A Vision For Transforming Aquatic Food Systems*, https://openknowledge.fao.org/server/api/core/bitstreams/9df19f53-b931-4d04-acd3-58a71c6b1a5b/content/sofia/2022/transforming-aquatic-based-food.html#:~:text=from%20climate%20change.-,Objectives%20of%20Blue%20Transformation,systems%2C%20and%20secure%20nutritional%20outcomes.

119 *Id.*

120 Rohana Subasinghe, Doris Soto, and Jiansan Jia, *Global Aquaculture and Its Role in Sustainable* Development, REVIEWS IN AQUACULTURE, 1 (1) (2009), 2-9.

121 Doris Soto, *Integrated Mariculture: A Global Review*, FAO Technical Paper No. 529 (2009).

122 Simon Goddek, et.al. (eds.) *Aquaponics Food Production Systems: Combined Aquaculture and Hydroponic Production Technologies For the Future* (Springer Open: 2019); Carmelo Maucieri et al., *Hydroponic Systems and Water Management In Aquaponics: A Review*, ITALIAN JOURNAL OF AGRONOMY, 13 (1) (2018), 1012.

123 See Christopher Costello et al., *The Future of Food from the Sea*, in Jane Lubchenci and Peter M, Haugan (eds.) *The Blue Compendium: From Knowledge to Action for a Sustainable Ocean Economy* (Springer: 2023, 2024), 1, https://doi.org/10.1007/978-3-031-16277-0.

124 FAO, *The State of World Fisheries and Aquaculture : Blue Transformation in Action* (2024), xxi https://openknowledge.fao.org/server/api/core/bitstreams/f985caed-cc7a-457e-8107-7ce16c6ef209/content.

and equitability of distribution are considered crucial to achieving Sustainable Development Goals 1 (no poverty) and 2 (zero hunger). However, increasing scholarship on aquatic food security has lamented that most of the emphasis on aquaculture as a major economic and food-producing sector has largely focused on economic and ecological aquaculture issues, and neglected the human and social dimensions of the sector.[125] There is, therefore, the need to incorporate human, social and rights-based considerations into aquaculture (mariculture and aquaponics) development, in a manner which can incorporate notions of justice and equity, including the idea of blue justice and its relevance in aquaculture.[126]

The increased production in the aquaculture, mariculture and aquaponics sector is now a fundamental part of the blue economy, including the grassroots level,[127] and as an alternative for blue injustices which cause displacements of small-scale-fishing livelihoods.[128] Recognizing the need to develop a framework, which can both draw on international instruments and inspire national policies and legislation to eliminate injustices in fisheries and aquaculture value chains, the FAO, for example, has in 2024 adopted Guidelines for Sustainable Aquaculture (GSA).[129] These Guidelines comprise principles and practices that all countries and stakeholders can use to promote the Blue Transformation Principles, and is a targeted effort to incorporate the application of human rights into the aquaculture (mariculture and aquaponics) sector. A critical ingredient of the Blue Transformation are notions of justice and equity, which are incorporated in the blue justice paradigm, and consider issues of gender equality and youth engagement in aquaculture, as well as the incorporation of Indigenous, Afro-descendant, and local ecological knowledge. The absence of a rights-based approach in aquaculture poses challenges to aquatic food security, and like fisheries crimes, IUU fishing and other transnational organized crimes will undermine the rights of small-scale fishers guaranteed under international human rights law, such as the livelihood and food rights.

---

[125] C. Brugere, et al., *Humanizing Aquaculture Development: Putting Social and Human Concerns at the Center of Future Aquaculture Development,* JOURNAL OF THE WORLD AQUACULTURE SOCIETY, 54 (2) (2023), 482-526.

[126] *Id.*

[127] See for example, Corin Bailey et al., *Rural Poverty in the Caribbean: Assets, Social Exclusion and Agricultural Livelihoods,* Case Study, FAO (2024), 24, https://openknowledge.fao.org/server/api/core/bitstreams/cf2c9abb-be9e-42ea-a2a4-f483c927f588/content.

[128] See for example, Lancaster Salmon et al., *supra* note 60.

[129] FAO, Guidelines for Sustainable Aquaculture, FAO Committee On Fisheries (July 8-12, 2024), https://openknowledge.fao.org/server/api/core/bitstreams/b87a56eb-749d-4e76-b952-413708c021e0/content.

Accordingly, for small-scale fisheries, including small-scale aquaculture, mariculture and aquaponics production systems to be "socially responsible," there must be an equal emphasis on social performance criteria, as there is currently on environmental performance criteria. This requires a comprehensive consideration which transcends the general framing of civil and political human rights, to one which applies economic, social and cultural rights.[130] Additionally, given the prominent role of private actors in the fishing industry, the role of the State in regulating, supervising, and overseeing the business and human rights principles is crucial to stemming instances of human rights violations.[131] In the Caribbean and Latin American Region, the judgment of the Inter-American Court of Human Rights in *Miskito Divers v Honduras*[132] has been a turning point in delineating clear business and human rights standards to be met by states and companies.[133] The benefits of this approach can make inroads into addressing human rights violations such as slavery and human trafficking common in distant water fishing, which the Copenhagen Declaration aims to address. Further, business and human rights principles safeguard rights which have been lagging in small-scale fishing, such as the right to decent work,[134] food and nutrition security[135] for present and future generations, and can also meet legal and ethical standards for welfare of animals, people and

---

130 Lydia C. L. Teh et al., *The Role of Human Rights in Implementing Socially Responsible Seafood*, PLOS ONE, 14 (1) (2019), e0210241.

131 See for example, the *United Nations Guiding Principles on Business and Human Rights, Implementing the United Nations "Protect, Respect and Remedy" Framework* (2011), https://www.ohchr.org/sites/default/files/documents/publications/guidingprinciplesbusinesshr_en.pdf; U.N. Working Group on the Issue of Human Rights and Transnational Corporations and Other Business Enterprises, Investors, Environmental, Social and Governance Approaches and Human Rights, A/HRC/56/55 (May 02, 2024), https://www.ohchr.org/en/documents/thematic-reports/ahrc5655-investors-environmental-social-and-governance-approaches-and (accessed November 29, 2024).

132 Inter-American Court of Human Rights, *Case of the Miskito Divers (Lemoth Morris et al.) v Honduras*, Judgement of August 31, 2021, https://www.corteidh.or.cr/docs/casos/articulos/seriec_432_ing.pdf (accessed November 29, 2024).

133 Maysa Zorob and Hector Candray, Justice for Miskito Divers: A Turning Point for Business and Human Rights Standards from the Inter-American Court of Human Rights, OPEN GLOBAL RIGHTS (March 21, 2022), https://www.openglobalrights.org/justice-for-miskito-divers-a-turning-point-for-business-and-human-rights-standards/.

134 Gabrielle Lout et al., *Decent Work in a Seascape of Livelihoods: Regional Evaluation of the Shrimp and Groundfish Fishery of the Guianas-Brazil Shelf*, MARINE POLICY, 144 (2022), 105231.

135 See for example, United Nations in the Caribbean, *FAO Calls on Governments and Organizations to Commit to Guaranteeing the Right to Food in Latin America and the Caribbean* (October 9, 2024), https://caribbean.un.org/en/281144-fao-calls-governments-and-organizations-commit-guaranteeing-right-food-latin-america-and.

environment.[136] Blue justice must be oriented, in theory and practice, to address these and related intersections effectively.

Both blue justice and human rights frameworks emphasize protecting the rights of individuals and communities, including their access to resources and participation in decision-making processes. While the human rights lens is broader, encompassing a wide range of civil, political, economic, social, and cultural rights, the blue justice framework focuses specifically on fisheries and marine governance. Accordingly, the human rights framework often relies on legal instruments and mechanisms to enforce rights, as opposed to the blue justice framework, which may incorporate a wider range of approaches, including community-based management and participatory governance. The following indices can be used to measure fisheries crimes and efforts to combat them:

1. Equitable and Inclusive Measures: Assessing whether measures to combat fisheries crimes are fair and inclusive, ensuring all stakeholders, including small-scale fishers and coastal communities, are considered.
2. Participatory Governance: Evaluating the extent to which small-scale fishers and coastal communities are involved in decision-making processes related to fisheries governance and the implementation of measures to combat fisheries crimes.
3. Respect for Livelihood Rights: Ensuring measures to combat fisheries crimes do not undermine the livelihood rights of small-scale fishers and coastal communities, and that alternative livelihood options are provided where necessary.
4. Balance Between Competing Rights: Assessing whether measures strike a balance between the rights of different stakeholders, including small-scale fishers, industrial fishers, and other marine resource users.
5. Effectiveness of Enforcement: Evaluating the effectiveness of enforcement mechanisms in addressing fisheries crimes, including the use of monitoring, control, and surveillance (MCS) systems.
6. Impact on Human Rights: Assessing the impact of measures to combat fisheries crimes on the human rights of small-scale fishers and coastal communities, including their rights to food, work, and a healthy environment.

---

[136] Simon Jennings et al., *Aquatic Food Security: Insights Into Challenges and Solutions From An Analysis of Interactions Between Fisheries, Aquaculture, Food Safety, Human Health, Fish And Human Welfare, Economy and Environment*, FISH AND FISHERIES, 17 (4) (2016), 893-938.

7. Sustainability of Marine Resources: Evaluating the impact of measures on the sustainability of marine resources, ensuring they contribute to the long-term viability of fish stocks and marine ecosystems.

The blue justice and human rights lens, therefore provides a comprehensive framework for addressing fisheries crimes in a manner that promotes equity, sustainability, and the protection of the rights and interests of small-scale fishers and coastal communities. By using these indices to measure fisheries crimes and efforts to combat them, we can ensure that our approaches are fair, inclusive, and effective in promoting a just and sustainable fisheries sector.[137]

There has accordingly been a paradigm shift from the approach in binding legal instruments mentioned in the previous Section, to one with an expanded scope through several of the soft-law instruments.[138] Collectively, these instruments are primarily concerned with regulating the access to, use, and management of fishery resources, but lack binding power and leave gaps in several crucial areas related to access rights of small-scale fishers to fishery resources and fishing grounds. These gaps have intensified in the face of pressures from fisheries crimes,[139] diminishing the opportunities for achieving sustainability in marine and inland SSF, and the recognition of the contribution of fisheries to people and societies. Within this context, blue justice, as a contemporary global paradigm, aims to integrate food security, local and global economic growth, biodiversity conservation with other sustainable development objectives. In an effort to acknowledge the potential and diversity of small-scale artisanal fisheries and aquaculture, the United Nations General Assembly declared 2022 as the International Year of Artisanal Fisheries and Aquaculture (IYAFA 2022).[140] Guided by the IYAFA Global Action Plan (GAP),[141] the overall

---

[137] Bugeja Said and Isaacs, *supra* note 113.

[138] Notably the FAO Code of Conduct for Responsible Fisheries, *supra* note 69, Articles 6.18, 7.2.2(c), 7.6.6, 8.4.8, 8.11.3, 9.4.2, 10.1.3; U.N. Economic and Social Council, *Kyoto Declaration on Fisheries and Food Security*, E/CN.17/1996/29 (March 6, 1996), Paras 2 and 17, https://openknowledge.fao.org/items/43d41c7b-7226-4a74-8421-8b3a08d6ec9f

[139] Mary Ann Palma, Martin Tsamenyi, and William Edeson. *Promoting Sustainable Fisheries: The International Legal and Policy Framework to Combat Illegal, Unreported and Unregulated Fishing*, Martinus Nijhoff Publishers (2010).

[140] FAO, About the International Year of Artisanal Fisheries and Aquaculture, https://www.fao.org/artisanal-fisheries-aquaculture-2022/about/en/#:~:text=IYAFA%202022%20aims%20to%20raise,new%20and%20strengthen%20existing%20partnerships (accessed November 29, 2024).

[141] Food and Agricultural Organisation of the United Nations, International Year of Artisanal Fisheries and Aquaculture 2022, Global Action Plan, https://openknowledge.fao.org/server/api/core/bitstreams/b7255e14-ebc6-4a63-b5a5-d46d2a050f0a/content (accessed November 29, 2024).

goal of the Year was to reinforce the U.N. Decade of Family Farming,[142] and empower small-scale artisanal fisheries and aquaculture (including mariculture and aquaponics) systems to secure a sustainable future utilizing mutually reinforcing pillars of work.[143]

The shift of focus in resource governance and use is a clear consequence of FAO's work in developing the 2015 Voluntary Guidelines for Securing Sustainable Small-Scale Fisheries in the Context of Food Security and Poverty Eradication (SSF Guidelines),[144] as well as the proliferation globally, of instruments such as the FAO's 2012 The Voluntary Guidelines on the Responsible Governance of Tenure of Land, Fisheries and Forests in the Context of National Food Security (VGGT Guidelines),[145] the 2018 United Nations Declaration on the Rights of Peasants and Other People Working in Rural Areas (UNDROP)[146] and the 2007 United Nations Declaration on the. Rights of Indigenous Peoples (UNDRIP).[147] Unlike traditional international fisheries instruments, this quartet adopts a distinctive approach centered on a human-rights-based approach (HRBA), within the construct of an ecosystem approach to fisheries (EAF).[148] Despite being voluntary, and therefore soft law, the SSF provides a fundamental role as a framework through which states can align their law and policy in a more equitable and sustainable manner. The Guidelines complement, rather than conflict with existing rights and obligations which states have both at international (and regional) law[149] and accordingly can support a diverse range of rights, including the right to participation in decision-making and management,[150] access to justice and the right to an

---

[142] FAO/IFAD, United Nations Decade of Family Farming (2019 – 2028), *Introducing the UN Decade of Family Farming*, https://www.fao.org/family-farming-decade/home/en/ (accessed November 29, 2024).

[143] Food and Agriculture Organization of the United Nations (FAO). *The International Year of Artisanal Fisheries and Aquaculture (IYAFA 2022)*. Rome: FAO, 2021. Available at https://www.fao.org/in-action/globefish/news-events/news/news-detail/The-International-Year-of-Artisanal-Fisheries-and-Aquaculture-%28IYAFA-2022%29-/en.

[144] SSF Guidelines, *supra* note 62.

[145] FAO, *Voluntary Guidelines on the Responsible Governance of Tenure of Land, Fisheries and Forests in the Context of National Food Security*, https://openknowledge.fao.org/items/609a716c-464c-4454-9222-78f5e7cd23f7 (accessed November 29, 2024).

[146] United Nations Declaration on the Rights of Peasants and Other People Working in Rural Area, A/HRC/RES/39/12 (September 28, 2018), https://digitallibrary.un.org/record/1650694?ln=en&v=pdf.

[147] United Nations Declaration on the Rights of Indigenous Peoples, A/HRC/RES/61/295 (September 13, 2007), https://www.un.org/esa/socdev/unpfii/documents/DRIPS_en.pdf

[148] SSF Guidelines, *supra* note 62.

[149] *Id.*

[150] *Id.*, Paras. 3.1, 5.15 – 5.18, 8.2.

effective remedy,[151] the right to equality and non-discrimination at the national (marginalized groups within SSF communities)[152] regional and international[153] level, the right to basic services and decent standard of living,[154] and the right to decent work.[155] As such, the Guidelines build upon the combination of hard and soft law, which have progressively shaped international fisheries law (IFL), but go beyond the scope of traditional fisheries instruments by integrating both social and environmental concerns.

Combining both elements into the management of fisheries has pervaded ocean governance policy and dialogue,[156] and evolved into the rights-based approach, which is advocated by small-scale fishers and their supporters.[157] Therefore, in addition to supporting the visibility and recognition of the SSF sector, the SSF Guidelines promote socially inclusive SSF by incorporating prominently in their framework, elements for an equitable distribution of fishing rights. This is essential, especially for groups who may be doubly marginalized within the SSF sector, such as women, children, traditional, indigenous and Afro-descendant peoples.[158] While not detracting from the importance of any other marginalized groups, the SSF Guidelines also underscore the importance of recognizing the substantial role played by women in fisheries the world over.[159]Another significant and notable feature of

---

[151] *Id.*, Para 5.11.

[152] SSF Guidelines, *supra* note 62, Paras 3.1, 8.

[153] *Id.*, Paras. 3.1, 5.9, 7.10, 8.

[154] *Id.*, Para 6.2 (services) and generally (food).

[155] *Id.*, Para. 6.

[156] Allison K. Barner et al., *Solutions For Recovering and Sustaining the Bounty of the Ocean: Combining Fishery Reforms, Rights-based Fisheries Management, and Marine Reserves*, OCEANOGRAPHY, 28 (2) (2015), 252-263; Mads Barbesgaard, *Blue Growth: Savior or Ocean Grabbing?*, JOURNAL OF PEASANT STUDIES, 45 (1), (2018), 130-149.

[157] See, Philippa J. Cohen et al., *Securing a Just Space for Small-Scale Fisheries in the Blue Economy*, FRONTIERS IN MARINE SCIENCE, 6 (2019), 171; World Forum of Fisher Peoples (WFFP), World Forum of Fish Harvesters & Fish Workers (WFF), and International Planning Committee for Food Sovereignty (IPC), *A Call for Global Action to Support Small-Scale Fishers, Fish Workers, and Their Communities* (2016), https://www.fao.org/fileadmin/user_upload/COFI/COFI34/observers/AgendaItem8-IPC.pdf (accessed November 29, 2024); Edward H. Allison, Ratana Chuenpagdee, and John Kurien, *Small-Scale Fisheries and Aquaculture: A Vulnerable Livelihoods Perspective*, in R. Quentin Grafton et al., *Handbook of Marine Fisheries Conservation And Management*, Oxford University Press (2012), 404-418.

[158] Alana Malinde S. N. Lancaster, *Decolonising Tenure Rights in the CARICOM & OECS Caribbean: [Re]-assessing the Role of International Legal Instruments*, ASIAN JOURNAL OF INTERNATIONAL LAW (2025) 15 (1), 1 – 45 (forthcoming)

[159] SSF Guidelines, *supra* note 62, Para 8.1 – 8.4.

the SSF Guidelines, is their reinforcement of the core principles of the 2012 VGGT Guidelines, by underscoring the importance of protecting all forms of legitimate tenure rights.[160] This emphasis on tenure by the SSF is imperative, as tenure is fundamental to ensuring access to waters and fishing grounds under national jurisdiction, to achieving equitable outcomes, as well as to engage in redistributive reform.[161] In the Caribbean for example, the importance of these features is even more acute, as tenure issues are exacerbated by the specter of the Region's colonial past, often to the detriment of fishers and other coastal users.[162] This can often marginalize small-scale fishers by impacting critical aspects of their livelihood, such as landing sites in the case of Barbados[163] or the designation of their fishing grounds as a no-take zone, as in the case of Mayreau.[164] Often, these actions lead fishers to be vulnerable to fisheries crime because of their unique skill sets, as illustrated in the previous examples of the Rocky Point fishing community in Jamaica[165] and the island of Old Providence in Columbia.[166]

In South Africa, the implementation of the Small-Scale Fisheries Policy in 2012 was a result of extensive advocacy and legal action by small-scale fishers and their representatives. This policy aims to recognize and protect the rights of SSF fishers, ensuring their participation in decision-making processes and access to marine resources. SSF fishers have also been involved in community-based monitoring programs, where they report illegal fishing activities and

---

[160] *Id.*, Para. 5.1, 5.4

[161] *Id.*, Para. 5.8. See Elisa Morgera and Julia Nakamura, *Shedding a Light on the Human Rights of Small-scale Fishers: Complementarities and Contrasts between the UN Declaration on Peasants' Rights and the Small-Scale Fisheries Guidelines,* in Mariagrazia Alabrese et al., *The United Nations' Declaration On Peasants' Rights,* 1 ed., Routledge (2022); Sumudu Atapattu, Carmen G. Gonzalez, and Sara L. Seck (eds.), *THE CAMBRIDGE HANDBOOK OF ENVIRONMENTAL JUSTICE AND SUSTAINABLE DEVELOPMENT,* Cambridge University Press (2021).

[162] Lancaster, *supra* note 158; Tim P. Clark and Andrés M. Cisneros-Montemayor, *Colonialism and the Blue Economy: Confronting Historical Legacies to enable Equitable Ocean* Development, ECOLOGY AND SOCIETY, 29 (3) (2024); Ryan S. Mohammed et al., *Colonial Legacies Influence Biodiversity Lessons: How Past Trade Routes and Power Dynamics Shape Present-Day Scientific Research and Professional Opportunities for Caribbean Scientists,* THE AMERICAN NATURALIST, 200 (1), (2022), 140-155.

[163] Lancaster, *supra* note 158.

[164] Lancaster Salmon et al., *supra* note 60.

[165] Witbooi, *supra* note 53.

[166] BBC News, *supra* note 54.

contribute to data collection efforts.[167] The Namibian government has implemented the National Plan of Action for Small-Scale Fisheries (NPOA-SSF) 2022-2026, which aims to enhance the contribution of SSF fishers to sustainable fisheries management. International cooperation and legislative reforms are essential to effectively combat fisheries crimes and promote the sustainable use of marine resources. SSF fishers have been actively involved in initiatives to combat fisheries crimes through community-based surveillance and reporting. For example, in Jamaica, SSF fishers have participated in the Fisheries Management and Development Fund, which supports community-based monitoring and enforcement efforts.[168] Additionally, the Caribbean Regional Fisheries Mechanism (CRFM) has worked with SSF fishers to enhance their capacity to monitor and report illegal fishing activities.[169]

While in the nascent stages, the blue justice approach is, therefore, infiltrating the governance of small-scale fisheries in Africa and the Caribbean. In the upcoming years, African and Caribbean States will need to capitalize on the regional and international approaches to blue justice to consolidate more comprehensive national frameworks.

VI. Conclusion

Fisheries crimes remain a significant manifestation of blue crimes globally, and as illustrated in our comparative assessment, take different, and often unique forms across the oceans between Africa and the Caribbean. While the overarching approach in both regions has been to address fisheries and blue crimes through approaches primarily underpinned by punitive or criminal law mechanisms, it is patent that this strategy is falling short internationally, regionally and nationally, often to the detriment of small-scale fishers. While we acknowledge that the scale and scope of fisheries crimes require the criminal enforcement approach favored by the UNODC, there are gaps which need to be filled by the blue justice approach, given the importance of fisheries and aquaculture to achieving multiple Sustainable Development Goals (SDGs).

---

167 Government of South Africa, *Policy for the Small Scale Fisheries Sector in South Africa*, Department of Agriculture, Forestry and Fisheries (February 20, 2012), http://www.dalrrd.gov.za/phocadownloadpap/Policy_Documents/Policy%20for%20the%20%20Small%20Scale%20Fisheries%20Sector%20in%20South%20Africa.pdf (accessed September 29, 2024).

168 Garfield L. Angus, *Fisheries Management Fund in Healthy Position*, Jamaica Information Service, (October 27, 2016), https://jis.gov.jm/fisheries-management-fund-healthy-position/ (accessed September 29, 2024).

169 *Caribbean Community Common Fisheries Policy*, *supra* note 102, Articles 4.3 (d), 14.3 (a), 20.1 (d).

Within this context, many of the global instruments often utilized to address fisheries crimes have not been successful in addressing the impacts on small-scale fishers and other coastal users, nor safeguarding their rights. The same can be said of many national laws, which are often steeped in colonial inequities. On the other hand, regional instruments, most notably the Ålesund Resolution, are increasingly endeavoring to stem the gap by incorporating human rights-based approaches, and indeed, it was this regional response to fisheries crime which led this perspective to percolate into the global instruments such as the Copenhagen Declaration. This Declaration, which broadly reconceptualizes the lens through which fisheries crime is addressed in both the international and national context, has led to a unified response including its endorsement by African and Caribbean States. Additionally, the Declaration sets out to address blue justice in fisheries crimes within the transnational context, and as we have highlighted in this Chapter, this approach can be supported by instruments which pivot the approach of international fisheries law from one of solely a governance approach, to one guided by human rights and the ecosystem approach to fisheries. This new paradigm is fundamental to complementing the current approach to fisheries crimes, and closely aligns small-scale fisheries in Africa and the Caribbean within the framework of the Sustainable Development Goals.

Bibliography

African Charter on Maritime Security and Safety and Development in Africa (Lomé Charter) (October 15, 2016), https://au.int/en/treaties/african-charter-maritime-security-and-safety-and-development-africa-lome-charter.

African Defense Forum, Human Trafficking Victims Discovered on Shadowy Fishing Vessels in Namibia, Adf Magazine (October 11, 2022), https://adf-magazine.com/2022/10/human-trafficking-victims-discovered-on-shadowy-fishing-vessels-in-namibia/.

African Union, *2050 Africa's Integrated Maritime Strategy (2050 AIM Strategy)* (2012), https://www.nairobiconvention.org/clearinghouse/sites/default/files/2050%20Africa%E2%80%99s%20Integrated%20Maritime%20%28AIM%29%20Strategy.pdf.

African Union Commission and NEPAD Planning and Coordinating Agency, *Policy Framework and Reform Strategy for Fisheries and Aquaculture in Africa* (May 2014), https://au.int/sites/default/files/documents/30266-doc-au-ibar_-_fisheries_policy_framework_and_reform_strategy.pdf.

African Union Inter-African Bureau for Animal Resources. *Policy Brief on Strategies for Institutional Coordination Between RECs and RFBs and Strengthening Their Relationships with NSAs* (2022), http://repository.au-ibar.org/bitstream/handle/123456789/1508/Policy%20Brief%20%20on%20strategies%20for%20institutional%20coordination%20%28Final%20Version%202%29141022.pdf?sequence=1

David J. Agnew et al., *Estimating the Worldwide Extent of Illegal Fishing,* PLOS ONE 4 (2) (2009): e4570, doi:10.1371/journal.pone.0004570.

Agreement Concerning Co-Operation in Suppressing Illicit Maritime and Air Trafficking in Narcotic Drugs and Psychotropic Substances in the Caribbean Area (Treaty of San José) (April 10, 2003), Article 25, https://zoek.officielebekendmakingen.nl/trb-2003-82.pdf (accessed November 29, 2024).

Agreement under the United Nations Convention on the Law of the Sea on the Conservation and Sustainable Use of Marine Biological Diversity of Areas Beyond National Jurisdiction (June 19, 2023), https://documents.un.org/doc/undoc/ltd/n23/177/28/pdf/n2317728.pdf.

Edward H. Allison, Ratana Chuenpagdee, and John Kurien, *Small-Scale Fisheries and Aquaculture: A Vulnerable Livelihoods Perspective,* in R. Quentin Grafton et al., Handbook of Marine Fisheries Conservation and Management, Oxford University Press (2012), 404-418.

Garfield L. Angus, *Fisheries Management Fund in Healthy Position,* Jamaica Information Service, (October 27, 2016), https://jis.gov.jm/fisheries-management-fund-healthy-position/ (accessed September 29, 2024).

Sumudu Atapattu, Carmen G. Gonzalez, and Sara L. Seck (eds.), The Cambridge Handbook of Environmental Justice and Sustainable Development, Cambridge University Press (2021). https://doi.org/10.1017/9781108555791.

Corin Bailey et al., *Rural Poverty in the Caribbean: Assets, Social Exclusion and Agricultural Livelihoods,* Case Study, FAO (2024), 24, https://openknowledge.fao.org/server/api/core/bitstreams/cf2c9abb-be9e-42ea-a2a4-f483c927f588/content.

Barbados, *Fisheries (Management) Regulations 1998,* s. 2, https://www.fao.org/faolex/results/details/en/c/LEX-FAOC018057 (accessed September 29, 2024).

Barbados, *Fisheries (Sea Egg Closed Season) Notice, 2015,* https://www.barbadoslawcourts.gov.bb/assets/content/pdfs/annuals/statutoryinstrumentsannual/sIs2015/SI2015No72.pdf, (accessed November 29, 2024).

Mads Barbesgaard, *Blue Growth: Savior or Ocean Grabbing?*, Journal of Peasant Studies, 45 (1), (2018), 130-149. https://doi.org/10.1080/03066150.2017.1377186.

Allison K. Barner et al., *Solutions For Recovering and Sustaining the Bounty of the Ocean: Combining Fishery Reforms, Rights-based Fisheries Management, and Marine Reserves,* Oceanography, 28 (2) (2015), 252-263. https://doi.org/10.5670/oceanog.2015.51.

BBC News, *Fishrot: The Corruption Scandal Entwining Namibia and Iceland,* (February 6, 2023), https://www.bbc.com/news/world-africa-64526018.

BBC News, *The Island Where Men Are Disappearing* (October 12, 2015), https://www.bbc.com/news/magazine-34487450 .

Dyhia Belhabib and U. Rashid Sumaila, T*he Blue Economy–Cultural Livelihood–Ecosystem Approach: The Case of Africa,* Frontiers in Marine Science 7 (2020), 586, https://doi.org/10.3389/fmars.2020.00586.

Benguela Current Convention, *Overview of the Benguela Current Convention,* https://www.benguelacc.org/bcc-overview/ (accessed September 29, 2024).

Nathan J. Bennett et al., *Blue Growth and Blue Justice: Ten Risks and Solutions for the Ocean Economy*, Marine Policy 125 (2021), 104387. https://doi.org/10.1016/j.marpol.2020.104387.

Nathan J. Bennett et al., *Environmental (in) justice in the Anthropocene ocean*, Marine Policy 147 (2023), 105383, https://doi.org/10.1016/j.marpol.2022.105383.

Nathan J. Bennett et al., *Towards a Blue Justice Framework: Integrating Social Equity and Environmental Sustainability in Marine Conservation*, Marine Policy 87 (2018), 194-204. https://doi.org/10.1016/j.marpol.2017.10.023.

Blue Justice, The International Declaration on Transnational Organised Crime in the Global Fishing Industry (the Copenhagen Declaration) (October 15, 2018) https://bluejustice.org/copenhagen-declaration/.

Jessica L. Blythe, et al., *Blue justice: A review of emerging scholarship and resistance movements*, Cambridge Prisms: Coastal Futures 1 (2023): e15. https://doi.org/10.1017/cft.2023.4.

Shekar Bose, *Law Enforcement, Compliance, and Fisheries Sustainability* in Laith A. Jawad (ed), The Arabian Seas: Biodiversity, Environmental Challenges and Conservation Measures (Springer Nature) (2021), 829-844. https://doi.org/10.1007/978-3-030-51506-5_35.

C. Brugere, et al., *Humanizing Aquaculture Development: Putting Social and Human Concerns at the Center of Future Aquaculture Development*, Journal of the World Aquaculture Society, 54 (2) (2023), 482-526. https://doi.org/10.1111/jwas.12959.

Christian Bueger and Timothy Edmunds, *Blue Crime: Conceptualising Transnational Organised Crime at Sea*, MARINE POLICY 119 (2020),104067, https://doi.org/10.1016/j.marpol.2020.104067.

Caribbean Community, *Caribbean Community Common Fisheries Policy (CCCFP)*, https://caricom.org/documents/12304-cccf-policy.pdf (accessed September 29, 2024).

Carlos A. Cruz Carillo, *The Advisory Jurisdiction of ITLOS: From Uncertainties to Opportunities for Ocean Governance*, in Froukje Maria Platjouw and Alla Pozdnakova (eds), The Environmental Rule of Law for Oceans, Designing Legal Solutions (Cambridge University Press) (2023). https://doi.org/10.1017/9781009253741.

Christine M. Chinkin, *The Challenge of Soft Law: Development and Change in International Law*, The International and Comparative Law Quarterly, 38(4) (1989), 850–66. http://www.jstor.org/stable/759917. https://doi.org/10.1093/iclqaj/38.4.850.

Tim P. Clark and Andrés M. Cisneros-Montemayor, *Colonialism and the Blue Economy: Confronting Historical Legacies to enable Equitable Ocean* Development, Ecology and Society, 29 (3) (2024). https://doi.org/10.5751/ES-15122-290304.

CLME+ Project, Catalysing Implementation of the Strategic Action Programme for the Sustainable Management of Shared Living Marine Resources in the Caribbean and North Brazil Shelf Large Marine Ecosystems, https://www.clmeproject.org/ (accessed September 29, 2024).

Philippa J. Cohen et al., *Securing a Just Space for Small-Scale Fisheries in the Blue Economy*, Frontiers in Marine Science, 6 (2019), 171. https://doi.org/10.3389/fmars.2019.00171.

Christopher Costello et al., *The Future of Food from the Sea*, in Jane Lubchenci and Peter M, Haugan (eds) The Blue Compendium, From Knowledge to Action for a Sustainable Ocean Economy, Springer (2023, 2024), 1, https://doi.org/10.1007/978-3-031-16277-0.

Shelly-Ann Cox, Sea Egg Season Remains Closed, Barbados Fisheries Division (September 3, 2023), https://www.fisheries.gov.bb/sea-egg-season-remains-closed/.

Janice Cumberbatch, *Case Study of the Folkestone Marine Park and Reserve, Barbados*, Canari Technical Report No. 281, Caribbean National Resources Institute (CANARI) (2001), https://tools.thecpag.org/sites/default/files/2021-02/Case%20Study%20of%20the%20Folkestone%20Marine%20Park%20and%20Reserve%20Barbados.pdf.

Eve de Coning and Emma Witbooi, *Towards a new' fisheries crime' paradigm: South Africa as an Illustrative Example*, Marine Policy 60 (2015), 208-215, https://doi.org/10.1016/j.marpol.2015.06.024.

Environmental Justice Foundation, *A Human Rights Lens on the Impacts of Industrial Illegal Fishing and Overfishing in Ghana* (2021), https://ejfoundation.org/resources/downloads/EJF-DIHR-socio-economic-report-2021-final.pdf.

European Institute for International Law and International Relations, *The Blue Economy and its Related Crimes* (June 8, 2023), https://www.eiir.eu/strategic-affairs/international-economy/the-blue-economy-and-its-related-crimes/.

Lucia Fanning, Robin Mahon, and Patrick McConney, *Focusing on Living Marine Resource Governance: The Caribbean Large Marine Ecosystem and Adjacent Areas Project*, Coastal Management 37 (3-4) (2009), 219-234. https://doi.org/10.1080/08920750902851203

Fisheries Committee for the West Central Gulf of Guinea, *About Us: Fisheries Committee for the West Central Gulf of Guinea*, https://fcwc-fish.org/about-us (accessed September 29, 2024).

Fisheries Committee for the West Central Gulf of Guinea, *Regional MCS Centre – Fisheries Committee for the West Central Gulf of Guinea*, https://fcwc-fish.org/regional-mcs-centre (accessed September 29, 2024).

Food and Agricultural Organization of the United Nations, *About the International Year of Artisanal Fisheries and Aquaculture*, https://www.fao.org/artisanal-fisheries-aquaculture-2022/about/en/#:~:text=IYAFA%202022%20aims%20to%20raise,new%20and%20strengthen%20existing%20partnerships (accessed November 29, 2024).

Food and Agriculture Organization of the United Nations. *Agreement on Port State Measures to Prevent, Deter and Eliminate Illegal, Unreported and Unregulated Fishing* (November 22, 2009), https://www.fao.org/fileadmin/user_upload/legal/docs/037t-e.pdf.

Food and Agricultural Organization of the United Nations, *Blue Transformation in Brief: Advancing Aquatic Ecosystems for Prosperity and Well-being* (2023), https://openknowledge.fao.org/server/api/core/bitstreams/ac40a573-c505-4f1d-a5a2-422e0eaf7a45/content#.

Food and Agricultural Organization of the United Nations, *Blue Transformation: FAO's Work on Aquatic Food Systems*, https://openknowledge.fao.org/server/api/core/bitstreams/39ef1d5b-0bee-4c31-9883-1325a44c48a8/content#.

Food and Agricultural Organization, *Blue Transformation: A Vision For Transforming Aquatic Food Systems*, https://openknowledge.fao.org/server/api/core/bitstreams/9df19f53-b931-4d04-acd3-58a71c6b1a5b/content/sofia/2022/transforming-aquatic-based-food.html.

Food and Agriculture Organization of the United Nations, *Code of Conduct for Responsible Fisheries* (1995), https://www.fao.org/3/v9878e/v9878e00.htm.

Food and Agricultural Organization of the United Nations, *Guidelines for Sustainable Aquaculture*, FAO Committee on Fisheries (July 8 – 12, 2024), https://openknowledge.fao.org/server/api/core/bitstreams/b87a56eb-749d-4e76-b952-413708c021e0/content.

Food and Agriculture Organization of the United Nations, *The International Year of Artisanal Fisheries and Aquaculture (IYAFA 2022)*. Rome: FAO, 2021. Available at https://www.fao.org/in-action/globefish/news-events/news/news-detail/The-International-Year-of-Artisanal-Fisheries-and-Aquaculture-%28IYAFA-2022%29-/en.

Food and Agricultural Organization of the United Nations, *The State of World Fisheries and Aquaculture: Blue Transformation in Action* (2024), xxi https://openknowledge.fao.org/server/api/core/bitstreams/f985caed-cc7a-457e-8107-7ce16c6ef209/content.

Food and Agriculture Organization of the United Nations, *Voluntary Guidelines for Flag State Performance* (2015), https://openknowledge.fao.org/server/api/core/bitstreams/903d8997-7bc8-4c88-8d93-e6f57cf5609d/content.

Food and Agriculture Organization of the United Nations, *Voluntary Guidelines on the Responsible Governance of Tenure of Land, Fisheries and Forests in the Context of National Food Security*, https://openknowledge.fao.org/items/609a716c-464c-4454-9222-78f5e7cd23f7 (accessed November 29, 2024).

Food and Agriculture Organization of the United Nations. *Voluntary Guidelines for Securing Sustainable Small-Scale Fisheries in the Context of Food Security and Poverty Eradication*, FAO (2015), https://www.fao.org/3/a-i4356en.pdf.

Food and Agricultural Organization of the United Nations/IFAD, United Nations Decade of Family Farming (2019 – 2028), *Introducing the UN Decade of Family Farming*, https://www.fao.org/family-farming-decade/home/en/ (accessed November 29, 2024).

Miguel G García-Revillo, *International Tribunal for the Law of the Sea (ITLOS)*, Yearbook of International Environmental Law, 29 (2018), 381–383. https://doi.org/10.1093/yiel/yvz058.

William C. Gilmore, *Agreement Concerning Co-operation in Suppressing Illicit Maritime and Air Trafficking in Narcotic Drugs and Psychotropic Substances in the Caribbean Area, 2003*, The Stationery Office (2005), 8.

GNA, *Closed Season: The Woes of Women and Children in Fishing Communities*, MyJoyOnline (July 30, 2023), https://www.myjoyonline.com/closed-season-the-woes-of-women-and-children-in-fishing-communities/#google_vignette (accessed September 29, 2024).

Simon Goddek, et.al. (eds.), Aquaponics Food Production Systems: Combined Aquaculture and Hydroponic Production Technologies For the Future, Springer Open, (2019). https://doi.org/10.1007/978-3-030-15943-6.

Government of South Africa, *Policy for the Small Scale Fisheries Sector in South Africa*, Department of Agriculture, Forestry and Fisheries (February 20, 2012), http://www.dalrrd.gov.za/phocadownloadpap/Policy_Documents/Policy%20for%20the%20%20Small%20Scale%20Fisheries%20Sector%20in%20South%20Africa.pdf (accessed September 29, 2024).

Government of St. Vincent and the Grenadines, *Fisheries Regulations 1987*, https://natlex.ilo.org/dyn/natlex2/r/natlex/fe/details?p3_isn=3608 (accessed September 29, 2024).

Maria Hauck and Neville A. Sweijd, *A Case Study of Abalone Poaching in South Africa and its Impact on Fisheries Management*, Ices Journal of Marine Science, 56 (6), (1999), 1024-1032. https://doi.org/10.1006/jmsc.1999.0534.

Maria Hauck and Merle Sowman, *Poaching, Security and the State in South Africa: Evolving Perspectives on Abalone Crime*, Journal of Southern African Studies, 46 (4) (2020), 707-724. https://doi.org/10.1080/03057070.2020.1795225.

High Level Panel on a Sustainable Ocean Economy, The International Declaration on Transnational Organized Crime in the Global Fishing Industry and the Blue Justice Initiative, https://action.oceanpanel.org/initiative/norway/the-international-declaration-on-transnational-organized-crime-in-the-global-fishing-industry-and-the-blue-justice-initiative/ (accessed September 29, 2024).

Daniel Hoggarth, *Tobago Cays Marine Park 2007-2009 Management Plan*, Organisation of Eastern Caribbean States and Environment and Sustainable Development Unit (2007).

Inter-American Court of Human Rights, *Case of the Miskito Divers (Lemoth Morris et al.) v Honduras*, Judgement of August 31, 2021, https://www.corteidh.or.cr/docs/casos/articulos/seriec_432_ing.pdf (accessed November 29, 2024).

International Labour Organization, *Work in Fishing Convention, 2007 (No. 188)* (2007), https://www.ilo.org/dyn/normlex/en/f?p=NORMLEXPUB:12100:0::NO::P12100_ILO_CODE:C188.

International Tribunal for the Law of the Sea, *Advisory Opinion in Case No. 31, Request Submitted to the Tribunal by the Commission of Small Island States on Climate Change and International Law*, ITLOS (May 21, 2024), https://www.itlos.org/fileadmin/itlos/documents/cases/31/Advisory_Opinion/C31_Adv_Op_21.05.2024_orig.pdf.

International Tribunal for the Law of the Sea, *International Agreements Conferring Jurisdiction on the Tribunal*, https://www.itlos.org/en/main/jurisdiction/international-agreements-conferring-jurisdiction-on-the-tribunal/.

International Tribunal for the Law of the Sea, *Request for Advisory Opinion Submitted by the Sub-Regional Fisheries Commission (SRFC Advisory Opinion), Advisory Opinion* (2 April 2015), paras. ¶¶ 54–56, https://www.itlos.org/index.php?id=252. https://doi.org/10.5305/intelegamate.54.5.0890.

Interpol, *International Law Enforcement Cooperation in the Fisheries Sector: A Guide for Law Enforcement Practitioners*, Interpol General Secretariat (2018), https://www.interpol.int/Crimes/Environmental-crime/Fisheries-crime.

IPPR, FIAM International & ICJ, *Human Rights Violations, Transnational Corporations and a Scandal in the Fishing Industry, CIVIC264* (March 31, 2022), https://www.civic264.org.na/images/pdf/2022/3/Fishrot-humanrightsimpact_1.pdf

Martin Isaacs, *The Role of Fisheries Crime in the Blue Economy,* Marine Policy 104 (2019), 123-130, doi:10.1016/j.marpol.2019.02.005.

Moenieba Isaacs, *Fisheries crime, Human Rights and Small-Scale Fisheries in South Africa: A Case of Bigger Fish to Fry,* Marine Policy 105 (2019): 158-168, https://doi.org/10.1016/j.marpol.2018.12.023

Moenieba Isaacs, *Is The Blue Justice Concept a Human Rights Agenda?,* African Portal: Policy Brief, 54 (2019), 1–5. http://hdl.handle.net/10566/5087.

Simon Jennings et al., *Aquatic Food Security: Insights Into Challenges and Solutions From An Analysis of Interactions Between Fisheries, Aquaculture, Food Safety, Human Health, Fish And Human Welfare, Economy and Environment,* Fish and Fisheries, 17 (4) (2016), 893-938. https://doi.org/10.1111/faf.12152.

Svein Jentoft et al. (eds), Blue Justice: Small-Scale Fisheries in a Sustainable Ocean Economy, Springer Nature (2022). https://doi.org/10.1007/978-3-030-89624-9

Svein Jentoft and Ratana Chuenpagdee, *Interactive Learning and Governance Transformation for Securing Blue Justice for Small-Scale Fisheries,* Administration and Society 54 (7) (2022), 1255-1282. https://doi.org/10.1177/00953997211073947.

Alana Malinde S. N. Lancaster, *A Sea of Challenges, But an Ocean of Possibilities: Examining the Nexus between Maritime Security & Safeguarding the Rights of Ocean-dependent Populations in Caribbean Small Island Developing States,* Caribbean Law Review 22 (2) (2025) (forthcoming).

Alana Malinde S. N. Lancaster, *Full Seas, Floods & Fortunes? Fathoming The Impact of the ITLOS Advisory Opinion to the Future of Climate Justice for Climate Vulnerable Populations in Large Ocean States* in Ezio Costa Costa Cordella and Pilar Moraga Sariego (eds.), States Responsibilities in the Climate Crisis: Legal Standards and Global Litigation (Tirant Lo Blanch), (2024).

Alana Malinde S. N. Lancaster, *Decolonising Tenure Rights in the CARICOM & OECS Caribbean: [Re]-assessing the Role of International Legal Instruments,* Asian Journal of International Law (2025) 15 (1), 1 – 45 (forthcoming).

Alana Malinde S. N. Lancaster et al., *De La Pesca al Cultivo del Medio Marino: El Caso Exitoso de la Gestión Comunitaria en Mayreau, Cayos de Tobago y San Vincente y Las Granadinas,* in Lina María Saavedra-Díaz y Maria Claudia Díazgranados, Comunidades Con Voz: El Futuro de La Pesca Artesanal En Latino America Y E Caribe, Editoral Madgalena/Conservation International Foundation/NORAD/Universidad del Magdalena (2022), 1 – 33, https://editorial.unimagdalena.edu.co/Editorial/Publicacion/4236.

Gabrielle Lout et al., *Decent Work in a Seascape of Livelihoods: Regional Evaluation of the Shrimp and Groundfish Fishery of the Guianas-Brazil Shelf,* Marine Policy 144 (2022), 105231. https://doi.org/10.1016/j.marpol.2022.105231.

Robin Mahon and Michael B. Mascia, The Barbados (Alias Folkestone) Marine Reserve, Barbados: A Late Bloomer?, *Gulf and Caribbean Research* 14.2 (2003): 171-180. https://doi.org/10.18785/gcr.1402.14.

Robin Mahon and Christopher Parker, *Barbados Sea Eggs, Past, Present, Future*, Fisheries Management Plan, Public Information Document No. 1, Fisheries Division, Ministry of Agriculture and Rural Development, Barbados (1999), https://www.fisheries.gov.bb/content/files/2023/09/Mahon_1999_sea_eggs_past_present_future.pdf.

Carmelo Maucieri et al., *Hydroponic Systems and Water Management In Aquaponics: A Review*, Italian Journal of Agronomy 13 (1) (2018), 1012. https://doi.org/10.4081/ija.2017.1012.

Channing Mavrellis, *The Serious Impacts of Fisheries Crime*, Global Financial Integrity (October 22, 2018), https://gfintegrity.org/the-serious-impacts-of-fisheries-crime/.

Patrick McConney, Hazel A. Oxenford, and Milton Haughton, Management in the Gulf and Caribbean: Mosaic or Melting Pot?, Gulf and Caribbean Research, 19 (2) (2007), 103-112, https://aquila.usm.edu/cgi/viewcontent.cgi?article=1422&context=gcr. https://doi.org/10.18785/gcr.1902.13.

Patrick McConney, Robin Mahon and Christopher Parker, Barbados Case Study: The Sea Egg Fishery, CCA/CERMES/MRAG (2003), https://citeseerx.ist.psu.edu/document?repid=rep1&type=pdf&doi=de4673fa0523742322cf3ce72ca3a8ce262a9358.

Elizabeth Mendenhall, *Advancing the International Law of the Sea to Address Illegal, Unreported, and Unregulated Fishing Future Fisheries Management*, Issue Brief, Mercatus Center (October 18, 2023), https://www.mercatus.org/research/policy-briefs/advancing-international-law-sea-address-illegal-unreported-and-unregulated. https://doi.org/10.2139/ssrn.4608523.

Dana D. Miller, and U. Rashid Sumaila, *Flag Use Behavior and IUU Activity within the International Fishing Fleet: Refining Definitions and Identifying Areas of Concern*, Marine Policy 44 (2014), 204-211, https://doi.org/10.1016/j.marpol.2013.08.027.

Ryan S. Mohammed et al., *Colonial Legacies Influence Biodiversity Lessons: How Past Trade Routes and Power Dynamics Shape Present-Day Scientific Research and Professional Opportunities for Caribbean Scientists*, The American Naturalist, 200 (1), (2022), 140-155. https://doi.org/10.1086/720154.

Elisa Morgera and Julia Nakamura, *Shedding a Light on the Human Rights of Small-scale Fishers: Complementarities and Contrasts between the UN Declaration on Peasants' Rights and the Small-Scale Fisheries Guidelines*, in Mariagrazia Alabrese et al., The United Nations' Declaration on Peasants' Rights, 1 ed., Routledge (2022). https://doi.org/10.2139/ssrn.3850133.

Nature Crime Alliance, *Why Multisector Collaboration is Critical in the Fight Against Illegal Fishing* (September 27, 2024), https://naturecrimealliance.org/multi-sector-action-critical-to-fight-illegal-fishing/.

Holly J. Niner et al., *Reflections on the Past, Present, and Potential Futures of Knowledge Hierarchies in Ocean Biodiversity Governance*, Frontiers in Marine Science 11 (2024), https://doi.org/10.3389/fmars.2024.1347494.

Nordic Council of Ministers, *Nordic Minister Statement on Transnational Organized Fisheries Crime*, (June 28, 2017), https://www.norden.org/en/declaration/nordic-minister-statement-transnational-organized-fisheries-crime.

Marieke Norton, *The Militarisation of Marine Resource Conservation and Law Enforcement in the Western Cape, South Africa*, Marine Policy 60 (2015), 338-344, https://doi.org/10.1016/j.marpol.2014.09.007.

Samuel Nyavor et al., *Compensation Payment for Fisherfolk During Closed-Season Fishing: Lessons from Small-Scale Fisherfolk in Ghana*, Cogent Social Sciences, 9 (2) (2023), https://doi.org/10.1080/23311886.2023.2282502

Ifesinachi Okafor-Yarwood, *The Cyclical Nature of Maritime Security Threats: Illegal, Unreported and Unregulated Fishing as a Threat to Human and National Security in the Gulf of Guinea*, African Security, 14 (2) (2021), 123-146, doi:10.1080/19392206.2021.1982241.

Sara Orofino et al., *Opportunities and Challenges for Improving Fisheries Management Through Greater Transparency in Vessel Tracking*, ICES Journal of Marine Science, 80 (4), (2023), 675-689. https://doi.org/10.1093/icesjms/fsad008

Victor Owusu et al., *Factors Influencing Compliance of Closed Fishing Season: Lessons from Small-Scale Coastal Fisheries in the Central Region of Ghana*, Humanities and Social Science Communications 10 (2023), 20, https://doi.org/10.1057/s41599-023-01513-4

Mary Ann Palma, Martin Tsamenyi, and William Edeson, Promoting Sustainable Fisheries: The International Legal and Policy Framework to Combat Illegal, Unreported and Unregulated Fishing, Martinus Nijhoff Publishers (2010). https://doi.org/10.1163/ej.9789004175754.i-341.

Khemraj Parsram, Barbados Case Study: The Sea Egg Fishery, A Summary of Lessons Learnt, CCA/CERMES (2004), https://assets.publishing.service.gov.uk/media/57a08cbded915d3cfd00159c/R8317Barb2.pdf.

Efthymios Papastavridis, The Interception of Vessels on the High Seas, Hart Publishing Limited (2013), 221.

Gohar A. Petrossian, *Preventing Illegal, Unreported and Unregulated (IUU) Fishing: A Situational Crime Prevention Approach*, Biological Conservation 189 (2015), 39-48, https://doi.org/10.1016/j.biocon.2014.09.005.

Jonathan Pugh, *Speaking Without Voice: Participatory Planning, Acknowledgment, and Latent Subjectivity in Barbados*, Annals of the Association of American Geographers, 103 (5) (2013), 1226 – 1281. https://doi.org/10.1080/00045608.2012.706571

Republic of Ghana, *Fisheries Act 2002*, https://faolex.fao.org/docs/pdf/gha34737.pdf (accessed September 29, 2024).

Republic of Namibia, *Marine Resources Act, 2000*, https://www.fao.org/faolex/results/details/en/c/LEX-FAOC044344/ (accessed September 29, 2024).

Republic of South Africa, *Marine Living Resources Act 1998*, ss. 44 (1) (a); 58(1) (b), https://www.fao.org/faolex/results/details/en/c/LEX-FAOC015984/ (accessed September 29, 2024).

Revised Treaty of Chaguaramas Establishing the Caribbean Community including the CARICOM Single Market and Economy, https://caricom.org/documents/4906-revised_treaty-text.pdf (accessed September 29, 2024).

Alba Garcia Rodriguez and Lucia M. Fanning, *Assessing Marine Protected Areas Effectiveness: A Case Study with the Tobago Cays Marine Park*, Open Journal of

Marine Science 7 (3) (2017), 379-408. https://doi.org/10.4236/ojms.2017.73027.

Rules of the International Tribunal for the Law of the Sea (October 28, 1997; amended September 25, 2018), Art. 138, https://www.itlos.org/fileadmin/itlos/documents/basic_texts/Itlos_8_E_17_03_09.pdf.

SafeSeas, Panel - *Towards a 'Blue' Criminology: How Should We Study Transnational Organised Crime at Sea?* SafeSeas (December 2, 2021), https://www.safeseas.net/panel-towards-a-blue-criminology-how-should-we-study-transnational-organised-crime-at-sea/.

Alicia Bugeja Said and Moenieba Isaacs, Blue Justice: Small-Scale Fisheries in a Sustainable Ocean Economy (Springer Nature), 2021.

Tajudeen Sanni, *SDG 14: Life under water,* in Ralf Michaels, Verónica Ruiz Abou-Nhim and Hans van Loon (eds), The Private Side of Transforming Our World – UN Sustainable Development Goals 2030 and the Role of Private International Law, https://www.intersentiaonline.com/publication/the-private-side-of-transforming-our-world-un-sustainable-development-goals-2030-and-the-role-of-p/16 (accessed November 15, 2024).

Kenneth Sherman, *The Large Marine Ecosystem Concept: Research and Management Strategy for Living Marine Resources,* Ecological Applications, 1(4) (1991), 349-360. https://doi.org/10.2307/1941896.

Bertha Simmons and Patrick McConney, *Tobago Cays Marine Park: Are The Conditions for Successful Co-Management Likely to be Met?,* Ceremes Technical Report No. 6, Centre for Resources Management and Environmental Studies (Ceremes) (2006), 10, https://www.cavehill.uwi.edu/cermes/docs/technical_reports/simmons_2006_tcmp_co_management_conditions_ctr_06.aspx.

Doris Soto, *Integrated Mariculture:* A Global Review, FAO Technical Paper No. 529 (2009).

André Standing, *Criminality in Africa's Fishing Industry: A Threat to Human Security, ISS Africa Report,* (June 6, 2017), https://africacenter.org/publication/criminality-africa-fishing-industry-threat-human-security/.

Statute of the International Tribunal for the Law of the Sea (December 10, 1982), Article 20, 21.

Tim Stephens and Donald R Rothwell, *The LOSC Framework for Maritime Jurisdiction and Enforcement 30 Years On,* The International Journal of Marine and Coastal Law, 27 (2012, 701 – 709, https://openresearch-repository.anu.edu.au/server/api/core/bitstreams/ba3eead3-8499-4409-b7d5-7257e5ced471/content. https://doi.org/10.1163/15718085-12341250.

Gunnar Stølsvik, *The Development of the Fisheries Crime Concept and Processes to Address It in the International Arena,* Marine Policy 99 (2019), 243-249, doi:10.1016/j.marpol.2018.12.027.

Rohana Subasinghe, Doris Soto, and Jiansan Jia, *Global Aquaculture and Its Role in Sustainable* Development, Reviews in Acquaculture, 1 (1) (2009), 2-9. https://doi.org/10.1111/j.1753-5131.2008.01002.x.

Sub-Regional Fisheries Commission, http://spcsrp.org/en (accessed September 29, 2024).

U. Rashid Sumaila et al., *Illicit Trade in Marine Resources: Impacts on Economies, Ecosystems, and Fisheries Management*, Nature Communications, 11 (1), (2020), 1-12, https://doi.org/10.1038/s41467-020-17721-2.

Judith Swan, *Fisheries Crime: Bridging the Conceptual Gap and Practical Response*, Marine Policy 134 (2022), 104791, https://doi.org/10.1016/j.marpol.2021.104791.

Lydia C. L. Teh et al., *The Role of Human Rights in Implementing Socially Responsible Seafood*, PLOS ONE, 14 (1) (2019), e0210241. https://doi.org/10.1371/journal.pone.0210241

TMT, *West Africa Task Force: TMT Targeting Illegal Fishing and Associated Crime*, https://www.tm-tracking.org/west-africa-task-force (accessed September 29, 2024).

Treaty Establishing the Regional Security System (RSS Agreement) (March 5, 1996), Article 4 (1), https://assets.ctfassets.net/1yxaau1iba16/6XjfOwHdA6XB32aQiYCPci/e5bb5fae403657a184a22562d37d302f/Treaty_Establishing_the_RSS.pdf (accessed September 29, 2024).

UIA, *Regional Fisheries Advisory Commission for the Southwest Atlantic*, https://uia.org/s/or/en/1100001222 (accessed September 29, 2024).

United Nations, *Agreement for the Implementation of the Provisions of the United Nations Convention on the Law of the Sea of 10 December 1982 Relating to the Conservation and Management of Straddling Fish Stocks and Highly Migratory Fish Stocks* (December 4, 1995), https://www.un.org/oceancapacity/unfsa.

United Nations, *Transforming Our World: The 2030 Agenda for Sustainable Development*, A/RES/70/1 (October 21, 2015), https://sdgs.un.org/2030agenda.

United Nations Convention on the Law of the Sea, 1833 U.N.T.S. 397 (November 16, 1994), https://www.un.org/depts/los/convention_agreements/texts/unclos/unclos_e.pdf.

United Nations Declaration on the Rights of Indigenous Peoples, A/HRC/RES/61/295 (September 13, 2007), https://www.un.org/esa/socdev/unpfii/documents/DRIPS_en.pdf.

United Nations Declaration on the Rights of Peasants and Other People Working in Rural Area, A/HRC/RES/39/12 (September 28, 2018), https://digitallibrary.un.org/record/1650694?ln=en&v=pdf.

U.N. Economic and Social Council, *Kyoto Declaration on Fisheries and Food Security*, E/CN.17/1996/29 (March 6, 1996), Paras 2 and 17, https://openknowledge.fao.org/items/43d41c7b-7226-4a74-8421-8b3a08d6ec9f.

UNEP, *Factsheet: The Protocol on Specially Protected Areas and Wildlife in the Wider Caribbean (SPAW): Tobago Cays Marine Park*, UNEP/CEP/CAR SPAW RAC/CaMPAM, https://www.car-spaw-rac.org/IMG/pdf/factsheet_stvincent_grenadine_tobago_cays.pdf (accessed September 29, 2024).

United Nations General Assembly, *Cooperation between the United Nations and the Caribbean Community*, A/RES/53/17 (16 November 1998), para 15.

United Nations General Assembly, *Oceans and the Law of the Sea*, A/RES/63/111 (December 5, 2008), paras. 98-105, https://sdgs.un.org/documents/ares63111-oceans-and-law-sea-19229.

United Nations General Assembly, *Oceans and the Law of the Sea*, A/RES/72/72 (December 5, 2017), para. 98, https://documents.un.org/doc/undoc/gen/n17/421/83/pdf/n1742183.pdf.

United Nations General Assembly, *Sustainable Fisheries, Including Through the 1995 Agreement for the Implementation of the Provisions of the United Nations Convention on the Law of the Sea of 10 December 1982 Relating to the Conservation and Management of Straddling Fish Stocks and Highly Migratory Fish Stocks, and Related Instruments*, A/RES/63/112 (December 5, 2008), para. 59, https://sdgs.un.org/documents/ares63112-sustainable-fisheries-incl-throug-19230.

United Nations Guiding Principles on Business and Human Rights, Implementing the United Nations "Protect, Respect and Remedy" Framework (2011), https://www.ohchr.org/sites/default/files/documents/publications/guidingprinciplesbusinesshr_en.pdf.

United Nations in the Caribbean, *FAO Calls on Governments and Organizations to Commit to Guaranteeing the Right to Food in Latin America and the Caribbean* (October 9, 2024), https://caribbean.un.org/en/281144-fao-calls-governments-and-organizations-commit-guaranteeing-right-food-latin-america-and.

United Nations Office on Drugs and Crime (UNODC), *Transnational Organized Crime in the Fishing Industry, UNODC* (2011), https://www.unodc.org/documents/human-trafficking/Issue_Paper_-_TOC_in_the_Fishing_Industry.pdf.

United Nations Office on Drugs and Crime (UNODC), *Transnational Organized Crime in the Fishing* Industry: *Focus on: Trafficking in Persons Smuggling of Migrants Illicit Drugs Trafficking*, UNODC (2011), https://www.unodc.org/documents/human-trafficking/Issue_Paper_-_TOC_in_the_Fishing_Industry.pdf.

United Nations Office on Drugs and Crime (UNODC), *Fisheries Crime: Bringing to Light the Perfect Storm of Illegal Activities in the Fishing* Sector, UNODC, https://www.unodc.org/documents/about-unodc/Campaigns/Fisheries/focus_sheet_PRINT.pdf (accessed September 29, 2024).

United Nations Working Group on the Issue of Human Rights and Transnational Corporations and Other Business Enterprises, Investors, Environmental, Social and Governance Approaches and Human Rights, A/HRC/56/55 (May 02, 2024), https://www.ohchr.org/en/documents/thematic-reports/ahrc5655-investors-environmental-social-and-governance-approaches-and (accessed November 29, 2024).

Julio Jorge Urbina, *Towards an International Legal Definition of the Notion of Fisheries Crime*, Marine Policy 119 (2020): 104067, https://doi.org/10.1016/j.marpol.2022.105214.

Hennie van As, *Poaching of Marine Living Resources: Can the Tide Be Turned?*, South African Journal of Science, 120 (1-2) (2024), 1-5, https://doi.org/10.17159/2413-3108/2020/i69a8351.

Emma Witbooi, *Criminality and Resilience: An Assessment of Organized Crime in Jamaica*, Research Report, Global Initiative Against Transnational Organized Crime (February 2020), https://globalinitiative.net/wp-content/uploads/2020/02/Jamaica-report.26.02.v1.pdf. https://doi.org/10.1038/s41586-020-2913-5.

Giselle Vigneron, *Compliance and International Environmental Agreements: A Case Study of the 1995 United Nations Straddling Fish Stocks Agreement,* Geo. Int'l Entl. L. Rev, 10, (1997), 581.

Julia Weston, *The International Tribunal for the Law of the Sea: Its Wide Jurisdiction and Potential to Analyse Current Law of the Sea,* Czech Yearbook of International Law, XIII (2022), 211 – 234.

Emma Witbooi et al., *Organised Crime in the Fisheries Sector,* in Jane Lubchenci and Peter M, Haugan (eds) The Blue Compendium, From Knowledge to Action for a Sustainable Ocean Economy, Springer (2023, 2024), 593, https://doi.org/10.1007/978-3-031-16277-0.

Emma Witbooi et al., *Organised Crime in the Fisheries Sector Threatens a Sustainable Ocean* Economy, Nature, 588, 48 – 56 (2020), https://www.nature.com/articles/s41586-020-2913-5.

Emma Witbooi et al., *Organised Crime in the Fisheries Sector,* Washington, DC: World Resources Institute, 2020), https://oceanpanel.org/blue-papers/organised-crime-associated-fisheries.

World Bank, Oceans, Fisheries and Coastal Economies, World Bank Group (April 3, 2024), https://www.worldbank.org/en/topic/oceans-fisheries-and-coastal-economies (accessed September 29, 2024).

World Forum of Fisher Peoples (WFFP), World Forum of Fish Harvesters & Fish Workers (WFF), and International Planning Committee for Food Sovereignty (IPC), *A Call for Global Action to Support Small-Scale Fishers, Fish Workers, and Their Communities* (2016), https://www.fao.org/fileadmin/user_upload/COFI/COFI34/observers/AgendaItem8-IPC.pdf (accessed November 29, 2024).

Minna Yu and Xinyu Liu, *A New Approach to Combating Illegal, Unreported, and Unregulated Fishing: Analysis of the WTO Agreement on Fisheries* Subsidies, Marine Development 2 (1), 10 (2024). https://doi.org/10.1007/s44312-024-00023-4.

Maysa Zorob and Hector Candray, Justice for Miskito Divers: A Turning Point for Business and Human Rights Standards from the Inter-American Court of Human Rights, Open Global Rights (March 21, 2022), https://www.openglobalrights.org/justice-for-miskito-divers-a-turning-point-for-business-and-human-rights-standards/.

Chapter 5

The End of Piracy: Towards Legal Reform for the First International Crime

Dr Mark Chadwick
Nottingham Trent University

Abstract: In 2019 the ILC announced the inclusion of the prevention and repression of piracy and armed robbery at sea as part of its long-term program of work, this being an area that, it was considered, would benefit from study, codification and progressive development. Piracy is often considered the original international crime whose universal criminalization has, by many accounts, acted as a catalyst for the expansion of international criminal law to include genocide, crimes against humanity, and war crimes. The modern definition of the offense, though, is archaic, ambiguous, prone to manipulation and frequently unhelpful, making it ripe for reconsideration.

This chapter will trace the historical development of the crime of high-seas piracy and the values represented in the present legal definition. Against this backdrop, piracy will be framed in its modern context, with the various problems inherent in the definition examined and exposed, from law enforcement and judicial perspectives. The final part of the chapter will analyze the ILC's proposals and consider options for the future of the oldest international crime.

Keywords: International Law Commission, piracy, Sea Shepard, U.N. Security Council Chapter VII, private ends requirement, Harvard draft, UNCLOS Article 101.

Introduction

> Despite the extensive amount of international, regional and national law [in relation to piracy], there remain important issues of international

> law that are uncertain or underdeveloped, which could benefit from study, codification, and progressive development.[1]

High-seas piracy is the original international crime. Since the time of Cicero, writing in the first century BC,[2] pirates have been denounced as "the bitterest and most dangerous enemy [...], the common enemy of all peoples," or "*communes hostes omnium.*"[3] In the centuries since, pirates have preyed upon and impeded the open commerce of the oceans, often presenting themselves as subversive anti-civilizational rebels.[4] In so doing, piracy became a prime candidate for international proscription, prompting the innovation of universal jurisdiction, an exceptional principle that permits any State to intercept and prosecute anybody who has committed the offense (as defined in international law), regardless of nationality. Universal jurisdiction, while continuing to apply to piracy today, is otherwise restricted only to the most serious crimes of international concern by analogy to the precedent established by high-seas piracy. So, then, the crime of genocide, crimes against humanity, war crimes, and the crime of aggression are similarly subject to universal jurisdiction[5] on the basis that such heinous offenses, in turn, undermine universally recognized standards of international law, as underpinned and informed by human rights considerations in the post-Nuremberg legal order.[6] Without the historical antipathy towards (and gradual

---

[1] International Law Commission, *Report of the International Law Commission* (Seventy-first session, A/74/10, 2019), Annex C (*Prevention and repression of piracy and armed robbery at sea*, drafted by Yacouba Cissé), para 10.

[2] Writing in IN VERREM, 70BC, and DE OFFICIIS, 44BC.

[3] CICERO, IN VERREM Book II, 4.21 and 5.76 (C.D. Yonge trans, George Bell & Sons 1903) (70BC). The term "*hostes humani generis*" is more commonly used, in academic texts, to describe pirates and their relationship with the international community.

[4] MARK CHADWICK, PIRACY AND THE ORIGINS OF UNIVERSAL JURISDICTION: ON STRANGER TIDES 70-72 (Brill, 2018).

[5] See *e.g.* Restatement (Third) of the Foreign Relations Law of the United States s404 (1988); STEPHEN MACEDO et al., THE PRINCETON PRINCIPLES ON UNIVERSAL JURISDICTION (Princeton University, 2001); Case Concerning Application of the Convention on the Prevention and Punishment of the Crime of Genocide (Bosnia and Herzegovina v. Serbia and Montenegro), 2007 I.C.J. 43 (Feb. 2007); Jorgić v. Germany (Application no. 74613/01), 2007 European Court of Human Rights, paras 68-70; 1949 Geneva Conventions, Articles 49/50/129/146 of Conventions I-IV, respectively; TRIAL INTERNATIONAL, UNIVERSAL JURISDICTION ANNUAL REVIEW 2024 (2024); Kenneth C. Randall, *Universal Jurisdiction under International Law,* 66 TEX. L. REV. 785 (1987-88); Michael P. Scharf, *Universal Jurisdiction and the Crime of Aggression,* 53 HARV. INT'L L.J. 358 (2012); Maximo Langer, *Universal Jurisdiction is Not Disappearing,* 13 J. INT'L CRIM. JUST. 245 (2015).

[6] Christian Tomuschat, *The Legacy of Nuremberg,* 4 J. INT'L CRIM. JUST. 830, 840 (2006).

proscription of) high-seas piracy, we would need to look elsewhere for the foundations of international criminal law. In this way, pirates might be seen as catalysts for the project of international criminal law, the original *hostes humani generis* and a "constitutive exception" to the civilizational norms against which States, and the international community at large, have defined their own prevailing values.[7]

Notwithstanding the influence that high seas piracy has exerted on the development of international (criminal) law, the fight against piracy has often proved to be problematic in modern times, largely due to the rigid way in which it is defined at an international level. The international definition of high seas piracy is set out in Article 101 of the 1982 UNCLOS, this also being recognized as the definition of piracy in customary international law.[8] The 1982 definition establishes various "contingencies"[9] of piracy that must be met in order for an act to meet the definition. These are:

- The act must involve "illegal acts of violence or detention, or any act of depredation";
- The act must be "committed for private ends," and "by the crew or the passengers of a private ship";
- The act must occur on the high seas (here defined as including the exclusive economic zones of States, but excluding territorial seas or internal waters);
- The act must originate from one "ship" and be targeted against another "ship."

These strict delineations are problematic, particularly given that the requirement of a "motive for the crime of piracy [...] has often been left rather unclear"[10] due to the vagueness of the "private ends" requirement and also given that "restricting the characterization of acts of piracy to those that take place on the high seas is [...] out of step with modern forms of piracy, which defy borders

---

[7] Gerry Simpson, *Piracy and the Origins of Enmity* in TIME, HISTORY AND INTERNATIONAL LAW 219, 223 (Matthew Craven, Malgosia Fitzmaurice & Maria Vogiatzi eds, Martinus Nijhoff 2007).

[8] United Nations Convention on the Law of the Sea, art. 101, 1833 U.N.T.S. 397, Dec. 10 1982. See *e.g.* ROBIN GEISS & ANNA PETRIG, PIRACY AND ARMED ROBBERY AT SEA 41 (OUP, 2011); DOUGLAS GUILFOYLE, SHIPPING INTERDICTION AND THE LAW OF THE SEA 30 (Cambridge, 2011); U.N. Security Council Resolution 2020 (2011), preambular 7; *United States v. Dire* 680 F.3d 446 (4th Cir. 2012).

[9] Dino Kritsiotis, *The Contingencies of Piracy*, 41 CAL. W. INT'L L.J. 305 (2011).

[10] International Law Commission, *First report on prevention and repression of piracy and armed robbery at sea* (74th Session, A/CN.4/758, 2023), ¶47.

and boundaries at sea."[11] Accordingly, acts committed for a "public," "political," or "ideological" motive would, it appears, fail to meet the definition of piracy, while acts *resembling* piracy but which are committed in coastal regions (by most accounts, the most common *locus* of piratical acts today)[12] would similarly not, technically, satisfy the definition. This seems incongruous given that the consequences for the *victims* of the offense, and the implications for States seeking to control piracy, would be largely the same in either event (provided the sovereignty of other States is respected), regardless of the motive behind the act or the geographic location in which it is committed.[13] Indeed, very few crimes indicate the need for a particular motive as a key definitional component ("terrorism," by most accounts, being an exception)[14] while, similarly, crimes don't tend to be defined in terms of a particular *locus delicti.* Acts *resembling* piracy that fail to meet the Article 101 definition are generally classed as instances of armed robbery at sea.[15]

Definitional issues are problematic not only from a practical (law-enforcement) perspective[16] but also from a legal perspective, given that further relevant provisions in UNCLOS are dependent on the Article 101 definition being met, including a vaguely defined "duty to cooperate to the fullest extent in the repression of piracy" (Article 100), and the "activation" of universal jurisdiction in relation piracy, permitting States to "seize" suspected pirate ships, arrest those on board, and "decide upon the penalties to be imposed" (Article 105), regardless of the identity of the perpetrators or victims. Peculiarly, there is no specific obligation on States to criminalize piracy within their domestic codes (though many have).[17]

---

[11] *Id.* at ¶ 45.

[12] See, *e.g.*, International Commercial Crime Services & International Maritime Bureau, *Piracy and Armed Robbery against Ships; Report for the Period 1 January – 30 September 2024*, Oct. 2024 (available on request); *IMB Piracy and Armed Robbery Map*, ICC COMMERCIAL CRIME SERVICES, https://www.icc-ccs.org/piracy-reporting-centre/live-piracy-map.

[13] Aaron Honniball, *Private Political Activists and the International Law Definition of Piracy: Acting for Private Ends*, 36 ADEL. L. REV. 279, 281 (2015).

[14] Marcello Di Filippo, *The definition(s) of terrorism in international law* in RESEARCH HANDBOOK ON INTERNATIONAL LAW AND TERRORISM 2 (Ben Saul ed, Edward Elgar 2020).

[15] International Maritime Organisation, Resolution A.1025(26), *Code of Practice for the Investigation of Crimes of Piracy and Armed Robbery against Ships*, adopted 2 December 2009, Annex, para 2.2.

[16] ROBERT C. MCCABE, MODERN MARITIME PIRACY: GENESIS, EVOLUTION AND RESPONSES 27-28 (Routledge, 2018).

[17] *Id.* at 28; ILC, *supra* note 10, parts II-VI.

The shortcomings in the international definition of piracy have been overcome in two main ways. Firstly, from 2008 until 2022, a series of United Nations Security Council Resolutions, issued using Chapter VII powers, authorized States to "[e]nter the territorial waters of Somalia for the purpose of repressing acts of piracy and armed robbery at sea,"[18] given the "threat that acts of piracy [...] pose to the prompt, safe and effective delivery of humanitarian aid to Somalia, the safety of commercial maritime routes, and to international navigation."[19] This practice remained, though, specific to the situation in Somalia and was not extended to other parts of the world, such as, for example, the Gulf of Guinea, which at the time was similarly impacted by rampant piracy.[20]

Secondly, the 1988 Convention on the Suppression of Unlawful Acts against the Safety of Maritime Navigation (SUA) plugs several gaps inherent in the international definition of piracy by establishing a right for ratifying States to claim jurisdiction over a broad range of offenses at sea, dispensing with the rigid spatial or motivational requirements established by UNCLOS.[21] The SUA Convention is, today, widely ratified, with 168 State Parties at the time of writing.[22] Unlike UNCLOS, however, the Convention does not grant a universal jurisdiction to States, instead establishing territorial, national, passive personality and protective forms of jurisdiction, exercisable by those States that have ratified the agreement.[23] Although, in principle, the broad approach to crime at sea renders the definitional nuances presented by UNCLOS to be somewhat moot,[24] its more restrictive jurisdictional regime represents a step back from the universal repression of what, historically, has been a ubiquitous menace.

Notwithstanding these initiatives, several issues remain, given the apparently patchwork approach to crime at sea, definitional dilemmas, jurisdictional gaps,

---

[18] U.N. Security Council Resolution 1816 (2008), para 7(a); see also Resolution 1918 (2010) requiring States to "criminalise piracy under their domestic laws and favourably consider the prosecution of suspected [...] pirates apprehended off the coast of Somalia."

[19] UNSC Res 1816 (2008), *Id.* at para 2.

[20] *Id.* at para 9; see also UNSC Resolution 2018 (2011).

[21] Convention on the Suppression of Unlawful Acts against the Safety of Maritime Navigation, art. 3, 1678 U.N.T.S. 201, Mar. 10, 1988.

[22] As of 23 December 2024; data *via Status of Conventions*, INTERNATIONAL MARITIME ORGANIZATION, www.imo.org/en/About/Conventions/Pages/StatusofConventions.aspx.

[23] *Supra* note 21, art. 6. On the different forms of jurisdiction available to States in international law see MALCOLM N. SHAW, INTERNATIONAL LAW, chapter 11 (9th ed., CUP, 2021).

[24] José Luis Jesus, *Protection of Foreign Ships against Piracy and Terrorism at Sea: Legal Aspects*, 18 INT'L J. MARINE & COASTAL L. 363, 378 (2003).

and lack of clarity regarding State obligations. Thus, "[l]ike a tattered quilt that has been patched too many times, the international legal framework governing piracy is worn and inadequate, with legislative stitching [...] barely keeping it from coming apart at the seams."[25] We are returned, then, to the opening quote, and proposals announced by the International Law Commission to consider the potential for reform.[26]

This chapter will examine the potential for reforming the international legal regime governing the proscription of high seas piracy, and the form that this might best take. It will do so by, first, examining the historic rationale for the rigid definition of piracy, with a focus on, first, the "private ends" and, second, the "high seas" requirements. The historical study assists in setting out the nature of the crime of piracy: how and why the proscription has evolved as it has, and how this informs the present definition. Such a study also serves as a necessary grounding for any future reform, as it enables us to test whether the historical considerations that have informed the definition remain pertinent to attempts to define and restrain piracy today, and whether the issues in the definition have any chance of being overcome. Against this background, the chapter will move to demonstrate the challenges inherent in the present-day legal regime, again particularly as created by the defining and unique criteria that give rise to the offense. The chapter will then draw on the rich history of piracy and modern-day issues to reach suggestions for potential ways forward, while taking into account the place of "piracy" within the broader framework of relevant international law.

The definition of piracy in UNCLOS Article 101 is informed by centuries of State practice and rooted in historic interpretations of the threat that it poses. On studying the evolution of the offense, it becomes apparent that the seemingly problematic "private ends" and "high seas" requirements are essential and fundamental to it, serving to delineate it from purely domestic (non-international) offenses and, on the other hand, from State-administered or State-sponsored acts. This section explores, in greater detail, the historical logic behind the unusual definition, in turn informing the propriety and utility of potential future reforms. The focus is on the aforementioned "private ends"

---

[25] JAY BAHADUR, THE PIRATES OF SOMALIA: INSIDE THEIR HIDDEN WORLD 168 (Vintage, 2011).

[26] Laurence Teillet, *'If you were waiting for the opportune moment, that was it' – The International Law Commission's first report fails to address the pitfalls of piracy's definition*, INTERNATIONAL LAW BLOG (May 22, 2023), https://internationallaw.blog/2023/05/22/if-you-were-waiting-for-the-opportune-moment-that-was-it-the-international-law-commissions-first-report-fails-to-address-the-pitfalls-of-piracys-definit/, for an appraisal of the ILC's initial report.

and "high seas" requirements, these arguably being the most problematic aspects of the UNCLOS definition.

I. The "Private Ends" Requirement

As an initial starting point, it will be useful to consider the immediate history of UNCLOS Article 101, to ascertain any interpretive prompts that may be available.[27] The content of the provision is directly derived from the 1932 "Draft Convention on Piracy," as researched and compiled by academics working at Harvard University (henceforth, "the Harvard Draft").[28] Although never itself adopted, the contents went on to form the basis of the 1958 Geneva Convention on the High Seas, the relevant parts of which remained unchanged for adoption into the 1982 UNCLOS – hence a largely unbroken lineage from the contents of the 1932 draft through to the present-day definition of piracy. Prepared at a time when piracy was thought to be largely obsolete,[29] the Harvard Draft was pursued as a largely academic exercise, an initiative on the part of Harvard Law School to inform any potential future treaty following the abandonment of a similar codification project by the League of Nations.[30] The meticulous academic approach is clearly visible through the commentaries to the draft, with a dense portfolio of meticulously researched cases, laws and legal scholarship informing the contents – from a range of different jurisdictions and languages, and often reaching back by many decades, if not centuries. The rich academic quality of the approach, however, betrays the lack of concrete *practical* considerations which negotiating State representatives might have sought to consider in the ordinary course of treaty drafting. The end result is that the draft is characterized by the accretion of historical legal perspectives and philosophies on piracy rather than by practicalities, making it an intriguing but problematic predecessor to the relevant provisions of UNCLOS.[31]

In terms of the "private ends" requirement, the Harvard Draft introduces the requirement that, in order to be defined as such, a pirate must act "for private

---

[27] *Supra* note 13, at 291-292.

[28] *Draft Convention on Piracy, with Comments* 26 AM. J. INT'L L. supplement, 764 (1932).

[29] Edward D. Dickinson, *Is the Crime of Piracy Obsolete?* 38 HARV. L. REV. 334 (1924-25).

[30] McCabe, *supra* note 16, 26, noting that "the terminology of the UNCLOS definition borrowed heavily from the Harvard draft [...] and as such did not take in to account contemporary geo-political sensibilities or realities." The earlier League of Nations sanctioned Report, 9 February 1926, commonly known as *The Matsuda Draft*, had initially suggested that "piracy consists in sailing the seas for private ends without authorisation from the Government of any State with the object of committing depredations upon property or acts of violence against persons."

[31] BARRY HART DUBNER, THE LAW OF INTERNATIONAL SEA PIRACY – DEVELOPMENTS IN INTERNATIONAL LAW 57 (Martinus Nijhoff, 1980); Geiss & Petrig, *supra* note 8.

ends," adding that this must be "without *bona fide* purpose of asserting a claim of right."[32] There are some clues in the accompanying commentary that assist in the interpretation of this statement, notably that "pirates are a menace to the interests of every state which has access to the sea, and therefore this traditional conception seems to justify in favor of all [...] states a common legal right, and perhaps reciprocal duties, to prevent piracies and to punish pirates."[33] Elsewhere, the drafters link this analysis to ongoing fisheries disputes,[34] by suggesting that

> it is important to exclude [from the ambit of piracy] specifically cases of violence committed in asserting a claim of right, which should not be assimilated to piracy, or at any rate, could not be assimilated by common consent of all states. Perhaps quarrels of fishermen of different nationalities will cause most cases of this type.[35]

The term "claim of right," then, seems to require a form of authorization, most likely by a State (with "quarrels of fisherman" likely to be rooted in State disagreements over access to resources at sea). In turn, then, by operating in the absence of a "*bona fide* purpose of asserting a claim of right" pirates would, by definition, operate outside the purview of the State and would lack any claim to act with lawful (State-issued) authority.[36] Acts of piracy, then, "are done under conditions which render it impossible or unfair to hold any State responsible for their commission"[37] while representing "an offense against the whole body of civilized states, not against any particular one of them."[38] Just as piracy, by definition, operates within the void created by an *absence* of State sanction, it is *all* States – each one equally injured by piracy – that possess a common legal right to curtail it.

---

[32] *Supra* note 28, at 743. See also Kevin Jon Heller, *Judge Kozinski's 'Rich History' of Piracy*, OPINIO JURIS (Feb. 27, 2013), https://opiniojuris.org/2013/02/27/judge-kozinskis-rich-history-of-piracy/.

[33] *Id.* at 769.

[34] See *e.g.*, Fisheries Case (UK v. Norway), 1951 I.C.J. 3 (Dec. 1951) (noting that incidents informing the dispute dated from 1911).

[35] *Supra* note 28, at 809.

[36] Dubner, *supra* note 31, at 67.

[37] *Supra* note 28, at 771, WILLIAM EDWARD HALL, A TREATISE ON INTERNATIONAL LAW 310-311 (8th ed., OUP, 1924). Several extracts from other academic sources consolidate this approach.

[38] *Id.*, at 772-773, citing T.J. LAWRENCE, THE PRINCIPLES OF INTERNATIONAL LAW, 232-243 (5th ed., 1913).

While the history of the clause may be of some assistance, it is not particularly determinative,[39] and, in any case, does not provide exhaustive criteria to cover the situations in which the provision might apply. Indeed, academic commentaries highlight a range of overlapping approaches to the dilemma, each of which appears to be compelling, yet problematic, in its own way. The subsequent analysis will now consider, in turn, the various interpretations of the "private ends" contingency.

A. "Private Ends" as the Absence of State Authorization

As a starting point, it is apparent that State-sponsored acts cannot constitute "private ends" and therefore, by definition, cannot be considered acts of piracy. This is clear enough from the prior discussion of the Harvard Draft, though this approach is further re-emphasized in UNCLOS. Article 102, for instance, stipulates that

> The acts of piracy, as defined in article 101, committed by a warship [o]r government ship [...] whose crew has mutinied and taken control of the ship [...] are assimilated to acts committed by a private ship [...].[40]

The flipside of this provision is that acts committed by States (led by "warships" or "government ships"), for as long as the link with the State remains intact (*i.e.*, where no mutiny has taken place), cannot be assimilated to acts of piracy.

This qualification is inherent to the offense, differentiating acts of piracy from acts of State. The line of differentiation, however, has not always been clear-cut. Long since outlawed at the international level,[41] the practice of "privateering" referred to the common tendency among States (from at least the thirteenth century through to the nineteenth century)[42] to issue "letters of marque" to private seamen, permitting them to plunder the vessels or ports of others in the State's name, or even to act as "pirate hunters" themselves. Infamous privateers

---

[39] Douglas Guilfoyle, *Political Motivation and Piracy: What History Doesn't Teach Us About Law, EJIL:TALK!* (June 17, 2013), https://www.ejiltalk.org/political-motivation-and-piracy-what-history-doesnt-teach-us-about-law/.

[40] See also Article 107 which classifies "warships" together with any ships "clearly marked and identifiable as being on government service and authorized to that effect."

[41] Privateering has been proscribed since the Declaration of Paris, 1856, reproduced in ADAM ROBERTS & RICHARD GUELFF (EDS), DOCUMENTS ON THE LAWS OF WAR 48-49 (3d ed., OUP, 2000).

[42] Chadwick, *supra* note 4, at 55.

included such historical figures as Francis Drake,[43] Henry Morgan,[44] Bartolomeu Português,[45] Alonso de Contreras,[46] and Captain Kidd.[47] The parameters set by letters of marque were often the subject of abuse, however, with the result that many of these figures were as renowned for their acts of clear-cut piracy as they were for their authorized acts of State force-by-proxy.[48]

The fine line of sovereign authorization remained, in principle, vital to how privateering and piracy were defined. Thus, even while States openly engaged in larcenous pirate-like activities,[49] pirates *stricto sensu*, as agents of unsanctioned chaos, remained outside the ambit of ordered, Westphalian civilization and, as such, were considered a threat to that order.[50] Operating outside the system of State sanction, pirates represented a primordial, plunderous form of politics, seeking "to challenge assertions of sovereignty with counter-assertions of independent polity"[51] whereas "privateer[s], conversely, when acting within his commission, [were] part of the system."[52] The identity of the actor, rather than the nature of the act, was (and remains) the overriding consideration.[53]

The separation between State (or privateer) and pirate is engrained in the scholarship of renowned early scholars of international law such as Alberico Gentili and Hugo Grotius. Gentili, for instance, cautioned that war, and acts

---

[43] ANGUS KONSTAM, PIRACY: THE COMPLETE HISTORY 54 (Osprey, 2008).

[44] NEVILLE WILLIAMS, CAPTAINS OUTRAGEOUS: SEVEN CENTURIES OF PIRACY 128 (Barrie and Rockcliff, 1961).

[45] ALEXANDER EXQUEMELIN, THE BUCCANEERS OF AMERICA 64-69 (Henry Powell trans, Swan Sonnenschein, 1898) (1678).

[46] ALONSO DE CONTRERAS, THE LIFE OF CAPTAIN ALONSO DE CONTRERAS: KNIGHT OF THE MILITARY ORDER OF ST. JOHN, NATIVE OF MADRID (Catherine Phillips trans, A.A. Knopf, 1926).

[47] RICHARD ZACKS, THE PIRATE HUNTER: THE TRUE STORY OF CAPTAIN KIDD (Headline, 2002).

[48] Morgan, for instance, led a brutal attack on the Spanish city of Panama between 1670 and 1671, an act that was "contrary to the King's express commands", with Morgan briefly removed from his Admiralty post in Jamaica, but was later knighted and appointed governor (Williams, *supra* note 44, at 128). Captain Kidd violated the terms of the commission he had been granted to reign in piracy in the Indian Ocean piracy by instead becoming a pirate himself (*Id.*).

[49] JEAN-DENIS G. G. LEPAGE, MEDIEVAL ARMIES AND WEAPONS IN WESTERN EUROPE: AN ILLUSTRATED HISTORY 120 (McFarland, 2014).

[50] Chadwick, *supra* note 4, at 58-59.

[51] Emily Sohmer Tai, *Marking Water: Piracy and Property in the Pre-Modern West* in SEASCAPES 205 (Jerry H. Bentley, Renate Bridenthal & Kären Wigen eds, University of Hawaii Press, 2007).

[52] Chadwick, *supra* note 4, at 64.

[53] *Id.* at 62.

committed in its execution, such as plunder, could only be "waged by sovereigns"[54] whereas, conversely, "pirates and brigands" ("*piratis et latrunculis*") instead were within jurisdiction of States and could claim no independent right to wage wars of their own.[55] Grotius referred to a certain class of pirates ("*praedones*") as "persons who without any legitimate cause usurp authority to wage public war,"[56] their status as archvillains of the sea exacerbated by preying on the sacrosanct State right to access the seas freely and to engage in commerce thereon.[57]

This core consideration, of the separation between pirate and State, has remained a defining feature of piracy throughout the centuries. In 1718, when sentencing the captured pirate Stede Bonnett (whose own incompetent exploits would become the stuff of legend),[58] the judge chided him that "the power of the sword not being committed into your hands by any lawful authority, you were not empowered to use any force."[59] Two centuries later, Judge Moore, in his dissenting opinion at the Permanent Court of International Justice in the *Lotus* case, would echo similar ideas:

> acts of piracy by law of nations [...] are done under conditions which render it impossible or unfair to hold any State responsible for their commission; [...] a pirate either belongs to no State or organized political society, or by the nature of the act he has shown his intention and his power to reject the authority of that to which he is properly subject.[60]

The more recent (2013) judgment of the US Ninth Circuit Court of Appeal in the case *Institute of Cetacean Research v. Sea Shepherd Conservation Society* somewhat rigidly defined "acts taken for private ends as those not taken on behalf of a state."[61]

---

54 DE JURE BELLI LIBRI TRES, Chapter 3 (John C. Rolfe trans, Clarendon Press, 1933) (1598).
55 *Id.* at 15 and 20.
56 DE JURE PRAEDAE, 447 (Martine Julia van Ittersum trans, Liberty Fund Inc, 2006) (1604).
57 Chadwick, *supra* note 4 at 95-99.
58 CAPTAIN CHARLES JOHNSON, A GENERAL HISTORY OF THE ROBBERIES AND MURDERS OF THE MOST NOTORIOUS PIRATES 54 (David Cordingly ed, Conway Maritime Press, 1988) (1724).
59 *Bonnet's Trial*, 15 State Trials (Howell) 1231, 1235 (Am. Vice Adm. 1718) (UK).
60 S. S. Lotus (Fr. v. Turk.), 1927 P.C.I.J. (ser. A) No. 10 (Sept. 7), dissenting opinion of Judge Moore, 69, para. 5.
61 *Institute of Cetacean Research and ors v. Sea Shepherd Conservation Society and Watson*, Appeal judgment, 725 F3d 940 (9th Cir 2013).

That piracy, by definition, entails acts committed by non-State actors appears to be clear-cut, then, and universally agreed.[62] This is generally thought to extend also to excluding acts committed by recognized insurgents, in circumstances where they attack the ships of their own government, on the basis that they "exercise a limited form of public power" and "have the recognized capacity at international law to become a lawful government."[63] Violence at sea, in such circumstances, falls more appropriately within the remit of the laws of armed conflict. Where such actors attack vessels belonging to other States, however, they would be deemed acts of piracy under this approach, given these would not be legitimate objectives in pursuit of the "revolutionary" cause.[64]

A further question remains, however, over not only the identity of the actor but also as to the underlying motive, and whether the term "private ends" also requires that a pirate be driven by personal (as opposed to public or political) desires. Existing scholarship and domestic case law outline two potential approaches to this issue: firstly, the "private/public dichotomy" adopts the approach that "private ends" defines "private" as being purely the inverse of *public* motive and is solely dependent on whether an act is authorized by the State (or, by many accounts, by a recognized insurgent/belligerent movement); the second approach, the "private/political dichotomy," expresses the idea that acts of violence carried out with any kind of "political" motive cannot properly be defined as piracy but that, instead, piracy is of necessity *apolitical*, thereby placing a key emphasis on the factors which drive the offense.[65] These positions will be considered in turn.

B. "Private Ends" as (Purely) Identity: The Private/Public Dichotomy

The private/public dichotomy adopts the broad view that the term "private ends" "simply emphasize[s] that the violence involved lacks state sanction or authority,"[66] so that "[t]he test of piracy lies not in the pirate's subjective motivation, but in the lack of public sanction for his or her acts."[67] According

---

[62] Mark Chadwick, *Time to Fix a Sinking Ship? Rethinking the International Law of High Seas Piracy*, LAW.COM (June 22, 2021), https://www.law.com/international-edition/2021/06/22/time-to-fix-a-sinking-ship-rethinking-the-international-law-of-high-seas-piracy/; Jon Bellish, *More Great Piracy Facts in U.S. Courts: Private Ends Edition, EJIL:TALK!* (Feb 28, 2013), https://www.ejiltalk.org/more-great-piracy-facts-in-u-s-courts-private-ends-edition/.

[63] Guilfoyle, *Shipping Interdiction, supra* note 8 at 35.

[64] *Id.* at 33 and 40. See also Hall, *supra* no37 at 312, noting that "acts which are allowed in war, when authorized by a politically organized society, are not piratical."

[65] See, in particular, Honniball, *supra* note 13 at 285-288, and Guilfoyle, *id.* at 34-35.

[66] Guilfoyle, *id.* at 42.

[67] *Id.* at 36.

to this view, piracy represents an infringement of "the monopoly of states over legitimate violence," with the perpetrators "deliberately operating outside the law of a state-based system and committing unauthorized acts which impinge upon it."[68] "Put simply," Guilfoyle concludes on the matter, "the words 'for private ends' must be understood broadly. All acts of violence that lack state sanction are acts undertaken 'for private ends.'"[69]

The approach finds support in the aforementioned Ninth Circuit *Sea Shepherd* case,[70] while supporters of this line of reasoning also point to the terminology in UNCLOS Article 102,[71] which explicitly distinguishes between "government" and "private" ships, as well as to some historical precedents in which unrecognized insurgents had been classified as "pirates."[72] The commentary to the Harvard Draft, while failing to provide a direct explanation, can be interpreted as defining "private ends" as excluding only acts carried out by States or by recognized insurgents.[73] A similar but more nuanced approach was adopted by the Belgian Court of Cassation in the *Castle John* case,[74] which suggested that the requirement for "private ends" (here defined as "personal" ends) precluded acts carried out by States or targeted *against* specific States; in this case, the actions of Greenpeace in protesting the dumping of toxic chemicals were regarded as being an instance of piracy, being "purely in support of a personal point of view concerning a particular problem, even if they reflected a political perspective."[75]

The public/private dichotomy approach has the advantage of being relatively straightforward to administer and enables courts to bypass complex issues of motive (which, as previously noted, is not generally an essential element of a criminal offense). As Guilfoyle suggests, there is a certain workable

---

[68] *Id.* at 37.

[69] *Id.*

[70] *Supra* note 61.

[71] Eugene Kontorovich, *Yes, Sea Shepherd Engages in Piracy Under International Law*, THE VOLOKH CONSPIRACY (Feb. 27, 2013), https://volokh.com/2013/02/27/yes-sea-sheperd-engages-in-piracy-under-international-law/; but see, *contra*, Honniball, *supra* note 13 at 289.

[72] Maggie Gardner, *Piracy Prosecutions in National Courts*, 10 J. INT'L CRIM. JUST. 797, 808-809 (2012).

[73] *Supra* note 28 at 798; Guilfoyle, *Shipping Interdiction, supra* note 8 at 33.

[74] *Castle John and Nederlandse Stichting Sirius v. NV Mabeco and NV Parfin*, 77 INT'L LAW REPORT 537 (Court of Cassation of Belgium) (1986).

[75] Samuel Pyeatt Menefee, *The Case of The Castle John, or Greenbeard The Pirate?: Environmentalism, Piracy and the Development of International Law* 24 CAL. W. INT'L L.J. 1 (1993), and Honniball, *supra* note 13 at 313-314. See also *The Republic v. Abdukar Ahmed and five others*, Supreme Court of the Seychelles, July 14 2011.

functionality to this approach in that "lack of [State] authority is a question that may be tested objectively and without reference to subjective motives."[76]

The approach is a poor fit, however, for the actual wording of Article 101, with the choice of the term "ends" ("an outcome worked toward,"[77] in plain English) an apparent direction to a subtler approach than State (or insurgent) *versus* non-State, this being difficult to reconcile with objective conceptions of authority and factual circumstance.[78] Judging the meaning of Article 101 within its historical context also renders this approach difficult to justify, as will be discussed shortly.

C. "Private Ends" as Motive: The Private/Political Dichotomy

The second approach to the interpretation of "private ends" requires an inquiry into the motivations behind a given act of "piracy," which must, by definition, be *apolitical.*[79] Advancing the private/political dichotomy, José Luis Jesus, former President of the International Tribunal for the Law of the Sea, opines that the "private ends" contingency "seems to exclude sheer politically motivated acts directed at ships or their crew from the definition of piracy," adding that this would include "terrorist acts."[80]

Proponents of this line of argumentation find support in the 1926 "Matsuda Draft" which states, overtly, that "acts committed with a purely political object will not be regarded as constituting piracy."[81] This line of reasoning appears to

---

[76] Guilfoyle, *Shipping Interdiction, supra* note 8 at 42.

[77] "End," MERRIAM-WEBSTER, https://www.merriam-webster.com/dictionary/end.

[78] Honniball, *supra* note 13 at 289-290, demonstrating myriad usages of the term "private" throughout UNCLOS. Indeed, the choice of language in different language versions of UNCLOS would also seem to render the approach untenable: in French, the relevant term is "*agissant á des fins privées*", which would commonly translate into English as "acting for private purposes", alluding to motive rather than identity.

[79] Proponents include: Kevin Jon Heller, *supra* note 32, and *Why Political Ends are Public Ends, Not Private Ends,* OPINIO JURIS (Mar. 1, 2013), https://opiniojuris.org/2013/03/01/a-final-word-about-politically-motivated-piracy/; Samuel Pyeatt Menefee, *Foreign Naval Intervention in Cases of Piracy: Problems and Strategies* 14 INT'L J. MARINE & COASTAL L. 353, 357 (1993); Tina Garmon, *Reconciling the Law of Piracy and Terrorism in the Wake of September 11th,* 27 TUL. MAR. L.J. 257, 258-259 (2002); Malvina Halberstam, *Terrorism on the High Seas: The Achille Lauro, Piracy, and IMO Convention on Maritime Safety* 82 AM. J. INT'L L. 269, 272 (1988); Ömer F Direk, Martin D. A. Hamilton, Karen S. Openshaw & Patrick C. R. Terry, *Somalia and the Problem of Piracy in International Law* 4 *USAK Y.B. OF INT'L POLITICS AND LAW* 223, 234 (2011).

[80] *Supra* note 24 at 378, by reference to the terrorist seizures of the *Santa Maria* in 1961 and the *Achille Lauro* in 1985.

[81] *Supra* note 30, and see also Honniball, *supra* note 13 at 291.

find further support from the later Harvard Draft, which suggested that attacks by politically motivated "unrecognized revolutionaries" would not be "cases falling under the common jurisdiction of all states as piracy by the traditional law, but [rather] special cases of offences for which the perpetrators may be punished by an offended state as it sees fit." [82]

It has been suggested that the term "unrecognized revolutionaries" is intended to refer to anti-colonial struggles and exclude these from the scope of the term "piracy,"[83] though the broad terminology could possibly encapsulate a wider range of politically motivated violence. Certainly, in circumstances where application of the laws of armed conflict is warranted,[84] it would be inappropriate to regard the pirates involved as being "pirates" if engaged in violence at sea. Rather, "pirates do not acquire a combatant status [under the laws of armed conflict], and the use of force against pirates must be directed at arresting them and not at putting them hors de combat, including killing them, as can be done with enemy combatants."[85]

Under the most expansive reading of this approach, as advocated by Jesus,[86] violence at sea inspired by any form of political motive would exclude them from the ambit of the crime of piracy. Pirates, then, would be defined by their lack of political motive, which in turn renders them an indiscriminate threat to all States, "a menace to the international maritime commerce for the protection of whose security every civilized State is to some extent interested in intervening so far as its power permits."[87] This approach would exclude acts of terrorism and lower-intensity political violence (not meeting the thresholds for

---

[82] *Supra* note 28 at 857 (with further clarifications at 798), though see, *contra*, Guilfoyle, *Political Motivation supra* note 39, suggesting a limited reading of this provision. Others opine that by omitting specific discussion of "political motives" in the Harvard Draft, as compared with the Matsuda Draft, is evidence of this concept's rejection: Eugene Kontorovich, *'Private ends' in the Travaux Préparatoires of the Law of the Sea Treaty*, THE VOLOKH CONSPIRACY (Feb. 28 2013), https://volokh.com/2013/02/28/private-ends-in-the-travaux-preparatoires-of-the-law-of-the-sea-treaty/.

[83] George R. Constantinople, *Towards a New Definition of Piracy: The Achille Lauro Incident* 26 VA. J. INT'L L. 723, 735-737 (1986); Markiyan Z. Kulyk, *Piracy, Hijacking and Armed Robbery Against Ships* in III THE IMLI MANUAL ON INTERNATIONAL MARITIME LAW 393 (David Joseph Attard et al. ed, OUP 2016).

[84] See YORAM DINSTEIN, NON-INTERNATIONAL CONFLICTS IN INTERNATIONAL LAW, Chapter 3 (CUP, 2021).

[85] International Law Institute (*Institut de Droit International*), 11th Commission (2022), *Piracy, Present Problems* 170-171. See also GUILFOYLE, SHIPPING INTERDICTION, *supra* note 8 at 33 and 40.

[86] *Supra* note 24 at 378.

[87] *The Matsuda Draft*, *supra* note 30.

applying the laws of armed conflict) from the definition of piracy. While this paradigm is more in keeping with the relevant foundational texts and is a better fit for the actual language found in UNCLOS, it is problematic in its application. In the lack of a specific definition of "apolitical," the risk is that *any* action can be seen to be political in some form.

For instance, even for actors we might consider to be definitive examples of pirates, we would likely struggle to paint them as genuinely *apolitical* actors. The wave of pirates operating out of Somalia throughout the 2000s and 2010s, for example, was initially driven by recriminations linked to over-fishing and the dumping of toxic waste in Somali waters,[88] so their motivation could be said to be, at least in part, linked to the protection of their region – an "end" that seems inherently "political" in scope.[89] Moreover, the money acquired from ransoms or pirated goods is often linked to funding for terrorism, or broadly to "a political movement [which] may profit from piracy to enrich its party and give it greater power in its struggle."[90] In such cases, it becomes difficult to draw a clear conclusion as to motive and how such acts ought to be characterized.[91] Indeed, this grey area may even obfuscate the identities of the infamous pirates of the Golden Age, who claimed to "declar[e] war against the whole world,"[92] with infamous pirate "Black" Sam Bellamy once proclaiming himself "a free prince [with] authority to make war on the whole world."[93] Again, it is difficult to class the actions of these most paradigmatic of pirates as being genuinely "piratical" under the broadest reading of the "private ends" contingency, rendering the private/political dichotomy, without qualification, to be somewhat problematic. Arguably, then, "an interpretation of the notion of 'private ends' to exclude any kind of action by private individuals motivated by political, ideological, religious or environmental reasons could easily open the way to undue justifications of acts of violence at sea."[94]

---

[88] Bahadur, *supra* note 25 at Chapter 4; Sara McLaughlin Mitchell & Cody J. Schmidt, *Insecure fisheries: How illegal, unreported, and unregulated fishing affects piracy* 41 CONFLICT MANAGEMENT AND PEACE SCIENCE 313 (2023).

[89] Though see Nicole Stillwell, *Robbers or Robinhoods: A Study of the Somali Piracy Crisis and a Call to Develop an International Framework to Combat Maritime Terrorism* 7 LOY. MAR. L.J. 127, 131 (2009) noting that this position has since shifted, with the more recent actions of Somali pirates now more difficult to attribute to a "political" motive.

[90] A. A. Flagel, *The Revival of International Piracy*, PhD thesis submitted to University of New Caledonia (2013), 110.

[91] ILC, *supra* note 10 at 48.

[92] Johnson, *supra* note 58 at 134.

[93] Cited in C. R. Pennell, *Brought to Book: Reading about Pirates* in BANDITS AT SEA: A PIRATES READER 3, 9 (Pennell ed, NYU Press, 2001).

[94] Institute of International Law, *supra* note 85 at 197.

The problem is alluded to by the Harvard drafters who, dubious of "the fancy that piracy traditionally involves a declaration of hostility to the social order of the whole world"[95] suggest that

> every consideration of certainty in prosecution and of assured protection in places outside the territory of all States argues that the jurisdiction to seize and to punish a [a pirate] should not depend on whether [...] he intended to attack only the citizens of certain states and their ships and other property, or to prey on the people and commerce of all nations indiscriminately. Such matters of collateral intent of an offender (often uncertain and indistinct) and of his transactions other than those involved in the case at hand, are very unsatisfactory as elements in a basis of State jurisdiction.[96]

This caution re-emphasizes the potential issues arising from a narrow approach to "private ends" which would exclude, from the ambit of piracy, acts committed for political purposes and, again, places the crime of piracy in an unconventional category of offenses characterized by underlying motive. An analysis of the "private ends" requirement that is more robustly rooted in the history of the crime of piracy and how it has been regarded by scholars and by States provides us with a further option, and it is to this that we turn now.

D. "Confederated Only to Do Mischief": A Grotian Approach to "Private Ends"

A better, more common sense, approach may be to root the definition of "private ends" within its historical context and evolution. Hugo Grotius, for instance, developed a nuanced approach to the definition of piracy, in turn informed by anxieties about the risk posed to emergent Westphalian civilization. This approach underpins subsequent approaches to piracy in courtrooms around the world and informs much of the material relied upon by the Harvard drafters in formulating the "private ends" requirement.[97]

In *De Jure Praedae* (1604), Grotius defines certain pirates as "*praedones*" in the original Latin, describing them as "persons who without any legitimate cause usurp authority to wage public war."[98] This characterization seemingly subscribes to the private/public dichotomy approach to "private ends," with pirates deemed to be such wherever they act without the cover of State

---

[95] *Supra* note 28 at 804.

[96] *Id.* at 803.

[97] For insights into this evolution see Chadwick, *supra* note 4 at Chapters 4 and 5.

[98] *Supra* note 56 at 447.

sanction.[99] Elsewhere, however, Grotius paints a more complex picture. He goes on to identify a further class of pirates, "*piratae*," who are described as persons "who despoil others through privately exercised force and without urgent reasons to do so."[100] Further explanation is provided, with Grotius clarifying that *piratae* could be identified by establishing motive ("the end sought")[101] and, further, that such individuals were lacking in "honor, [...] since by audacious but unwarlike devices they turn public loss into private gain, a course of conduct clearly incompatible not only with justice but also with fortitude, the virtue wherein legitimate enemies vie with one another."[102] Rather than serving any kind of feasibly meritorious purpose, an attack by *piratae* "neither weakens the enemy to any appreciable extent nor advances the interests of his own side."[103] The analysis shifts the defining feature of the pirate from his lack of State authority, towards an identity that combines status *and* purpose ("motive," "ends") with the latter rooted in self-aggrandizement and enrichment rather than the advancement of "common good," however so defined.

In his 1625 *magnum opus, De Jure Belli ac Pacis*, Grotius expands on this notion by suggesting that pirates

> are associated *on the account of their crimes*; but [States], though sometimes not wholly guiltless, *do associate for the peaceable enjoyment of their own rights*[.][104]

Heavily influenced by the works of Cicero,[105] Grotius goes on to add that there is a great difference "between a nation, however wicked, and those who, not making a body of people, are confederated only to do mischief."[106] His conceptualization thus impugns the very nature and purpose of such piratical groups, who "associate on the account of their crimes"[107] and serve no public or virtuous purpose, instead representing a primordial, archaic, plunder-based form of quasi-political organization.

---

99 A similar line of reasoning is advanced by Alberico Gentili in his influential *De Jure Belli Libri Tres* (1589); see Chadwick, *supra* note 4 at Chapter 4.
100 *Supra* note 56 at 447. In the translation used, both terms are translated into English as "pirate" or sometimes "freebooter", albeit not consistently.
101 *Id.* at 455.
102 *Id.* at 449.
103 *Id.*
104 *Supra* note 54, Book III, Chapter III, s. II.
105 *Supra* notes 2 and 3, and see also Chadwick, *supra* note 4 at Chapter 2.
106 *Supra* note 54, III.XIX.III.
107 *Supra* note 54, III.III.II.

Grotius thus centralizes the nature or *raison d'etre* of pirate bands as their unique defining feature. The pirate not only does not represent a State, but he/she outwardly undermines it by existing purely for selfish, private gain. Pirates represented speculation rather than "honorable" or "virtuous" public or societal furtherance, while simultaneously disturbing the open commerce between States and the sanctity of the free and open sea. Pirates, left unchecked, were a genuine civilizational threat, the flipside of the "civilized" Westphalian European State order, being instead "confederated only to do mischief."[108]

Grotius' pronouncements rippled through the ages, informing anti-pirate purges in the early 1700s.[109] At *Houghling's Trial*, in 1700, for instance, pirates were denounced as "beasts of prey, and [...] worse than the worst of enemies, for they are governed by no laws of nations or arms [and are] enemies of all mankind,"[110] while at Captain Kidd's trial, in 1701, the judge concluded that pirates were "*hostes humani generis*, the enemies to all mankind, but [...] especially so to those that depend upon trade."[111] The 1705 *Tryal of Captain Thomas Green* (of an English citizen in a Scottish court, prior to the Acts of Union) held that "it is obvious how heinous [pirates] are, [being] in a perpetual war with every State [...]. Pirates extinguish humanity in themselves, and prey upon men only, especially upon traders."[112] The language draws closely on that espoused by Grotius and intimates that the identity of piracy is not merely informed by their lack of State authority but that, rather, they represent a subversive, anti-civilizational, indiscriminate threat (as particularly emphasized, in *Kidd* and *Green*, with the explicit recognition of the hazard posed to traders). These are the origins of the "private ends" requirement.

Later scholars such as Emmerich de Vattel and William Blackstone played further on these historical narratives, lamenting the pirate, respectively, as "violat[ing] all public security and declar[ing] themselves the enemies of the human race," and as having "reduced himself afresh to the savage state of nature by declaring war against all mankind, [so that] every community hath a right, by the rule of self-defense, to inflict [...] punishment on him." Beyond the seemingly harsh rhetoric, pirates were regarded as a genuine universal menace,

---

108 *Id.* See also Harvard Draft, *supra* note 28 at 566, and Virginia W. Lunsford, PIRACY AND PRIVATEERING IN THE GOLDEN AGE NETHERLANDS 137 (Palgrave Macmillan, 2005).

109 Chadwick, *supra* note 4 at Chapter 5.

110 As related in Williams, *supra* note 44 at 134.

111 *Kidd's Trial*, 14 Howell's State Trials 123 (1701).

112 *Tryal of Captain Thomas Green and his crew*, 14 Howell's State Trials 1199 (1705).

"a physical and ontological threat"[113] to civilization – a status that tracked with Golden Age pirates' own conception of themselves.[114]

A two-part test emerges from this "Grotian paradigm" of piracy for the purpose of ascertaining whether the "private ends" contingency is satisfied. The test requires (i) an *identity* element and; (ii) an *impact* element (indiscriminate threat). The two are intertwined, with the identity of the actor likely to inform the pattern of violence.

In terms of point (i), identity, pirates represent "a universally belligerent quasi-political force and a *sui generis* criminal operating beyond all borders," underwritten by archaic, State-subversive ideals.[115] On the face of it, following this approach, perpetrators of violence at sea who are States, or State-sponsored, or are engaged in an insurgency against a government, could not be pirates, given that they would satisfy Grotius' test of "associat[ing] for the peaceable enjoyment of their own rights"; in other words, serving some wider societal purpose. The requirement is simultaneously one of both identity and motive or purpose. Arguably, at its most basic level, Grotius intended purely to exclude States and insurgents from the ambit of piracy, and this may be the neatest solution, given that the "test" here is somewhat arcane (a seventeenth-century academic text is, after all, unlikely to provide a practical basis for modern-day law enforcement).

This leaves us with a couple of grey areas to work through. Firstly, consider the situation where an insurgent (who is, perhaps, seeking to overthrow a colonial power) begins to attack merchant vessels belonging to other, neutral, States. Strictly speaking, given that Grotius by implication excluded insurgents from the class of actors who could commit piracy, the result is that this would not be treated as piracy. Insurgents, in these circumstances, wouldn't fall into that class of actors that "associate on the account of their crimes" or, by their nature, undermine civilizational values – even if their targets are selected indiscriminately. Their actions could be amply (and more appropriately) dealt with elsewhere under international law, such as through application of relevant laws of armed conflict or under domestic criminal law.

Secondly, this conception of private ends may not always be straightforward when dealing with acts of terrorism at sea, given that politically motivated but clearly criminal violence does not fit cleanly either within, or outside, Grotius' conception. Indeed, it is questionable as to whether to whether those

---

[113] Andrew Dilts, *To Kill a Thief: Punishment, Proportionality and Criminal Subjectivity in Locke's Second Treatise* 40 POLITICAL THEORY 58, 60 (2012).
[114] *Supra* note 95 and associated text.
[115] Chadwick, *supra* note 4 at 150.

committing acts of terrorism would, under Grotius' conception, "associate for the peaceable enjoyment of their own rights" (even though it also seems conceptually difficult to class them as operating at the behest of "private" motives), and if this were not to be the case, they *could* be classed as pirates. This classification, however, is generally likely to be negated by the subsequent requirement of indiscriminate *animus*, given that terrorists seeking a particular outcome are likely, by definition, to have specific targets in mind, and that if the actions only impact a single State (or specific group thereof) it would fail to meet the criteria.[116]

For point (ii), impact, the pirates' *modus operandi* will be pivotal to the enquiry. The pirate identity manifests itself through its indiscriminate nature, requiring some enquiry into targeting strategy. Pirates emanate

> an antagonism that cannot be defined as that of one individual with respect to another or of one political association with respect to another. Such an antagonism [...] appears not as particular but as general; it is often represented as 'universal.'[117]

In so doing, pirates undermine trade and cut against more developed, post-Westphalian premises of civilization, in a manner that affects all States (and, by extension, all individuals) equally. Indeed, the Harvard Draft (citing Grotius directly in places) suggests that "pirates are a menace to the interests of every state which has access to the sea, and therefore this traditional conception seems to justify in favor of all [...] states a common legal right, and perhaps reciprocal duties, to prevent piracies and to punish pirates."[118] On these bases, acts that target particular States would not be conceived as piratical, in that they do not harm us all equally and would not engender universal ire. Indeed, the fact that universal jurisdiction has developed concomitantly with the definition of the offence, thereby permitting *all* States to arrest and prosecute those committing piracy, further cements the suggestion that piracy, to be so, must occur indiscriminately.[119]

This approach to "private ends" presents a cleaner solution than either of the existing approaches outlined above, while drawing on both, yet with greater nuance and drawing more closely on the history of how piracy has been

---

116 Conceptual problems may nevertheless still arise where piracy is conducted indiscriminately but to raise money for terrorist operations, as alluded to previously.
117 DANIEL HELLER-ROAZEN, THE ENEMY OF ALL: PIRACY AND THE LAW OF NATIONS 11 (Zone Books, 2009).
118 *Supra* note 28 at 769.
119 Chadwick, *supra* note 4 at 155-156.

perceived and has developed as an international crime. Where perpetrators don't meet the criteria, perhaps because their grudge is targeted at a single or limited group of States, their cases can be dealt with as instances of armed robbery at sea, falling short of the definition of piracy *stricto sensu*, and left to those States that possess relevant bases of jurisdiction.

Notwithstanding the concerns in the Harvard Draft about a preoccupation with pirates as "*hostes humani generis*" and the "fancy" of pirates declaring war against the world,[120] the drafters nevertheless concede that

> the opposition to bringing under the common jurisdiction offences against the interests of a single state, and the insistence on some international factual element in the definition of piracy, are strong enough to make it expedient to exclude from the definition of piracy offences which involve only ships and territory under the ordinary jurisdiction of one State and which are not incidents of an enterprise with purposes of wider scope. In all these cases of piracy, then, there is an element which engages the interest of the international community[.][121]

In line with this guidance, the application of the "Grotian paradigm," then, would seem to resolve much of the misunderstanding and hand-wringing over the proper application of the "private ends" contingency, reconciling the terminology with the historicity of piracy and linking universal jurisdiction back to the indiscriminate violence that it originally developed in conjunction with.

E. "Private Ends": A Continued Unsuitability

Following from the foregoing analysis, we might reconcile the underlying rationale for the "private ends" contingency, contained in Article 101, as rooted in ancient concepts of pirates as civilizational rebels or Stateless "outsiders," posing an indiscriminate threat to all States and, in so doing, warranting a unanimous response from all States (today framed as universal jurisdiction).

While the first component of this approach rules out acts carried out by States or insurgents, the element of "indiscriminate act" is a measurable determinant that can be applied in order to assess whether acts by other actors should properly be considered as being high seas piracy within the terms of Article 101. In this way, those who we commonly think of as being pirates today, such as those operating out of Somalia, would meet the definition, in that they

---

120 *Supra* note 28 at 804.
121 *Id.* at 807-808.

attack passing trade without discrimination. Although perhaps acting in pursuance of deep-seated political motives (albeit not, perhaps, of an anti-civilizational character) linked to illegal overfishing or the dumping of toxic waste, or even as a direct consequence of Somalia's calamitous political situation,[122] on application of Grotius' principles, there is no immediate or obvious "virtuous" outcome from such acts.[123] Subsequently, their targets are not selected on the basis of identity, politics or ideology, but are, rather, indiscriminately selected based on practical considerations.[124] Conversely, sea-robbers selecting specific targets, such as insurgents or terrorists targeting a particular State (or group thereof), or eco-activists such as Sea Shepherd or Greenpeace, do not act indiscriminately, and cannot properly be considered "pirates."[125]

In this way, the approach to "private ends" can be reconciled with the various source texts and historical contexts in a way that avoids absurd results such as that found in the *Sea Shepherd* case while also avoiding the complications that would arise from having to analyze the specific motivations behind any given act of ship-on-ship violence at sea. The approach is, moreover, true to the rich lineage of the offense.

The "Grotian approach," however, remains problematic, as do all of the various conceptions of the "private ends" contingency. It still requires the ascertaining of the nature and/or motive of the actor involved, this being an unusual criterion for defining any offense, and one that is likely to create a level of subjectivity in how it will be applied, creating the possibility of abuse. Moreover, the approach is still likely to leave grey areas to be worked out, such as the questions of whether terrorism at sea,[126] or acts such as "petro-piracy"

---

122 Jade Lindley, Somali Piracy: A Criminological Perspective 47 (Routledge, 2016) noting that "[t]he common motivator into piracy for many Somalis transitioned from grievance to greed. While pirates initially attacked vessels because of grievances over depleted fish stocks, increased success and high ransom payments switched their motivation to greed."

123 *Supra* note 102.

124 Lindley, *supra* note 122 at 61-62, noting that piracy results from "the convergence of a suitable target, a motivated offender and the absence of capable guardianship" and that "[s]ince the *modus operandi* of Somali pirates is to attack steaming vessels, slow and low vessels are at greatest risk of attack."

125 Though see, *contra*, the approach taken by Honniball, *supra* note 13 at 321-323, suggesting *inter alia* that "[t]he action of Sea Shepherd is not directed against a particular state but rather all [illegal] whaling by any people, anywhere for any reason."

126 Discussed in section 1d, *supra*.

(whereby pirates specifically target oil tankers),[127] or acts with mixed motives,[128] could properly be considered piracy. More fundamentally, the issue with any of the approaches to the "private ends" contingency will always be the creation of a two-tier system for dealing with crimes at sea, with piracy subject to universal jurisdiction, but armed robbery at sea left to affected States to deal with – a distinction that is based largely on the underlying identity or motive of the perpetrator (or, as the next section will explore, the location where the offense is committed). The two-tier approach is problematic for victims, and for the State enforcement arms looking to contain violence at sea. Notwithstanding the range of different approaches, then, it may be that more radical change is needed to better govern how crime at sea is monitored and thwarted.

II. The High Seas Contingency

The *locus delicti* of high-seas piracy is a constitutive part of how the offense is defined under international law. Article 101 of UNCLOS defines piracy as taking place either "on the high seas" or "outside the jurisdiction of any State." The term "high seas" is, here, somewhat misleading, however, as the term here covers *all* maritime zones beyond a State's twelve nautical mile territorial waters,[129] hence, violence committed in the exclusive economic zones of States can constitute piracy provided the various other contingencies are met. Conversely, this means that acts of violence committed in the internal waters of States, or in territorial or archipelagic waters, will *not* be high seas piracy as defined in international law, but instead instances of armed robbery at sea" and subject to the jurisdiction of the territorial State, in addition to any others that might possess relevant (non-universal) jurisdiction. The idea that *locus delicti* can determine whether a given crime has been committed (regardless of whether *actus reus* and *mens rea* can be established) is somewhat unique, while also being logically discordant. In order to avoid being classed as a pirate under international law, and thereby swerving the potential exercise of universal jurisdiction, a perpetrator need only be mindful of where, on the seas, he or she is. Again, for victims of such violence, the distinction makes little difference.

As with the similarly exceptional "private ends" requirement, there are sound historical and underlying legal reasons for this restriction, as discussed below. Nevertheless, the territorial delimitation of piracy can lead to undesirable results. As the ILC reports,

---

127 Martin N. Murphy, Petro-Piracy: Oil and Troubled Waters, 57 ORBIS 424 (2013).
128 ILC, *supra* note 10 at para 48.
129 By virtue of UNCLOS Article 58(2); see also "Enrica Lexie" Incident, Italy v India, Award, PCA Case No 2015, May 21 2020, para. 979.

> Defining piracy based on a geographical criterion by linking it exclusively to the high seas is restrictive[.] [...] Once the elements of piracy are found to be present, the crime scene should have no consequences for the legal characterization of the acts. The same illegal acts should lead to the same characterization of the crime, regardless of whether the perpetrators passed from one maritime zone to another.[130]

The Report goes on to note that violence at sea occurs, today, more often "along coastlines, being committed in ports and their approaches,"[131] situations that technically would not constitute piracy as defined in Article 101 of UNCLOS. Rather, "where the attack takes place within the territory of a State, including its territorial sea, the general rule should be applied that it is a matter for the State affected to take the necessary measures for the repression of the acts committed within its territory."[132] The issues that might arise here are readily apparent:

> pirates committing crimes in the high seas know that by staying in the high seas or the exclusive economic zone, they may be pursued and captured by any state on the basis of universal criminal jurisdiction. To avoid that situation, they typically will quickly move, after an act of piracy, to the nearest territorial sea of a State to escape pursuit by foreign vessels. Moreover, the fact that many States do not have the capacity to control their territorial sea encourages pirates to move their operations in these waters by raiding and attacking ships waiting their turn to enter a port.[133]

As such, there are discrepancies in terms of how the law may be applied (or even *which* law may be applied), with the potential for gaps in enforcement in situations where the territorial State is unable to take preventive or restraining action.

The "high seas" contingency forms an inescapably core element of what it means to be a "pirate," namely that by usurping the common good of the high seas, pirates are thereby perceived as an indiscriminate and universal enemy,

---

130 ILC, *supra* note 10 at para 45.

131 *Id.* and see also resources cites *supra* note 12.

132 United Nations, YEARBOOK OF THE INTERNATIONAL LAW COMMISSION, 282 (1956); quoted by International Law Institute, *supra* note 85 at 200.

133 ILC, *supra* note 10 at para 23, citing Joseph M Isanga, *Countering Persistent Contemporary Sea Piracy: Expanding Jurisdictional Regimes* 59 AM. U. L. REV. 1267, 1273 (2010).

hostes humani generis.[134] Interestingly, however, the strict geographic delimitation of piracy is a relatively recent delimitation. The history of piracy is replete with examples of "pirates" raiding ports or operating in coastal waters, where the strict legal concepts of "high seas" or "territorial waters" would have been anachronistic.

In May 1718, for instance, the notorious pirate Edward Teach (more famously known as Blackbeard) blockaded Charleston harbor "for five or six days" and captured numerous passing vessels "all which being done in the face of the town [...] so that the trade of this place was totally interrupted."[135] Blackbeard only left the town alone upon receipt of a "chest of medicines," upon which he "let go the ships and the prisoners having first taken out of then in gold and silver, about 1,500 pound sterling, besides provisions and other matters."[136] These acts evidently took place within the territorial waters of the British colony of Carolina, apparently even being visible from Charleston. Yet there was apparently never any doubt that Blackbeard's actions were instances of piracy.[137] Similarly, in January 1722, Bartholomew Roberts attacked the port of Ouidah (in what is, today, Benin), "the wealthiest harbour in West Africa."[138] Roberts "sailed in, trumpets fanfaring, drums rolling, a black flag at the mizzenmast[.] [...] The eleven ships at anchor instantly struck their colors and the captains hurried ashore with their money hoping that the pirates would be content with the litter of goods and chattels that had been left behind."[139] The episode led to a tense standoff between the town and Roberts' crew. Again, historians do not tend to doubt that this was one amongst many instances of piracy carried out by Roberts during a lengthy and illustrious career.

The notion of a territorial sea began to emerge from the early 1600s, initially as a "cannon shot" rule based on the distance into the sea that a State could enforce its laws by force.[140] This had crystallized into a "three-mile" rule by the turn of the twentieth century[141] and has, today, become formalized into a 12

---

[134] Chadwick, *supra* note 4 at 155-156.

[135] Johnson, *supra* note 58 at 48.

[136] *Id.* at 49.

[137] Vail Stewart Rumley, *300 years later, judge upholds Blackbeard's guilty verdict,* WASHINGTON DAILY NEWS (Oct. 19, 2018), www.thewashingtondailynews.com/2018/10/19/300-years-later-judge-upholds-blackbeards-guilty-verdict.

[138] AUBREY BURL, BLACK BARTY: THE REAL PIRATE OF THE CARIBBEAN 219 (Sutton Mill, 2006).

[139] *Id.*

[140] Wyndham L. Walker, *Territorial Waters: The Cannon Shot Rule* 22 BRIT. Y.B. OF INT'L L. 210 (1945).

[141] Bernard G. Heinzen, *The Three-Mile Limit: Preserving the Freedom of the Seas* 11 STAN. L. REV. 597 (1959).

nautical mile territorial sea, accepted by the vast majority of States.[142] The view taken by the Harvard drafters was that the high seas requirement was an intrinsic part of the definition of piracy. Quoting international law scholar Lassa Oppenheim, the drafters subscribe to the view that

> Piracy in territorial waters has as little to do with international law as other robberies within the territory of a State. Piracy is, and has always been, a crime against the safety of traffic on the open sea, and therefore it cannot be committed anywhere else than on the open sea.[143]

The underpinning rationale, then, is similar to that which informs the "private ends" requirement. Pirates were not simply everyday criminals breaking domestic laws; rather, by commanding ships, with their own rules, existing beyond the reach of State jurisdictions and threatening to "invade" merchant vessels, they were defiant proto-States, actively seeking to subvert State-made law and posing an existential threat to the mercantilist European States. Piracy gains strength from "the fundamental fact of the lack of government control," so that in the lack of effective enforcement mechanisms, pirates hope "to commit their crimes with impunity from State-made law,"[144] as per Guilfoyle's view that pirates infringed on "the monopoly of States over legitimate violence."[145] The extra-territorial, extra-jurisdictional *locus* was a key part of what made pirates *hostes humani generis* and a heinous, universal threat.[146]

Moreover, it was by operating at sea that pirates were perceived as indiscriminately targeting all trade, and so harming the interests of all States. At the 1696 trial of Henry Avery's crew, the prosecutor opened by suggesting that "piracy so much exceeds theft or robbery at land [...] for suffer pirates and the commerce of the world must cease," later adding that "in the case of a robbery on the land, we know who is to pay for it; but in a robbery at sea, it

---

142 Rudiger Wolfrum, *The Emerging Customary law of marine zones: State practice and the Convention on the law of the sea* 18 NETHS Y.B. OF INT'L L. 121 (1987).

143 *Supra* note 28 at 789, quoting LASSA OPPENHEIM, INTERNATIONAL LAW (4th ed., Longmans, Green & Company, 1905). The earlier Matsuda Draft (*supra* note 30) had similarly suggested that "[w]hen pirates choose as the scene of their acts of sea-robbery a place common to all men and when they attack all nations indiscriminately, their practices become harmful to the international community of all States. They become the enemies of the human race."

144 Willard B. Cowles, *Universality of Jurisdiction over War Crimes* 33 CALIF. L. REV. 177, 193 (1945).

145 *Shipping Interdiction, supra* note 8 at 37.

146 Chadwick, *supra* note 4 at 156-160.

often happens that innocent persons bear the loss of what these men do,"[147] linking the crime to its humanitarian consequences and the difficulty experienced by States in containing it. Thus, piracy was perceived as targeting all of humankind, when carried out indiscriminately, in a way that robbery on land could not. Once the territorial sea became recognized as a formal part of a State's territory, this applied to coastal regions by analogy.

Since the advent of the Harvard Draft, and subsequent reinforcing of the territorial sea in UNCLOS, the notion of the pirate as the universal offender has become enshrined in a precise geography (similarly to the way in which piracy is also defined in terms of identity or motive). Moving from the vague assertion that pirates constitute a worldwide menace, the offense can be discerned using measurable data. Moreover, the rule also plays a role in protecting State sovereignty over the territorial sea, by effectively barring navies of other States from entering their jurisdiction. As such, "[s]eizing a ship within the territorial sea of another State, and arresting people on board who have committed acts corresponding to piracy, whether or not the acts occurred in that territorial sea, would be a violation of the sovereignty of that State."[148] There is no right of "hot pursuit" permitting navies to chase pirates into the territorial waters of other States.[149]

The history and background of the "high seas" contingency may be logical, then, but the implications are largely impractical, for the reasons spelled out earlier. With a majority of violence at sea taking place in ports or otherwise in territorial seas, the definition of piracy and mechanisms available for dealing with it have become redundant in many cases.[150] The flipside of the "high seas" requirement is that we become reliant on the territorial State to deal with violent "pirate-like" crimes committed in territorial waters, given the non-availability of universal jurisdiction that would permit other States to arrest and prosecute. Armed robbery at sea in territorial waters may be just as difficult to police as piracy *stricto sensu*, with the potential for gaps in enforcement where the territorial State does not have the resources or capacity to respond.[151] In the case of Somalia, for instance, prior to the U.N. Security Council intervention,

---

147 *Rex v Dawson*, 13 *Howell's State Trials* 451 (1696). Avery himself was never apprehended.

148 Institute of International Law, *supra* note 85 at 200.

149 UNCLOS, *supra* note 8 at Article 111(3).

150 *Supra* note 12; see also Honniball, *supra* note 13 at 18.

151 Institute of International Law, *supra* note 85 at 157, "noting the lack of capability of some coastal States to comply with their responsibility to ensure safety of navigation in the territorial sea and to take effective steps, within their territory, including internal waters, to prevent acts of piracy and other acts of violence at sea and activities connected with such acts."

the ongoing conflict and weak governance were instrumental in allowing piracy and armed robbery at sea to flourish.[152] Indonesia provides an example of where the "high seas" requirement has created difficulties for an archipelagic State; faced with a significant increase in armed robberies taking place in territorial waters throughout the 1990s and 2000s, "Indonesia was unable to tackle the problem unilaterally due in part to a paucity of naval assets and financial resources."[153]

Even where the perpetrators leave the territorial waters where the crime was committed, and sail back onto the high seas, then the majority of other States would not possess jurisdiction to arrest or detain them (notwithstanding the possibility of arrest following an extradition request from another State that does possess jurisdiction, such as *via* an Interpol "red notice").[154]

III. The End of Piracy? On the Inadequacies of the Present Definition and Suggestions Towards Reform

This chapter opened with a quote by the International Law Commission, which had chosen to place the study of high-seas piracy on its long-term agenda due to "important issues of international law that are uncertain or underdeveloped."[155] Notwithstanding (or perhaps because of) piracy's ancient history and lineage, it has become clear how and why this may be the case.

The unusual "contingencies" of piracy exist for good reason, as we have explored, and the chapter has endeavored to explore these and explain how (especially in the case of the "private ends" requirement) they might be better interpreted. The histories that they reveal are, at once, fascinating and revelatory in terms of what they tell us about the evolution of international criminal law, with the universal proscription of piracy since becoming a catalyst for the broader expansion of universal jurisdiction (and arguably international criminal law in general).

In terms of its practical usage, though, the definition is flawed and problematic. Notably, the issues of requiring that pirates operate for "private ends" and that the offense occurs on the high seas create considerable issues in terms of defining the crime and, by extension, applying it to events that take place. The unusual (though explainable) emphasis on identity or motive, and

---

152 Bahadur, *supra* note 25 at Chapter 2; see *supra* note 8 for details of U.N. Security Council intervention.
153 McCabe, *supra* note 16 at 277.
154 For a prominent example, see Alex Boyd & Adrienne Murray, *Anti-whaling activist Paul Watson released from jail in Greenland,* BBC News (Dec. 17, 2024).
155 *Supra* note 1.

on the *locus delicti*, create distinctive loopholes through which seaborne criminals may, metaphorically, flee. Yet, from victimological, criminological, and enforcement perspectives, the existence of such loopholes is nonsensical. One scholar has gone so far as to suggest that:

> The utility of UNCLOS as a counter-piracy mechanism [is] particularly limited. [...] Despite presenting a codified legal definition of maritime piracy and urging all nations to cooperate in the repression of piracy, UNCLOS, it is argued, weakened counter-piracy activities rather than enhanced them. The introduction of territorial sea limits [...] paradoxically undermined the potential efficacy of Article 101.[156]

Moreover, the chapter only provides a limited snapshot of the broader issues in the international legal regime relevant to piracy, with issues over international cooperation,[157] State willingness to arrest and prosecute,[158] and State (non-)implementation of relevant domestic laws[159] being among other areas that are ripe for closer consideration.

Article 101 is perhaps best regarded as a "museum piece" for international criminal law, a kind of fascinating, antique relic that has, somehow, managed to survive – but not in a way that is useful in the modern world. To most extents, and especially given the advent of the SUA Convention,[160] the definition of high seas piracy is, arguably, largely redundant.

A number of options present themselves:

A. Strengthen / Clarify UNCLOS

The least disruptive or progressive approach would be to ensure there is amply clear interpretive guidance layered upon the relevant provisions in UNCLOS, while taking appropriate steps to attempt to address any adequacies as and where they arise.

An interpretive approach has been taken by the *Institut de Droit International* (Institute for International Law) in a 2022 resolution, creating "a number of understandings [...] that would be considered as a natural interpretation of the

---

[156] McCabe, *supra* note 16 at 26-27.
[157] Chadwick, *supra* note 4 at 101.
[158] Jack Lang, *Report of the Special Adviser to the Secretary-General on Legal Issues Related to Piracy off the Coast of Somalia* 13, Jan. 25, 2011.
[159] McCabe, *supra* note 16 at 276.
[160] *Supra* note 21.

UNCLOS provisions in the light of subsequent international practice"[161] such as, for example, by confirming that "[a]cts committed by or under the authority of a State do not constitute piracy under Article 101 of the UNCLOS."[162] This may be useful, but does not of itself serve to address the underlying disagreements over the scope of the offense (particularly in terms of how "private ends" is defined), nor does it address the seeming two-tier system of enforcement that the rigid definition of piracy (in opposition to robbery at sea) gives rise to. The underlying issues, therefore, would remain.

In terms of addressing issues as they arise, a potential approach is to essentially "waive" the existence of a State's territorial sea using appropriate international mechanisms, as was done by having the U.N. Security Council in the context of Somalia.[163] This is an approach that, given the right circumstances, might also work well elsewhere, but it is unlikely to be a panacea in all situations and, moreover, would rely on *ad hoc* interventions to respond to established issues while also being susceptible to the internal political wranglings of the Security Council.

Another approach may be to adopt an additional protocol to UNCLOS that would, where circumstances similar to those experienced in Somalia arise, permit State navies to enter the territorial waters of another State in order to control piracy outbreaks. However, the rights ceded by States in ratifying such a protocol would need to be intermittently turned on and off as circumstances require, while other States may use the situation to abuse the sovereign territorial rights under the guise of combating piracy. Otherwise, the situation that resembles intervention by invitation,[164] which shouldn't need an additional protocol in order to be viable – indeed, such a protocol might lead to unnecessary complications.

B. Revise UNCLOS

The approach of the ILC to considering options for "codification, and progressive development"[165] of the law has been to propose amendments to the existing relevant provisions of UNCLOS via a series of "draft articles" (which could, equally, be issued in such a way that they exist separately of UNCLOS in

---

[161] Institute of International Law, *supra* no85 at 177. Much of the content relates to State cooperation and to the human rights of suspects.

[162] *Id.* at 233.

[163] *Supra* note 8.

[164] Shaw, *supra* note 23 at 1011-1013.

[165] *Supra* note 1.

a separate treaty).[166] The approach has, at the time of writing, been somewhat subtle, with "no clarification on how the private ends requirement should be interpreted, [...] none of the above-mentioned issues [...] addressed or resolved."[167] Perhaps, though, this should not be surprising. Any changes to UNCLOS would need to be enacted *via* a rigorous amendment process, requiring "ratification or accession by two-thirds of the States Parties" and which would in any case "not affect the enjoyment by other States Parties of their rights or the performance of their obligations under this Convention."[168] Such an approach is likely to be time-consuming and create further complexity and confusion, given the different legal regimes that will be in effect for different States.[169] The same problems would be likely to arise were the provisions to be adopted into a new treaty.

In any case, in terms of reform, there are good reasons why the various contingencies of piracy are in place, each of which is informed by the history of the offense and is properly integral to the definition. Regardless, certainly waiving the "high seas" contingency does not seem to be an option, given the entrenchment of the territorial sea rule and the impression that such a development would strip back the sovereign and jurisdictional rights of States.[170]

C. "Retire" Article 101 UNCLOS

The most logical (if perhaps somewhat radical) proposal would be to effectively "retire" the piracy provisions in UNCLOS and move away from the device of "piracy" as the principal means for maintaining order at sea. As the chapter has shown, the iconoclastic definition of piracy is soundly rooted in historical developments of a world-making order. And yet, in the modern world, with its

---

166 The ILC has, though, clarified that "[a]s the topic unfolds, it may become clearer whether the topic is an appropriate one for the development of new convention, in which case draft articles would remain the proper form for the Commission's work. If, however, it becomes apparent that the topic is best developed simply as guidance to States with respect to implementation of existing international obligations, then the outcome might be changed to 'conclusion' or 'guidelines'" (*supra* no1, para 35). The draft articles are contained in two reports that have been issued at the time of writing: the "First Report", *supra* note 10, and *Second Report*, document A/CN.4/770, issued Mar. 4, 2024.

167 Teillet, *supra* note 26.

168 UNCLOS, *supra* note 8 at Article 136(1).

169 On the existing perceived complexity, see McCabe, *supra* note 16 at 276.

170 Institute of International Law, *supra* no85 at 203, noting that "[a]part from the localized and temporary situation of Somalia, States are careful to preserve one of the fundamental aspects of the present regime of piracy, that is to preserve their jurisdiction over crimes committed in their territorial sea and to prevent interventions therein by other States to exercise universal jurisdiction."

multifaceted politics and complex zoning of maritime areas, the definition ceases to have practical value: save, perhaps, in confirming the potential heinousness or piracy.

Other forms of regulation already exist; the SUA, for example, provides a reasonably cohesive global option for managing crime at sea without the nuanced constraints of UNCLOS. The Convention permits ratifying States to arrest and, subsequently, extradite or prosecute, individuals committing various forms of violence.[171] Going one step further than UNCLOS, the Convention obliges States to criminalize the listed acts.[172] The Convention applies in all cases where the suspects' vessel navigates beyond the territorial sea of a single State,[173] while the motive of the perpetrator is not a relevant consideration, thereby obviating the "private ends" issue and applying to both "private" and politically motivated acts alike, the only qualification being that the convention does not apply to State vessels.[174] Ratifying States are, in Article 6, granted flag-state jurisdiction, territorial (sea) jurisdiction, nationality-based jurisdiction (extending to acts committed by residents of the State), passive personality jurisdiction and protective jurisdiction.[175] Critically, Article 6(4) creates an *aut dedere aut judicare* obligation by requiring States to "take such measures as may be necessary to establish its jurisdiction [...] where the alleged offender is present in its territory and it does not extradite him to any of the State Parties which have established their jurisdiction [...]."[176] Further, Article 10 obliges the custodial State "without exception whatsoever and whether or not the offence was committed in its territory, to submit the case without delay to its competent authorities for the purpose of prosecution."[177]

In requiring contracting States to take action in relation to any suspect in their custody who may have committed any of the acts of violence at sea (and who is linked to any other contracting State *via* the forms of jurisdiction listed in Article 6), the Convention creates a form of treaty-based universal jurisdiction,[178] limited only in terms of the number of ratifying States; though

---

[171] *Supra* note 21 at Article 3. A 2005 Protocol extends the convention to attacks against fixed platforms on the continental shelf.

[172] *Id.* at Article 5.

[173] *Id.* at Article 4.

[174] *Id.* at Article 2.

[175] *Id.* at Article 6, and see also Shaw, *supra* note 23 at Chapter 11.

[176] *Id.* Article 8 subsequently sets out the process of "delivery" of the suspect from the custodial State to the State with jurisdiction.

[177] *Id.*, Article 10.

[178] David Freestone, *The 1988 International Convention for the Suppression of Unlawful Acts against the Safety of Maritime Navigation*, 3 INT'L J. ESTUARINE & COASTAL L. 305 (1988).

the SUA is now widely ratified, with 168 States parties at the time of writing. An enforcement gap nevertheless remains in that the convention is "not intended to justify the stopping and boarding of vessels, and the apprehension of individuals, in circumstances which would traditionally be contrary to international law, e.g., on the high seas or in the EEZ of another state or on a ship exercising the right of innocent passage."[179] It would, therefore, be difficult for State ships to enact an arrest at sea, unless their own interests are affected, though the extensive ratification figures and wide jurisdictional provisions make it likely that perpetrators of the proscribed acts will ultimately face justice.

The SUA, arguably, largely addresses significant gaps and ambiguities left by the UNCLOS provisions on piracy and will become increasingly effective as it moves toward universal ratification. Now may be time to move towards the more practical model promised by the SUA, rather than to continue sweating over the narrow definition of piracy in UNCLOS. It may be time, finally, to abandon the pirates to the Museum of International Law.

Bibliography

1949 Geneva Conventions: Geneva Convention for the Amelioration of the Condition of the Wounded and Sick in Armed Forces in the Field (GC I), Aug. 12, 1949, 75 U.N.T.S. 31; Geneva Convention for the Amelioration of the Condition of Wounded, Sick and Shipwrecked Members of Armed Forces at Sea (GC II), Aug. 12, 1949, 75 U.N.T.S. 85; Geneva Convention Relative to the Treatment of Prisoners of War (GC III), Aug. 12, 1949, 75 U.N.T.S. 135; Geneva Convention Relative to the Protection of Civilian Persons in Times of War (GC IV), Aug. 12, 1949, 75 U.N.T.S. 287.

Jay Bahadur, The Pirates of Somalia: Inside Their Hidden World (Vintage, 2011).

Jon Bellish, *More Great Piracy Facts in U.S. Courts: Private Ends Edition*, Ejil: Talk! (Feb 28, 2013), https://www.ejiltalk.org/more-great-piracy-facts-in-u-s-courts-private-ends-edition/.

Bonnet's Trial, 15 State Trials (Howell) 1231, 1235 (Am. Vice Adm. 1718).

Alex Boyd & Adrienne Murray, *Anti-whaling activist Paul Watson released from jail in Greenland*, BBC News (Dec. 17, 2024).

Aubrey Burl, Black Barty: The Real Pirate of the Caribbean 219 (Sutton Mill, 2006).

Castle John and Nederlandse Stichting Sirius v. NV Mabeco and NV Parfin, 77 Int'l Law Report 537 (Court of Cassation of Belgium) (1986). https://doi.org/10.1017/CBO9781316152058.054.

Case Concerning Application of the Convention on the Prevention and Punishment of the Crime of Genocide (Bosnia and Herzegovina v. Serbia and Montenegro), 2007 I.C.J. 43 (Feb. 2007).

[179] *Id.* at 311.

Mark Chadwick, Piracy and the Origins of Universal Jurisdiction: On Stranger Tides (Brill, 2018). https://doi.org/10.1163/9789004390461.

Mark Chadwick, *Time to Fix a Sinking Ship? Rethinking the International Law of High Seas Piracy,* Law.com (June 22, 2021), https://www.law.com/international-edition/2021/06/22/time-to-fix-a-sinking-ship-rethinking-the-international-law-of-high-seas-piracy/.

Cicero, In Verrem (C.D. Yonge trans, George Bell & Sons 1903) (70BC).

George R. Constantinople, *Towards a New Definition of Piracy: The Achille Lauro Incident* 26 Va. J. Int'l L. 723 (1986).

Convention on the Suppression of Unlawful Acts against the Safety of Maritime Navigation, art 3, 1678 U.N.T.S 201, Mar. 10, 1988.

Willard B. Cowles, *Universality of Jurisdiction over War Crimes* 33 Calif L. Rev. 177 (1945). https://doi.org/10.2307/3477334.

Alonso De Contreras, The Life of Captain Alonso De Contreras: Knight of the Military Order of St. John, Native of Madrid (Catherine Phillips trans, A.A. Knopf, 1926).

De Jure Belli Libri Tres, Chapter 3 (John C. Rolfe trans, Clarendon Press, 1933) (1598).

De Jure Praedae, 447 (Martine Julia van Ittersum trans, Liberty Fund Inc, 2006) (1604).

Edward D. Dickinson, *Is the Crime of Piracy Obsolete?* 38 Harv. L. Rev. 334 (1924-25). https://doi.org/10.2307/1328811.

Marcello Di Filippo, *The definition(s) of terrorism in international law* in Research Handbook on International Law and Terrorism 2 (Ben Saul ed, Edward Elgar 2020). https://doi.org/10.4337/9781788972222.00008.

Andrew Dilts, *To Kill a Thief: Punishment, Proportionality and Criminal Subjectivity in Locke's Second Treatise* 40 Political Theory 58 (2012). https://doi.org/10.1177/0090591711427000.

Yoram Dinstein, Non-International Conflicts In International Law, Chapter 3 (CUP, 2021). https://doi.org/10.1017/9781108864091.

Ömer F. Direk et al., *Somalia and the Problem of Piracy in International Law* 4 USAK Y.B. of Int'l Politics and Law 223 (2011).

Draft Convention on Piracy, with Comments 26 AM J. Int'l L. supplement, 764 (1932). https://doi.org/10.2307/2213753.

Barry Hart Dubner, The Law of International Sea Piracy – Developments in International Law (Martinus Nijhoff, 1980). https://doi.org/10.1163/9789004636187.

"End," Merriam-Webster, https://www.merriam-webster.com/dictionary/end.

"Enrica Lexie" Incident, *Italy v India,* Award, PCA Case No 2015, May 21 2020.

Alexander Exquemelin, The Buccaneers of America (Henry Powell trans, Swan Sonnenschein, 1898) (1678).

Fisheries Case (*UK v. Norway*), 1951 I.C.J. 3 (Dec. 1951).

A. Flagel, *The Revival of International Piracy,* PhD thesis submitted to University of New Caledonia (2013).

David Freestone, *The 1988 International Convention for the Suppression of Unlawful Acts against the Safety of Maritime Navigation*, 3 Int'l J. Estuarine & Coastal L. 305 (1988).

Maggie Gardner, *Piracy Prosecutions in National Courts*, 10 J. Int'l Crim. Just. 797 (2012). https://doi.org/10.1093/jicj/mqs045.

Tina Garmon, *Reconciling the Law of Piracy and Terrorism in the Wake of September 11th*, 27 Tul. Mar. L.J. 257 (2002).

Robin Geiss & Anna Petrig, Piracy and Armed Robbery at Sea (OUP, 2011). https://doi.org/10.1093/acprof:oso/9780199609529.001.0001.

Alberico Gentili, De Jure Belli Libri Tres (John C. Rolfe trans, Clarendon Press, 1933) (1598).

Hugo Grotius, De Jure Praedae (Martine Julia van Ittersum trans, Liberty Fund Inc, 2006) (1604).

Douglas Guilfoyle, *Political Motivation and Piracy: What History Doesn't Teach Us About Law*, Ejil: Talk! (June 17, 2013), https://www.ejiltalk.org/political-motivation-and-piracy-what-history-doesnt-teach-us-about-law/.

Douglas Guilfoyle, Shipping Interdiction and the Law of the Sea (Cambridge, 2011).

Malvina Halberstam, *Terrorism on the High Seas: The Achille Lauro, Piracy, and IMO Convention on Maritime Safety* 82 Am. J. Int'l L. 269 (1988). https://doi.org/10.2307/2203189.

William Edward Hall, A Treatise on International Law (8th ed., OUP, 1924).

Bernard G. Heinzen, *The Three-Mile Limit: Preserving the Freedom of the Seas* 11 Stan L. Rev. 597 (1959). https://doi.org/10.2307/1226663.

Kevin Jon Heller, *Why Political Ends are Public Ends, Not Private Ends*, Opinio Juris (Mar. 1, 2013), https://opiniojuris.org/2013/03/01/a-final-word-about-politically-motivated-piracy.

Kevin Jon Heller, *Judge Kozinski's 'Rich History' of Piracy*, Opinio Juris (Feb. 27, 2013), https://opiniojuris.org/2013/02/27/judge-kozinskis-rich-history-of-piracy/.

Daniel Heller–Roazen, The Enemy of All: Piracy and the Law of Nations 11 (Zone Books, 2009).

Aaron Honniball, *Private Political Activists and the International Law Definition of Piracy: Acting for Private Ends*, 36 Adel L. Rev. 279 (2015).

IMB Piracy and Armed Robbery Map, ICC Commercial Crime Services, https://www.icc-ccs.org/piracy-reporting-centre/live-piracy-map.

Institute of Cetacean Research and ors v. Sea Shepherd Conservation Society and Watson, Appeal judgment, 725 F3d 940 (9th Cir 2013).

International Commercial Crime Services & International Maritime Bureau, *Piracy and Armed Robbery against Ships; Report for the Period 1 January – 30 September 2024*, Oct. 2024.

International Law Commission, *Report of the International Law Commission* (Seventy-first session, A/74/10, 2019), Annex C (*Prevention and repression of piracy and armed robbery at sea*, drafted by Yacouba Cissé), *First report on prevention and repression of piracy and armed robbery at sea* (74th Session, A/CN.4/758, 2023) and *Second report*, A/CN.4/770, issued Mar. 4, 2024.

International Law Commission, *First report on prevention and repression of piracy and armed robbery at sea* (74th Session, A/CN.4/758, 2023).

International Law Institute (*Institut de Droit International*), 11th Commission (2022), *Piracy, Present Problems.*

International Maritime Organization, Resolution A.1025(26), *Code of Practice for the Investigation of Crimes of Piracy and Armed Robbery against Ships,* adopted 2 December 2009.

International Maritime Organization, *Status of Conventions,* www.imo.org/en/About/Conventions/Pages/StatusofConventions.aspx.

Joseph M. Isanga, *Countering Persistent Contemporary Sea Piracy: Expanding Jurisdictional Regimes* 59 Am. U. L. Rev. 1267 (2010).

Jose Luis Jesus, *Protection of Foreign Ships against Piracy and Terrorism at Sea: Legal Aspects,* 18 Int'l J. Marine & Coastal L. 363 (2003). https://doi.org/10.1163/092735203770223585.

Captain Charles Johnson, A General History of the Robberies and Murders of the Most Notorious Pirates (David Cordingly ed, Conway Maritime Press, 1988) (1724).

Jorgić v. Germany (Application no. 74613/01), 2007 European Court of Human Rights.

Kidd's Trial, 14 Howell's State Trials 123 (1701).

Dino Kritsiotis, *The Contingencies of Piracy,* 41 Cal. W. Int'l L. J. 305 (2011).

Angus Konstam, Piracy: The Complete History (Osprey, 2008).

Eugene Kontorovich, *'Private ends' in the Travaux Préparatoires of the Law of the Sea Treaty,* The Volokh Conspiracy (Feb. 28 2013), https://volokh.com/2013/02/28/private-ends-in-the-travaux-preparatoires-of-the-law-of-the-sea-treaty.

Eugene Kontorovich, *Yes, Sea Shepherd Engages in Piracy Under International Law,* The Volokh Conspiracy (Feb. 27, 2013), https://volokh.com/2013/02/27/yes-sea-sheperd-engages-in-piracy-under-international-law/.

Markiyan Z. Kulyk, *Piracy, Hijacking and Armed Robbery Against Ships* in III The ILMI Manual on International Maritime Law 393 (David Joseph Attard et al. ed, OUP 2016).

Jack Lang, *Report of the Special Adviser to the Secretary-General on Legal Issues Related to Piracy off the Coast of Somalia* 13, Jan. 25, 2011.

Maximo Langer, *Universal Jurisdiction is Not Disappearing,* 13 J. Int'l Crim. Just. 245 (2015).

T. J. Lawrence, The Principles of International Law (5th ed., 1913). https://doi.org/10.1093/jicj/mqv009.

Jean-Denis G. G. Lepage, Medieval Armies and Weapons in Western Europe: An Illustrated History (McFarland, 2014).

Jade Lindley, Somali Piracy: A Criminological Perspective (Routledge, 2016). https://doi.org/10.4324/9781315563053.

Virginia W. Lunsford, Piracy and Privateering in the Golden Age Netherlands (Palgrave Macmillan, 2005). https://doi.org/10.1057/9781403979384.

Stephen Macedo et al., The Princeton Principles on Universal Jurisdiction (Princeton University, 2001).

Robert C. McCabe, Modern Maritime Piracy: Evolution and Responses (Routle dge, 2018). https://doi.org/10.4324/9781315163550.

Sara Mitchell McLaughlin & Cody J. Schmidt, *Insecure fisheries: How illegal, unreported, and unregulated fishing affects piracy* 41 Conflict Management and Peace Science 313 (2023). https://doi.org/10.1177/07388942231174174

Samuel Pyeatt Menefee, *Foreign Naval Intervention in Cases of Piracy: Problems and Strategies* 14 Int'l L.L. Marine & Coastal L. 353 (1993). https://doi.org/10.1163/157180899X00183.

Samuel Pyeatt Menefee, *The Case of The Castle John, or Greenbeard The Pirate?: Environmentalism, Piracy and the Development of International Law* 24 Cal. W. Int'l L.J. 1 (1993).

Martin N. Murphy, Petro-Piracy: Oil and Troubled Waters, 57 Orbis 424 (2013). https://doi.org/10.1016/j.orbis.2013.05.011.

Lassa Oppenheim, International Law (4th ed., Longmans, Green & Company, 1905).

C. R. Pennell, *Brought to Book: Reading about Pirates* in Bandits at Sea: A Pirates Reader 3 (Pennell ed, NYU Press, 2001).

Kenneth C. Randall, *Universal Jurisdiction under International Law,* 66 Tex. L. Rev. 785 (1987-88).

The Republic v. Abdukar Ahmed and five others, Supreme Court of the Seychelles, July 14 2011.

Restatement (Third) of the Foreign Relations Law of the United States s404 (1988).

Rex v Dawson, 13 *Howell's State Trials* 451 (1696).

Adam Roberts & Richard Guelff (eds), Documents on the Laws of War (3d ed., OUP, 2000).

Vail Stewart Rumley, *300 years later, judge upholds Blackbeard's guilty verdict,* Washington Daily News (Oct. 19, 2018), www.thewashingtondailynews.com/2018/10/19/300-years-later-judge-upholds-blackbeards-guilty-verdict.

Malcolm N. Shaw, International Law (9th ed., CUP, 2021).

S. S. Lotus (*France v. Turkey*), 1927 P.C.I.J. (ser. A) No. 10 (Sept. 7).

Michael P. Scharf, *Universal Jurisdiction and the Crime of Aggression,* 53 Harv. Int'l L. J. 358 (2012).

Gerry Simpson, *Piracy and the Origins of Enmity* in Time, History and International Law 219 (Matthew Craven, Malgosia Fitzmaurice & Maria Vogiatzi eds, Martinus Nijhoff 2007). https://doi.org/10.1163/ej.9789004154810.i-255.55.

Nicole Stillwell, *Robbers or Robinhoods: A Study of the Somali Piracy Crisis and a Call to Develop an International Framework to Combat Maritime Terrorism* 7 Loy. Mar. L.J. 127, 131 (2009).

Emily Sohmer Tai, *Marking Water: Piracy and Property in the Pre-Modern West* in Seascapes 205 (Jerry H. Bentley, Renate Bridenthal & Kären Wigen eds, University of Hawaii Press, 2007). https://doi.org/10.2307/j.ctt6wr35q.16.

Laurence Teillet, *'If you were waiting for the opportune moment, that was it' – The International Law Commission's first report fails to address the pitfalls of piracy's definition,* International Law Blog (May 22, 2023), https://internationallaw.blog/2023/05/22/if-you-were-waiting-for-the-opportune-moment-t hat-was-it-the-international-law-commissions-first-report-fails-to-address-the-pitfalls-of-piracys-definit/.

Christian Tomuschat, *The Legacy of Nuremberg*, 4 J. Int'l Crim. Just. 830 (2006). https://doi.org/10.1093/jicj/mql051.

Trial International, Universal Jurisdiction Annual Review 2024 (2024).

Tryal of Captain Thomas Green and his crew, 14 Howell's State Trials 1199 (1705).

United Nations, II Yearbook of the International Law Commission, 282 (1956).

United Nations Convention on the Law of the Sea, art. 101, 1833 U.N.T.S. 397, Dec. 10, 1982.

U.N. Security Council Resolution 1816 (2008).

U.N. Security Council Resolution 1918 (2010).

U.N. Security Council Resolution 2018 (2011).

U.N. Security Council Resolution 2020 (2011).

United States v. Dire 680 F.3d 446 (4th Cir. 2012).

Wyndham L. Walker, *Territorial Waters: The Cannon Shot Rule* 22 Brit. Y. B. of Intl'l L. 210 (1945).

Neville Williams, Captains Outrageous: Seven Centuries of Piracy (Barrie and Rockcliff, 1961).

Rudiger Wolfrum, *The Emerging Customary law of marine zones: State practice and the Convention on the law of the sea* 18 Neths. Y. B. of Intl'l L. 121 (1987). https://doi.org/10.1017/S0167676800001690.

Richard Zacks, The Pirate Hunter: The True Story of Captain Kidd (Headline, 2002).

Chapter 6

The Gibe III Dam- Genocide against the El Molo People?

Ronald Rogo

University of Nairobi

Christine Okidi

Human Rights Practitioner

Abstract: This chapter presents a case study on the impact of development on water bodies, its effect on indigenous communities that have relied on them, and how international criminal law can come to their aid. The focus will be on the construction of the Gibe 3 Dam, the fourth largest hydroelectric dam in Africa, by the Ethiopian government on Omo River Lake Turkana basin region which hosts a total of 200,000 people divided into 8 ethnic groups namely: Turkana, Pokot, Watta, Rendile, Dassanach, Samburu and El Molo. The communities comprising pastoralists and fishers rely on the lake for fishing, drinking water, and water for their livestock. This chapter will specifically focus on the impact the Gibe 3 Dam is having on the El Molo, a small indigenous group who live around El Molo Bay. The authors will investigate whether international criminal law can provide some sort of relief given the imminent erasure of the El Molo community.

Keywords: Omo River, Lake Turkana, El Molo, Gibe Dam, livelihood, development.

Introduction

In 2006, the Ethiopian Government embarked on a project that involved constructing the Gibe III Dam on the banks of River Omo. The goals of the construction of the dam were ostensibly to generate power and to control the flow of the river in order to allow for large-scale irrigation farming. The government envisioned converting the surrounding land into sugarcane plantations. However, part of the effect of the project was that it reduced the flows of water into Lake Turkana in Kenya.[1] This subsequently also affected the ability of the El Molo people, a small indigenous community in Kenya, to continue with their traditional lifestyle.[2] The authors focus on this development and whether or not its effects can be interpreted as genocide against the El Molo people. This chapter presents a case study on the impact of development on indigenous communities that rely on rivers and lakes, focusing on the El Molo people who live around Lake Turkana, Kenya. It aims to offer a contextual analysis of how development projects affect these communities and highlight potential human rights violations associated with these initiatives. Development, devoid of community engagement, can hold negative implications for indigenous people's livelihoods, hence, critical reflection is needed.

The first section provides a contextual analysis of genocide from a historical perspective. It then breaks down the term into the different elements and their meanings. The second section considers the process of construction of Gibe III Dam on Omo River, the main source of water for Lake Turkana, and provides context on the construction of the dam. Lastly, the third section examines the effect of the development on the El Molo community who heavily relied on the lake for their livelihood.

I. Definition of Genocide

The word genocide is, perhaps, one of the most dreaded words. In the minds of most, it creates images of mass killings and destruction of millions of people. It is used to define "the most aggravated form of crime against humanity.[3] The word was initially invented by Raphael Lemkin, a Polish lawyer, as he struggled to describe the actions of the Nazi regime against the Jews during World War II.

---

[1] Lake Turkana is located in Kenya's northern desert area around the border with Ethiopia. It is Kenya's largest lake that entirely lies within its borders. It is also the world's largest permanent lake in a desert and the largest alkaline lake. Most of its water inflows come from River Omo in Ethiopia. *See* D.S. AVERY, LAKE TURKANA & THE LOWER OMO: HYDROLOGICAL IMPACTS OF MAJOR DAM AND IRRIGATION DEVELOPMENTS (Univ. of Oxford, 2012); *see also* W. O. OJWANG ET AL., "LAKE TURKANA: WORLD'S LARGEST PERMANENT DESERT LAKE (KENYA)," IN THE WETLAND BOOK, EDS. C. FINLAYSON ET AL. (SPRINGER, DORDRECHT, 2016).

[2] The El Molo are a small Cushitic community living on the shores of Lake Turkana. They are currently the smallest ethnic community in Kenya and have traditionally survived by fishing on the lake and hunting crocodiles and hippos on the lake. See Purity Kiura, *Africa 101 Last Tribes: El Molo,* https://www.101lasttribes.com/tribes/el_molo.html (accessed December 5, 2024).

[3] WILLIAM SCHABAS, AN INTRODUCTION TO THE INTERNATIONAL CRIMINAL COURT, 3rd ed. (New York: Cambridge University Press 2007).

The holocaust by the Nazi catalyzed his efforts to define this crime that resulted in elimination of parts of protected groups.[4]

Loosely, the word genocide is created by merging two Greek terms *genos (a people)* and *çide* (kill)[5] Thus, the crime of genocide mainly describes the act of targeting and destroying a huge part of a population that is protected. It is the crime of targeted homicide magnified many times over. The UN General Assembly Resolution 96(1) defined genocide as "a denial of the right of existence of entire human groups, as homicide is the denial of the right to live of individual human being."[6] More particularly, thanks to the efforts of Lemkin, the Convention on the Prevention and Punishment of the Crime of Genocide ("the Genocide Convention"), which came into operation in 1951, has a more specific definition:

> 'genocide' means any of the following acts committed with intent to destroy, in whole or in part, a national, ethnical, racial or religious group, as such: (a) Killing members of the group; (b) Causing serious bodily or mental harm to members of the group; (c) Deliberately inflicting on the group conditions of life calculated to bring about its physical destruction in whole or in part; (d) Imposing measures intended to prevent births within the group; (e) Forcibly transferring children of the group to another group.[7]

Article 3 of the Genocide Convention then lists the various levels of responsibilities for any actions of genocide: acts of genocide, conspiracy to commit genocide, direct and public incitement to commit genocide, attempt to commit genocide and complicity in genocide.[8] In other words, one does not have to be directly involved in the actual act of killing or destruction of a member of a protected group in order to be culpable of genocide. Publicly inciting another person to engage in genocidal acts, for example, could amount

---

[4] JOHN QUIGLEY, THE GENOCIDE CONVENTION: AN INTERNATIONAL LAW ANALYSIS (Hampshire: Ashgate Publishing Limited 2006).

[5] *Id.;* Thomas Simon, *Defining Genocide*, WISCONSIN INTERNATIONAL LAW JOURNAL, Volume 15, 243-256 (1996-1997); Dominik Schaller, *From Lemkin to Clooney: The Development and State of Genocide Development and State of Genocide Studies*, GENOCIDE STUDIES AND PREVENTION: AN INTERNATIONAL JOURNAL, 6(3), 245-256 (2011); Julia Rappaport, *Where Did the Word "Genocide" Come From?*, FACING HISTORY AND OURSELVES (2014) https://www.facinghistory.org/ideas-week/where-did-word-genocide-come. (accessed November 9, 2024).

[6] GA Res. 96(I), A/RES/96 (December 11, 1946).

[7] Convention on the Prevention and Punishment of the Crime of Genocide, art 2, Dec. 9, 1948, S. Exec. Doc. O, 81-1 (1949), 78 U.N.T.S. 277.

[8] *Id.*, art 3.

to an act of genocide. The same for an individual who attempts, but fails, to destroy the members of a protected group. Article 4 of the Genocide Convention removes any form of judicial protection from prosecution to all public officials, irrespective of their status ("whether they are constitutionally responsible rulers, public officials or private individuals").[9]

II. Elements of the Offence of Genocide

A. Intention to destroy

The crime of genocide requires a double *mens rea:* the initial *mens rea* against the particular individual(s) harmed and a second *mens rea* (special intent) against the particular group that is protected. This is because the crime of genocide is seen as a crime that simultaneously targets the victims, the protected groups to which they belong and human diversity at different levels.[10] This requirement of double *mens rea is* perhaps one of the most important elements of the offense of genocide and, without it, the charges will definitely fail. It is also important to note that the fact that the intended or presumed desire of the perpetrator is not met does not mean that the intent to commit genocide is not met. Only the desire and the actions of the perpetrator to meet this desire are relevant-not the end result.[11]

The first requirement for *mens rea* is easier to prove. Most domestic criminal jurisdictions in most states require the forbidden act (*actus reus*) to be accompanied by the requisite mental state (*mens rea)* in order for the accused person to be charged and convicted for a criminal offense. The second *mens rea* is what makes the crime of genocide distinct from other crimes.[12]

---

[9] *Id.*, art 4.

[10] ROBERT CRYER, AN INTRODUCTION TO INTERNATIONAL CRIMINAL LAW & PROCEDURE, 2nd ed. (New York: Cambridge University Press 2010); *See also* Payam Akhavan, *The Crime of Genocide in the ICTR Jurisprudence,* JOURNAL OF INTERNATIONAL CRIMINAL JUSTICE, 3(4), 989-1006 (2005); *see also* Claus Kreb, *The Crime of Genocide under International Law,* INTERNATIONAL CRIMINAL LAW REVIEW, Volume 6, 461-502, 471 (2006).

[11] Paola Gaeta, *Genocide,* in Schabas, ed. ROUTLEDGE HANDBOOK OF INTERNATIONAL CRIMINAL LAW 109 (New York: Taylor & Francis Group 2011); *see also* GUÉNAËL METTRAUX, *Special Genocidal Intent/Dolus Specialis,* in INTERNATIONAL CRIMES: LAW AND PRACTICE: VOLUME I: GENOCIDE (Oxford Academic 2019); *see also* Kai Ambos, *What does 'intent to destroy' in genocide mean?,* INTERNATIONAL REVIEW OF THE RED CROSS, 91(876), 835-851, 835 (2006).

[12] Prosecutor v. Jean Paul Akayesu (1998) ICTR-96-4-T; Akhavan, *supra* note 10; Marko Milanovic, *State Responsibility for Genocide,* THE EUROPEAN JOURNAL OF INTERNATIONAL LAW, 17(3), 553-604, 558 (2006).

At a most basic level, the intention to destroy a protected group indicates an intention or desire to eliminate, in whole or in part, the protected group. In *Akayesu* it was described as "a psychological relationship between the physical result and the mental state of the perpetrator."[13] This could, for example, be shown through communication expressing hatred towards the group and the need for its ultimate destruction.[14] There is therefore, a targeting of the members of the group by the perpetrator. In concrete terms, for any of the acts set out under Article 2(2) of the Statute to be a constitutive element of genocide, the act must have been committed against one or several individuals, because such individual or individuals were members of a specific group, and specifically because they belonged to this group. Thus, the victim is chosen not because of his individual identity, but rather on account of his membership of a national, ethnical, racial or religious group. Accordingly, the individual is victimized not in their personal capacity, but as a representative of a protected group. As such, the crime of genocide is directed primarily against the group as a collective entity, rather than against the individual alone.

At a more technical level is another important consideration: is this second *mens rea* only found in situations where there is a specific communicated goal of destruction of the protected group? What about in instances where the perpetrator who has not expressed a desire for the destruction of a protected group but however operates without care about the foreseeable consequences of his or her actions. Can the court infer the second *mens rea* from the negligent actions of the accused person? With regard to the crime of genocide, the offender is culpable only because he knew *or should have known* that his actions would destroy a protected group, in whole or in part.

In the *Akayesu* case, the court stated that the perpetrator was guilty of genocide "because he knew or should have known that the act committed would destroy, in whole or in part, a group."[15] It proceeded to state that due to the difficulty in establishing this special intent to destroy a group, the court could consider other additional circumstances, such as "the scale of atrocities committed, their general nature, in a region or a country."[16] This special intent could also be inferred "from the perpetration of acts which violate, or which the perpetrators themselves consider to violate the very foundation of the group."[17] Similarly, the ITCY interpreted the intention to destroy a group as

---

[13] Akayesu, *supra* note 12, ¶ 518.

[14] United Nations, *Addressing Hate Speech Through Education: A Guide for Policy Makers* (U.N. Educ., Sci. & Cultural Org. 2023).

[15] Akayesu, *supra* note 12, ¶ 520.

[16] *Id.*,¶ 523.

[17] *Id.*, ¶ 524.

deriving "from the combined effect of speeches or projects laying the groundwork for and justifying the acts, from the massive scale of their destructive effect and from their specific nature, which aims at undermining what is considered to be the foundation of the group."[18] In *Jelisic*, the prosecutor argued that the "intent to destroy" is satisfied if the accused "knows that his acts will inevitably, or even only probably, result in the destruction of the group," even if the accused did not "seek the destruction."[19] This reflects the view of the UN Commission on Human Rights which also reported that an intent to destroy a group may be inferred from "actions or omissions of such a degree of criminal negligence or recklessness that the defendant must reasonably be assumed to have been aware of the consequences of his conduct." Similarly, it has been stated that if the foreseeable consequences of an act are, or seem likely to be, the destruction of a group, then the requirements of the special intent have been met.[20]

From this, one can surmise that being able to reasonably foresee the natural consequences of an act as the destruction or the likely destruction of a group and, nevertheless, continue in pursuit of those goals, would be interpreted as an intention to destroy a group wholly or in part. An express desire to destroy the group-whether or not communicated-need not be expressly proven by the prosecution. The intent can be proven by circumstantial evidence.[21] This position reflects most domestic legislation regarding the requirement for *mens rea*. The term can, therefore, be loosely interpreted to include situations other than where there was an expressed desire for the ultimate end. Recklessness for example, in the actions by the accused person can often be an indicator of the intention to destroy. Quigley describes this as a situation of "willful blindness" where one should be aware about the likely effect of his actions but fails to inquire on the consequences.[22] Similarly, he describes a situation where "the actor understands that a particular consequence will follow and consciously

---

[18] Radovan Karadzic, Raiko Mladic Case (n.d.) Decision of Trial Chamber 1, ICTY, Cases Nos. IT-95-5-R61 and IT-95-18-R61, ¶ 94.

[19] Prosecutor v. Goran Jelisic (Trial Judgement), IT-95-10-T, ICTY, December 14, 1999.

[20] Katherine Goldsmith, *The Issue of Intent in the Genocide Convention and Its Effect on the Prevention and Punishment of the Crime of Genocide: Toward a Knowledge-Based Approach*, GENOCIDE STUDIES AND PREVENTION: AN INTERNATIONAL JOURNAL 5(3) (2010), available at: https://digitalcommons.usf.edu/cgi/viewcontent.cgi?article=1092&context=gsp; *see also* Ambos, *supra* note 11.

[21] Indicators of such intent include the scale of atrocities committed, their general nature, in a region or a country, the fact of deliberately and systematically targeting victims on account of their membership of a particular group. See Mettraux, *supra note* 11. *See also* Ambos, *supra* note 11.

[22] Quigley, *supra* note 4, 119.

allows that result to occur, albeit without desiring that result."[23] Thus, in the *Jelisic* case, the court found the accused guilty, notwithstanding his personality or the seemingly random character of his killings. This would involve a culpability level lower than "knowledge," but akin to "recklessness."[24] However, it is important to note that in this situation, the existence of intent should be "the only inference that could reasonably be drawn."[25]

In the case concerning the Application of the Convention on the Prevention and Punishment of the Crime of Genocide (*Bosnia and Herzegovina v. Serbia and Montenegro*), the ICJ recognized that a 'higher authority' may possess genocidal intent, whether within the Army of the Republika Srpska or at the level of the Respondent itself.[26] This intent was found not to be made out on the facts.[27] The ICJ seemingly, as a matter of law, admitted to the possibility of a specific intent on the part of the Respondent, either on the basis of a concerted plan or on the basis that the events reviewed in the pleadings and evidence presented revealed a consistent pattern of conduct which could only point to the existence of a specific intent.

B. in whole or in part, a national, ethnical, racial or religious group, as such

It has been stated that while the individual victim is the direct victim of an act of genocide, the ultimate victim is usually the group.[28] In the *Krstic* case, the ICTY Trial Chamber emphasized this point stating that the ultimate victim of genocide is the group.[29] There is, therefore, a need for these groups to be protected. After much negotiations, the Convention settled on the four protected groups: national group, ethnic group, racial group, and religious group. While there were many other groups that required some mention in the group the main consideration was to mainly consider 'stable and permanent

---

[23] *Id.* at 116.

[24] *Id.* at 115.

[25] *Application of the Convention on the Prevention and Punishment of the Crime of Genocide* (Croatia v. Serbia), Judgment, 2015 I.C.J. Rep. (Feb. 3)., ¶148.

[26] *Case Concerning the Application of the Convention on the Prevention and Punishment of the Crime of Genocide* (Bosn. & Herz. v. Serb. & Montenegro), Judgment, 2007 I.C.J. 43, ¶ 371 (Feb. 26).

[27] *Id.* ¶, 376.

[28] Gaeta, *supra* note 11, 109.

[29] *Krstic,* Trial Chamber, August 2, 2001, ¶ 561: "[T]he victims of genocide must be targeted *by reason* of their membership in a group... The intent to destroy a group as such, in whole or in part, presupposes that the victims were chosen by reason of their membership in the group whose destruction was sought. Mere knowledge of the victims' membership in a distinct group on the part of the perpetrators is not sufficient to establish an intention to destroy the group as such."

group.'[30] However, even the determination of who belongs to these groups has been difficult. This is especially true in situations where the language of the perpetrator and the victims are almost similar. For example, one of the tasks of the Darfur Commission was to determine whether the Fur, Massalit, and Zaghawa groups were distinct groups that could qualify as protected groups-separate from the groups of their attackers.[31] This was because these three groups largely shared the same language and religious practices. The Commission relied on a very subjective and non-scientific way of differentiating the victim from the perpetrator: the perception of the victims as either African or Arab to differentiate the two groups.[32] One would expect that with such a serious offense, the distinction ought to be clear and unequivocal. Robert Cryer, however, proposed a mixture of both objective and subjective standards to determine a group: "assessed on a case-by-case basis by reference to the objective particulars of a given social or historical context, and by the subjective perceptions of the perpetrators."[33]

C. Deliberately inflicting on the group conditions of life calculated to bring about its physical destruction in whole or in part

The ICC Elements of Crimes interpret the term "conditions of life" as including but "not necessarily restricted to, deliberate deprivation of resources, indispensable for survival, such as food or medical services, or systematic expulsion from, homes." The term 'calculated' means that "there must be a deliberate effort to impose conditions of life that are generally extraneous for the sole purpose of destruction of the group."[34] This does not mean that there must be a guaranteed outcome-only that there is such a conscious decision. The challenge, however, arises when the intention for physical destruction arises in lack of care for the physical environment. What happens in a situation where, although the perpetrator does not show clear intent, but there is knowledge that the end result is the destruction of the group? For example, the Truth and Justice Commission in Paraguay held that there was no evidence of genocide for acts such as sterilization and executions

---

30 Cryer, *supra* note 10, 209.

31 Darfur International commission of Inquiry, 25 January 2005. *Report of the International Commission of Inquiry on Darfur to the United Nations Secretary General*, Geneva.

32 Cryer, *supra* note 10, 212.

33 *Id.* at 213.

34 Prosecutor v. Radislav Krstic (Appeal Judgement), IT-98-33-A, ICTY, April 19, 2004, available at: https://www.refworld.org/jurisprudence/caselaw/icty/2004/en/33340.

against the Aché People.[35] The Commission held there was no evidence of intention to destroy the group.[36] However, a similar Commission in Guatemala took an opposing view on the situation affecting the Mayan population. Destruction of goods and crops, forced displacements and destruction of cultural elements were seen as indicators of such intention to destroy the Mayan.[37] The actions of the Brazil government in failing to prevent deforestation of Amazon-leading to escalation of violence and killing of tribal leaders and the survival of the communities in the forest- were viewed as a mode of genocide.[38] This was described as "environmental cleansing"- the deliberate manipulation and misuse of the environment so as to subordinate groups based on characteristics such as race, ethnicity, nationality, religion and so forth.[39] Similarly, in *Prosecutor v. Radislav Krstić*[40] the court agreed to consider the destruction of mosques and buildings belonging to members of a group as evidence of intent to destroy the group. This ruling underscores that the destruction of cultural and religious buildings can be considered as part of the evidence to establish the intent to destroy a protected group, a key element in proving genocide.

Inflicting group conditions of life could include the imposition of a 'modern' lifestyle to replace what one would consider as a 'traditional and backward' lifestyle.[41] Therefore, intentionally affecting the natural habitat of a people while knowing that it would affect the indigenous communities and making it impossible for the group to continue sustaining itself could be evidence of such intention to destroy the group.[42] It does not matter whether such intention was motivated by the need for political or economic development since the

---

[35] Emmanuel Guematcha, *Genocide Against Indigenous Peoples: The Experiences of the Truth Commisisons of Canada & Guatemala,* THE INTERNATIONAL INDIGENOUS POLICY JOURNAL, 10(2) (2019).

[36] *Id.*

[37] *Id.* at 12.

[38] Aurelie Lopez, *The Protection of Environmentally-Displaced Persons In International Law,* ENVIRONMENTAL LAW, 37, No. 2, 365-409, 232 (Spring 2007).

[39] Mark Drumbl, *Oral intervention of Mark A. Drumbl, The International responses to the environmental impacts of war,* GEO. INT'L ENVTL. L. REV., Volume 17, 565 (2005).

[40] Krstic, ¶ 580.

[41] Y Eski discusses how genocide involves not just physical but also sociocultural annihilation. This includes the destruction of cultural identities and traditions by forced assimilation or the imposition of a different lifestyle. *See* Y. Eski, *An existentialist victimology of genocide?* In Y. ESKI (ED.), GENOCIDE AND VICTIMOLOGY, 6-22 (Routledge Taylor & Francis Group 2020).

[42] Quigley, *supra* note 4, 111-112.

motive does not negate the intent.[43] An example provided is building the road and related industrial activities and, thereby affecting the ecology of a forest and the source of food. This, in turn, results in the death of the community due to lack of food but also introduction of other diseases that the community does not have a natural immunity to. In the end, even if the perpetrator is pursuing a goal different from destruction of the victim group, they would still be held liable.[44] There is no need to prove that the perpetrator bore some ill will against the victims.[45] However, forcing the migration of a people, by itself, is not sufficient to deduce an intention to destroy the group.[46] It is important that the conditions of life are actually intended to cause the destruction of the group-whether or not the group is actually destroyed.[47]

II. 'Development' on rivers as a source of genocidal activities

The concept of rivers as a unit for development emerged in the late 19th and early 20th centuries.[48] The concept was boosted by technological changes in dam construction at the beginning of the twentieth century. This led to a primary focus on the construction of large dams in the late twentieth century, resulting in an increase from 5,000 dams in 1950 to 45,000 in 2000.[49] Dams are now considered long-term avenues for meeting needs such as hydropower generation, flood control and water storage for irrigation, amongst other multiple benefits such as export earnings from the sale of electricity and job creation.[50]

While dams have contributed to economic growth in the twentieth century, the services and benefits they provide have come at a cost. Human interventions in the water cycle have placed many rivers and river basins under growing stress. Interventions such as construction of dams and the resultant large-scale irrigation, and interruption of natural flow of water generally have

---

[43] *Id.* at 122. In the *Kristic* case, it was held that "The intent to destroy a group as such must be the only, or at least the primary, motive for the acts committed. However, it is not necessary to prove that the perpetrator had no other motive" [ICTY, Prosecutor v. Radislav Krstić, IT-98-33-T, Trial Chamber, August 2, 2001, ¶ 571] 6.

[44] Quigley, *supra* note 4, 124-125.

[45] *Id.* at 202-203.

[46] Cryer, *supra* note 10, 216.

[47] Gaeta, *supra* note 11, 109.

[48] MOLLE FRANCOIS, DEVELOPMENT TRAJECTORIES OF RIVER BASINS: A CONCEPTUAL FRAMEWORK. (Colombo: International Water Management Institute 2003).

[49] WORLD COMMISSION ON DAMS, DAMS AND DEVELOPMENT: A NEW FRAMEWORK FOR DECISION-MAKING (s.l.: Earthscans Publications 2000).

[50] Edson Severnini, *The Power of Hydroelectric Dams: Historical Evidence from the United States over the Twentieth Century,* THE ECONOMIC JOURNAL, Volume 133, Issue 649, 420–459 (January 2023), https://doi.org/10.1093/ej/ueac059.

unexpected third-party effects elsewhere in the river. This section provides an overview of the problems associated with large dams from a human rights perspective.

Communities have depended on rivers for livelihood, habitat and the sustaining ecological functions they provide, and throughout history alterations to rivers by human beings have affected riverine communities in varying ways. As a result, the construction of dams has come with negative side effects. These include displaced communities, which has, in turn, led to conflicts for the few resources.[51] Large dam projects have also resulted in the loss of the wildlife habitat, loss of species, destruction of downstream fishing activities, loss of cultural heritage of the people, among others.[52] In addition, flash floods destroy crops and kill people downstream. The ones who survive then get displaced and then live in poverty.[53] Extreme situations also include earthquakes that result from filling of dams and destroying the already constructed houses[54] The impact on the ecosystem is seen more as negative rather than positive.[55]

The absence of effective policies on forced displacement is one of the most important concerns when it comes to construction of large dams. Around 40-80 million people are estimated to have been displaced by the construction of dams.[56] Most of them are indigenous or tribal peoples and their land is usually targeted for major projects such as major dams, mines, and for dumping of

---

[51] Oscar Mwangi, *Hydropolitics, Ecocide and Human Security in Lesotho: A Case Study of the Lesotho Highlands Water Project,* JOURNAL OF SOUTHERN AFRICAN STUDIES, 33(1), 3-17, 5 (2007); *See* Yousra Mohamed Khir Alla & Lee Liu, *Impacts of Dams on the Environment: A Review,* INTERNATIONAL JOURNAL OF ENVIRONMENT, AGRICULTURE AND BIOTECHNOLOGY, 6(1), 64-74 (2021); *See also* Petro Kotze, *The world's dams: Doing major harm but a manageable problem?* (2022), https://news.mongabay.com/2022/04/the-worlds-dams-doing-major-harm-but-a-manageable-problem/.

[52] *Id.* at 5. See also Regina M. Paulose, *Crouching tiger, hidden dragon: hydropower and crimes against humanity* in REGINA M. PAULOSE (ED), GREEN CRIMES AND INTERNATIONAL CRIMINAL LAW, 257-294 (Vernon Press 2021).

[53] Johnstone Barbara Rose, *Chixoy Dam Legacies: The Struggle to Secure Reparation and the Right to Remedy in Guatemala,* WATER ALTERNATIVES, 3(2), 341-361, 344 (2010).

[54] Earth Island Institute, *376 Killed. Did World Bank Know?,* EARTH ISLAND JOURNAL, 11, No. 3, 18 (Summer 1996); *See* Mina Parvizishad, *Analyzing the Impact of Large Dams on Seismicity Patterns,* ARCHIVES OF HYDRO-ENGINEERING AND ENVIRONMENTAL MECHANICS, 68(1), 3-17 (2021).

[55] Mwangi, *supra* note 51.

[56] Michelle Hay et al., *Dam-Induced Displacement and Resettlement: A Literature Review,* FUTURE DAMS Working Paper 004 (September 2019), available at: https://hummedia.manchester.ac.uk/institutes/gdi/publications/workingpapers/futuredams/futuredams-working-paper-004-hay-skinner-notron.pdf.

toxic waste.[57] Perhaps the most obvious effect of displacement is the loss of their land, forest, fishing grounds and grazing lands.[58] As a result of their dislocation, the victims have lost their main source of income and livelihood. Forced relocations in the name of development also jeopardize the survival of the displaced, especially as the majority of those displaced are from minority communities. Large dams are, therefore, seen as a huge risk to their security.[59]

The indigenous people are the worst prepared to compete in the labor and financial markets, the large majority being unable to speak any of the national languages.[60] Their displacement is also likely to cause a loss of livelihoods, eroded health, severe food insecurity, loss of identity and dignity. In addition, these populations have a very strong attachment to their land. Their land is not just a commodity that can be sold or bought in the open market. Instead, it is the source of life for these communities.[61] And "if land enables Indigenous life, the dispossession or contamination of those lands threatens Indigenous life."[62] Any attempt to change the way they use their land is immediately interpreted as an act of genocide.[63] For example, when the Awash Valley program in Ethiopia

---

[57] T. B. Goldtooth, *Continuing threats to Indigenous people's sovereignty and survival*, RACE, POVERTY & THE ENVIRONMENT, Vol. 11, No. 1, 9-12 (Summer 2004).

[58] WORLD COMMISSION ON DAMS, DAMS, INDIGENOUS PEOPLES, CAPE TOWN: SECRETARIAT OF THE WORLD COMMISSION ON DAMS (1999).

[59] Mwangi, *supra* note 51, See also Regina M. Paulose, *Hydropower and Human Rights: Revisiting the World Commission on Dams Report*, INDIAN JOURNAL OF PROJECTS, INFRASTRUCTURE AND ENERGY LAW (December 17, 2021), https://ijpiel.com/index.php/2021/12/17/hydropower-and-human-rights-revisiting-the-world-commission-on-dams-report/.

[60] ILO, *Indigenous People in a Changing World of Work: Exploring Indigenous peoples economic and social rights through the Indigenous Navigator*, ILO (May 17, 2021), https://www.ilo.org/publications/indigenous-peoples-changing-world-work-exploring-indigenous-peoples

[61] "Land provides sustenance for current and future generations; it is connected to spiritual beliefs, traditional knowledge and teachings; it is fundamental to cultural reproduction." OECD, *The importance of land for Indigenous economic development*, in LINKING INDIGENOUS COMMUNITIES WITH REGIONAL DEVELOPMENT IN CANADA, OECD Publishing (Paris: January 21, 2020), https://doi.org/10.1787/fc2b28b3-en.
See also Belay et al., *Land Use and Land Cover Changes in Awash National Park, Ethiopia: Impact of Decentralization on the Use and Management of Resources*, OPEN JOURNAL OF ECOLOGY, 4, 950-960 (2014) doi: 10.4236/oje.2014.415079.

[62] Kaitlin Reed, *We Are a Part of the Land and the Land Is Us*, HUMBOLDT JOURNAL OF SOCIAL RELATIONS, No. 42, Special Issue 42 (2020), https://digitalcommons.humboldt.edu/hjsr/vol1/iss42/4/.

[63] World Commission on Dams, *supra* note 58; *See also* Lauren Eichler, *Ecocide Is Genocide: Decolonizing the Definition of Genocide*, GENOCIDE STUDIES AND PREVENTION: AN INTERNATIONAL JOURNAL, 14(2), 104-121 (2020).

led to loss of the forest grazing lands, from the perspective of the local population, the dam was a form of punishment from God.[64]

As if this is not enough, there is an obvious failure on the part of the promoters to factor in relevant issues such as the distinctiveness of the affected population, the need to get prior informed consent, failure to recognize and measure the impact on the loss of the land on the people, and lack of adequate compensation, if any.[65] For example, in Lesotho, where the people were displaced by the Lesotho Highlands Water Project, they were only promised groceries for fifteen years as compensation.[66] Lastly, any attempts to oppose the displacement of the population and construction of dams are faced with brute force. Another example can be found in Guatemala, where it is reported that 326 people were killed by agents of the government of Guatemala for opposing the construction of the Chixoy dam.[67]

Some scholars have therefore considered the displacement of the indigenous and tribal peoples due to development projects as a "developmental genocide," "cultural genocide," or "ethnocide."[68] This describes "the deliberate and systematic destruction of a culture."[69] This can be done by the imposition of the oppressor's national pattern on the oppressed group, forced assimilation, destruction of cultural symbols, and the disruption of traditional practices and relationships with the land.[70] Unlike traditional genocide, which often involves direct physical violence, developmental genocide can involve indirect harms that compromise the quality of life and the ability of a group to maintain its identity. This form of genocide is mediated by projects such as the construction

---

[64] World Commission on Dams, *supra* note 58, 21.

[65] *Id.*

[66] Earth Island Institute, *supra* note 54, 18. While the amount of compensation is not supported elsewhere, there is proof of its inadequacy and delay in payment. *See* Fiona Darroch et al., *Dams, Displacement, And Communal Compensation: A Lesotho Highlands Legal Case*, UNIVERSITY OF BOTSWANA LAW JOURNAL, 28, 122-175 (2020).

[67] Earth Island Institute, *supra* note 54, 18. Other sources have different numbers of fatalities. For example, others state that the massacres "resulted in the deaths of 444 of the 791 members of the Río Negro community" (B.R. Johnston, *Chixoy dam legacies: The struggle to secure reparation and the right to remedy in Guatemala*, WATER ALTERNATIVES 3(2): 341-361 (2010).

[68] David Goyes, *Genocide And Ecocide In Four Colombian Indigenous Communities: The Erosion Of A Way Of Life And Memory*, THE BRITISH JOURNAL OF CRIMINOLOGY, 61(4), 965-984 (2021); Alana Tiemessen, *Cultural Genocide in Law & Politics*, in OXFORD RESEARCH ENCYCLOPEDIA OF INTERNATIONAL STUDIES (Oxford University Press 2024).

[69] Dallas Browne, Cultural *Genocide*, in SALEM PRESS ENCYCLOPEDIA (2019).

[70] Goyes, *supra* note 68. See also Regina M. Paulose, *Death by a Thousand Cuts? Green Tech, Traditional Knowledge, and Genocide*, GENOCIDE STUDIES PREVENTION JOURNAL, Vol 16, Article 6 (2022) 1: 40–59. DOI: https://doi.org/10.5038/1911-9933.16.1.1881.

of dams whose effect is to displace indigenous communities and destroy their traditional ways of life.[71]

In cases in which minorities are forcibly resettled in order to free their traditional land and rivers for economic development, the purpose of the displacement might be to further economic development. However, it goes without saying that a project may have more than one purpose. For example, the actions taken against Paraguay's Northern Aché population between 1962 and 1972. The state, in a bid to make way for mining, farming, ranchers and timber industry for transnational companies, was complicit in the killing of half of the Aché population.[72]

The construction of the Chixoy Dam in Guatemala is a prominent example of human rights abuse that occurred as a result of development of dams. When the water levels from the dam rose, ten communities by the river basin were initially displaced and then destroyed by massacre. They were later forcibly hunted down and displaced by the government.[73] The government had militias that targeted anyone opposed to the dam and labeled them as part of the pro-guerilla movement, hence providing an excuse for the massacres.[74] The violence against the Rio Negro inhabitants included rape of women, torture, enforced disappearances, strangulation, and death by machetes.[75] Finally, in September 1982, 35 orphaned children from Río Negro were among 92 people machine-gunned and burned to death in a village near the Dam. The survivors were then forcibly evicted from their homes, and moved to a grossly inadequate resettlement site. Filling of the reservoir began soon after this final massacre. Complaints filed in the Inter-American Commission on Human Rights showed that 444 of the 791 members of the Rio Negro community were killed.[76]

---

[71] Goyes, *supra* note 68.

[72] Mark Münzel, *The Aché Indians: Genocide in Paraguay.*, Copenhagen: INTERNATIONAL WORK GROUP FOR INDIGENOUS AFFAIRS (1973), https://www.iwgia.org/images/publications//Ache_Doc1.pdf.

[73] Johnston, *supra* note 67.

[74] Jaroslave Colajacomo, *The Chixoy Dam: The Maya Achi' Genocide: The Story of Forced Displacement,* Cape Town: WORLD COMMISSION OF DAMS, 4 (1999), http://rio-negro.info/che/doc/ChixoyDam_StoryOfForcedResettlement.pdf.

[75] Bret Thiele and Mayra Gomez, *Genocide in Guatemala: The Roles of the World Bank and Inter-American Development Bank,* INDIGENOUS LAW BULLETIN, 6(13), 8 (2005), https://classic.austlii.edu.au/au/journals/IndigLawB/2005/43.html.

[76] Johnston, *supra* note 67, 343.

The displacement and violence also led to the destruction of cultural practices and traditional knowledge.[77] Elderly community members, who were the custodians of traditional knowledge, were targeted and killed. Medicinal plants, traditional healing systems, and other cultural practices were lost as communities were forced to leave their ancestral land.[78] In summary, the Chixoy Dam project acted as a catalyst for the genocide and human rights abuses against the Maya Achi people, facilitated by the Guatemalan military government.

In Brazil, there was a similar claim that the construction of the Bel Monte dam had disposed of the indigenous communities and had led to ethnocide by "the cultural and environmental damage done to the Xingu region."[79]

The link between construction of the dams and genocide is therefore evident where it is accompanied by forced displacement, violence and destruction of the indigenous communities.

III. Case Study of the Ethiopian people & El Molo on River Omo

The Omo River is a lifeline for the riverine indigenous communities of southwest Ethiopia and the indigenous community residing on the southeastern shores of Lake Turkana.[80] Among these are the El Molo, which is one of the smallest ethnic groups in Kenya. The El Molo is mainly a fishing community that relies on fish for their livelihood.[81]

In 2006, the Ethiopian Government embarked on one of its most ambitious projects: the construction of the Gibe III Dam on the banks of River Omo.[82] The goals of the construction of the dam were to generate power and secondly to

---

[77]Jaroslave Calajacomo *Maya Achi: the Story of a Forced Displacement,* CULTURAL SURVIVAL (2010), https://www.culturalsurvival.org/publications/cultural-survival-quarterly/maya-achi-story-forced-resettlement.

[78] *Id.*

[79] Zoe Sullivan, *Brazil's dispossessed: Belo Monte dam ruinous for indigenous cultures,* MONGABAY(December 8, 2016), https://news.mongabay.com/2016/12/brazils-dispossessed-belo-monte-dam-ruinous-for-indigenous-cultures/.

[80] Claudia Carr, *Humanitarian Catastrophe & Regional Armed Conflict Brewing in the Transborder Region of Ethiopia, Kenya & South Sudan: The Proposed Gibe III Dam in Ethiopia,* UNIVERSITY OF CALIFORNIA AT BERKELEY: AFRICAN RESOURCES WORKING GROUP (2012), https://assets.survivalinternational.org/documents/1282/gibe-iii-dam-report-carr-arwg.pdf.

[81] Purity Kiura, *El molo: The forgotten people of Lake Turkana,* SABINET GATEWAY; PROJECT, ENDANGERED LANGUAGES *EL MOLO* (2013), https://www.endangeredlanguages.com/lang/4124 (accessed November 30, 2024).

[82] Nate Olson, *Gibe III,* https://www.canr.msu.edu/news/gibe-iii (accessed November 30, 2024).

control the flow of the river in order to allow for large-scale irrigation farming. The government envisioned converting the surrounding land to sugarcane plantations. In a speech in Jinka, the capital of South Omo Zone, in January 2011 the Prime Minister, Meles Zenawi, stated, "[e]ven though this area [the Lower Omo] is known as backward in terms of civilization, it will become an example of rapid development."[83] Objections to the construction of the dam centered around anticipated devastating environmental, social, and economic impacts on the communities and ecosystems dependent on the Omo River and Lake Turkana.[84] For example, in Kenya, the dam was expected to reduce the flow of water into Lake Turkana, which receives 90% of its water from the River Omo.[85] In addition, since Lake Turkana runs in the mainly dry northern Kenya it is the main source of water for most of the inhabitants in the region. This situation is magnified by the fact that most of these inhabitants are pastoralists who keep cattle. Around 200,000 pastoralists within the lower Omo basin would likely face devastation.[86] The biomass and the fisheries on the lake were also likely to be negatively affected by the dam.[87]

The Government of Ethiopia, however, failed to conduct an environmental and social impact assessment on the project or to consult with local populations. These are fundamental requirements for such a large-scale project in order to build trust and manage expectations, especially among the local communities.[88] Effective community engagement is no longer just a statutory requirement but a critical component of successful infrastructure development. The UNDRIP, for example, mandates the states to obtain the free, prior and informed consent of the indigenous people before any significant

---

[83] Sabine Troeger, *Just Societal Transformation: Perspectives of Pastoralists in the Lower Omo Valley in Ethiopia*, in Oguge (ed.) AFRICAN HANDBOOK OF CLIMATE CHANGE ADAPTATION, 2447-2467, 2458 (Springer 2021), https://doi.org/10.1007/978-3-030-45106-6_265.

[84] The Environment Protection Authority only approved the project two years after the construction had started. However, environmental and human rights activists have criticized these documents for their poor preparation and their belated release after construction began. *See* AIDDATA, *Project 34447*, https://china.aiddata.org/projects/34447/ (accessed December 27, 2024).

[85] Sean Avery, *Lake Turkana & the Lower Omo: Hydrological Impacts of Major Dam & Irrigation Developments* 10, AFRICAN STUDIES CENTRE, UNIVERSITY OF OXFORD (2012), https://www.africanstudies.ox.ac.uk/research-projects/lake-turkana-and-the-lower-omo-hydrological-impacts-of-major-dam-and-irrigation-de.

[86] *Id.*, at. 1-4.

[87] *Id.* at 6.

[88] Arden Lunay, *Constructing better infrastructure outcomes with community engagement*, ARTICULOUS, https://articulous.com.au/infrastructure-engagement/.

projects that could affect them are implemented.[89] This recognizes that the indigenous people also have a right to self-determination. This includes the right to decide how the property that they hold will be utilized. Since this right is inherent and not gifted by the state, it cannot also be taken away by ignoring the voices of the local community.[90]

Furthermore, the environmentalists were concerned about the negative environmental and social impact the construction of the dam would bring about. Key among these were likely seismic activities due to the size and magnitude of the project and massive landslides. According to the Africa Resources Working Group, the construction of the Gibe III dam on the Omo River, which the Indigenous and local communities are dependent on for their livelihood, would lead to massive economic and cultural losses, with the resultant widespread severe hunger, disease and loss of life on a regional scale.[91]

Despite all these concerns raised by a number of environmental actors and indigenous activists the Gibe III Dam was constructed and opened in October 2015. This eventually led to the relocation of indigenous and local communities who live in the vicinity of the sugar plantations into permanent sedentary villages under the Ethiopian government's infamous "villagization" program. Under this program, people were to be moved into sedentary villages and provided with schools, hospitals, and other infrastructure.[92]

---

[89] "States shall consult and cooperate in good faith with the indigenous peoples concerned through their own representative institutions in order to obtain their free, prior and informed consent before adopting and implementing legislative or administrative measures that may affect them." UN Declaration on the Rights of Indigenous People, Art 19, Sep. 13, 2007, G.A. Res. 61/295, U.N. Doc. A/RES/61/295.

[90] *See* THE INTERNATIONAL ALLIANCE OF INDIGENOUS AND TRIBAL PEOPLE OF THE TROPICAL FORESTS & THE INDIGENOUS PEOPLES' FOUNDATION FOR EDUCATION AND ENVIRONMENT, *Handbook on Free, Prior and Informed Consent For Practical Use by Indigenous Peoples' Communities* (September 2021), https://www.un-redd.org/sites/default/files/2021-09/FPIC_Handbook_Final%20(80337).pdf.

[91] Africa Resources Working Group, *A Commentary on the Environmental, Socio-economic and Human Rights Impact of the Proposed Gibe III Dam in the Lower Omo River Basin of Ethiopia,* FOREST PEOPLES (January 2009), https://www.forestpeoples.org/sites/fpp/files/publication/2010/08/ethiopiahydroelecimpactsarwgjan09eng.pdf.

[92] United Nations Human Rights Council, *Communication Report of Special Procedures: Communications Sent 1 December 2010 to 31 May 2011; Replies Received 1 February 2011 to 31 July 2011,* New York: United Nations General Assembly, A/HRC/18/51, September 9, 2011, https://www.ohchr.org/sites/default/files/Documents/HRBodies/SP/A.HRC.18.51.pdf.

The construction of Gibe III also brought two types of changes: first, traditional livelihoods based on flood-retreat cultivation were significantly eroded. Secondly, the indigenous communities have been left greatly impoverished.[93]

IV. Impact on the El Molo

The El Molo community in Kenya is no exception. The construction of the Gibe III dam on the River Omo has significantly reduced the water flow to Lake Turkana, their main source of livelihood.[94] In some calculations, the dam has caused a reduction of up to 60 to 70 percent of Omo River flow volume and inflow to Lake Turkana.[95] This extreme drop in river waters would quickly cause the collapse of Indigenous riverine and lakeside survival systems, producing mass starvation, accompanied by region-wide violent conflict over disappearing food resources.[96]

With the reduced inflow of freshwater due to the dam,[97] the salinity of Lake Turkana is increasing, leading to a decline in fish populations. The reduced inflows of water have also affected the breeding grounds of the fish and affected their ability to multiply as they otherwise would. This directly threatens the El Molo's primary source of food and income, making it increasingly difficult for them to sustain their traditional way of life.[98] For example, it is estimated that the number of fish caught by each fisherman has reduced from fifteen to one per day.[99] This, in turn, has also affected the economic stability of the community. Where in the past the community would supply four trucks of fish every month, it currently only supplies one track. Such dire economic

---

[93] OAKLAND INSTITUTE, *How they Tricked Us: Living with the Gibe III Dam and Sugarcane Plantations in South West Ethiopia* (June 10, 2019), https://www.oaklandinstitute.org/gibe-dam-sugarcane-plantations-southwest-ethiopia.

[94] Avery, *supra* note 85, p. 6.

[95] AFP, *We are Divided: Lake upsets life for tiny Kenyan El Molo tribe* (2022), https://nation.africa/kenya/counties/turkana/lake-turkana-upsets-life-for-tiny-el-molo-tribe-3924692.

[96] Carr, *supra* note 80.

[97] The estimates are that Lake Turkana has lost around 10-20 meters of water since the construction of the Dam. *See* Sean Avery, *What Future for Lake Turkana? The Impact of Hydropower and Irrigation Development on the World's Largest Desert Lake,* AFRICAN STUDIES CENTER, UNIVERSITY OF OXFORD (2013), https://www.mursi.org/pdf/copy3_of_pastoral-livelihoods.pdf/view.

[98] Fredrick Mugira, *Life After Gibe III Construction: Kenya's Smallest Tribe Struggles to Survive as Lake Turkana Water Recedes,* WATER JOURNALISTS AFRICA, November 9, 2017, https://infonile.org/en/2017/11/life-after-gibe-iii-dam-construction-kenyas-smallest-tribe-struggles-to-survive-as-lake-turkana-water-recedes/ .

[99] *Id.*

conditions, in turn, have affected the ability of the community to access education, healthcare and resulted in early deaths among the population.[100] In addition, the effect of the dam on the fishing habitat has had an impact on the survival of the El Molo.[101] In addition, the El Molo practiced traditional farming practices such as reverse agriculture which relied on the natural flooding cycles on the lake.[102] These natural floods have, however, been disrupted by the construction of the dam. This, in turn, has further impeded the ability of the El Molo to feed themselves by growing traditional crops.

Another effect of the reduced resources is increased competition between the El Molo and other communities that rely on Lake Turkana for basic needs like food and water. The increased competition has, in turn, led to tensions and armed conflict among these communities.[103] According to the UN Human Rights Council, the dam has introduced "competition over land and resources has resulted in periodic conflicts among these groups,"[104] Being the smallest community among the number, the El Molo are thereby more exposed to attacks from their neighbors. In addition, their natural areas of hiding from attacks by their enemies on islets on the lake have also been interfered with and left them exposed and vulnerable.[105]

The dam has also affected the quality of the water in Lake Turkana. First, the reduced inflows from the Omo have increased the salinity of the water and rendered them unfit for consumption. Secondly, there has been an increased amount of fluoride in the water, which has exposed the El Molo to "crippling skeletal fluorosis."[106] In addition, the industries upstream pollute the stream and the Lake with chemical wastes and affect the health of the people downstream.

The El Molo is also suffering as the dam has increased the "crippling cultural heritage and traditional knowledge that is also related to fishing."[107] The Lake

---

[100] *Id.*

[101] Carr, *supra* note 80.

[102] CLIMATE DIPLOMACY, *Security Implications of the Gilgel Gibe III Dam in Ethiopia* (2023), https://climate-diplomacy.org/case-studies/security-implications-gilgel-gibe-iii-dam-ethiopia.

[103] BUSINESS DAILY, *Is Gibe 111 dam a poisoned chalice for the Turkana?* (2010), https://www.businessdailyafrica.com/bd/corporate/health/is-gibe-111-dam-a-poisoned-chalice-for-the-turkana--1958916.

[104] Human Rights Council, 2011. *Communication Report of Special Procedures: Communications Sent 1 December 2010 to 31 May 2011; Replies Received 1 February 2011 to 31 July 2011*, New York: United Nations General Assembly, 54. Also see CLIMATE DIPLOMACY, *supra* note 850.

[105] Kiura, *supra* note 2.

[106] Avery, *supra* note 97, 18.

[107] Mugira, *supra* note 98. See also Carr, *supra* note 80.

has served as a source of special religious and cultural activities for the community.[108] Fishing was not just an economic activity but a social, cultural and religious activity. Hunting of hippos and crocodiles on the lake also involved a lot of communal activities that resulted in praising the heroes, eating together, and thanking the ancestors. Fishing activities also offered opportunities to make implements such as traditional rafts, harpoons, and woven baskets to catch the fish in shallow baskets.[109] However, as the external pressures caused by the dam threaten their fishing lifestyle, these traditional practices are also in danger of being lost.

Conclusion

In conclusion, the resultant effects of the construction of the Gibe III Dam raise serious concerns of "cultural genocide" among the El Molo.[110] The significant loss of a source of livelihood has no doubt led to an unnecessary loss of life among them. In addition, the disruption of their traditional livelihood by the dam and the resulting impoverishment of their lives suggests a deliberate neglect or recklessness on the part of the funders of the dam. There had been various studies that had forewarned about this likely consequence to the El Molo. Some even stated that up to 200,000 lives of the surrounding communities would be severely and adversely threatened by diminished fish stocks, leading to food insecurity.[111] They also showed how there was a lack of consideration of the needs of the indigenous economies and of "the barest survival needs."[112] of the communities around the region. In addition, the developers were informed the dam would introduce "an options squeeze"[113] that would also take away all the alternative options for survival and exacerbate inter-communal conflict.

In effect, the cumulative effects of the dam currently threaten the existence of the El Molo people. Admittedly, it is difficult to show any prior deliberate plans or desire for destruction of the El Molo by the Ethiopian government. However, it is also clear that those implementing the dam project continued with its construction with little care about the foreseeable effect and consequences of their actions. It is also clear that this dam has now added to

---

108 Human Rights Council, *supra* note 104.
109 Kiura, *supra* note 2.
110 It is important to note that although Raphael Lemkin initially considered cultural destruction of the identity of a group as amounting to genocide, the final text of the 1948 Genocide Convention does not include cultural genocide.
111 Africa Resources Working Group, *supra* note 91; Carr, *supra* note 80.
112 *Id.*
113 *Id.*

the level of exposure and risk of extinction of Kenya's smallest ethnic community. Like the view by the Commission in Guatemala regarding the Mayan population, the continued destruction of livelihoods and cultural elements of the El Molo should be taken as indicators of such intention to destroy them. Indeed, their continued loss of lives and livelihoods indicates a troubling lack of care and concern for their lives. One could, therefore, argue that the promoters and funders of the dam "knew *or should have known*" that their actions would destroy the El Molo. The prior independent environmental impact assessment reports act as a good pointer to this recklessness. The only way for future 'development' and 'cultural genocide'- such as that of the El Molo-to can be prevented is for governments to be held accountable for such reckless action.

Bibliography

AFP, *We are Divided: Lake upsets life for tiny Kenyan El Molo tribe* (2022), https://nation.africa/kenya/counties/turkana/lake-turkana-upsets-life-for-tiny-el-molo-tribe-3924692.

Africa Resources Working Group, *A Commentary on the Environmental, Socio-economic and Human Rights Impact of the Proposed Gibe III Dam in the Lower Omo River Basin of Ethiopia,* Forest Peoples (January 2009), https://www.forestpeoples.org/sites/fpp/files/publication/2010/08/ethiopiahydroelecimpactsarwgjan09eng.pdf.

Aiddata, *Project 34447,* https://china.aiddata.org/projects/34447/ (accessed December 27, 2024).

Payam Akhavan, *The Crime of Genocide in the ICTR Jurisprudence,* Journal of International Criminal Justice, 3(4), 989-1006 (2005). https://doi.org/10.1093/jicj/mqi060.

Yousra Mohamed Khir Alla & Lee Liu, *Impacts of Dams on the Environment: A Review,* International Journal of Environment, Agriculture and Biotechnology, 6(1), 64-74 (2021). https://doi.org/10.22161/ijeab.61.9

Kai Ambos, *What does 'intent to destroy' in genocide mean?,* International Review of the Red Cross, 91(876), 835-851, 835 (2006). https://doi.org/10.1017/S1816383110000056.

Application of the Convention on the Prevention and Punishment of the Crime of Genocide (*Croatia v. Serbia*), Judgment, 2015 I.C.J. Rep. (Feb. 3)., ¶ 148.

D. S. Avery, Lake Turkana & the Lower Omo: Hydrological Impacts of Major Dam and Irrigation Developments (Univ. of Oxford, 2012).

Sean Avery, *Lake Turkana & the Lower Omo: Hydrological Impacts of Major Dam & Irrigation Developments* 10, African Studies Centre, University of Oxford (2012), https://www.africanstudies.ox.ac.uk/research-projects/lake-turkana-and-the-lower-omo-hydrological-impacts-of-major-dam-and-irrigation-de.

Sean Avery, *What Future for Lake Turkana? The Impact of Hydropower and Irrigation Development on the World's Largest Desert Lake,* African Studies Center, University of Oxford (2013), https://www.mursi.org/pdf/copy3_of_pastoral-livelihoods.pdf/view.

Belay et al., *Land Use and Land Cover Changes in Awash National Park, Ethiopia: Impact of Decentralization on the Use and Management of Resources,* Open Journal of Ecology, 4, 950-960 (2014) doi: 10.4236/oje.2014.415079. https://doi.org/10.4236/oje.2014.415079.

Dallas Browne, Cultural *Genocide,* in Salem Press Encyclopedia (2019).

Business Daily, *Is Gibe 111 dam a poisoned chalice for the Turkana?* (2010), https://www.businessdailyafrica.com/bd/corporate/health/is-gibe-111-dam-a-poisoned-chalice-for-the-turkana--1958916.

Claudia Carr, *Humanitarian Catastrophe & Regional Armed Conflict Brewing in the Transborder Region of Ethiopia, Kenya & South Sudan: The Proposed Gibe III Dam in Ethiopia,* University of California at Berkeley: African Resources Working Group (2012).

Case Concerning the Application of the Convention on the Prevention and Punishment of the Crime of Genocide (*Bosnia & Herz. v. Serbia & Montenegro),* Judgment, 2007 I.C.J. 43, ¶ 371 (Feb. 26).

Climate Diplomacy, *Security Implications of the Gilgel Gibe III Dam, Ethiopia.* https://climate-diplomacy.org/case-studies/security-implications-gilgel-gibe-iii-dam-ethiopia.

Jaroslave Colajacomo, *Maya Achi: the Story of a Forced Displacement,* Cultural Survival (2010), https://www.culturalsurvival.org/publications/cultural-survival-quarterly/maya-achi-story-forced-resettlement.

Jaroslave Colajacomo, *The Chixoy Dam: The Maya Achi' Genocide: The Story of Forced Displacement,* Cape Town: World Commission of Dams, 4 (1999), http://rio-negro.info/che/doc/ChixoyDam_StoryOfForcedResettlement.pdf.

Convention on the Prevention and Punishment of the Crime of Genocide, art 2, Dec. 9, 1948, S. Exec. Doc. O, 81-1 (1949), 78 U.N.T.S. 277.

Robert Cryer, An Introduction to International Criminal Law & Procedure, 2nd ed. (New York: Cambridge University Press 2010).

Darfur International commission of Inquiry, 25 January 2005. *Report of the International Commission of Inquiry on Darfur to the United Nations Secretary General,* Geneva.

Fiona Darroch et al., *Dams, Displacement, And Communal Compensation: A Lesotho Highlands Legal Case,* University of Botswana Law Journal, 28, 122-175 (2020).

Mark Drumbl, *Oral intervention of Mark A. Drumbl, The International responses to the environmental impacts of war,* Geo. Int'l Envtl. L. Rev., Volume 17, 565 (2005).

Earth Island Institute, *376 Killed. Did World Bank Know?,* Earth Island Journal, 11, No. 3, 18 (Summer 1996).

Lauren Eichler, *Ecocide Is Genocide: Decolonizing the Definition of Genocide,* Genocide Studies and Prevention: An International Journal, 14(2), 104-121 (2020). https://doi.org/10.5038/1911-9933.14.2.1720.

Y. Eski, *An existentialist victimology of genocide?* In Y. Eski (Ed.), Genocide and Victimology, 6-22 (Routledge Taylor & Francis Group 2020). https://doi.org/10.4324/9780429458675-2.

Molle Francois, Development Trajectories of River Basins: A Conceptual Framework. (Colombo: International Water Management Institute 2003).

Paola Gaeta, *Genocide*, in Schabas, ed. Routledge Handbook of International Criminal Law 109 (New York: Taylor & Francis Group 2011).

Katherine Goldsmith, *The Issue of Intent in the Genocide Convention and Its Effect on the Prevention and Punishment of the Crime of Genocide: Toward a Knowledge-Based Approach*, Genocide Studies and Prevention: An International Journal 5(3) (2010), available at: https://digitalcommons.usf.edu/cgi/viewcontent.cgi?article=1092&context=gsp. https://doi.org/10.1353/gsp.2010.0018.

T. B. Goldtooth, *Continuing threats to Indigenous people's sovereignty and survival*, Race, Poverty & the Environment, Vol. 11, No. 1, 9-12 (Summer 2004).

David Goyes, *Genocide And Ecocide In Four Colombian Indigenous Communities: The Erosion Of A Way Of Life And Memory*, The British Journal of Criminology, 61(4), 965-984 (2021). https://doi.org/10.1093/bjc/azaa109.

Emmanuel Guematcha, *Genocide Against Indigenous Peoples: The Experiences of the Truth Commisisons of Canada & Guatemala*, The International Indigenous Policy Journal, 10(2) (2019). https://doi.org/10.18584/iipj.2019.10.2.6.

Michelle Hay et al., *Dam-Induced Displacement and Resettlement: A Literature Review*, Future DAMS Working Paper 004 (September 2019), available at: https://hummedia.manchester.ac.uk/institutes/gdi/publications/workingpapers/futuredams/futuredams-working-paper-004-hay-skinner-notron.pdf.

The International Alliance of Indigenous and Tribal People of the Tropical Forests & the Indigenous Peoples' Foundation for Education and Environment, *Handbook on Free, Prior and Informed Consent For Practical Use by Indigenous Peoples' Communities* (September 2021), https://www.un-redd.org/sites/default/files/2021-09/FPIC_Handbook_Final%20(80337).pdf.

International Labour Organization, *Indigenous People in a Changing World of Work: Exploring Indigenous peoples economic and social rights through the Indigenous Navigator* (May 17, 2021), https://www.ilo.org/publications/indigenous-peoples-changing-world-work-exploring-indigenous-peoples.

Barbara Rose Johnston, *Chixoy Dam Legacies: The Struggle to Secure Reparation and the Right to Remedy in Guatemala*, Water Alternatives, 3(2), 341-361, 344 (2010).

Radovan Karadzic, Raiko Mladic Case (n.d.) Decision of Trial Chamber 1, ICTY, Cases Nos. IT-95-5-R61 and IT-95-18-R61, ¶ 94.

Purity Kiura, *Africa 101 Last Tribes: El Molo*, https://www.101lasttribes.com/tribes/el_molo.html (accessed December 5, 2024).

Purity Kiura, *El molo: The forgotten people of Lake Turkana*, Sabinet Gateway; Project, Endangered Languages *El Molo* (2013), https://www.endangeredlanguages.com/lang/4124 (accessed November 30, 2024).

Petro Kotze, *The world's dams: Doing major harm but a manageable problem?* (2022), https://news.mongabay.com/2022/04/the-worlds-dams-doing-major-harm-but-a-manageable-problem/.

Claus Kreb, *The Crime of Genocide under International Law*, International Criminal Law Review, Volume 6, 461-502, 471 (2006). https://doi.org/10.1163/157181206778992287.

Aurelie Lopez, *The Protection Of Environmentally-Displaced Persons In International Law*, Environmental Law, 37, No. 2, 365-409, 232 (Spring 2007).

Arden Lunay, *Constructing better infrastructure outcomes with community engagement,* Articulous, https://articulous.com.au/infrastructure-engagement/.

Guénaël Mettraux, *Special Genocidal Intent/Dolus Specialis,* in International Crimes: Law and Practice: Volume I: Genocide (Oxford Academic 2019). https://doi.org/10.1093/law/9780198843115.001.0001.

Marko Milanovic, *State Responsibility for Genocide,* The European Journal of International Law, 17(3), 553-604, 558 (2006). https://doi.org/10.1093/ejil/chl019.

Fredrick Mugira, *Life After Gibe III Construction: Kenya's Smallest Tribe Struggles to Survive as Lake Turkana Water Recedes,* Water Journalists Africa, November 9, 2017, https://infonile.org/en/2017/11/life-after-gibe-iii-dam-construction-kenyas-smallest-tribe-struggles-to-survive-as-lake-turkana-water-recedes/.

Mark Münzel, *The Aché Indians: Genocide in Paraguay.,* Copenhagen: International Work Group for Indigenous Affairs (1973), https://www.iwgia.org/images/publications//Ache_Doc1.pdf.

Oscar Mwangi, *Hydropolitics, Ecocide and Human Security in Lesotho: A Case Study of the Lesotho Highlands Water Project,* Journal of Southern African Studies, 33(1), 3-17, 5 (2007). https://doi.org/10.1080/03057070601136509.

Oakland Institute, *How they Tricked Us: Living with the Gibe III Dam and Sugarcane Plantations in South West Ethiopia* (June 10, 2019), https://www.oaklandinstitute.org/gibe-dam-sugarcane-plantations-southwest-ethiopia.

OECD, *The importance of land for Indigenous economic development,* in Linking Indigenous Communities with Regional Development in Canada, OECD Publishing (Paris: January 21, 2020), https://doi.org/10.1787/fc2b28b3-en.

Nate Olson, *Gibe III,* https://www.canr.msu.edu/news/gibe-iii (accessed November 30, 2024).

W. O. Ojwang et al., "Lake Turkana: World's Largest Permanent Desert Lake (Kenya)," in The Wetland Book, eds. C. Finlayson et al. (Springer, Dordrecht, 2016). https://doi.org/10.1007/978-94-007-6173-5_254-1.

Mina Parvizishad, *Analyzing the Impact of Large Dams on Seismicity Patterns,* Archives of Hydro-Engineering and Environmental Mechanics, 68(1), 3-17 (2021). https://doi.org/10.1515/heem-2021-0001.

Regina M. Paulose, *Crouching tiger, hidden dragon: hydropower and crimes against humanity* in Regina M. Paulose (ed), Green Crimes and International Criminal Law, 257-294 (Vernon Press 2021).

Regina M. Paulose, *Death by a Thousand Cuts? Green Tech, Traditional Knowledge, and Genocide,* Genocide Studies Prevention Journal, Vol 16, Article 6 (2022) 1: 40–59. DOI: https://doi.org/10.5038/1911-9933.16.1.1881.

Regina M. Paulose, *Hydropower and Human Rights: Revisiting the World Commission on Dams Report,* Indian Journal of Projects, Infrastructure and Energy Law (December 17, 2021), https://ijpiel.com/index.php/2021/12/17/hydropower-and-human-rights-revisiting-the-world-commission-on-dams-report/.

Prosecutor v. Goran Jelisic (Trial Judgement), IT-95-10-T, ICTY, December 14, 1999.

Prosecutor v. Jean Paul Akayesu (1998) ICTR-96-4-T.

Prosecutor v. Radislav Krstic (Appeal Judgement), IT-98-33-A, ICTY, April 19, 2004, available at: https://www.refworld.org/jurisprudence/caselaw/icty/2004/en/33340.

John Quigley, The Genocide Convention: An International Law Analysis (Hampshire: Ashgate Publishing Limited 2006).

Julia Rappaport, *Where Did the Word "Genocide" Come From?*, Facing History and Ourselves (2014) https://www.facinghistory.org/ideas-week/where-did-word-genocide-come (accessed November 9, 2024).

Kaitlin Reed, *We Are a Part of the Land and the Land Is Us*, Humboldt Journal of Social Relations, No. 42, Special Issue 42 (2020), https://digitalcommons.humboldt.edu/hjsr/vol1/iss42/4/. https://doi.org/10.55671/0160-4341.1131.

William Schabas, An Introduction to the International Criminal Court, 3rd ed. (New York: Cambridge University Press 2007). https://doi.org/10.1017/CBO9780511801440.

Dominik Schaller, *From Lemkin to Clooney: The Development and State of Genocide Development and State of Genocide Studies*, Genocide Studies and Prevention: An International Journal, 6(3), 245-256 (2011). https://doi.org/10.1353/gsp.2011.0132.

Edson Severnini, *The Power of Hydroelectric Dams: Historical Evidence from the United States over the Twentieth Century*, The Economic Journal, Volume 133, Issue 649, 420–459 (January 2023), https://doi.org/10.1093/ej/ueac059.

Thomas Simon, *Defining Genocide*, Wisconsin International Law Journal, Volume 15, 243-256 (1996-1997).

Zoe Sullivan, *Brazil's dispossessed: Belo Monte dam ruinous for indigenous cultures*, Mongabay (December 8, 2016), https://news.mongabay.com/2016/12/brazils-dispossessed-belo-monte-dam-ruinous-for-indigenous-cultures/.

Bret Thiele and Mayra Gomez, *Genocide in Guatemala: The Roles of the World Bank and Inter-American Development Bank*, Indigenous Law Bulletin, 6(13), 8 (2005), https://classic.austlii.edu.au/au/journals/IndigLawB/2005/43.html.

Alana Tiemessen, *Cultural Genocide in Law & Politics*, in Oxford Research Encyclopedia of International Studies (Oxford University Press 2024). https://doi.org/10.1093/acrefore/9780190846626.013.762.

Sabine Troeger, *Just Societal Transformation: Perspectives of Pastoralists in the Lower Omo Valley in Ethiopia*, in Oguge (ed.) African Handbook of Climate Change Adaptation, 2447-2467, 2458 (Springer 2021), https://doi.org/10.1007/978-3-030-45106-6_265.

United Nations, *Addressing Hate Speech Through Education: A Guide for Policy Makers* (U.N. Educ., Sci. & Cultural Org. 2023).

UN Declaration on the Rights of Indigenous People, Art 19, Sep. 13, 2007, G.A. Res. 61/295, U.N. Doc. A/RES/61/295.

United Nations General Assembly Resolution 96(I), A/RES/96 (December 11, 1946).

United Nations Human Rights Council, *Communication Report of Special Procedures: Communications Sent 1 December 2010 to 31 May 2011; Replies*

Received 1 February 2011 to 31 July 2011, New York: United Nations General Assembly, A/HRC/18/51, September 9, 2011, https://www.ohchr.org/sites/default/files/Documents/HRBodies/SP/A.HRC.18.51.pdf.

World Commission on Dams, Dams and Development: A new Framework for Decision-Making (s.l.: Earthscans Publications 2000).

World Commission on Dams, Dams, Indigenous Peoples, Cape Town: Secretariat of the World Commission on Dams (1999).

Chapter 7

The Intersection of Iran's Water Crisis and Criminal Law: A Legal and Environmental Analysis

Dr. Shabnam Moinipour

Human Rights Expert

Abstract: This chapter explores the complex interplay between Iran's water crisis and criminal law, framing the crisis as a significant legal challenge. It examines the historical context and development of water management laws, key regulations, and the roles of various regulatory bodies, while identifying gaps and inconsistencies that impede effective governance.

The analysis highlights water-related crimes associated with water mismanagement, including illegal wells, industrial pollution, and inefficiencies in agricultural water use. It discusses the challenges of prosecuting these offenses in the face of widespread corruption and an underground economy. The roles of the state and corporations in exacerbating the crisis are scrutinized, underscoring the urgent need for accountability and legal reform.

The assessment of enforcement and judicial response reveals issues like corruption and a lack of specialized expertise, which complicate community involvement. The chapter concludes with proposals for comprehensive legal reforms aimed at strengthening enforcement mechanisms, enhancing judicial independence, and promoting ethical governance in water management. By integrating human rights considerations and addressing the needs of marginalized populations, this analysis aims to lay the groundwork for sustainable water governance in Iran, emphasizing the critical connection between environmental and criminal law.

Keywords: Islamic Republic of Iran, water crisis, water governance, IRGC, corruption, Integrated Water Resources Management, Human Rights Impact Assessments (HRIA), water activists.

I. Understanding Iran's Water Crisis as a Legal Challenge

Water crisis in Iran has emerged to be one of the most pressing challenges the nation is grappling with. The implications of this water crisis are far-reaching, affecting the environment, economy, and social stability. Iran was once recognized for its advanced water management systems. Agricultural and permanent settlements were once supported by the ancient qanat system, which tapped "alluvial aquifers at the heads of valleys" and conducted the water "along underground tunnels by gravity."[1] The severe water shortages, driven by a combination of factors such as climate change, decades of mismanagement, over-extraction, and rapid population growth, threaten the livelihood of millions. The aforementioned factors have led to the depletion of vital groundwater reserves and caused lakes and rivers to shrink and fertile lands to desertify. The environmental and technical aspects of Iran's water crisis are documented to some extent. However, what remains underexplored is the intersection of Iran's water crisis with criminal law, which this chapter aims to address.

This chapter seeks to shed light on the critical role criminal law plays in both contribution to and potential alleviation of the water crisis in Iran. This is because the blame for the water crisis cannot solely be placed on environmental misfortunes. Water crisis is deeply intertwined with legal failings, corrupt practices, and illicit activities, stemming from regulatory gaps and weak enforcement, that exacerbate the situation. Conservation and distribution are not the only components of water management in Iran. Individuals, corporations, and state officials are all involved actors in a legal battlefield whose actions could constitute serious crimes. Illegal wells, unauthorized water diversion, black market for water resources have proliferated, destabilizing communities and deepening the crisis. These along with pollution, corruption, and the mismanagement of resources, face legal repercussions. However, enforcement is inadequate and inconsistent. This complex legal landscape raises critical questions: How can criminal law be effectively utilized to address water-related offenses? What role does corruption within state institutions play in undermining water governance? And how do legal frameworks balance the enforcement of water laws with the rights and needs of the population? This chapter will explore these complexities in detail, examining the ways in which criminal law intersects with Iran's water crisis. It will analyze specific cases of water mismanagement, corruption, and water-related crimes, highlighting the legal challenges and opportunities for reform. By understanding the role of criminal law in this context, the broader implications

---

[1] UNESCO, *The Persian qanat.* [online] (2016), https://whc.unesco.org/en/list/1506/.

of Iran's water crisis and how legal interventions might contribute to a more sustainable and just future for the country's water resources can be better appreciated and considered.

A. Historical Context and Development of Water Laws in Iran Pre and Post-1979 Revolution

The legal management of water in Iran has a deep historical foundation. Traditional systems like qanats—underground channels developed centuries ago to transport water from aquifers—exemplified sustainable water management practices deeply embedded in Iranian culture.[2] These systems were governed through "community-based coordination mechanisms" that ensured fair distribution and maintenance.[3] However, with rapid population growth and urbanization, along with many other causes,[4] Iran's approach to water management shifted dramatically. The introduction of large-scale dam projects, industrial expansion, and modern irrigation methods in the 20th century, particularly after the 1979 Islamic Revolution, brought significant changes to the legal framework governing water resources.[5]

Modern water laws in Iran began to take shape in the 1950s, with the main one being the introduction of the Water Nationalization Act of 1968, which declared all water resources—rivers, lakes, underground waters, and rainwater—to be public property under the state's control. This law marked a turning point, centralizing water management under state authority and eliminating traditional local control. The Act aimed to regulate water use, prevent unauthorized extraction, and ensure equitable distribution. However, the state's centralized control often failed to adapt to local needs and environmental realities, leading to inefficiencies and conflicts.[6]

After the 1979 Islamic Revolution in Iran, water management systems experienced substantial transformations, reflecting the broader socio-political

---

[2] Nilou Vakil, *The Cultural Landscape of the Persian Qanat*, in THE ROUTLEDGE HANDBOOK OF CULTURAL LANDSCAPE HERITAGE IN THE ASIA-PACIFIC 420 (K.D. Silva et al. eds., Routledge 2022).

[3] S. Nourikia, and N. Zivdar, *Participatory management of traditional urban water infrastructures in Iran: The case of Tehran historic qanat*, SPOOL 7(2), 95 (2020).

[4] Jamil Zargan and Seyed Mohammad Waez-Mousavi, *Water crisis in Iran: Its intensity, causes and confronting strategies*, INDIAN JOURNAL OF SCIENCE AND TECHNOLOGY 9(44), 3 (2020).

[5] REZA TALEBI, HYDROPOLITICS AND WATER ISSUES AFTER THE IRANIAN REVOLUTION (1979-2021) 15,165 (Merve Hatemi, trans. Turkey: Qobustan Publishing 2023).

[6] Assad Tavakoli, *Nationalization and efficient management of water resources in Iran*, JOURNAL OF WATER RESOURCES PLANNING AND MANAGEMENT 113(4), 523, 525 (1987).

upheavals. The revolution's ideology framed many pre-revolutionary policies, including water laws, as remnants of the Shah's regime, which were perceived as unjust and disconnected from the values of the revolutionary populace, particularly the *Mostaz'afin* ("oppressed"). This mindset led to the dismissal of previous water regulations and the push for new legislation. The Ministry of Energy, tasked with developing revised laws, argued that pre-revolution laws prioritized industrial growth over agricultural self-sufficiency, contradicting revolutionary priorities.[7]

Post-revolution, Iran witnessed the introduction of several significant laws aimed at addressing water management and environmental issues, each shaped by the political and social context of the time. The Fair Water Distribution Law of 1983 was introduced during a post-revolutionary era marked by efforts at reconstruction alongside the ongoing challenges posed by the Iran-Iraq War. It aimed to consolidate control over water resources and address issues stemming from rapid urbanization and agricultural expansion, aligning with the state's post-war reconstruction goals.[8] While the law provided a legal framework for water management, including rights to water usage and equitable distribution, it ultimately exacerbated the water crisis. The state's focus on so-called "social justice" led to the legalization of previously illegal water extraction and usage without adequate consideration for sustainability, resulting in groundwater depletion and pollution.[9]

Originally enacted before the revolution, the Environmental Protection and Enhancement Act of 1974 was amended in 1992 to modernize its provisions in light of post-revolutionary environmental challenges. These amendments emphasized the importance of environmental protection alongside economic development, seeking to integrate environmental considerations into development planning, including water management.[10] However, despite good intentions, enforcement remained weak, and environmental priorities often took a backseat to urgent economic needs. This dynamic contributed to ongoing environmental degradation, including water quality issues and habitat destruction.

---

[7] Ehsan Nabavi *(Ground) Water Governance and Legal Development in Iran, 1906–2016,* MIDDLE EAST LAW AND GOVERNANCE 9, 1, 56-57 (2017).

[8] Shahryar Ershad Sarabi, *Impacts of institutional arrangements on the adaptive capacity of the Urmia Lake basin* (Thesis) INTERNATIONAL INSTITUTE OF URBAN MANAGEMENT OF ERASMUS UNIVERSITY ROTTERDAM, 22-23 (2018).

[9] Nabavi, *supra* note 7, at 57-58.

[10] MINISTRY OF HEALTH AND MEDICAL EDUCATION, *Environmental Protection and Enhancement Act of 1974,* https://health.bpums.ac.ir/UploadedFiles/xfiles/File/M-Behdashti/rule/behdasht%20mohit/hefazat%20va%20behsazi.pdf.

In 2005, Iran passed the Water Independence of Provinces Law as part of its broader strategy to address growing water scarcity and improve water management across the country. This law aimed to decentralize water management and empower provincial governments and water companies to take charge of their own water resources. Despite the decentralization efforts, the Ministry still held significant authority over critical areas, including the approval of extensive studies in various basins, the establishment of policies for water resource development, allocation of water to different sectors, management of inter-basin water transfers, and the assessment of water's economic value. This new regulatory framework encouraged competition among water companies, leading to an increase in conflicts between provinces. The Zayandehrood river basin emerged as one of the most contentious areas, highlighting the discrepancy between the Fair Water Distribution Law and the Water Independence of Province Law.[11]

The *Ta'een-i Taklif* (Determination of Responsibilities) Law of 2010 emerged as Iran faced a severe water crisis, marked by mounting challenges from climate change, urbanization, and population growth. This legislation effectively granted legal status to owners of previously illegal wells, allowing them to obtain licenses[12] for water extraction.[13] As a result, what had once been deemed unlawful activities were transformed into legitimate enterprises, creating a scenario where former violators became recognized stakeholders with rights to water resources. This decision sparked significant debate, as it appeared to endorse past infractions while raising concerns about sustainable water management and equity among users.

While these laws simultaneously seek to regulate and control water resources, they also legitimize practices that undermine those very regulations. In other words, the laws surrounding water management in Iran, particularly the *Ta'een-i Taklif* of 2010, present a contradiction that can inadvertently encourage criminal behavior. By legitimizing previously illegal wells and granting licenses to those who had violated water extraction regulations, the laws create a perception that unlawful practices can lead to eventual acceptance and reward. This undermines the rule of law and sets a troubling precedent, where individuals may feel incentivized to bypass regulations in the hope of future legalization, ultimately jeopardizing sustainable water management and exacerbating environmental challenges.

---

[11] Ehsan Nabavi, *Failed policies, falling aquifers: Unpacking groundwater overabstraction in Iran*, WATER ALTERNATIVES, 11(3), 705 (2018).

[12] Nabavi, *supra* note 11, at 705.

[13] Sarabi, *supra* note 8, at 27.

The contradictory nature of these laws not only fosters an environment conducive to criminal behavior but also complicates the broader policy making landscape in Iran. For instance, there are complexities between the government and the Islamic Consultative Assembly (Parliament) when it comes to policy making on water issues. According to Talebi Somehsaraie and Asadi,[14] there is a tendency for divergence between the two institutions—while the Assembly often focuses on facilitating groundwater extraction, the government prioritizes reducing financial burdens and streamlining responsibilities. This divergence, along with opposition from government experts to certain Assembly proposals, has hindered the effective approval of laws meant to facilitate sustainable water use. Even in cases where there was some alignment between the two bodies, it did not necessarily lead to better outcomes for water sustainability and resource protection.

B. Regulatory Bodies and their Roles

The laws concerning water management in post-revolution Iran are closely tied to the regulatory bodies established to oversee their implementation and enforce compliance. Each of these laws created frameworks that required coordination among various state agencies and regulatory authorities, which played crucial roles in managing the country's water resources. Several state bodies are responsible for overseeing water management in Iran, each with distinct but sometimes overlapping mandates. The relationship between Iran's water management laws and the key regulatory bodies—the Ministry of Energy, the Department of Environment (DoE), the Ministry of Agricultural Jihad and Regional Water Companies, the Ministry of Health and Medical Education, and the Ministry of Construction Jihad all have contributed to the challenges faced in managing water resources and implementing policies effectively.[15]

The Ministry of Energy is primarily responsible for water supply and distribution. Under the Fair Water Distribution Law of 1983, this ministry played a crucial role in defining water rights, overseeing allocation, and managing national water infrastructure.[16] However, while it was tasked with promoting equitable distribution and sustainable practices, the ministry often faced challenges due to competing priorities, particularly the government's focus on agricultural self-sufficiency. This led to increased water extraction without

---

[14] M. Talebi Somehsaraie, M.Asadi, *Sociological investigation of institutional convergence in the approval of the most important water laws in Iran*, MAJLIS AND RAHBORD (2024), doi: 10.22034/mr.2024.16771.5802.

[15] M. Saatsaz, *A historical investigation on water resources management in Iran*, ENVIRONMENT, DEVELOPMENT AND SUSTAINABILITY, 22, 1766 (2020).

[16] Sarabi, *supra* note 8, at 26.

adequate consideration for long-term sustainability, exacerbating issues like groundwater depletion. In addition, the transition of the management of groundwater to a centralized system, often lacking adequate understanding of local hydrological conditions, resulted in reduced transparency and limited oversight from local communities. Consequently, it created opportunities for corruption, allowing influential individuals to secure well permits through undue influence and bribery.[17]

The DoE, established to address environmental concerns, has a pivotal role in enforcing the Environmental Protection and Enhancement Act. It was amended several times to integrate environmental considerations into development planning, including water management. The DoE was tasked with monitoring environmental impacts and ensuring compliance with regulations.[18] However, it often struggled with limited authority and budget constraints, hindering its ability to enforce laws effectively.[19] The lack of synergy between the DoE and the Ministry of Energy further complicated efforts to achieve both environmental protection and efficient water resource management.

The Ministry of Agricultural Jihad is yet another regulatory body responsible for managing all activities related to agriculture. In total, there are 31 organizations functioning under the ministry, one in each province in Iran.[20] This Ministry aims to enhance agricultural productivity, which often requires significant water resources. Consequently, its demands for water are in conflict with the environmental objectives of the DoE and the resource management strategies of the Ministry of Energy. The Ministry of Construction Jihad, established in 1980, was also meant to reduce poverty and inequality through construction of infrastructure, including structures for water distribution and filtration systems but failed to manage demand and promote users' self-management. The Ministry of Health and Medical Education was also tasked with establishing drinking-water quality standards, as well as monitoring and regulating water quality parameters from the source to the consumer.[21]

---

[17] F. Molle and A. Mamanpoush, *Scale, governance and the management of river basins: A case study from Central Iran*, GEOFORUM, 43(2), 291. (2012).

[18] Hossein Moradi, *Biodiversity, climate change and environmental impact assessment* (Thesis) UNIVERSITY OF ZURICH, 87 (2009).

[19] K. Madani, *Water management in Iran: What is causing the looming crisis*, JOURNAL OF ENVIRONMENTAL STUDIES AND SCIENCES, 4(2014), 323.

[20] H. Zanjanian et al., *Influential third party on water right conflict: A Game Theory approach to achieve the desired equilibrium* (case study: Ilam dam, Iran), JOURNAL OF ENVIRONMENTAL MANAGEMENT, 214, 285 (2018).

[21] Saatsaz, *supra* note 15, at 1766-67.

Regional water companies, such as the Water and Wastewater Company, operate at a more localized level and are essential for implementing national water policies on the ground. They manage water distribution and infrastructure within specific regions and are crucial in operationalizing the *Ta'een-i Taklif* (Determination of Responsibilities) Law of 2010. This law aims to foster community involvement and promote sustainable practices, requiring effective coordination between regional water companies and higher-level regulatory bodies. According to Zanjanian et al., "[t]he Jihad Agriculture Organization and the Water and Wastewater Company must distribute the delivered water to final users."[22] However, these companies often face bureaucratic inefficiencies and lack the necessary resources and training to implement sustainable practices effectively. Their operations are frequently hampered by inadequate funding and support from the Ministry of Energy, limiting their capacity to address local water management challenges.

After the revolution, Iran's policy to decentralize water resource management aimed to replace the Shah's centralized model with a structure reflecting Islamic values of equity and stewardship. However, the fragmented system involving multiple ministries and departments introduced inefficiency and disorganization. The creation of redundant bureaucracies, paired with inconsistent and convoluted laws, undermined effective governance. This shift, intended to prove the superiority of Islamic ideology over the Shah's policies, instead exacerbated water management challenges, contributing significantly to the crisis seen today.

C. Gaps and Inconsistencies in the Legal Framework

The legal framework governing water management in Iran exhibits significant gaps and inconsistencies that hinder effective governance and sustainable resource management. For instance, the Fair Water Distribution Law of 1983, the 2005 Water Independence of Provinces, and the *Ta'een-i Taklif* Law of 2010 each tackle distinct aspects of water management but fail to establish a cohesive framework. This disconnect results in overlapping jurisdictions and poor coordination among regulatory bodies, ultimately leading to confusion and inefficiencies in policy implementation.

The Fair Water Distribution Law of 1983 primarily focuses on the allocation and usage rights of water resources, emphasizing the regulation of water supply and distribution. While it set the groundwork for national oversight of water resources, it did not effectively integrate environmental considerations or address sustainable practices. The *Ta'een-i Taklif* Law of 2010 sought to

[22] Zanjanian, *supra* note 20, at 284.

promote integrated water resource management and address some of these deficiencies. However, despite its intention to create a holistic framework, it often operates in isolation from the earlier laws. For example, while it encourages community participation and the sustainable use of water resources, it does not explicitly align with the allocation rights established by the Fair Water Distribution Law of 1983. This leads to scenarios where local communities are encouraged to manage resources sustainably but are simultaneously constrained by outdated allocation rights that favor certain agricultural interests, leading to conflicts and non-compliance.[23]

Furthermore, overlapping jurisdictions exacerbate these challenges. Different regulatory bodies, such as the Ministry of Energy, the DoE, and local water authorities,[24] pursue conflicting objectives.[25] For instance, while the Ministry of Agricultural Jihad prioritizes water extraction to meet agricultural demands, the DoE seeks to impose restrictions to protect ecosystems and water quality. This misalignment results in duplicated efforts, where both agencies invest resources in monitoring the same water bodies but with divergent goals. To that end, an agricultural project might proceed with little oversight from the DoE, even if it threatens local ecosystems, due to a lack of coordination and clear jurisdictional authority.

Additionally, the fragmentation of laws has led to inefficient use of resources. Regulatory authorities often engage in redundant monitoring and compliance efforts, creating confusion among stakeholders. For instance, if a regional water company enforces specific water usage regulations but lacks support or guidance from the Ministry of Energy or the DoE, the resulting policies may differ significantly, leading to inconsistent practices across regions. Such inconsistencies can undermine trust in regulatory frameworks, making it more challenging to achieve compliance and fostering resistance among users who may feel unfairly targeted by fluctuating regulations.

There are also significant gaps in addressing emerging challenges such as climate change, population growth, and urbanization.[26] While the Comprehensive Water Law of 2010 aimed to promote integrated water resource management, it has not adequately incorporated adaptive strategies necessary for responding to changing environmental conditions. For example, the law does not sufficiently account for water conservation measures in light of decreasing rainfall and increasing demand, exacerbating stress on already

---

[23] Nabavi, *supra* note 11, at 703-705.

[24] Molle and Mamanpoush, *supra* note 17, at 286.

[25] Sarah Lerech Zilberberg, *The water crisis in Iran: Heightening instability*, STRATEGIC ASSESSMENT, 26(3), 54 (2023).

[26] Zargan and Waez-Mousavi, *supra* note 4, at 1.

scarce resources. This failure to adapt to climate change demonstrates a critical oversight in the legal framework, as Iran faces severe environmental challenges that require urgent and innovative responses.

Inadequate public participation and transparency further compound these issues. The legal framework does not sufficiently encourage stakeholder engagement in decision-making processes related to water management. This lack of public involvement has led to policies that do not reflect the needs and experiences of local communities, undermining the legitimacy and effectiveness of regulations. Moreover, the opacity in how decisions are made has fostered mistrust among stakeholders, discouraging compliance and collaboration.[27] The insufficient engagement with stakeholders also highlights the unprofessionalism in policymaking, which contributes to the fragmented legal landscape. Without meaningful consultation with local communities and experts, policymakers often miss critical insights that could inform more coherent and effective regulations. For example, community feedback regarding water usage and local ecological conditions is essential for developing sustainable policies. When this input is disregarded, the resulting regulations may lack practicality and relevance, leading to non-compliance and further exacerbating the water crisis.

Lastly, the legal framework struggles with outdated provisions that fail to reflect current realities.[28] Many laws do not account for technological advancements in water management, such as modern irrigation techniques (e.g., drip irrigation) and optimal water recycling technologies, which could significantly improve efficiency and sustainability.[29] This disconnect between legal frameworks and contemporary practices limits the ability of regulatory bodies to promote innovation and adopt best practices in water management. In addition, the gaps and inconsistencies in Iran's legal framework for water management create significant obstacles to achieving sustainable resource management.

What's more, disintegrated decision-making and a fragmented water governance structure are major challenges, which have occurred because knowledgeable experts operate in isolation without cohesive collaboration. The problem is exacerbated by a governance system involving too many stakeholders and an undesirable hierarchy, which hinders effective coordination

---

[27] Zilberberg, *supra* note 25, at 50.

[28] Lena Horlemann and Parisa Jafari Berenji, *Participation in water management in Iran.* IN: S. MOHAJERI & L. HORLEMANN (EDS.), REVIVING THE DYING GIANT. 52, 58 (Switzerland: Spring, Cham 2017).

[29] Georg Meran et al., *The Economics of Water: Rules and Institutions,* 43, 57 (Springer, Cham 2021).

and management of water resources. In essence, the governance model, rather than technological deficits, is the core issue.[30]

The political environment in which policymakers operate can also hinder their ability to create a coherent legal framework. When decisions are driven by political agendas[31] rather than sound scientific principles,[32] contrasting policies may be implemented. The interplay of "various policies, actions, and driving factors, which are devised at a regime level, can lead to different outcomes," shaped by the complexities of governance structures.[33]

In Iran, there is also an obvious lack of accountability and transparency within the policymaking process, which compounds these challenges. When policymakers operate without sufficient oversight, their lack of expertise and unprofessional behavior can perpetuate a fragmented regulatory environment, where laws exist in theory but fail to be effectively applied in practice.[34] This has led to a situation where incoherent regulations persist, further complicating enforcement and management efforts.

D. Enforcement Mechanisms and Challenges

The inconsistencies in the enforcement of regulations exacerbate water crisis challenges, as some regions experience strict oversight while others operate with little to no enforcement. This uneven application of laws creates a perception of inequity, leading to frustration among stakeholders and fostering non-compliance. For example, agricultural areas receive more lenient treatment concerning water extraction, undermining efforts to promote sustainable practices. Local authorities often lack the necessary training and resources to implement national policies effectively, contributing to further inconsistencies

---

[30] Madani, *supra* note 19, at 321.

[31] An example is the decision to build the Gotvand Dam on the Karun River. Despite warnings from environmental experts about the high salinity of nearby geological formations, which risked contaminating the water supply, the project was pushed forward to fulfill political goals, such as showcasing infrastructure development and securing contracts for politically connected companies. After its completion, the dam's reservoir interacted with salt domes, significantly increasing the salinity of the water. This has caused severe harm to downstream agriculture and drinking water supplies, directly contradicting sustainable water management principles and creating long-term environmental and economic challenges.

[32] S. Amiri et al., *Salinity management in the world's most saline dam reservoir: The Gotvand Reservoir, Iran.* EARTH AND SPACE SCIENCE OPEN ARCHIVE, II-III. (2023).

[33] Nishtman Karimi et al., *The Water Management Regime in Western Iran: A Retrospective Analysis through a Hybrid Transitions Framework*, SUSTAINABILITY, 13(3323), 2. (2021).

[34] P. Azadi, *Governance and development in Iran*, STANFORD IRAN 2040 PROJECT. STANFORD UNIVERSITY, 26. (2019).

in enforcement. Such inconsistencies have led to ambiguities, which in turn create challenges for higher levels of the justice system, making it difficult for judges and other officials to enforce the law effectively.[35]

In addition, the fragmented system under which regulatory bodies operate, leading to overlapping responsibilities and insufficient coordination, makes enforcement efforts complicated and creates gaps in accountability.[36] A major issue is the pervasive corruption and bribery that undermines regulatory processes. For instance, officials tend to accept bribes in exchange for permits allowing illegal water extraction or disregard for pollution regulations.[37] This has not only eroded public trust in regulatory bodies but also has perpetuated unsustainable practices, as violators operate with impunity. Additionally, the lack of resources and technical capacity within these agencies significantly hampers their ability to monitor compliance effectively. For example, many regional water companies lack the necessary tools and personnel to conduct regular inspections of water quality and usage, which has led to unchecked pollution and over-extraction of groundwater. In addition, as Pooya Azadi puts it, enforcement of the law is unpredictable and is "heavily reliant on the political conditions and interests of the state."[38]

Moreover, judicial inefficiency and political interference further complicate enforcement efforts. Iran's judiciary is often slow to respond to environmental violations, and when cases are brought to court, they are often subject to political influences that prioritize short-term economic gains over long-term sustainability. An illustrative example is the case of illegal dam constructions, where political connections sometimes allow developers to bypass regulatory scrutiny and continue operations, despite clear violations of environmental laws. Together, these challenges not only impede the enforcement of existing laws but also contribute to the deterioration of water resources, exacerbating the ongoing water crisis in the country.[39] For instance, over-extraction from the Zayandeh Rood has led to severe ecological damage, partly due to insufficient regulatory enforcement and corruption.

As a way of addressing the water crises, the state has, in recent years, introduced various plans and projects, such as the Groundwater Resources

---

[35] Nabavi, *supra* note 11, at 715-717.

[36] H. Hamidifar, *Water crisis in Iran: Causes, consequences, and solutions,* in Chibueze Izah, S., Chidozie Ogwu, M., Loukas, A., and Hamidifar, H. (Eds.) WATER CRISES AND SUSTAINABLE MANAGEMENT IN THE GLOBAL SOUTH, 98. (Singapore: Spring 2024).

[37] P. Azadi, *The structure of corruption in Iran,* STANFORD IRAN 2040 PROJECT. STANFORD UNIVERSITY 2. (2020).

[38] Azadi, *supra* note 34, at 25.

[39] Nabavi, *supra* note 11, at 716.

Reclamation and Balancing Plan, which includes 15 projects,[40] alongside other[41] current and future water scarcity adaptation programs.[42] However, these initiatives often fail to achieve their intended outcomes due to the very enforcement challenges outlined above. Corruption, weak regulatory measures, and inconsistent implementation significantly undermine the success of these programs. For instance, resources allocated to improving irrigation systems or building desalination plants are frequently misused or diverted, while a lack of accountability allows poorly executed projects to go unchecked.

Ultimately, the success of these programs hinges on cohesive laws, strengthening governance, enhancing enforcement mechanisms, addressing systemic corruption, and introducing educational initiatives and awareness campaigns.[43] Without these foundational changes, even the most ambitious plans will struggle to tackle the root causes of water scarcity, leaving Iran's water crisis unresolved.[44]

E. Broader Implications of Weak Enforcement and Judicial Response

The consequences of weak enforcement extend beyond mere environmental degradation; they also exacerbate social tensions within affected communities. As water shortages become more acute, frustration and desperation rise, leading to heightened public disillusionment with state institutions. This erosion of trust translates into widespread anger, resulting in protests and civil unrest as citizens demand accountability and action from their leaders. In a context where communities feel their basic needs are being ignored, the potential for social conflict increases significantly, threatening not only the stability of local governance but also national security. Water-related protests have become a frequent occurrence in Iran, particularly in regions most affected by water scarcity, such as Khuzestan, Isfahan, Sistan and Baluchistan, and Fars

---

40 Regional Water Company of Qazvin, *Groundwater Resources Reclamation and Balancing Plan*, available at: https://www.qzrw.ir/st/212 (last visited October 23, 2024).

41 Hamidifar, *supra* note 36, at 95.

42 ISNA, A Serious Crisis in the Country/Take the Depletion of Groundwater Resources Seriously (September 17, 2024), https://www.isna.ir/news/1403062717453/یک-بحران-جدی-در-کشور-کاهش-منابع-آب-زیرزمینی-را-جدی-بگیرید .

43 S. Amiri and M. Mazaheri, *Challenges arising from excessive groundwater extraction in the country, an examination of the current conditions, and the land subsidence crisis*, Monthly Reports of the Research Center of the Islamic Consultative Assembly, 31(2), 7 (2023).

44 A. Khaleghi, A. and H. Rashnavadi, *The Iran criminal legislative policy for the preservation of water Resources with regard to the international instruments*, Journal of Criminal Law Research, 1(3), 139 (2013).

Provinces.[45] The response that the Islamic Republic of Iran increasingly turns to is repression, aiming to quell dissent through arrests, intimidation, and the criminalization of activism. Authorities often frame water activists and protestors as "threats to national security, accusing them of inciting unrest, spreading false information, or colluding with foreign entities." This strategy serves to delegitimize genuine grievances while discouraging further public mobilization. Water activists and environmentalists have faced surveillance, arbitrary detention, and harsh sentences under vague and broadly defined charges such as "acting against national security," "propaganda against the state," "espionage," or "spreading corruption on earth"—a charge that carries the death penalty.[46] These charges allow the state to suppress environmental advocacy without addressing the underlying causes of public discontent.

The challenges in enforcement and judicial response to water-related offenses in Iran highlight the deep-seated institutional and legal weaknesses that underpin the country's water crisis. Fragmented governance, political interference, judicial corruption, and insufficient penalties for water-related crimes create an environment where laws are routinely flouted, accountability is elusive, and genuine grievances are hampered. Addressing these challenges requires comprehensive reforms that enhance regulatory capacity, promote judicial independence, and foster greater public engagement in water management.

Besides judicial independence, the interplay between weak enforcement and social unrest, also highlights the urgent need for a more robust and credible judicial system that can effectively respond to environmental and water-related violations from the outset, not in the aftermath. Strengthening enforcement mechanisms is not merely an environmental imperative; it is also essential for maintaining social stability and restoring public confidence in the rule of law. When communities see that violations are addressed and that accountability is upheld, it fosters a sense of fairness and cooperation, encouraging compliance with regulations. Conversely, continued regulatory failure will likely deepen the cycle of crisis, with the environment suffering and social cohesion unraveling.

---

45 Zilberberg, *supra* note 25, at 46, 47.

46 ARTICLE 19, *Iran: Decline for free expression requires increased support for UN scrutiny* (March 2019), https://www.article19.org/wp-content/uploads/2019/03/HRC40-Briefing-Iran-AS-FINAL.pdf.

II. Water-Related Crimes and Water Mismanagement

Environmental mismanagement has played a central role in deepening Iran's water crisis, turning what was once a manageable scarcity issue into a severe and complex national emergency. Misguided policies, poor regulatory oversight, and rampant illegal activities have pushed Iran's water resources to the brink of collapse. As P.H. Gleick[47] points out, water resources are particularly vulnerable targets due to their irreplaceable nature. Water-related crimes—ranging from unauthorized drilling and illegal water extraction to industrial pollution and overuse of agricultural chemicals—are not only damaging ecosystems but also undermining the nation's legal efforts to conserve water. According to Mattioli, Segato, and Capello, water-related crimes are "often recorded under other offences like fraud, corruption, theft..."[48] as no established definition of what constitutes a water-related crime exists hence complicating legal discourse.[49]

The European Union Network for the Implementation and Enforcement of Environmental Law,[50] however, defines water/soil crime as "any punishable contravention or violation of the limits on human behavior as imposed by national criminal legislation, against surface, and groundwater, or against water services or against soil." This also includes "any intentional act that can potentially harm or damage the water." It also defines water/soil-related crime as "any punishable contravention or violation of the limits on human behavior as imposed by national criminal legislation, which uses surface, and groundwater, or water services or soil, as a means for committing other crimes."

This section explores the key water-related crimes contributing to water mismanagement in Iran, highlighting specific cases, the legal implications of these actions, and the challenges in prosecuting offenders under the current legal framework.

A. Illegal Wells and Unauthorized Water Extraction

One of the most pervasive water-related crimes in Iran is the illegal drilling of wells and unauthorized extraction of groundwater. In a country where over 60% of water use is sourced from underground aquifers, the uncontrolled exploitation of these resources poses a dire threat to their sustainability. Despite

---

47 P.H. Gleick, *Water and terrorism.* WATER POLICY, 8, 482 (2006).

48 L. Segato et al., "Water Crimes within Environmental Crimes," in *Water, Governance, and Crime Issues*, ed. K. Eman, G. Meško, L. Segato, and M. Migliorini (Cham, Switzerland: Springer, 2020), 32.

49 K. Eman et al., *Water crimes and policing*, JOURNAL OF CRIMINAL JUSTICE AND SECURITY. 19(2), 107. (2017).

50 IMPEL, *Project Water Crimes*, EUROPEAN UNION NETWORK FOR THE IMPLEMENTATION AND ENFORCEMENT OF ENVIRONMENTAL LAW, Report number: 2019/11, 2.

regulations requiring permits for drilling, the proliferation of wells, both legal and illegal, has surged dramatically.[51] According to a 2018 announcement by Ghasem Taghizadeh, the Deputy Minister of Agriculture, the number of wells increased from 60,000 to approximately 800,000, with 430,000 classified as illegal.[52] This trend continues unabated, particularly in agricultural and rural areas where water scarcity is most acute, driven by persistent incentives that encourage such activities[53] and exacerbate violations.[54,55] The Islamic Republic's long-standing focus on achieving agricultural self-sufficiency has often led to a permissive stance toward illegal wells. Although recent years have seen some unauthorized wells sealed and a small number of violators brought to court, progress in addressing these widespread violations has been slow.[56]

Over-extraction of resources, such as groundwater, has led to significant subsidence. When excessive amounts of water are removed from underground aquifers, the soil above can lose its support structure, causing the ground to sink. This process occurs as the voids left by the withdrawn water are not adequately filled, leading to a gradual collapse of the surrounding earth. The result can be serious, including damage to buildings, roads, and infrastructure, as well as changes to natural water flows and ecosystems. The cumulative impact of subsidence worsens the issues associated with the water crisis, as sinking ground diminishes overall water storage capacity and intensifies pressure on already limited water resources.[57]

The legal response to illegal well drilling has been largely ineffective. While the law prescribes penalties, including fines and the sealing of unauthorized wells, enforcement remains weak due to corruption, lack of resources, and political pressures. Farmers, often desperate to sustain their livelihoods, frequently bypass legal channels and drill wells without permits, driven by the immediate need for water. They have also learnt "over the years that if they

---

[51] Nabavi, *supra* note 11, at 704-705.

[52] M. Salami, *The water crisis and decline of legitimacy in Iran*, TRENDS RESEARCH & ADVISORY, October 6, 2022, https://trendsresearch.org/insight/the-water-crisis-and-decline-of-legitimacy-in-iran/?srsltid=AfmBOooyLew9N1EJnaDKlbKSYySXjNgpjD_Mwc-QvrjYwaLjsQ7Fd1fu.

[53] M. Al-Aloosy, *Water insecurity: Iran's formidable threat*, THE WASHINGTON INSTITUTE (2022), https://www.washingtoninstitute.org/policy-analysis/water-insecurity-irans-formidable-threat.

[54] FINANCIAL TRIBUNE, *Dilemma of illegal water wells*, July 12, 2019, https://financialtribune.com/articles/energy/98887/dilemma-of-illegal-water-wells.

[55] N. Badisar and M.S. Ahmadi, *Rules governing groundwater (wells) resources in Iran*, IRANIAN WATER RESEARCHES JOURNAL, 12(2), 77 (2018).

[56] Salami, *supra* note 52.

[57] Hamidifar, *supra* note 36, at 90.

break the law and bypass regulations, later they can negotiate with authorities to get exempted from the penalties, and also get a licence for their well."[58] In 2006, a new program was initiated by the regional water authorities to curb the rampant proliferation of illegal wells. They started collaborating with the "military, judicial, and other relevant authorities to close and, in some cases, destroy existing illegal wells." However, they faced significant social pushback. In light of this resistance, the parliament, guided by the Commission established under Article 90 of the Constitution, decided to halt the initiative. This decision echoed a similar one made two decades prior when the Fair Water Distribution law was enacted.[59]

As was discussed, the *Ta'een Taklif* law also aimed to address the status of unlicensed wells. This legislation directed the Ministry of Energy to grant abstraction permits for illegal wells that had been established prior to 2005. Like the earlier Fair Water Distribution law, this measure was a response to the growing number of unlicensed wells and the demands from local communities for water to support agriculture. Additionally, the law mandated that water usage at all agricultural wells be metered according to their licensing, placing the responsibility for the procurement and installation of meters on the Ministry of Energy. However, progress in implementing these measures has been slow and, in some regions, barely noticeable.[60]

One prominent case illustrating the severity of this issue occurred in Fars Province, where illegal wells have led to the significant depletion of groundwater, causing severe land subsidence and the collapse of farmlands. For instance, farmers have been extracting groundwater from depths of up to 450 meters to irrigate crops, while in Chaharmahal and Bakhtiari Province, water is pumped from 600 meters to irrigate trees and grow crops. In regions like Kermanshah and Mazandaran, farmers continue to draw groundwater for rice cultivation despite ongoing drought conditions.[61] Despite local efforts to close unauthorized wells, enforcement has been inconsistent, with many wells reopening shortly after being sealed. This ongoing cycle highlights the challenges in effectively curbing illegal water extraction, as the economic pressures on farmers often outweigh the legal consequences.

---

[58] Nabavi, *supra* note 12, at 716.
[59] Nabavi, *supra* note 12, at 705.
[60] *Id.*
[61] Nabavi, *supra* note 12, at 710-11.

B. Dam Construction and River Diversion Projects

Iran's aggressive pursuit of dam construction and river diversion projects, aimed at addressing water shortages and boosting agricultural output, has often backfired, causing significant ecological damage and worsening water scarcity. While dams are designed to regulate water flow and store water for times of drought, many projects have been poorly planned, lacking comprehensive environmental impact assessments. As a result, they have disrupted natural water systems, depleted downstream water supplies, and contributed to the drying of critical ecosystems like Lake Urmia and the Gavkhouni Wetland. Once one of the largest lakes in the world, Lake Urmia has drastically diminished in size. The Islamic Republic of Iran started constructing multiple dams around the lake in the 1990s, gradually diverting its water. The beneficiaries of these initiatives included the Islamic Revolutionary Guard Corps (IRGC) contractors, associates of the Ministry of Energy, and major agribusinesses, all of whom profited as the lake shrank. The lake has now been transformed into salt, contributing to Iran's suffocating dust storms.[62]

The construction of the Gotvand Dam on the Karun River, the KaniSib Dam, and tunnel to divert water to Lake Urmia and other similar initiatives illustrate the environmental and legal failings of the dam and water diversion projects in Iran.[63] The Gotvand Dam, for instance, was built with inadequate consideration of the geological conditions; the dam's reservoir sits on salt beds, causing salinization of the water and rendering it unsuitable for agriculture and drinking.[64]

Since 1979, Iran has erected 647 operational dams, averaging about 14 new dams each year. In stark contrast, prior to the revolution, the country had only seven ancient dams and 13 modern ones.[65] According to Iran's Water Resources Management Company, by 2022, the country had a total of 1,366 dams: 647 operational, 146 under construction, and 573 in the planning phase.[66] In 2016,

---

[62] IRAN ACTION GROUP, *Outlaw regime: A Chronicle of Iran's Destructive Activities* (2018), https://www.state.gov/wp-content/uploads/2018/12/Iran-Report.pdf.

[63] Mehdi Ketabchy, *Investigating the impacts of the political system components in Iran on the existing water bankruptcy*, SUSTAINABILITY, 13(13657), 5-6 (2021).

[64] Morteza Sharif and Saeid Hamzeh, *Investigating the effect of Gotvand Dam on changes in soil salinity and vegetation cover of downstream lands of the dam using satellite imagery and spectral indices*, ENVIRONMENTAL SCIENCES, 19(4), 225 (2022).

[65] Afshin Shahi, *Drought: The Achilles heel of the Islamic Republic of Iran*, ASIAN AFFAIRS, 50(1), 24 (2019).

[66] Mohammad Sadegh Talebi, *Water crisis in Iran and its security consequences*, JOURNAL OF HYDRAULIC STRUCTURES, 8(4), 23 (2022).

Iran was ranked among the top three dam-building nations in the world,[67] and as of 2024, Iran's Minister of Energy, Ali-Akbar Mehrabian, noted that Iran remains among the top four countries globally in dam construction.[68]

Authorities take pride in these rankings despite the nation's severe economic hardship, escalating water crisis, and environmental degradation. Following the end of the Iran-Iraq war, dam-building became the state's symbol of "advancement and 'self-sufficiency.'" The IRGC, which operates under the authority of the Supreme Leader, who is the highest-ranking figure in the Iranian political and religious hierarchy, was given immense power to take on dam construction projects[69] among other economic projects.[70] The IRGC and its units, such as Khatam al-Anbiya,[71] an engineering arm of the IRGC,[72] began profiting financially from these initiatives. However, many of these structures have proven ineffective and due to corruption and mismanagement, the IRGC has contributed to ongoing drought and water crisis. In numerous cases, these projects have exacerbated environmental issues and further depleted water resources for marginalized communities already facing hardships.[73]

Despite clear evidence of environmental damage and violations of environmental protection laws, legal accountability for the mismanagement of these projects has been minimal, with little recourse for affected communities. The ultimate beneficiary of these initiatives and projects is Iran's Supreme Leader, first Ayatollah Khomeini and subsequently Ayatollah Khamenei, both serving as Commander-in-Chief of the IRGC, among other agencies. Holding an "unlimited term of service and unaccountability," the Supreme Leader—along with numerous high-ranking officials directly or indirectly appointed by him— has perpetuated centralization of the political system, abuse of power, and a complete disregard for democratic legal norms and frameworks.[74]

---

[67] Kaveh Madani et al., *Iran's socio-economic drought: Challenges of a water-bankrupt nation*, IRANIAN STUDIES, 49(6): 1001 (2016).

[68] MOJNEWS, *Iran ranked among 4 main dam builder countries in the world* (May 21, 2024) https://www.mojnews.com/Section-economy-4/555642-iran-ranked-among-main-dam-builder-countries-in-the-world.

[69] Shahi, *supra* note 65, at 23-24.

[70] Madani, *supra* note 68, at 1000.

[71] *Khatam-al Anbiya* Construction Headquarters is an engineering arm of the IRGC in Iran, involved in large-scale infrastructure projects.

[72] IRNA, *62 dams were built by the Khatam-al Anbiya Construction Headquarters* (June 1, 2024) https://www.irna.ir/news/85484863/۶۲-سد-توسط-قرارگاه-ساز□دگی-خاتم-الا□بیا-ساخته-□د.

[73] Iran Action Group, *supra* note 62.

[74] Ketabchy, *supra* note 63, at 3.

C. The Underground Water Economy: Black Markets and Illicit Trade

The underground economy, often referred to as the "shadow", "hidden," or "black" economy, encompasses all economic activities that operate outside the formal, regulated financial and legal systems and "include conscious efforts to avoid official detection."[75] While these activities are generally unreported to authorities, untaxed, and unregulated, they fulfill various market demands where formal systems fall short or impose restrictive controls. In many countries, the underground economy involves a range of goods and services, from unlicensed labor and counterfeit goods to the illicit trade of natural resources. Its drivers are diverse and typically stem from high unemployment rates, stringent state regulations, economic crises, and a lack of access to essential capabilities, goods and services, among other things.[76]

Iran's post-war emphasis on food security, aimed at achieving agricultural self-sufficiency, inadvertently led to the proliferation of illegal practices related to land and water use. Following the Iran-Iraq war, national policies prioritized the domestic production of critical crops such as wheat, barley, and rice, making agriculture a cornerstone of the country's development strategy.[77]

This strategy led to vast areas of new farmland coming under cultivation and an increase in the drilling of deep wells, largely to support irrigation. However, the agricultural sector was ill-equipped to support the intensified production demands due to technological and economic constraints. To meet these ambitious targets, successive administrations indirectly permitted the over-appropriation of resources by tolerating unregulated land expansion and water extraction.[78] This approach, combined with Iran's heavy reliance on agriculture—consuming 80-90% of the country's water supply— and the impact of prolonged droughts, pushed many farmers and rural communities to resort to unauthorized wells for irrigation.[79]

This surge in illegal groundwater exploitation resulted in an annual overdraft of approximately five billion cubic meters. Today, of Iran's 658,000 total water wells, an estimated 300,000 operate without legal authorization. This lack of regulation has given rise to an underground economy and black markets,

---

[75] M.H. Fleming et al., *The shadow economy,* JOURNAL OF INTERNATIONAL AFFAIRS, 53(2) 387 (2020).

[76] S. Rasouli Firooz Abadi et al., *Examining the effective social and economic factors on underground economy,* MEDITERRANEAN JOURNAL OF SOCIAL SCIENCES, 6(3), 527-28 (2015).

[77] Hamidifar, *supra* note 36, at 86.

[78] Saatsaz, *supra* note 15, at 1767.

[79] Omid Zamani et al., *Limiting and timing water supply for agricultural production – The case of the Zayandeh-Rud River Basin, Iran,* AGRICULTURAL WATER MANAGEMENT, 222, 323 (2019).

particularly in areas facing acute shortages or where rationing measures have been implemented, where illegally extracted water is sold at high prices, allowing wealthier farmers and industries to maintain access while smaller farms[80] and rural communities face restrictions.[81] Vendors illegally extract water from groundwater sources or private wells and then transport and sell it at inflated prices to individuals and businesses in need. This underground trade is particularly active during the summer months, when demand peaks due to higher temperatures and agricultural needs. In some regions, tanker trucks filled with illicit water to distribute to households or businesses, creating a secondary economy that operates outside the state-controlled water supply network. This unregulated trade exacerbates inequality, as those who can afford to pay the black-market prices have access to water, while low-income households are left with limited or no options.[82]

Masoud Moradian, Deputy of Operations and Water Development at the Kohgiluyeh and Boyer-Ahmad Water and Wastewater Company, outlined several unauthorized practices in water use. These include illegal water usage by bypassing or directly accessing the supply line before it gets to the meter, or reselling water to neighboring properties without authorization. Tampering with water meters is also a significant issue; examples include removing or disabling meters, altering mechanisms to lower recorded consumption (such as breaking the glass, pouring boiling water, or adjusting internal screws), or installing non-standard or illegal meters. Additional violations involve direct water pumping without intermediary storage tanks, unauthorized changes to the agreed water usage capacity, or increasing the number of units served by a single connection. Infrastructure-related offenses, such as unauthorized plumbing connections to adjacent properties, improper installation of fixtures, or misusing water connections for purposes that differ from the original approval (e.g., commercial use of residential connections), exacerbate the issue. These activities result in wasted water, financial losses for the water company, and disrupted services for compliant users, with repair costs ultimately borne by the public.[83]

The underground economy in Iran includes unregulated activities, such as smuggling and unchecked middleman operations, which undermine economic

---

[80] KHABARBAN, *Fars Roundtable: Examining the Black Market for Water and the Necessity of Establishing a Legal Market for It in Iran* (2023), https://38493096.khabarban.com.

[81] Saatsaz, *supra* note 15, at 1767.

[82] REGIONAL WATER COMPANY OF TEHRAN, Seizure of an unauthorized water-selling tanker in Pakdasht. (2020), https://thrw.ir/cs/News/118/3677.

[83] BORNA NEWS, Examples of violations and unauthorized water usage (2022), https://borna.news/fa/news/1287223/مصادیق-تخلفات-و-مصارف-غیر-مجاز-آبی.

efficiency and exacerbate instability. In the agricultural sector, for instance, there are seven brokers for every producer, leading to significant price discrepancies—cheap farm products become excessively expensive for consumers.[84] Farmers face critical challenges, including the dominance of intermediaries, insufficient state support, and inadequate infrastructure for agricultural distribution. Middlemen reap the largest profits, leaving producers with minimal returns despite their labor-intensive efforts. Issues such as delayed government payments for crops, rising costs of chemical fertilizers and pesticides, and challenges in securing export markets exacerbate the farmers' struggles.[85] The water crisis exacerbates the role and influence of middlemen in agricultural markets. As water scarcity increases, farmers face higher production costs and reduced yields due to the limited availability of irrigation water or the necessity of investing in alternative water sources. This vulnerability makes farmers more reliant on middlemen, who often exploit the situation by purchasing crops at extremely low prices under the pretext of market uncertainties or production risks.

Middlemen, who typically have better access to resources and networks, capitalize on the farmers' inability to store or market their produce effectively. The lack of efficient water management systems and state-supported distribution networks amplifies this dependency, allowing intermediaries to dominate the supply chain and reap the majority of profits. This dynamic not only undermines farmers' livelihoods but also distorts market pricing, creating inefficiencies that could further stress agricultural productivity and sustainability amidst the water crisis.

In addition to state policies that have led the country to this crisis, the growth of Iran's underground water economy is also fueled by weak regulatory enforcement and inadequate legal deterrents. Despite having laws to regulate groundwater extraction,[86] Iran's enforcement agencies often lack the resources, technical capacity, and sometimes the political backing to effectively police illegal wells and groundwater usage. Corruption among local officials further fuels the problem, with some accepting bribes to overlook unauthorized wells

---

84 PISHKHAN, The dominance of middlemen in the underground economy (2020), https://www.pishkhan.com/news/192635.

85 ISNA, *From water shortages to profits for middlemen* (November 14, 2024) https://www.isna.ir/news/1403081409967/%D8%A7%D8%B2-%DA%A9%D9%85%D8%A8%D9%88%D8%AF-%D8%A2%D8%A8-%D8%AA%D8%A7-%D8%B3%D9%88%D8%AF%DB%8C-%DA%A9%D9%87-%D9%86%D8%B5%DB%8C%D8%A8-%D8%AF%D9%84%D8%A7%D9%84%D8%A7%D9%86-%D9%85%DB%8C-%D8%B4%D9%88%D8%AF.

86 Sanaz Alasti, *Legislation on Use of Water in Agriculture: Iran* (2013), https://tile.loc.gov/storage-services/service/ll/llglrd/2013417719/2013417719.pdf.

or illegal water transactions. The penalties for water-related offenses are often too lenient to serve as effective deterrents, especially for larger landowners or industrial operations that can absorb these fines as operational costs. Consequently, the lack of meaningful repercussions has made it difficult to curb illegal activities in the water sector,[87] allowing the underground water economy to flourish.[88]

III. State and Corporate Accountability in Water Mismanagement

State and corporate entities have played significant roles in Iran's water crisis, often prioritizing economic growth, industrial development, and political agendas over sustainable water management. The state, as the primary regulator, water distributor, and developer of infrastructure projects, bears substantial responsibility for the mismanagement of water resources. At the same time, corporate actors, including state-owned enterprises, private industries, and agricultural businesses, frequently engage in practices that exacerbate water scarcity, pollution, and environmental degradation. The lack of accountability mechanisms for these powerful actors has allowed harmful practices to persist, with profound consequences for Iran's environment and communities. This section explores the role of the state and corporate entities in water mismanagement, examining legal frameworks, specific cases, and the challenges in enforcing accountability.

A. Challenges and Consequences of Water Management in Iran

Unlike other resources, water is fundamental to all life, and its depletion or over-commercialization has immediate and severe consequences for human and ecological systems. Hence, Iran's approach to water management presents a complex and increasingly untenable "double-edged sword" situation. In a country where water scarcity is reaching critical levels, privatization of water rights empowers firms, contractors, stakeholders, and companies to prioritize profit over sustainable use and public welfare, leading to restricted access for lower-income communities and a reduction in overall availability due to profit-driven over-extraction.[89] This "crime against water" occurs when private ownership leads to resource depletion without accountability, altering both the quantity and quality of the water supply and driving up prices to the extent that water becomes financially exclusive. This renders it accessible only to those

---

[87] Saatsaz, *supra* note 15, at 1773.

[88] Helena Du Rées, *Can criminal law protect the environment*, JOURNAL OF SCANDINAVIAN STUDIES IN CRIMINOLOGY AND CRIME PREVENTION, Vol. 2, 123 (2001).

[89] Armaghan Omrani, *Water management in Iran*, Thesis. FACULTY OF ECONOMIC & MANAGEMENT ODISEE, UNIVERSITY OF APPLIED SCIENCE, 72 (2013).

who can afford it, creating "financial exclusion" for many Iranians—especially vulnerable rural populations—whose livelihoods depend on affordable water for agriculture and daily living. Given these risks, privatization exacerbates inequality and undermines both food security and social stability in Iran.[90]

Yet, the alternative—leaving management of water resources under complete state control—poses its own set of challenges. While, in principle, state management should work in the public's interest, the reality in Iran complicates this notion. The Islamic Republic has faced persistent criticisms over inefficiencies, corruption, and a lack of responsiveness to citizens' needs. In theory, a state-run water system would prioritize equitable access, resource sustainability, and long-term planning. However, the Islamic Republic of Iran has struggled to implement effective regulatory frameworks or adopt necessary reforms, leading to widespread issues like illegal well drilling, poor infrastructure maintenance, and insufficient oversight. This weak regulatory environment has allowed the over-extraction of water and the continued exploitation of groundwater reserves, with little accountability. As a result, even under state control, water resources remain vulnerable to misuse, exacerbating environmental degradation and water scarcity.

Thus, Iran's current water crisis exemplifies a situation where neither privatization nor sole state control offers a clear solution. The privatization of water has deepened socio-economic divides, while the state's poor track record in resource management has raised serious doubts about its ability to ensure sustainable and fair access to water. Resolving this double-edged problem requires a new model of governance that emphasizes transparency, community involvement, and stricter regulation of both private and public actors. Such a model would need to balance resource sustainability with equitable access, ensuring that water remains affordable and available to all while protecting Iran's already stressed water reserves from further depletion.

B. Corporate Accountability: Industrial and Agricultural Mismanagement

Corporate actors, including both private companies and state-owned enterprises, are major contributors to Iran's water mismanagement. Industries such as petrochemicals, steel manufacturing, and mining are notorious for their high-water consumption and pollution, often operating with little regard for environmental regulations.[91] Similarly, large agricultural enterprises, many of which are linked to powerful state or military organizations, engage in

---

[90] Rob White & Katja Eman, *Green Criminology, Water Issues, Human Rights and Private Profit*, in WATER, GOVERNANCE, AND CRIME ISSUES 10 (Katja Eman et al. eds., Springer 2020).
[91] Omrani, *supra* note 89, at 21,71-72.

unsustainable water use practices, exacerbating water scarcity and environmental degradation.

Industrial pollution is a pervasive problem, with factories frequently discharging untreated or inadequately treated wastewater into rivers, lakes, and groundwater sources. According to Akbarzadeh et al., "the untreated discharge of municipal, industrial, and agricultural wastewaters in Iran has created serious pollution of the water resources and environment."[92] Despite regulations requiring industries to implement pollution control measures, compliance is often poor, and enforcement is inconsistent.[93] For example, steel plants in Isfahan Province have been repeatedly cited for polluting the Zayandeh River, contributing to severe water quality degradation[94] and impacting local agriculture and drinking water supplies.[95] However, efforts to hold these companies accountable have been stymied by their economic importance and political connections, which often shield them from meaningful legal consequences.[96]

In agriculture, corporate accountability is equally problematic. Stakeholders of large-scale agribusinesses, many of whom are commercial farmers seeking "to turn agriculture into an income-generating enterprise," often disregard water management regulations, engaging in practices that deplete water resources at unsustainable rates.[97] The cultivation of water-intensive crops in arid regions, excessive use of groundwater, and inefficient irrigation methods are widespread issues that have been exacerbated by the lack of regulatory oversight and accountability.

One illustrative case of the challenges surrounding corporate accountability is the agricultural expansion in Sistan and Baluchistan Province, where more

---

92 Abbas Akbarzadeh et al., *Municipal wastewater treatment in Iran: Current situation, barriers and future policies*, JOURNAL OF ADVANCES IN ENVIRONMENTAL HEALTH RESEARCH, 11(1), 60-71, 60 (2023).

93 H. Reza Shiravand, *Laws and legal safeguards governing the handling of air pollution in the industrial city of Arak in Iran, and its comparison with international norms*, JOURNAL OF FUNDAMENTAL AND APPLIED SCIENCES, 9(1S), 870 (2017).

94 Mahdi Hashemi Beni et al., *Water-energy nexus approach for optimal design of hybrid cooling system in direct reduction of iron plant*, JOURNAL OF CLEANER PRODUCTION, 287(2021), 5 (2020).

95 Ali Esmaeili et al., *A geochemical survey of heavy metals in agricultural and background soils of the Isfahan industrial zone, Iran*, CATENA, 121, 97 (2014).

96 Michael Scollon, *Iran's environmental standards, polluted reality mix like oil and water*, RADIO FREE EUROPE (May 1, 2023), https://www.rferl.org/a/iran-environmental-standards-pollution-smog/32385813.html.

97 Fatemeh Karandish et al., *Agro-economic and socio-environmental assessments of food and virtual water trades of Iran*, SCIENTIFIC REPORTS, 11:15022, 10 (2021).

than 50 state-backed agribusinesses and water-intensive industries, such as steel and cement factories, operate with little regard for environmental regulations. These enterprises have led to over-extraction of groundwater, causing severe water shortages for local communities. Despite clear evidence of environmental harm and non-compliance with water use regulations, these powerful economic actors continue to operate with impunity, reflecting a failure of the state to enforce laws and hold corporations accountable. While the Islamic Republic has simultaneously invested public funds to support agricultural production and provided subsidies to prevent internal displacement and anti-government protests, the region's reliance on water-intensive farming practices, such as wheat and watermelon cultivation, and the absence of economic diversification have intensified its vulnerability. With 94 percent of the province's water used for agriculture—35–40 percent of which is wasted—the dependence of farming communities on scarce resources like those from the Helmand River underscores the need for stricter enforcement and corporate responsibility to address the growing environmental and socio-economic crisis.[98]

C. Legal and Governance Challenges in Addressing Iran's Water Crisis

Iran's escalating water crisis is deeply intertwined with challenges in legal enforcement and prosecution, which hinder the country's ability to effectively manage and protect its water resources. Although Iran has established environmental laws intended to regulate water use,[99] these frameworks are often outdated and lack the specificity required to address modern challenges like climate change, rapid urban expansion, and agricultural demand. These, combined with corruption and political interference, often protect powerful offenders, including state-affiliated companies and influential individuals, from facing the full extent of the law. The influence of powerful groups in Iran, often referred to as the "water mafia," has hindered effective decision-making and governance in addressing the country's water challenges.[100] Regulatory agencies lack the independence, resources, and will and political power necessary to conduct thorough investigations and enforce penalties, leading to a culture of impunity. Judicial inefficiency further hampers efforts to address

---

[98] MINORITY RIGHTS GROUP, *Iran: Baluch people running out of water due to unfair water management*, Minority and Indigenous Trends 2023: Focus on water, 226 (2023).

[99] Alasti, *supra* note 86.

[100] Allan Hassaniyan, *Iran's water policy: Environmental injustice and peripheral marginalisation*, PROGRESS IN PHYSICAL GEOGRAPHY, 48(3), 423 (2024); KHABARBAN, *Thirteen counties in Sistan and Baluchistan face absolute water scarcity and the drying up of 292 water wells / How is the revival of the Zayandehrud River possible?* (2024), https://40792607.khabarban.com/.

water-related crimes. Courts are often reluctant to prioritize environmental cases, and when cases do proceed, they are frequently bogged down by procedural delays and insufficient legal expertise in environmental law. The lack of clear legal definitions for certain environmental offenses also complicates the prosecution process, making it difficult to hold violators accountable under existing statutes.

Although water is not explicitly recognized as an independent human right in international treaties, international human rights law imposes obligations on states to ensure access to safe drinking water for all. These obligations encompass providing a sufficient supply of safe water for essential personal and domestic uses, including drinking, sanitation, laundry, food preparation, and hygiene. Additionally, states are required to progressively guarantee access to adequate sanitation, which is vital not only for human dignity and privacy but also for safeguarding water quality. Iran's constitution also implies a general responsibility for the state to provide safe drinking water and sanitation.[101] However, the country's lack of accountability mechanisms and failure to address human rights violations, including those related to water rights, perpetuates a culture of impunity. This undermines the effectiveness of both Iran's constitutional commitments and the human rights instruments it has ratified.[102]

This culture of impunity makes it ripe for officials responsible for regulating water resources to accept bribes or engage in favoritism, leading to uneven resource allocation and the continuation of harmful practices.[103] Corruption within local governments allows unauthorized agricultural expansion and illegal water extraction, practices that drain already scarce water supplies and erode the integrity of legal frameworks. The lack of transparency around water data and decision-making processes also makes it difficult for the judiciary and prosecutors to hold powerful actors accountable. Iran's Supreme Leader appoints the head of the judiciary, who is responsible for overseeing Iran's court system, appointing judges, and enforcing legal and religious guidelines within the judiciary. This individual has significant influence over Iran's legal landscape, including the power to interpret and enforce laws in ways that align with the Supreme Leader's directives. This appointment system ensures that the judiciary remains aligned with the values and objectives of the Supreme

---

[101] Office of the United Nations High Commissioner for Human Rights, *The Human Rights Fact Sheet No. 35*, 7 (2010), https://www.ohchr.org/sites/default/files/Documents/Publications/FactSheet35en.pdf.
[102] A. Shaheed, Report of the Special Rapporteur on the Situation of Human Rights in the Islamic Republic of Iran, U.N. Doc. A/HRC/22/56 (2013).
[103] Shahi, *supra* note 65, at 24.

Leader, which can impact the handling of cases, including those that involve the environment. This structure centralized authority within the Supreme Leader's office and reinforces the judiciary's role as a supporting pillar of the Islamic Republic's political framework, hence limiting judicial independence.

This climate of limited accountability discourages adherence to water regulations and weakens the rule of law in Iran's environmental sector. Consequently, regulatory bodies and the judiciary often do not hold violators accountable for illegal water use, over-extraction of groundwater, and unauthorized well drilling. Legal gaps, compounded by limited judicial expertise in environmental law and judicial independence, have created a system where violations frequently go unchecked.[104] Furthermore, legal penalties for water-related violations are often too lenient to serve as meaningful deterrents, especially for influential actors with significant financial and political resources. This has created a situation in which the penalties for illegal water use are insufficient to deter future violations, perpetuating unsustainable practices that further stress Iran's water supply.[105]

There is also a significant gap between law and practice in terms of environmental restoration and compensation for damages. Even when penalties are imposed, they rarely include measures to remediate the environmental harm caused, leaving polluted rivers, dried wetlands, and depleted aquifers with little hope of recovery. According to Segato, Mattioli, and Capello,

> [t]he root causes of environmental crimes vary greatly: these are primarily the low risks and high profits in an environment made permissive by poor governance and widespread corruption, minimal budget allocated to police, prosecution and courts, inadequate institutional support, political interference and low employee morale, as well as minimal benefits to local communities. The situation is especially critical when it comes to support for prosecution and courts/the judiciary in many developing countries.[106]

Restrictions on civil society and environmental activism also limit public oversight and accountability, effectively silencing voices that might otherwise advocate for more sustainable practices. In Iran, environmental activists who speak out against water mismanagement risk prosecution, which discourages

---

104 Zahra Mahmoudi Kordi et al., *Analyzing the environmental democracy in international law and Iran's legal system*, INTERNATIONAL LAW REVIEW, 40(69), 207 (2023).
105 Flora Heidari et al., *Legal system governing on water pollution in Iran*, JOURNAL OF GEOSCIENCE AND ENVIRONMENTAL PROTECTION, 5(9), 55 (2017).
106 Segato, *supra* note 48, at 34-35.

public discourse and minimizes grassroots efforts to address the crisis. As an example, in 2019, an Iranian revolutionary court sentenced six environmental experts from the Persian Wildlife Heritage Foundation, detained since January 2018, to prison terms of 4 to 10 years following an unfair trial where they were denied access to the full evidence against them.[107]

D. Systemic Corruption and Legal Barriers to Accountability

Prosecuting corruption and water-related crimes in Iran faces significant legal and institutional barriers. The intertwined nature of political power, economic interests, and regulatory agencies often shields offenders from accountability. Investigations into corruption are frequently hindered by lack of transparency, bureaucratic inertia, and the reluctance of authorities to confront powerful individuals or entities involved in illegal activities. While "international human rights law does not prescribe an exact formula for domestic mechanisms of redress and accountability," the Islamic Republic is obligated to establish an accountability system that is, at a minimum, "accessible, impartial, transparent, and effective."[108]

The legal and institutional frameworks in Iran have proven inadequate in holding state and corporate actors accountable for water mismanagement, largely due to several interrelated factors. One significant issue is weak regulatory oversight; agencies such as the Ministry of Energy and the Department of Environment lack the independence and enforcement capacity necessary for effective monitoring and regulation of water usage.[109] Budget constraints, political interference, and bureaucratic inefficiencies further undermine their ability to hold violators accountable.

The judiciary in Iran also operates within a complex political framework that significantly undermines its independence, despite constitutional provisions theoretically guaranteeing autonomy.[110] The head of the judiciary, as noted, is

---

[107] HUMAN RIGHTS WATCH, Iran: Environmentalists Sentenced (Unfair Trial; Continued Due Process Violations) (2019), https://www.hrw.org/news/2019/11/22/iran-environ mentalists-sentenced.

[108] Office of the United Nations High Commissioner for Human Rights, *supra* note 101, at 38.

[109] Zilberberg, *supra* note 25, at 50.

[110] Article 156: The judiciary is an independent power, the protector of the rights of the individual and society, responsible for the implementation of justice, and entrusted with the following duties: 1) Investigating and passing judgement on grievances, violations of rights, and complaints; the resolving of litigation; the settling of disputes; and the taking of all necessary decisions and measures in probate matters as the law may determine; 2) restoring public rights and promoting justice and legitimate freedoms; 3) supervising

appointed by the Supreme Leader, while the head of the Supreme Court is subsequently appointed by the head of the judiciary.[111] This structure underscores the judiciary's lack of independence, as it is effectively subordinate to the Supreme Leader. The independence of Iran's courts is similarly compromised within this political framework.

The head of judiciary serves a five-year term, which can be renewed indefinitely, fostering minimal accountability.[112] Political pressure on judges is pervasive, particularly in revolutionary courts handling politically sensitive cases, where rulings are often influenced by the interests of the ruling elite. Judges in these courts frequently face pressure to deliver verdicts aligned with the interests of powerful authorities, further diminishing the courts' independence. This lack of judicial and institutional autonomy is exacerbated by the intertwining of religious authority and legal processes, enabling interpretations of Islamic jurisprudence that serve political objectives rather than ensuring justice. Consequently, both the judiciary and the courts in Iran lack the necessary safeguards to function as independent and impartial arbiters of the law. Ultimately, environmental crimes are of "secondary importance compared to other public crimes" in Iran. As such prosecutors fail to pay attention to environmental crime cases.[113]

Legal proceedings against corrupt officials or major players in the underground water economy are rare but when they do occur, they often result in lenient sentences that fail to deter future crimes. The complex and opaque nature of water-related corruption also makes it difficult for prosecutors to build strong cases, as key evidence is often concealed or manipulated. Additionally, there is a lack of specialized legal frameworks specifically targeting water theft and corruption within the water sector. Existing laws are often too broad or insufficiently detailed, leaving significant loopholes that allow offenders to evade prosecution. Efforts to strengthen legal responses have

---

the proper enforcement of laws; 4) uncovering crimes; prosecuting, punishing, and chastising criminals; and enacting the penalties and provisions of the Islamic penal code; 5) taking suitable measures to prevent the occurrence of crime and to reform criminals.

[111] Abbas Mirshekari and Mohsen Salami, *A comparative study of the supreme court of Iran and the United States of America*, SOCIETY, DEVELOPMENT AND COMMERCIAL LAW REVIEW, 1(1), 38 (2023).

[112] *Id.* at 38.

[113] Ahmad Shohani et al., *Prevention and suppression of environmental crimes in the [sic] light of the actions of non-governmental organizations in the Iranian legal system*, RESEARCH JOURNAL OF ECOLOGY AND ENVIRONMENTAL SCIENCES, 1, 8 (2021).

been sporadic, and proposed reforms frequently stall due to resistance from vested interests.

Corruption, water theft, and the underground economy represent some of the most insidious challenges to water management in Iran. These activities not only exacerbate the water crisis but also undermine the rule of law and public trust in state institutions. Ultimately, Iran's legal and regulatory environment, hindered by systemic corruption, political interference, and inadequate enforcement mechanisms, fosters an environment where water-related crimes thrive unchecked. This pervasive lack of accountability has transformed resource management into a system dominated by powerful, state-aligned entities, laying the groundwork for a deeper issue: the criminalization of governance itself and the monopolization of resources by those in power. This alarming trend illuminates how Iran's governance structure has come to resemble an organized criminal network, further entrenching environmental degradation and social inequality across the country.

E. Criminalized Governance and Resource Monopoly in Iran

The Islamic Republic of Iran exhibits characteristics akin to an organized criminal network that wields political power to maintain control, monopolize resources, and suppress opposition. Much like traditional organized criminal groups, the Islamic Republic of Iran relies on systematic threats, violence, bribery, and state-sanctioned extortion to uphold its influence across society. Through its various security apparatuses, such as the IRGC and intelligence services, the Islamic Republic of Iran has constructed a parallel state structure that exerts coercive power over critical economic and social sectors, all while maintaining impunity. This system effectively mirrors how organized crime infiltrates political structures, instilling fear to establish dominance within communities and presenting "a direct threat to... social structures."[114] In its initial definition, the Federal Bureau of Investigation (FBI) defined organized crime as,

> [a]ny group having some manner of a formalized structure and whose primary objective is to obtain money through illegal activities. Such groups maintain their position through the use of actual or threatened violence, corrupt public officials, graft, or extortion, and generally have

---

114 Katja Eman & Rob White, *Water and Organised Crime*, in WATER, GOVERNANCE, AND CRIME ISSUES 49 (Katja Eman et al. eds., Springer 2020).

a significant impact on the people in their locales, region, or the country as a whole.[115]

Even though the FBI's definition of organized crime has evolved over the years to address transnational criminal activities,[116] including cross-border operations, corruption, and resource exploitation, with the Islamic Republic of Iran also aligning with these expanded parameters, for the purposes of this chapter, the earlier FBI definition is utilized to focus on Iran's domestic governance crisis. This earlier definition emphasizes formalized structures, the use of violence and corruption, and significant localized impacts, which aptly describe the regime's internal operations and control mechanisms.[117]

One of the most profound impacts of this criminalized state structure is visible in the control and exploitation of natural resources, particularly water. Following years of mismanagement, rapid depletion, and weak regulation, Iran faces a severe water crisis, exacerbated by corrupt practices and environmental crime. Iran's governance over water resembles organized crime's exploitative behavior: the state and affiliated bodies, such as the IRGC, often treat water resources as private assets rather than public goods, neglecting sustainable management in favor of profit-driven extraction. This has led to a black market for water and a surge in unauthorized water extraction. Similar to organized criminal groups engaged in environmental crimes globally, Iran's ruling entities prioritize short-term gains, degrading environmental resources in ways that drive up prices and limit access to those who can afford it, [118] thus leaving marginalized communities increasingly vulnerable.[119]

However, prosecuting corruption and water-related crimes within this framework presents one of the biggest legal challenges in Iran. Because entities like the IRGC not only hold considerable economic influence but also operate under state protection as part of the organized criminal system, legal

---

[115] Gregory F. Treverton et al., *Organized Crime and Terrorism*, FILM PIRACY, ORGANIZED CRIME, AND TERRORISM, RAND CORPORATION, 12 (2009).

[116] Federal Bureau of Investigation (FBI) (2024) Transnational Organized Crime. [online] Available at: https://www.fbi.gov/investigate/transnational-organized-crime (last visited: November 29, 2024).

[117] Treverton, *supra* note 115, at 12.

[118] Eman, *supra* note 114, at 49.

[119] Interpol, *Strategic Report: Environment, Peace and Security – A Convergence of Threats*, INTERPOL-UN ENVIRONMENT (2016) https://www.interpol.int/content/download/5088/file/INTERPOL-UNEP%2520Strategic%2520Report%2520-%2520Environment, %2520Peace%2520and%2520Security%2520-%2520A%2520Convergence%2520of%2520Threats.pdf&ved=2ahUKEwirypfHx4GKAxXpUkEAHV_jGEYQFnoECBIQAQ&usg=AovVaw2CW5lyn8msr_KUnLWIya5f.

accountability for resource exploitation and environmental degradation is minimal. High-level individuals and organizations involved in illegal water extraction or land monopolization are often shielded by political connections, making it virtually impossible for enforcement agencies to pursue action. Iran's judiciary itself is compromised by the centralized power structure, lacking the independence necessary to take on cases involving influential figures tied to the state. Even if evidence of corruption or environmental crime surfaces, weak legal deterrents and regulatory gaps allow such practices to continue unabated. Attempts to strengthen environmental or anti-corruption laws frequently encounter resistance from those benefiting from the current system, fostering a cycle where resource crimes and corruption remain pervasive.[120]

Moreover, the repression of dissent and limited transparency in the legal system further entrench these challenges. Those who expose corrupt practices or criticize unsustainable resource management face severe risks, while judicial officials may avoid pursuing cases involving powerful actors due to fears of professional or personal repercussions. This lack of accountability allows state-affiliated networks to persist in exploiting resources without oversight, deepening both the environmental crisis and economic inequalities within the country.

Thus, Iran's water crisis and broader environmental degradation are not merely the result of poor policy but are rooted in a systemic criminalization of governance itself. The state functions as a criminal enterprise, wielding its political dominance to secure economic monopolies, repress opposition, and extract resources for profit rather than public benefit. This dual structure of criminalized governance and entrenched corruption presents a formidable obstacle to legal enforcement, eroding both the environment and social welfare. Overcoming these challenges would require a transformation in Iran's governance model—one that introduces genuine accountability, transparency, and reforms to restore sustainable resource management and legal integrity. Without these changes, the Islamic Republic of Iran will continue to operate as an organized crime entity, using its power to exploit resources at the expense of its people and environment.

Reduced availability of freshwater, tensions over trans-boundary basins, water's strategic relevance for public safety and state security, widespread corruption and corporate interests, unequal distribution of resources, and large-scale investments in highly corrupt countries are the key drivers of criminal activities.[121]

---

120 Eman, *supra* note 114, at 49.

121 Segato, *supra* note 48, at 32.

IV. Proposals for Legal Reforms

Addressing Iran's water crisis effectively requires significant legal and institutional reforms to enhance water management, improve enforcement, and ensure accountability. The current legal framework and enforcement mechanisms are insufficient to tackle the complexities of water scarcity and environmental degradation.

A unified definition of water crimes is critical to overcoming fragmented enforcement mechanisms and fostering effective water governance in Iran. Without a clear and standardized definition, efforts to identify, prosecute, and penalize activities such as illegal water extraction, diversion, and pollution remain inconsistent and ineffective. This ambiguity weakens both national and international enforcement measures, allowing offenders to exploit regulatory gaps. Developing a common definition would ensure clarity, bolster legal accountability, and create a foundation for coordinated responses to water-related offenses. Furthermore, the incorporation of water crimes into international criminal law conventions is necessary to establish uniform criminalization standards and expand jurisdiction to prevent offenders from evading justice by exploiting jurisdictional loopholes.[122] By aligning Iran's water governance framework with international standards and fostering cross-border cooperation, these reforms would strengthen accountability and contribute to the sustainable management of shared water resources, ensuring that water crimes are addressed comprehensively and equitably.

This section outlines several other key proposals for legal reforms aimed at strengthening Iran's water governance, improving the judicial response to environmental and water crimes, and fostering sustainable water use.

A. The Need For Strengthening Accountability Mechanisms

To effectively address the ongoing water crisis in Iran and promote sustainable resource management, strengthening accountability mechanisms for both state and corporate actors is crucial. To strengthen accountability mechanisms in Iran's water management, any advocacy for reform must align with the broader priorities of the regime, such as national security, economic resilience, and maintaining control through centralized governance. While environmental stewardship may not be a core element of the Supreme Leader's vision, themes of resource protection and self-sufficiency resonate with the state's broader narrative of safeguarding national assets and reducing dependency on external

---

[122] *Id.* at 43.

actors. Framing reforms around these priorities can increase the likelihood of acceptance within the current political structure.

Public engagement, often constrained by political restrictions, could focus on culturally acceptable channels such as mosques, local councils, and community organizations aligned with state-approved initiatives. This approach provides a platform for promoting water conservation and management without appearing confrontational. Similarly, judicial reforms, like specialized environmental law training for judges and establishing environmental courts, could be framed as technical efficiency improvements rather than systemic overhauls, reducing resistance from entrenched interests.

Corporate Social Responsibility (CSR) standards offer another avenue. Encouraging industries, including those tied to the IRGC, to adopt sustainable practices could begin with pilot projects in sectors directly impacted by water scarcity. Highlighting the economic benefits of sustainability may incentivize compliance. Additionally, digital tools for monitoring water usage can enhance transparency without directly challenging political power, with pilot programs demonstrating their effectiveness as a first step. International collaboration, particularly with organizations providing technical expertise, could be framed as apolitical and focused purely on national benefit, avoiding perceptions of foreign interference. While comprehensive systemic reform remains constrained, these carefully designed, incremental steps, aligning with the regime's priorities and emphasizing shared national benefits, could foster meaningful improvements in accountability mechanisms.

B. Strengthening Enforcement Mechanisms

Effective enforcement is paramount for ensuring compliance with water regulations and addressing violations that threaten Iran's already strained water resources. To achieve this, legal reforms must focus on enhancing the capacity and authority of regulatory agencies while improving the enforcement of environmental laws. Empowering regulatory bodies such as the Ministry of Energy and the Department of Environment would require overcoming significant political interference, as these agencies currently operate under the influence of powerful state institutions, including IRGC and entities aligned with the Supreme Leader. While granting these agencies greater independence is ideal, a more pragmatic approach would involve framing reforms as efforts to enhance national security and self-reliance—core tenets of the regime's narrative. Increasing funding is crucial to enhance their operational capabilities, allowing for better training, recruitment of skilled personnel, and development of technical expertise. This would enable these agencies to conduct regular inspections and monitor water use effectively, ensuring stricter compliance with existing regulations.

Investing in advanced monitoring technologies—such as remote sensing, satellite imagery, and real-time data systems—is more feasible given Iran's demonstrated capacity for technological development, particularly in areas tied to national security. Framing these investments as tools for safeguarding critical resources against overexploitation and external threats could garner support from key stakeholders, despite financial constraints due to international sanctions. Financing could involve reallocating resources or fostering partnerships with domestic technology firms. Reliable data from these technologies would facilitate prompt identification of violations, trend analysis, and informed policymaking, significantly strengthening enforcement efforts.

Legal reforms should also include increasing penalties for water-related offenses to serve as a strong deterrent against violations. Establishing more stringent penalties—such as higher fines, criminal sanctions, and remedial measures—could align with the government's broader emphasis on law enforcement and control. However, such measures must be carefully implemented to avoid targeting powerful state or semi-state entities that are often the largest violators. Enhancing public reporting mechanisms and whistleblower protection is equally critical but requires strategic framing. Implementing systems that encourage citizen participation in monitoring and reporting violations could be positioned as community empowerment initiatives, aligning with the regime's occasional calls for public involvement in governance. Strong legal safeguards would need to be put in place to protect whistleblowers from retaliation and address the public's deep-seated fear of retribution.

While these measures face significant hurdles in Iran's centralized and authoritarian context, strategically aligning reforms with national priorities and emphasizing their potential to bolster Iran's internal resilience and resource security could improve their chances of success. Together, these reforms would strengthen enforcement mechanisms, foster public trust in regulatory bodies, and pave the way for more sustainable and equitable management of Iran's water resources.

The Role of Public Perception, Community Engagement, and Human Rights in Water GovernancePublic perception and community engagement are critical factors influencing the enforcement of water regulations in Iran. The prevailing lack of trust in regulatory bodies and the judiciary significantly affects communities' willingness to comply with environmental laws or cooperate with enforcement actions. Many individuals harbor a deep-seated distrust of authorities, fueled by widespread perceptions of corruption, inefficiency, and political bias within enforcement agencies. This skepticism undermines public confidence in environmental governance and leads many communities to view regulatory actions as inconsistent or unjustly targeted. Such perceptions foster resentment and resistance, complicating efforts to engage these communities in sustainable water management practices. When residents believe that enforcement measures are arbitrary or biased, their compliance with legal requirements diminishes, further exacerbating issues of water mismanagement.

Adopting a human rights-based approach to water governance could play a transformative role in addressing these challenges. Viewing safe drinking water and sanitation as legal entitlements, rather than as charity, shifts the paradigm to place individuals at the center of water management policies. This approach empowers marginalized communities and informs them of their rights while holding governments accountable for the equitable distribution of water resources. Although this framework does not automatically resolve complex policy issues like financing or delivery, it establishes international standards that guide political and economic decisions about water allocation. Prioritizing access for the most vulnerable populations ensures that no group is excluded, and resources are allocated to address the needs of those facing discrimination or lack of access.[123]

However, community participation in decision-making processes must be approached with caution to avoid inadvertently marginalizing vulnerable members of the community, such as women or persons with disabilities. Efforts to promote inclusivity and empowerment should ensure that all voices are heard, and special attention must be paid to creating spaces where these groups can actively contribute to discussions on water and sanitation. By addressing power imbalances within communities, participation can become more equitable and meaningful, aligning with the principles of a human rights-based approach.[124]

A core characteristic of this approach is its focus on accountability, which emphasizes the obligations of the duty-bearer, i.e., the State, "to ensure access to safe drinking water and sanitation" for all rights-holders. In practice, this means developing laws, policies, institutions, administrative procedures, and mechanisms of redress to promote and protect access to these essential resources.[125] In Iran, integrating these accountability measures into water governance would help rebuild public trust in regulatory bodies and foster greater compliance with environmental laws. Public education campaigns and legal protections for whistleblowers could further enhance community

---

[123] Office of the United Nations High Commissioner for Human Rights, *supra* note 101, at 15-17.

[124] *Id.*

[125] *Id.*

engagement by fostering a culture of shared responsibility and active participation in sustainable water management.

Ultimately, incorporating human rights principles into water governance would not only improve enforcement and compliance but also ensure that all community members, particularly the most vulnerable, have a meaningful role in safeguarding water resources for future generations. This paradigm shift would strengthen the foundation for equitable, sustainable, and inclusive water management in Iran.

C. Comprehensive Water Management Legislation

To effectively tackle the multifaceted nature of Iran's water crisis, comprehensive water management legislation is imperative. Such legislation must integrate various aspects of water governance, encompassing resource allocation, conservation, pollution control, and ecosystem protection. A unified water law is essential to consolidate existing regulations and fill the gaps currently present in water governance. This proposed law should establish a clear framework for water rights and management, providing guidelines for equitable allocation among various users while ensuring that regulatory bodies operate in a coordinated manner. By integrating principles of sustainability, the legislation should ensure that water use remains within renewable limits, thereby protecting both the resource and the ecosystems dependent on it.

Adopting Integrated Water Resources Management (IWRM)[126] principles within the legislation[127] can further enhance the effectiveness of water governance.[128] IWRM emphasizes a holistic approach, recognizing the interconnectedness of surface water, groundwater, and the ecosystems that rely on these resources. The legislation should mandate the development of integrated management plans that address critical issues such as water scarcity,

---

[126] Integrated Water Resources Management (IWRM) is "a process that promotes the coordinated development and management of water, land and related resources, in order to maximize the resultant economic and social welfare in an equitable manner without compromising the sustainability of vital ecosystems," as defined by the Global Water Partnership. The Dublin Statement on Water and Sustainable Development established the foundational principles of Integrated Water Resources Management, emphasizing freshwater's finite nature, participatory management, women's central role, and water's recognition as an economic good.

[127] Tinashe Lindel Dirwai et al., *Water resource management: IWRM strategies for improved water management. A systematic review of case studies of East, West and Southern Africa.* PLoS ONE 16(5): 2 (2021).

[128] Global Water Partnership, *Integrated water resources management,* Technical advisory committee (TAC) background paper no. 4, 36 (Stockholm, Sweden: Global Water Partnership, 2000).

pollution, and the impacts of climate change. These plans should involve all relevant stakeholders, including local communities, governmental bodies, and environmental organizations, in the decision-making process. By fostering collaboration among diverse interests,[129] IWRM can promote more equitable and effective water management outcomes.[130]

Additionally, the new legislation should establish environmental flow requirements to maintain the ecological health of rivers, wetlands, and lakes. By setting minimum flow levels, the law would ensure that sufficient water is allocated to sustain ecosystems, protect biodiversity, and support natural processes. This provision is crucial, as healthy ecosystems not only provide essential services such as water purification and flood regulation but also enhance the overall resilience of communities facing environmental changes. By prioritizing both human and ecological needs in water management, comprehensive legislation can help build a more sustainable future for Iran, ultimately mitigating the water crisis while fostering a harmonious relationship between people and their environment.

D. Reforming the Judicial System

Reforming the judiciary to effectively address water mismanagement and environmental crimes necessitates tackling the pervasive political interference by powerful entities such as the IRGC and state-affiliated networks. Establishing specialized environmental courts or tribunals could still be a valuable step, but their independence and effectiveness would require significant protections against influence from entrenched political and military interests. These courts must be insulated from the broader judiciary's vulnerabilities, operating with a mandate to prioritize environmental sustainability and public welfare. Staffed with judges trained in environmental law and shielded from undue external pressures, such courts could serve as a beacon of expertise and fairness in navigating complex water-related cases. However, achieving this level of independence would demand careful framing of these reforms, potentially presenting them as efforts to align with broader global environmental standards or as non-threatening administrative advancements.

Promoting judicial independence in Iran is deeply challenging, given the regime's control over judicial appointments and operations. While transparency and accountability in judicial selection are ideal goals, a more realistic approach would involve incremental reforms, such as improving the professionalism

---

[129] Meran, *supra* note 29, at 23-26.

[130] M. Xie, *Integrated water resources management (IWRM) – Introduction to principles and practices*, WORLD BANK INSTITUTE 4-7 (2006). https://www.pacificwater.org/userfiles/file/IWRM/Toolboxes/introduction%20to%20iwrm/IWRM%20Introduction.pdf.

of judicial appointments by emphasizing environmental expertise and technical competence as non-political criteria. Strengthening legal training for judges and prosecutors in environmental law, water management, and international standards could be framed as part of Iran's national development priorities, avoiding direct confrontation with political power centers.

To ensure that judicial remedies are effective, an independent and functioning judiciary is vital. Judges and lawyers must be able to conduct their work impartially, on the basis of facts and in accordance with the law, without any improper influences, threats or interference. Members of the judiciary, lawyers and other legal professionals must be competent to perform their role and accountable for their performance.[131]

Enhancing access to justice for marginalized communities suffering from environmental harm is critical but fraught with difficulties in a context where dissent is repressed. Simplifying legal procedures and expanding access to legal aid would benefit affected individuals, but these measures must be implemented with caution to avoid provoking backlash from state actors. Providing avenues for affected parties to seek remediation for environmental damage through non-confrontational or community-based mechanisms could complement judicial reforms, fostering public engagement without directly challenging the regime's authority.

Ultimately, while these reforms face significant obstacles under the current system, framing them in a way that aligns with nationalistic rhetoric or non-political development goals could increase their feasibility. Incremental progress in empowering environmental courts, enhancing legal expertise, and fostering public participation could create foundational changes that contribute to addressing Iran's water crisis within its challenging political landscape.

E. Promoting Sustainable Water Use and Innovation

Legal reforms must also prioritize promoting sustainable water use and fostering innovation in water management practices to effectively address Iran's water challenges. One key approach is incentivizing water efficiency and conservation through targeted policies. By implementing subsidies for water-saving technologies, such as drip irrigation systems and efficient appliances, the state can encourage both households and agricultural sectors to adopt practices that significantly reduce water consumption. Additionally, supporting sustainable agricultural practices, such as crop rotation and drought-resistant varieties, can further optimize water use. Regulations that mandate efficient

---

[131] Office of the United Nations High Commissioner for Human Rights, *supra* note 101, at 42.

water use across different sectors will complement these incentives, ensuring that water resources are managed wisely and sustainably.[132]

Supporting research and innovation in water management is another crucial aspect of legal reforms. Investing in research initiatives focused on developing new technologies and practices can yield innovative solutions to persistent water challenges.[133] Legal frameworks should facilitate funding for research projects that explore advanced irrigation techniques, wastewater recycling, and desalination technologies. Moreover, pilot projects that test these innovations in real-world settings can provide valuable insights and data on their effectiveness. By fostering an environment that encourages experimentation and the adoption of best practices, Iran can improve water use efficiency and enhance environmental protection, contributing to more resilient water systems.[134]

Encouraging public-private partnerships (PPPs) is essential for improving water management and infrastructure, particularly in developing countries like Iran. Legal reforms should establish frameworks that facilitate collaboration between state agencies, private sector entities, civil society organizations, practitioners, experts, and academics, while proactively addressing potential pitfalls such as the exclusion of vulnerable groups, undue influence or control by specific entities (agency capture), accountability challenges, and indeterminate outcomes.[135] These partnerships can leverage the strengths and resources of each sector, with private companies bringing innovative technologies and funding, and state agencies providing regulatory support and access to public infrastructure. By promoting collaboration and shared responsibility, Iran can enhance its capacity to tackle water scarcity and foster sustainable practices that benefit both the environment and local communities.

However, successful PPPs implementation in the water and wastewater infrastructure (WWI) sector requires effective risk management, as risks can lead to project delays and increased costs. A study of PPPs projects in Iran identified 35 critical risks, including material cost fluctuations, contradictions in state policies, and project suspensions due to political instability. Proper risk assessment is essential to prioritize risks such as delays in fund payments and

---

[132] Taize Yu et al., *Benefits of Crop Rotation on Climate Resilience and Its Prospects in China*, AGRONOMY, 12(436), 10 (2022).

[133] *Id.*, at 12-13.

[134] B. Menin, *Innovative technologies for large-scale water production in arid regions: Strategies for sustainable development*, JOURNAL OF APPLIED MATHEMATICS AND PHYSICS, 12, 2539-2540 (2024).

[135] Manisha Verma, *Role of the state in partnerships with the private sector*, *JOURNAL OF DEVELOPMENT POLICY AND PRACTICE*, 1(1): 53 (2016).

unstable state economic programs. By integrating these findings, policymakers can develop comprehensive regulatory frameworks and transparent selection criteria, mitigating risks and boosting private sector investment in WWI projects.[136] Ultimately, combining strong risk management with effective legal and regulatory frameworks will create a more dynamic and adaptive water governance system, vital for addressing Iran's water challenges and ensuring the successful implementation of PPPs in the sector.

V. Ethical Considerations and Human Rights Issues

The water crisis in Iran intersects with numerous ethical considerations and human rights issues, reflecting the profound impacts of water mismanagement on vulnerable populations and the environment. Addressing these concerns requires a nuanced understanding of the ethical responsibilities of various stakeholders, the human rights implications of water policies, and the need for justice and equity in water governance. This section explores the key ethical and human rights issues related to Iran's water crisis, including the impacts of water mismanagement on marginalized communities, access to water as a fundamental right, and the ethical implications of state and corporate actions.

A. Impacts on Marginalized and Vulnerable Populations

Water mismanagement in Iran disproportionately impacts marginalized and vulnerable populations, including rural communities, ethnic minorities, and low-income groups. These populations, mainly in Sistan and Baluchistan, Chaharmahal and Bakhtiari, Lorestan, Khuzestan, Kurdistan are often the most severely affected by water scarcity, pollution, and the environmental degradation that arise from inadequate water governance due to systematic policies that keep these provinces "impoverished and underdeveloped."[137] As water becomes scarcer, these communities struggle to maintain their way of life, leading to increased poverty and social unrest due to the "mismanagement, corruption, and ethnic favouritism."[138]

Ethnic and regional minorities, such as the Arabs in Khuzestan, Kurds in western Iran, and Baluchis in Sistan and Baluchistan, often experience compounded challenges related to water access and environmental degradation. Historical marginalization and political neglect have left these communities

---

[136] Leila Moradi Shahdadi et al., *Determining the critical risk factors of implementing public–private partnership in water and wastewater infrastructure facilities: Perspectives of private and public partners in Iran*, BUILDINGS, 13(2735), 17-18 (2023).
[137] Hassaniyan, *supra* note 100, at 427.
[138] *Id.*, 424; N. Kowsar, *A thirsty reality: Iran's dire water situation*, ATLANTIC COUNCIL (2024), https://www.atlanticcouncil.org/blogs/iransource/iran-water-environment-us-policy/.

particularly vulnerable to water-related issues. They frequently encounter systemic barriers that limit their access to essential resources, exacerbated by discriminatory policies that are centralist and prioritize the needs of more dominant groups. This situation has manifested itself as environmental racism, where the adverse effects of water mismanagement disproportionately burden these minorities. As a result, they often find themselves facing not only water scarcity but also increased pollution and environmental hazards, deepening their socio-economic challenges.[139]

Low-income and informal settlements, including slums and informal housing areas, further illustrate the disparities in water access. Residents of these areas, particularly migrants such as Afghan refugees, typically suffer from inadequate water infrastructure and sanitation services, leaving them reliant on unreliable and often contaminated water sources. This situation poses significant health risks, exacerbating existing socio-economic inequalities. The lack of access to clean water can lead to waterborne diseases and other health issues, disproportionately affecting low-income populations who may lack the resources to seek medical care.[140] Addressing these disparities requires targeted interventions aimed at improving water access and infrastructure in underserved areas.

In Iran, such systemic inequalities are deeply rooted in criminalized governance and resource monopolies that prioritize the interests of the powerful while neglecting marginalized populations. These structural failures not only deprive vulnerable communities of essential resources but also create an environment where economic desperation pushes individuals toward illegal activities, including environmental crimes. Eman and White describe environmental crime as "a high-profit and low-risk activity," driven by demand for environmental commodities and weak enforcement mechanisms. They highlight that "environmental crime is extremely lucrative but with comparatively low risk due to several situational factors on local, national, and global levels."[141] At the local level, environmental crimes often serve as an "alternative to poverty for disadvantaged populations," offering a vital source of income amid systematic neglect. This interplay between economic necessity and weak enforcement mechanisms underscores the persistent and complex nature of environmental crime.[142]

---

[139] Hassaniyan, *supra* note 100, at 423.
[140] Ali Hosseini et al., *Urban disparities and quality of life among Afghan refugees living in informal settlements in Mashhad, Iran*, APPLIED RESEARCH QUALITY LIFE, 18, 1075 (2023).
[141] Rob White & Katja Eman, Green Criminology, Water Issues, Human Rights and Private Profit, in Water, GOVERNANCE, AND CRIME ISSUES 10 (Katja Eman et al. eds., Springer 2020).
[142] Eman, *supra* note 114, at 49.

B. Access to Water as a Fundamental Human Right

Access to clean and safe water is universally recognized as a fundamental human right, essential for health, dignity, and well-being. The UN General Assembly explicitly affirmed this right in 2010, emphasizing that access to water is critical for the realization of other human rights, including the right to life, health, and an adequate standard of living.[143] Access to safe drinking water and sanitation are not only universally acknowledged as basic human rights but are also derived from the right to an adequate standard of living under Article 11(1) of the International Covenant on Economic, Social and Cultural Rights (ICESCR), to which Iran is a state party. By ratifying the ICESCR, Iran has committed to fulfilling its obligations to ensure access to safe drinking water and sanitation for all its citizens.

Violations of Article 11(1) of the ICESCR, which guarantees the right to an adequate standard of living, including access to water, can result in legal and criminal accountability in Iran. When the Islamic of Republic of Iran fails to uphold these obligations—whether through gross negligence, corruption, or deliberate actions that deprive citizens of their right to water—such violations may intersect with criminal law. Since state authorities or private actors engage in corrupt practices that obstruct access to safe drinking water and fail to address water-related health risks, they can be held liable under Iran's national laws, including those concerning criminal negligence, misconduct, or violations of public health standards. Furthermore, such actions can potentially activate international legal mechanisms, particularly as the denial of water access is widespread, systemic, and used as a tool of discrimination or punitive measures against specific populations, thereby violating Iran's international human rights obligations.

In Iran, the right to water and sanitation is enshrined in national laws and policies, yet significant disparities in access and quality persist across the country. "International human rights law obliges States to work towards achieving universal access to water and sanitation," prioritizing the needs of those most vulnerable and disadvantaged.[144] The Committee on Economic, Social and Cultural Rights, in its General Comment No. 15, along with the work of the Special Rapporteur on the human right to safe drinking water, outlines key elements of the rights to water and sanitation that guide the implementation

---

[143] G.A. Res. 64/292, *The Human Right to Water and Sanitation,* U.N. Doc. A/RES/64/292 (July 28, 2010) 2.

[144] U.N. Office of the High Comm'r for Human Rights, About Water and Sanitation: OHCHR and the Right to Water and Sanitation (2024).Available at: https://www.ohchr.org/en/water-and-sanitation/about-water-and-sanitation#:~:text=On%2028%20July%202010%2C%20the,RES%2F64%2F292.

by States. These elements include: the availability of water, ensuring sufficient and continuous supply for personal and domestic uses such as drinking, food preparation, washing clothes, and hygiene, with adequate sanitation facilities available nearby; accessibility, ensuring water and sanitation facilities are physically accessible to all, particularly vulnerable groups like persons with disabilities, women, children, and older persons; affordability, ensuring that water services are affordable for all, without anyone being denied access due to inability to pay; quality and safety, ensuring water is free from harmful microorganisms, chemicals, and hazards that threaten health, while sanitation facilities must be safe and prevent contamination; and acceptability, ensuring water and sanitation facilities are "culturally acceptable and appropriate, and sensitive to gender, life-cycle and privacy requirements."[145]

Recognizing and fulfilling the human right to water, as mandated by international law and reinforced by Iran's obligations as a state party to the ICESCR, is essential not only for individual well-being but also for fostering social cohesion and sustainable development across the nation.

C. Ethical implications of state and corporate actions

The actions and decisions of both state and corporate actors carry significant ethical implications, especially when economic interests are prioritized over environmental and social concerns. State actors, including state officials and policymakers, hold an ethical obligation to prioritize the well-being of citizens and the protection of natural resources. When decisions lead to the over-extraction of water, environmental degradation, or the displacement of communities for development projects, these actions must be critically examined for their ethical ramifications. This means evaluating whether such actions uphold values such as justice, fairness, and respect for human rights or whether they result in harm, inequality, or neglect of long-term sustainability. By assessing the moral consequences of their decisions, state actors can ensure that their actions align with the principles of good governance and social responsibility.

However, the presence of corruption and conflicts of interest within state institutions and regulatory bodies can severely undermine ethical governance, contributing to the mismanagement of water resources. When regulatory agencies succumb to political or economic pressures, they often fail to enforce laws impartially, prioritizing the interests of powerful actors over the public good. This environment can foster a culture of impunity where ethical standards are compromised, leading to further exploitation of natural resources

---

[145] *Id.*

and exacerbating inequalities. Addressing corruption and conflicts of interest is crucial for ensuring that water governance remains ethical and focused on the welfare of all citizens.

Corporate actors, particularly those involved in water-intensive industries such as mining, agriculture, and manufacturing, also bear ethical responsibilities. These corporations must actively work to mitigate their environmental impact and respect human rights. Sustainable water management practices should be at the forefront of their operations, with companies adopting strategies that avoid contributing to water scarcity or pollution. Additionally, corporations can utilize human rights impact assessments (HRIAs) to systematically identify, address, and mitigate the potential and actual impacts of their activities on the rights of local communities, including the right to water and sanitation. HRIAs provide a structured framework for analyzing how corporate projects may affect human rights, enabling companies to adopt preventive measures, remediate harms, and align their operations with international human rights standards.

Furthermore, corporations need to be mindful of the social impacts their activities have on local communities, engaging with residents and considering their needs and concerns. Ethical business practices include transparency in operations, meaningful community engagement, and efforts to reduce water usage and overall environmental footprint. By incorporating tools such as HRIAs into their operations, corporations can not only fulfill their ethical obligations but also build trust and enhance their reputation among consumers and stakeholders. These efforts demonstrate a commitment to human rights, environmental sustainability, and the equitable treatment of all affected populations.

To achieve sustainable and just water governance, actions must also be rooted in moral principles that go beyond regulatory compliance. A robust system of oversight can ensure adherence to ethical standards, but it is equally important to cultivate a deeper, intrinsic commitment to moral responsibility among both duty-bearers and rights-holders. Through spiritual education and ethical training, both groups can be guided to make moral choices even in the absence of external enforcement. When individuals internalize the values of justice, compassion, and accountability, they are more likely to prioritize the well-being of all as well as the environment, paving the way for a truly equitable and sustainable society.

D. Human Rights Violations Related to Water Activism

Water activism in Iran, which often involves challenging state policies or corporate practices, can lead to severe human rights violations, including the suppression of free speech, arbitrary detention, and violence against activists.

One of the most pressing issues is the criminalization of activism. Activists who dare to speak out against water mismanagement or environmental degradation frequently find themselves facing serious repercussions. Authorities often label their actions as inciting unrest, spreading propaganda, or acting against national security, using these charges to silence dissent and intimidate those advocating for water justice. This criminalization not only undermines the right to freedom of expression and assembly but also restricts public discourse on critical environmental issues, stifling the collective efforts needed to address the water crisis in Iran.

Moreover, harassment and violence against environmental and water activists are alarmingly common. Many activists experience threats, intimidation, and physical attacks as a direct response to their efforts to challenge the status quo. This systemic violence serves to instill fear in those who would otherwise engage in advocacy, effectively stifling broader movements aimed at addressing water-related issues and promoting sustainable water management practices. Such actions represent a profound violation of human rights, undermining not only the individual rights of activists but also the overall health of civil society, which relies on the ability to critique and hold authorities accountable.

The detention of activists under harsh conditions further illustrates the human rights violations inherent in this context. Many individuals face lengthy prison sentences for non-violent protests or advocacy efforts, which can amount to severe breaches of their rights. The lack of fair trials, due process, and protections against torture or ill-treatment is particularly concerning. Such conditions violate fundamental rights that should be upheld for all individuals, including those engaged in environmental activism. The repercussions of these actions extend beyond individual cases, creating a chilling effect that discourages others from speaking out or participating in the fight for water justice. In this environment, addressing water mismanagement and advocating for sustainable practices become increasingly difficult, highlighting the urgent need for reforms that protect activists and uphold human rights in Iran.

E. Promoting Human Rights and Ethical Water Governance

To effectively address the ethical and human rights issues associated with Iran's water crisis, several key measures can be implemented to promote human rights and ethical governance. First and foremost, strengthening human rights protections is critical. Legal and policy reforms should incorporate robust safeguards for human rights, particularly the right to water, freedom of expression, and protection against discrimination. It is essential that these rights are upheld within the context of water governance and activism, as doing so lays the groundwork for promoting justice and equity across affected communities.

Encouraging transparent and inclusive governance practices is another vital measure. Water management decisions should be made with careful consideration of their ethical and social impacts, which necessitates the involvement of affected communities in decision-making processes. Providing access to information and fostering accountability for both state and corporate actions can help build trust and ensure that the needs of marginalized groups are adequately addressed. This inclusive approach not only empowers communities but also enhances the legitimacy and effectiveness of water governance.

Supporting human rights and environmental advocacy is crucial for addressing water-related issues and fostering ethical governance. Creating safe spaces for activism, offering legal support to defenders of water rights, and actively addressing any retaliation or repression faced by activists are essential steps in this direction. By protecting those who speak out against injustices, the government can foster a more vibrant civil society that contributes to sustainable water management and accountability.

Lastly, promoting international collaboration and standards can provide valuable guidance for domestic reforms and practices. Engaging with international human rights frameworks and environmental standards can help elevate local efforts and ensure they align with global best practices. Collaboration with international organizations, human rights groups, and environmental NGOs can offer insights, resources, and support for advancing human rights and ethical water governance. This holistic approach can facilitate a transformation in how water resources are managed in Iran, ensuring that the needs and rights of all citizens are respected and upheld.

Conclusion: Integrating Criminal Law Into Water Governance

Iran's water crisis is not merely an environmental issue but a deeply rooted legal and ethical challenge, intertwined with systemic mismanagement, corruption, and neglect of fundamental human rights. The country's water governance framework reveals significant gaps in legislation, enforcement mechanisms, and judicial accountability, exacerbating the crisis. Addressing these deficiencies requires a multi-faceted approach that integrates criminal law as a core component of water governance while emphasizing sustainability, equity, and human rights.

Criminal law can be effectively utilized to address water-related offenses by incorporating strong legal sanctions against illegal activities such as unauthorized water extraction, the illicit trade in water, and environmentally harmful projects like dam construction that damage ecosystems and displace communities. Criminal penalties for these offenses would serve as a deterrent, ensuring that violators—whether state actors, corporate entities, or individuals—are held accountable. This would also involve holding corporate actors responsible for practices that deplete water resources or cause pollution, demanding that companies implement sustainable water management practices and respect human rights. Criminal law should not only punish violations but also ensure systemic accountability, focusing on restoring justice for affected communities and holding those in power accountable for their role in exacerbating the crisis.

Corruption within state institutions plays a crucial role in undermining water governance in Iran. When regulatory bodies are compromised by political and economic pressures, they often fail to enforce water laws impartially, giving rise to a culture of impunity where illegal water extraction, water mismanagement, and environmental degradation thrive unchecked. Corruption distorts decision-making processes, often prioritizing the interests of powerful state actors and corporations over the public good. This fosters a governance environment where water resources are mismanaged, and the rights of the population, particularly marginalized groups, are disregarded. Addressing corruption through robust anti-corruption measures and judicial reforms is vital to restoring trust in state institutions and ensuring that water governance is transparent, equitable, and focused on the public welfare.

Legal frameworks in Iran must strike a balance between the enforcement of water laws and the protection of the rights and needs of the population. While it is essential to strengthen enforcement mechanisms to tackle water mismanagement, it is equally important that these laws are designed with an awareness of human rights, ensuring equitable access to water for all citizens, especially vulnerable and marginalized groups. Legal reforms must include provisions for public participation in water governance, enabling communities to be involved in decision-making processes that directly impact their access to water. The integration of human rights principles, such as access to water as a fundamental human right, should guide these reforms. By ensuring that state and corporate actions are held to account through criminal law while respecting human rights, Iran can work toward a more just and sustainable water governance system.

Complete regime change in Iran is often considered a potential solution to address the country's deeply rooted governance issues, including environmental crisis and water mismanagement. Such a shift could dismantle entrenched structures of corruption and patronage that hinder sustainable resource management, opening pathways for transparent, accountable, and reform-oriented governance. A new political system might prioritize environmental stewardship, judicial independence, and equitable access to natural resources. However, regime change alone does not guarantee success and is fraught with complexities. Transitional periods often bring instability, during which entrenched interests may resist reforms, and new governance structures face challenges in asserting authority. Without mechanisms for transitional justice to hold past offenders accountable and strong institutional frameworks to enforce laws and protect citizens' rights, a new regime risks perpetuating the same issues under different leadership. Powerful entities like the IRGC and other vested interests are likely to resist changes that threaten their control, further complicating the process. While regime change could be a step toward addressing Iran's environmental challenges, sustainable progress demands not only political change but also inclusive governance practices, strengthened accountability mechanisms, and a commitment to human rights.

Ultimately, the integration of criminal law into water governance is not only a legal imperative but also a moral and ethical one. Sustainable solutions require fostering a culture of accountability and integrity, where state and corporate actors act in the public interest, even in the absence of external oversight. This vision demands comprehensive reforms to Iran's legal and judicial frameworks, prioritizing ethical water governance, public participation, and innovative approaches to resource management. By addressing the water crisis through a lens that incorporates criminal law, human rights, and environmental ethics, Iran can chart a path toward sustainable and equitable water governance for future generations.

Bibliography

S. Rasouli Firooz Abadi et al., *Examining the effective social and economic factors on underground economy*, Mediterranean Journal of Social Sciences, 6(3), 527-528 (2015). https://doi.org/10.5901/mjss.2015.v6n3p525.

Abbas Akbarzadeh et al., *Municipal wastewater treatment in Iran: Current situation, barriers and future policies*, Journal of Advances in Environmental Health Research, 11(1), 60-71, 60 (2023). https://doi.org/10.34172/jaehr.2023.08.

M. Al-Aloosy, *Water insecurity: Iran's formidable threat,* The Washington Institute (2022), https://www.washingtoninstitute.org/policy-analysis/water-insecurity-irans-formidable-threat.

Sanaz Alasti, *Legislation on Use of Water in Agriculture: Iran* (2013), https://maint.loc.gov/law/help/water-law/iran.php.

S. Amiri et al., *Salinity management in the world's most saline dam reservoir: The Gotvand Reservoir, Iran.* Earth and Space Science Open Archive, II-III. (2023).

S. Amiri and M. Mazaheri, *Challenges arising from excessive groundwater extraction in the country, an examination of the current conditions, and the land subsidence crisis,* Monthly Reports of the Research Center of the Islamic Consultative Assembly, 31(2), 7 (2023). https://doi.org/10.22541/essoar.169774539.99039742/v1.

Article 19, *Iran: Decline for free expression requires increased support for UN scrutiny* (March 2019), https://www.article19.org/wp-content/uploads/2019/03/HRC40-Briefing-Iran-AS-FINAL.pdf.

P. Azadi, *Governance and development in Iran*, Stanford Iran 2040 Project. Stanford University, 26. (2019).

P. Azadi, *The structure of corruption in Iran*, Stanford Iran 2040 Project. Stanford University 2. (2020).

N. Badisar and M.S. Ahmadi, *Rules governing groundwater (wells) resources in Iran*, Iranian Water Researches Journal, 12(2), 77 (2018).

Mahdi Hashemi Beni et al., *Water-energy nexus approach for optimal design of hybrid cooling system in direct reduction of iron plant*, Journal of Cleaner Production, 287(2021), 5 (2020). https://doi.org/10.1016/j.jclepro.2020.125576.

Borna News, Examples of violations and unauthorized water usage (2022), https://borna.news/fa/news/1287223/مصادیق-تخلفات-و-مصارف-غیر-مجاز-آبی.

Tinashe Lindel Dirwai et al., *Water resource management: IWRM strategies for improved water management. A systematic review of case studies of East, West and Southern Africa.* PLoS ONE 16(5): p. 2 (2021). https://doi.org/10.1371/journal.pone.0236903.

Helena Du Rées, *Can criminal law protect the environment*, Journal of Scandinavian Studies in Criminology and Crime Prevention, Vol. 2, 123 (2001). https://doi.org/10.1080/140438501753737606.

Katja Eman et al., *Water crimes and policing*, Journal of Criminal Justice and Security. 19(2), 107. (2017). https://doi.org/10.1007/978-3-030-44798-4.

Katja Eman & Rob White, *Water and Organised Crime*, in Water, Governance, and Crime Issues 49 (Katja Eman et al. eds., Springer 2020)

Ali Esmaeili et al., *A geochemical survey of heavy metals in agricultural and background soils of the Isfahan industrial zone, Iran*, CATENA, 121, 97 (2014). https://doi.org/10.1016/j.catena.2014.05.003.

Federal Bureau of Investigation (FBI), Transnational Organized Crime (2024). [online] Available at: https://www.fbi.gov/investigate/transnational-organized-crime.

Financial Tribune, *Dilemma of illegal water wells*, July 12, 2019, https://financialtribune.com/articles/energy/98887/dilemma-of-illegal-water-wells.

M. H. Fleming et al., *The shadow economy*, Journal of International Affairs, 53(2) 387 (2020).

P. H. Gleick, *Water and terrorism.* Water Policy, 8, 482 (2006). https://doi.org/10.2166/wp.2006.035.

Global Water Partnership, *Integrated water resources management.* Technical advisory committee (TAC) background paper no. 4. Stockholm, Sweden: Global Water Partnership, p. 36 (2000).

H. Hamidifar, *Water crisis in Iran: Causes, consequences, and solutions*, in Chibueze Izah, S., Chidozie Ogwu, M., Loukas, A., and Hamidifar, H. (Eds.) Water crises and sustainable management in the Global South, 98. (Singapore: Spring 2024). https://doi.org/10.1007/978-981-97-4966-9_3.

Allan Hassaniyan, *Iran's water policy: Environmental injustice and peripheral marginalisation*, Progress in Physical Geography, 48(3), 423 (2024). https://doi.org/10.1177/03091333241252523.

Flora Heidari et al., *Legal system governing on water pollution in Iran*, Journal of Geoscience and Environmental Protection, 5(9), 55 (2017).

Lena Horlemann and Parisa Jafari Berenji, *Participation in water management in Iran*. In: S. Mohajeri & L. Horlemann (eds.), Reviving the Dying Giant. 52, 58 (Switzerland: Spring, Cham 2017). https://doi.org/10.1007/978-3-319-54922-4_4.

Ali Hosseini et al., *Urban disparities and quality of life among Afghan refugees living in informal settlements in Mashhad, Iran*, Applied Research Quality Life, 18, 1075 (2023). https://doi.org/10.1007/s11482-022-10133-0.

Human Rights Watch, Iran: Environmentalists Sentenced (Unfair Trial; Continued Due Process Violations) (2019), https://www.hrw.org/news/2019/11/22/iran-environmentalists-sentenced.

IMPEL, *Project Water Crimes*, European Union Network for the Implementation and Enforcement of Environmental Law, Report number: 2019/11, 2.

INTERPOL-UN Environment (2016). Strategic Report: Environment, Peace and Security – A Convergence of Threats. Available at: https://www.google.com/url?sa=t&source=web&rct=j&opi=89978449&url=https://www.interpol.int/content/download/5088/file/INTERPOL-UNEP%2520Strategic%2520Report%2520-%2520Environment,%2520Peace%2520and%2520Security%2520-%2520A%2520Convergence%2520of%2520Threats.pdf&ved=2ahUKEwirypfHx4GKAxXpUkEAHV_jGEYQFnoECBIQAQ&usg=AOvVaw2CW5lyn8msr_KUnLWIya5f.

Iran Action Group, *Outlaw regime: A Chronicle of Iran's Destructive Activities* (2018), https://www.state.gov/wp-content/uploads/2018/12/Iran-Report.pdf.

IRNA (2024) 62 dams were built by the Khatam-al Anbiya Construction Headquarters. [online] Available at: https://www.irna.ir/news/85484863/سد-توسط-قرارگاه-ساز□دگی-خاتم-الا□بیا-ساخته-□د-۶۲.

ISNA, A Serious Crisis in the Country/Take the Depletion of Groundwater Resources Seriously (2024), https://www.isna.ir/news/1403062717453/یک-بحران-جدی-در-کشور-کاهش-منابع-آب-زیرزمینی-را-جدی-بگیرید.

ISNA (2024b) From water shortages to profits for middlemen, https://www.isna.ir/news/1403081409967/%D8%A7%D8%B2-%DA%A9%D9%85%D8%A8%D9%88%D8%AF-%D8%A2%D8%A8-%D8%AA%D8%A7-%D8%B3%D9%88%D8%AF%DB%8C-%DA%A9%D9%87-%D9%86%D8%B5%DB%8C%D8%A8-%D8%AF%D9%84%D8%A7%D9%84%D8%A7%D9%86-%D9%85%DB%8C-%D8%B4%D9%88%D8%AF.

Fatemeh Karandish et al., *Agro-economic and socio-environmental assessments of food and virtual water trades of Iran*, Scientific Reports, 11:15022, 10 (2021). https://doi.org/10.1038/s41598-021-93928-9.

Nishtman Karimi et al., *The Water Management Regime in Western Iran: A Retrospective Analysis through a Hybrid Transitions Framework*, Sustainability, 13(3323), 2. (2021). https://doi.org/10.3390/su13063323.

Mehdi Ketabchy, *Investigating the impacts of the political system components in Iran on the existing water bankruptcy*, Sustainability, 13(13657), 5-6 (2021). https://doi.org/10.3390/su132413657.

A Khaleghi and H. Rashnavadi, *The Iran criminal legislative policy for the preservation of water Resources with regard to the international instruments*, Journal of Criminal Law Research, 1(3), 139 (2013).

Khabarban, *Thirteen counties in Sistan and Baluchistan face absolute water scarcity and the drying up of 292 water wells / How is the revival of the Zayandehrud River possible?* (2024), https://40792607.khabarban.com.

Khabarban, *Fars Roundtable: Examining the Black Market for Water and the Necessity of Establishing a Legal Market for It in Iran* (2023), https://38493096.khabarban.com.

Zahra Mahmoudi Kordi et al., *Analyzing the environmental democracy in international law and Iran's legal system*, International Law Review, 40(69), 207 (2023).

N. Kowsar, *A thirsty reality: Iran's dire water situation*, Atlantic Council (2024), https://www.atlanticcouncil.org/blogs/iransource/iran-water-environment-us-policy/.

Kaveh Madani et al., *Iran's socio-economic drought: Challenges of a water-bankrupt nation*, Iranian Studies, 49(6): 1001 (2016). https://doi.org/10.1080/00210862.2016.1259286. https://doi.org/10.1007/s13412-014-0182-z.

Kaveh Madani, *Water management in Iran: What is causing the looming crisis*, Journal of Environmental Studies and Sciences, 4(2014), 323.

B. Menin, *Innovative technologies for large-scale water production in arid regions: Strategies for sustainable development*, Journal of Applied Mathematics and Physics, 12, 2539-2540 (2024). https://doi.org/10.4236/jamp.2024.127150.

Georg Meran et al., The Economics of water: Rules and institutions, 43, 57 (Switzerland: Springer, Cham 2021). https://doi.org/10.1007/978-3-030-48485-9.

Ministry of Health and Medical Education, *Environmental Protection and Enhancement Act of 1974*, https://health.bpums.ac.ir/UploadedFiles/xfiles/File/M-Behdashti/rule/behdasht%20mohit/hefazat%20va%20behsazi.pdf.

Minority Rights Group, *Iran: Baluch people running out of water due to unfair water management*, Minority and Indigenous Trends 2023: Focus on water, 226 (2023).

Abbas Mirshekari and Mohsen Salami, *A comparative study of the supreme court of Iran and the United States of America*, Society, Development and Commercial Law Review, 1(1), 38 (2023).

MojNews, *Iran ranked among 4 main dam builder countries in the world* (May 21, 2024) https://www.mojnews.com/Section-economy-4/555642-iran-ranked-among-main-dam-builder-countries-in-the-world.

F. Molle and A. Mamanpoush, *Scale, governance and the management of river basins: A case study from Central Iran*, Geoforum, 43(2), 291. (2012). https://doi.org/10.1016/j.geoforum.2011.08.004.

Hossein Moradi, *Biodiversity, climate change and environmental impact assessment* (Thesis) University of Zurich, 87 (2009).

Ehsan Nabavi, *(Ground)Water Governance and Legal Development in Iran, 1906–2016*, Middle East Law and Governance 9, 1, 56-57 (2017).

Ehsan Nabavi, *Failed policies, falling aquifers: Unpacking groundwater overabstraction in Iran*, Water Alternatives, 11(3), 705 (2018). https://doi.org/10.1163/18763375-00901005.

S. Nourikia, and N. Zivdar, *Participatory management of traditional urban water infrastructures in Iran: The case of Tehran historic qanat*, Spool 7(2), 95 (2020).

Armaghan Omrani, *Water management in Iran*, Thesis. Faculty of Economic & Management Odisee, University of Applied Science, 72 (2013).

Pishkhan, The dominance of middlemen in the underground economy (2020), https://www.pishkhan.com/news/192635.

Regional Water Company of Qazvin, *Groundwater Resources Reclamation and Balancing Plan*, available at: https://www.qzrw.ir/st/212.

Regional Water Company of Tehran, Seizure of an unauthorized water-selling tanker in Pakdasht. (2020), https://thrw.ir/cs/News/118/3677.

M. Saatsaz, *A historical investigation on water resources management in Iran*, Environment, Development and Sustainability, 22, 1766 (2020). https://doi.org/10.1007/s10668-018-00307-y.

M. Salami, *The water crisis and decline of legitimacy in Iran*, Trends Research & Advisory, October 6, 2022, https://trendsresearch.org/insight/the-water-crisis-and-decline-of-legitimacy-in-iran/?srsltid=AfmBOooyLew9N1EJnaDKlbKSYySXjNgpjD_Mwc-QvrjYwaLjsQ7Fd1fu.

Shahryar Ershad Sarabi, *Impacts of institutional arrangements on the adaptive capacity of the Urmia Lake basin* (Thesis), International Institute of Urban Management of Erasmus University Rotterdam, 22-23 (2018).

Michael Scollon, *Iran's environmental standards, polluted reality mix like oil and water*, Radio Free Europe (May 1, 2023), https://www.rferl.org/a/iran-environmental-standards-pollution-smog/32385813.html.

L. Segato et al., *Water crimes within environmental crimes*, in K. Eman, G. Meško, L. Segato, L., and Migliorini, M. (eds.) Water, Governance, and Crime Issues. p. 32. (Springer, Switzerland 2020). https://doi.org/10.1007/978-3-030-44798-4_3.

Afshin Shahi, *Drought: The Achilles heel of the Islamic Republic of Iran*, Asian Affairs, 50(1), 24 (2019). https://doi.org/10.1080/03068374.2019.1567100.

Leila Moradi Shahdadi et al., *Determining the critical risk factors of implementing public-private partnership in water and wastewater infrastructure facilities: Perspectives of private and public partners in Iran*, Buildings, 13(2735), 17-18 (2023). https://doi.org/10.3390/buildings13112735.

A. Shaheed, Report of the Special Rapporteur on the situation of human rights in the Islamic Republic of Iran A/HRC/22/56 (2013), [online] Available at: https://www.ohchr.org/sites/default/files/Documents/Countries/IR/A-HRC-22-56_en.pdf.

Morteza Sharif and Saeid Hamzeh, *Investigating the effect of Gotvand Dam on changes in soil salinity and vegetation cover of downstream lands of the dam using satellite imagery and spectral indices*, Environmental Sciences, 19(4), 225 (2022). https://doi.org/10.52547/envs.2021.1014.

H. Reza Shiravand, *Laws and legal safeguards governing the handling of air pollution in industrial city of Arak in Iran, and its comparison with international norms,* Journal of Fundamental and Applied Sciences, 9(1S), 870 (2017). https://doi.org/10.4314/jfas.v9i1s.738.

Ahmad Shohani et al., *Prevention and suppression of environmental crimes in the [sic] light of the actions of non-governmental organizations in the Iranian legal system,* Research Journal of Ecology and Environmental Sciences, 1, 8 (2021). https://doi.org/10.31586/rjees.2021.097.

M. Talebi Somehsaraie, M.Asadi, *Sociological investigation of institutional convergence in the approval of the most important water laws in Iran,* Majlis and Rahbord (2024), doi: 10.22034/mr.2024.16771.5802.

Mohammad Sadegh Talebi, *Water crisis in Iran and its security consequences,* Journal of Hydraulic Structures, 8(4), 23 (2022).

Reza Talebi, Hydropolitics and water issues after the Iranian Revolution (1979-2021) 15,165 (Merve Hatemi, trans. Turkey: Qobustan Publishing 2023).

Assad Tavakoli, *Nationalization and efficient management of water resources in Iran,* Journal of Water Resources Planning and Management 113(4), 523, 525 (1987). https://doi.org/10.1061/(ASCE)0733-9496(1987)113:4(522).

Gregory F. Treverton et al., *Organized Crime and Terrorism,* Film Piracy, Organized Crime, and Terrorism, RAND Corporation, 12 (2009).

UNESCO, *The Persian qanat.* [online] (2016), https://whc.unesco.org/en/list/1506/.

United Nations General Assembly, G.A. Res. 64/292, *The Human Right to Water and Sanitation,* U.N. Doc. A/RES/64/292 (July 28, 2010)

UN Office of the High Commissioner for Human Rights (OHCHR), About Water and Sanitation: OHCHR and the Right to Water and Sanitation (2024), https://www.ohchr.org/en/water-and-sanitation/about-water-and-sanitation#:~:text=On%2028%20July%202010%2C%20the,RES%2F64%2F292.

UN Office of the United Nations High Commissioner for Human Rights (OHCHR) (2010) The Human Rights Fact Sheet No. 35. [online], https://www.ohchr.org/sites/default/files/Documents/Publications/FactSheet35en.pdf.

Nilou Vakil, *The Cultural Landscape of the Persian Qanat,* in The Routledge Handbook of Cultural Landscape Heritage in the Asia-Pacific 420 (K.D. Silva et al. eds., Routledge 2022). https://doi.org/10.4324/9781003099994-31.

Manisha Verma, *Role of the state in partnerships with the private sector, Journal of Development Policy and Practice,* 1(1): 53 (2016). https://doi.org/10.1177/2455133315613229.

Rob White & Katja Eman, *Green Criminology, Water Issues, Human Rights and Private Profit,* in Water, Governance, and Crime Issues 10 (Katja Eman et al. eds., Springer 2020). https://doi.org/10.1007/978-3-030-44798-4_1.

M. Xie, *Integrated water resources management (IWRM) – Introduction to principles and practices,* World Bank Institute 4-7 (2006). https://www.pacificwater.org/userfiles/file/IWRM/Toolboxes/introduction%20to%20iwrm/IWRM%20Introduction.pdf.

Taize Yu et al., *Benefits of Crop Rotation on Climate Resilience and Its Prospects in China,* Agronomy, 12(436), 10 (2022). https://doi.org/10.3390/agronomy12020436.

Omid Zamani et al., *Limiting and timing water supply for agricultural production – The case of the Zayandeh-Rud River Basin, Iran*, Agricultural Water Management, 222, 323 (2019). https://doi.org/10.1016/j.agwat.2019.05.047.

H. Zanjanian et al., *Influential third party on water right conflict: A Game Theory approach to achieve the desired equilibrium* (case study: Ilam dam, Iran), Journal of Environmental Management, 214, 285 (2018). https://doi.org/10.1016/j.jenvman.2018.03.023.

Jamil Zargan and Seyed Mohammad Waez-Mousavi, *Water crisis in Iran: Its intensity, causes and confronting strategies*, Indian Journal of Science and Technology 9(44), 3 (2020). https://doi.org/10.17485/ijst/2016/v9i44/100632.

Sarah Lerech Zilberberg, *The water crisis in Iran: Heightening instability*, Strategic Assessment, 26(3), 54 (2023).

Chapter 8

Blue Justice: Blue Crimes and Corporate Accountability under International Criminal Law

Henna J. Shah

Public International Law Attorney

Abstract: In an increasingly interconnected world shaped by globalization, industrialization, and technological development, corporations have become more embedded in our society and personal lives. Although society benefits from corporations—they spur economic activity, inspire innovation, and encourage competition—their activities can have negative consequences. For example, corporations can be involved in and commit international crimes such as supplying weapons in furtherance of armed conflicts, providing services that exacerbate abuse, and illegally exploiting natural resources. Generally, corporations are involved in international crimes in three ways: (1) direct involvement in international crimes as a primary perpetrator or via acts constituting aiding and abetting; (2) indirect involvement by knowingly benefiting from crimes committed by others; and (3) passive involvement when their presence and participation in a country's economy contributes to a State or non-State actor's commission of abuses in that country.

A corporation's criminal activities are not siloed to land operations. As most corporations rely on water, rivers, and oceans for resources and shipping, corporations can commit "blue crimes." This chapter provides an overview on how and why corporations should be held accountable for blue crimes under international criminal law. This chapter begins with introducing the concepts of corporate accountability and blue crimes generally. Part I will then explain and define the term blue crime and what types of actions amount to a blue crime. Next, Part II will discuss corporate accountability under international law. This part will discuss why the current soft law instruments pertaining to corporate accountability are ineffective for holding corporations accountable for international crimes; explain that because the international criminal courts are created and defined by treaty, soft law instruments are ineffective for holding corporations accountable; and provide an overview of prominent case law discussing corporate accountability. Then, Part III will describe the relationship between blue crimes and corporate accountability under international law. In particular, this part will explain how a blue crimes case could be brought before the International Criminal Court (ICC) and provide a case study of a blue crimes prosecution in the United States implicating international law. Subsequently, Part IV will provide recommendations for holding corporations accountable for blue crimes under international law. These recommendations include expanding the ICC's definition of personal jurisdiction to include corporations and creating blue crimes and corporate accountability treaties using an international human rights law and international criminal law perspective. Lastly, this chapter will conclude by reflecting on the importance of holding corporations accountable for blue crimes under international criminal law.

Keywords: ICC, corporate accountability, blue crimes definition, OECD, UN Guiding Principles on Business and Human Rights, Corporate Social Responsibility, UNTOC

Introduction

In an increasingly interconnected world shaped by globalization, industrialization, and technological development, corporations have become more embedded in our society and personal lives. Although society benefits from corporations—they spur economic activity, inspire innovation, and encourage competition—their activities can have negative consequences. For example, corporations can be involved in and commit international crimes such as supplying weapons in furtherance of armed conflicts, providing services that exacerbate abuse, and illegally exploiting natural resources.

Generally, corporations are involved in international crimes in three ways: (1) direct involvement in international crimes as a primary perpetrator or via acts constituting aiding and abetting; (2) indirect involvement by knowingly benefiting from crimes committed by others; and (3) passive involvement when their presence and participation in a country's economy contributes to a State or non-State actor's commission of abuses in that country. Yet, despite the immense influence corporations have, the number of cases in which business actors–individuals and legal entities—have been legally held accountable for their involvement in international crime is marginal compared to the number of cases reported by victims, civil society organizations, States, and UN agencies of corporate human rights abuses.

A corporation's criminal activities are not siloed to land operations. As most corporations rely on water, rivers, and oceans for resources and shipping, corporations can commit "blue crimes." Transnational organized crime at sea, commonly referred to as "blue crimes," is not defined by international law via treaty or international agreement. Rather, scholars in this area have agreed that blue crimes are "[s]erious organi[z]ed crimes or offen[s]es that take place transnationally, on, in or across the maritime domain and cause or have the potential to inflict significant harms."[1] This conceptualization stems from the definition of "transnational organized crime" in the United Nations Convention against Transnational Organized Crime (UNTOC).

This chapter provides an overview of how and why corporations should be held accountable for blue crimes under international criminal law. Part I of this chapter will introduce the concepts of corporate accountability and blue crimes generally. Part II will then explain and define the term blue crime and what types of actions amount to a blue crime. Next, Part III will discuss corporate accountability under international law. This part will discuss why the current soft law instruments pertaining to corporate accountability are ineffective for holding corporations accountable for international crimes; explain that because the international criminal courts are created and defined by treaty, soft law instruments are ineffective for holding corporations accountable; and provide an overview of prominent case law discussing corporate accountability. Then, Part IV will describe the relationship between blue crimes and corporate accountability under international law. In particular, this part will explain how a blue crimes case could be brought before the International Criminal Court (ICC) and provide a case study of a blue crimes prosecution in the United States implicating international law. Subsequently, Part V will provide recommendations for holding corporations accountable for blue crimes under international law. These recommendations include expanding the ICC's definition of personal jurisdiction to include corporations and creating blue crimes and corporate accountability treaties using an international human rights law and international criminal law perspective. Lastly, this chapter will conclude by reflecting on the importance of holding corporations accountable for blue crimes under international criminal law in Part VI.

---

[1] Christian Bueger & Timothy Edmunds, *Blue crime: Conceptualising transnational organised crime at sea*, Marine Policy 119 (2020), https://www.safeseas.net/wp-content/uploads/2022/11/Bueger-and-Edmunds-2020-Blue-Crime.pdf.

I. What are Blue Crimes?

Transnational organized crime at sea, commonly referred to as "blue crimes," has only recently become the subject of major security issues and political attention.[2] The subject was first addressed by the United Nations (UN) Security Council in 2019.[3] Under the title of "Transnational organised crime at sea as a threat to international peace and security," the U.N. Security Council's discussions centered on the impact of maritime crime.[4] For example, during the debate, the United States advocated that "all countries should be deploying a broad range of tools: diplomatic, economic, social, military, intelligence, law enforcement, and judicial to tackle this problem," and that "all States that have not yet done so [should] ratify the [United Nations Convention against Transnational Organized Crime and its protocols]" and "ensure that their domestic laws appropriately criminalize the core offenses listed in the convention and its protocols."[5] Although representatives agreed that blue crimes significantly decrease international peace and security, the meeting did not result in any official statements or formal conclusions.[6]

On December 7, 2023, the U.N. Security Council held a ministerial-level open debate on "Transnational organized crime, growing challenges and new threats" under the "Threats to international peace and security" agenda item.[7] Of note, Malta highlighted the importance of the UNTOC in combating existing and emerging forms of transnational crime. Specifically, Malta stated that it "is especially aware of challenges and difficulties posed by maritime crime and trafficking at sea. Arms and drug trafficking, smuggling of migrants and trafficking in human beings are among the most concerning threats."[8]

---

[2] *Id.*

[3] *Id.*, Ambassador Jonathan Cohen, Acting Permanent Representative to the U.S. Mission to the United Nations, *Remarks at a U.N. Security Council Open Debate on Transnational Organized Crime at Sea as a Threat to International Peace and Security*, UNITED STATES MISSION TO THE UNITED NATIONS (Feb. 5, 2019), https://usun.usmission.gov/remarks-at-a-un-security-council-open-debate-on-transnational-organized-crime-at-sea-as-a-threat-to-international-peace-and-security/.

[4] Bueger & Edmunds, *supra* note 1.

[5] Ambassador Cohen, *supra* note 3.

[6] Bueger & Edmunds, *supra* note 1.

[7] *Open Debate on Transnational Organised Crime*, SECURITY COUNCIL REPORT (Dec. 6, 2023), https://www.securitycouncilreport.org/whatsinblue/2023/12/open-debate-on-transnational-organised-crime.php.

[8] *Security Council Adopts Presidential Statement on Transnational Organized Crime, Urges States to Ramp Up Cooperation, Laws, Borders to Combat It*, United Nations Meetings Coverage and Press Releases (Dec. 7, 2023), https://press.un.org/en/2023/sc15516.doc.htm.

Moreover, Malta urged that "[c]limate change and other environmental threats deserve the Council's attention, as organized criminal groups take advantage of such vulnerabilities"[9] and "multidimensional and tailored responses"[10] are necessary. This debate concluded with the U.N. Security Council adopting a presidential statement which

> expresse[d] its serious concern over the increase of drug trafficking, smuggling of migrants, trafficking in persons and illicit trafficking and smuggling of small arms and light weapons by land, air and sea, and other criminal activities by organized criminal groups and networks which undermine the authority of States and threaten peace and security in many regions of the world.[11]

Unfortunately, the presidential statement neglected to discuss blue crimes specifically.

Despite the lack of discussion of blue crimes at the international level, scholars have agreed that "blue crimes" are conceptualized to be "[s]erious organised crimes or offences that take place transnationally, on, in or across the maritime domain and cause or have the potential to inflict significant harms."[12] This definition, created by Christian Bueger and Timothy Edmunds, stems from the definition of transnational organized crime in the UNTOC. Per Article 2(a) of the UNTOC, an "organized criminal group" is a "structured group of three or more persons, existing for a period of time and acting in concert with the aim of committing one or more serious crime or offences established in accordance with [the UNTOC], in order to obtain, directly or indirectly, a financial or other material benefit."[13] Furthermore, the UNTOC defines a "serious crime" in Article 2(b) as "conduct constituting an offence punishable by a maximum deprivation of liberty of at least four years or a more serious penalty,"[14] and provides in Article 3(2) that an offence is transnational in nature if:

---

[9] *Id.*

[10] *Id.*

[11] *U.N. Security Council, Statement by the President of the Security Council, U.N. Doc. S/PRST/2023/6 (2023).*

[12] Bueger & Edmunds, *supra* note 1.

[13] United Nations Convention against Transnational Organized Crime art. 2(a), *opened for signature* Nov. 15, 2000, 2225 U.N.T.S. 209 (entered into force Sep. 29, 2003).

[14] *Id.* at art. 2(b).

a) It is committed in more than one State;

b) It is committed in one State but a substantial part of its preparation, planning, direction or control takes place in another State;

c) It is committed in one State but involves an organized criminal group that engages in criminal activities in more than one State; or

d) It is committed in one State but has substantial effects in another State.[15]

According to Bueger and Edmunds,

> [t]he UNTOC definition has a number of notable features. First, it suggests that organised crime is: a) structured in some way; i.e. it implies identifiable patterns and processes of behaviour within and between criminal groups; b) enduring, in the sense that these patterns and processes persist (though may also adapt) over time; c) collaborative, in the sense that three or more members of a criminal group act in concert; d) purposive, in that they do so with the specific aim of committing serious crimes; and e) profit seeking in that such crimes are expected to have a financial or material benefit of some sort. It also implies that organised crime is considered to be transnational only if it implicates two states or more.[16]

Furthermore, there are three main categories of blue crimes, each of which has a particular relationship with the sea and its objects of harm.[17] The first category of blue crimes is crimes against mobility.[18] This category targets the forms of circulation on the sea and movement of goods, such as shipping, supply chains, and maritime trade.[19] The second category of blue crimes relates to criminal flows, as the sea is often used as a conduit for criminal activities like smuggling.[20] As blue crimes in this category are associated with criminal flows, they are sometimes called "transit crimes" because they "concern the movement of illicit commodities or the illegal movement of people from their source

---

[15] *Id.* at art. 3(2).
[16] Bueger & Edmunds, *supra* note 1.
[17] *Id.*
[18] *Id.*
[19] *Id.* The target sites of crimes against mobility are primarily the ship and the port, with the harmed objects being ships, commodities, and their crew. Wider transport infrastructures and supply chains are also targeted by crimes against mobility.
[20] *Id.* Blue crimes under the category of criminal flows consist of crimes that take place across the sea.

location to their markets or destinations, while avoiding detection, entry controls, customs inspections, taxation or other forms of regulation."[21] Lastly, the third category of blue crimes is crimes that inflict harm on the sea itself and the resources it provides.[22] These crimes are typically environmental crimes that "take place in the sea and target the marine environment itself, including natural resources or installations and objects in the sea,"[23] and are crimes of the anthropocene such that "they take place in the context of human activities that engage and interact with the environment of the oceans themselves."[24]

II. What is Corporate Accountability?

Unlike the terms "responsibility" and "liability," the term "accountability" is not defined in public international law. According to the Draft Articles on Responsibility of States for Internationally Wrongful Acts, "[e]very internationally wrongful act of a State entails the international responsibility of that State."[25] Thus, "the term 'international responsibility' covers the new legal relations which arise under international law by a reason of the internationally wrongful act of a State."[26] On the other hand, the term "liability" does not have as straightforward a definition as the term "responsibility." Civil law "expresses the notion of 'liability' in terms of 'responsibility' or 'civil responsibility.'"[27] As such, "'State responsibility' refers to a State's responsibility under international law in general, whereas 'international liability' denotes a State's 'civil responsibility,' or obligation to pay compensation or make reparations for injuries that non-nationals suffer outside its national boundaries as a result of activities within its territory or under its control."[28] Therefore, a State's international liability is prompted under international law and national law in situations involving transnational relations.[29] As the term "accountability" denotes a relationship that

---

21 *Id.*

22 *Id.*

23 *Id.* Illegal resource exploitation and crimes against maritime infrastructures are the core types of crimes included in this category.

24 *Id.*

25 Draft Articles on Responsibility of States for Internationally Wrongful Acts, art. 1, *in* Report of the International Law Commission on the Work of its Fifty-third Session, UN GAOR, 56th Sess., Supp. No. 10, at 43, UN Doc. A/56/10 (2001), https://legal.un.org/ilc/texts/instruments/english/commentaries/9_6_2001.pdf.

26 *Id.* at 32.

27 Sompong Sucharitkul, *State Responsibility And International Liability Under International Law*, 18 Loyola of Los Angeles Int'l & Vomp. L. J. 821, 822 (1996).

28 *Id.*

29 *Id.*

is more than "responsibility," but less than "liability," one must look at soft law principles and case law to understand the term.

A. Soft Law Instruments are Ineffective for Holding Corporations Accountable for International Crimes

The United Nations Guiding Principles on Business and Human Rights

The primary instrument for holding corporations accountable under international law is the UN Guiding Principles on Business and Human Rights (UN Guiding Principles). Adopted in 2011 with overwhelming support by States and corporations,[30] the UN Guiding Principles provide "a global standard of expected conduct for all business enterprises where they operate" and elaborate on the implications of existing standards and practices for States and corporations.[31] As a soft law instrument, the UN Guiding Principles lack any binding legal obligations or enforcement mechanisms, thereby making it a toothless legal instrument. Without mandatory rules and responsibilities, efficient monitoring, or enforcement mechanisms, like sanctions, the UN Guiding Principles lack the ability to hold corporations accountable for their international crimes.[32] Thus, even though the UN Guiding Principles are the main source of international law governing corporate accountability, they are wholly ineffective as it is a soft law instrument with no mandatory requirements.

The Conventions of the International Labour Organization

The Conventions of the International Labour Organization (ILO) are similarly based on human rights and the belief that corporations must respect certain social and environmental standards. Founded in 1919 and becoming a specialized agency of the UN in 1946, the ILO was created with the aim of improving international labor and standards.[33] As stated in its declarations, the fundamental principles of the ILO are freedom of association and the right to collective bargaining, elimination of all forms of forced labor or bonded labor,

---

[30] The support by States and corporations is largely attributable to the absence of any binding legal obligations or enforcement mechanisms in the UN Guiding Principles.

[31] *Guiding Principles on Business and Human Rights*, OFFICE OF THE UNITED NATIONS HIGH COMMISSIONER FOR HUMAN RIGHTS (2011), https://www.ohchr.org/documents/publications/guidingprinciplesbusinesshr_en.pdf.

[32] Photeine Lambridis, *Corporate Accountability: Prosecuting Corporations for the Commission of International Crimes of Atrocity*, 53 N.Y.U. J. OF INT'L. & POL. 144, 149 (2021).

[33] *ILO: International Labour Organization*, UNITED NATIONS OFFICE OF THE SECRETARY-GENERAL'S ENVOY ON YOUTH, https://www.un.org/youthenvoy/2013/08/ilo-international-labour-organization/#:~:text=The%20ILO%20was%20created%20in,agency%20of%20the%20United%20Nations.

ending child labor, and eliminating discrimination in the workplace.[34] Additionally, the ILO is based on the tripartite principle.[35] Under the tripartite principle, "employers' and employees' representatives are equally positioned with respect to the governments of the ... [M]ember [S]tates in the ILO."[36] Although the ILO Conventions only address States, the "Tripartite Declaration of Principles concerning Multinational Enterprises and Social Policy" (Tripartite Declaration) addresses corporations.[37] According to the Tripartite Declaration, all Parties "should contribute to the realization of the ILO Declaration on Fundamental Principles and Rights at Work by adhering to the General Declaration of Human Rights and correlating international pacts ratified by the UN General Assembly, as well as the ILO's Constitution and its basic principles."[38]

Under the ILO's Constitution and the Declaration of Fundamental Principles' rules of procedure, ILO members have a duty "to deliver on annual reports regarding the implementation of their obligations."[39] Accordingly, every ILO Member State can register complaints against Member States or corporations at the ILO for nonfulfillment of obligations prescribed in the Convention or in the Fundamental Principles.[40] Following such a complaint, a Commission of Inquiry writes a report, makes recommendations, and determines the timeframe for implementing said recommendations.[41] Unfortunately, the ILO procedures have a limited benefit for victims of international crimes because they provide victims with intermediate access—individual victims nor civil society organizations are able to initiate proceedings or be involved in this

---

[34] ILO Declaration on Fundamental Principles and Rights at Work, *adopted* 1998, https://www.ilo.org/sites/default/files/2024-04/ILO_1998_Declaration_EN.pdf.

[35] *Tripartite Declaration of Principles concerning Multinational Enterprises and Social Policy*, INTERNATIONAL LABOUR ORGANIZATION (2022), https://www.ilo.org/media/365271/download.

[36] Wolfgang Kaleck & Miriam Saage-MaaB, *Corporate Accountability for Human Rights Violations Amounting to International Crimes, in* CORPORATE ACCOUNTABILITY FOR INTERNATIONAL CRIME, 8 J. OF INT'L CRIM. JUST. 699, 711 (2010).

[37] *Tripartite Declaration of Principles concerning Multinational Enterprises and Social Policy, supra* note 35. The Tripartite Declaration of Principles concerning Multinational Enterprises and Social Policy aims to "encourage the positive contribution which multinational enterprises can make to economic and social progress and to minimize and resolve the difficulties to which their various operations may give rise."

[38] Wolfgang Kaleck & Miriam Saage-MaaB, *supra* note 36 (citing *Tripartite Declaration of Principles concerning Multinational Enterprises and Social Policy, supra* note 35, at art. 8.

[39] Wolfgang Kaleck & Miriam Saage-MaaB, *supra* note 36 (citing Constitution of the International Labour Organization. art. 22 (1919).

[40] Constitution of the ILO, *supra* note 39, at arts. 24, 26 (1919).

[41] *Id.* at art. 29.

process.[42] Only ILO Member States and representatives of employers and employees are able to be involved in this complaint process.[43]

The Guidelines for Multinational Enterprises on Responsible Business Conduct of the Organisation for Economic Co-operation and Development

In 1976, the Guidelines for Multinational Enterprises on Responsible Business Conduct (Guidelines for Multinational Enterprises) were issued by thirty Member States of the Organisation for Economic Co-operation and Development (OECD).[44] These Guidelines make explicit recommendations, but are not legally binding; refer to the ILO core labor standards; and provide recommendations for corporations to fulfill human and labor rights while also abiding by environmental protection, consumer protection, corruption, taxation, and disclosure of information regulations.[45] However, these recommendations only pertain to corporations whose headquarters are located in Member States that have ratified the Guidelines for Multinational Enterprises.[46] Therefore, complaints can only be brought against companies from those countries.[47]

Additionally, the Guidelines for Multinational Enterprises also provide Procedural Guidance. The Procedural Guidance provides a dispute settlement procedure wherein complaints against individual companies for not adhering to the Guidelines can be filed before a National Contact Point, which every Member State is obligated to create.[48] Unlike ILO proceedings, civil society organizations have access to the OECD procedure. Thus, the OECD complaint procedure is more accessible for victims and their representatives.[49]

---

[42] Wolfgang Kaleck & Miriam Saage-MaaB, *supra* note 36.
[43] Wolfgang Kaleck & Miriam Saage-MaaB, *supra* note 36.
[44] *U.S. National Contact Point for the OECD Guidelines for Multinational Enterprises*, U.S. Department of State, https://www.state.gov/u-s-national-contact-point-for-the-oecd-guidelines-for-multinational-enterprises/#:~:text=for%20Multinational%20Enterprises%20.-,The%20OECD%20Guidelines%20for%20Multinational%20Enterprises,fundamental%20principle%20of%20the%20Guidelines.
[45] *OECD Guidelines for Multinational Enterprises on Responsible Business Conduct*, ORGANISATION FOR ECONOMIC CO-OPERATION AND DEVELOPMENT (2023), https://www.oecd-ilibrary.org/deliver/81f92357-en.pdf?itemId=%2Fcontent%2Fpublication%2F81f92357-en&mimeType=pdf.
[46] Wolfgang Kaleck & Miriam Saage-MaaB, *supra* note 36, at 712.
[47] *Id.*
[48] *Id.* (citing *Procedural Guidance of the OECD Guidelines for Multinational Enterprises on Responsible Business Conduct*, No. 1 (revision 2000), OECD Ministerial decision of June 2000.).
[49] Wolfgang Kaleck & Miriam Saage-MaaB, *supra* note 36, at 712.

If a complaint is deemed worthy of examination, the National Contact Point will open a consultation process and attempt mediation between the parties.[50] In the event that the parties involved are not able to resolve their differences, the National Contact Point can issue a final statement.[51] However, the final statements can be limited as the National Contact Point does not have to attribute accountability.[52] Moreover, the National Contact Point cannot impose sanctions.[53] Nonetheless, the statement does contain recommendations for how to implement the Guidelines for Multinational Enterprises.[54]

The United Nations Global Compact

The United Nations Global Compact (Global Compact) is another soft law instrument. The Global Compact provides numerous voluntary corporate citizenship initiatives.[55] However, unlike the ILO Conventions or OECD Guidelines, the Global Compact was not created by Member States via negotiations of an international treaty. Rather, it was initiated by the U.N. General Secretary Kofi Annan in cooperation with UN agencies and business actors.[56]

Although the UN General Assembly "unanimously passed the resolution in support of increased cooperation between the UN and the private sector, thereby endorsing the Global Compact, the latter does not have the status of an UN agency or any other standards setting body."[57] Instead, it serves as more of a "forum for education and dialogue between the different stakeholders in the field of business and human rights," and "aims for the cooperative integration of corporations into the work of the UN and its specialized agencies to promote

---

[50] *Procedural Guidance of the OECD Guidelines for Multinational Enterprises on Responsible Business Conduct, supra* note 48, *Commentary on the Procedural Guidance of the OECD Guidelines for Multinational Enterprises on Responsible Business Conduct* (revision 2000), § 17.

[51] Wolfgang Kaleck & Miriam Saage-MaaB, *supra* note 36, at 712.

[52] *Id.*

[53] *Id.*

[54] *Commentary on the Procedural Guidance of the OECD Guidelines for Multinational Enterprises on Responsible Business Conduct, supra* note 50, at § 18.

[55] Wolfgang Kaleck & Miriam Saage-MaaB, *supra* note 36, at 713.

[56] *Id.* U.N. Secretary General Kofi Annan described the Global Compact as an initiative created to "safeguard sustainable growth within the context of globalization by promoting a core set of universal values which are fundamental to meeting the socio-economic needs of the world's people now and in the future." *Secretary-General proposes Global Compact on Human Rights, Labour, Environment, in Address to World Economic Forum in Davos,* UN Press Release SG/SM/6881, 1 February 1999.

[57] Wolfgang Kaleck & Miriam Saage-MaaB, *supra* note 36, at 713.

the realization of human rights and other common interests of the international community."[58]

B. Since International Criminal Courts are Created and Defined by Treaty, Soft Law Instruments are Ineffective for Holding Corporations Accountable for International Crimes

It is clear that when it comes to the involvement of corporations in international crimes, voluntary self-restrictions are inadequate. In addition to soft law instruments having no or limited enforcement mechanisms, the ineffectiveness of soft law in holding corporations accountable for international crimes is also attributable to the fact that in international criminal law, both *mens rea* and *actus reus* are required for an offense to rise to the level of an international crime. In simple terms, the *mens rea* is the "guilty mind" and the *acuts reus* is the "guilty act."[59] The requirements of the *mens rea* and *actus reus* for a particular crime are detailed in the elements of the crime. These elements are typically found in treaties. For example, the Convention on the Prevention and Punishment of the Crime of Genocide defines the crime of genocide in Article 2[60] and the Convention against Torture and Other Cruel, Inhuman or Degrading Treatment of Punishment defines torture in Article 1.[61] As such, international criminal law is primarily treaty-based rather than normative-based.

International criminal courts are also treaty-based. In fact, every international court, either permanent or ad hoc, was created by a treaty. The Rome Statute established the ICC in 1998 to prosecute genocide, war crimes, crimes against humanity and crimes of aggression,[62] and ad hoc courts such as the International Criminal Tribunal for the former Yugoslavia (ICTY) and the International Criminal Tribunal for Rwanda (ICTR) were established by the Statute of the ICTY and the Statute of the ICTR, respectively.[63] Accordingly, it

---

58 *Id.*

59 William Schabas, *Mens Rea, Actus Reus, and the Role of the State, in* Unimaginable Atrocities: Justice, Politics, and Rights at the War Crimes Tribunals (Mar. 2012).

60 Convention on the Prevention and Punishment of the Crime of Genocide art. 2, Dec. 9, 1948, S. Exec. Doc. O, 81-1 (1949), 78 U.N.T.S. 277.

61 Convention against Torture and Other Cruel, Inhuman or Degrading Treatment or Punishment art. 1, Dec. 10, 1984, 1465 U.N.T.S. 85, 113; S. Treaty Doc. No. 100-20 (1988); 23 I.L.M. 1027 (1984).

62 Rome Statute of the International Criminal Court, 2187 U.N.T.S. 90, *entered into force* July 1, 2002.

63 *See* Statute of the International Criminal Tribunal for the former Yugoslavia, S.C. Res. 827 (May 25, 1993), Statute of the International Tribunal for Rwanda, S.C. Res. 955 (Nov. 8, 1994).

should be no surprise that soft law is an insufficient mechanism to hold corporations accountable for their crimes.[64]

C. Overview of Prominent Case Law Discussing Corporate Accountability

As depicted in case law, individuals within a corporation and the corporation itself, depending on the jurisdiction and whether a corporation is deemed a legal entity, can be held criminally liable for crimes occurring in the process of "doing business."[65] When taking office as the Chief Prosecutor of the ICC, Luis Moreno Ocampo announced that he would consider business leaders as accomplices in international crimes.[66] However, the ICC has yet to prosecute a corporation for any international crime apart from the "business" of conscripting and enlisting child soldiers under the age of fifteen years.[67] To date, there have been no indictments concerning business activities.[68]

In principle, no business activity is truly "neutral." In theory, corporations could be indicted and prosecuted for accessory liability to the commission of an international crime. Possible situations where this may arise include a corporation providing raw materials, any kind of semi-finished products, end-products like weapons, goods, services for personal, technical, and logistic assistance, information, cash, credit, and banking facilitates for the commission of a crime.[69] As well, corporations may have accessorial liability even if they buy resources. It is not uncommon to buy mineral resources, like blood diamonds, that fuel and protract armed conflict and gross human rights violations.[70]

The idea of holding corporate actors accountable for their involvement via the corporation for international crimes took prominence after the Second World War (World War II). Although "the main objective of the Trial of the Major

---

[64] Lambridis, *supra* note 32.

[65] Wolfgang Kaleck & Miriam Saage-MaaB, *supra* note 36, at 700.

[66] Statement made by Mr. Luis Moreno-Ocampo at the ceremony for the solemn undertaking of the Chief Prosecutor of the ICC of Jun. 16, 2003 (ICC-OTP 2003), available at https://www.icc-cpi.int/NR/rdonlyres/D7572226-264A-4B6B-85E3-2673648B4896/143585/030616_moreno_ocampo_english.pdf (visited Dec. 11, 2024).

[67] Kyle Rex Jacobson, *Doing Business with the Devil: The Challenges of Prosecuting Corporate Officials whose Business Transactions Facilitate War Crimes and Crimes against Humanity*, 56 AIR FORCE L. REV. 167, 167 (2005).

[68] *Id.*

[69] The Report of the International Commission of Jurists' Expert Panel on Corporate Complicity in International Crimes (ICJ Expert Panel), *Corporate Criminality & Legal Accountability, Vol. 2: Criminal Law and International Crimes*, at 19, 37–43.

[70] Hans Vest, *Business Leaders and the Modes of Individual Criminal Responsibility under International Law, in* CORPORATE ACCOUNTABILITY FOR INTERNATIONAL CRIME, 8 J. OF INT'L CRIM. JUST. 851, 852 (2010).

War Criminals before the International Military Tribunal (IMT) at Nuremberg was to hold individual high-ranking civilian and military officials accountable for the Nazi regime's systematic human rights crimes,"[71] the "prosecutors acknowledged that the owners and directors of large German companies played a key role in supporting and facilitating the Nazi regime and its crimes."[72] In three cases of the "Subsequent Nuremberg Trials before [United States] Military Tribunals,"[73] high-ranking corporate officers and owners of the IG Farben trust, the Flick trust, and the Krupp firm were indicted for crimes against humanity, war crimes, complicity in the crime of aggression and mass murder, and aiding and abetting murder, cruelties, brutalities, torture, atrocities, and other inhuman acts committed by the Schutzstaffel, commonly referred to as the "SS."[74] As well, in the 1946 *Zyklon B* case, a British Military Tribunal convicted Bruno Tesch and Karl Weinbacher, businessmen, for aiding and abetting murder.

These and other post-World War II cases are important because they demonstrate that "civil actors were held accountable for using their positions in economic, military or state institutions to participate in the Nazi regime's crimes."[75] In the following sections, this chapter will provide brief case studies that shed light on the definition of "corporate accountability" under international criminal law.

United States v. Friedrich Flick et al.

In *United States v. Friedrich Flick*, some of the defendants were members of the "Circle of Friends of Himmler," which consisted of bankers, industrialists, government officials, and SS officers.[76] Originally set up to be an advisory committee on economic issues, the Circle's members were soon thereafter invited to attend dinners and social events, like visiting concentration camps, in exchange for donations to a personal fund of the SS.[77] Friedrich Flick and Otto Steinbrink, two prominent industrialists, were charged for "aiding and abetting criminal activities of the SS" for providing "extensive financial and

---

[71] Wolfgang Kaleck & Miriam Saage-MaaB, *supra* note 36, at 701.

[72] *Id.* (citing Jonathan A. Bush, *The Prehistory of Corporations and Conspiracy in International Law: What Nuremberg Really Said*, 109 COLUM. L. REV. 1094, 1094-1262 (2009)).

[73] Wolfgang Kaleck & Miriam Saage-MaaB, *supra* note 36, at 701.

[74] *Id.*

[75] *Id.* at 702.

[76] *United States v. Friedrich Flick et al., Trials of War Criminals before the Nuremberg Military Tribunals under Control Council Law No. 10*, TWC, Vol. VI (Washington, DC: U.S. Government Printing Office, 1949-1953).

[77] *Id.*

other support."[78] The United States Military Court found Flick and Steinbrink guilty and held that "one who knowingly contributes to the support [of a criminal organization] must ... be deemed to be, if not a principle, certainly an accessory to such crimes."[79] In its reasoning, the Court stated that it would be a "strain upon credibility to believe that [Himmler] needed or spent annually a million *Reichsmark* solely for cultural purposes or that the members of the Circle could reasonably believe that he did."[80]

United States v. Ernest von Weizaecker et al. ("Ministries" case)

In *United States v. Ernest von Weizaecker*, commonly referred to as the "*Ministries*" case, Defendant Karl Rasche was a member of the board of directors of the Dresdner Bank. He was charged for financially supporting the Circle of Friends of Himmler and granting loans to "various SS enterprises which employed large numbers of inmates of concentration camps, and also to Reich enterprises and agencies engaged in the so-called resettlement program."[81] Regarding the loans made by Dresdner Bank to SS enterprises, the U.S. Military Tribunal held that Rasche could "well be condemned from a moral standpoint," but his conduct could "hardly be said to be a crime" as the accused only tried to generate a net profit.[82] As for the financial support of enterprises that were mainly created to exploit slave labor with knowledge of that purpose, the Court reached the opposite judgment.[83]

Trial of Bruno Tesch and two others ("Zyklon B" Case)

In 1946, in the *Trial of Bruno Tresch and two others*, commonly referred to as the "*Zyklon B*" case, a British Military Tribunal convicted the businessmen, Bruno Tesch and Karl Weinbacher, for aiding and abetting murder. Tesch, the owner of the Hamburg, Germany-based company, Testa, his deputy, Weinbacher, and the chief gassing technician, Joachim Drosihn, were charged with having "made themselves accessories before the fact" by distributing large amounts of prussic acid for pest control and murdering extermination camp inmates.[84] In

---

[78] *Id.*

[79] *Id.*

[80] *Id.*

[81] *United States v. Ernst von Weizsaecker et al.*, TWC, Vol. XIV (Washington, DC: U.S. Government Printing Office, 1949-1953).

[82] *Id.*

[83] *Id.*

[84] *Trial of Bruno Tesch and two others, Law Reports of Trials of War Criminals* (LRTWC), Vol. I (London: H.M.S.O, 1947-1949).

this case, the British Military Tribunal was asked to determine whether "the accused knew of the purpose to which their gas was being put."[85]

According to the Court, the prosecution proved beyond a reasonable doubt that Tesch and Weinbacher acted with the requisite knowledge.[86] Although they were not physically present at the concentration camps where the gassing occurred, they were sentenced to death by hanging.[87] Drosihn was acquitted of all charges.[88]

Public Prosecutor v. Van Anraat

In 2005, the District Court of The Hague convicted the businessman Frans van Anraat for aiding and abetting war crimes for supplying more than 1,100 tons of chemical thiodiglycol (TDG) to the Iraqi government under Saddam Hussein's regime. TDG is combined with chemicals for the production of mustard gas, which was used in massacres against Kurdish minorities in Iraq. The Court found that van Anraat's sale of those chemicals contributed to the deaths of the Kurds and found him criminally liable for providing essential assistance to Saddam Hussein with the knowledge that his product would be used to commit human rights abuses.[89] He was convicted for aiding and abetting war crimes, but acquitted for the charge of complicity in genocide because there was no sufficient proof that, at the time of delivering TDG, van Anraat had actual knowledge of Saddam Hussein's intent to destroy, in part, the Kurdish population.[90]

III. The Relationship between Blue Crimes and Corporate Accountability

Unlike genocide, war crimes, crimes against humanity, and crimes of aggression, blue crimes have not been officially defined by treaty or the ICC. As discussed in Part I of this chapter, the definition commonly accepted for blue crimes comes from the scholarship of Bueger and Edmunds. Relying heavily on the definition of transnational organized crime in the UNTOC, Bueger and Edmunds defined blue crimes as "[s]erious organised crimes or offences that take place transnationally, on, in or across the maritime domain and cause or

---

[85] *Id.*

[86] *Id.*

[87] *Id.*

[88] *Id.* The reasons for the acquittal remain uncertain. Drosihn may have been acquitted due to his inferior position not allowing him to influence business operations or due to lack of knowledge, or both.

[89] *Public Prosecutor v. Van Anraat*, LJN AU8685, The Hague District Court (Dec. 23, 2005).

[90] *Id.*

have the potential to inflict significant harms."[91] Moreover, as discussed in Part II of this chapter, there is no official definition for the term "corporate accountability." Based on soft law instruments and case law, one can infer that actions amounting to corporate accountability are more wrongful than actions that prompt "international responsibility," but less wrongful than actions that create "international liability." Accordingly, it comes as no surprise that there have been no prosecutions of corporations for blue crimes under international criminal law. As international criminal law requires a crime to have both a *mens rea* and an *actus reus*[92] to hold corporations accountable for committing blue crimes, the elements of the crime must be clearly defined, which is typically done via treaty or international agreement.

A. Bringing a Blue Crimes Case Before the International Criminal Court

Even if blue crimes were defined via treaty or international agreement, for blue crimes to be prosecuted and corporations to be held accountable under international criminal law, the court must have jurisdiction over the case, the case must be admissible, and moving forward with the case would be in the interest of justice.[93] As the ICC is the only permanent international criminal court, the following analysis is based on the ICC's case requirements.

Jurisdictional Analysis of the International Criminal Court

First, the ICC must have temporal jurisdiction.[94] This means that the ICC can only exercise jurisdiction over crimes committed after July 1, 2002—the date that the Rome Statute went into force.[95] If the alleged crime occurred prior to this date, then the case cannot move forward at the ICC.[96]

Second, the ICC must have territorial jurisdiction.[97] The ICC can only exercise jurisdiction in the territory of States Parties, non-States Parties that consent to jurisdiction, or non-States Parties that are referred to the Court by the U.N. Security Council.[98] If the alleged crime occurred in a State that does not meet any of these requirements, the ICC cannot move forward with the case.[99]

---

91 Bueger & Edmunds, *supra* note 1.

92 *See* Part II, Section B of this chapter.

93 Rome Statute of the International Criminal Court, *supra* note 62, at art. 11.

94 *Id.*

95 *Id.*

96 *Id.* at art. 12.

97 *Id.*

98 *Id.*

99 *Id.*

Third, the ICC must have subject matter jurisdiction.[100] Under the Rome Statute, the ICC has subject matter jurisdiction over a case if the alleged crime is a war crime, crime against humanity, genocide, or crime of aggression.[101] If the alleged crime does not fall within one of these definitions, the case cannot move forward at the ICC.[102]

Lastly, the ICC must have personal jurisdiction.[103] The ICC can only investigate and prosecute "natural persons" who are over the age of eighteen.[104] As such, the ICC cannot investigate or prosecute governments, corporations, political parties, or rebel movements. However, it may investigate individuals who are members of these groups. Moreover, the ICC can only exercise jurisdiction over nations from a State within the Court's jurisdiction: State Party, non-State Party that consents to jurisdiction, or non-State Party that was referred to the Court by the U.N. Security Council.[105]

Admissibility Analysis of the International Criminal Court

Even if the ICC has temporal, territorial, subject matter, and personal jurisdiction over a case, the Rome Statute still limits the types of cases that are deemed "admissible" at the ICC. Before a case can be brought before the ICC, the ICC Prosecutor must determine whether another court, domestic or international, is properly investigating and prosecuting the alleged crimes (this principle is called "complementarity"),[106] and whether the alleged crimes are the gravest of crimes (this principle is called "gravity").[107]

Under the principle of "complementarity," the ICC "complements" other courts that have jurisdiction over the alleged crimes.[108] This principle makes the ICC "a court of last resort." Thus, the ICC Prosecutor must determine if another court is "genuinely able and willing" to investigate and prosecute the case, or already has.[109] If another court is properly investigating and prosecuting the alleged crimes, the ICC cannot move forward with the case.[110]

---

100 *Id.* at art. 5.
101 *Id.*
102 *Id.*
103 *Id.* at art. 25
104 *Id.* at arts. 25–26.
105 *Id.* at art. 12.
106 *Id.* at art. 17
107 *Id.*
108 *Id.* at art. 1, 17.
109 *Id.* at art. 1, 17.
110 *Id.* at art. 1, 17.

Furthermore, per the "gravity" principle, the alleged crimes must be the gravest of atrocity crimes.[111] The ICC Prosecutor determines the gravity by looking at the scale, nature, manner, and impact of the alleged crime.[112] For example, in *The Prosecutor v. Abdallah Banda Abakaer Nourain*, the ICC charged Sudanese rebels Abdallah Banda Abakaer Nourain and Saleh Mohammed Jerbo Jamus with the killing of twelve African Union peacekeepers in 2007.[113] Despite the relatively small number of deaths, the Court found that the crime was an attack on the millions of civilians the peacekeepers were sent to protect, and, thus, met the gravity threshold.[114]

Interest of Justice Analysis of the International Criminal Court

Finally, even when the jurisdictional and admissibility requirements are met, the ICC Prosecutor has the discretion to determine whether moving forward with the case serves the "interests of justice."[115] The ICC Prosecutor may decide not to move forward with an investigation or prosecution if he or she decides that there are substantial reasons to believe that it would not be in the interests of justice.[116]

B. Case Study: Blue Crimes Prosecution in the United States & International Law

As discussed above, corporations cannot be held accountable via prosecution at the ICC because they are not "natural persons." Accordingly, the ICC lacks personal jurisdiction over corporations. However, that is not the case in domestic law.

Recently, in the United States, two companies were prosecuted for blue crimes. In the case *United States v. Prive Overseas Marine et al.*, a court sentenced Prive Shipping Denizcilik Ticaret and Prive Overseas Marine to four-year terms of probation[117] and to pay $2 million in criminal penalties, which includes a $500,000 community service payment for coastal environment projects.[118] In this case, Abdurrahman Korkmaz, a Turkish citizen and master of the Motor Tanker PS Dream, a Panama-flagged chemical tanker, and its

---

[111] *Id.* at art. 17.

[112] *Id.* at art. 17.

[113] *The Prosecutor v. Abdallah Banda Abakaer Nourain*, ICC-02/05-03/09 (Mar. 7, 2011).

[114] *Id.*

[115] Rome Statute of the International Criminal Court, *supra* note 62, at art. 17.

[116] *Id.*

[117] *United States v. Prive Overseas Marine et al.*, No. 2:24-CR-00073, 00074 (E.D. La. 2024). The four-year term of probation includes terms to implement an environmental compliance plan with audit, inspection, and reporting requirements.

[118] *Id.*

operator ordered the crew to perform an overboard discharge of the residual oil tank's contents.[119] Over several days, the crew used a portable pump to empty the tank before arriving in New Orleans, Louisiana, and failed to report the conduct in the ship's oil record books.[120] As well, Korokmaz gave false statements to the United States Coast Guard inspectors in an attempt to conceal the discharge.[121] The two companies pleaded guilty to conspiracy, knowingly violating the Act to Prevent Pollution from Ships, and obstruction of justice related to the falsification of the tanker's Oil Record Book.[122] Not only did the dumping of oil-contaminated waste violate domestic law, but this action also did not comply with Annex I, entitled the "Prevention of Pollution by Oil," of the International Convention for the Prevention of Pollution from Ships—an international treaty that regulates oil pollution from ships.[123] Moreover, the falsified logs, presented to the United States Coast Guard during its inspection of the ship, were intended to conceal the fact that the crew had dumped oil-contaminated waste overboard. As stated by Assistant Attorney General Todd Kim of the United States Department of Justice Environment and Natural Resources Division, "[m]aritime laws regulating pollution from ships are intended to ensure that ocean waters are not used as dumping grounds."[124]

IV. Recommendations for Holding Corporations Accountable for Blue Crimes under International Criminal Law

Even after the establishment of the Nuremberg Principles, the enforcement of international criminal law is a rare exception. Although international crimes are committed in numerous regions of the world—for example, apartheid in South Africa, dictatorships in Latin America, war crimes in countries like Korea and Vietnam, and armed conflicts in countries such as Indonesia and the Philippines—there are very little efforts to hold perpetrators accountable. As there is almost absolute impunity for direct perpetrators, it is unlikely that other actors, such as corporations, would ever be held accountable directly or indirectly for their blue crimes under the present international criminal law regime.

---

119 *Id.*

120 *Id.*

121 *Id.*

122 *Id.*

123 *Id.*

124 *Companies that Own and Operate Oil Tanker Plead Guilty to Environmental Crimes*, U.S. DEPARTMENT OF JUSTICE OFFICE OF PUBLIC AFFAIRS (May 21, 2024), https://www.justice.gov/opa/pr/companies-own-and-operate-oil-tanker-plead-guilty-environmental-crimes.

A. Expanding the International Criminal Court's Definition of Personal Jurisdiction to Include Corporations

As discussed in Part III, the ICC only has personal jurisdiction over natural persons.[125] As a result, governments, corporations, political parties, or rebel movements cannot be prosecuted at the ICC for their crimes.[126] To allow for corporate accountability under international criminal law, the ICC should broaden its definition of personal jurisdiction to include entities that are not natural persons. This expansion of personal jurisdiction would be in line with the personal jurisdiction requirements of many countries.

At first, the United States was the only apparent venue for disputes between victims of crimes and corporations.[127] Beginning in the 1960s, human rights and civil rights organizations in the United States began holding U.S. military personnel and individuals residing in the United States accountable for their actions and involvement in international crimes.[128] Since the criminal law system of the United States provides little opportunity for crime victims to be involved in the proceedings, organizations brought civil lawsuits to claim compensation.[129] This, in turn, provided the possibility for victims to claim punitive damages and attracted a broader public audience to the case.[130]

In the early 1990s, human rights and civil rights organizations brought cases under the Alien Tort Claims Act (ATCA) against business entities and corporations for their involvement in international crimes.[131] The ATCA is a jurisdictional statute that allows federal courts to hear civil tort suits.[132] These ATCA cases against corporations in the United States raised public awareness

---

125 Rome Statute of the International Criminal Court, *supra* note 62, at arts. 25–26.

126 *Id.*

127 Anita Ramasastry, *Mapping the Web of Liability: The Expanding Geography of Corporate Accountability in Domestic Jurisdictions*, https://media.business-humanrights.org/media/documents/files/reports-and-materials/Anita-Ramasastry-commentary.pdf.

128 Kaleck & Saage-MaaB, *supra* note 36, at 702.

129 *Id.*

130 *Id.*

131 *Id.*

132 *Sosa v. Alvarez-Machain*, 542 U.S. 692, 713-714 (2004). Federal subject matter jurisdiction is established when (1) an alien sues (2) for a tort that is (3) committed in violation of the law of nations, or of a treaty of which the United States is a signatory. *Flores v. Southern Peru Copper Corp.*, 414 F.3d 233, 242 (2d Cir. 2003). The United States Supreme Court has restricted the application of the ATCA to violations of international crimes that amount to *jus cogens* norms as it held that federal courts cannot recognize "violations of any international law norm with less definite content and acceptance among civilized nations." *Sosa v. Alvarez-Machain*, 542 U.S. 692, 725 (2004).

considerably about the role of corporations in international crimes.[133] For example, in 1997, Shell was sued for allegedly aiding and abetting the military government in its extrajudicial execution of environmental activists in the Ogoni oil region in Nigeria.[134] Likewise, in California, a lawsuit was brought by Burmese villagers alleging that Unocal Corporation had aided and abetted the Myanmar junta in its use of forced labor to clear lands and build roads and infrastructure to further an oil pipeline located in Myanmar.[135]

Outside of the United States, corporations can be prosecuted for violating international criminal law in national courts.[136] In many countries, there is no distinction between natural persons, humans, legal persons, and corporations.[137] The ability to prosecute corporations for crimes in domestic courts has become a growing trend across the globe.[138]

In 2006, the Fafo Institute for Applied International Studies, a Norwegian research institute, published a study entitled "Commerce, Crime and Conflict."[139] This study showed that among the eleven countries surveyed—Australia, Belgium, Canada, France, India, Japan, the Netherlands, Norway, South Africa, the United Kingdom, and the United States—there is a prevailing practice of applying criminal liability to legal persons.[140] In five countries—Argentina, Germany, Indonesia, Spain, and Ukraine—the jurisprudence did not recognize this type of liability as a conceptual matter.[141] In fact, according to the study, in Argentina and Indonesia, the national legislature ignored conceptual issues and adopted specific statutes making legal persons liable for important crimes such as environmental crimes, commercial crimes, corruption, and terrorism.[142]

These findings of state practice of prosecuting and holding corporations accountable for their crimes are significant. For corporations to be held accountable for committing crimes, namely blue crimes, at the international level, the ICC must expand the scope of its definition of personal jurisdiction to include legal persons in addition to natural persons. As the only permanent international criminal court, the expansion of its definition of personal

---

133 Kaleck & Saage-MaaB, *supra* note 36, at 702.

134 Ramasastry, *supra* note 127.

135 *Id.*

136 *Id.*

137 *Id.*

138 *Id.*

139 *Id.*

140 *Id.*

141 *Id.*

142 *Id.*

jurisdiction could trigger a cascading effect whereby other criminal courts, such as future ad hoc international criminal courts and current domestic criminal courts, may also expand their personal jurisdiction definitions to include corporations. This would result in corporations being held accountable under international criminal law for their blue crimes, provided that the blue crime committed fits within the definition of an already existing international crime, i.e., war crime, crime against humanity, crime of aggression, or genocide.

B. Creating Blue Crimes and Corporate Accountability Treaties using an International Human Rights Law and International Criminal Law Perspective

Although the UN Guiding Principles on Business and Human Rights, the ILO Conventions, and the Guidelines for Multinational Enterprises on Responsible Business Conduct of the OECD provide a good first step for addressing corporate accountability via soft law, the current international criminal law framework does not adequately address corporate accountability nor prosecution of blue crimes. Accordingly, the global community needs to invest in two new international treaties that focus on (1) holding corporations accountable for international crimes generally and (2) defining blue crimes.

First, a treaty should be created that addresses corporate accountability. This treaty should require action by States to create mandatory provisions that impose specific obligations on individuals operating a corporation and the corporation itself to act in accordance with international criminal law and international human rights law. This new treaty would provide that corporations and business entities have the same rights and responsibilities under international law as natural persons. As such, this would equate a legal entity, here, a corporation, to that of a natural person regarding what they can and cannot do under international human rights and international criminal law. Although this would make natural persons and legal entities the same under the eyes of the law, this would ensure that corporations are not treated more or less favorably than humans in terms of accountability measures and prosecutions.

Second, a treaty should be created that defines blue crimes. Similar to human rights treaties that are devoted to defining and criminalizing a particular wrongdoing and ill act, such as the Convention on the Prevention and Punishment of the Crime of Genocide and the Convention against Torture and Other Cruel, Inhuman or Degrading Treatment or Punishment, a treaty should be created to define and criminalize blue crimes. As discussed in Part I of this chapter, blue crimes can take on a variety of forms; they can be crimes relating to the circulation on the sea and movement of goods,[143] criminal flows,[144] and crimes that inflict harm on the sea itself and the resources it provides.[145] Accordingly, this new treaty should provide concrete definitions of the different types of blue crimes and the elements of each blue crime. Without having clear elements of what intent (*mens rea*) and action (*actus reus*) constitute each type of blue crime, a corporation cannot be held accountable or prosecuted for their actions.

Conclusion

As a society, we are conditioned to believe that crimes can only be committed by humans. Very rarely do we see on the news, reports about corporations or business entities being found guilty of crimes. However, corporations are equally as culpable of committing international crimes as humans.

Given the interconnectedness of this world, corporations are at the helm of economic activity, innovation, and competition. In producing or delivering their products and services, corporations often rely on water, rivers, and oceans for resources and transportation. As such, they are increasingly becoming perpetrators of blue crimes.

The current international criminal law framework does not allow for corporations to be held accountable for blue crimes. This is mainly because international criminal law has not defined corporate accountability, except for in non-enforceable soft law instruments, and blue crimes have not been adequately defined in international law via treaties or international agreements. Without these pertinent definitions and enforcement mechanisms, it comes as no surprise that corporations can commit blue crimes without repercussion.

To hold corporations accountable for their blue crimes, the ICC should expand its definition of personal jurisdiction to include corporations. Currently, the ICC only has personal jurisdiction over natural persons. By expanding the scope of its personal jurisdiction definition to include legal entities, it would be able to prosecute corporations for international crimes. Additionally, the global community needs to create two new international

---

143 Bueger & Edmunds, *supra* note 1. The target sites of crimes against mobility are primarily the ship and the port, with the harmed objects being ships, commodities, and their crew. Wider transport infrastructures and supply chains are also targeted by crimes against mobility.

144 *Id.* Blue crimes under the category of criminal flows consist of crimes that take place across the sea.

145 *Id.*

treaties that focus on (1) holding corporations accountable for international crimes generally and (2) defining blue crimes.

The time has long come for the international community to hold corporations accountable for their actions. By doing so, we are not only protecting our basic human rights, but are ensuring that future generations are protected from the international crimes committed and facilitated by corporations.

Bibliography

Christian Bueger & Timothy Edmunds, *Blue crime: Conceptualising transnational organised crime at sea*, Marine Policy 119 (2020), https://www.safeseas.net/wp-content/uploads/2022/11/Bueger-and-Edmunds-2020-Blue-Crime.pdf. https://doi.org/10.1016/j.marpol.2020.104067.

Jonathan A. Bush, *The Prehistory of Corporations and Conspiracy in International Law: What Nuremberg Really Said*, 109 Colum. L. Rev. 1094, 1094-1262 (2009).

Ambassador Jonathan Cohen, Acting Permanent Representative to the U.S. Mission to the United Nations, *Remarks at a U.N. Security Council Open Debate on Transnational Organized Crime at Sea as a Threat to International Peace and Security*, United States Mission to the United Nations (Feb. 5, 2019), https://usun.usmission.gov/remarks-at-a-un-security-council-open-debate-on-transnational-organized-crime-at-sea-as-a-threat-to-international-peace-and-security/.

Convention against Torture and Other Cruel, Inhuman or Degrading Treatment or Punishment, Dec. 10, 1984, 1465 U.N.T.S. 85, 113; S. Treaty Doc. No. 100-20 (1988); 23 I.L.M. 1027 (1984).

Convention on the Prevention and Punishment of the Crime of Genocide, Dec. 9, 1948, S. Exec. Doc. O, 81-1 (1949), 78 U.N.T.S. 277.

Draft Articles on Responsibility of States for Internationally Wrongful Acts, *in* Report of the International Law Commission on the Work of its Fifty-third Session, UN GAOR, 56th Sess., Supp. No. 10, at 43, UN Doc. A/56/10 (2001), https://legal.un.org/ilc/texts/instruments/english/commentaries/9_6_2001.pdf.

Flores v. Southern Peru Copper Corp., 414 F.3d 233, 242 (2d Cir. 2003).

International Criminal Court, Statement made by Mr. Luis Moreno-Ocampo at the ceremony for the solemn undertaking of the Chief Prosecutor of the ICC of Jun. 16, 2003 (ICC-OTP 2003), available at https://www.icc-cpi.int/NR/rdonlyres/D7572226-264A-4B6B-85E3-2673648B4896/143585/030616_moreno_ocampo_english.pdf.

ICJ Expert Panel, The Report of the International Commission of Jurists' Expert Panel on Corporate Complicity in International Crimes, *Corporate Criminality & Legal Accountability, Vol. 2: Criminal Law and International Crimes*, at 19, 37–43.

ILO, Declaration on Fundamental Principles and Rights at Work, *adopted* 1998, https://www.ilo.org/sites/default/files/2024-04/ILO_1998_Declaration_EN.pdf.

ILO, *Tripartite Declaration of Principles concerning Multinational Enterprises and Social Policy* (2022), https://www.ilo.org/media/365271/download.

ILO, United Nations Office of the Secretary-General's Envoy on Youth, https://www.un.org/youthenvoy/2013/08/ilo-international-labour-organization/#:~:text=The%20ILO%20was%20created%20in,agency%20of%20the%20United%20Nations.

Kyle Rex Jacobson, *Doing Business with the Devil: The Challenges of Prosecuting Corporate Officials whose Business Transactions Facilitate War Crimes and Crimes against Humanity*, 56 Air Force L. Rev. 167, 167 (2005).

Wolfgang Kaleck & Miriam Saage-MaaB, *Corporate Accountability for Human Rights Violations Amounting to International Crimes, in* Corporate Accountability for International Crime, 8 J. of Int'l Crim. Just. 699, 711 (2010). https://doi.org/10.1093/jicj/mqq043.

Photeine Lambridis, *Corporate Accountability: Prosecuting Corporations for the Commission of International Crimes of Atrocity*, 53 N.Y.U. J. of Int'l. & Pol. 144, 149 (2021).

Organisation for Economic Co-operation and Development, *Commentary on the Procedural Guidance of the OECD Guidelines for Multinational Enterprises on Responsible Business Conduct* (revision 2000), § 17.

Organisation for Economic Co-operation and Development, *OECD Guidelines for Multinational Enterprises on Responsible Business Conduct* (2023), https://www.oecd-ilibrary.org/deliver/81f92357-en.pdf?itemId=%2Fcontent%2Fpublication%2F81f92357-en&mimeType=pdf.

Organisation for the Economic Co-operation and Development, *Procedural Guidance of the OECD Guidelines for Multinational Enterprises on Responsible Business Conduct*, No. 1 (revision 2000), OECD Ministerial decision of June 2000).

Public Prosecutor v. Van Anraat, LJN AU8685, The Hague District Court (Dec. 23, 2005).

Anita Ramasastry, *Mapping the Web of Liability: The Expanding Geography of Corporate Accountability in Domestic Jurisdictions*, https://media.business-humanrights.org/media/documents/files/reports-and-materials/Anita-Ramasastry-commentary.pdf.

Rome Statute of the International Criminal Court, 2187 U.N.T.S. 90, *entered into force* July 1, 2002.

William Schabas, *Mens Rea, Actus Reus, and the Role of the State, in* Unimaginable Atrocities: Justice, Politics, and Rights at the War Crimes Tribunals (Mar. 2012). https://doi.org/10.1093/acprof:oso/9780199653072.001.0001.

Security Council Report, *Open Debate on Transnational Organised Crime* (Dec. 6, 2023), https://www.securitycouncilreport.org/whatsinblue/2023/12/open-debate-on-transnational-organised-crime.php.

Sompong Sucharitkul, *State Responsibility And International Liability Under International Law*, 18 Loyola of Los Angeles Int'l & Vomp. L. J. 821 (1996).

Sosa v. Alvarez-Machain, 542 U.S. 692, 713-714 (2004). https://doi.org/10.1643/OT-04-143.

International Criminal Court, Statement made by Mr. Luis Moreno-Ocampo at the ceremony for the solemn undertaking of the Chief Prosecutor of the ICC of Jun. 16, 2003 (ICC-OTP 2003), available at https://www.icc-cpi.int/NR

/rdonlyres/D7572226-264A-4B6B-85E3-2673648B4896/143585/030616_moreno_ocampo_english.pdf (visited Dec. 11, 2024).

Statute of the International Criminal Tribunal for the former Yugoslavia, S.C. Res. 827 (May 25, 1993).

Statute of the International Tribunal for Rwanda, S.C. Res. 955 (Nov. 8, 1994).

United Nations Convention against Transnational Organized Crime, *opened for signature* Nov. 15, 2000, 2225 U.N.T.S. 209 (entered into force Sep. 29, 2003).

United Nations Meetings and Press Releases, *Security Council Adopts Presidential Statement on Transnational Organized Crime, Urges States to Ramp Up Cooperation, Laws, Borders to Combat It* (Dec. 7, 2023), https://press.un.org/en/2023/sc15516.doc.htm.

United Nations Press Release, *Secretary-General proposes Global Compact on Human Rights, Labour, Environment, in Address to World Economic Forum in Davos*, SG/SM/6881, 1 February 1999.

United Nations Office of the High Commissioner for Human Rights, *Guiding Principles on Business and Human Rights* (2011), https://www.ohchr.org/documents/publications/guidingprinciplesbusinesshr_en.pdf.

U.N. Security Council, Statement by the President of the Security Council, U.N. Doc. S/PRST/2023/6 (2023).

United States Department of Justice of Public Affairs, *Companies that Own and Operate Oil Tanker Plead Guilty to Environmental Crimes* (May 21, 2024), https://www.justice.gov/opa/pr/companies-own-and-operate-oil-tanker-plead-guilty-environmental-crimes.

United States Department of State, *U.S. National Contact Point for the OECD Guidelines for Multinational Enterprises*, https://www.state.gov/u-s-national-contact-point-for-the-oecd-guidelines-for-multinational-enterprises/#.

United States v. Ernst von Weizsaecker et al., TWC, Vol. XIV (Washington, DC: US Government Printing Office, 1949-1953).

United States v. Friedrich Flick et al., Trials of War Criminals before the Nuremberg Military Tribunals under Control Council Law No. 10 (TWC), Vol. VI (Washington, DC: US Government Printing Office, 1949-1953).

United States v. Prive Overseas Marine et al., No. 2:24-CR-00073, 00074 (E.D. La. 2024).

The Prosecutor v. Abdallah Banda Abakaer Nourain, ICC-02/05-03/09 (Mar. 7, 2011).

Trial of Bruno Tesch and two others, Law Reports of Trials of War Criminals (LRTWC), Vol. I (London: H.M.S.O, 1947-1949).

Hans Vest, *Business Leaders and the Modes of Individual Criminal Responsibility under International Law, in* Corporate Accountability for International Crime, 8 J. of Int'l Crim. Just. 851, 852 (2010). https://doi.org/10.1093/jicj/mqq032.

Chapter 9

The Depths of Impunity: International Criminal Law and Crimes on the High Seas

Major Vy Thuy Nguyen[1]
Judge Advocate, U.S. Army

Abstract: This chapter considers whether the ICC is an appropriate forum to prosecute crimes committed on the high seas. It considers inherent enforcement problems and current dispute resolution mechanisms related to the international law of the sea. It then relies on ICC decisions to identify issues relating to the exercise of the court's jurisdiction for crimes committed at sea over both flagged and stateless vessels. This article will therefore analyze the inherent gaps in accountability efforts arising from the Rome Statute of the ICC in view of the UNCLOS.

Keywords: ICC, UNCLOS, stateless and flagged vessels, jurisdiction, maritime law, Rohingya, Hague Conventions, mutual legal assistance.

Introduction

The environment in which States attempt to investigate and enforce laws beyond their maritime zones is complex. Maritime law emerged around the

---

[1]** The views expressed in this chapter are those solely of the author and do not reflect, nor should be construed, to be the official policy or views of the U.S. Department of Defense or U.S. Department of the Army.
See, e.g., Convention against Illicit Traffic in Narcotic Drugs and Psychotropic Substances, Dec. 20, 1988, 1582 U.N.T.S. 95; Convention for the Suppression of Unlawful Acts against Safety of Maritime Navigation, Mar. 10, 1988, 1678 U.N.T.S. 1; Convention against Transnational Organized Crime, Nov. 15, 2000, 2225 U.N.T.S. 209; Protocol against the Smuggling of Migrants by Land, Sea and Air, Nov. 15, 2000, 2241 U.N.T.S. 507; *see also Maritime Crime*, INTERNATIONAL CRIMINAL POLICE ORGANIZATION (2024) [hereinafter INTERPOL], https://www.interpol.int/en/Crimes/Maritime-crime (last visited Sep. 26, 2024); *IMB Piracy Reporting Centre*, INT'L COM. CRIME SERVICES, https://www.icc-ccs.org/index.php/piracy-reporting-centre (last visited Dec. 2, 2024).

concepts of freedom and sovereignty within the harsh conditions and expansive nature of the high seas. What resulted was a patchwork of intentionally broad agreements that accommodate varied applications and interpretations such that enforcement depends on consent, collaboration, de-confliction, resourcing, and specialized expertise. The legal and practical gaps inherent in such a patchwork contribute to the sentiment that there is lawlessness on the high seas. Nevertheless, attempts at cooperative enforcement have sought to address two categories of maritime crimes: (i) threats to merchant vessels and seafarers (e.g., piracy, kidnapping, armed robbery) and (ii) transnational crimes (e.g., organized crime groups trafficking drugs, persons, and weapons). Other areas whose regulatory framework is continually developed relate to military activity, including weapons transport, and prevention of terrorist activities.

No similar maritime protocols exist specifically for the core international crimes of genocide, crimes against humanity, war crimes, or the crime of aggression. This raises a number of concerns. For example, where core international crimes are committed, or peremptory norms (jus cogens) are violated on the high seas, who has the authority or bears the responsibility to prevent or punish? Are discretionary national processes the best avenue for justice? Is the ICC able or necessary to prosecute these crimes when they are committed on the high seas?

This chapter considers the scope of the ICC's ability to prosecute crimes committed on the high seas. It provides a broad overview of maritime and international criminal law before considering ICC case studies. It does not consider crimes committed within the maritime zones of a State, disputed or otherwise, nor does it seek to provide a comprehensive discussion of all facets of maritime enforcement. It also does not engage in the morality or legitimacy of ICC prosecution. It merely offers the narrow conclusion that the exercise of ICC jurisdiction is appropriate in very few instances and feasible in even fewer.

For purposes of this chapter, the following terms will be used: "maritime zones" refer to a State's internal waters, territorial sea, contiguous zone, and exclusive economic zone; "high seas" refer to the waters beyond and not including maritime zones; "flagged vessels" refer to vessels registered under the laws of a State; and "stateless vessel" refers to vessels (i) not registered under the laws of any State, (ii) that sail under flags of two or more States, or (iii) that changes flags during navigation; and "peremptory norms (jus cogens)" refer to prohibitions on genocide, crimes against humanity, slavery, racial discrimination, piracy, and use of armed force except for self-defense.[2] These definitions may differ from treaty language but are used in this manner to focus the discussion.

I. Overview of Maritime Law

The doctrine of freedom of the high seas and principle of flag state sovereignty is at the heart of maritime law. The key international instrument is the 1982 UNCLOS, which entered into force on November 16, 1994, codifying customary international law related to ocean usage and sovereignty generally.[3] It specifically guarantees the freedom to navigate and overflight and, subject to certain conditions, to lay submarine cables and pipelines, construct artificial islands and other installations, fish, and conduct scientific research.[4] States have the exclusive authority to exercise jurisdiction over their flagged vessels,[5] vessels located within its ports, and vessels within its maritime zones. The general rule is that no State may exercise jurisdiction over foreign vessels on the

---

[2] *See* Vienna Convention on the Laws of Treaties art. 53, May 23, 1969, 1155 U.N.T.S. 331 (defining a peremptory norm of general international law as a norm accepted and recognized by the international community of States as a whole as a norm from which no derogation is permitted and which can be modified only by a subsequent norm of general international law having the same character.); Rep. of the Int'l Law Comm'n, 73rd Sess., Apr. 18-Jun. 3, Jul. 4-Aug. 5, 2022, 43, U.N. Doc. A/77/10; GAOR, 77th Sess., Supp. No. 10 (2022); *Start Your Research: (6) Peremptory Norms of International Law (Jus Cogens)*, PEACE PALACE LIBRARY, https://peacepalacelibrary.nl/start-your-research-6-peremptory-norms-international-law-jus-cogens (last visited Oct. 6, 2024); *see generally Analytical Guide to the Work of the International Law Commission: Peremptory norms of general international law (Jus cogens)*, INT'L LAW COMM'N (Jul. 5, 2024), https://legal.un.org/ilc/guide/1_14.shtml (last visited Oct. 6, 2024); Ulf Linderfalk, *The Effect of Jus Cogens Norms: Whoever Opened Pandora's Box, Did You Ever Think About the Consequences?*, 18 EUR. J. INT'L L. 853 (2007), https://academic.oup.com/ejil/article/18/5/853/398659 (last visited Dec. 5, 2024).

[3] UNCLOS superseded the 1958 UN Convention on the High Seas (UNCHS). *See* UNCHS, Apr. 29, 1958, 450 U.N.T.S. 11; UNCLOS, Oct. 12, 1982, 1833 U.N.T.S. 397; *see generally United Nations Convention on the Law of the Sea (UNCLOS): Living Resources Provision*, R4774, CONG. RES. SERVICE (Jul. 15, 2024), https://crsreports.congress.gov/product/pdf/R/R47744 (last visited Nov. 23, 2024).

[4] UNCLOS art. 87.

[5] *See S. S. Lotus (Fr. v. Turk.)*, 1927 P.C.I.J. (ser. A) No. 10 (Sep. 7, 1927), https://www.worldcourts.com/pcij/eng/decisions/1927.09.07_lotus.htm (last visited Oct. 6, 2024) ("The collision which occurred on August 2nd, 1926, between the S. S. Lotus, flying the French flag, and the S. S. Boz-Kourt, flying the Turkish flag, took place on the high seas: the territorial jurisdiction of any State other than France and Turkey therefore does not enter into account.").

high seas.[6] It is important to keep in mind though, that stateless vessels are not entitled to these freedoms; to be entitled to these freedoms, vessels must be registered under a flag state.[7]

Nevertheless, there are exceptions to the general rule of non-interference on the high seas. The authority to interdict foreign vessels on the high seas is provided in specific situations in the UNCLOS as well as through bilateral agreements.[8] Those situations may confer the right to board, to inspect certain documents, to search and seize persons or property, to detain persons or the vessel itself, or to pull the vessel to port, for example. Notably, a warship that encounters on the high seas a foreign ship which it has "reasonable ground for suspecting" is stateless, may be justified in boarding it to verify its documents.[9]

However, the right to carry out interdiction is not limitless, nor may a State have the right to carry out each of these interventions in every situation.[10] The right to engage in hot pursuit of another vessel, for example, only belongs to

(i) a warship, military aircraft, or other ship or aircraft on government service specifically authorized to that effect,

(ii) until it reaches the territorial sea of its own State or a third State,[11] and

---

[6] *See, e.g.*, UNCLOS art. 97(3) (No arrest or detention of the ship, even as a measure of investigation, shall be ordered by any authorities other than those of the flag State).

[7] *See id.* at art. 92(2).

[8] *See, e.g.*, Agreement between the United States and Tuvalu Concerning Operational Cooperation to Suppress Illicit Transnational Maritime Activity (Sep. 9, 2011), https://www.state.gov/wp-content/uploads/2019/02/11-909-Tuvalu-Maritime-Interdiction.pdf (last visited Sep. 29, 2024); Agreement between the United States and the United Kingdom of Great Britain and Northern Ireland (Jul. 13, 1998), https://www.state.gov/wp-content/uploads/2020/02/00-1030-United-Kingdom-Maritime-Mtrs-Shiprider-Carib-and-Bermuda.pdf (last visited Dec. 2, 2024).

[9] UNCLOS art. 110.

[10] *See, e.g., Maritime Counterdrug and Alien Migrant Interdiction Operation Manual – COMDTINST M16247.4A – Table of Contents*, U.S. COAST GUARD (2012), *available at* https://www.governmentattic.org/46docs/USCGcdamioTOC_2012.pdf (last visited Dec. 2, 2024).

[11] UNCLOS art. 111(3); *see also Claim of the British Ship "I'm Alone" v. United States* (1933), 3 R.I.A.A. 1609, 29 A.J.I.L. 326, https://legal.un.org/riaa/cases/vol_III/1609-1618.pdf (last visited Nov. 23, 2024) (finding no justification for a United States Coast Guard vessel during hot pursuit to *intentionally* sink in the Gulf of Mexico a Canadian vessel suspected of engaging in a conspiracy to smuggle liquor into the United States). *But see United States v. F/V Taiyo Maru, Number 28, SOI 600*, 395 F. Supp. 413 (D. Me. 1975) (finding U.S. Coast Guard seizure of a Japanese vessel on the high seas following hot pursuit from the contiguous zone was not in violation of Article 23 of the 1958 Convention on the High

(iii) when it has "good reason to believe" the foreign vessel has violated the laws and regulations of that State.[12]

In recent decades, States have worked together to further prevent, deter, and punish mutual threats on the high seas. They may enter into bilateral or multilateral agreements, for example, to assist each other with training, resourcing, and joint operations. As discussed in other chapters of this book, they have also ratified various protocols including those addressing piracy, migrant smuggling, as well as IUU fishing. Multilateral institutions further facilitate those operations through technical assistance, capacity building, and direct participation.

After interdiction on the high seas, the authority to criminally prosecute individuals generally remains with the vessel's flag State or State of which the alleged perpetrator is a national. This can prove complex where the crew, passenger, and/or vessel possess different nationalities. Consider also for example, article 97, UNCLOS that provides, in relevant part:

> 1. In the event of a collision or any other incident of navigation concerning a ship on the high seas, involving the penal or disciplinary responsibility of the master or of any other person in the service of the ship, no penal or disciplinary proceedings may be instituted against such person except before the judicial or administrative authorities either of the flag State or of the State of which such person is a national.
>
> . . .
>
> 3. No arrest or detention of the ship, even as a measure of investigation, shall be ordered by any authorities other than those of the flag State.

The UNCLOS also addresses maritime dispute resolution mechanisms, whose exercise of jurisdiction are consent-based. State parties to the UNCLOS may elect to seek recourse or settlement of disputes through the ITLOS, ICJ, and/or PCA or other arbitral tribunals designated to resolve specific issues.[13] Some elect only ITLOS, others elect only arbitral tribunals, and still, some others elect

---

Seas, sanctioned by domestic law, and conformed with prevailing consensus of international law and practice).

[12] UNCLOS art. 111(1).

[13] *See* UNCLOS Declarations and Reservations; *see generally* Statute of the International Tribunal for the Law of the Sea, Dec. 10, 1982, 1833 U.N.T.S. 561.

all three with preference for one over the others.[14] Notably, unless the parties otherwise agree, the jurisdiction of ITLOS is mandatory in cases relating to the prompt release of vessels and crew under article 292, UNCLOS and to provisional measures pending the constitution of an arbitral tribunal under article 290, paragraph 5, UNCLOS.[15] No express provision provides for the holdings in each case to be precedential, but in practice, their dicta and underlying principles are persuasive guidance. These proceedings result in awards such as those settling maritime delimitation, not adjudging individual criminal responsibility.[16]

II. Overview of International Criminal Law

The concept of individual criminal responsibility under international law emerged at the end of the nineteenth century and rapidly evolved in the twentieth century. The term "core international crimes" has come to be understood as genocide, crimes against humanity, war crimes, and the crime of aggression. The key conventions relating to these core international crimes include: (i) 1899, 1907, and 1954 Hague Conventions;[17] (ii) 1949 Geneva Conventions;[18] (iii) 1948 UN Convention on the Prevention and Punishment of

---

[14] UNCLOS Declarations and Reservations, *compare* Austria *and* Belgium *and* Croatia *and* Hungary *and* Montenegro (preferring ITLOS over other forums), *with* Denmark (choosing the ICJ and refusing arbitral tribunal), *with* the Netherlands (choosing only the ICJ), *with* Honduras (choosing the ICJ and reserving the right to accept ITLOS on a case-by-case basis), *with* Australia *and* Congo *and* Ecuador *and* Estonia *and* Finland *and* Italy *and* Latvia *and* Lithuania *and* Mexico *and* Togo (accepting without requiring one forum having precedence over another), *with* Algeria (requiring prior agreement to submit a dispute to the ICJ), *with* Cuba (expressly refusing to accept ICJ jurisdiction).

[15] *The Tribunal*, ITLOS, https://www.itlos.org/en/main/the-tribunal/the-tribunal/ (last visited Sep. 29, 2024).

[16] *See, e.g.*, Bay of Bengal Maritime Boundary Arbitration (Bangladesh v. India), Case No. 2010-16 (Perm. Ct. Arb. 2014); Sovereignty and Maritime Delimitation in the Red Sea (Eritrea v. Yemen) Award of the Arbitral Tribunal in the First Stage of the Proceedings, Case No. 1996-04 (Perm. Ct. Arb. 1998); *see generally* United Nations, *Reports of International Arbitral Awards*, CODIFICATION AND PROGRESSIVE DEVELOPMENT OF INTERNATIONAL LAW, https://legal.un.org/riaa/ (last visited Dec. 6, 2024).

[17] *See Hague Conventions*, INTERNATIONAL COMMITTEE OF THE RED CROSS (2024), https://casebook.icrc.org/a_to_z/glossary/hague-conventions (last visited Dec. 6, 2024).

[18] Geneva Convention for the Amelioration of the Condition of the Wounded and Sick in Armed Forces in the Field (GC I), Aug. 12, 1949, 75 U.N.T.S. 31; Geneva Convention for the Amelioration of the Condition of Wounded, Sick and Shipwrecked Members of Armed Forces at Sea (GC II), Aug. 12, 1949, 75 U.N.T.S. 85; Geneva Convention Relative to the Treatment of Prisoners of War (GC III), Aug. 12, 1949, 75 U.N.T.S. 135; Geneva Convention

the Crime of Genocide ("Genocide Convention"), which entered into force on January 12, 1951;[19] (iv) 1984 UN Convention Against Torture and Other Cruel, Inhuman or Degrading Treatment or Punishment ("Torture Convention"), which entered into force on June 26, 1987;[20] and (v) The Rome Statute of the ICC ("Rome Statute"), which entered into force on July 1, 2002.[21]

While the 1907 Hague Conventions on Enemy Merchant Ships and on Restrictions of the Right of Capture address protections for neutral and enemy ships encountered on the high seas during hostilities, the remaining conventions neither contemplate nor provide for the exercise of jurisdiction over foreign or stateless vessels on the high seas.[22] The Genocide Convention makes no mention of jurisdiction over vessels, though its Article VIII provides that "any contracting party may call upon the competent organs of the UN to take such action under the Charter of the UN as they consider appropriate for the prevention and suppression of acts of genocide." The Torture Convention requires States to take measures necessary to establish jurisdiction over offenses committed "on board a ship . . . registered in that State."[23] As discussed later in this chapter, article 12(2)(a) of the Rome Statute requires flag state consent as a precondition for the exercise of its jurisdiction over crimes committed on a vessel.

Of note, while there continues to be grassroot support and diplomatic efforts, there is currently no international convention for the prevention and punishment of crimes against humanity.[24] Nevertheless, States have the

---

Relative to the Protection of Civilian Persons in Times of War (GC IV), Aug. 12, 1949, 75 U.N.T.S. 287.

19 Genocide Convention, Dec. 9, 1948, 78 U.N.T.S. 277.

20 Torture Convention, Oct. 12, 1984, 1465 U.N.T.S. 85.

21 Rome Statute, Jul. 17, 1998, 2187 U.N.T.S. 3. *See also* Amendments on the crime of aggression to the Rome Statute, Jun. 11, 2010, Resolution RC/Res.6 (entered into force Jul. 17, 2018), https://treaties.un.org/doc/source/docs/RC-Res.6-ENG.pdf (last visited Dec. 2, 2024) (activating the ICC's jurisdiction over the crime of aggression); *see generally* G.A. Res. 3314 (XXIX), U.N. Doc. A/RES/3314 (XXIX) (Dec. 14, 1974); U.N. Audiovisual Library of Int'l Law, *Definition of Aggression: General Assembly Resolution 3314 (XXIX)* (2008), https://legal.un.org/avl/pdf/ha/da/da_ph_e.pdf (last visited Dec. 2, 2024).

22 *See, e.g.*, Hague Convention (XI) on Restrictions on the Right of Capture art. 1; Hague Convention (VI) on Enemy Merchant Ships art. 3.

23 Torture Convention art. 5. Moreover, the jus cogens norms are also identified within the core treaties and so create *erga omnes partes* obligations on states, giving all state a right of standing before the ICJ to initiate action. *See, e.g.*, Barcelona Traction, Light and Power Company, Limited (Belgium v. Spain), Judgment, 1970 I.C.J. 4, ¶¶ 33-34 (Feb. 5).

24 Draft articles on Prevention and Punishment of Crimes Against Humanity, INTERNATIONAL LAW COMMISSION (2019), https://legal.un.org/ilc/texts/instruments/english/draft_articl es/7_7_2019.pdf (last visited Dec. 2, 2024);Global: Amnesty Int'l, *UN General Assembly*

primary responsibility for preventing and punishing core international crimes.[25] In other words, they have the positive obligation to criminalize these offenses in their own laws to establish jurisdiction over these crimes and allow for their extraterritorial application.[26] And indeed, some States have criminalized crimes against humanity in the absence of a specific treaty dealing with this particular crime.[27] As has been done with more frequency in the last decade for core international crimes, even if a State is unable or unwilling to prosecute the perpetrator of a core international crime, another State could prosecute under universal jurisdiction or other national laws with extraterritorial application.

There has also been the addition of the Ljubljana-Hague Convention on International Cooperation in the Investigation and Prosecution of the Crime of Genocide, Crimes Against Humanity, War Crimes and other International Crimes ("Ljubljana-Hague Convention"), which was prepared outside United Nations processes but is currently open for signature. The Ljubljana-Hague Convention was prepared in recognition of the importance of individual State participation in the fight against impunity of these core international crimes. Its drafters sought to facilitate international cooperation for domestic investigation and prosecution of core international crimes.[28] In fact, the Mutual Legal Assistance and Extradition (MLA) Initiative emerged after 2011 to address legal gaps in State-to-State mutual legal assistance and extradition for

---

must open formal negotiations on Crimes Against Humanity Convention (Oct. 9, 2024), https://www.amnesty.org/en/latest/news/2024/10/un-negotiations-crimes-against-humanity-convention/ (last visited Dec. 2, 2024).

[25] *See, e.g.*, Genocide Convention art. VI ("Persons charged with genocide shall be tried by a competent tribunal of the State in the territory of which the act was committed, or by such penal tribunal as may have jurisdiction.").

[26] Genocide Convention art. I (imposing positive obligation to prevent and punish); Torture Convention art. 2 ("Each State Party shall take effective legislative, administrative, judicial or other measures to prevent acts of torture in any territory under its jurisdiction."); Torture Convention art. 5 (requiring States to take measures necessary to establish jurisdiction over offenses committed in "any territory under its jurisdiction or on board a ship or aircraft registered in that State," "when the alleged offender is a national of that State," "when the victim is a national of that State if that State considers it appropriate," and "where the alleged offender is present in any territory under its jurisdiction" and the State does not extradite him.).

[27] Philippine Act on Crimes Against International Humanitarian Law, Genocide, and Other Crimes Against Humanity, Rep. Act No. 9851 (Dec. 11, 2009), *available at* https://lawphil.net/statutes/repacts/ra2009/ra_9851_2009.html; Establishing the Ad Hoc Human Rights Court, Law No. 26 (2000) (Indonesia), *available at* https://policehumanrightsresources.org/content/uploads/2019/07/Law-26-2000-Act-on-the-Human-Rights-Courts-2000-Eng.pdf?x39143.

[28] The Ljubljana-Hague Convention art. 1.

national adjudication of these crimes.[29] In 2023, the Convention was adopted by consensus with the participation of sixty-eight States and observation of seven international organizations.[30] Its article 8 provides, "Each State Party shall take such measures as necessary to establish its jurisdiction over the crimes to which this Convention applies . . . [w]hen the crimes are committed in any territory under its jurisdiction or on board a vessel or aircraft registered in that State." However, it too confers no right to intervene in a foreign or stateless vessel nor creates a positive obligation to act on the high seas.[31]

III. The Rome Statute and Its Limits

Proposals for a collective process for prosecuting enemy officers and leaders for war crimes and defining the laws of humanity arose after World War I at the 1919 Paris Peace Conference. Efforts continued in the interwar period through and after World War II, but stalled during the Cold War before reinvigorating in the 1990s.[32] During this period, the pursuit of international criminal justice developed exponentially through the passage of multilateral treaties such as the Convention against Genocide, the operation of the Nuremberg and Far East Tribunals, as well as the International Criminal Tribunals for Rwanda and the Former Yugoslavia. With its entry into force, the Rome Statute established the ICC as the first permanent international criminal court.[33]

The Rome Statute narrowly defines the ICC's competence with respect to temporal, personal, and subject matter jurisdiction. Temporally, it has authority over crimes committed after July 1, 2002. In recognition of the State's primary role in the exercise of criminal jurisdiction, the ICC was designed to be

---

[29] Republic of Slovenia, *MLA (Mutual Legal Assistance and Extradition) Initiative*, MINISTRY OF FOREIGN AND EUROPEAN AFFAIRS, https://www.gov.si/en/registries/projects/mla-initiative/#:~:text=The%20Ljubljana%2DThe%20Hague%20Convention,against%20humanity%20and%20war%20crimes. (last visited Dec. 5, 2024).

[30] "MLA Diplomatic Conference: List of Participants," MLA/INF.1 (May 26, 2023), https://www.gov.si/assets/ministrstva/MZEZ/projekti/MLA-pobuda/List-of-Participants.pdf (last visited Oct. 6, 2024).

[31] *Id.*

[32] *See generally* John H. Currie, Craig Forcese, and Valerie Oosterveld, International Law: Doctrine, Practice, and Theory, Irwin Law (2007), pp. 890-945.

[33] Rome Statute art. 1; "With Today's Entry into Force of Rome Statute of Global Court, Speakers Hail 'Day of Hope' for Seekers of Justice," L/3007, UNITED NATIONS (Jul. 1, 2002), https://press.un.org/en/2002/l3007.doc.htm (last visited Nov. 23, 2024); Ban Ki-Moon, "Secretary-General Marks Entry into Force of Rome Statute by Hailing International Criminal Court As Centrepiece Of World Criminal Justice System," SG/SM/11067-L/T/4405, UNITED NATIONS (Jul. 2, 2007), https://press.un.org/en/2007/sgsm11067.doc.htm (last visited Nov. 23, 2024).

a court of last resort (e.g., to act when a State is unable or unwilling) and its work limited to situations referred to it by the U.N. Security Council and by State parties to the Rome Statute.[34] Unlike the ICJ, it is intended to adjudge individual criminal responsibility, not collective (i.e., state-level responsibility).[35] However, key to the Rome Statute is consent to jurisdiction. The drafters considered the Security Council as a solution for issues arising from a lack of consent by a non-party to the Rome Statute:

> It was also noted that the Court could not exercise jurisdiction in relation to States not party to the Statute. This, it was agreed, could become a particularly difficult issue when the State not party was the custodial State or its cooperation was indispensable to the prosecution. For this reason, some delegations were of the view that it would be proper for the Security Council to have a role which was respectful of the independence of the Court in humanitarian situations.[36]

Furthermore, with respect to subject matter, the ICC "investigates and, where warranted, tries individuals charged with the gravest crimes of concern to the international community[.]."[37] Article 5 provides that those crimes are genocide, crimes against humanity, war crimes, and the crime of aggression.[38] It is important to understand how high a threshold must be met, however, as that the drafters did not intend for every single war crime to warrant

---

[34] Rome Statute arts. 14-15.

[35] *Compare* Application of Convention on Prevention and Punishment of Crime of Genocide (Bosn. & Herz. v. Serb. & Montenegro, Judgment, 2007 I.C.J. 43, ¶ 417 (Feb. 26) (finding "no organs of the [former Republic of Yugoslavia] . . . or persons acting on its instructions or under its effective control, directly and publicly incited the commission of genocide in Srebrenica . . . or anywhere else on the territory of Bosnia and Herzegovina"), *with* Prosecutor v. Radislav Krstić, Case No. IT-98-33, Judgment and Sentence, ¶¶ 598-99, 727 (Aug. 2, 2001), https://www.icty.org/x/cases/krstic/tjug/en/krs-tj010802e.pdf (finding the defendant guilty of genocide in Srebrenica).

[36] Preparatory Committee on the Establishment of an International Criminal Court, Report of the Informal Group on Procedural Questions, Fair Trial and rights of the Accused, ¶ 128 (Aug. 27, 1996) [hereinafter, 1996 Informal Group Report], https://www.legal-tools.org/doc/e75432/pdf/ (last visited Nov. 19, 2024); Report of the International Law Commission on the work of its forty-sixth session, 2 May - 22 July 1994, General Assembly, Forty-ninth Session Supplement No.10 (A/49/10), pp. 22 ¶ 67-68 (1994) [hereinafter, 1994 ILC Report] (considering Security Council action as a "substitute" for the State consent requirement).

[37] "About the Court," INTERNATIONAL CRIMINAL COURT, https://www.icc-cpi.int/about/the-court (last visited Sep. 27, 2024).

[38] Rome Statute art. 5.

submission to the ICC; it must be of sufficient serious international concern.[39] Considering even the chapeau elements for crimes against humanity, which require a "widespread and systematic attack." Thus, a single serious incident, without more, would not ordinarily fall within the ICC's competence.

Consider for example, Houthi rebel attacks on merchant and commercial vessels in the Red Sea since November 19, 2023. On January 10, 2024, the U.N. Security Council adopted a resolution condemning those attacks.[40] Of central concern for Security Council members was whether the acts implicated the principle of freedom of navigation and waterway vital to the free flow of global commerce or if it was a part of a larger conflict.[41] While the Houthi rebels' stated purpose for these attacks was in support of the Palestinians against Israeli-linked vessels, many of the vessels targeted had no apparent link.[42] Moreover, the first vessel to reportedly sink because of these attacks was the cargo ship Rubymar.[43] M/V Rubymar was flagged in Belize, operated by a Lebanese firm,

---

[39] *See* 1996 Informal Group Report, *supra* note 36; *see also* 1994 ILC Report, *supra* note 36:

> There were also suggestions that the court should have discretion to decline to exercise its jurisdiction if the case was not of sufficient gravity or could be adequately handled by a national court. This suggestion was explained in terms of ensuring that the court would deal solely with the most serious crimes, it would not encroach on the functions of national courts, and it would adapt its caseload to the resources available. In this context, attention was drawn to the experience of the European Court of Human Rights.

. . .

> Another characteristic of "suppression conventions" (such as the United Nations Convention against Illicit Traffic in Narcotic Drugs and Psychotropic Substances . . . is that they cover a wide range of conduct, much of which, taken in isolation in the context of a single prosecution for a breach is not of any substantial international concern. If the court's jurisdiction is to be appropriately limited, either the treaties in question would have to be excluded altogether (which in the case of the Convention mentioned above would be undesirable) or other jurisdiction-limiting provisions need to be devised.

[40] S.C. Res. 2722, ¶ 1, U.N. Doc. S/RES/2722 (Jan. 10, 2024).

[41] U.N. SCOR, 79th Sess., 9527th mtg., U.N. Doc. S/PV.9527 (Jan. 10, 2024).

[42] *Who are the Houthis and why are they attacking Red Sea ships?*, BBC News (Mar. 15, 2024), https://www.bbc.com/news/world-middle-east-67614911 (last visited Dec. 4, 2024).

[43] Lipika Pelham, *Cargo ship attacked by Houthis sinks off Yemen coast*, BBC NEWS (Mar. 2, 2024), https://www.bbc.com/news/world-middle-east-68457445 (last visited Dec. 4, 2024); Avi Scharf, *The Full Map: All Ships Attacked by Yemen's Houthis in the Red Sea*,

and its registered owner was Golden Adventure Shipping in the British port of Southampton.[44] And at least two coastal States on the Red Sea, Jordan and Djibouti, are parties to the Rome Statute and have utilized the referral process to the ICC.[45] And yet, despite the multifaceted international implications, whether these attacks would constitute a qualifying crime within the court's jurisdiction remains debatable,[46] particularly with respect to whether the acts appeared to be systemic or grave enough.[47]

Since its establishment over two decades ago, the ICC has yet to engage in deep analyses of maritime dimensions. It has not, for example, considered crimes exclusively occurring on the high seas or in disputed territorial waters, crimes beginning in the territorial waters of a non-party State and ending in those same waters or on the high seas, or crimes occurring on a stateless vessel or vessel registered to a non-party State in those same waters. In fairness, this may be largely due to the factual allegations that have been brought before it, which do not require the court to consider those dimensions. However, notably, the only crimes the drafters explicitly considered in connection with vessels or the high seas were terrorism and large-scale drug-trafficking.[48]

HAARETZ (Jan. 15, 2024), https://www.haaretz.com/israel-news/security-aviation/2024-01-15/ty-article-magazine/30-attacks-all-red-sea-ships-targeted-by-the-houthis/0000018c-5df7-d6f9-afbc-5dff7a430000 (last visited Dec. 4, 2024).

44 Lipika Pelham, *supra* note 43.

45 *See Statement of the Prosecutor of the International Criminal Court, Karim A.A. Khan KC, on the Situation in the State of Palestine: receipt of a referral from five States Parties*, ICC (Nov. 17, 2023) https://www.icc-cpi.int/news/statement-prosecutor-international-criminal-court-karim-aa-khan-kc-situation-state-palestine (last visited Dec. 6, 2024) (including Djibouti).; *see generally State of Palestine – Situation in the State of Palestine ICC-01/18*, ICC, https://www.icc-cpi.int/palestine (last visited Dec. 4, 2024).

46 *See, e.g.*, Magne Frostad, *Houthi Attacks on Merchant Vessels in the Red Sea*, LIEBER INSTITUTE WEST POINT (Jun. 10, 2024), https://lieber.westpoint.edu/houthi-attacks-merchant-vessels-red-sea/ (last visited Dec. 4, 2024).

47 Magne Frostad, *Security at Sea: Houthi Attacks and the Global Impact with Magne Frostad (Part 2)*, National Security Law Today Podcast (Episode 336) (Aug. 28, 2024), *available at* https://www.americanbar.org/groups/law_national_security/nslt/security-at-sea-part-2/?login (last visited Sep. 26, 2024); Magne Frostad (Jun. 10, 2024), *supra* note 46.

48 *See, e.g.*, 1994 ILC Report *supra* note 36 at 37 ¶ (9), p. 41 ¶ (22), 68 (referencing the United Nations Convention against Illicit Traffic in Narcotic Drugs and Psychotropic Substances); *see also* Preparatory Committee on the Establishment of an International Criminal Court, 16 March-3 April 1998, Report of the Inter-Sessional Meeting from 19 to 30 January in Zutphen, Netherlands, UN Doc. A/AC.249/1998/L.13 (Feb. 4, 1998), https://www.legal-tools.org/doc/7ba9a4/pdf/ (last visited Nov. 19, 2024) ("[(b) the State on the territory of which the act [or omission] in question occurred [or if the crime was

IV. Case Study: Rohingya and Myanmar-Bangladesh

A maritime-related prosecution arose in the Situation in Bangladesh/Myanmar wherein Myanmar, as a non-party to the Rome Statute, continues to contest the court's jurisdiction. Over the course of the conflict, Rohingya refugees have fled by boat across the Bay of Bengal to reach safety in Bangladesh[49] and, in recent years, across the Andaman Sea to Indonesia or Malaysia.[50] In 2022 alone, "More than 3,500 . . . Rohingya attempted deadly sea crossings in 39 boats," resulting in over 300 people dying or missing at sea.[51]

In November 2019, the ICC Pre-Trial Chamber III granted the Prosecution's request to open an investigation, finding a reasonable basis to believe that "since at least 9 October 2016, members of the Tatmadaw, jointly with other security forces and with some participation of local civilians, may have committed coercive acts that could qualify as the crimes against humanity of deportation (article 7(1)(d) of the Rome Statute) against the Rohingya population.[52] Pre-Trial Chamber III found "a reasonable prosecutor could believe that coercive acts towards the Rohingya forced them to flee to Bangladesh, which may amount to the crime against humanity of

---

committed on board a vessel or aircraft, the State of registration of that vessel or aircraft;]"); *see generally* Melanie O'Brien, *Where Security Meets Justice: Prosecuting Maritime Piracy in the International Criminal Court*, CAMBRIDGE UNIVERSITY PRESS (Nov. 19, 2013), https://www.cambridge.org/core/journals/asian-journal-of-international-law/article/abs/where-security-meets-justice-prosecuting-maritime-piracy-in-the-international-criminal-court/ADA5F3BC6254BCC1E5E87CF2F71205E1 (last visited Nov. 21, 2024) (analyzing the potential of ICC prosecution of pirates).

49 UN Refugee Agency, *Rohingya Refugee Crisis Explained*, https://www.unrefugees.org/news/rohingya-refugee-crisis-explained/ (last visited Aug. 25, 2024).

50 Mitra Salima Suryono, *Rohingya Refugees Risk Dangerous Sea Route to Indonesia in Search of Safety and Freedom*, UNHCR (Apr. 25, 2024), https://www.unhcr.org/us/news/stories/rohingya-refugees-risk-dangerous-sea-route-indonesia-search-safety-and-freedom (last visited Sep. 26, 2024); Zsombor Peter, "Rohingya Refugees Fleeing Bangladesh by Boat This Year Top 2022 Number," Voice of America News (Dec. 2, 2023), https://www.voanews.com/a/rohingya-refugees-fleeing-bangladesh-by-boat-this-year-top-2022-number/7381473.html (last visited Aug. 25, 2024).

51 A.B.A. Res. 503 (Feb. 5, 2024), https://www.americanbar.org/content/dam/aba/directories/policy/midyear-2024/503-midyear-2024.pdf (last visited Dec. 4, 2024) (citing UNHCR, *Steep increase in deadly boat journeys reflects Rohingyas' desperation* (Jan. 17, 2023), https://news.un.org/en/story/2023/01/1132517).

52 "Decision Pursuant to Article 15 of the Rome Statute on the Authorisation of an Investigation into the Situation in the People's Republic of Bangladesh/Republic of the Union of Myanmar," No: ICC-01/19 (Nov. 14, 2019) [hereinafter, PTC III Rohingya Decision].

deportation."[53] On November 27, 2024, the ICC Prosecutor reportedly filed an application for the warrant of arrest against Acting President Min Aung Hlaing for the crimes against humanity of deportation and persecution of the Rohingya, committed in Myanmar and in part in Bangladesh.[54]

A. Deportation as a Crime Against Humanity

Turning first to the text of the Rome Statute, deportation may constitute a crime against humanity under Article 7 when it is committed "as part of a widespread or systematic attack directed against any civilian population, with knowledge of the attack."[55] "Deportation" is defined as forced displacement of the persons concerned by expulsion or other coercive acts from the area in which they are lawfully present, without grounds permitted under international law.[56] The crime of deportation has two elements, the first of which requires "the perpetrator deported or forcibly transferred, without grounds permitted under international law, one or more persons to another State or location, by expulsion or other coercive acts."[57]

B. Pre-Trial Chamber I's Destination Analysis

On September 6, 2018, the ICC Pre-Trial Chamber I considered the ICC Prosecutor's Request for a Ruling on Jurisdiction under Article 19(3) of the Statute. In its decision, Pre-Trial Chamber I distinguished "deported" from "transfer" as linked to the destination of "another State," meaning that, provided that all other requirements are met, only the displacement of persons lawfully residing in an area to another State amounts to deportation.[58]

---

[53] *Id.*

[54] *Statement of ICC Prosecutor Karim A.A. Khan KC: Application for an arrest warrant in the situation in Bangladesh/Myanmar*, INTERNATIONAL CRIMINAL COURT (Nov. 27, 2024), https://www.icc-cpi.int/news/statement-icc-prosecutor-karim-aa-khan-kc-application-arrest-warrant-situation-bangladesh (last visited Dec. 2, 2024).

[55] Rome Statute art. 7(1). Unlawful deportation may also constitute a war crime under Article 8 of the Rome Statute as a grave breach of the Geneva Conventions of 12 August 1949, particularly when it is committed as part of a plan or policy or as part of a large-scale commission of such crime.

[56] Rome Statute art. 7(2)(d).

[57] Elements of Crimes, INTERNATIONAL CRIMINAL COURT (2013), https://www.icc-cpi.int/sites/default/files/Publications/Elements-of-Crimes.pdf (last visited Aug. 25, 2024).

[58] Decision on the "Prosecution's Request for a Ruling on Jurisdiction under Article 19(3) of the Statute," No. ICC-RoC46(3)-01/18 (Sep. 6, 2018) [hereinafter, PTC I Rohingya Decision].

From a plain reading of the text, such a restrictive interpretation is not required. The words at issue are delineated in brackets for the reader's convenience:

> The perpetrator [deported] or [forcibly transferred], without grounds permitted under international law, one or more persons to another [State] or [location], by expulsion or other coercive acts.[59]

The text's construction permits a reading that deportation could be "to another . . . location." The text does not provide, for example, that the perpetrator [deported], without grounds permitted under international law, one or more persons to another [State] or [forcibly transferred], without grounds permitted under international law, one or more persons to another [location].

Moreover, Pre-Trial Chamber I's interpretation carries consequences beyond this case; this factual predicate of destination creates a jurisdictional gap in the maritime context. If deportation from a non-party State occurs across the high seas on that State's flagged vessel without ever entering another State party's territorial waters or without evidence of the perpetrator's knowledge or intent of that destination, then the ICC would not have jurisdiction. Said another way, the ICC could not exercise jurisdiction if the evidence before the court was merely that the victims were carried on a vessel registered with a non-party State which crossed into or remained on the high seas.

This gap might have been avoided if origin (i.e., expulsion *from* a State's territory) was the Element's meaningful factual predicate and the less restrictive reading of deportation were permitted (i.e., to another [location]). Then, if the crime required the victims to originate from and within a State's territory and then were forced to go "to another location" *outside that originating State territory*, the element could be satisfied once the victims crossed in or remained in the high seas.

C. Pre-Trial Chamber III's Expulsion Analysis

Approximately one year later, the ICC Pre-Trial Chamber III decided on the ICC Prosecutor's request for authorization to investigate, wherein she cited a suggestion that crossing any international border would suffice.[60] It appeared

---

[59] Elements of Crimes, *supra* note 57, art. 7(1)(d).

[60] *Situation in the People's Republic of Bangladesh / Republic of The Union of Myanmar*, ICC-01/19, Request for authorization of an investigation pursuant to article 15, n.217 (Jul. 4, 2019), https://www.icc-cpi.int/sites/default/files/CourtRecords/CR2019_03510. PDF (citing *Prosecutor v. William Samoei Ruto and Joshua Arap Sang*, ICC-01/09-01/11-373, Decision on the Confirmation of Charges Pursuant to Article 61(7)(a) and (b) of the

as if the Chamber accepted this formulation for purposes of the "expulsion or other coercive acts" clause of deportation:

> [T]the first element of deportation may be carried out by the perpetrator either by physically removing the deportees or by coercive acts that cause them to leave the area where they were lawfully present. In such a situation, the victims' behavior or response as a consequence of the coercive environment is required to be established for the completion of the crime. If the victims refused to leave the area despite the coercive environment or they did not cross **an international border,** it would constitute forcible transfer or an attempt to commit the crime of deportation.[61]

Read expansively, if the Rohingya did not cross an international border as they fled, then the court could exercise jurisdiction over the perpetrators for attempted deportation. Here again, the practical considerations and improbability of investigation where attempted deportation begins and ends in the territory of a non-party State remain.

D. Preconditions to the Exercise of Jurisdiction under Article 12(2)(a) of the Rome Statute

Article 12(2) of the Rome Statute provides that where a case is referred to the Prosecutor by a State Party or the Prosecutor initiates investigations proprio motu on the basis of information on crimes within the jurisdiction of the Court:

> [T]he Court may exercise its jurisdiction if one or more of the following States are Parties to this Statute or have accepted the jurisdiction of the Court in accordance with paragraph 3:

Rome Statute, para. 245 (Jan. 23, 2012) (suggesting that deportation requires a causal link between the conduct of the perpetrator and the victims' departure from the place where they were lawfully present and then crossing an international border)); *see also* "Amicus Curiae Observations by the International Commission of Jurists (pursuant to Rule 103 of the Rules)," No. ICC-RoC46(3)-01/18 (Jun. 18, 2018).

[61] "The term "forcibly" is not restricted to physical force, but may include threat of force or coercion, such as that caused by fear of violence, duress, detention, psychological oppression or abuse of power against such person or persons or another person, or by taking advantage of a coercive environment." Elements of Crimes, INTERNATIONAL CRIMINAL COURT, n.12 (2013), https://www.icc-cpi.int/sites/default/files/Publications/Elements-of-Crimes.pdf (last visited Aug. 25, 2024).

(a) The State on the territory of which the conduct in question occurred or, if the crime was committed on board a vessel or aircraft, the State of registration of that vessel or aircraft.

(b) The State of which the person accused of the crime is a national.

In its decision, Pre-Trial Chamber I determined it may exercise jurisdiction under this over acts of deportation (expulsion or other coercive acts) initiated in a non-party State (Myanmar) and completed in a State Party to the Statute (Bangladesh) by virtue of victims crossing the border to a State.[62]

Similarly, Pre-Trial Chamber III determined the court had jurisdiction based on objective, ubiquity, and constitutive elements of territoriality principles. It reasoned Bangladesh was a State Party and (i) the crime was completed in Bangladesh; (ii) took place in whole or in part in Bangladesh; or (iii) one or more elements of the crime of deportation occurred in Bangladesh, respectively. Satisfied that a "territorial link" to a State party existed, which satisfied article 12(2)(a), the Chamber declined to "formulate abstract conditions for the Court's exercise of territorial jurisdiction for all potentially transboundary crimes contained in the Statute."

E. Maritime Implications

Neither Pre-Trial Chamber I nor Pre-Trial Chamber III's decision accounted for flag state jurisdiction. In fact, while observing that article 12(2)(a) referred to vessels and aircraft, Pre-Trial Chamber III wrote that there was "no apparent reason why the threshold for territorial jurisdiction would be different based on whether the location of the conduct/crime is on land or vessel/aircraft."[63]

The author would offer that the first apparent reason why the threshold would be different is because there can be no territorial link on the high seas. Consistent with the doctrine of the freedom of the high seas, the high seas belong to no one. Consider when a non-party State's vessel leaves its territory and enters the high seas. There, its crew, acting pursuant to a government policy, commits a core international crime within the court's jurisdiction. If the vessel remains on the high seas, who could prosecute those crimes? Based on a territorial link test, not the ICC.

The next apparent reason is textualist. Article 12(2)(a) contains two clauses: the first, dependent on a "territorial link"; and the second, dependent on the state of registration. A plain reading of the text includes the word "or" suggesting

---

62 PTC I Rohingya Decision, *supra* note 58.

63 PTC III Rohingya Decision, *supra* note 52.

a disjunctive reading followed by a comma, indicating distinction from the first clause of article 12(2)(a). The clauses at issue are delineated in brackets and the word and punctuation at issue are emphasized for the reader's convenience:

> [The State on the territory of which the conduct in question occurred] **or,** [if the crime was committed on board a vessel or aircraft, the State of registration of that vessel or aircraft].

This reading supports the understanding that the "territorial link" test is separate from that required for crimes committed on vessels or aircraft.

What is less clear is whether the clauses are mutually exclusive. As mentioned above, if a crime is committed on board a non-party State's vessel on the high seas, only the second clause could apply. But if a crime is committed on board a non-party State's vessel on the territory of a State party, does the State party's territorial link satisfy the requisite precondition for the exercise of jurisdiction? Or is the "territorial link" irrelevant because the crime occurred on a vessel? If the latter, then only the state of registration clause governs. In other words, the clauses are mutually exclusive.

Article 12(2)(a)'s chapeau paragraph supports the mutually exclusive interpretation. It contemplates, in relevant part, the unlikely scenario where a non-party State may consent to the exercise of the court's jurisdiction. For the "territorial link" clause, that right to accept the court's jurisdiction would belong to the State on whose territory the conduct in question occurred. For the state of registration clause, the right would belong to the state of registration of the vessel on which the conduct in question occurred. Continuing with our hypothetical and applying the state of registration clause, if the non-party State's vessel remains on the high seas, the ICC could have jurisdiction if the non-party State consents. It is worth considering the improbability of this occurrence, however; applied to the Rohingya, if Myanmar was the State of registration of the vessel carrying the Rohingya on the high seas, then the ICC could not exercise jurisdiction without Myanmar's consent.

Now, what if the crime was committed and completed on a non-party State's vessel in that non-party State's territory and then crossed into a State party's territorial waters? Or what if while on the high seas the crime is committed and completed on a stateless or non-party State's vessel that subsequently enters a State party's territorial waters? Would the vessel's presence in the State party's territorial waters satisfy the precondition for the exercise of the court's jurisdiction?[64] Arguably, the "territorial link" test would not be satisfied because the crime (i) was completed in the non-party State's territory/on the high seas, not in the territory of a State party; (ii) took place in whole or in part in the non-party State's territory/on the high seas, not in the territory of a State party; and (iii) none of the elements of the crime occurred in the territory of a State party.

Even assuming the "territorial link" was satisfied in these scenarios, the principle of flag-state sovereignty favors the interpretation that the clauses should be mutually exclusive. A look at the work of the ILC in the context of international liability may be a useful comparison. In the same session that the ILC considered proposals for a permanent criminal court, it considered the related concept of international liability for injurious consequences arising out of acts not prohibited by international law. In that report, the ILC explained that it used the terms "jurisdiction" and "control," rather than "territory" alone to account for:

> [C]rimes committed in locations where there is no territorial link between a State and that activity for example, activities taking place in outer space or on the high seas. The most common example is the jurisdiction of the flag State over a ship. The four Conventions on the law of the sea adopted at Geneva in 1958 and the United Nations Convention on the Law of the Sea have covered many jurisdictional capacities of the flag State.[65]

While the legal concepts and underlying public interests for the court's jurisdiction and State liability are distinct, it is nevertheless fair to consider that the absence of the terms "control" and "territory" in the state registration clause of article 12(2)(a) of the Rome Statute was deliberate. In other words, territory and control are insufficient (even impossible in the context of the high seas) to meet the precondition for the ICC's exercise of jurisdiction over crimes

---

[64] *See generally* UNCLOS article 27 (generally prohibiting arrest and investigation of crimes committed on board foreign ships in or before entering the state's territorial waters); Anna Petrig, *Coastal State Jurisdiction in the Territorial Sea and the Protection of People on Board Foreign-Flagged Vessels*, EJIL:TALK! (Dec. 10, 2024), https://www.ejiltalk.org/coastal-state-jurisdiction-in-the-territorial-sea-and-the-protection-of-people-on-board-foreign-flagged-vessels/?fbclid=IwY2xjawHIkPNleHRuA2FlbQIxMQABHTCX56jUWf4pPDQT_B8cwAJ0hZut37e-ETJMZ537Wc2q_gxYs5X8EjbQWg_aem_5WkhYfk_Rw-pt8bc56XH0Q (last visited Dec. 13, 2024); Antonios Tzanakopoulos, *Coastal State Jurisdiction in the Territorial Sea and Transnational Organised Crime*, UNODC (Dec. 10, 2023), https://papers.ssrn.com/sol3/papers.cfm?abstract_id=4659926 (last visited Dec. 13, 2024).

[65] 1994 ILC Report, *supra* note 36 at 163 ¶¶ (13)-(17); *see also id.* at 165 ¶ 8 (considering transboundary harms such as pollution).

committed on a vessel. This interpretation appears to be most consistent with the customary recognition of exclusive flag-state jurisdiction.

With that said, a consequence of the mutually exclusive interpretation is a continued gap in protections for victims of crimes committed on stateless vessels, such as the Rohingya who are routinely subject to placement on stateless vessels and trafficked.[66] Even assuming the crimes are of sufficient serious international concern, neither Article 12(2)(a) nor any other article in the Rome Statute specifically grants jurisdiction to the court for crimes committed on stateless vessels. Instead, it is silent with respect to stateless vessels whether they (i) are not registered under the laws of any State, (ii) sail under flags of two or more States, or (iii) change flags during navigation. This presents an opportunity for consideration of a comprehensive framework to address jurisdiction over stateless vessels. Less ambitious actions may be an amendment that makes clear a State party's territorial link is sufficient for the court to exercise jurisdiction over crimes committed on a stateless vessel. Or, whereas the UNCLOS confers rights and protections for flagged vessels, the Rome Statute ought to have the explicit grant of jurisdiction over vessels who sail under two or more States flags or who change flags during navigation.

G. Implications for State Cooperation and Assistance

As gaps remain in the court's ability to prosecute crimes on the high seas and in the maritime context generally, the importance of leveraging national processes should not be overlooked. In the hypotheticals posed wherein a stateless or non-party State may enter the territorial waters of a State party and a non-party State of registration declines to accept the court's jurisdiction, a State party may still interdict in accordance with its national laws, just not on behalf of the ICC.[67] Of course, what a State may legislate (by sovereign right) differs from what it must

---

[66] *See, e.g.*, "Navy, Army Officers Charged with Human Trafficking," Thai Anti-Trafficking Action (Sep. 21, 2015), https://www.thaianti-humantraffickingaction.org/Home/2015/09/21/navy-army-officers-charged-with-human-trafficking/ (last visited Nov. 21, 2024); Marcia Robiou, *A New Report Sheds Light on an International Rohingya Trafficking Network*, PBS (Apr. 5, 2019), https://www.pbs.org/wgbh/frontline/article/a-new-report-sheds-light-on-an-international rohingya-trafficking-network/; *Sold Like Fish*, Fortify Rights and SUHAKAM (Mar. 2019), https://www.fortifyrights.org/downloads/Fortify%20Rights-SUHAKAM%20-%20Sold%20Like%20Fish.pdf.

[67] *See, e.g.*, U.S. Coast Guard, *Coast Guard offloads more than $14 million in illegal narcotics interdicted by Royal Navy partners in Caribbean Sea*, JOINT INTERAGENCY TASK FORCE SOUTH (Aug. 21, 2024), https://www.jiatfs.southcom.mil/News/News-Article-View/Article/3879860/ (last visited Dec. 5, 2024); *About OCDETF*, U.S. DEPT. OF JUSTICE ORGANIZED CRIME DRUG ENFORCEMENT TASK FORCES (Oct. 2, 2023), https://www.justice.gov/ocdetf/about-ocdetf (last visited Dec. 5, 2024).

do (positive obligation by agreement or customary international law) or must refrain from doing (negative obligation by the same).

Nevertheless, in theory, if the threshold crime were to occur on the high seas on a stateless vessel, then any State could have the authority to inspect and board the vessel to verify its stateless status. The scope of the intervening State's authority with respect to searches, seizures, and pull to port for the purpose of preventing and punishing the commission of core international crimes could be proscribed in a mutual assistance or cooperation agreement with the ICC. While not the subject of this chapter, it will be essential for cooperation to consider and develop uniform standards and protocols for evidence collection and preservation, seizure and transfer, and so on.

In turn, it might be fair that such vessels acting on behalf of the court or pursuant to an ICC arrest warrant be afforded certain protections and immunities from civil liability or suit before forums such as the ICJ, ITLOS, or an arbitral tribunal.[68] Would those protections then apply to vessels whose flag state is not a party of the ICC but nonetheless has *ergo omnes* responsibility to prevent and punish violations of a jus cogens (i.e., non-derogable) norm? Similarly, to ensure the ICC's jurisdiction does not compete with ITLOS on matters such as those relating to prompt release of vessels and crew under Article 292, UNCLOS, the parties should develop agreements that would allow for the ICC's criminal jurisdiction to preempt ITLOS claims (i.e., a rule of primacy), rather than permit concurrent jurisdiction.[69]

Then, there is the lingering issue of resourcing. The ICC does not have its own ships or aircraft authorized to pursue, board, inspect, seize, search, detain, transfer, etc. As with crimes committed on land, the ICC must rely on State assistance. But unique to the maritime context is the status requirement for effecting certain acts of interdictions. Recall, for example, that hot pursuit is a right limited to a warship, military aircraft, or other ship or aircraft on government service specifically authorized to that effect. To carry out an arrest warrant or interdict on the high seas pursuant to the request of the ICC Prosecutor, the intervening vessel must be specifically authorized to do so and the scope of that authority clearly defined.

---

68 *See, e.g.*, Reparation for injuries Suffered in the Service of the United Nations, Advisory Opinion, 1949 I.C.J. 17 (Apr. 1949).

69 *See* Horst Fischer, *Concurrent Jurisdiction: Developments and Issues, in* TREATY ENFORCEMENT AND INTERNATIONAL COOPERATION IN CRIMINAL MATTERS 56, 57-60 (Rodrigo Yepes-Enríquez & Lisa Tabassi eds., 2002).

Conclusion

As with any other crime on the high seas, the ability to prosecute core international crimes on the high seas is difficult. But the political will, precedent, and continued efforts toward collective enforcement on the high seas for other crimes prove it is not impossible. Nevertheless, while in theory, the ICC is precisely designed to be a court of last resort, the text of the Rome Statute is too narrow to punish perpetrators of crimes committed on stateless vessels or on a non-party State's flagged vessel on the high seas. And as the court is largely dependent on consent for the exercise of jurisdiction, collective effort should focus on continuing to enable by developing and supporting the capacity and will for national adjudications, including through the exercise of universal jurisdiction. A critical step will include the development of a comprehensive framework, whether created by treaty or mutual legal assistance agreements with the ICC, clarifying positive and negative obligations, or incorporating maritime concepts into existing conventions and protocols.

Bibliography

American Bar Association, Res. 503 (Feb. 5, 2024), https://www.americanbar.org/content/dam/aba/directories/policy/midyear-2024/503-midyear-2024.pdf.

Agreement between the United States and the United Kingdom of Great Britain and Northern Ireland (Jul. 13, 1998), https://www.state.gov/wp-content/uploads/2020/02/00-1030-United-Kingdom-Maritime-Mtrs-Shiprider-Carib-and-Bermuda.pdf.

Agreement between the United States and Tuvalu Concerning Operational Cooperation to Suppress Illicit Transnational Maritime Activity (Sep. 9, 2011), https://www.state.gov/wp-content/uploads/2019/02/11-909-Tuvalu-Maritime-Interdiction.pdf.

Amnesty International Global, *UN General Assembly must open formal negotiations on Crimes Against Humanity Convention* (Oct. 9, 2024), https://www.amnesty.org/en/latest/news/2024/10/un-negotiations-crimes-against-humanity-convention/.

Application of Convention on Prevention and Punishment of Crime of Genocide (*Bosn. & Herz. v. Serb. & Montenegro*, Judgment, 2007 I.C.J. 43, ¶ 417 (Feb. 26).

Barcelona Traction, Light and Power Company, Limited (*Belgium v. Spain*), Judgment, 1970 I.C.J. 4, ¶¶ 33-34 (Feb. 5).

Bay of Bengal Maritime Boundary Arbitration (Bangladesh v. India), Case No. 2010-16 (Perm. Ct. Arb. 2014).

BBC News, *Who are the Houthis and why are they attacking Red Sea ships?*, News (Mar. 15, 2024), https://www.bbc.com/news/world-middle-east-67614911.

Claim of the British Ship "I'm Alone" v. United States (1933), 3 R.I.A.A. 1609, 29 A.J.I.L. 326, https://legal.un.org/riaa/cases/vol_III/1609-1618.pdf.

Congressional Research Service, *United Nations Convention on the Law of the Sea (UNCLOS): Living Resources Provision*, R4774 (Jul. 15, 2024), https://crsreports.congress.gov/product/pdf/R/R47744.

Convention against Illicit Traffic in Narcotic Drugs and Psychotropic Substances, Dec. 20, 1988, 1582 U.N.T.S. 95.

Convention against Transnational Organized Crime, Nov. 15, 2000, 2225 U.N.T.S. 209.

Convention for the Suppression of Unlawful Acts against (SUA), Mar. 10, 1988, 1678 U.N.T.S. 221.

Convention for the Suppression of Unlawful Acts against Safety of Maritime Navigation, Mar. 10, 1988, 1678 U.N.T.S. 1.

John H. Currie, Craig Forcese, and Valerie Oosterveld, International Law: Doctrine, Practice, and Theory, Irwin Law (2007).

Daniele Fabris, *Crimes Committed at Sea and Criminal Jurisdiction: Current Issues of International Law of the Sea Awaiting the 'Enrica Lexie' Decision*, 9 Amsterdam Law Forum 5 (2017), https://amsterdamlawforum.org/articles/292/files/submission/proof/292-1-581-1-10-20200122.pdf. https://doi.org/10.37974/ALF.292.

Horst Fischer, *Concurrent Jurisdiction: Developments and Issues*, *in* Treaty Enforcement and International Cooperation in Criminal Matters 56, 57-60 (Rodrigo Yepes-Enríquez & Lisa Tabassi eds., 2002).

Fortify Rights and SUHAKAM, *Sold Like Fish* (Mar. 2019), https://www.fortifyrights.org/downloads/Fortify%20Rights-SUHAKAM%20%20Sold%20Like%20Fish.pdf.

Magne Frostad, *Houthi Attacks on Merchant Vessels in the Red Sea*, Lieber Institute West Point (Jun. 10, 2024), https://lieber.westpoint.edu/houthi-attacks-merchant-vessels-red-sea/.

Magne Frostad, *Security at Sea: Houthi Attacks and the Global Impact with Magne Frostad (Part 2)*, National Security Law Today Podcast (Episode 336) (Aug. 28, 2024), *available at* https://www.americanbar.org/groups/law_national_security/nslt/security-at-sea-part-2/?login.

Genocide Convention, Dec. 9, 1948, 78 U.N.T.S. 277.

Hague Convention (VI) on Enemy Merchant Ships art. 3.

Hague Convention (XI) on Restrictions on the Right of Capture art. 1.

Hague Conventions, International Committee of the Red Cross (2024), https://casebook.icrc.org/a_to_z/glossary/hague-conventions; Geneva Convention for the Amelioration of the Condition of the Wounded and Sick in Armed Forces in the Field (GC I), Aug. 12, 1949, 75 U.N.T.S. 31; Geneva Convention for the Amelioration of the Condition of Wounded, Sick and Shipwrecked Members of Armed Forces at Sea (GC II), Aug. 12, 1949, 75 U.N.T.S. 85; Geneva Convention Relative to the Protection of Civilian Persons in Times of War (GC IV), Aug. 12, 1949, 75 U.N.T.S. 287.

In the Matter of The Italian Republic v. The Republic of India (The "Enrica Lexie" Incident), Award, PCA Case No. 2015-28 (May 21, 2020), https://pcacases.com/web/sendAttach/16500.

International Commercial Crime Services, *IMB Piracy Reporting Centre*, https://www.icc-ccs.org/index.php/piracy-reporting-centre.

International Criminal Court, "About the Court," https://www.icc-cpi.int/about/the-court (last visited Sep. 27, 2024).

International Criminal Court, Decision on the "Prosecution's Request for a Ruling on Jurisdiction under Article 19(3) of the Statute," No. ICC-RoC46(3)-01/18 (Sep. 6, 2018).

International Criminal Court, "Decision Pursuant to Article 15 of the Rome Statute on the Authorisation of an Investigation into the Situation in the People's Republic of Bangladesh/Republic of the Union of Myanmar," No: ICC-01/19 (Nov. 14, 2019).

International Criminal Court, Elements of Crimes (2013), https://www.icc-cpi.int/sites/default/files/Publications/Elements-of-Crimes.pdf.

International Criminal Court, *Situation in the People's Republic of Bangladesh / Republic of The Union of Myanmar*, ICC-01/19, Request for authorization of an investigation pursuant to article 15, n.217 (Jul. 4, 2019), https://www.icc-cpi.int/sites/default/files/CourtRecords/CR2019_03510.PDF.

International Criminal Court, *State of Palestine – Situation in the State of Palestine ICC-01/18*, ICC, https://www.icc-cpi.int/palestine.

International Criminal Court, *Statement of ICC Prosecutor Karim A.A. Khan KC: Application for an arrest warrant in the situation in Bangladesh/Myanmar* (Nov. 27, 2024), https://www.icc-cpi.int/news/statement-icc-prosecutor-karim-aa-khan-kc-application-arrest-warrant-situation-bangladesh.

International Criminal Court, *Statement of the Prosecutor of the International Criminal Court, Karim A.A. Khan KC, on the Situation in the State of Palestine: receipt of a referral from five States Parties* (Nov. 17, 2023) https://www.icc-cpi.int/news/statement-prosecutor-international-criminal-court-karim-aa-khan-kc-situation-state-palestine.

International Commission of Jurists, "Amicus Curiae Observations by the International Commission of Jurists (pursuant to Rule 103 of the Rules)," No. ICC-RoC46(3)-01/18 (Jun. 18, 2018).

International Law Commission, *Analytical Guide to the Work of the International Law Commission: Peremptory norms of general international law (Jus cogens)* (Jul. 5, 2024), https://legal.un.org/ilc/guide/1_14.shtml.

International Law Commission, Draft articles on Prevention and Punishment of Crimes Against Humanity (2019), https://legal.un.org/ilc/texts/instruments/english/draft_articles/7_7_2019.pdf.

International Law Commission, Report of the International Law Commission on the work of its forty-sixth session, 2 May - 22 July 1994, General Assembly, Forty-ninth Session Supplement No.10 (A/49/10) (1994).

International Law Commission, "U.N. Security Council resolution underscores role of INTERPOL in securing maritime piracy prosecutions," 73rd Sess., Apr. 18-Jun. 3, Jul. 4-Aug. 5, 2022, ¶ 43, U.N. Doc. A/77/10.

International Maritime Organization, *Maritime Security* (last visited Dec. 2, 2024).

INTERPOL, *Maritime Crime* (2024), https://www.interpol.int/en/Crimes/Maritime-crime.

INTERPOL, "U.N. Security Council resolution underscores role of INTERPOL in securing maritime piracy prosecutions," (Apr. 13, 2011), https://www.interpo

l.int/en/News-and-Events/News/2011/UN-Security-Council-resolution-underscores-role-of-INTERPOL-in-securing-maritime-piracy-prosecutions (last visited Nov. 23, 2024).

ITLOS, *The Tribunal*, https://www.itlos.org/en/main/the-tribunal/the-tribunal/.

Ban Ki-Moon, "Secretary-General Marks Entry into Force of Rome Statute by Hailing International Criminal Court As Centrepiece Of World Criminal Justice System," SG/SM/11067-L/T/4405, United Nations (Jul. 2, 2007), https://press.un.org/en/2007/sgsm11067.doc.htm.

Ulf Linderfalk, *The Effect of Jus Cogens Norms: Whoever Opened Pandora's Box, Did You Ever Think About the Consequences?*, 18 Eur. J. Int'l L. 853 (2007), https://academic.oup.com/ejil/article/18/5/853/398659. https://doi.org/10.1093/ejil/chm044.

MLA, "MLA Diplomatic Conference: List of Participants," MLA/INF.1 (May 26, 2023), https://www.gov.si/assets/ministrstva/MZEZ/projekti/MLA-pobuda/List-of-Participants.pdf (last visited Oct. 6, 2024).

Melanie O'Brien, *Where Security Meets Justice: Prosecuting Maritime Piracy in the International Criminal Court*, Cambridge University Press (Nov. 19, 2013), https://www.cambridge.org/core/journals/asian-journal-of-international-law/article/abs/where-security-meets-justice-prosecuting-maritime-piracy-in-the-international-criminal-court/ADA5F3BC6254BCC1E5E87CF2F71205E1.

PBS News Hour, *How Slavery and Murder Goes Unpunished on the High Seas* (Jul. 28, 2015), https://www.pbs.org/video/how-slavery-and-murder-goes-unpunished-on-the-high-seas-1445298401/.

Peace Palace Library, *Start Your Research: (6) Peremptory Norms of International Law (Jus Cogens)*, https://peacepalacelibrary.nl/start-your-research-6-peremptory-norms-international-law-jus-cogens.

Lipika Pelham, *Cargo ship attacked by Houthis sinks off Yemen coast*, BBC News (Mar. 2, 2024), https://www.bbc.com/news/world-middle-east-68457445.

Zsombor Peter, "Rohingya Refugees Fleeing Bangladesh by Boat This Year Top 2022 Number," Voice of America News (Dec. 2, 2023), https://www.voanews.com/a/rohingya-refugees-fleeing-bangladesh-by-boat-this-year-top-2022-number/7381473.html.

Anna Petrig, *Coastal State Jurisdiction in the Territorial Sea and the Protection of People on Board Foreign-Flagged Vessels*, EJI: Talk! (Dec. 10, 2024), https://www.ejiltalk.org/coastal-state-jurisdiction-in-the-territorial-sea-and-the-protection-of-people-on-board-foreign-flagged-vessels/?fbclid=IwY2xjawHIkPNleHRuA2FlbQIxMQABHTCX56jUWf4pPDQT_B8cwAJ0hZut37e-ETJMZ537Wc2q_gxYs5X8EjbQWg_aem_5WkhYfk_Rw-pt8bc56XH0Q.

Philippine Act on Crimes Against International Humanitarian Law, Genocide, and Other Crimes Against Humanity, Rep. Act No. 9851 (Dec. 11, 2009), *available at* https://lawphil.net/statutes/repacts/ra2009/ra_9851_2009.html.

Preparatory Committee on the Establishment of an International Criminal Court, 16 March-3 April 1998, Report of the Inter-Sessional Meeting from 19 to 30 January in Zutphen, Netherlands, UN Doc. A/AC.249/1998/L.13 (Feb. 4, 1998), https://www.legal-tools.org/doc/7ba9a4/pdf/.

Preparatory Committee on the Establishment of an International Criminal Court, Report of the Informal Group on Procedural Questions, Fair Trial and rights of the Accused, ¶ 128 (Aug. 27, 1996) [hereinafter, 1996 Informal Group Report], https://www.legal-tools.org/doc/e75432/pdf/.

Protocol against the Smuggling of Migrants by Land, Sea and Air, Nov. 15, 2000, 2241 U.N.T.S. 507.

Protocol against the Smuggling of Migrants by Land, Sea and Air, supplementing the United Nations Convention against Transnational Organized Crime, G.A. Res. 55/25, Annex III, U.N. GAOR, 55th Sess., U.N. Doc. A/RES/55/25 (Nov. 15, 2000).

Prosecutor v. Radislav Krstić, Case No. IT-98-33, Judgment and Sentence, ¶¶ 598-99, 727 (Aug. 2, 2001), https://www.icty.org/x/cases/krstic/tjug/en/krs-tj010802e.pdf.

Prosecutor v. William Samoei Ruto and Joshua Arap Sang, ICC-01/09-01/11-373, Decision on the Confirmation of Charges Pursuant to Article 61(7)(a) and (b) of the Rome Statute, para. 245 (Jan. 23, 2012).

Himanil Raina, *Attacks on Merchant Shipping: Which State has the Right to Respond in Self-Defence?*, Articles of War (Apr. 15, 2024), https://lieber.westpoint.edu/attacks-merchant-shipping-which-state-has-right-respond-self-defence/.

Reparation for injuries Suffered in the Service of the United Nations, Advisory Opinion, 1949 I.C.J. 17 (Apr. 1949).

Republic of Indonesia, Establishing the Ad Hoc Human Rights Court, Law No. 26 (2000) (Indonesia), *available at* https://policehumanrightsresources.org/content/uploads/2019/07/Law-26-2000-Act-on-the-Human-Rights-Courts-2000-Eng.pdf?x39143.

Republic of Slovenia, *MLA (Mutual Legal Assistance and Extradition) Initiative*, Ministry of Foreign and European Affairs, https://www.gov.si/en/registries/projects/mla-initiative/#:~:text=The%20Ljubljana%2DThe%20Hague%20Convention,against%20humanity%20and%20war%20crimes.

Marcia Robiou, *A New Report Sheds Light on an International Rohingya Trafficking Network*, PBS (Apr. 5, 2019), https://www.pbs.org/wgbh/frontline/article/a-new-report-sheds-light-on-an-internationalrohingya-trafficking-network/.

Rome Statute, Jul. 17, 1998, 2187 U.N.T.S. 3.

Rome Statute, Amendments on the crime of aggression to the Rome Statute, Jun. 11, 2010, Resolution RC/Res.6 (entered into force Jul. 17, 2018), https://treaties.un.org/doc/source/docs/RC-Res.6-ENG.pdf.

S. S. Lotus (Fr. v. Turk.), 1927 P.C.I.J. (ser. A) No. 10 (Sept. 7, 1927), https://www.worldcourts.com/pcij/eng/decisions/1927.09.07_lotus.htm.

Avi Scharf, *The Full Map: All Ships Attacked by Yemen's Houthis in the Red Sea*, HAARETZ (Jan. 15, 2024), https://www.haaretz.com/israel-news/security-aviation/2024-01-15/ty-article-magazine/30-attacks-all-red-sea-ships-targeted-by-the-houthis/0000018c-5df7-d6f9-afbc-5dff7a430000.

Sovereignty and Maritime Delimitation in the Red Sea (*Eritrea v. Yemen*) Award of the Arbitral Tribunal in the First Stage of the Proceedings, Case No. 1996-04 (Perm. Ct. Arb. 1998).

Statute of the International Tribunal for the Law of the Sea, Dec. 10, 1982, 1833 U.N.T.S. 561.

Mitra Salima Suryono, *Rohingya Refugees Risk Dangerous Sea Route to Indonesia in Search of Safety and Freedom*, UNHCR (Apr. 25, 2024), https://www.unhcr.org/us/news/stories/rohingya-refugees-risk-dangerous-sea-route-indonesia-search-safety-and-freedom.

Thai Anti-Trafficking Action, "Navy, Army Officers Charged with Human Trafficking," (Sep. 21, 2015), https://www.thaianti-humantraffickingaction.org/Home/2015/09/21/navy-army-officers-charged-with-human-trafficking/ (last visited Nov. 21, 2024).

The Ljubljana - The Hague Convention on International Cooperation in the Investigation and Prosecution of the Crime of Genocide, Crimes Against Humanity, War Crimes and Other International Crimes, adopted in Ljubljana on May 26, 2023.

Torture Convention, Oct. 12, 1984, 1465 U.N.T.S. 85.

Antonios Tzanakopoulos, *Coastal State Jurisdiction in the Territorial Sea and Transnational Organised Crime*, UNODC (Dec. 10, 2023), https://papers.ssrn.com/sol3/papers.cfm?abstract_id=4659926 (last visited Dec. 13, 2024). https://doi.org/10.2139/ssrn.4857439.

United Nations, *Reports of International Arbitral Awards*, Codification and Progressive Development of International Law, https://legal.un.org/riaa/.

United Nations, "With Today's Entry into Force of Rome Statute of Global Court, Speakers Hail 'Day of Hope' for Seekers of Justice," L/3007 (Jul. 1, 2002), https://press.un.org/en/2002/l3007.doc.htm.

United Nations Audiovisual Library of Int'l Law, *Definition of Aggression: General Assembly Resolution 3314 (XXIX)* (2008), https://legal.un.org/avl/pdf/ha/da/da_ph_e.pdf.

United Nations Convention on the High Seas (UNCHS), Apr. 29, 1958, 450 U.N.T.S. 11, UNCLOS, Oct. 12, 1982, 1833 U.N.T.S. 397.

United Nations General Assembly, GAOR, 77th Sess., Supp. No. 10 (2022).

United Nations General Assembly, G.A. Res. 3314 (XXIX), U.N. Doc. A/RES/3314 (XXIX) (Dec. 14, 1974).

United Nations General Assembly, G.A. Res. 57/142, ¶ 17, U.N. Doc. A/RES/57/142 (Feb. 26, 2003). https://doi.org/10.1159/000071504.

UNHCR, *Steep increase in deadly boat journeys reflects Rohingyas' desperation* (Jan. 17, 2023), https://news.un.org/en/story/2023/01/1132517.

United Nations Office on Drugs and Crime, "Maritime Crime: About Us," https://www.unodc.org/unodc/en/piracy/index.html.

United Nations Office on Drugs and Crime, "Publications & Resources," https://www.unodc.org/unodc/en/piracy/resources_Template.html.

United Nations Office on Drugs and Crime, *Maritime Crime: A Manual for Criminal Justice Practitioners* (2019), https://www.unodc.org/documents/Maritime_crime/19-02087_Maritime_Crime_Manual_Second_Edition_ebook.pdf.

United Nations Refugee Agency, *Rohingya Refugee Crisis Explained*, https://www.unrefugees.org/news/rohingya-refugee-crisis-explained/.

United Nations Security Council, S.C. Res. 2722, ¶ 1, U.N. Doc. S/RES/2722 (Jan. 10, 2024).

United Nations SCOR, 79th Sess., 9527th mtg., U.N. Doc. S/PV.9527 (Jan. 10, 2024).

United States v. F/V Taiyo Maru, Number 28, SOI 600, 395 F. Supp. 413 (D. Me. 1975).

U.S. Coast Guard, *Coast Guard offloads more than $14 million in illegal narcotics interdicted by Royal Navy partners in Caribbean Sea*, Joint Interagency Task Force South (Aug. 21, 2024), https://www.jiatfs.southcom.mil/News/News-Article-View/Article/3879860/.

U.S. Coast Guard, *Maritime Counterdrug and Alien Migrant Interdiction Operation Manual – COMDTINST M16247.4A – Table of Contents*, U.S. Coast Guard (2012), *available at* https://www.governmentattic.org/46docs/USCGcdamioTOC_2012.pdf.

U.S. Department of Homeland Security, *Fiscal Year 2020 Report to Congress: Counter-Drug Operations* (Aug. 14, 2020), https://www.dhs.gov/sites/default/files/publications/uscg_-_counter-drug_operations.pdf.

U.S. Department of Justice Organized Crime Drug Enforcement Task Forces, *About OCDETF* (Oct. 2, 2023), https://www.justice.gov/ocdetf/about-ocdetf.

U.S. Department of State, "Aumoana Regional Law Enforcement Initiative Announced in Nuku'alofa Tonga," (Sep. 5, 2024), https://www.state.gov/aumoana-regional-law-enforcement-initiative-announced-in-nukualofa-tonga/

Vienna Convention on the Laws of Treaties art. 53, May 23, 1969, 1155 U.N.T.S. 331.

List of Contributors

Zoi Aliozi

Dr. Zoi Aliozi is an international academic, lawyer-scholar-activist, a climate justice and human rights educator, and an award-winning philosopher. Prior to her academic pursuits, she practiced criminal law, bringing a wealth of practical experience to her scholarly endeavors. With a rich academic background, Dr. Aliozi has accumulated more than a decade of experience in climate justice and human rights education across international universities. Her expertise is lauded for insightful connections between law, philosophy, and activism. Beyond academia, Dr. Aliozi is actively engaged in influential climate action projects, emphasizing her steadfast commitment to promoting climate justice. Her notable contributions include offering her expertise in the creation of the 'Maastricht Principles for the Rights of Future Generations', and serving as a Climate Justice expert research evaluator for Horizon Europe under the European Commission; notably, she currently serves as an EU Climate Pact Ambassador. Dr. Aliozi's multifaceted career exemplifies her dedication to advancing climate justice, human rights, law, and philosophy, on both scholarly and practical fronts.

Mark Chadwick

Dr Mark Chadwick is a Principal Lecturer in Law at Nottingham Trent University, where he teaches and researches International Criminal Law. He holds a PhD from the University of Nottingham for a thesis focusing on the historical development of universal jurisdiction in relation to piracy and, more recently, in relation to serious international crimes such as genocide, crimes against humanity and war crimes. Mark's PhD was subsequently developed into a monograph, *Piracy and the Origins of Universal Jurisdiction: On Stranger Tides?* (BRILL, 2019), which provides an invaluable historical and legal examination of our relationship with high-seas piracy, drawing on influences from literature, culture and philosophy.

Mark has also published in various journals and blogs, particularly on the topic of universal jurisdiction, and has presented widely at many academic conferences. He has worked as an intern at the International Criminal Court, the International Bar Association and the Human Rights Law Centre (Nottingham) and has served several times as a judge for the IBA International Criminal Court Moot Court, held annually in The Hague. In 2019, he appeared on the Netflix documentary series "*Explained*", for an episode focusing on the phenomenon of piracy.

Bolanle Erinosho

Bolanle Erinosho is a Senior Lecturer at the Law School, University of Derby. She was the Co-country Director for the One Ocean Hub at the University of Cape Coast in Ghana. She has a Ph. D in International Environmental Law from the University of Sheffield in the United Kingdom. She teaches and researches in the areas of environment, oceans law and governance.

Hashali Hamukuaya

Hashali Hamukuaya is a Research Fellow at the University of South Africa. He has contributed to diverse, high-profile projects, including combating fisheries crime with FishForce, enhancing ocean biodiversity governance with the One Ocean Hub, and shaping South Africa's maritime economy at the South African International Maritime Institute (SAIMI). At SAIMI, Hashali led research proposal development, managed the Think Tank, and played an important role in Operation Phakisa, a national initiative to unlock South Africa's ocean economy. Currently serving as Research Development and Monitoring Manager at the Sustainable Seas Trust, Hashali leads efforts to promote sustainable practices in the blue economy across Africa.

Alana Malinde S. N. Lancaster

Alana Malinde S. N. Lancaster is a Guyanese-Barbadian environmental, energy & human rights lawyer, academic and natural resources specialist. She is currently a Lecturer in International Environmental & Energy Law and Head of Environmental Law, Ocean Governance & Climate Justice Unit (ELOG&CJ Unit) of the Faculty of Law at the University of the West Indies. Alana is also a Co-Investigator with the UKRI GCRF-funded One Ocean Hub, and serves as the Regional Deputy Director of the Global Network for Human Rights and the Environment for the Caribbean Region. She has been a Member of the International Law Association Caribbean Branch for 9 years and currently serves as the Association's Honorary Treasurer.

Academically, Alana specializes in international, regional (CARICOM & OECS) and comparative marine environmental law. This includes climate law, international human rights law, maritime security at sea, the law of the blue economy and international energy law. Alana's latest research projects include a co-edited Research Handbook on Climate Justice, to be published by Edward Elgar in 2025, and an upcoming book chapter by Vernon Press on ocean-based solutions as tools for achieving climate justice for vulnerable States and peoples.

Over 2022 and 2023, she contributed to the international consultations on the Zero Draft Of General Comment 26 on children's rights and the environment, with a special focus on climate change; and the Report of the Special Rapporteur on Climate Change and the Environment focused on loss and damage, and the ongoing advisory opinions on climate change in front of the International Tribunal for the Law of the Sea (ITLOS), the International Court of Justice (ICJ), the Inter-American Court of Human Rights (IACtHR) and the African Commission of Human and Peoples' Rights (ACHPR). She has also produced research and policy pieces on the expansion of human rights and the marine environment; oceans and planetary health, with an emphasis on [de]colonization and gender in environmental issues affecting women, girls, children, Indigenous and Afro-descendant, displaced, migrant and LGBTIQA+ peoples.

Regionally, Alana has supported The University of the West Indies with the drafting and implementation of the institution's Climate Action Plan & Climate Justice Strategy and provides support to the Barbados' Coordinating Committee and National Working Group for the GEF Islands Child Project, a five-year project which aims to strengthen the mechanisms for the environmentally sound management of chemicals, plastics and wastes in the Caribbean. This includes support in the negotiations on the global treaty to end plastics pollution, and in developing Barbados' National Ocean Policy.

Shabnam Moinipour

Dr. Shabnam Moinipour is a scholar and advocate with a focus on human rights and social justice. She holds a Ph.D. in human rights. Her work centers on critical human rights issues, with particular attention to challenges faced by marginalized populations.

Dr. Moinipour has published significant works that explore institutionalized discrimination and the barriers to achieving equity, particularly in the context of Iran. She is the author of several publications, including a book entitled *Human Rights, Iranian Migrants, and State Media: From Media Portrayal to Civil Reality*. Her scholarly contributions delve into the structural and systemic factors that perpetuate human rights violations and inequality, offering nuanced analyses that inform both policy and practice in human rights advocacy. Dr. Moinipour is also an experienced educator, having taught courses on human rights and social research methods at leading institutions such as the School of Advanced Study, University of London.

In addition to her academic work, Dr. Moinipour actively supports human rights initiatives through her role as Program Director at the Centre for Supporters of Human Rights. Dr. Moinipour emphasizes the importance of bridging academia and civil society, fostering a collaborative approach to human rights education and advocacy. She highlights the need to apply academic knowledge in practical ways to address real-world challenges and drive meaningful change.

Vy. T. Nguyen

Major (MAJ) Vy T. Nguyen holds a JD/MA from the American University Washington College of Law (WCL) and School of International Service and Honours BA from the University of Toronto. She is admitted to the Virginia State Bar.

MAJ Nguyen is the current Vice-Chair of publications for the ABA ILS International Criminal Law Committee. She is also an Alumni Council member for the WCL War Crimes Research Office and serves on active duty as a Government Appellate Attorney.

In 2020, MAJ Nguyen deployed to Afghanistan as the Command Judge Advocate for the Train, Advise, Assist Command—South and Kandahar Airfield in support of the NATO Resolute Support and USFOR-A Operation Freedom's Sentinel missions. Her other notable military assignments included Chief of National Security Law for the 10th Mountain Division (LI) and Fort Drum, Trial Defense Counsel in Vilseck, Germany, and Military Justice Advisor for the 10th Combat Aviation Brigade and 10th Mountain Division Sustainment Brigade. In 2022, she was selected as the U.S. Army recipient of the Judge Advocates Association-ABA Outstanding Young Military Lawyer Award.

Prior to military service, MAJ Nguyen served as a Department of Justice Honors Attorney Advisor at the Krome (Detained) Immigration Court. As a student, she worked for the Chairperson of the UN Committee Against Torture, Trial Chamber III at the International Criminal Tribunal for the Former Yugoslavia, and the Center for the Prevention of Genocide at the U.S. Holocaust Memorial Museum. In 2015, she was selected as a finalist for the Presidential Management Fellows (PMF) Program.

Christine Okidi

Christine Okidi is a legal professional with expertise in criminal justice, human rights, and public interest litigation. She has a strong focus on research, advocacy, and policy development, driving impactful legal and social change. Christine holds an LL. B degree from the University of Nairobi and a Postgraduate Diploma from the Kenya School of Law.

Regina M. Paulose

Regina M. Paulose is an attorney focusing on international criminal law, based in the United States. She serves on the Executive Committee of the American Bar Association International Law Section's International Criminal Law Committee. She is the editor and a contributor to People's Tribunals, Human Rights and the Law (Routledge) and Green Crimes and International Criminal Law (Vernon Press). She is the Executive Director of The Common Good Foundation, Inc.

Pierpaolo Petrelli

Dr. Pierpaolo Petrelli, an Associate Professor at O.P. Jindal Global University, exemplifies a distinguished career in international law and criminal justice. With a rich academic background from prestigious institutions, including a Doctorate of Juridical Science in International Criminal Law from Case Western Reserve University, Petrelli has honed his expertise in areas such as international humanitarian law, human rights law, transnational terrorism, and refugee law.

His career encompasses significant roles in academia and legal practice. As an educator, he has developed and taught courses in Public International Law, International Criminal Law, and International Courts and Tribunals, fostering comprehensive knowledge and critical thinking skills among his students. His commitment to education extends beyond the classroom, as he serves as an Associate Dean, facilitating international internships and actively participating in university and community programs.

Petrelli's legal prowess is further accentuated in his consultancy and research roles. His involvement in legal counsel positions demonstrates a deep-seated ability in intricate legal analysis and effective client advocacy. His research endeavors, particularly in documenting and analyzing war crimes and crimes against humanity, reflect his unwavering dedication to applying legal acumen to global challenges.

In addition to his professional roles, Petrelli has contributed to the legal field through scholarly publications, highlighting his research on the crime of aggression and other significant international law topics. His work reflects a deep understanding of the intricacies of international criminal law and a dedication to advancing knowledge in this field.

Pierpaolo Petrelli's career trajectory showcases a harmonious blend of academic rigor, practical legal experience, and a profound commitment to justice and human rights. His contributions to international law, both in theory and practice, make him a significant voice in contemporary legal discussions and an inspiring figure for future legal scholars and practitioners.

Ronald Rogo

Ronald Rogo has a Master's degree in ICL from the University of Torino, Italy. He has taught ICL at the University of Nairobi, Kenya. He has co-written a number of articles, including Ronald Gordon Rogo, *'People's Tribunals and Truth Commissions'*, in Regina Menachery Paulose (ed) People's Tribunals, Human Rights and the Law: Searching for Justice (2020), Routledge, 40-59, Regina Menachery Paulose and Ronald Gordon Rogo, *Addressing Colonial Crimes through Reparations: The Mau Mau, Herero and Nama* (2018), State Crime Journal Vol. 7, No. 2, State Crime and Colonialism (Autumn 2018), 369-388, Lina Laurinaviciute, Regina Paulose and Ronald Rogo, *The Forgotten: The Armenian Genocide 100 Years,* in Morten Bergsmo, Cheah Wui Ling And Yi Ping (eds) Historical Origins of International Criminal Law: Volume 1 (Torkel Opsahl Academic EPublisher, Brussels, 2014), 379-406.

Tajudeen Sanni

Dr. Tajudeen Sanni received his LLB (Ahmadu Bello University), BL (Nigerian Law School). LLM (University of Ilorin), LLM (Liverpool John Moore University), and LLD (Nelson Mandela University). Tajudeen was a One Ocean Hub-funded Research Fellow, Chair in Law of the Sea and Development in Africa, at the Institute for Coastal and Marine Research, Nelson Mandela University, South Africa. He is currently an Associate Professor and Head at the Center for Transformative Environmental and Marine Law, Faculty of Shariah and Law, Villa College, Male, Maldives. At the same institution, he is a module leader for the University of West of England LLB and LLM programs.

Henna J. Shah

Henna J. Shah holds a Juris Doctor from Wake Forest University School of Law and a Master of Laws in International Human Rights from Northwestern University Pritzker School of Law. She also received a Bachelor of Science and Arts in Biology, a Certificate in Business Foundations, and a Minor in Government from The University of Texas at Austin. Her legal experience includes working for the United Nations, the United States Government, non-governmental organizations, and legal clinics all over the world. She has held leadership positions with the American Bar Association, American Society of International Law, and Federal Bar Association, and is a member of Wake Forest University School of Law's Rose Council. Her legal practice and scholarship focus on public international law, specifically international human rights law, international criminal law, international humanitarian law, international transportation law, aviation law, and outer space law.

Lu Shegay

Lu Shegay is the co-founder of the Institute of Animal Law of Asia and professor of law, she has earned her LL.B degree at KIMEP University School of Law (Kazakhstan) and her LL.M degree at Lewis & Clark Law School (Portland, Oregon). Twice Ambassador of the Center for Animal Law Studies, Lewis & Clark Law School, under the initiative Global Ambassador Program, Lu worked on projects on aquatic animals and animal abuse in Kazakhstan. She also serves as a permanent judge in the Jessup International Law Moot Court Competition. Lu contributed to the draft of the Animal Welfare Law of Kazakhstan, has published a chapter on animals in agriculture in *Animal Law in Kazakhstan, Russia, and Worldwide,* and her upcoming publication is the chapter on animal law in Kazakhstan in *Global Animal Law* (Oxford University Press).

Index

D

E

F

G

H

I

J

K

L

M

N

V

W

Z

www.ingramcontent.com/pod-product-compliance
Lightning Source LLC
LaVergne TN
LVHW020413220926
848484LV00018B/2565/J
* 9 7 9 8 8 8 1 9 0 2 4 0 7 *